Landmark Papers in Economic Fluctuations, Economic Policy and Related Subjects

The Foundations of 20th Century Economics

Prefaces by: Mark Blaug

Professor Emeritus, University of London, UK
Professor Emeritus, University of Buckingham, UK
Visiting Professor, University of Amsterdam, The Netherlands
Visiting Professor, Erasmus University of Rotterdam, The Netherlands

1. Landmark Papers in Economic Growth
   Selected by Robert M. Solow

2. Landmark Papers in Economic Fluctuations, Economic Policy and Related Subjects
   Selected by Lawrence R. Klein

Future titles will include:

Landmark Papers in General Equilibrium Theory, Social Choice and Welfare
Selected by Kenneth J. Arrow and Gérard Debreu

Landmark Papers in Economics, Politics and Law
Selected by James M. Buchanan

Landmark Papers in Macroeconomics
Selected by James Tobin

Wherever possible, the articles in these volumes have been reproduced as originally published using facsimile reproduction, inclusive of footnotes and pagination to facilitate ease of reference.

For a list of all Edward Elgar published titles visit our site on the World Wide Web at
http://www.e-elgar.co.uk

Landmark Papers in Economic Fluctuations, Economic Policy and Related Subjects

Selected by

Lawrence R. Klein

Benjamin Franklin Professor of Economics Emeritus
University of Pennsylvania, USA

THE FOUNDATIONS OF 20TH CENTURY ECONOMICS

An Elgar Reference Collection
Cheltenham, UK • Northampton, MA, USA

Published by
Edward Elgar Publishing Limited
Glensanda House
Montpellier Parade
Cheltenham
Glos GL50 1UA
UK

Edward Elgar Publishing, Inc.
136 West Street
Suite 202
Northampton
Massachusetts 01060
USA

A catalogue record for this book is available from the British Library.

Library of Congress Cataloging in Publication Data

Landmark papers in economic fluctuations, economic policy, and related subjects /
selected by Lawrence R. Klein.
p. cm. — (An Elgar reference collection) (The Foundations of 20th century economics ; 2)
Includes bibliographical references and index.
1. Business cycles—History—20th century. 2. Economic policy—History—20th century.
3. Economics—History—20th century. I. Klein, Lawrence Roberts. II. Series. III. Series:
The Foundations of 20th century economics ; 2

HB3714 .L28 2002
338.5'42'0904—dc21 200104028

ISBN 1 84064 470 2

Printed and bound in Great Britain by MPG Books Ltd, Bodmin, Cornwall

Contents

Acknowledgements

The editor and publishers wish to thank the authors and the following publishers who have kindly given permission for the use of copyright material.

American Economic Association for articles: Irving Fisher (1911), '"The Equation of Exchange", 1896–1910', *American Economic Review*, **4** (3), June, 296–305; Evsey D. Domar (1944), 'The "Burden of the Debt" and the National Income', *American Economic Review*, **XXXIV**, December, 798–827; Jacob Marschak (1947), 'Economic Structure, Path, Policy, and Prediction', *American Economic Review*, Supplement, **XXXVII** (2), May, 81–4; Paul H. Douglas (1948), 'Are There Laws of Production?', *American Economic Review*, **XXXVIII** (1), March, 1–41; William Brainard (1967), 'Uncertainty and the Effectiveness of Policy', *American Economic Review*, Supplement, **LVII** (2), May, 411–25.

American Statistical Association for article: Irving Fisher (1923), 'The Business Cycle Largely a "Dance of the Dollar"', *Journal of the American Statistical Association*, **XVIII** (144), December, 1024–8.

Blackwell Publishers Ltd for articles: Knut Wicksell (1907), 'The Influence of the Rate of Interest on Prices', *Economic Journal*, **XVII** (66), June, 213–20; R.F. Kahn (1931), 'The Relation of Home Investment to Unemployment', *Economic Journal*, **XLI** (162), June, 173–98; Joan Robinson (1933), 'A Parable on Savings and Investment', *Economica*, **39**, February, 75–84; Oskar Lange (1938), 'The Rate of Interest and the Optimum Propensity to Consume', *Economica*, **V**, February, 12–32; R.F. Harrod (1939), 'An Essay in Dynamic Theory', *Economic Journal*, **49** (193), March, 14–33 and 'Errata', *Economic Journal*, **49** (194), June, 377; N. Kaldor (1940), 'A Model of the Trade Cycle', *Economic Journal*, **L** (197), March, 78–92; P. de Wolff (1941), 'Income Elasticity of Demand, a Micro-Economic and a Macro-Economic Interpretation', *Economic Journal*, **LI**, April, 140–45; D.G. Champernowne (1953), 'A Model of Income Distribution', *Economic Journal*, **LXIII** (250), June, 318–51; A.W. Phillips (1957), 'Stabilisation Policy and the Time-Forms of Lagged Responses', *Economic Journal*, **LXVII** (266), June, 265–77; A.W. Phillips (1958), 'The Relation Between Unemployment and the Rate of Change of Money Wage Rates in the United Kingdom, 1861–1957', *Economica*, **XXV**, New Series, November, 283–99; A.B. Atkinson (1997), 'Bringing Income Distribution in From the Cold', *Economic Journal*, **107** (441), March, 297–321.

Blackwell Publishers Ltd and the University Institute of Social and Economic Research Association for article: Bert G. Hickman, Robert M. Coen and Michael D. Hurd (1975), 'The Hickman-Coen Annual Growth Model: Structural Characteristics and Policy Responses', *International Economic Review*, **16** (1), February, 20–37.

Econometric Society for articles and excerpt: Eugen Slutzky (1937), 'The Summation of Random Causes as the Source of Cyclic Processes', *Econometrica*, **5** (2), April, 105–46; Leonid Hurwicz (1944), 'Stochastic Models of Economic Fluctuations', *Econometrica*, **12** (2), April, 114–24; Leonid Hurwicz (1946), 'Theory of the Firm and of Investment', *Econometrica*, **14** (2), April, 109–36; R.M. Goodwin (1951), 'The Nonlinear Accelerator and the Persistence of Business Cycles', *Econometrica*, **19** (1), January, 1–17; P.J. Verdoorn (1951), 'On an Empirical Law Governing the Productivity of Labor', *Econometrica*, **19** (2), April, 209–10; P.J. Verdoorn (1956), 'Complementarity and Long-Range Projections', *Econometrica*, **24** (4), October, 429–50; Michio Morishima (1960), 'Economic Expansion and the Interest Rate in Generalized von Neumann Models', *Econometrica*, **28** (2), April, 352–63; Edmond Malinvaud (1969), 'Capital Accumulation and Efficient Allocation of Resources', in Kenneth J. Arrow and Tibor Scitovsky (eds) *Readings in Welfare Economics*, Volume XII, 645–81.

Elsevier Science Ltd for article: Leif Johansen (1972), 'On the Optimal Use of Forecasts in Economic Policy Decisions', *Journal of Public Economics*, **1** (1), April, 1–24.

International Monetary Fund for article: Paul S. Armington (1969), 'A Theory of Demand for Products Distinguished by Place of Production', *International Monetary Fund Staff Papers*, **XVI** (1), March, 159–76.

The Estate of Michał Kalecki for excerpts: Michał Kalecki (1990), 'A Macro-dynamic Theory of Business Cycles', in Jerzy Osiatyński (ed.), *The Collected Works of Michał Kalecki*, Volume I, Oxford: Clarendon Press, 120–38; Michał Kalecki (1990), 'A Theory of the Business Cycle', in Jerzy Osiatyński (ed.), *The Collected Works of Michał Kalecki*, Volume I, Oxford: Clarendon Press, 529–57.

Macmillan Press Ltd for article: J.M. Keynes (1937), 'The General Theory of Employment', *Quarterly Journal of Economics*, **51** (2), February, 209–23.

MIT Press Journals for articles: Abba P. Lerner (1944), 'Interest Theory – Supply and Demand for Loans or Supply and Demand for Cash', *Review of Economic Statistics*, **26** (2), May, 88–91; R.M. Goodwin (1950), 'A Non-linear Theory of the Cycle', *Review of Economics and Statistics*, **XXXII** (4), November, 316–20; William J. Baumol (1952), 'The Transactions Demand for Cash: An Inventory Theoretic Approach', *Quarterly Journal of Economics*, **66** (4), November, 545–56.

Review of Economic Studies Ltd for articles: Joan Robinson (1933), 'The Theory of Money and the Analysis of Output', *Review of Economic Studies*, **1**, October, 22–6; J.J. Polak (1939), 'International Propagation of Business Cycles', *Review of Economic Studies*, **VI** (2), February, 79–99; Nicholas Kaldor (1941), 'Rationing and the Cost of Living Index', *Review of Economic Studies*, **VIII**, June, 185–7; J.v. Neumann (1945), 'A Model of General Economic Equilibrium', *Review of Economic Studies*, **XIII** (1), 1–9.

Social Research for article: Abba P. Lerner (1943), 'Functional Finance and the Federal Debt', *Social Research*, **10** (1), February, 38–51.

Springer Verlag GmbH & Co. KG for article: R.F. Harrod (1937), 'Studies in the Theory of Economic Expansion', *Zeitschrift fiir Nationalökonomie*, **VIII** (4), August, 494–8.

Every effort has been made to trace all the copyright holders but if any have been inadvertently overlooked the publishers will be pleased to make the necessary arrangement at the first opportunity.

In addition the publishers wish to thank the Library of the London School of Economics and Political Science, the Marshall Library of Economics, Cambridge University, B & N Microfilm, London and the Library of Indiana University at Bloomington, USA for their assistance in obtaining these articles.

Preface

Mark Blaug

The computer revolution of the 1960s ushered in a golden period of econometric model-building, particularly the big econometric model with hundreds or even thousands of equations describing the workings of different sectors and national areas of economic activity and the flows of consumer expenditure, business and government saving, private and public investment, transfer payments, the money supply, exports, imports, capital flows and so on, all of which were estimated simultaneously and used to forecast the performance of the economy. Some believe that the days of such large multi-equation econometric models are over, but there can be little doubt that the experience of large-scale model-building did much to improve the standards of econometric research. Lawrence Klein was constantly in the forefront of this development, being particularly associated with the so-called 'Brookings Econometric Model Project', the largest model of its kind in the 1960s. He was awarded the Nobel Prize in Economics in 1980 for this and other contributions to applied econometrics. Honours of this kind have been showered on him ever since the late 1950s: he was awarded the John Bates Clark Medal of the American Economic Association in 1959 and was President of the Econometric Society in 1960, the Eastern Economic Association in 1974, the American Economic Association in 1977 and the Atlantic Economic Society in 1990. He served as Chairman of the economic task force of Democratic Presidential Candidate Governor Carter.

Klein was born in Omaha, Nebraska in 1920. He received his bachelor's degree from the University of California, Berkeley in 1942 and his PhD from the Massachusetts Institute of Technology in 1944. He became a research associate at the Cowles Commission at the University of Chicago (1944–47), then at the National Bureau of Economic Research in New York (1948–51) and finally at the Survey Research Center of the University of Michigan (1949–54), where he taught from 1950. In 1954 he left the USA in protest against the activities of the McCarthy Committee for a position as Senior Research Officer and later Reader in Econometrics at the Oxford Institute of Statistics. In 1958 he returned to America to take up a professorship at the University of Pennsylvania, where he remained until his retirement from teaching in 1991.

In 1947, he published his first book, *The Keynesian Revolution* (Macmillan, 1947; 2nd ed., 1966), an early study of the process whereby Keynes had moved from the arid formulae of his *Treatise* (1930) to the more promising line of advance in his *General Theory* (1936); this is a subject which was subsequently re-examined with the aid of new evidence from Keynes' *Collected Writings* by Don Patinkin and others without, however, diminishing the impact of Klein's first and greatest book. It was followed a few years later by a major piece of macroeconomic model-building, *Economic Fluctuations in the United States, 1921–1941* (Wiley, 1950), which in turn gave way to a still more ambitious *Econometric Model of the United States, 1929–1952* (Wiley, 1955), co-authored with A.S. Goldberger, followed by a complementary *Econometric Model of the United Kingdom*, with R.J. Ball and others (Basil Blackwell, 1961). *The Brookings Model* (Wiley, 1975), co-edited with G. Fromm, reviews some of the findings of this and other large-scale American econometric models and tests their comparative performance during the preceding ten years. He summed up his lifetime effort at macroeconomic modelling with a recent *History of Macroeconomic Model-Building,* co-authored and co-edited with R.G. Bodkin and K. Marwah (Edward Elgar, 1991).

Klein has long been concerned with improving the teaching of econometrics and his *Textbook of Econometrics* (Row, Peterson, 1962) has continued to hold its own in a field that has recently seen an explosion of competing material; see also his *Lectures in Econometrics* (North Holland, 1983). A subsequent book, *The Economics of Supply and Demand* (Johns Hopkins University Press, 1983), marks a break in his work: it takes a new critical look at the Keynesian ideas that Klein has adhered to all his life and attempts to take account of the new supply-side of economics associated with the Reagan administration, not in the vulgar sense of the Laffer curve but in the sense of industry-specific programmes rather than sole reliance on broad macropolicies. One of his enduring legacies is Project LINK (the international linkage of national economic models), which brings together model builders from both developed and developing countries in the construction and continual refinement of a set of equations across countries to express the linkages between national economies; even now, 30 years after its inception, the LINK Project is still a vital feature of model-building around the world.

Mark Blaug
University of Amsterdam

Introduction

Lawrence R. Klein

The scholarly inquiries into main economic events of the last century – their underlying causes, their indirect policy responses, and the creation of appropriate methods of logical treatment – brought forth stunning advances in our subject. In my search for 'Landmark' papers in this century of expansion of economics as a scholarly discipline, I looked for papers that sparked my interest in the subject as a student in the late 1930s and early 1940s and as a teacher-researcher in the entire second half of the century.

I set some ground rules for my choices. Since the participants in the 'Landmark' selections are Nobel Laureates in Economic Sciences, I did not want to include their works, although some had clearly sparked my interest, coming from teachers, supervisors and esteemed colleagues, but the Laureates have had ample opportunity for discussing their own professional careers (as in successive annual editions of Les Prix Nobel), have been frequently the subject of Festschriften, and have appeared in several other biographical or autobiographical works.

I confined my selections to other economists who, by their papers, had significantly contributed to my own career.

An explanation of my list of 40 'Landmark' contributions follows:

Chapters 1 and 2

Bill Phillips had a remarkable life as a war prisoner, machine builder, and novel thinker about economic dynamics. I first met him when I was in Oxford and had just recently estimated equations relating wage rate change to unemployment. As in Phillips' case, I also looked upon these equations as market-clearing relationships between price (wage-rate of labor) and excess supply (unemployment). His original findings caught on in the economics literature but has become distorted from its original meaning. Phillips' work encouraged me to probe more deeply into the specification and estimation of this relationship.

I had earlier been exposed to Phillips' hydraulic machine but regarded it as too slow and cumbersome to be useful, either in teaching or research, but was intrigued by his drawing on the engineering literature of control systems for insight into policies designed for economic stabilization. Soon after I left Oxford for Pennsylvania, I found myself supervising dissertations that implemented Phillips-type stabilization policies.

Later generations of control engineers have drawn upon developments in computer science to bring Phillips' ideas to finer degrees of sophistication.

Chapters 3 and 4

Michał Kalecki had many admirers, but his insight as an early econometrician and macroeconomic thinker was under appreciated. In the early years of Econometric Society meetings in Europe, his models of business cycles fully anticipated, by independent thinking, the ideas of Keynes for interpreting the problems of the 1930s. If one looks separately at his thinking about the investment-orders relationship, the velocity-interest relationship, and savings-income relationship it is clear that he had all the pieces of a fully integrated Keynesian macro model in place. Among economic analysts this should be clear but, among financiers, politicians, journalists and businessmen, he lacked the convincing arguments that Keynes could put forward.

Kalecki's econometric methodology lacked finesse, but he was right. His sharp intuition ran ahead of his formalism and my advice to readers is to study his contributions to the literature of macroeconomic business-cycle analysis for his early insight into what was needed in order to understand the conditions of the interwar period.

In his work at Oxford on wartime policy, at the UN in postwar reconstruction or recovery, on post World War II growth/development, and even on the theory of income distribution his insight stood out.

Chapter 5

Evsey Domar is often remembered for his contribution to macroeconomic growth theory in models that are independently similar to Harrod's extension of static/domestic Keynesian models.

When, however, the world became disturbed over the build-up of US public debt during the 1980s and the world's debt crisis at the same time in many developing countries, students of the postwar recovery literature in the United States had only to recall Evsey Domar's treatment of the debt burden as a race between interest rates and economic growth rates. The same kinds of elegant formulas interpret the domestic problems for the United States and for such developing countries nations as Argentina, Brazil and Mexico (the ABM) during the so-called 'lost decade' of the 1980s. The reductions of the same identities to relationships between the rate of interest and the rate of economic expansion (GDP or trade volume) showed where the problem areas occurred. Just as Evsey Domar's beautiful formulation of 1944, for the domestic economy, showed up again in the international economy in the 1980s, it is bound to become relevant again in future debt problems, but the next generation of scholars ought not to overlook the lasting truths of Domar's analysis at mid century.

Chapters 6 and 7

Roy Harrod was not only an interpreter of Keynes, he also made important extensions of the Keynesian system of analysis. Keynes propounded a framework for analysis of a depressed economy, but it was a *General Theory* and applicable to other phases of the business cycle. It was up to Harrod, and also Domar (oceans away) to formalize a Keynesian system to include analysis of growth.

Harrod stated that one should 'think dynamically' and built a model from the same kind of reasoning about non-static macroeconomic relationships. In today's scheme of things economists reason a great deal about the economy's growth rate – its warranted and its natural rate of growth – and also its shorter run dynamic fluctuations about the realized growth rate. Harrod and Domar independently worked out the basic macroeconomic relationships for sustained expansion or growth, and this analysis, although extended further, still draws on their breakthrough insights. Harrod, as early as the late 1930s, was able to combine both the multiplier and accelerator principles from a specification of a savings and an investment relationship. He then went on to show policy implications that link monetary policy, influencing the interest rate, with fiscal policy, in the form of public works expenditures that sound very much like today's discussion for economic stabilization. At the policy level, he even had the intuitive foresight to distinguish between effects on the short-term interest rate (the modern monetary *instrument*) and the long-term interest rate, which is more important for capital formation, but which can have a life of its own.

Chapters 8 and 9

It is evident that a Cambridge University group, surrounding Keynes, was jointly participating in developing a theoretical system, partly from 1) general discussions of macroeconomic behavioral analysis, 2) partly from mathematical formulation and, 3) eventually from statistical measurement in the form of national income accounting. Joan Robinson used the first of the three approaches cited above. In early 1933 she published a paper that analyzed saving and investment flows in the macroeconomy, very much in terms of the approach used by Keynes in his *Treatise on Money*, in which the level of aggregate output, in some sense of aggregative national income measurement, was assumed to be given. Then, in the paper published later in the year she looked at saving and investment flows in relation to the determination of aggregate output, which is simply another way of looking at the same national accounting aggregate, namely national income.

While all their concepts are clearly understood at the present time, they posed new and difficult-to-understand ideas in the early 1930s. As I have remarked above, Kalecki also came to the same enlightened conclusions earlier, in the implicit framework of a mathematical system. At the same time, Ragnar Frisch was writing economic-political tracts in Norway in which he was also using the same kind of reasoning, based on what later became the 'paradox of thrift', that is, if the population tries collectively to save more, they are likely to end up saving less. In my listing of 'Landmark' papers, I do not include Frisch's contribution because he, together with Tinbergen, shared the first prize in memory of Nobel. On the occasion of the 100th anniversary of Frisch's death, I had the opportunity of showing his early perception at a memorial seminar meeting in Oslo.

Chapter 10

There were several precursors or contemporaries of Keynes who shared his ideas about reviving the depressed world economy, especially in Europe or North America. None, however, was so important as Richard Kahn. The multiplier concept was a key factor in showing how macroeconomic policy could be used, according to the Keynesian way of looking at things, for economic stabilization at elevated levels of activity, presumably the levels at full employment.

Today, we know much more about the political difficulties of using fiscal policy in democratic society, about military Keynesianism, about the importance of the manner in which fiscal policy is implemented, and about the dynamics of fiscal policy in multi-period implementation. These are important refinements but it was a major step forward to be able to illustrate and demonstrate the workings of fiscal policy, as Richard Kahn in fact spelled out in his celebrated paper. It is important for the subsequent generations of economists to know how these ideas came into being.

Chapter 11

This volume is entirely concerned with papers and not books. While Keynes wrote a 'Landmark' book, that is not a suitable reference under the present circumstances, and it surely would be a serious omission if Keynes were not included in a 'Landmark collection' for the 20th century. His thinking dominated economic discussion of much of the second half of the 20th century.

Many of his close followers are included in this listing (Kahn, Robinson, Harrod, Kaldor, Lange, Lerner and probably others) but, for a purely Keynesian contribution as a paper, I have selected the 1937 article in the *Quarterly Journal of Economics*, for it was here that he acknowledged a point made by Leontief that his system lacked the fundamental mathematical property of homogeneity-in-prices in order to produce a model that permitted equilibrium at less than full employment. I, personally, do not like that interpretation, but it is used a great deal by some of Keynes' outstanding supporters, especially by Don Patinkin, who took the argument into the discussion of general equilibrium systems with money as a variable.

I cite this paper of Keynes, because I think that the argument is very important, but I prefer to work with homogeneous systems that admit a solution with less than full employment because of the non-existence of full employment solutions. It is a system in which the relevant equations do not admit a solution in an appropriate quadrant in the steady state solution.

In this paper the editors of the *Quarterly Journal of Economics* had Keynes responding to critics of his newly published *General Theory*. In addition to Leontief cited above, the critics were Taussig, Robertson and Viner. Keynes addressed each piece of criticism individually but went on to summarize the essential points of his entire book in a compact scholarly article. He analyzed the propensity to consume, interest sensitivity of investment and the liquidity preference theory of interest. He then produced what I, as an econometrician would call a neat and crucial (verbal) reduced-form expression for output as a whole in the form of a function of those individual building blocks of his whole system, including a very good explanation of the role of expectations. For a publication in early 1937, this was an insightful exposition.

Chapters 12 and 13

Dynamic macroeconomic models are usually specified as linear systems. In econometrics, linearity is assumed both in the space of parameters and the space of variables. When economists first studied dynamic models, it made sense to start with linear systems. They admit of complete solutions with explicit properties that can be related to familiar economic concepts and are comparatively easy to express in closed mathematical form. Richard Goodwin was a pioneer in introducing non-linear models into dynamic macroeconomics. For some interesting non-linear systems it is possible to find solutions in closed mathematical form. Such systems have rich properties beyond those found in linear systems. In particular, they depend, for some properties, on initial conditions and are capable of generating maintained oscillations ('the business cycle') without necessarily dying out, especially under stochastic perturbation.

At the empirical statistical level, the advances in computation have made non-linearities much more tractable, and there is no compelling reason to assume linearity, especially in places where such an assumption is not plausible.

Richard Goodwin's research papers are truly pioneering in this respect, but there are other researchers who have subsequently dealt effectively with non-linearity.

Chapter 14

Slutzky's paper on the summation of random shocks (to an economic system) is truly remarkable and serves as a fundamental contribution to the theory of maintained oscillation. Slutzky showed how successive moving averages of random number sequences are capable of generating curves with trigonometric cycles. This is fundamental, because the solution to dynamic equation systems of econometrics can be shown to have a component that does indeed perform moving average operations on random disturbances to equations of interrelated economic behavior.

Other statisticians have independently come to the same conclusions (Yule, Moran, Frisch and others), but Slutzky opened our eyes to such possibilities at an early stage and in such a way as to fit well with the specification of stochastic dynamic equation systems of economics. It is possible, and of utmost importance, to go beyond tractable linear econometric systems. Conditions for maintained cycles can be explained more easily with Slutzky's than with any other specifications.

Chapter 15

After Abraham Wald, Kenneth Arrow, Gerard Debreu and others, showed how general equilibrium theory went far beyond the mere counting of equations and variables to show why solutions exist for economic systems of equations to determine prices and quantities throughout the whole economy, it was left to mathematical economists such as John von Neumann, Edmond Malinvaud and others to show how such solutions move through time. John von Neumann made his contribution at a very early stage and then went on to tackle other problems, many of which were far removed from economic systems.

Malinvaud extended general equilibrium theory to a state with productive capital accumulation, using direct and indirect processes of production on the supply side. He related supply to future consumption on the demand side, observing requirements for efficient production and consumer welfare. In his dynamic system he introduced the interest rate to discount the future. These results are theoretical, but they lay groundwork for realizing dynamic equilibrium in realistic expansionary movement of an economy.

Chapter 16

Leif Johansen had one of the best minds in economics during the second half of the 20th century, when his contributions were unfortunately cut short by his death in 1982. He left his mark on many subjects, but one of his best papers was to put economic policy decisions in a generalized framework. It is not surprising that he treated decision making for policy in the manner of Tinbergen, clearly distinguishing between instrument and target. Many contemporary policy analyses treat these two distinct aspects in a loose and confusing way, forgetting where the power of control lies. In this paper, Johansen provides guidelines for decision making for cases of equality between instruments and targets and also cases where one exceeds or falls short of the other. An important feature of his analysis is to introduce present uncertainty into the process because the instruments are not fixed with precision, and the hitting of targets is certainly subject to error. Johansen provides a calculus to deal with present uncertainty.

Chapter 17

When control theorists argued for their technique for stabilizing engineering systems, they did not allow fully for uncertainty – in the measurement of economic magnitudes, in the ability to control economic instruments, or in the ability to attain target values. In short, they did not view the macroeconomic system as stochastic and thought, in many cases, that it would be straightforward to control the economy, even with great precision. William Brainard showed how various forms of uncertainty effect the manner and degree of attempts at economic control. In some configurations of sources of uncertainty, he showed that policy makers should put forward their economic prescriptions modestly when the uncertainty factors are very strong. This idea seems to be quite evident, but had not been properly recognized in the discussions of use of control theory methods for economic policy formation.

Chapters 18 and 19

The scholars who designed econometric inference in macrodynamic models, following Jan Tinbergen, immediately chose to specify equation systems as linear multivariate relationships in finite difference form; this was a close analogue to linear differential equation systems that were well known in mathematical and scientific circles. Abraham Wald and Henry Mann generalized the econometric treatment together with Haavelmo's breakthrough discoveries about the properties of simultaneous equations in econometrics. Leonid Hurwicz showed the importance of retaining the stochastic specification in place and accounting for its transformation when reducing a system of dynamic relations to some derived form, either a fully or semi-reduced form. The stochastic properties may be altered in the derived form. This becomes even more significant if there are important non-linearities in the original specification.

At the stage of building empirical models for econometric analysis of economic systems it is important to make a careful specification of the underlying theoretical model and show how it is related to the model that is being empirically estimated and tested. Hurwicz showed how investment behavior, based on the economic theory of the firm, forms the appropriate underlying theory for empirical studies of investment activity.

Chapter 20

Vienna and Budapest were fertile grounds for the development of mathematical economics, and John von Neumann was outstanding in bringing fresh views of a mathematical physicist into the development of general equilibrium theory. He used the mathematics of fixed-point theorems to show the existence of general equilibrium with efficient economic production.

Among approaches to the formulation and solution, in the sense of existence, of the general equilibrium system, von Neumann's article is path-breaking in that it is a dynamic system that grows, but has two unusual features, namely, that growth is balanced among all producing sectors and that little attention is paid to the demand side of the economy except to impose the unrealistic condition that workers do not save (they spend all their income) and employers do not spend on consumer goods (they save all their income). He obtained an elegant relationship by showing that the balanced growth rate equals the real interest rate. Later theorists have generalized von Neumann's results, but it was a remarkable step forward at an early stage of 20th century thinking, and had to be discovered and put in reprinted form for a wider audience.

Chapter 21

The Cowles Commission approach to econometrics was shaped by a team effort, which began from different original contributions by Haavelmo, Koopmans, Mann/Wald, Hurwicz, Anderson, Rubin and others. The whole activity, lasting over several years, was orchestrated at the beginning by Jacob Marschak (not the beginning of Cowles Commission activity, but the beginning of their distinctive approach to model building for forecasting, policy analysis and theory testing).

Marschak explains the objective: to use a scientific, scholarly approach to formulate and estimate the structure of a national economy all the way from microeconomic behavior to macroeconomic performance. Such systems were dynamic and stochastic. He aimed to use such estimated structural models to devise policies that could guide the national economy, and some major parts of it, towards postwar (World War II) recovery and expansionary development. The ultimate goal was the *Path* of expansion extrapolated from the *Path* of history; the estimated model was used for *Prediction*; and the choice of *Policy* was to be based on consideration of alternative *Predictions* that used different *Policy* assumptions.

The first application of this reasoning was aimed for prediction and policy for re-conversion after the end of World War II, made for the Committee for Economic Development and for Alfred Cowles who had civic financial responsibilities.

Chapters 22 and 23

In a semi-reduced form, the simplest Keynesian model, combining the multiplier and accelerator relationships can be shown, in the linear case, to have two kinds of plausible dynamic solutions: indefinite expansion, or damped trigonometric oscillation. Since it is generally believed that business cycles have non-damped oscillatory behavior, there has been a search for models that can produce limit cycles, that is, un-damped periodic fluctuations. One way of obtaining this result is to introduce random disturbances in linear, damped systems of oscillation. The disturbances are capable of keeping the cycle alive, as Slutzky and others have shown. One alternative approach has been followed by Kaldor, and, as indicated in another contribution to this collection of 'Landmark' papers, in articles by Richard Goodwin. Kaldor, in 1940, introduced other types of nonlinearity that are capable of producing limit cycles. His technique was graphical, but I, with student collaboration, have estimated empirical functions of Kaldor's types, and they can produce limit cycles. In the strictly linear case, there are some models that have limit cycles as special cases, but these do not have finite variance of oscillation. A model of Kaldor's type, if disturbed in a probability sense, can be shown to have stable variance. His paper is extremely profound and important for business cycle analysis.

During World War II, some British economists argued that rationing was not properly taken into account for calculating the economists' concept of the cost of living. It is essentially due to the fact that standard index number practices do not adjust for the quality deterioration that accompanies rationing. In fact, Kaldor's discussion of this issue inspired me to estimate formulas for calculating a 'true' cost of living index, and, out of that research effort, I, with Herman Rubin, found that the linear expenditure system lent itself readily to such index construction.

Chapter 24

The Hickman-Coen growth model (with the collaboration of Michael Hurd) went beyond the usual range of considerations that characterized models to study effective demand, in the spirit of Keynes' *General Theory*. Such models explained the national expenditure, as the sum of types of expenditure and some assorted equations for money demand (liquidity preference) and wage determination (Phillips curve). Hickman, Coen and Hurd went further and devoted much attention to the supply side of the macroeconomy, by introducing consistent factor demand equations and an aggregate production function. They also allowed for an open economy and some longer run growth effects.

Although this basic paper was published in 1975, Hickman and Coen have maintained this model, updated the data base, added new features and are still using it to analyze macroeconomic problems in the 21st century.

Chapter 25

Knut Wicksell introduced an interesting distinction between an actual rate of interest and the natural rate, the latter being the rate that equalizes the demand for loan capital with the supply of savings. The distinction between the two concepts, one directly observable (actual rate) and the other being implicitly indirect and not plainly observable, is much like the modern distinction between the observed and natural rates of unemployment. The latter concept is also not directly measurable. In fact, poor estimates of the natural rate of unemployment have seriously called into question some central bankers' devices for monetary policy. Wicksell argued that discrepancy between the actual and natural rates of interest would cause prices, money balances and velocity of circulation to change. When the actual rate is high relative to the natural rate, the price level would tend to fall. These are interesting ideas that merit more careful econometric testing, in the context of a comprehensive macro model. In this early Landmark paper, Wicksell used the term *normal level* instead of natural rate.

Chapters 26 and 27

One of the first great American economists, probably even the first, was Irving Fisher, who made many contributions to our discipline. While he is mostly referenced now for his work on index numbers (the Fisher 'ideal' index) he was prominent at an early stage with views on the theory and application of interest rate concepts, inflation and business cycles.

The quantity theory of money displayed in the equation of exchange was an early triumph. As Fisher laid out this equation, it is little more than an identity – a truism – but to formulate interesting identities in economics, a great deal of understanding and economic intuition is required. Fisher's truism was

$$MV + M1\,V1 = PT$$

M = currency in circulation *at* an *instant* of time
V = velocity or turnover of M, *during* a *period* of time
M1 = checkable deposits *at* an *instant* of time
V1 = velocity or turnover of M1 *during* a *period* of time
P = price index
T = volume of economic activity (trade)

In discussing statistical measurement of each of the five determinants of P, Fisher noted the very small range of variation (1896–1910) of V and the moderate, but not tiny, variation of V1. Had he been led into the technological revolution of banking/finance after 1980 he would have seen the great drift and volatility of these velocity concepts, which make the equations of exchange a not-very-helpful identity now. But it did convey economic sense to Fisher in the early part of the 20th century, particularly when agricultural and other seasonal influences dominated much of the economic statistics of the times. Fisher's excursion into measurement and careful definition of major economic magnitudes was basic for first steps.

Irving Fisher sought stabilization of prices, that is containment or elimination of inflation, as a means for conquering the business cycles. His views of the 1920s, in many respects, are like those of monetary policy makers now (early 21st century) who regard their main, or only, objective to be to hold down inflation so that the price level is virtually stabilized. Although this is a one-sided approach to general stabilization, it is argued by monetary specialists that control of inflation leads to control over the macroeconomic growth rate. Price stability is practically an end for them. In Fisher's case, stabilization of the price level leads not only to good performance in the real economy, but also to exchange rate stability.

Chapter 28

J.J. Polak, who worked with Tinbergen at the League of Nations, took an interesting step forward in fashioning the first international macro models. His database was miniscule in comparison with figures on many detailed items in economic-social accounts of more than a hundred countries that are routinely available today. Polak had to work with data for only eight major countries. Although the international linkage was known to exist and to be instrumental in understanding the economic movements of the world economy there were few, if any, systematic bilateral compilations, as we know them at annual, quarterly, or even monthly frequencies now.

Inspired by the formal modeling of individual national economies (US, UK, Netherlands and others), Polak devised a credible, but rudimentary, world model prior to World War II. After the War, after Bretton Woods and the formation of multinational institutions such as IMF, World Bank, United Nations and others, Polak put together a more detailed and more comprehensive system. He formulated an empirical world model, with international linkage displayed in some scores or hundreds of equations, and it was essentially the inspirational source for world models that are routinely used today, consisting of thousands of relationships at the bilateral level of linkage.

Chapter 29

In the design of large multilateral equation systems for the empirical depiction of international linkages there must necessarily be equation specifications that allow for major accounting identities (such as, world exports = world imports, or the world current account balance is truly zero, or countries' import prices depend on partner countries' export prices) and also adhere to an economical parameterization. Paul Armington was an early exponent of the use of world trade matrices, by some broad commodity groupings, the ability to form subgroup totals for countries that worked especially well together, and enable empirical researchers to establish cross relationships among commodity groups as well as geographical groups and yet be very sparing of use of 'degrees-of-freedom'. He accomplished this feat by devising elegant relationships within parametric families, one of which was coming into prominence, known as constant-elasticity-of-substitution (CES) equations for trade relationships. At a later stage, following Armington's ideas, Lawrence Lau and Bert Hickman of Stanford were able to formulate export and import equations that were specified so as to insure that main accounting identities were automatically satisfied. In many respects, the CES specification is a generalization of the more limited linear expenditure systems (LES).

Chapters 30 and 31

Productivity growth, especially for the medium term to long run (that is, within decades and between decades) has been challenging for quantitative economists to estimate productivity prospects. P. Verdoorn studied long term productivity trends and formulated novel relationships. A basic finding was that productivity showed close long-run relationship with cumulative production, as distinct from current production. His ideas have proved to be important for the approach based on 'learning by doing'. In his paper he found close correlation between current output and the history of (integral of) output. His papers formed the basis of discussions at contemporary meetings of the Econometric Society in Europe.

Chapter 32

No sooner had Keynes published the *General Theory*, with an exposition of one of the main pillars, the propensity to consume, in simple aggregative terms – aggregate consumer spending and aggregate spendable income – than critics noted the absence of an explicit role for income distribution. One of the first of these critical papers was that by Pieter de Wolff. It was, however, constructive criticism and very perceptive about a wider problem, namely that of aggregation, to bridge the gap between microeconomic foundations and macroeconomics; for that is what distribution theory is all about.

Pieter de Wolff was not the first person to sense the implication of the aggregation problem, but his exposition was clear, concise and gave explicit treatment to the role of distribution functions. He looked at a micro function, such as an Engel Curve in a family budget sample and integrated that relation over the range of the distribution of income. He explained the outcome in terms of the parametric structure of the distribution function. In the strictly linear case, this can be straightforward in passing from micro to macro, but Engel Curve specifications are rarely strictly linear. He also indicated the complications when the distribution function depends on two or more parameters.

There is another twist to the contribution of de Wolff, namely that Paul Samuelson, in a search for the first person to use the term *macroeconomics* – a standard subheading for the teaching of elementary economic principles – was led by Hendrik Houthakker to de Wolff's paper, but the title of the 1941 article wrote the expressions as Micro-Economic and Macro-Economic, using hyphens. Samuelson attributed the use of Macroeconomics to me in an article published in 1946, but I believe that a search of the critical literature in the *General Theory* will reveal the use of Macroeconomics earlier than 1946.

Chapter 33

Economists have observed income (size) distributions for many different countries, different time periods, different stages of economic development and have been able to provide a good picture of typical distributions to fit time and place, but David Champernowne has gone a step further and studied why a typical income distribution is found – skewed, with a long tail at the high end of the income range. Champernowne described a stochastic process about how people and money incomes move about and showed how a given popular family of distribution functions could be generated by the process. He showed why we accept, in many cases, the Pareto distribution as a typical income distribution for a national community.

Subsequently, researchers have devised alternative standard processes that can generate Pareto distributions or other distributions such as the lognormal distribution or even the 5-parameter Champernowne distribution. The particular article selected in this 'Landmark collection' has been the source of many fruitful investigations of income (or wealth) distributions and provides a better analytical basis for choosing one or another parametric representation.

Chapter 34

William Baumol was able to draw some conclusions about average behavior with respect to the holding of cash balances for transaction purposes, apart from speculative or precautionary purposes. He developed results from analogies to those found in business behavior for inventory holding of stocks of goods. In the simplest case he assumed a steady spending stream, matched by corresponding withdrawals of cash at regularly spaced intervals. For these extreme assumptions, he showed that the rational individual, given the price level, will demand cash in proportion to the square root of the value of transactions.

This result from inventory theory is generalized to take account of inventory funds that are not used and finds that the sums remaining will vary at a compromise rate, between the square root of transactions and another term that changes by less than the transaction level.

He made interesting comparisons with Irving Fisher, Wicksell and Edgeworth. The latter two suggested that banks' precautionary holdings of cash grow in line with the square root of transactions, in line with Baumol's more formal derivation.

Chapter 35

Within a few years after the publication of Keynes' *General Theory*, there were several attempts to formulate mathematical models of the macroeconomic system that was implied by the literary exposition of Keynes. In fact, as I indicated in connection with Kalecki's anticipatory work, it was already being done, prior to formal publication. Among the various mathematical formulations, Oskar Lange's is the most attractive, rivaled only by J.R. Hicks' independent effort. Hicks' model is not listed here, since he was a very early Nobel Laureate in economics.

Oskar Lange set out macroeconomic behavioral relations to display the interrelationship among the three Keynesian pillars – the consumption function (propensity to consume), the investment function (propensity to invest), and the demand for money (liquidity preference function). He suggested that either money supply or the interest rate could be chosen as the exogenous instrument of the central bank. At the present time, central bankers aim closely at the very short-term interest rate as their exogenous target, but their main instrument is the reserve position of private banks, which is very close to a money supply concept.

To me, Lange's 'Landmark paper' is mainly interesting as a first step in model specification, a very big first step indeed, especially in the 1930s. It is not nearly so interesting in terms of the title words 'Optimum Propensity to Consume'.

Chapters 36 and 37

Abba Lerner played an important role in interpreting Keynes' macroeconomic thinking in the *General Theory*, in ways that tried to clarify issues that were puzzling to many economists. In Lerner's treatment of Functional Finance, he focused attention on maintaining a favorable level of output and employment, and argued against being concerned about the burden of the national debt associated with fiscal policy for high-level employment. He argued that a *domestically* held debt is not a burden but does raise some distributional issues. Foreign held debt is a different matter. Fiscal policy should be financed on a functional basis for economic performance, regardless of domestic debt. As long as debt is domestically held, it does not impoverish a nation and should not stand in the way of choice of an appropriate fiscal policy.

The discussion surrounding Keynes' treatment of money holding, interest rate determination and the conduct of monetary policy for economic stabilization was confusing to many economists. Lerner argued that the confusion between acceptance of a loanable-funds theory of interest rate determination and a liquidity-preference theory stemmed from a failure to distinguish between partial and general equilibrium and also a failure to distinguish between an analysis of stocks versus one dealing with flows. He pointed out that simple equating of supply and demand for flows, as in the loanable-funds theory to determine the interest rate failed to consider at least as many as three or four variables in a market for stocks rather than flows.

Central banks have eventually (now, 2001) come round to Lerner's position. They set targets for their main interest rate variable, at very short term, and engage in market operations on banks' reserve positions (in terms of stocks) in order to realize their target values, knowing full well that other variables of the type that Lerner was concerned with, may not achieve the full macroeconomic results that they are (or should be) targeting at the same time that they are targeting a short-term interest rate.

Chapter 38

The historical accounts of the development of econometrics in the 20th century pay all too little attention to the extreme importance of Paul Douglas's contributions on the supply side. More attention is devoted to the early estimates of demand functions, but for understanding growth, technical change and inflation control over the trade cycle, analysis of the conditions of production are of the utmost importance. Paul Douglas spent more than two decades examining production and factor input statistics for many countries, industries, time periods, and cross-sections. In his Presidential address to the American Economic Association he stressed common findings in many investigations. On his work, countless econometricians have built or extended studies of productivity growth, capacity utilization and 'the laws of production'. Many of the deep problems of econometrics surfaced in this field, starting with Douglas's own work and those of his collaborator, Charles Cobb. These encompass identification, degree of returns to scale, factor demand, multi collinearity and, most recently, *sustainable* development.

Chapter 39

Anthony Atkinson devoted much of his scholarly research and teaching to problems of inequality, particularly from the standpoint of functional (factorial) and size distribution of income. He contributed significantly to the technical issues of measurement, but in his Presidential address to the Royal Economic Society he summed up the situation with respect to inequality at the end of the 20th century, noting that the subject had been marginalized for many years since the beginning of the century but was now getting some fresh recognition, especially since his own country exhibited a marked increase in inequality during the closing decade.

His analysis covers dispersion and inequality in earnings, returns from capital and transfers. He does not claim to have final conclusions about reasons for trends and episodes of inequality, but he does lay out the subject in an appealing way and lets the reader know that it will be necessary to take political and other variables that are not strictly economic into account in order to gain a full understanding of the role of transfers.

Chapter 40

There has always been a degree of unease about the properties that von Neumann found in his model of general equilibrium growth, with all sectors expanding at fixed proportions. The expansion rate for the economy turns out to be the real interest rate. Michio Morishima lists the following assumptions imposed by von Neumann: constant returns to scale, abundant labor availability, wages totally consumed and capitalist income wholly reinvested each period. Morishima relaxes the last three assumptions and has more plausible conditions. The working population grows at a finite rate; workers' propensity to consume is less than unity (and also depends on prices); capitalists consume a fraction of their income (and also respond to price changes). Morishima finds, for a positive interest rate, that the output of each sector expands at a rate, which is the product of the interest rate and the capitalists' average propensity to save.

Morishima goes on to relate his findings to those of Marx, Walras, Kaldor and Harrod. He, thus, neatly pulls together many loose threads in the balanced growth literature.

[1]

STABILISATION POLICY AND THE TIME-FORMS OF LAGGED RESPONSES[1]

IN an earlier article[2] I used a number of dynamic process models to illustrate the operation of certain types of stabilisation policy. In setting up the models I assumed that each lagged response was of the particular time-form known as an exponential lag. I pointed out[3] that other time-forms would probably give better representations of the real responses in an economic system, but did not introduce these more realistic lag forms into the models owing to the difficulty of solving the high-order differential equations to which they would have led.

Since then the National Physical Laboratory and Short Brothers and Harland, Ltd., have allowed me to use their electronic simulators, by means of which the time responses of quite complex systems with a variety of lag forms can be found very rapidly.[4] In addition, I have become more familiar with the frequency-response method of analysis based on the Nyquist stability criterion. This is a graphical method which not only enables considerable information to be obtained about the dynamic properties of a system without solving the differential equation of the system, but also gives valuable insight into the ways in which the dynamic properties would be altered if the relationships and lag forms in the system were modified or additional relationships included.[5]

A study, using frequency-response analysis and electronic simulators, of the properties of models in which the lags are given more realistic time-forms has shown that the problem of stabilisation is more complex than appeared to be the case when attention was confined to the simpler lag forms used in

[1] I wish the thank Professor R. G. D. Allen, Professor J. E. Meade, Professor Lionel Robbins and Mr. R. H. Tizard for helpful comments on an earlier draft of this paper.

[2] " Stabilisation Policy in a Closed Economy," ECONOMIC JOURNAL, June 1954, pp. 290–323.

[3] *Ibid.*, p. 292.

[4] I am indebted to the Director of the National Physical Laboratory and to Short Brothers and Harland, Ltd., for permission to use the simulators. At the National Physical Laboratory, where most of the work was carried out, Mr. D. V. Blake operated the simulator and gave invaluable help and advice. I benefited greatly from discussions with him and am most grateful to him for his willing co-operation. I also wish to thank Mr. E. Lloyd Thomas, Mr. R. J. A. Paul and Mr. P. A. R. Wright of Short Brothers and Harland, Ltd., for their assistance. The possibility of using electronic simulators for studying problems of economic regulation was suggested to me by Mr. R. H. Tizard.

[5] There is an extensive literature on the use of frequency-response methods in the analysis and synthesis of engineering systems. See, for example, H. M. James, N. B. Nichols and R. S. Phillips, *Theory of Servomechanisms* (New York: McGraw-Hill Book Co., 1947) and G. S. Brown and D. P. Cambell, *Principles of Servomechanisms* (New York: John Wiley and Sons, 1948). For a brief description of the methods with some applications to economic problems see A. Tustin, *The Mechanism of Economic Systems* (London: William Heinemann, Ltd., 1954), especially Chapter III. See also R. G. D. Allen, " The Engineers' Approach to Economic Models," *Economica*, May 1955, and R. G. D. Allen, *Mathematical Economics* (London: Macmillan and Co. Ltd., 1956), Chapters 8 and 9.

my earlier article. In this study a number of alternative models were first analysed by the frequency-response method, and the effects of variations in the lag forms and the values of the parameters on the stability of the models were investigated. Some of the models were then set up on the electronic simulators, disturbances were applied and the resulting time paths of the variables were found. In the present article two of the models which were studied are described and their dynamic properties illustrated by recordings from the electronic simulators.

I. A Multiplier Model with Error Correction

The first model is shown diagrammatically in Fig. 1, which is similar to Fig. 10 of my earlier article [1] except that the accelerator relationship has

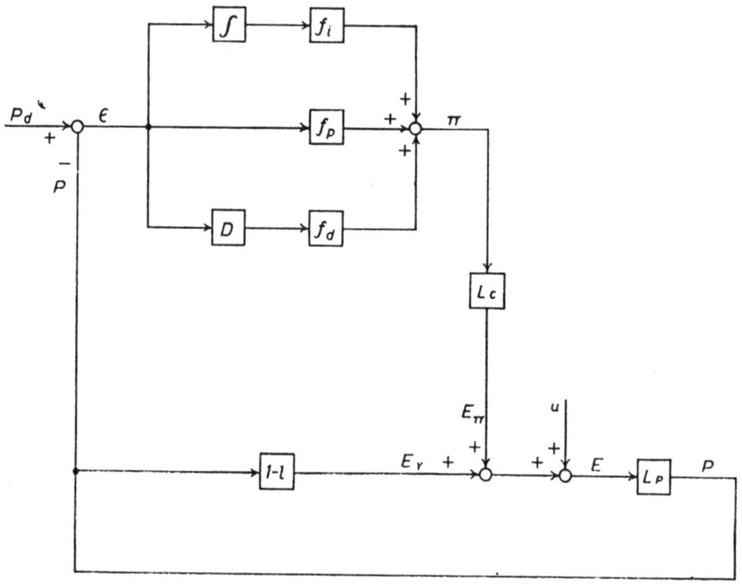

Fig. 1

been omitted. The lines in the diagram represent the variables of the system, measured as deviations from initial equilibrium values. Relationships between variables are indicated by the symbols in the squares, the arrows showing the causal direction of the relationships. The lower closed loop in the diagram represents a simple multiplier model. It is assumed that aggregate real income or production, P, responds to changes in aggregate real demand, E, through the lag relationship L_P. Changes in aggregate demand are analysed into three components, E_Y, E_π and u. E_Y denotes those changes in demand which are related to changes in income through the

[1] *Op. cit.*, p. 306.

marginal propensity to spend $1-l$. We shall give l, the " marginal leakage " from the circular flow of income, the value 0·25, so that the multiplier is 4·0. E_π is the policy demand, *i.e.*, it is the amount by which aggregate demand is increased or decreased as a direct result of action taken by the regulating authorities for the purpose of stabilising the system. All changes in aggregate demand caused by changes in factors other than income and stabilisation policy are included in the variable u.

The relationships shown at the top of the diagram represent an error-correction type of stabilisation policy. The actual level of production is subtracted from the desired level of production, P_d, giving the error in production,[1] ϵ. It is assumed that the regulating authorities are able to make continuous adjustments in the strength of the correcting action they take but that there is a distributed time lag, L_c, between changes in the strength of the correcting action and the resulting changes in policy demand. The amount by which policy demand would be changed as a direct result of the policy measures if they operated without time lag will be called the potential policy demand, π, the amount by which it is in fact changed as a direct result of policy measures is the actual policy demand E_π.

The basic problem in stabilising production is to relate the actual policy demand to the error in production in such a way that errors caused by unpredicted disturbances are corrected as quickly and smoothly as possible.[2] For a given correction lag the problem reduces to that of finding the most suitable way of relating the potential policy demand to the error in production. In my earlier article [3] I argued that to obtain satisfactory regulation of a system it is usually necessary for the potential policy demand to be made the sum of three components, one component depending on the error itself, one depending on the time integral of the error and the third depending on the time derivative (or rate of change) of the error. That is, the relationship should be of the form $\pi = f_p\epsilon + f_i\int\epsilon dt + f_d\frac{d\epsilon}{dt}$, where f_p, f_i and f_d are parameters which I called respectively the proportional, integral and derivative correction factors. This relationship is represented by the three loops at the top of Fig. 1, the symbol $\int$ indicating integration with respect to time and D indicating differentiation with respect to time.

We shall consider three different forms of the production lag L_P. These are illustrated by curves (*a*), (*b*) and (*c*) of Fig. 2, which show hypothetical time paths of the response of production to a unit step fall in demand occurring at time $t = 0$. With lag form (*a*) the rate of change of production at any

[1] The error is here defined to be P_d-P rather than $P-P_d$ as in my earlier article. In the literature on regulating systems the error in a variable is usually defined as the desired value minus the actual value.

[2] If reliable and frequent measurements of aggregate demand were available the potential policy demand could also be related to the error in demand. This would permit a more rapid correction of errors in production caused by shifts in aggregate demand.

[3] *Op. cit.*, pp. 293–303.

time is proportional to the difference between demand and production at that time. We call this an exponential lag and define the time constant of the lag as the reciprocal of the factor of proportionality; for the response shown in curve (*a*) the time constant is 0·25 year. The exponential lag form is very convenient for mathematical treatment, but it implies a more rapid response in the early stages of an adjustment than is likely to be typical of economic behaviour. The time path of adjustment shown in curve (*b*) of Fig. 2 is probably more realistic. This time path is obtained if the lag is

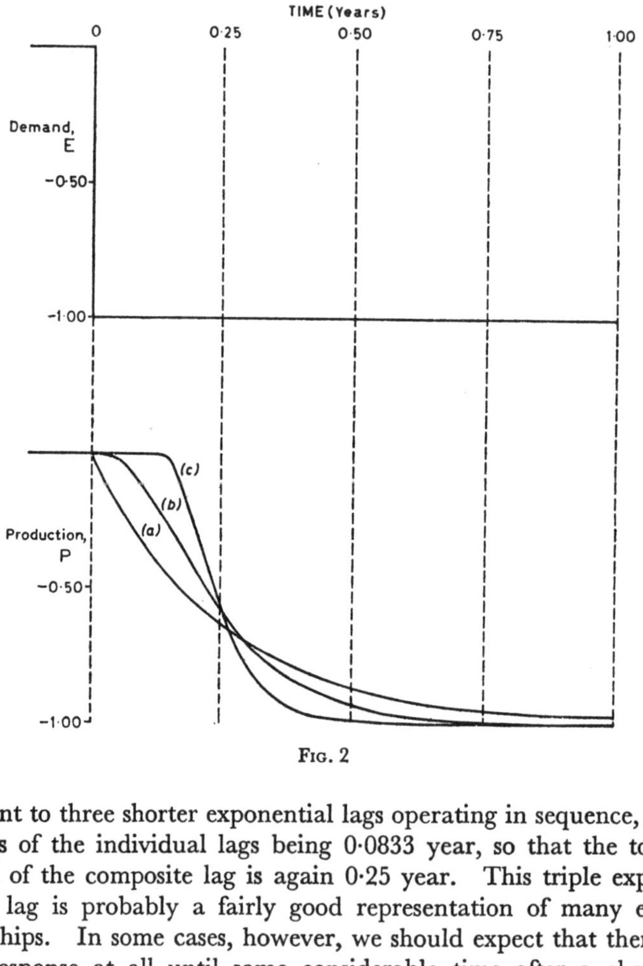

FIG. 2

equivalent to three shorter exponential lags operating in sequence, the time constants of the individual lags being 0·0833 year, so that the total time constant of the composite lag is again 0·25 year. This triple exponential form of lag is probably a fairly good representation of many economic relationships. In some cases, however, we should expect that there would be no response at all until some considerable time after a change had occurred, the time path of the adjustment being somewhat like that shown in curve (*c*) of Fig. 2. We shall call an interval during which there is no response at all a time delay, to distinguish it from the exponential type of lag in which a continuous gradual adjustment takes place. The adjustment path in curve (*c*) results from a lag which is equivalent to a sequence consisting of a time delay of 0·125 year and three exponential lags each with a time constant of 0·0417 year, the total time constant of the composite lag again being 0·25 year.

The time forms which we shall use for the correction lag will be similar to those shown in Fig. 2, except that the time scale will be doubled. Thus lag form (*a*) for the correction lag will be a single exponential lag with a time

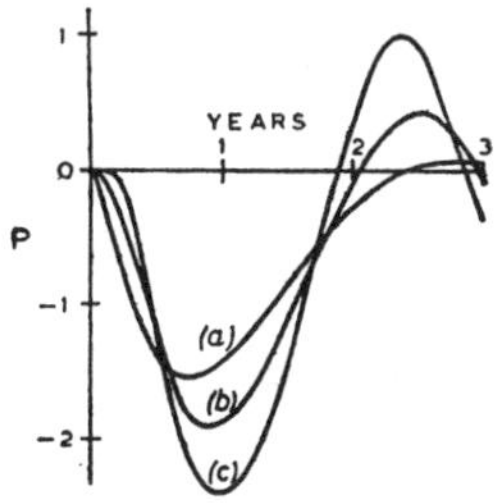

FIG. 3

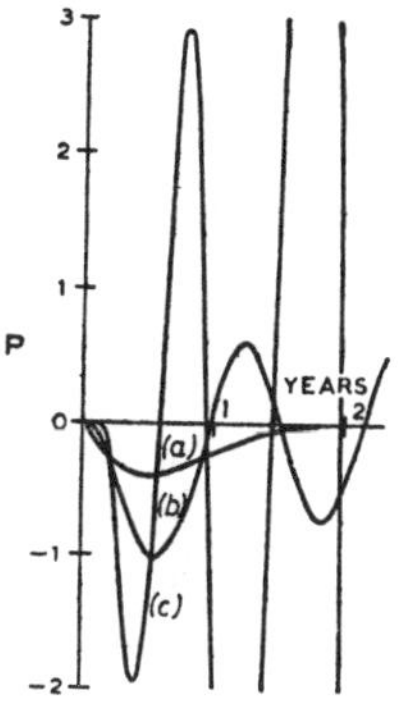

FIG. 4

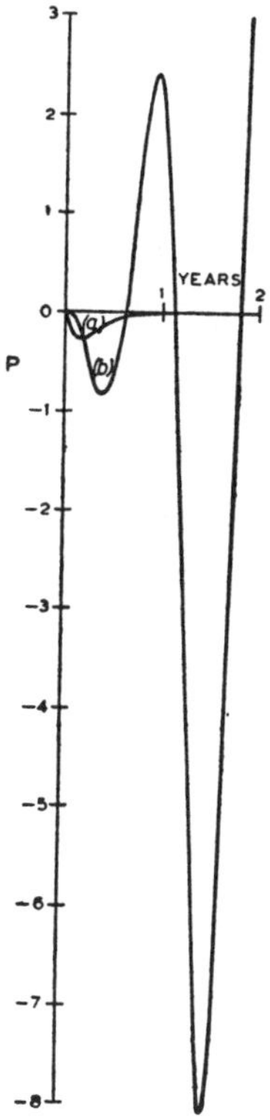

FIG. 5

constant of 0·50 year, lag form (*b*) will be a sequence of three exponential lags, each with a time constant of 0·167 year, and lag form (*c*) will be a sequence consisting of a time delay of 0·25 year and three exponential lags, each with a time constant of 0·0833 year.

Figs. 3, 4 and 5 reproduce recordings from the electronic simulators showing the response of production to a unit step change in the variable u applied negatively at time $t = 0$, for different combinations of correction factors and lag forms. The responses shown in Fig. 3 are obtained when the proportional correction factor f_p is 0·5, the integral correction factor f_i is

0·5 and the derivative correction factor f_d is zero. When both the production and the correction lags are of form (*a*) the response is that shown in curve (*a*).[1] When the lags are changed to form (*b*), the rest of the system remaining the same, the response is that shown in curve (*b*). When the lags are of form (*c*) the response shown in curve (*c*) is obtained. In the case now being considered, with proportional and integral correction factors of 0·5, the " overshoot " which occurs in the response when the lags are of form (*b*) or (*c*) can be eliminated by introducing a small amount of derivative correction. When the lags are of form (*b*) the overshoot is eliminated if the derivative correction factor is raised from zero to about 0·06; when they are of form (*c*) a derivative correction factor of about 0·09 is required to prevent overshoot in the response.

Curves (*a*), (*b*) and (*c*) of Fig. 4 show the responses obtained with lag forms (*a*), (*b*) and (*c*) respectively when both the proportional and the integral correction factors are 2·0 and the derivative correction factor is 0·5. With the higher values of the proportional and integral correction factors the system has become less stable, and even when the lags are of form (*a*) some derivative correction is needed to prevent an oscillatory response. When the lags are of form (*b*) the system is on the verge of instability. Nor can the response be improved by adjustment of the derivative correction factor. Any appreciable increase or decrease in its value makes the system completely unstable. When the corrective action has some effect fairly quickly, as is the case when the lags are of form (*a*), the use of derivative correction is a powerful method of reducing or eliminating fluctuations. But when the corrective action does not have much effect until some considerable time after it is applied, as is the case when the lags are of form (*b*) and still more when they are of form (*c*), derivative correction is less effective in reducing oscillations, and indeed if used excessively it will introduce an additional cycle of high frequency. When the proportional and integral correction factors are 2·0 and the lags are of form (*c*) the system is unstable for all values of the derivative correction factor.

Curve (*a*) of Fig. 5 shows the response when both the proportional and integral correction factors are raised to 8·0 and the derivative correction factor is 1·0, the lags being of form (*a*).[2] With lags of form (*b*) the response becomes that shown in curve (*b*). With lags of form (*c*) the system is so violently unstable that it proved impossible to obtain a satisfactory recording of the response given by the electronic simulator. Adjustment of the derivative correction factor again fails to stabilise the system in this case when the lags are of form (*b*) or (*c*).

Figs. 3, 4 and 5 show that a comparatively small change in the time-

[1] This response was obtained mathematically in my earlier article and was shown as curve (*b*) o Fig. 7, p. 300.

[2] This response was also obtained mathematically in my earlier article and was shown as curve (*e*) of Fig. 7.

forms of the lags may have a great effect on the stability of a closed-loop control system, especially if the values of the correction factors are high. It is in fact only in the simplest systems in which there are not more than two lags, each of single exponential form, that it is possible to give any value, no matter how large, to one correction factor and then to find values for the other correction factors such that the system is stable and non-oscillatory. Any system in which there is time delay or a sequence of more than two lags of single exponential form, or in which any lag is equivalent to a sequence which includes a time delay or more than two single exponential lags, as is the case with lags of form (*b*) or (*c*), will be stable and non-oscillatory only if the values of the correction factors are kept sufficiently low. This limitation of permissible values of the correction factors implies a corresponding limit to the speed with which it is possible to correct an error caused by a disturbance.

It is not possible to make any completely general statement about the effect on the response of a closed-loop system of an alteration to one part of the system unless the remainder of the system is fully specified. It will, however, be found that except in very special cases which are most unlikely to occur in practice a reduction in the length of the correction lag brought about by a reduction in the time scale, the form of the lag remaining unchanged, increases the maximum values of the correction factors that can be used without causing instability, and so permits a more rapid correction of errors. A similar effect is produced, again except in very special cases, if the form of the correction lag is altered from form (*c*) through form (*b*) to form (*a*). As can be seen from Fig. 2, this implies that the maximum values of the correction factors that can be used without causing instability are increased if the interval between the time when an error occurs and the time when the corrective action *begins* to take effect is reduced, even if the time required for the full effect of the corrective action to be obtained is simultaneously increased. Thus it is important, both for obtaining rapid correction and for avoiding instability, that the corrective action should be adjusted continuously and quickly to changes in the error and that it should have some initial effect quickly; whether its full effect is obtained quickly or slowly is comparatively unimportant.[1]

We have seen from Fig. 3 that a cycle with a period of about three years occurs if the lags in our system are of form (*b*) or (*c*) and if the proportional and integral correction factors are 0·5 (which may perhaps be about the order of magnitude of these correction factors that can be attained in actual economic regulation) unless a small amount of derivative correction is also applied. Since the basic multiplier model which has been used so far is

[1] Justification of the above statements would require an extensive use of the frequency-response method of analysis and cannot be given here. The reader who wishes to acquire sufficient familiarity with the method to convince himself of their truth will find the necessary material in the works cited in footnote 5, p. 265.

non-oscillatory, this may properly be called a control cycle. A more adequate model of an economy might itself have cyclical properties, for example, inventory adjustments are likely to cause cycles with a period of three or four years. The question immediately arises whether the maximum values of the correction factors that can be used without causing instability are not further reduced when the system being controlled has oscillatory tendencies. This question is examined briefly in the next section.

II. An Inventory Model with Error Correction

A model with inventory adjustments is shown in Fig. 6. An " inventory demand," E_V, is now distinguished as an additional component of aggregate demand, total demand for purposes other than inventory adjustment being E_N. Thus $E = E_N + E_V$ and $E_N = E_Y + E_\pi + u$. We assume that any excess of the " non-inventory demand " E_N over aggregate production P is met by drawing on inventories, and any excess of production over non-inventory demand is added to inventories. Then the rate of change of inventories, $\frac{dV}{dt}$, is equal to $P - E_N$. Integration of $\frac{dV}{dt}$ with respect to time gives total inventories, V. Some part of the total inventories will be locked up in work in progress and essential stocks closely related to the level of production. These " minimum working inventories," which we shall call V_1, are assumed to be a constant proportion, w, of production. We shall give w the value 0·2, *i.e.*, we shall assume that minimum working inventories are equal to one-fifth of a year's production. Inventories held in excess of minimum working inventories will be called V_2, so that $V_2 = V - V_1$.[1] From precautionary and speculative motives businesses will wish to hold some inventories in excess of minimum working inventories, but the amount they wish to hold, which we shall call V_{2d} or the desired value of V_2, will not always be equal to the amount they are holding. In this simplified model we shall assume that V_{2d} is a lagged function of non-inventory demand and we shall give the magnitude of this dependence, s, the value 0·125 and assume that the lag, L_s, is of form (*b*) with a time constant of 0·75 year. (In fact, of course, V_{2d} will also be influenced by other factors, in particular by interest rates and expected rates of change of prices.) Subtracting V_2 from V_{2d} gives the " error in inventories," ϵ_V. We shall assume that the inventory demand, E_V, is a constant proportion, v, of the error in inventories and shall give v the value 2·0.

The only other change from the model shown in Fig. 1 is the addition of the demand lag, L_D, which, because of the fairly rapid adjustment of expenditure by wage-earners when their incomes change, we shall assume

[1] It will be noticed that the distinction made here between V_1 and V_2 corresponds closely to the distinction between working capital and liquid capital made by Keynes in Chapters 28 and 29 of the *Treatise on Money*. It is also analagous to his later distinction between M_1 and M_2 in monetary theory.

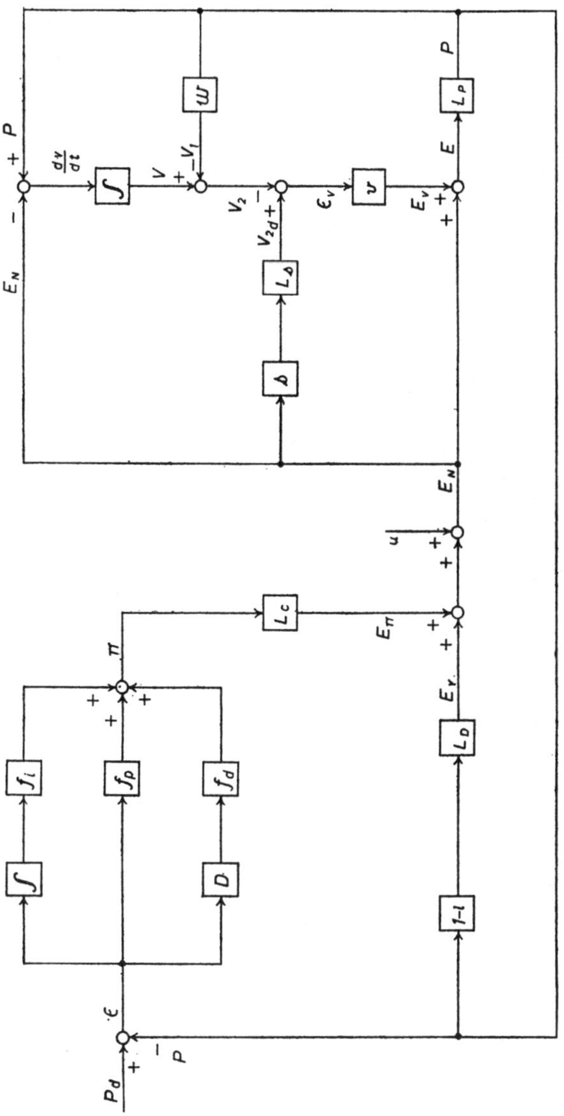

Fig. 6

to be of form (*a*) with a time constant of 0·125 year. We shall, however, give the marginal leakage, *l*, the value 0·4 instead of its previous value 0·25. This reduces the multiplier from 4·0 to 2·5, which is probably a more realistic value, and makes the system more stable. We assume a correction lag of form (*c*) with a total time constant of 0·5 year and a production lag of form (*b*) with a total time constant of 0·25 year.

When all three correction factors are zero the response of production to a unit step change in the variable *u*, applied negatively at time $t = 0$, is the damped inventory cycle shown in curve (*a*) of Fig. 7. If derivative correction only is applied the equilibrium position of the system is unchanged, so the error in production persists. With low values of the derivative correction factor the fluctuations in the response are reduced, but with

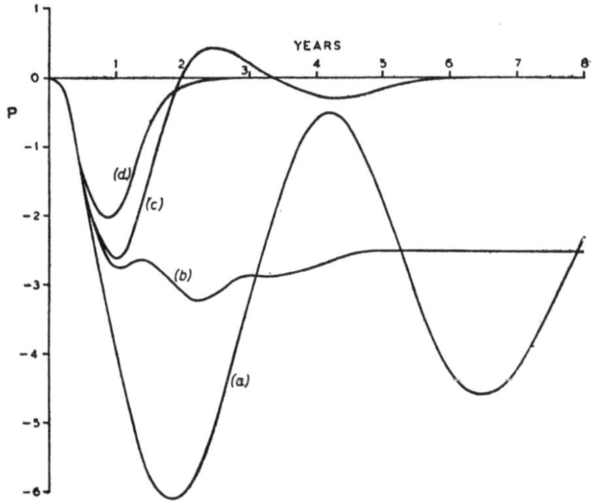

Fig. 7

higher values another cycle appears with a period of just over one year, and if the derivative correction factor is raised above 0·38 this cycle becomes explosive. Curve (*b*) of Fig. 7 shows the response when the derivative correction factor is 0·25.

If proportional correction only is applied, the fluctuations in the response are slightly reduced when the value of the proportional correction factor is very low, but if it is raised above 0·1 the fluctuations become worse again and the system becomes unstable when the proportional correction factor is raised above about 0·28. If any integral correction at all is applied alone the amplitudes of the fluctuations increase and the system becomes unstable if the integral correction factor is raised above about 0·08. Similarly, any combination of proportional and integral correction without the addition of derivative correction reduces the stability of the system and increases the magnitudes of the fluctuations unless the two correction factors have extremely low values, while if the values are extremely low the improvement in the response is negligible.

Even if derivative correction is included in the stabilisation policy, the speed with which an error can be corrected is rather limited. About the best response that can be obtained is that shown in curve (*c*) of Fig. 7. This response results when $f_p = 0{\cdot}3$, $f_i = 0{\cdot}4$ and $f_d = 0{\cdot}2$. Higher values of the correction factors worsen the response by reducing the stability of the system. If the correction lag is changed from form (*c*) to form (*b*), the time constant remaining at 0·5 years, the correction factors can be increased a

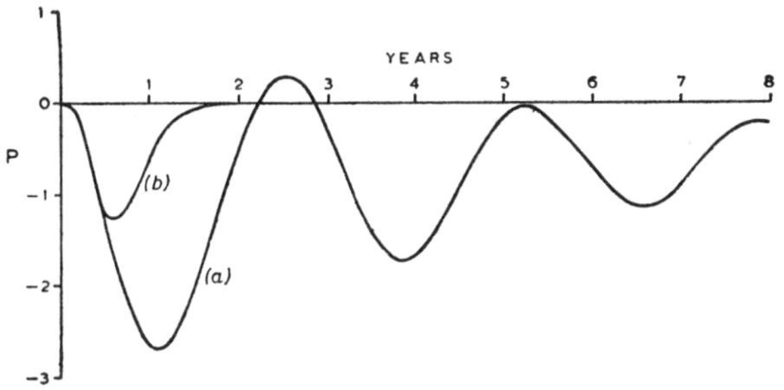

Fig. 8

little. The best response is then that shown in curve (*d*) of Fig. 7, the correction factors being $f_p = 0{\cdot}4$, $f_i = 0{\cdot}5$ and $f_d = 0{\cdot}3$.

If the correction lag is of form (*b*) with a total time constant of 0·25 year the best response is obtained when $f_p = 0{\cdot}9$, $f_i = 0{\cdot}9$ and $f_d = 0{\cdot}25$. It is shown as curve (*b*) of Fig. 8. It is of interest to note that even with this correction lag the stabilisation policy is not satisfactory unless it includes an element of derivative correction. If $f_d = 0$ about the best response that can be obtained is that shown in curve (*a*) of Fig. 8, the proportional and integral correction factors being 0·4 and 0·1 respectively. With either higher or lower values of f_p and f_i the fluctuations are of greater amplitude.

III. Conclusions

Because of the simplified nature of the models considered in this paper the results that have been obtained cannot be applied directly to the interpretation of actual economic situations. Indeed, one of the first lessons one learns from studying a variety of hypothetical models is that the problem of economic stabilisation is, even in principle, an extremely intricate one, and that a much more thorough investigation of both theoretical principles and empirical relationships would be needed before detailed policy recommendations could be justified. A few very elementary conclusions can, however, be drawn with some confidence.

The first is that the regulation of a system can be improved if the lengths of the time delays operating around the main control loop are reduced. The distinction between delays and lags should here be noticed. What is of primary importance is that the correcting action should be adjusted continuously and with the minimum possible delay to changes in the error and that the adjustments should quickly produce some initial effect. It does not matter very much if it takes a long time for the policy changes to have their full effect. In fact, it can be shown that if there is a long delay before corrective action is taken or before it begins to have an appreciable effect it is better that the effect, when it does come, should be gradual rather than sudden. The worst possible condition for regulating purposes is one in which the adjustment of policy demand to a change in the error is delayed for a considerable time and then effected quickly and abruptly.

A second conclusion is that it is usually necessary to include an element of derivative correction in a stabilisation policy if regulation is to be satisfactory. In other words, the potential policy demand should be made to depend not only on the magnitude of the current error and on the sum of the past errors,[1] but also on the rate of change of the error, or when observations are at discrete intervals on the difference between the last two observed values of the error. The longer the time delays in the responses around the main control loop, the less effective is derivative correction in reducing fluctuations. Nevertheless, the longer the delays, the more desirable it is that some derivative correction be used, since the delays reduce the stability of the system and so make it more important that whatever stabilising effect can still be obtained by derivative correction should not be foregone.

A third conclusion is that if the lags in the real economic system are at all similar to those we have used in the models it is unlikely that the period needed to restore any desired equilibrium conditions after an economy has experienced a severe disturbance could be much less than two years, even assuming that the regulating authorities use the policy which is most appropriate to the real system of relationships existing in the economy. As these relationships are not known quantitively, it is unlikely that the policy applied will be the most appropriate one, it may well cause cyclical fluctuations rather than eliminate them.

It is true that many relationships inherent in the real economic system have been omitted from our models and that some of the omitted relationships seem intuitively to be of a stabilising type. But intuitions about dynamic processes may be dangerously misleading and need to be carefully tested. Most of the inherent relationships which at first sight would seem

[1] The quantity to which integral correction is related is the integral, or sum, of all past errors. In practice a good approximation to integral correction would be obtained if the integral component of potential policy demand was made to depend on the sum of the errors over the past four or five years or on a weighted sum of these errors, the earlier errors being given less weight than the later one.

to have stabilising effects can be expressed in forms similar to the policy relationships in the models we have been using. If the lengths and forms of the time lags of these inherent relationships are also similar to those which we have assumed for the correction lag the effects of the inherent relationships will be similar to the effects of the policy relationships which we have already considered. The existence of inherent relationships which appear intuitively to be of a stabilising type may therefore reduce the amount of correction that needs to be applied deliberately by regulating authorities (particularly the proportional and integral elements of correction; it is difficult to think of any inherent relationship which is equivalent to the derivative element of a correction policy), but will not reduce the time required to restore equilibrium after a disturbance unless these relationships operate with shorter time lags and delays than we have been assuming. Nor do the additional inherent relationships make it more likely that cyclical fluctuations will be avoided. In fact, they make it less likely, since it becomes very difficult to judge what quantitative values should be given to the deliberate policy relationships when the system already contains numerous inherent relationships whose magnitudes and speeds of operation are unknown.

The main conclusion that must be drawn from this investigation is that much more research is needed in the general field of economic regulation. To throw light on the practical problems involved in regulating complex economic systems it is necessary to study the properties of more realistic models in which non-linear relationships, growth trends, multiple objectives and multiple disturbances are incorporated. The means for carrying out such studies are now becoming available and should be fully exploited. It is equally important that improved methods should be developed for estimating quantitatively the magnitudes and time-forms of economic relationships in order that the range of permissible hypothesis may be restricted more closely than is at present possible.

A. W. Phillips

London School of Economics.

[2]

The Relation Between Unemployment and the Rate of Change of Money Wage Rates in the United Kingdom, 1861–1957[1]

By A. W. Phillips

I. Hypothesis

When the demand for a commodity or service is high relatively to the supply of it we expect the price to rise, the rate of rise being greater the greater the excess demand. Conversely when the demand is low relatively to the supply we expect the price to fall, the rate of fall being greater the greater the deficiency of demand. It seems plausible that this principle should operate as one of the factors determining the rate of change of money wage rates, which are the price of labour services. When the demand for labour is high and there are very few unemployed we should expect employers to bid wage rates up quite rapidly, each firm and each industry being continually tempted to offer a little above the prevailing rates to attract the most suitable labour from other firms and industries. On the other hand it appears that workers are reluctant to offer their services at less than the prevailing rates when the demand for labour is low and unemployment is high so that wage rates fall only very slowly. The relation between unemployment and the rate of change of wage rates is therefore likely to be highly non-linear.

It seems possible that a second factor influencing the rate of change of money wage rates might be the rate of change of the demand for labour, and so of unemployment. Thus in a year of rising business activity, with the demand for labour increasing and the percentage unemployment decreasing, employers will be bidding more vigorously for the services of labour than they would be in a year during which the average percentage unemployment was the same but the demand for labour was not increasing. Conversely in a year of falling business activity, with the demand for labour decreasing and the percentage unemployment increasing, employers will be less inclined to grant wage increases, and workers will be in a weaker position to press for them, than they would be in a year during which the average percentage unemployment was the same but the demand for labour was not decreasing.

A third factor which may affect the rate of change of money wage rates is the rate of change of retail prices, operating through cost of living adjustments in wage rates. It will be argued here, however, that cost of living adjustments will have little or no effect on the rate of change of money wage rates except at times when retail prices are

[1] This study is part of a wider research project financed by a grant from the Ford Foundation. The writer was assisted by Mrs. Marjory Klonarides. Thanks are due to Professor E. H. Phelps Brown, Professor J. E. Meade and Dr. R. G. Lipsey for comments on an earlier draft.

forced up by a very rapid rise in import prices (or, on rare occasions in the United Kingdom, in the prices of home-produced agricultural products). For suppose that productivity is increasing steadily at the rate of, say, 2 per cent. per annum and that aggregate demand is increasing similarly so that unemployment is remaining constant at, say, 2 per cent. Assume that with this level of unemployment and without any cost of living adjustments wage rates rise by, say, 3 per cent. per annum as the result of employers' competitive bidding for labour and that import prices and the prices of other factor services are also rising by 3 per cent. per annum. Then retail prices will be rising on average at the rate of about 1 per cent. per annum (the rate of change of factor costs minus the rate of change of productivity). Under these conditions the introduction of cost of living adjustments in wage rates will have no effect, for employers will merely be giving under the name of cost of living adjustments part of the wage increases which they would in any case have given as a result of their competitive bidding for labour.

Assuming that the value of imports is one fifth of national income, it is only at times when the annual rate of change of import prices exceeds the rate at which wage rates would rise as a result of competitive bidding by employers by more than five times the rate of increase of productivity that cost of living adjustments become an operative factor in increasing the rate of change of money wage rates. Thus in the example given above a rate of increase of import prices of more than 13 per cent. per annum would more than offset the effects of rising productivity so that retail prices would rise by more than 3 per cent. per annum. Cost of living adjustments would then lead to a greater increase in wage rates than would have occurred as a result of employers' demand for labour and this would cause a further increase in retail prices, the rapid rise in import prices thus initiating a wage-price spiral which would continue until the rate of increase of import prices dropped significantly below the critical value of about 13 per cent. per annum.

The purpose of the present study is to see whether statistical evidence supports the hypothesis that the rate of change of money wage rates in the United Kingdom can be explained by the level of unemployment and the rate of change of unemployment, except in or immediately after those years in which there was a very rapid rise in import prices, and if so to form some quantitative estimate of the relation between unemployment and the rate of change of money wage rates. The periods 1861-1913, 1913-1948 and 1948-1957 will be considered separately.

II. 1861-1913

Schlote's index of the average price of imports[1] shows an increase of 12·5 per cent. in import prices in 1862 as compared with the previous

[1] W. Schlote, *British Overseas Trade from 1700 to the 1930's*, Table 26.

year, an increase of 7·6 per cent. in 1900 and in 1910, and an increase of 7·0 per cent. in 1872. In no other year between 1861 and 1913 was there an increase in import prices of as much as 5 per cent. If the hypothesis stated above is correct the rise in import prices in 1862 may just have been sufficient to start up a mild wage-price spiral, but in the remainder of the period changes in import prices will have had little or no effect on the rate of change of wage rates.

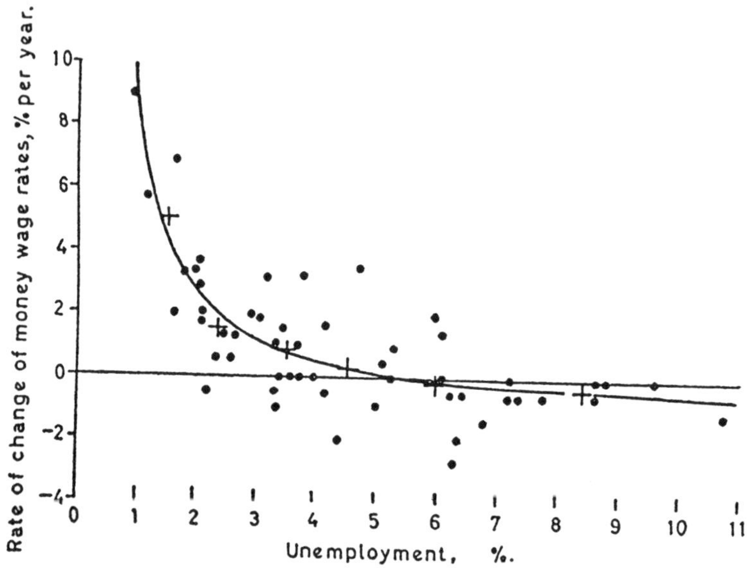

Fig.1. 1861 – 1913

A scatter diagram of the rate of change of wage rates and the percentage unemployment for the years 1861-1913 is shown in Figure 1. During this time there were 6½ fairly regular trade cycles with an average period of about 8 years. Scatter diagrams for the years of each trade cycle are shown in Figures 2 to 8. Each dot in the diagrams represents a year, the average rate of change of money wage rates during the year being given by the scale on the vertical axis and the average unemployment during the year by the scale on the horizontal axis. The rate of change of money wage rates was calculated from the index of hourly wage rates constructed by Phelps Brown and Sheila Hopkins,[1] by expressing the first central difference of the index for each year as a percentage of the index for the same year. Thus the rate of change for 1861 is taken to be half the difference between the index for 1862 and the index for 1860 expressed as a percentage of the index

[1] E. H. Phelps Brown and Sheila Hopkins, "The Course of Wage Rates in Five Countries, 1860-1939," *Oxford Economic Papers*, June, 1950.

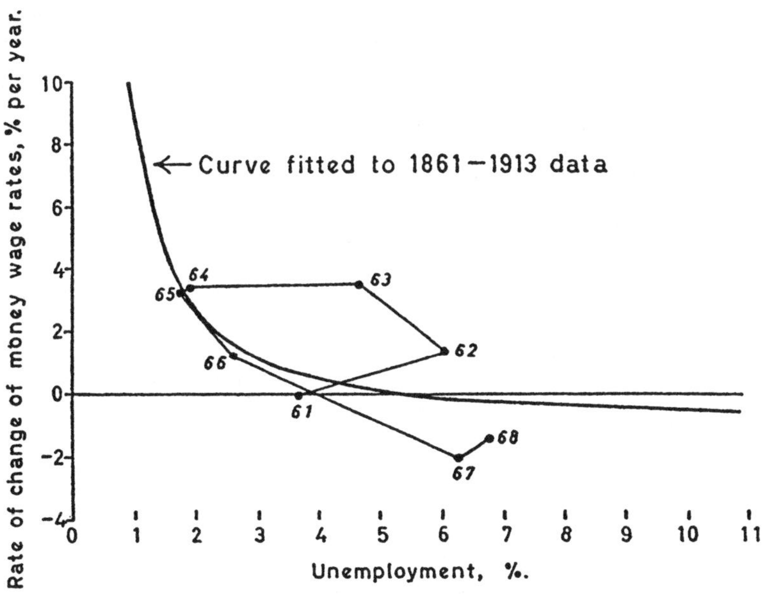

Fig. 2. 1861 — 1868

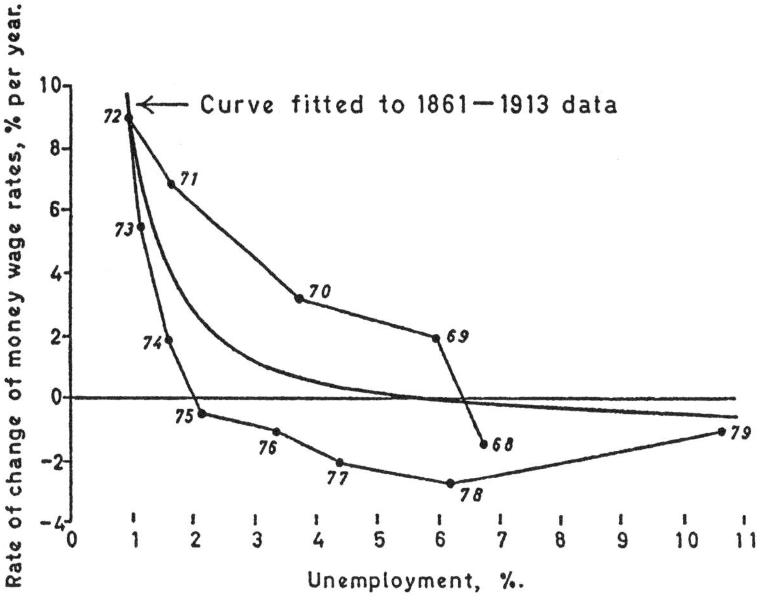

Fig. 3. 1868 — 1879

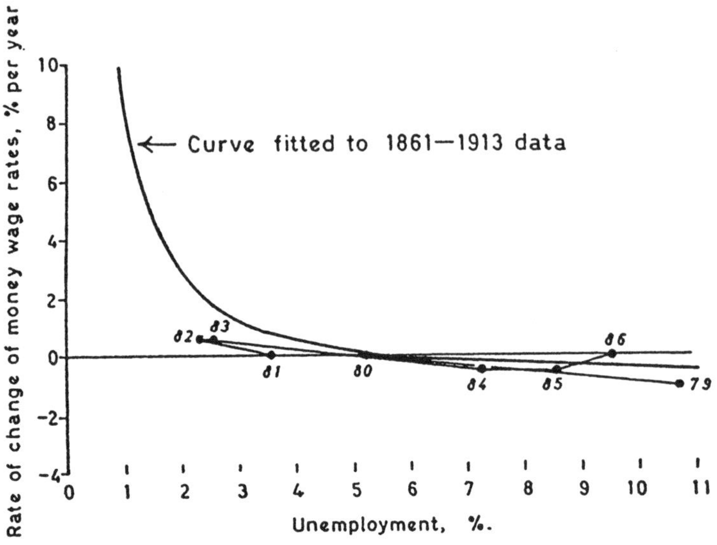

Fig. 4. 1879 – 1886

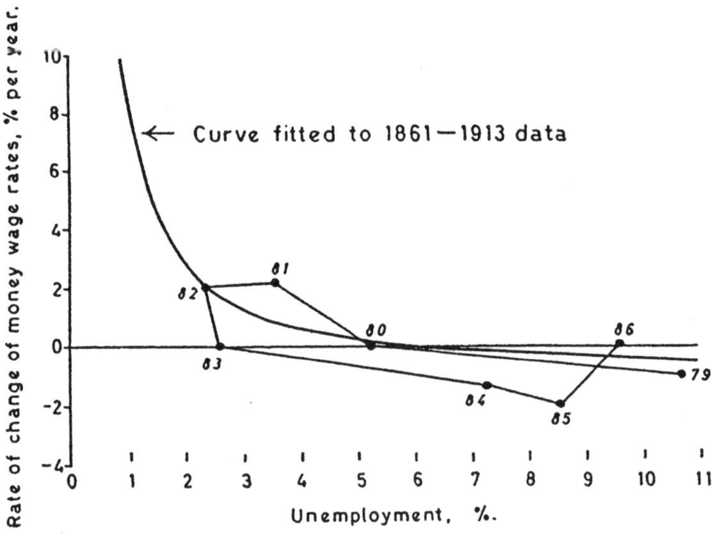

Fig. 4a. 1879–1886, using Bowley's wage index for the years 1881 to 1886

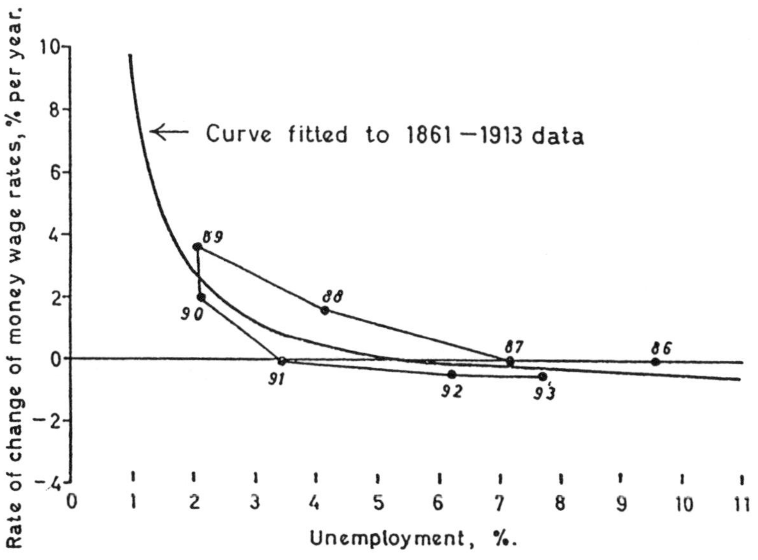

Fig.5. 1886 – 1893

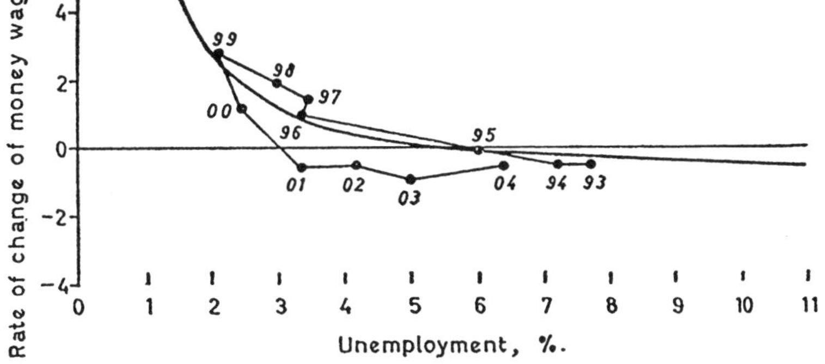

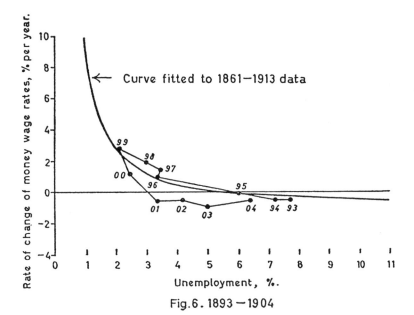

Fig.6. 1893 – 1904

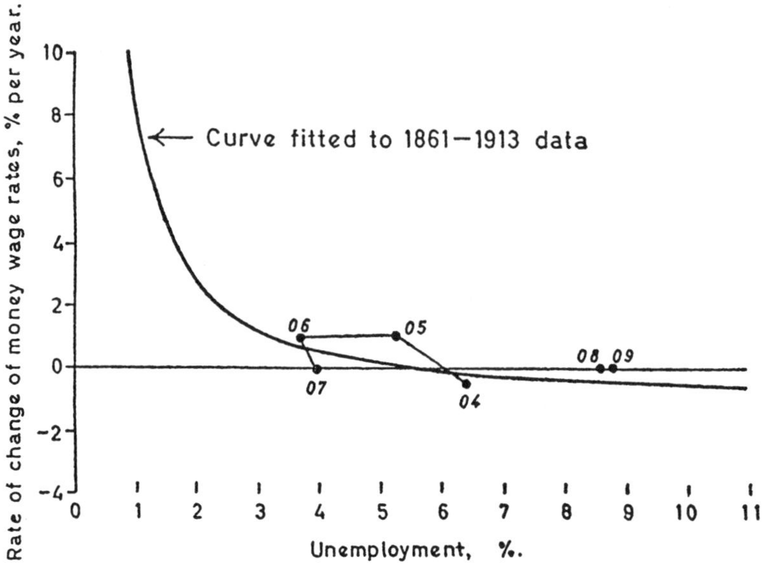

Fig. 7. 1904 — 1909

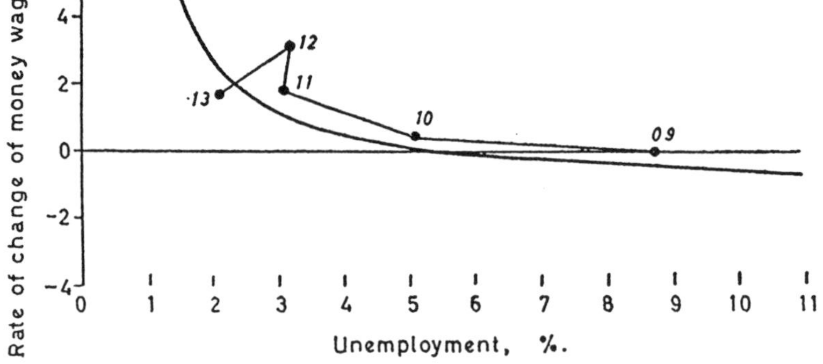

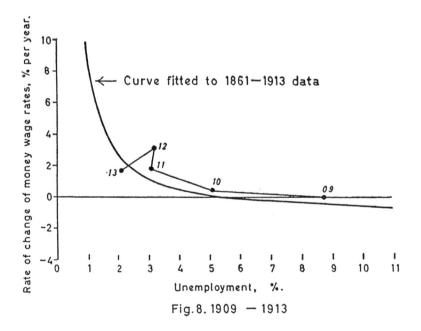

Fig. 8. 1909 — 1913

for 1861, and similarly for other years.[1] The percentage unemployment figures are those calculated by the Board of Trade and the Ministry of Labour[2] from trade union returns. The corresponding percentage employment figures are quoted in Beveridge, *Full Employment in a Free Society*, Table 22.

It will be seen from Figures 2 to 8 that there is a clear tendency for the rate of change of money wage rates to be high when unemployment is low and to be low or negative when unemployment is high. There is also a clear tendency for the rate of change of money wage rates at any given level of unemployment to be above the average for that level of unemployment when unemployment is decreasing during the upswing of a trade cycle and to be below the average for that level of unemployment when unemployment is increasing during the downswing of a trade cycle.

The crosses shown in Figure 1 give the average values of the rate of change of money wage rates and of the percentage unemployment in those years in which unemployment lay between 0 and 2, 2 and 3, 3 and 4, 4 and 5, 5 and 7, and 7 and 11 per cent. respectively (the upper bound being included in each interval). Since each interval includes years in which unemployment was increasing and years in which it was decreasing the effect of changing unemployment on the rate of change of wage rates tends to be cancelled out by this averaging, so that each cross gives an approximation to the rate of change of wages which would be associated with the indicated level of unemployment if unemployment were held constant at that level.

The curve shown in Figure 1 (and repeated for comparison in later diagrams) was fitted to the crosses. The form of equation chosen was

$$y + a = bx^c$$

or

$$\log (y + a) = \log b + c \log x$$

where y is the rate of change of wage rates and x is the percentage unemployment. The constants b and c were estimated by least squares using the values of y and x corresponding to the crosses in the four intervals between 0 and 5 per cent. unemployment, the constant a being chosen by trial and error to make the curve pass as close as possible to the remaining two crosses in the intervals between 5 and 11 per cent. unemployment.[3] The equation of the fitted curve is

$$y + 0{\cdot}900 = 9{\cdot}638x^{-1{\cdot}394}$$

or

$$\log (y + 0{\cdot}900) = 0.984 - 1{\cdot}394 \log x.$$

[1] The index is apparently intended to measure the average of wage rates during each year. The first central difference is therefore the best simple approximation to the average absolute rate of change of wage rates during a year and the central difference expressed as a percentage of the index number is an appropriate measure of the average percentage rate of change of wage rates during the year.

[2] *Memoranda upon British and Foreign Trade and Industrial Conditions* (Second Series) (Cd. 2337), B.P.P. 1905, Vol. 84; *21st Abstract of Labour Statistics, 1919–1933* (Cd. 4625), B.P.P. 1933–34, Vol. 26.

[3] At first sight it might appear preferable to carry out a multiple regression of y on the variables x and $\frac{dx}{dt}$. However, owing to the particular form of the relation

Considering the wage changes in individual years in relation to the fitted curve, the wage increase in 1862 (see Figure 2) is definitely larger than can be accounted for by the level of unemployment and the rate of change of unemployment, and the wage increase in 1863 is also larger than would be expected. It seems that the 12·5 per cent. increase in import prices between 1861 and 1862 referred to above (and no doubt connected with the outbreak of the American civil war) was in fact sufficient to have a real effect on wage rates by causing cost of living increases in wages which were greater than the increases which would have resulted from employers' demand for labour and that the consequent wage-price spiral continued into 1863. On the other hand the increases in import prices of 7·6 per cent. between 1899 and 1900 and again between 1909 and 1910 and the increase of 7·0 per cent. between 1871 and 1872 do not seem to have had any noticeable effect on wage rates. This is consistent with the hypothesis stated above about the effect of rising import prices on wage rates.

Figure 3 and Figures 5 to 8 show a very clear relation between the rate of change of wage rates and the level and rate of change of unemployment,[1] but the relation hardly appears at all in the cycle shown in Figure 4. The wage index of Phelps Brown and Sheila Hopkins from which the changes in wage rates were calculated was based on Wood's earlier index,[2] which shows the same stability during these years. From 1880 we have also Bowley's index of wage rates.[3] If the rate of change of money wage rates for 1881 to 1886 is calculated from Bowley's index by the same method as was used before, the results shown in Figure 4a are obtained, giving the typical relation between the rate of change of wage rates and the level and rate of change of unemployment. It seems possible that some peculiarity may have occurred in the construction of Wood's index for these years. Bowley's index for the remainder of the period up to 1913 gives results which are broadly similar to those shown in Figures 5 to 8, but the pattern is

between y and x in the present case it is not easy to find a suitable linear multiple regression equation. An equation of the form $y + a = bx^c + k\left(\frac{1}{x^m} \cdot \frac{dx}{dt}\right)$ would probably be suitable. If so the procedure which has been adopted for estimating the relation that would hold between y and x if $\frac{dx}{dt}$ were zero is satisfactory, since it can easily be shown that $\frac{1}{x^m} \cdot \frac{dx}{dt}$ is uncorrelated with x or with any power of x provided that x is, as in this case, a trend-free variable.

[1] Since the unemployment figures used are the averages of monthly percentages, the first central difference is again the best simple approximation to the average rate of change of unemployment during a year. It is obvious from an inspection of Fig. 3 and Figs. 5 to 8 that in each cycle there is a close relation between the deviations of the points from the fitted curve and the first central differences of the employment figures, though the magnitude of the relation does not seem to have remained constant over the whole period.

[2] See Phelps Brown and Sheila Hopkins, *loc. cit.*, pp. 264-5.

[3] A. L. Bowley, *Wages and Income in the United Kingdom since 1860*, Table VII, p. 30.

rather less regular than that obtained with the index of Phelps Brown and Sheila Hopkins.

From Figure 6 it can be seen that wage rates rose more slowly than usual in the upswing of business activity from 1893 to 1896 and then returned to their normal pattern of change ; but with a temporary increase in unemployment during 1897. This suggests that there may have been exceptional resistance by employers to wage increases from 1894 to 1896, culminating in industrial strife in 1897. A glance at industrial history[1] confirms this suspicion. During the 1890's there was a rapid growth of employers' federations and from 1895 to 1897 there was resistance by the employers' federations to trade union demands for the introduction of an eight-hour working day, which would have involved a rise in hourly wage rates. This resulted in a strike by the Amalgamated Society of Engineers, countered by the Employers' Federation with a lock-out which lasted until January 1898.

From Figure 8 it can be seen that the relation between wage changes and unemployment was again disturbed in 1912. From the monthly figures of percentage unemployment in trade unions[2] we find that unemployment rose from 2·8 per cent. in February 1912 to 11.3 per cent. in March, falling back to 3·6 per cent. in April and 2·7 per cent. in May, as the result of a general stoppage of work in coal mining. If an adjustment is made to eliminate the effect of the strike on unemployment the figure for the average percentage unemployment during 1912 would be reduced by about 0·8 per cent., restoring the typical pattern of the relation between the rate of change of wage rates and the level and rate of change of unemployment.

From a comparison of Figures 2 to 8 it appears that the width of loops obtained in each trade cycle has tended to narrow, suggesting a reduction in the dependence of the rate of change of wage rates on the rate of change of unemployment. There seem to be two possible explanations of this. First, in the coal and steel industries before the first world war sliding scale adjustments were common, by which wage rates were linked to the prices of the products.[3] Given the tendency of product prices to rise with an increase in business activity and fall with a decrease in business activity, these agreements may have strengthened the relation between changes in wage rates and changes in unemployment in these industries. During the earlier years of the period these industries would have fairly large weights in the wage index, but with the greater coverage of the statistical material available in later years the weights of these industries in the index would be reduced. Second, it is possible that the decrease in the width of the loops resulted not so much from a reduction in the dependence of wage

[1] See B. C. Roberts, *The Trades Union Congress, 1868-1921*, Chapter IV, especially pp. 158-162.

[2] *21st Abstract of Labour Statistics, 1919–1933, loc. cit.*

[3] I am indebted to Professor Phelps Brown for pointing this out to me.

changes on changes in unemployment as from the introduction of a time lag in the response of wage changes to changes in the level of unemployment, caused by the extension of collective bargaining and particularly by the growth of arbitration and conciliation procedures. If such a time lag existed in the later years of the period the wage change in any year should be related, not to average unemployment during that year, but to the average unemployment lagged by, perhaps, several months. This would have the effect of moving each point in the diagrams horizontally part of the way towards the point of the preceding year and it can easily be seen that this would widen the loops in the diagrams. This fact makes it difficult to discriminate at all closely between the effect of time lags and the effect of dependence of wage changes on the rate of change of unemployment.

III. 1913-1948

A scatter diagram of the rate of change of wage rates and percentage unemployment for the years 1913-1948 is shown in Figure 9. From 1913 to 1920 the series used are a continuation of those used for the period 1861-1913. From 1921 to 1948 the Ministry of Labour's index of hourly wage rates at the end of December of each year[1] has been used, the percentage change in the index each year being taken as a measure of the average rate of change of wage rates during that year. The Ministry of Labour's figures for the percentage unemployment in the United Kingdom[2] have been used for the years 1921-1945. For the years 1946-1948 the unemployment figures were taken from the *Statistical Yearbooks* of the International Labour Organisation.

It will be seen from Figure 9 that there was an increase in unemployment in 1914 (mainly due to a sharp rise in the three months following the commencement of the war). From 1915 to 1918 unemployment was low and wage rates rose rapidly. The cost of living was also rising rapidly and formal agreements for automatic cost of living adjustments in wage rates became widespread, but it is not clear whether the cost of living adjustments were a real factor in increasing wage rates or whether they merely replaced increases which would in any case have occurred as a result of the high demand for labour. Demobilisation brought increased unemployment in 1919 but wage rates continued to rise rapidly until 1920, probably as a result of the rapidly rising import prices, which reached their peak in 1920, and consequent cost of living adjustments in wage rates. There was then a sharp increase in unemployment from 2·6 per cent. in 1920 to 17·0 per cent. in 1921, accompanied by a fall of 22·2 per cent. in wage rates in 1921. Part of the fall can be explained by the extremely rapid increase in unemployment, but a fall of 12·8 per cent. in the cost of living, largely a result of falling import prices, was no doubt also a major factor. In 1922 unemployment was 14·3 per cent. and wage rates fell by 19·1 per cent. Although

[1] *Ministry of Labour Gazette*, April, 1958, p. 133.
[2] *Ibid.*, January, 1940 and subsequent issues.

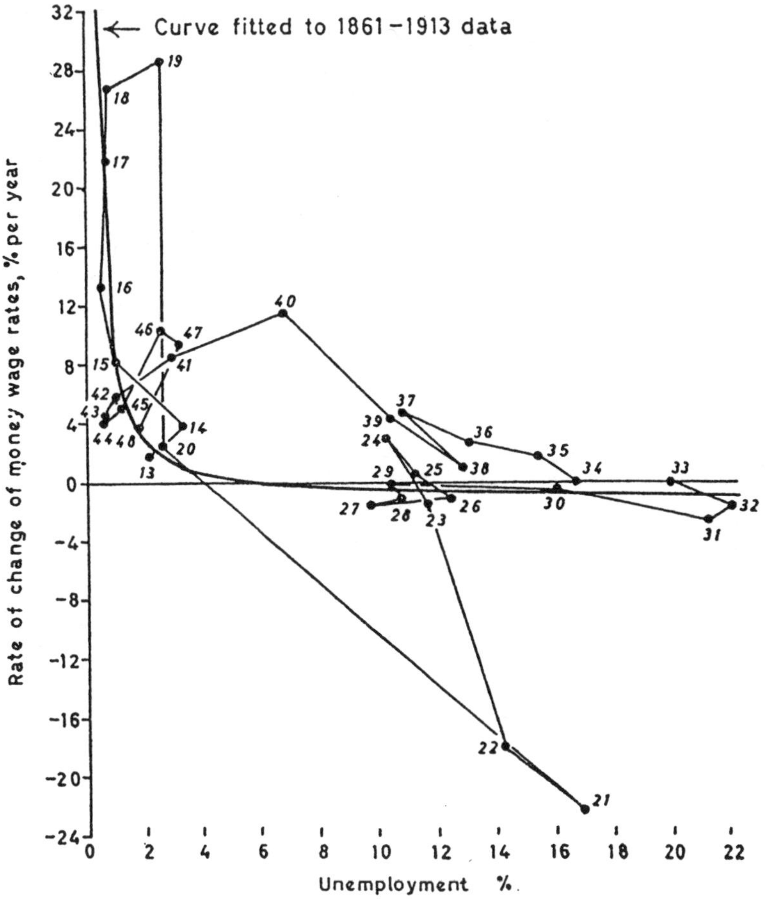

Fig. 9 1913 – 1948

unemployment was high in this year it was decreasing, and the major part of the large fall in wage rates must be explained by the fall of 17·5 per cent. in the cost of living index between 1921 and 1922. After this experience trade unions became less enthusiastic about agreements for automatic cost of living adjustments and the number of these agreements declined.

From 1923 to 1929 there were only small changes in import prices and in the cost of living. In 1923 and 1924 unemployment was high but decreasing. Wage rates fell slightly in 1923 and rose by 3·1 per cent. in 1924. It seems likely that if business activity had continued to improve after 1924 the changes in wage rates would have shown the usual pattern of the recovery phase of earlier trade cycles. However, the decision to check demand in an attempt to force the price level down in order to restore the gold standard at the pre-war parity of sterling prevented the recovery of business activity and unemployment remained fairly steady between 9·7 per cent. and 12·5 per cent. from 1925 to 1929. The average level of unemployment during these five years was 10·94 per cent. and the average rate of change of wage rates was −0·60 per cent. per year. The rate of change of wage rates calculated from the curve fitted to the 1861-1913 data for a level of unemployment of 10·94 per cent. is −0·56 per cent. per year, in close agreement with the average observed value. Thus the evidence does not support the view, which is sometimes expressed, that the policy of forcing the price level down failed because of increased resistance to downward movements of wage rates. The actual results obtained, given the levels of unemployment which were held, could have been predicted fairly accura ely from a study of the pre-war data, if anyone had felt inclined to carry out the necessary analysis.

The relation between wage changes and unemployment during the 1929-1937 trade cycle follows the usual pattern of the cycles in the 1861-1913 period except for the higher level of unemployment throughout the cycle. The increases in wage rates in 1935, 1936 and 1937 are perhaps rather larger than would be expected to result from the rate of change of employment alone and part of the increases must probably be attributed to cost of living adjustments. The cost of living index rose 3·1 per cent. in 1935, 3·0 per cent. in 1936 and 5·2 per cent. in 1937, the major part of the increase in each of these years being due to the rise in the food component of the index. Only in 1937 can the rise in food prices be fully accounted for by rising import prices; in 1935 and 1936 it seems likely that the policies introduced to raise prices of home-produced agricultural produce played a significant part in increasing food prices and so the cost of living index and wage rates. The extremely uneven geographical distribution of unemployment may also have been a factor tending to increase the rapidity of wage changes during the upswing of business activity between 1934 and 1937.

Increases in import prices probably contributed to the wage increases in 1940 and 1941. The points in Figure 9 for the remaining war years show the effectiveness of the economic controls introduced. After an increase in unemployment in 1946 due to demobilisation and in 1947 due to the coal crisis, we return in 1948 almost exactly to the fitted relation between unemployment and wage changes.

IV. 1948-1957

A scatter diagram for the years 1948-1957 is shown in Figure 10. The unemployment percentages shown are averages of the monthly unemployment percentages in Great Britain during the calendar years indicated, taken from the *Ministry of Labour Gazette*. The Ministry of Labour does not regularly publish figures of the percentage unemployment in the United Kingdom ; but from data published in the *Statistical Yearbooks* of the International Labour Organisation it appears that unemployment in the United Kingdom was fairly consistently about 0·1 per cent. higher than that in Great Britain throughout this period. The wage index used was the index of weekly wage rates, published monthly in the *Ministry of Labour Gazette*, the percentage change during each calendar year being taken as a measure of the average rate of change of money wage rates during the year. The Ministry does not regularly publish an index of hourly wage rates ;[1] but an index of normal weekly hours published in the *Ministry of Labour*

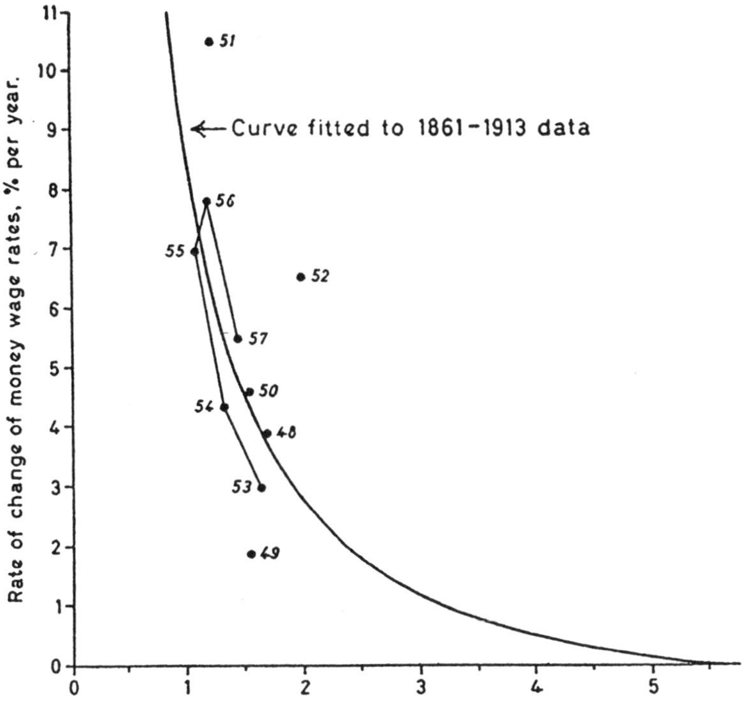

Fig. 10. 1948–1957

Gazette of September 1957 shows a reduction of 0·2 per cent. in 1948 and in 1949 and an average annual reduction of approximately 0·04 per cent. from 1950 to 1957. The percentage changes in hourly rates would therefore be greater than the percentage changes in weekly rates by these amounts.

It will be argued later that a rapid rise in import prices during 1947 led to a sharp increase in retail prices in 1948 which tended to stimulate wage increases during 1948, but that this tendency was offset by the

[1] An index of hourly wage rates covering the years considered in this section is, however, given in the *Ministry of Labour Gazette* of April, 1958.

policy of wage restraint introduced by Sir Stafford Cripps in the spring of 1948 ; that wage increases during 1949 were exceptionally low as a result of the policy of wage restraint ; that a rapid rise in import prices during 1950 and 1951 led to a rapid rise in retail prices during 1951 and 1952 which caused cost of living increases in wage rates in excess of the increases that would have occurred as a result of the demand for labour, but that there were no special factors of wage restraint or rapidly rising import prices to affect the wage increases in 1950 or in

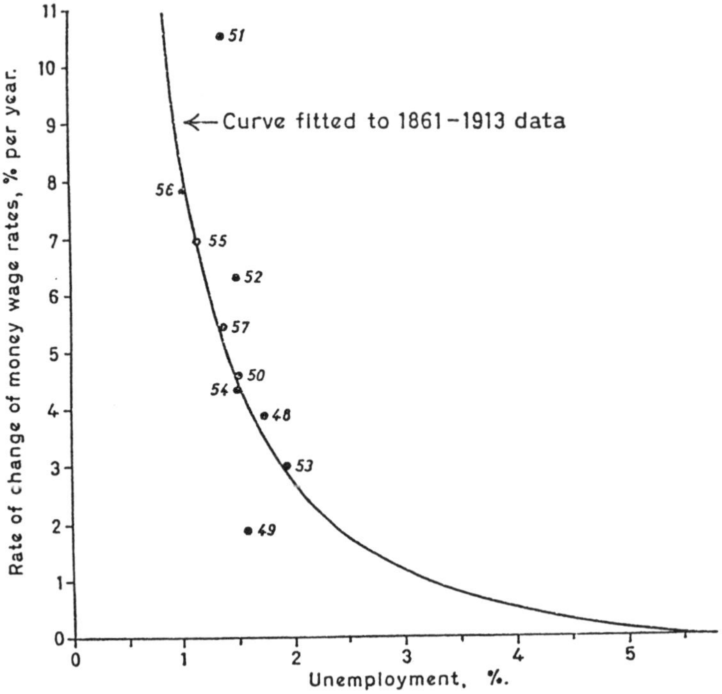

Fig. 11. 1948—1957, with unemployment lagged 7 months

the five years from 1953 to 1957. It can be seen from Figure 10 that the point for 1950 lies very close to the curve fitted to the 1861-1913 data and that the points for 1953 to 1957 lie on a narrow loop around this curve, the direction of the loop being the reverse of the direction of the loops shown in Figures 2 to 8. A loop in this direction could result from a time lag in the adjustment of wage rates. If the rate of change of wage rates during each calendar year is related to unemployment lagged seven months, i.e. to the average of the monthly percentages of unemployment from June of the preceding year to May of that year, the scatter diagram shown in Figure 11 is obtained. The loop has now disappeared and the points for the years 1950 and 1953 to 1957 lie closely along a smooth curve which coincides almost exactly with the curve fitted to the 1861-1913 data.

In Table 1 below the percentage changes in money wage rates during the years 1948-1957 are shown in column (1). The figures in column (2) are the percentage changes in wage rates calculated from the curve fitted to the 1861-1913 data corresponding to the unemployment percentages shown in Figure 11, i.e. the average percentages of unemployment lagged seven months. On the hypothesis that has been used in this paper, these figures represent the percentages by which wage rates would be expected to rise, given the level of employment for each year, as a result of employers' competitive bidding for labour, i.e. they represent the " demand pull " element in wage adjustments.

TABLE 1

	(1) Change in wage rates	(2) Demand pull	(3) Cost push	(4) Change in import prices
1947	..	..	..	20·1
1948	3·9	3·5	7·1	10·6
1949	1·9	4·1	2·9	4·1
1950	4·6	4·4	3·0	26·5
1951	10·5	5·2	9·0	23·3
1952	6·4	4·5	9·3	−11·7
1953	3·0	3·0	3·0	−4·8
1954	4·4	4·5	1·9	5·0
1955	6·9	6·8	4·6	1·9
1956	7·9	8·0	4·9	3·8
1957	5·4	5·2	3·8	−7·3

The relevant figure on the cost side in wage negotiations is the percentage increase shown by the retail price index in the month in which the negotiations are proceeding over the index of the corresponding month of the previous year. The average of these monthly percentages for each calendar year is an appropriate measure of the " cost push " element in wage adjustments, and these averages[1] are given in column (3). The percentage change in the index of import prices[2] during each year is given in column (4).

From Table 1 we see that in 1948 the cost push element was considerably greater than the demand pull element, as a result of the lagged effect on retail prices of the rapid rise in import prices during the previous year, and the change in wage rates was a little greater than could be accounted for by the demand pull element. It would probably have been considerably greater but for the co-operation of the trade unions in Sir Stafford Cripps' policy of wage restraint. In 1949 the cost element was less than the demand element and the actual change in

[1] Calculated from the retail price index published in the *Monthly Digest of Statistics*. The figure for 1948 is the average of the last seven months of the year.

[2] *Board of Trade Journal*.

wage rates was also much less, no doubt as a result of the policy of wage restraint which is generally acknowledged to have been effective in 1949. In 1950 the cost element was lower than the demand element and the actual wage change was approximately equal to the demand element.

Import prices rose very rapidly during 1950 and 1951 as a result of the devaluation of sterling in September 1949 and the outbreak of the Korean War in 1950. In consequence the retail price index rose rapidly during 1951 and 1952 so that the cost element in wage negotiations considerably exceeded the demand element. The actual wage increase in each year also considerably exceeded the demand element so that these two years provide a clear case of cost inflation.

In 1953 the cost element was equal to the demand element and in the years 1954 to 1957 it was well below the demand element. In each of these years the actual wage increase was almost exactly equal to the demand element. Thus in these five years, and also in 1950, there seems to have been pure demand inflation.

V. Conclusions

The statistical evidence in Sections II to IV above seems in general to support the hypothesis stated in Section I, that the rate of change of money wage rates can be explained by the level of unemployment and the rate of change of unemployment, except in or immediately after those years in which there is a sufficiently rapid rise in import prices to offset the tendency for increasing productivity to reduce the cost of living.

Ignoring years in which import prices rise rapidly enough to initiate a wage-price spiral, which seem to occur very rarely except as a result of war, and assuming an increase in productivity of 2 per cent. per year, it seems from the relation fitted to the data that if aggregate demand were kept at a value which would maintain a stable level of product prices the associated level of unemployment would be a little under 2½ per cent. If, as is sometimes recommended, demand were kept at a value which would maintain stable wage rates the associated level of unemployment would be about 5½ per cent.

Because of the strong curvature of the fitted relation in the region of low percentage unemployment, there will be a lower average rate of increase of wage rates if unemployment is held constant at a given level than there will be if unemployment is allowed to fluctuate about that level.

These conclusions are of course tentative. There is need for much more detailed research into the relations between unemployment, wage rates, prices and productivity.

The London School of Economics.

[3]

A Macro-dynamic Theory of Business Cycles[1] [1]

(1935)

I

In the following all our considerations concern an economic system *isolated and free of secular trend.* Moreover, we make with respect to that system the following assumptions.

1. We call real gross profit B the total real income of capitalists (businessmen and private capitalists), depreciation included, per unit of time. That income consists of two parts, that consumed and that accumulated:

$$B = C + A \tag{1}$$

Thus, C is the total volume of consumer goods consumed by capitalists, while A—if we disregard savings of workers, and their 'capitalistic' incomes—covers goods of all kinds serving the purpose of reproduction and expansion of fixed capital, as well as increment of stocks. We shall call A 'gross accumulation'.

The personal consumption of capitalists, C, is not very elastic. We assume that C is composed of a constant part, C_1, and a variable part proportional to the real gross profit λB:

$$C = C_1 + \lambda B \tag{2}$$

where λ is a small constant fraction.

From equations (1) and (2) we get:

$$B = C_1 + \lambda B + A$$

and

$$B = \frac{C_1 + A}{1 - \lambda} \tag{3}$$

[1] The term 'macro-dynamic' was first applied by Professor Frisch in his work 'Propagation Problems and Impulse Problems in Dynamics' (*Economic Essays in Honour of Gustav Cassel* (London, Cass, 1933)), to determine processes connected with the functioning of the economic system as a whole, disregarding the details of disproportionate development of special parts of that system.

i.e. the real gross profit B is proportional to the sum C_1+A of the constant part of the consumption of capitalists C_1 and of the gross accumulation A.

The gross accumulation A is equal to the sum of the production of capital goods and of the increment of stocks of all kinds.[2] We assume that the total volume of stocks remains constant all through the cycle. This is justified in so far as in existing economic systems which are totally or approximately isolated (the world, the USA) the total volume of stocks does not show any distinct cyclical variations. Indeed, while business is falling off, stocks of finished goods decrease, but those of raw materials and semi-manufactures rise; during recovery there is a reversal of these tendencies. From the above we may conclude that in our economic system the gross accumulation A is equal to the production of capital goods.

2. We assume further that the 'gestation period' of any investment is υ. Of course, this by no means corresponds to the reality; υ is merely the average of various actual durations of 'gestation periods', and our system in which υ is a constant value is to be considered as a simplified model of reality.

Whenever an investment is made, three stages can be discerned: (i) investment orders, i.e. all the orders for capital goods to serve the purpose of reproduction or expansion of industrial equipment; the total volume of such orders allocated per unit of time will be called I; (ii) production of capital goods; the volume of that production per unit of time, equal, as said above, to the gross accumulation, is called A; (iii) deliveries of finished industrial equipment; the volume of such deliveries per unit of time will be called L.[3]

The relation of L and I is simple. Deliveries L at the time t are equal to investment orders I at the time $t-\upsilon$:

$$L(t)=I(t-\upsilon) \tag{4}$$

($I(t)$ and $L(t)$ are investment orders and deliveries of industrial equipment at time t.)

[2] Industrial equipment in the course of construction is not included in 'stocks of all kinds'; thus change in the volume of industrial equipment in the course of construction is involved in the 'production of capital goods'.

[3] While A is the production of *all* capital goods, L is only that of *finished* capital goods. Thus, the difference $A-L$ represents the volume of industrial equipment in the course of construction, per unit of time.

The interrelationship of A and I is more complicated. Let us call W the total volume of unfilled investment orders at time t. As each investment needs the period υ to be filled, $1/\upsilon$ of its volume must be executed in a unit of time. Thus the production of capital goods must be equal to $1/\upsilon . W$:

$$A = \frac{W}{\upsilon} \tag{5}$$

As regards W, it is equal to the total of orders allocated during the period $(t-\upsilon, t)$. Indeed, since the gestation period of any investment is υ, no order allocated during the period $(t-\upsilon, t)$ is yet finished at the time t, while all the orders allocated before that period are filled. We thus obtain the equation:

$$W(t) = \int_{t-\upsilon}^{t} I(\tau)d\tau \tag{6}$$

According to equations (4) and (5) we get:

$$A(t) = \frac{1}{\upsilon}\int_{t-\upsilon}^{t} I(\tau)d\tau \tag{7}$$

($A(t)$ is the production of capital goods at the time t.)

Thus A at time t is equal to the average of investment orders $I(t)$ allocated during the period $(t-\upsilon, t)$.

3. Let us call K the volume of the existing industrial equipment. The increment of that volume within the given period is equal to the difference between the volume of deliveries of finished equipment and that of equipment coming out of use. If we denote by $K'(t)$ the derivative of K with respect to time, by $L(t)$ the volume of deliveries of industrial equipment per unit of time (as above), and by U the demand for restoration of equipment used up per unit of time, we get:

$$K'(t) = L(t) - U \tag{8}$$

We can assume that the demand for restoration of industrial equipment—U—remains constant all through the cycle. The volume of existing industrial equipment K shows, it is true, certain fluctuations: e.g. in the first part of the cycle K is above average (see Fig. 9), and one might think that the demand for restoration of equipment ought also to be above average. Yet it should be borne in mind that the new equipment is 'young' and its 'rate of mortality' very low, as the

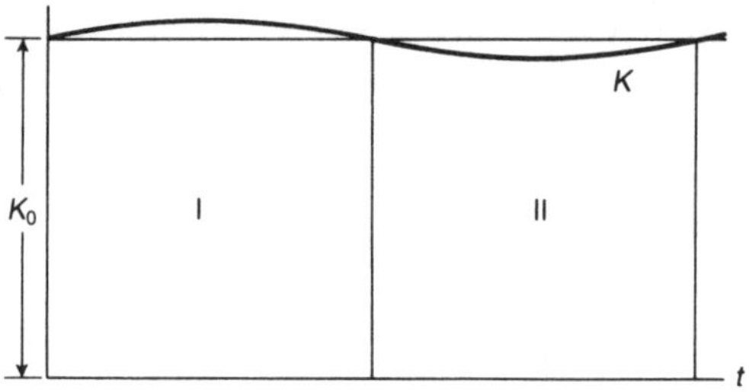

FIG. 9

average lifetime of industrial equipment is much longer than the duration of a cycle (15–30 years as against 8–12 years). Thus the fluctuations of the demand for restoration of equipment are of no importance, and may safely be disregarded.

4. The proportions of the investment activity at any time depend on the expected net yield. When the businessman invests capital k in the construction of industrial equipment, he will first evaluate the probable gross profit b, while deducting (i) the depreciation of the capital k, i.e. βk(β – the rate of depreciation); (ii) the interest on the capital k, i.e. pk (p – the interest rate); (iii) thc interest on the future working capital, the ratio of which to the invested capital k will be denoted by $\gamma - p\gamma k$. The probable yield of the investment will thus be:

$$\frac{b - \beta k - pk - p\gamma k}{k} = \frac{b}{k} - \beta - p(1 + \gamma)$$

The coefficients β and γ may be considered constant all through the cycle. p is the money rate at any given moment, b/k is the probable future yield evaluated after that of the existing enterprises. The volume of the existing industrial equipment is K, the total real gross profit is B. Thus the average real gross profit per unit of the existing fixed capital is B/K (that quotient will be called further gross yield B/K).

We may conclude that b/k is evaluated after B/K, and that investment activity is controlled by the gross yield B/K and the money rate p. As a matter of fact, the function of B/K and p is not the volume of investment orders I, but the ratio of that volume to that of industrial equipment K, i.e. I/K. In fact, when B and K rise in the same proportion, B/K remains unchanged, while I rises (probably) as did B

and K. Thus, we arrive at the equation:

$$\frac{I}{K}=f\left(\frac{B}{K'}p\right) \tag{9}$$

where f is an increasing function of B/K and a decreasing function of p.

It is commonly known that, except for financial panic (the so-called 'crises of confidence'), the market money rate rises and falls according to general business conditions. We make on that basis the following simplified assumption: the money rate p is an increasing function of the gross yield B/K.

From the assumption concerning the dependence of the money rate p on the gross yield B/K, and from (8), it follows that I/K is a function of B/K. As B is proportionate to C_1+A, where C_1 is the constant part of capitalist consumption and A the gross accumulation equal to the production of capital goods, we thus obtain:

$$\frac{I}{K}=\phi\left(\frac{C_1+A}{K}\right) \tag{10}$$

ϕ being, of course, an increasing function. We further assume that ϕ is a linear function, i.e. that:

$$\frac{I}{K}=m\frac{C_1+A}{K}-n$$

where the constant m is positive, ϕ being an increasing function. Multiplying both sides of the equation by K we get:

$$I=m(C_1+A)-nK \tag{11}$$

We have seen that between I (investment orders), A (gross accumulation equal to the production of capital goods), L (deliveries of industrial equipment), K (volume of existing industrial equipment), and time t, there are interrelationships:

$$L(t)=I(t-\upsilon) \tag{4}$$

$$A(t)=\frac{1}{\upsilon}\int_{t-\upsilon}^{t} I(\tau)d\tau \tag{7}$$

$$K'(t)=L(t)-U \tag{8}$$

resulting from techniques of capitalist production, and the relation

$$I=m(C_1+A)-nK \tag{11}$$

resulting from the interdependence between investments and yield of existing enterprises. From these equations the relation of I and t may be easily determined.

Let us differentiate (11) with respect to t:

$$I'(t) = mA'(t) - nK'(t) \tag{12}$$

Differentiating equation (7) with respect to t, we get:

$$A'(t) = \frac{I(t) - I(t-\upsilon)}{\upsilon} \tag{13}$$

and from (4) and (8):

$$K'(t) = I(t-\upsilon) - U \tag{14}$$

Putting into (12) values of $A'(t)$ and $K'(t)$ from (13) and (14), we have:

$$I'(t) = \frac{m}{\upsilon}[I(t) - I(t-\upsilon)] - n[(t-\upsilon) - U] \tag{15}$$

Denoting the deviation of $I(t)$ from the constant demand for restoration of industrial equipment U by $J(t)$:

$$J(t) = I(t) - U \tag{16}$$

we can transform (15) as follows:

$$J'(t) = \frac{m}{\upsilon}[J(t) - J(t-\upsilon)] - nJ(t-\upsilon)$$

or

$$(m + \upsilon n)J(t-\upsilon) = mJ(t) - \upsilon J'(t) \tag{17}$$

The solution of that equation will enable us to express $J(t)$ as a function of t and to find out which, if any, are the endogenous cyclical fluctuations in our economic system.

II

It may be easily seen that equation (17) is satisfied by the function $De^{\alpha t}$, where D is an arbitrary constant value and α a definite value which has to be determined. Replacing $J(t)$ by $De^{\alpha t}$, we get:

$$D(m + \upsilon n)e^{\alpha(t-\upsilon)} = Dme^{\alpha t} - D\alpha\upsilon e^{\alpha t}$$

and, dividing by $De^{\alpha t}$, we obtain an equation from which α can be determined:

$$(m+\upsilon n)e^{-\alpha\upsilon}=m-\alpha\upsilon \tag{18}$$

By simple transformations we get further:

$$e^{-m}(m+\upsilon n)e^{m-\alpha\upsilon}m-\alpha\upsilon$$

and setting

$$m-\alpha\upsilon=z \tag{19}$$

$$e^{-m}(m+\upsilon n)=l \tag{20}$$

we have

$$le^{z}=z \tag{21}$$

where z is to be considered as a complex number:

$$z=x+iy \tag{22}$$

Thus (19) can be given the following form:

$$\alpha=\frac{m-x}{\upsilon}-i\frac{y}{\upsilon} \tag{23}$$

and (21) can be transformed into:

$$x+iy=le^{x}(\cos y+i\sin y). \tag{24}$$

Adopting the method of Tinbergen,[4] we discern two cases: Case I, when $l>1/e$, and Case II, when $l\leqq 1/e$.

Case I. As Tinbergen has shown, in this case all the solutions will be complex numbers, and they will be infinite in number. Let us arrange them by increasing y_k:

$$\cdots x_k-iy_k, \cdots x_2-iy_2, x_1-iy_1, x_1+iy_1, x_2+iy_2 \cdots x_k+iy_k \cdots$$

(It is easy to see that when x_k+iy_k is a root of (24), that equation is also satisfied by x_k-iy_k).

From equation (23) we get values of α:

$$\alpha_k=\frac{m-x_k}{\upsilon}-i\frac{y_k}{\upsilon}$$

and

$$\alpha_{-k}=\frac{m-x_k}{\upsilon}+i\frac{y_k}{\upsilon}$$

[4] 'Ein Schiffbauzyklus?', *Weltwirtschaftliches Archiv*, 34/1.

Functions:

$$D_k e^{\alpha_k t} = D_k e^{(m - x_k)t/\upsilon}\left(\cos y_k \frac{t}{\upsilon} - i \sin y_k \frac{t}{\upsilon}\right)$$

and

$$D_{-k} e^{\alpha_{-k} t} = D_{-k} e^{(m - x - k)t/\upsilon}\left(\cos y_k \frac{t}{\upsilon} + i \sin y_k \frac{t}{\upsilon}\right)$$

satisfy (17).

The general solution of (17), which is at the same time a differential and a functional equation, depends upon the form of the function $J(t)$ in the initial interval $(0, \upsilon)$; that form is quite arbitrary. Yet we can develop (with sufficient approximation) the function $J(t)$ in the initial interval into the series $\Sigma D_k e^{\alpha_k t}$ where the constants D_k depend upon the form of the function $J(t)$ in the initial interval.[5] As functions $D_k e^{\alpha_k t}$ satisfy (17), the function $\Sigma D_k e^{\alpha_k t}$, which represents with sufficient approximation $J(t)$ in the initial interval, will be a general solution of (17).[6] That solution is, of course, a real one, and thus D_k and D_{-k} must be complex conjugate numbers, and $J(t)$ can be represented as follows:

$$J(t) = e^{(m - x_1)t/\upsilon}\left(F_1 \sin y_1 \frac{t}{\upsilon} + G_1 \cos y_1 \frac{t}{\upsilon}\right)$$
$$+ e^{(m - x_2)t/\upsilon}\left(F_2 \sin y_2 \frac{t}{\upsilon} + G_2 \cos y_2 \frac{t}{\upsilon}\right)\cdots \qquad (25)$$

On the basis of that solution we cannot yet say anything definite about the character of fluctuations of $J(t)$, as the constants F_k and G_k depend upon the form—unknown to us—of the function $J(t)$ in the initial interval. But here we can take advantage of the following circumstance. It may be inferred from Tinbergen's argument when he solves equation (24) that

$$x_1 < x_2,\ x_1 < x_3 \cdots \qquad (26)$$

Let us divide $J(t)$ by:

$$e^{(m - x_1)t/\upsilon}\left(F_1 \sin y_1 \frac{t}{\upsilon} + G_1 \cos y_1 \frac{t}{\upsilon}\right)$$

According to inequality (26), for a sufficiently great t the sum of all the

[5] Ibid., p. 158. [6] Ibid., p. 157.

expressions other than the first one will be equal to an arbitrarily small value ω:

$$\frac{J(t)}{e^{(m-x_1)t/\upsilon}\left(F_1 \sin y_1\frac{t}{\upsilon}+G_1 \cos y_1\frac{t}{\upsilon}\right)}=1+\omega$$

At a time sufficiently distant from the initial interval, the following equation will be true with an arbitrarily small relative error:

$$J(t)=e^{(m-x_1)t/\upsilon}\left(F_1 \sin y_1\frac{t}{\upsilon}+G_1 \cos y_1\frac{t}{\upsilon}\right) \tag{27}$$

That equation represents harmonic vibrations with an amplitude decreasing, constant, or increasing, according as $x_1 \gtreqless m$. Their period, and the degree of progression or degression they show, do not depend on the form of the function $J(t)$ in the initial interval. (It is worth mentioning that, as follows from Tinbergen's analysis, vibrations represented by (27) have a period longer than 2υ, while vibrations represented by the expressions on the right side of equation (25), which we dropped, have a period shorter than υ.)

If now we fix the origin of the time axis so as to equate $J(t)$ from (27) to zero for $t=0$, that equation will assume the form:

$$J(t)=F_1 e^{(m-x_1)t/\upsilon} \sin y_1\frac{t}{\upsilon}$$

or, taking into consideration (16):

$$I(t)-U=F_1 e^{(m-x_1)t/\upsilon} \sin y_1\frac{t}{\upsilon} \tag{28}$$

Case II. In that case (24) has two real roots, z_1'' and z_1'', among complex roots like $x_1 \pm iy$. As in the first case, we get here, for a time sufficiently distant from the initial interval:

$$J(t)=D_1' e^{(m-z_1')t/\upsilon}+D_1'' e^{(m-z_1'')t/\upsilon}$$

It follows from that equation that there are no cyclical vibrations.

The results of the above analysis can be summarized as follows. Cyclical variations occur in our economic system only when the following inequality is satisfied:

$$l>\frac{1}{e}$$

transformed by putting the value of l from (20) into:

$$m+\upsilon n>e^{m-1} \tag{29}$$

As we know, m is positive (see p. [124]). We can easily prove that a necessary, though insufficient, condition at which (29) is satisfied, i.e. there are cyclical variations, is that n be positive too.

Fluctuations of I at a time sufficiently distant from the initial interval $(0, \upsilon)$ will be represented by the equation:

$$I(t)-U=F_1e^{(m-x_1)t/\upsilon}\sin y_1\frac{t}{\upsilon} \tag{28}$$

The amplitude of fluctuations is decreasing, remains constant, or rises, according as $x_1 \gtreqless m$.

The period is equal to

$$T=\frac{2\pi}{y_1}\upsilon. \tag{30}$$

On the basis of equations

$$A(t)=\frac{1}{\upsilon}\int_{t-\upsilon}^{t} I(\tau)d\tau \tag{7}$$

and

$$L(t)=I(t-\upsilon) \tag{4}$$

we can show L and A as functions of t, and see that these values are fluctuating, like I, around the value U. K is obtained by integration of:

$$K'(t)=L(t)-U \tag{8}$$

It also fluctuates around a certain constant value, which we denote by K_0. The whole calculation will be given in section III below with respect to a particular case when the amplitude of fluctuations is constant.

III

If, while $x_1=m$, the amplitude of fluctuations remains constant, (28) assumes the form:

$$I(t)-U=a\sin y_1\frac{t}{\upsilon} \tag{31}$$

where a is the constant amplitude.

That case is of particular importance as its appears to be nearest to actual conditions. Indeed, in reality we do not observe any *regular* progression or regression in the intensity of cyclical fluctuations.

Putting the value of I from (31) into (7) and (4), we get

$$A-U=\frac{1}{\upsilon}\int_{t-\upsilon}^{t}\left(a\sin y_1\frac{\tau}{\upsilon}+U\right)d\tau-U$$

$$=a\frac{\sin\frac{y_1}{2}}{\frac{y_1}{2}}\sin y_1\frac{t-\frac{\upsilon}{2}}{\upsilon} \qquad (32)$$

and

$$L-U=a\sin y_1\frac{t-\upsilon}{\upsilon} \qquad (33)$$

From (8) and (33)

$$K'(t)=a\sin y_1\frac{t-\upsilon}{\upsilon}$$

Integrating:

$$K-K_0=a\frac{\upsilon}{y_1}\cos y_1\frac{t-\upsilon}{\upsilon} \qquad (34)$$

where K_0 is the constant around which K is fluctuating, equal here to the average volume of the industrial equipment K during a cycle.

In a similar way, the average values of I, A, and L during a cycle will be equal, in our case of constant amplitude, to the constant U around which I, A, and L are fluctuating.

Taking into consideration the condition of a constant amplitude $x_1=m$, we shall now get from (20) and (24):

$$\cos y_1=\frac{m}{m+\upsilon n} \qquad (35)$$

and

$$\frac{y_1}{\operatorname{tg} y_1}=m \qquad (36)$$

These equations allow us to determine y_1; moreover, they define the interrelationship of m and n.

Between m and n there is yet another dependency. They are both coefficients in the equation:

$$I = m(C_1 + A) - nK \tag{11}$$

which must be true for one-cycle averages of I and A equal to U, and for the average value of K equal to K_0:

$$U = m(C_1 + U) - nK_0$$

Hence:

$$n = (m - 1)\frac{U}{K_0} + m\frac{C_1}{K_0} \tag{37}$$

Thus, if values of U/K_0 and C_1/K_0 were given, we could determine m and n from (35), (36), and (37). U/K_0 is nothing else but the rate of depreciation, as U is equal to the demand for restoration of equipment, and K_0 is the average volume of that equipment. C_1 is the constant part of capitalist consumption. U/K_0 and C_1/K_0 may be roughly evaluated on the basis of statistical data. If we also knew the average gestation period of investments υ, we could determine y_1 and the duration of the cycle $T = 2\pi\upsilon/y$.

We evaluate the gestation period of investments υ on the basis of data of the German Institut für Konjunkturforschung. The lag between the curves of beginning and termination of building schemes (dwellings, industrial and public buildings) can be fixed at 8 months; the lag between orders and deliveries in the machinery-making industry can be fixed at 6 months. We assume that the average duration of υ is 0.6 years.

The rate of depreciation U/K_0 is evaluated on the basis of combined German and American data. On that of the German data, the ratio of depreciation to the national income can be fixed at 0.08. With a certain approximation, the same is true for the USA. Further, according to official estimates of the wealth of the USA in 1922, we set the amount of fixed capital in the USA at \$120 milliards (land excepted). The national income is evaluated at \$70 milliards for 5 years about 1922. The rate of depreciation would thus be 0.08 . 70/120, i.e. *c.* 0.05.

Most difficult is the *evaluation of* C_1/K_0. K_0 was fixed at \$120 milliards; C_1 is, as we know, the constant part of capitalist consumption. Let us evaluate first the average capitalist consumption in the USA in the period 1909–18. The total net profit in that period averaged, according to King, \$16 milliards deflated to the purchasing power of 1913. The average increment of total capital in that period is estimated by King at \$5 milliards. That figure includes workers' savings, but, on the other hand, \$16 milliards of profits also covers 'capitalistic' incomes of workers (use of own houses, etc.). Thus the difference, $16-5 = 11$ milliards of 1913 dollars, represents sufficiently accurately the consumption of capitalists (farmers included). The average national income in the period 1909–18 amounted to \$36 milliards at the purchasing power of 1913 (King). The ratio of capitalist consumption to the national income would thus be 0.3. As, further, the average income during 5 years around 1922 amounted, as mentioned, to \$70 milliards at current prices, capitalist consumption in these years may be estimated at \$21 milliards. Now, we have to determine the constant part of that consumption. In order to do that, we assume that when the volume of capitalists' gross profits deviates from the average by, say, $\pm 20\%$, the corresponding relative change in their consumption is but 5%, i.e. 4 times smaller. That assumption is confirmed by statistical evidence. Accordingly, the constant part of the consumption of capitalists, equal to $C_1 + \lambda B$ (see above; λ is a constant fraction, B – the total gross profit), amounts to $\frac{3}{4}$ of \$21 milliards, i.e. \$16 milliards. The ratio C_1/K_0 would then be 16/120 or *c.* 0.13.

Equations (35), (36), and (37), if we put:

$$\upsilon = 0.6 \quad \frac{U}{K_0} = 0.05 \quad \frac{C_1}{K_0} = 0.13$$

give:

$$\cos y_1 = \frac{m}{m + 0.6n}$$

$$\frac{y_1}{\operatorname{tg} y_1} = m$$

$$n = 0.05(m-1) + 0.13m$$

The solution of these equations gives

$$m = 0.95 \quad n = 0.121 \quad y_1 = 0.378$$

Thus, the duration of the cycle is

$$T = \frac{2\pi}{y_1}\upsilon = \frac{2\pi}{0.378}0.6 = 10.0$$

The figure of 10 years thus obtained as the duration of a cycle is supported by statistical evidence: 8 to 12 years.[7] It may be objected

[7] Shorter cycles can be considered as 'short-wave' fluctuations.

Table 5. *Dependence of the Duration of the Cycle on Changes of* υ, I_0/K_0, *and* C_0/K_0

υ	U_0/K_0	C_1/K_0	T
0.6	0.05	0.13	10.0
0.6	0.03	0.13	10.0
0.6	0.07	0.13	10.0
0.6	0.05	0.07	13.2
0.6	0.05	0.19	8.5
0.3	0.05	0.13	7.1
0.9	0.05	0.13	12.5

that values υ_1, U/K_0, C_1/K_0, on which our calculation was based, were but roughly estimated, and that the conformity between facts and theory can be merely a coincidence. Let us calculate T for such values of υ_1, U/K_0, C_1/K_0 as would be quite different from those previously taken (see Table 5).

We see that the value of U/K_0 plays no great role with respect to the result of our calculation. We see further that when values of C_1/K_0 and υ differ by almost 50% from those adopted before ($C_1/K_0=0.13$ and $U/K_0=0.05$), solutions for T move between 7 and 13 years. The actual duration of the cycle being, as already mentioned, 8 to 12 years, we can safely say that, irrespective of the degree of accuracy in estimating υ, U/K_0, C_1/K_0, there is no flagrant incongruity between the consequences of our theory and reality.

There is one more question to be dealt with. During the whole time we have considered, as stated at the very beginning of the study, an economic system free of secular trend. But a case when the trend is uniform, and when gross accumulation, capitalist consumption, and the volume of industrial equipment show the same rate of development, can be easily reduced to a state 'free of trend' simply by dividing all these values by the denominator of the trend. Interrelationships stated in our section I will remain true for these quotients, with the following changes.

1. The value U will be no longer equal to the demand for restoration of the used-up equipment, but it will cover as well the steady demand for the expansion of the existing equipment as a result of the uniform secular trend. Thus U/K_0 will be equal, not to the rate of depreciation, 0.05, but, assuming the rate of net accumulation equal, say, to 3%, to 0.08.

2. Also stocks of goods, previously considered constant, will increase in the same proportion under the influence of the trend. That steady increment of stocks per unit of time—let us call it C_2—will be a component of the gross profit B, now equal to $C + C_2 + A$, where C is personal capitalist consumption, C_1 the steady increment of stocks, and A the production of capital goods. If we now consider that, according to equation (2), capitalist consumption C is equal to $C_1 + \lambda B$, we see that B is proportional to $C_1 + C_2 + A$. The constant $C_1 + C_2$ will play in our considerations the same role as C_1 previously did. According to the official estimate of the national wealth of the USA, the volume of stocks of goods amounts to 0.3 of the volume of the industrial equipment, i.e. to $0.3 . K_0$. If the rate of net accumulation is 3%, C_2 will be $0.03 . 0.3 . K_0$. Hence, instead of $C_1/K_0 = 0.13$ we must take $(C_1 + C_2)/K_0 = 0.14$. From Table 5 we may easily see that both modifications—0.08 instead of 0.05 for U/K_0 and 0.14 instead of 0.13 for C_1/K_0—will have little effect on the result of the calculation of T.

We shall now determine, on the basis of (31), (32), (33), and (34), equations of curves I, A, L, and K, with $\upsilon = 0.6$ and $T = 10.0$:

$$\begin{aligned} I - U &= a \sin 0.63t \\ A - U &= 0.98a \sin 0.63\ (t - 0.3) \\ L - U &= a \sin 0.63\ (t - 0.6) \\ K - K_0 &= -1.59a \cos 0.63\,(t - 0.6) \end{aligned}$$

Assuming, in conformity with the above estimate, $U/K_0 = 0.05$, we find the following formulae for the relative deviations from the state of equilibrium:

$$\frac{I - U}{U} = \frac{a}{U} \sin 0.63t \tag{38}$$

$$\frac{A - U}{U} = \frac{a}{U} 0.98 . \sin 0.63\,(t - 0.3) \tag{39}$$

$$\frac{L - U}{U} = \frac{a}{U} \sin 0.63(t - 0.6) \tag{40}$$

$$\frac{K - K_0}{K_0} = -\frac{a}{U} 0.08 \cos 0.63(t - 0.6) \tag{41}$$

IV

Figure 10 represents the curves of investment orders I, of production of capital goods A, of deliveries of industrial equipment L, and of the

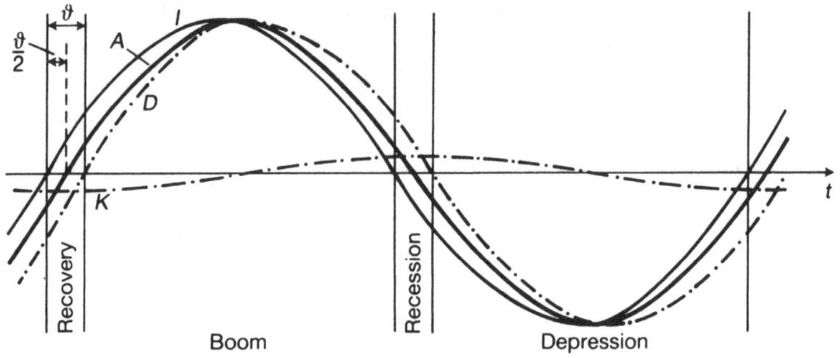

FIG. 10

volume of industrial equipment K, which correspond to formulae (38), (39), (40), and (41). Let us recall dependence (11), $I = m(C_1 + A) - nK$, whence it follows, if m and n are positive (see p. [129]), that the volume of investment orders is an increasing function of the gross accumulation equal to the production of capital goods, and a decreasing function of the volume of existing industrial equipment. Having these in mind, we can, on the basis of Fig. 10, explain the mechanism of the business cycle.

Recovery is the phase of the cycle of a length υ during which investment orders begin to exceed the demand for renewal of industrial equipment. But the actual volume of existing industrial equipment is not yet increasing, as deliveries of new equipment still remain below the demand for renewal of equipment.

The output of capital goods A, equal to the gross accumulation, is on the increase. Meanwhile, the volume of existing industrial equipment K is still on the decrease, and, as a result, investment orders rise rapidly.

During *prosperity* also, deliveries of equipment exceed the demand for renewal of the equipment, and thus the volume of the existing equipment is increasing. The rise of K at first hampers the rise of investment orders, and at last causes their drop. The output of capital goods follows suit, and begins to fall off in the second part of prosperity.

During *recession*, investment orders are below the level of the demand for renewal of the industrial equipment, but the volume of the existing industrial equipment K is still on the increase, since deliveries are still below the demand for renewal. As the volume of production of capital goods, equal to the gross accumulation A, continues to fall off, the volume of investment orders I, decreases rapidly.

During *depression*, deliveries of equipment are below the level of the demand for renewal of the equipment, and the volume of the existing equipment is dropping. The drop in K at first smoothes the downward tendency in investment orders, and then stimulates their rise. In the second part of depression the production of capital goods also begins to increase.

We have plotted investment orders, gross accumulation, and existing industrial equipment. But the fluctuations in the volume of the gross accumulation, which appear as a result of the functioning of the business cycle mechanism, must necessarily affect the movement of prices and the total volume of production. Indeed, the real gross profit B is, on the one hand, an increasing function of the gross accumulation A (B being proportional to $C_1 + A$, where C_1 is the constant part of capitalist consumption—see above) and, on the other hand, can be represented as a product of the general volume of production and of the profit per unit of production. In that way, the general volume of production and prices (or rather the ratio of prices to wages, determining the profit per unit of output) rises in the upward part of the cycle as the gross accumulation increases.

The interdependence of gross accumulation, equal to the production of capital goods, and the general movement of production and prices is realized in the following way. While the output of capital goods increases by a certain amount, in the general volume of production, beside that increment, there is another increment because of the increased demand for consumer goods on the part of workers recently hired by industries making capital goods.[8] The consequent increase in employment in industries making consumer goods results, in its turn, in an increase in the demand for consumer goods on the part of workers. As there is simultaneously a rise in prices, the new demand is but partly met by the new production. The remaining part of that demand is satisfied at the expense of the 'old' workers, whose real earnings suffer a reduction. The general level of production and prices must eventually rise, so as to provide for an increment of the real profit equal to the increment of the production of capital goods.

That description is incomplete in so far as it does not reckon with changes in the personal consumption of capitalists. That consump-

[8] We take for granted that there is a reserve army of unemployed.

tion, C, is dependent, to a certain extent, on the proportions of the total profit B, and increases in accordance with the gross accumulation A (from equations (2) and (3) it follows that $C = (C_1 + \lambda A)/(1+\lambda)$, where λ is a constant fraction). The increase in capitalist consumption has the same effect as the increase in production of capital goods: there is an increase in the volume of production of consumer goods for the use of capitalists; as a result, employment increases, stimulating an additional demand for consumer goods for the use of workers and, eventually, a further rise in production and prices.

The general level of production and prices must rise, eventually, so as to provide for an increment of the real profit equal to the increment of the production of capital goods and of the consumption of capitalists.

The question may still arise of where capitalists find the means to increase at the same time the production of capital goods and their own consumption. Disregarding the technical side of the money market, e.g. the variable demand for means of payment, we may say that these outlays are 'financing themselves'. Imagine, for instance, that some capitalists withdraw during a year a certain amount from their savings deposits, or borrow that amount at the central bank, in order to invest it in the construction of some additional equipment. In the course of the same year that amount will be received by other capitalists in the form of profits (since, according to our assumptions, workers do not save), and again put into a bank as a savings deposit or used to pay off a debt to the central bank. Thus the circle will close itself.

Yet in reality, just because of the technical side of the money market, which, as a matter of fact, forms its very nature, a credit inflation becomes necessary for two reasons.

The first is the fact that the curve I of investment orders does not coincide exactly with that of production of capital goods A, equal to the gross accumulation. When giving an investment order, the entrepreneur has to provide first some corresponding fund, out of which he will finance the filling of that order. At any time the corresponding bank account will be increased (per unit of time) by the amount I equal to the volume of orders allocated, and simultaneously decrease by an amount A spent on the production of capital goods.[9]

[9] The values concerned are not exactly the real values of I and A but corresponding amounts of money, calculated at current prices.

In that way, at any time investment activities require an amount I (per unit of time), namely: $I - A$ to form new investment reserves, and A to be spent on the production of capital goods. The amount actually spent, A, 'finances itself', i.e. returns to the bank in the form of realized profits, while the increment of investment reserves $I - A$ is to be created by means of a credit inflation.

Another reason for the inflation of credit is the circumstance that the increase in the production of capital goods or in capitalist consumption, i.e. increased profits, stimulates a rise in the general level of production and prices. This has the effect of increasing the demand for means of payment in the form of cash or current accounts, and to meet that increased demand a credit inflation becomes necessary.

[4]

A Theory of the Business Cycle[1]

M. Kalecki

Introduction

1. This paper, in which I attempt to give an analysis of investment processes, is closely allied to the Keynesian theory. The latter can be divided into two parts: (i) the determination of short-period equilibrium with a given capital equipment and with a given rate of investment; (ii) the determination of the rate of investment. In the section 'Short-Period Equilibrium' I give a representation of the first part of the Keynesian theory, arriving at its chief theorems in a slightly different way. In the following three sections I deal with the determination of the rate of investment, and there the results are fundamentally different from those of the Keynesian theory. These divergences are due to the important role played in my arguments by the time-lag between investment decisions and investment production, and also to a different treatment of the question of the inducement to invest. In the last section I show that the investment processes necessarily create a business cycle.

2. I assume in the whole paper that workers do not save (or dis-save). For the savings of workers certainly do not play an important part in the economic process, while to take them into consideration can often obscure some essential features of the capitalist economy. Therefore, it seems to me preferable to deal here with a system in which only capitalists (entrepreneurs and rentiers) save—exactly as is usually admitted in the assumption of a closed economy as being justifiable in a first approach. (I assume, also, in the whole paper a closed economic system.)

The second simplifying assumption I make concerns the wear and tear of fixed capital caused by its use in production. I assume that this 'extra wear and tear' is negligible and thus the total wear and tear is due to obsolescence. This assumption, contrary to the Keynesian conception of user-cost, does not imply an underestimation of its importance but is simply made to avoid complications inherent in this subject. I think, however, that this simplification will not affect the results of our analysis much.

[1] *Review of Economic Studies*, 4/2, 1936–7, pp. 77–97. We are grateful for permission to reproduce this article.

With this assumption, the only prime costs are those of labour and raw-materials. If we thus denote by the income of capitalists from an enterprise the difference between the value of its output and the value of prime costs, we find that this income is equal to the value of production minus the cost of labour and raw materials. We shall call the national income the sum of capitalists' and workers' incomes. It is easy to see that the national income is equal to the sum of the value of the output of all enterprises minus the value of the output of raw materials. But, hence, it follows that the national income is equal to the value of consumption, purchases of fixed capital equipment, and increase of stocks. The value of the purchases of fixed capital and the increase of stocks we shall call investment. It is clear that this is gross investment, and also that the income of capitalists means here their gross income, i.e. that from either the supplementary cost is not subtracted.

For both Keynes's theory and this paper, the notion of a given capital equipment is essential. The objection is often raised that it is wrong to assume a given capital equipment within a period, because the investment changes the equipment during this period. The answer is very simple: this period can be made so short that the change in the equipment is small enough not to affect the formation of output and income. For output and income are quantities measured per unit of time and thus are not dependent on the length of the period taken into consideration, whilst the change of equipment is, *ceteris paribus*, proportional to this length.

Short-Period Equilibrium

1. Output with a given capital equipment depends on the quantity of labour employed and on its distribution among the various sections of this equipment. In every enterprise employment is pushed to the point at which marginal revenue is equal to the marginal prime cost.

We shall represent the point of intersection of the marginal revenue and the marginal prime cost curves as follows. We subtract from both price and prime costs the cost of raw materials, and thus we obtain the so-called value added and labour costs respectively. We can now say that the output of an enterprise is given by the intersection of the curves of marginal value added and of marginal labour cost (see Fig. 36). Marginal value added and marginal labour cost are both expressed here in wage units.[1] We shall call short-time equilibrium a state in which the marginal labour cost curves and marginal value-added curves do not move. With a given capital equipment the curves of marginal labour cost are fixed. The establishment of short-time equilibrium with a given equipment will thus consist in the shift of marginal value-added curves.

The area $0ABC$ is the value added of the enterprise expressed in wage units, the hatched area is the income of the capitalists obtained from this enterprise, while the unhatched area is the income of the workers. Thus the sum of $0ABC$—areas of all enterprises—is the national income expressed in wage units, while the sum of the hatched areas is the total income of the capitalists, and that of the unhatched areas the total income of the workers. The national income is also equal to the value of total consumption and total investment, and, as we have

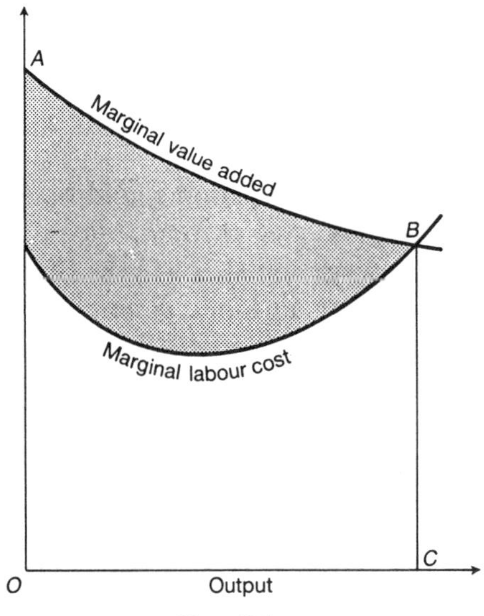

FIG. 36

[1] Keynes defines the wage-unit as follows: 'in so far as different grades and kinds of labour and salaried assistance enjoy a more or less fixed relative remuneration, the quantity of employment can be sufficiently defined for our purpose by taking an hour's employment of ordinary labour as our unit and weighting an hour's employment of special labour in proportion to its remuneration; i.e. an hour of special labour remunerated at double ordinary rates will count as two units. We shall call the unit in which the quantity of employment is measured the labour-unit; and the money-wage of a labour-unit we shall call the wage-unit' (*The General Theory of Employment*, p. 31).

assumed that the workers do not save, the sum of the unhatched areas covers the value of the consumption of the workers, while the sum of the hatched areas is the value of the consumption of the capitalists and of the investment.

We can now make clear the key position of the spending of the capitalists in the formation of short-time equilibrium. In such an equilibrium the marginal value-added curves remain by definition in a certain determined position. As we have just shown, the sum of the hatched areas is equal to the spending of the capitalists on consumption and investment, and the sum of the unhatched areas covers the consumption of the workers. There can be no spontaneous change in the spending of the workers, because they spend, by assumption, as much as they earn, but such changes of spending are quite possible for capitalists. Let us assume that the capitalists spend a given amount more than before per unit of time. Then there will be a shift in the marginal value-added curves until the sum of the hatched areas is equal to the increased spending by the capitalists for consumption and investment. As the sum of the hatched areas is also equal to the total income of the capitalists, the increase of their spending 'forces' their income to rise by the same amount.

It is clear that in the new short-period equilibrium the employment, the income of the workers, and therefore the value of their consumption (measured in wage units) is greater than before. Hence it follows that the demand for all kinds of investment and consumer goods, for both capitalists and workers, has risen, and thus a shift of the marginal value-added curves must have taken place in all industries.

We see now that the spending of the capitalists determines a position of marginal value-added curves such that the sum of the hatched areas, i.e. the incomes of the capitalists, is equal to the amount they spend. In this way the level of the spending of the capitalists (expressed in wage units) is the chief determinant of the short-period equilibrium and particularly of employment and income.

2. We have shown that the spending of the capitalists 'forces' a capitalist income which is equal to this spending. As the spending of the capitalists consists of their consumption and investment, and the income of the capitalists of their consumption and saving, it can also be said that the investment 'forces' saving to an amount which is equal to the amount of this investment. It is clear that in general the same capitalists do not invest and save: the investments of some create a saved income of an equal amount for others.

We assume now a definite capitalist propensity to consume, i.e. to every level of total capitalist income expressed in wage units there corresponds a definite distribution of this income between consumption and saving. It is clear that, in this way, to every level of saving there corresponds a definite level of capitalist consumption. Hence it can easily be concluded that the amount of investment expressed in wage units determines the total sum of the spending of capitalists; for the amount of investment I forces an equal amount of saving, and if capitalist consumption is, say, lower than the level C corresponding to the amount I of saving, then the capitalists will consume more; in this way they will push their income to the level $C+I$ at which the proportion between consumption C and saving I is in accordance with their propensity to consume.

3. We see now that the total investment I per unit of time expressed in wage units determines, *grosso modo*, the short-period equilibrium. For with a given propensity to consume there corresponds to I definite capitalist consumption C, and thus we have the total spending of the capitalists $C+I$ and its distribution between consumption and investment. To determine the short-period equilibrium in full detail we need, in addition to this, some knowledge of the kind of investments and the tastes of both capitalists and workers. If we assume these tastes as known, the only indeterminate element in the short-period equilibrium corresponding to the given amount I of spending on investments (in wage units) per unit of time is the distribution of this spending amongst various kinds of investment. But we can admit, I think, that the changes in the structure of investment expenses have no great importance for the general employment and national income Y expressed in wage units, and we can write, therefore, without making a considerable mistake:

$$Y=f(I)$$

f is here an increasing function and its shape is defined by the given capital equipment, capitalist propensity to consume, and the tastes of capitalists and workers. The derivative of this function:

$$\frac{dY}{dI}=f'(I)$$

is the Keynesian multiplier. If investment changes from the *given* level I

to the *given* level $I + \Delta I$—where ΔI is a small increment—then income will change from level Y to level $Y + \Delta I \cdot f'(I)$. This is the only question the multiplier answers and no other service can be required from it.

The Dynamic Process as a Chain of Short-Period Equilibrium

1. With given capital equipment, capitalist propensity to consume, and the tastes of both capitalists and workers, the amount of investment I expressed in wage units determines, as we have seen above, almost entirely the short-period equilibrium (the only indeterminate factor being the structure of investment) and particularly the amount of total employment and income. Thus it can now be asked: 'What determines investment?' Here a treatment of the subject called by Keynes 'inducement to invest' might be expected, but we postpone the examination of this problem to the next section, and now we propose to consider the matter from quite different point of view. We wish now to state that the present investment, i.e. the value of present investment output, is a result not of *present* but of *former* investment decisions, for, as we shall see immediately, a certain, relatively long, time is needed to complete the investment projects. This fact is of fundamental importance for the dynamics of an economic system. For the investments at a given moment fail to be a variable dependent on other factors acting at this moment, and become a datum inherited from the past like the capital equipment. (We assume that the investment decision is irrevocable in the course of construction of the particular object.) It is clear that the present phenomena are also a basis for investment decisions, which, however, will be relevant for the formation of investment output only in the future, and so on.

2. Let us now examine more closely the dependence of present investment output on former investment decisions. If it is known that two years, say, are needed to build a factory, then during two years from the moment of the investment decision 1/24 of this factory will be produced monthly. Now it is easily seen that the output of investment per unit of time is determined by the volume of investment orders not yet completed and the corresponding time spaces necessary to finish them. If, for instance, at the beginning of a month the building of a factory worth £1,000,000 is ordered for delivery 20 months hence; and besides this there remains to be completed half a factory the total value of which is £1,200,000 and time of building 12 months; then the value of orders to be finished is £1,000,000 and £600,000 respectively, whilst the time needed is 20 months and 6 months; thus the monthly investment output is (£1,000,000/20) + (£600,000/6) = £150,000. No difficulty arises in generalizing this formula. If we denote the parts of the investment orders not yet completed (reckoned at prices current at the given moment expressed in wage units) by $o_1, o_2 \ldots$ and the corresponding time needed by $\upsilon_1, \upsilon_2 \ldots$, the present level of investment is:

$$I = \sum \frac{o_k}{\upsilon_k}$$

Let us now denote the sum Σo_k of uncompleted parts of investment orders at a given moment by O. We define as the average time υ a time such as is needed to produce investment goods of the value O at a rate of investment $I = \Sigma (o_k/\upsilon_k)$. Thus we have:

$$\upsilon = \frac{O}{I} = \frac{\Sigma o_k}{\Sigma \dfrac{o_k}{\upsilon_k}}$$

It should be pointed out that υ is not the average time required for the completion of investment decisions (gestation period), but the average time required for finishing the orders, which are in diverse stages of construction; in this way υ is, roughly speaking, half the average gestation period, because at every moment there exist orders whose completion has just begun, is near to the end, or has reached an intermediate position. In reality υ is likely to be equal to a few months; it is certainly not a constant value, but it varies slowly within a narrow range (see the mathematical note at the end of this paper). We shall assume for the sake of simplicity that υ is constant; but it is easy to see that the argument can be reconstructed without any difficulty for the case of slowly varying υ (see n. 2 below). From the above equation it follows $I = O/\upsilon$, thus if υ is assumed to be constant the rate of investment is proportional to the value of the stock of uncompleted orders.

3. Let us now imagine that the time is divided into periods of the length υ, supposing that within every one of these periods the investment I does not change, i.e. that instead of a continuous time-curve we consider a 'stair line' inscribed in this curve (see Fig. 37). In a similar way, we imagine also that the change of capital equipment in a υ-period does not affect the short-time equilibrium in this period but in

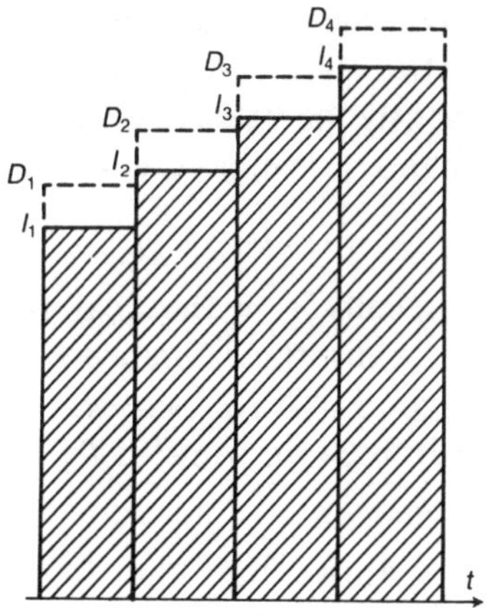

FIG. 37

the next. Thus as investment and capital equipment nearly define the short-period equilibrium output, income and prices also will prevail at a definite level during a υ-period and will change at the end of it.

At the beginning of period 1 we have a certain stock of uncompleted projects. The investment I in that period is equal to its current value divided by υ. Thus the value of investment goods $I_1 \upsilon$ produced in the period is just equal to the value of uncompleted parts of investment orders at the beginning of the period. Consequently the stock of uncompleted investment projects at the end of the υ-period is equal to the amount of investment decisions undertaken during this period.

If we thus denote the investment decisions per unit of time, i.e. the rate of investment decisions in period 1, by D_1 (reckoned at prices current during period 1 in wage units), the sum of uncompleted investment orders at the end of the period is equal to $D_1 \upsilon$. But *the investments per unit of time in period 2 reckoned at prices of period 1* are equal to this carry-over of orders from the first period divided by υ or $D_1 \upsilon / \upsilon = D_1$, i.e. *they are equal to the rate of investment decisions in the first period.*[2] Thus, if (as in Fig. 37) $D_1 > I_1$, the investment in period 2 reckoned at the prices of period 1 are larger than in the period 1. This

[2] The assumption about the constancy of υ was needed in order to demonstrate this proposition. But it is clear that it would be enough to assume that the difference between the length of two υ-periods following each other is negligible. Thus the assumption of the slow variation of υ is necessary but not its constancy. The latter is made only to simplify the exposition.

increased demand for investment goods will increase their prices (by an amount dependent on the state of equipment in investment goods industries) and consequently the value of investments in period 2. I_2 is thus, in turn, greater than D_1. We have, consequently, the inequality:

$$I_1 < D_1 < I_2$$

The difference $D_1 - I_1$ results from the 'real' increase of investment between periods 1 and 2, whilst the difference $I_2 - D_1$ is due to the rise in prices of investment goods.[3] If D_1 were less than I_1 the inequality would have changed its direction, whilst if $D_1 = I_1$ the investment I_2 would also be equal to I_1.

4. It follows from the above that the amount of investment I (measured in wage units) in a given υ-period is determined by the rate of investment decisions in the preceding period. Thus we can now imagine the dynamic process as a chain of short-period equilibria, each of them prevailing during time υ. Suppose we have in the initial υ-period a given amount of investment I_1 expressed in wage units, which on the basis of the capital equipment determines a short-period equilibrium. This state, which can be represented by the set of marginal value-added curves and marginal labour-cost curves of all enterprises, in conjunction with some other factors (principally the rate of interest), defines the rate of investment decisions D_1 in this period. But these decisions in turn determine the investment I_2 in period 2, and in that way also the new short-period equilibrium on the basis of the capital equipment, which has, of course, also changed in general as a result of wear and tear and of investments in the preceding period. Thus there is a new level of investment decisions and a further change in capital equipment caused by its wear and tear and by investments in the second period. As a result, we have again a new short-period equilibrium in the next period, and so on.

To be able to say more about the mechanism of the dynamic process, we must now examine the motives of investment decisions in order to show how the links of our chain are connected.

[3] As the result of changes in the prices of investment goods, a difference between the value of produced investment and the value of the corresponding orders will in general arise. Thus, if the prices have, say, risen, the entrepreneurs, who had given orders and obtain the investment objects at the old prices, make a relative gain, whilst the producers, whose marginal prime cost have undergone in the meantime a rise, suffer a relative loss.

The Inducement to Invest

1. In the Keynesian theory of inducement to invest, the fundamental notion is that of the marginal efficiency of an asset. Keynes defines it as the rate at which the prospective current returns (differences between revenues and effective expenditures) of an asset during its future 'life' have to be discontinued in order to obtain the present supply price of this asset. Keynes assumes that the greater the investment in a certain type of capital per unit of time, the less will be the marginal efficiency of the corresponding assets because of the rise of the supply prices of these assets. 'Now it is obvious that the actual rate of current investment will be pushed to the point where there is no longer any class of capital of which the marginal efficiency exceeds the current rate of interest.'[4] In other words, if at a given moment there is a gap between the marginal efficiency of the various assets and the rate of interest, the investment per unit of time will rise until the increase of the prices of investment goods caused by this will reduce the marginal efficiency of all assets to the level of the rate of interest.

There are two things lacking in this conception. First, it tells us nothing about the rate of investment decisions taken by entrepreneurs faced with *given* market prices of investment goods. It indicates only that, unless the marginal efficiency of all assets calculated on the basis of this level of prices of investment goods is equal to the rate of interest, a change of investment will take place which will transform the given situation into a new one, in which the marginal efficiency of various assets *is* equal to the rate of interest.

But a new trouble now arises. Let us assume that the rate of investment has really, say, risen so much that the new level of investment prices and the *initial* state of expectations give a marginal efficiency equal to the rate of interest. The increase of investment, however, will cause not only the prices of investment goods to rise, but also a rise of prices (or, more precisely, the upward shift of marginal revenue curves) and employment in all branches of trade. Thus, because 'the facts of the existing situation enter, in a sense disproportionately, into the formation of our long-term expectations',[5] the state of expectations will improve and the marginal efficiency of assets appears again higher than the rate of interest. Consequently equilibrium is not reached and investment continues to rise.

[4] *General Theory*, p. 136.

[5] Ibid., p. 148.

We see now that the Keynesian conception, which tells only how great investment will be if the given disequilibrium changes into an equilibrium, encounters a difficulty in this respect also, for it appears that the rise of investment does not lead to equilibrium at all (in any case, not to immediate equilibrium). I shall further try to give an outline of a different conception of inducement to invest which endeavours to find factors determining the amount of investment decisions corresponding to *every* definite state of long-term expectations, prices of investment goods, and rate of interest.

2. We start from the problem of uncertainty, which is also involved in Keynes's arguments. It can be gathered from his exposition that a certain amount has to be subtracted from the marginal efficiency of assets (calculated on the basis of the current prospective returns) to cover risk before comparing it with the rate of interest. We can express the same point in this manner: the gap between the marginal efficiency of assets calculated on the basis of the prospective current returns of these assets, which we shall call the prospective rate of profit, and the rate of interest, is equal to the risk incurred. But here we wish to draw attention to a point not considered by Keynes.

The rate of risk of every investment is greater the larger this investment is. If the entrepreneur builds up a factory, he incurs a certain risk of unprofitable business, and these losses, if any, will be more significant for him the greater proportion the investment considered bears to his wealth. But besides this, in sacrificing his reserves (consisting of deposits or securities) or taking credits, he exhausts his sources of capital, and if he should need this capital in the future he may be obliged to borrow at a high rate of interest because he has overdrawn the amount of credit considered by his creditors as normal. Thus both these aspects of risk incurred by investment show that the rate of risk must grow with the amount invested.

Now, I think we have the key to the problem of amount of investment decisions in a given economic situation in a certain period of time, for instance, in our υ-period. This amount is just so much as will equate the marginal risk to the gap between the prospective rate of profit and the rate of interest, both being given by the economic situation of the period in question. The greater the gap, the greater the sum of investment decisions in the period, for two reasons. First, the number of people undertaking investment increases, including the more timid entrepreneurs; and, secondly, each of them invests more.

3. In all this conception, however, an obscure point still remains. The entrepreneurs in the υ-period considered have taken so many investment decisions that any additional investment decision does not seem to them sufficiently attractive because of the growing risk. Will there, then, be no investment decision at all in the next υ-period if the gap between the prospective rate of profit and rate of interest remains at the same level as before? Certainly this is not the case. For the value of the investment in the second period—as we know from the preceding chapter—corresponds to the investment decisions in the first υ-period; further, the saving in the second period is equal to the investment in the second period; thus the capitalists as a body save in the second υ-period just the amount which they decided to invest in the first υ-period. To the money flow of investments there corresponds an equal money flow of savings, and if investment decisions of an equal amount should not be taken, an improvement in the security of wealth and liquidity for the entrepreneurs (who accumulate reserves or repay debts) would result at the end of the period; hence the marginal risk would be less than the gap between prospective rate of profit and the rate of interest. In this way, if the gap remains as supposed on the same level, a steady reinvestment of the same amount will take place. The flow of investment decisions continuously imposes the burden of risk on some capitalists, but the equal flow of savings relieves other capitalists from this burden.

If the gap between the prospective rate of profit and the rate of interest increases, the investment decisions in a υ-period will be pushed to the point at which the marginal risk is equal to the increased gap. If this gap does not change further, reinvestment of the new higher amount will take place in the following periods.

Thus we can now say that *the rate of investment decisions is an increasing function of the gap between the prospective rate of profit and the rate of interest.*[6]

Two Determinants of the Investment Decisions

1. We have shown that the rate of investment decisions is an increasing function of the difference between the prospective rate of

[6] This can also be deduced as follows. It can be concluded from the above that the burden of risk is created only by the existence of unrealized investment decisions. Thus this burden is, *ceteris paribus*, higher the larger the stock of uncompleted orders at the end of a given υ-period, which (see p. 536) is equal to $D\upsilon$. Or the marginal risk increases with the rate of investment decisions D and, consequently, so must the gap between the prospective rate of profit and the rate of interest needed to cover the risk.

profit[7] and the rate of interest. To find out the determinants of investment decisions we must analyse the factors on which this difference is dependent. We shall divide the analysis into two parts: in the first we assume a given capital equipment, in the second we examine the effects of changes in this capital equipment.

The prospective rate of profit is defined by the long-term expectations of returns and the supply prices of investment goods. It was mentioned above that the point of departure for estimating future returns is the present state of affairs. Thus it is the short-period equilibrium which chiefly determines the prospective rate of profit at the given moment. For in this short-period equilibrium we have given the system of marginal value-added curves, which describes the present state of affairs, while these curves and the marginal labour-cost curves in the investment goods industries give us the level of investment goods prices.

But with a given capital equipment the short-period equilibrium is determined by the rate of investment I, and so, consequently, is the prospective rate of profit. The change in the rate of investment I will affect the prospective rate of profit from two sides in opposite directions: the increase, say, of the investment will raise the marginal value-added curves and consequently improve expectations, but at the same time it will also increase the prices of investment goods. Thus we can say that the prospective rate of profit with a given capital equipment is a function of investment I, but we do not know, a priori, whether this function is increasing or decreasing.

2. We are now going to show that, with certain assumptions, the rate of interest can also be represented as a function of investment I. We know that, with a given capital equipment, both employment and the national income Y expressed in wage units are increasing functions of I. Here we shall also make a justifiable assumption that with the rise of employment the wage unit w increases in a definite way (due to a relative shortage of certain kinds of labour, improvement in the position of trade unions, and so on). Thus income expressed in terms of money Yw will increase in a definite way if the investment I rises. For the rise of I causes a rise of Y, while the increased employment pushes nominal wages to a higher level.

[7] It is clear that in general the prospective rates of profit in various industries are not equal. But we can define the general prospective rate of profit as such a rate which, if it were to prevail in all industries, would affect the rate of investment decisions in the same way as the given set of prospective rates of profit.

The greater the money income Yw the greater the demand for cash for transactions, which, with a constant amount of money in circulation, must cause the rate of interest to increase. In general, the amount of money in circulation will not remain constant because the banking system creates new money; but also, in that case, we can assume that this creation will be accompanied by a rise in the rate of interest because of the falling liquidity of banks.

We see thus that the rise of investment I increases the demand for cash and has in that way the tendency to raise the rate of interest. It is, however, not the only way in which the rate of interest is affected by change in investment I. The investment I as we know determines (with a given capital equipment) the short-period equilibrium and thus the general state of affairs. But the better this state of affairs the greater the lender's confidence;[8] and through this channel, therefore, the rise of investment has a tendency to lower the rate of interest.

Probably these two opposite stimuli will cause the rate of interest to fall initially with an increase of investment I, but after passing a minimum the rate will begin to rise when investment further increases. For at a low level of investment I, and thus of income Y, the elasticity of supply of money is high, while an improvement in business much affects the lender's confidence, and thus the rate of interest is likely to fall with the rise of investment. But at a high level of investment and income, as the supply of money has become more inelastic and the lender's confidence is less sensitive to a further rise in business activity, the increase of investment will, rather, cause the rate of interest to rise.

3. We have stated that both the prospective rate of profit and the rate of interest can be represented, with certain assumptions, as functions of investment I. Thus the rate of investment decisions which is an increasing function of the difference between the prospective rate of profit and the rate of interest is also the function of investment I.

$$D = \phi(I)$$

Hence it follows that in a given υ-period it is the level of investment which determines the rate of investment decisions and thus the investment in the next υ-period.

We cannot say a priori whether the function ϕ is increasing or decreasing. For the rise of I improves the expectations of returns, but at the same time raises the prices of investment goods and may also raise

[8] On the lender's confidence, see *General Theory*, pp. 144, 309.

(if I is sufficiently great) the rate of interest. But it is very probable that below a certain level of I this function *is* increasing. For if the level of investment is not relatively high, the marginal prime-cost curve in the investment goods production increases only slightly with output and, consequently, so do the prices of investment goods. The rate of interest, which initially falls with the increasing investment, also, after having passed the minimum within a certain interval, rises only slightly. Thus, before I reaches a certain rather high level it can be assumed that a rise in it affects investment decisions more by improvement of expectations than by raising prices of investment goods and the rate of interest.

We can now discover some further features of the function υ which is represented here in Fig. 38. We shall try to show that the curve MAN representing this function must cut the straight line $0L$, drawn at 45° through the zero point 0, and that the left part MA lies above, whilst the right part AN lies below $0L$. In other words, there exists a value of investment I_A to which corresponds a value of investment decisions D_A equal to I_A, while for investment lower than I_A we have $D > I$, and for investments higher than I_A the opposite, i.e. $D < I$. There are, a priori, three possible positions of the curve ϕ besides that shown in Fig. 38 (see Fig. 39). We shall show that they are unrealistic. It is easy to show that if the curve lies entirely above $0L$, or (which is the same) if D is always greater than I, we shall have an unlimited cumulative upward process. For if in a certain υ-period there corresponds to investment I a higher amount of investment decisions D, then in the next υ-period the investment will be higher; but because the curve ϕ lies above $0L$

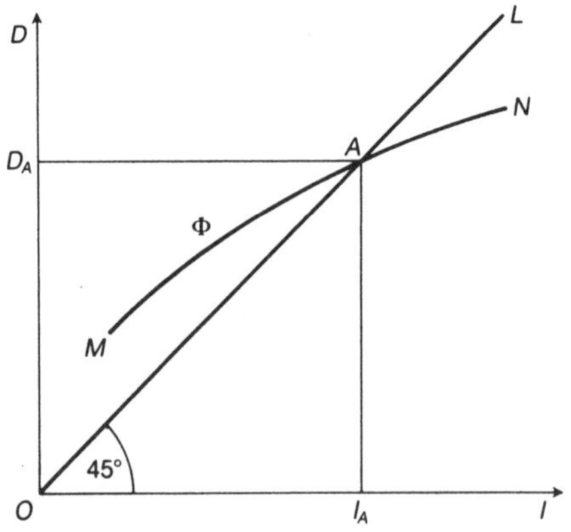

FIG. 38

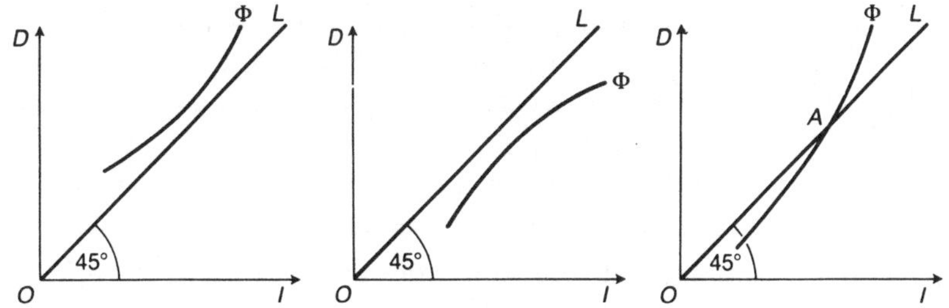

FIG. 39

the investment decisions in the second υ-period are again higher than the investment, and so on. In that way the investment would increase automatically without limit.

This is, however, impossible, for the limited amount of available labour does not permit investment and income to pass a certain level. What is the mechanism by which the cumulative process is stopped? In the neighbourhood of full employment the rise of nominal wages corresponding to every small increase of investment (measured in wage units) will be very sharp. It will cause a rapid rise of nominal income, of demand for money, and thus of the rate of interest. In that way the latter will soon reach the level at which investment decisions are equal to investment and thus there will be no tendency for a further rise of investment. But it all amounts to nothing more than the demonstration of the feature in question of the function ϕ. Because of the rapid rise of the rate of interest with the increased investment in the neighbourhood of full employment, the shape of this function must be such that the curve *MAN* cuts the straight line $0L$ at a point which cannot lie above the investment level corresponding to full employment. But it is clear that it may lie lower. For the investment in successive υ-periods may form a convergent series even without the restraining influence of the rate of interest.

4. We shall now demonstrate that the curve *MAN* cannot lie entirely below the straight line $0L$. In that case we should have an unlimited cumulative downward process. For if, in a certain υ-period, there corresponds to investment I a lower amount of investment decisions, it will cause a lower level of investment in the next period; but in that period D is again lower than I, and thus the downward process goes on. But, as in the case of the upward process, and unlimited movement is again impossible, though the factor which determines the limit is of quite a different nature.

The investment I by our definition is the value (expressed in wage units) of the purchases of fixed capital and the increase of stocks per unit of time. Thus it can be negative if the decrease of stocks is greater than the purchases of fixed capital, but, as we shall show at once, this negative value cannot fall below a certain level. We know that the capitalists' income is equal to their spending $C + I$ for consumer goods and investment. This income (from which supplementary costs are not subtracted) cannot be lower than zero, for otherwise the entrepreneurs would not produce at all. Thus we find that $C + I \geqq 0$ and consequently, $I \geqq -C$. Or the curve MAN must cut the straight line $0L$ at a point at which I is not lower than $-C$, where C is the capitalists' consumption in the case when their income is zero.

Now it is easy to see that the third position of the curve is also unrealistic; for if the investment is initially lower than the abscissa of A, we have an unlimited downward cumulative process, and if it is initially higher than the abscissa of A, an upward cumulative process goes on indefinitely. To summarize: we have stated three features of the function ϕ represented by the curve MAN:

(i) The curve MAN is initially ascending.

(ii) This curve cuts at point A the straight line $0L$ drawn through the zero point at 45°. The part MA of MAN lies above and the part AN below $0L$.

(iii) The investment I at this point of intersection A with OL is not higher than the investment level corresponding to full employment and not lower than $-C$, where C is capitalist consumption, when their income is zero.

5. We have up to now examined the dependence of the rate of investment decisions D on investment I assuming a given capital equipment. Now we are going in turn to analyse the influence of changes in this equipment on the investment decisions if the investment is given. In that way we shall be able to describe D as a function of both investment I and capital equipment.

We begin with the statement that, if investment I remains constant (capitalists' propensity to consume assumed as given), so also does total capitalists' spending $C + I$ and, consequently, total capitalists' income, which is equal to their spending. Thus, if the capacity of equipment, say, increases, it is easy to see that the state of affairs becomes worse. For if the same income is earned by capitalists on a greater number of factories the income on every factory is less. The new factories compete with the old ones, the downward shift of marginal value-added curves reduces capitalist income (hatched area on Fig. 34) in the old factories, and in that way a part of the total income of the capitalists $C + I$—being by assumption constant—is transferred to the new factories.

Thus it is clear that the increase of capital equipment with constant investment I, and thus with constant spending and income of the capitalists, must have a depressing effect on expectations. It is not certain, however, whether the prospective rate of profit will fall; for if the equipment is expanded also in investment goods industries, the prices of these goods will decline, and this may counterbalance the less favourable state of expectations.

We leave this case aside, however, from further exposition for the sake of simplicity[9] and thus assume that with constant capitalist spending the expansion of equipment causes the prospective rate of profit to fall.

The depressing effect of the increase of equipment on the prospective rate of profit stated here is also one of the fundamental propositions of the Keynesian theory. But it is considered there rather as a general principle which does not require to be proved. From our above argument it is clear that this law is valid only on the assumption of constant spending by capitalists (and in that case also with some additional assumption); if this spending increases in the same proportion as equipment, the prospective rate of profit has no tendency to fall.

Our proper aim was to state the influence of the change in capacity of equipment on investment decisions when capitalist spending re-

[9] It can be shown that this simplification does not affect the validity of the explanation of the business cycle given in the next section. The case left aside can occur only at the top of the boom when the supply of investment goods may become inelastic, because only on that condition will the increase of equipment producing these goods cause their prices to fall significantly. We should have then a situation in which investment does not rise (because it is the *top* of the boom), equipment expands, and the prospective rate of profit does not fall. This situation, however, could not last long. For the fall of the prices of investment goods would continuously increase the profitability of consumer goods industries at the expense of investment goods industries. Thus there would be a shift of investment activity from the latter to the former, the increase of consumer goods equipment would be accelerated, and that of investment goods equipment retarded; and this would cause the expected returns to fall more strongly than the prices of investment goods. The fall of the prospective rate of profit—which in our representation of the business cycle process in the next section accounts for the breaking down of the boom— would only be delayed; the economic system would stay longer at the top of the boom, to be, however, eventually overcome by the slump.

mains constant. The investment decisions are, as we know, an increasing function of the gap between the prospective rate of profit and the rate of interest. We have stated that (on certain assumptions) the prospective rate of profit falls when equipment is expanding. We have yet to examine what will happen to the rate of interest.

If the equipment expands with constant capitalist spending, the marginal value-added curves shift down, and the degree of employment in each factory diminishes. But this is accompanied by the fall of the relative share of the capitalists in value added in each factory[10] and, consequently, of the relative share of the capitalists in the national income. Since, however, their income, which equals their spending, is by assumption constant, this means that the national income must increase. Thus expansion of equipment with constant capitalist spending causes a rise of demand for cash, and, consequently an increase of the rate of interest.

From this and the depressing influence on the prospective rate of profit, it may be concluded that the increase of the capacity of equipment with the constant spending of the capitalists causes a reduction of the gap between the prospective rate of profit and the rate of interest, and thus a fall in investment decisions. But if the investment is constant, the spending of the capitalists is constant, too. Or we get: the greater the equipment with a constant investment I, the less the rate of investment decisions D.

The curve representing the function $D = \phi(I)$ is drawn on the assumption of a constant equipment. If the equipment changes, this curve will be shifted. And it follows from the above that it will be shifted down when the equipment increases. The greater the capacity of the equipment, the lower will be the position of the curve ϕ. In that way the family of curves ϕ represents the rate of investment decisions D as a function of two determinants—the rate of investment I and the volume of equipment [see Fig. 40].

The Business Cycle

1. Let us now, again, consider the dynamic process represented as a chain of short-period equilibria, each lasting a υ-period. To simplify the exposition we will examine this process in two stages: in the first we abstract the changes of capital equipment; in the second stage we take

[10] This is not strictly a rule, but the opposite case can be considered exceptional.

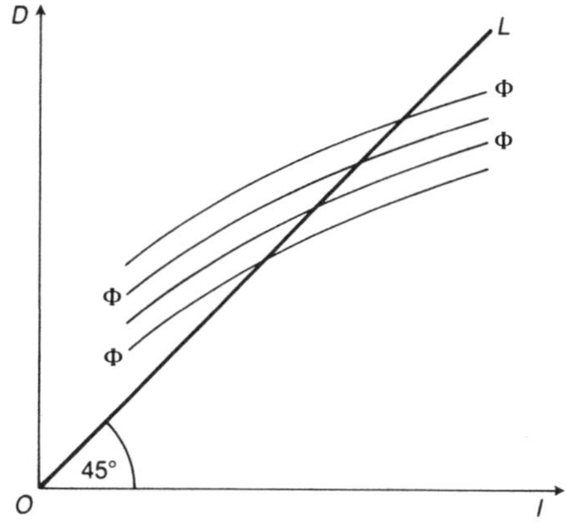

FIG. 40

into account also the influence of the changes which result from investment and wear and tear.[11]

Suppose the level of investment (expressed in wage units) in the first υ-period to be I_1 (see Fig. 41).

The curve ϕ on the left represents the dependence of the rate of investment decisions D on the investment I with a given equipment. Drawing a horizontal on the level I_1, we obtain first the point of intersection P_1 with $0L$, whose abscissa (being equal to the ordinate) is equal to I_1. Drawing the vertical through P_1 we obtain on the curve ϕ the point (I_1, D_1), whose ordinate is D_1—the rate of investment decisions corresponding to I_1—and thus that which will take place in the first υ-period.

The rate of investment decisions in the first υ-period is, as we see, higher than investment (we have so chosen our initial position). We know from the second section that the investment in the next υ-period reckoned at the prices of the first υ-period is equal to D_1. Thus, because $D_1 > I_1$ the real value of investment in the second υ-period is greater than in the first; this causes the prices of investment goods to increase, and we have:

$$I_1 < D_1 < I_2$$

where $D_1 - I_1$ is the real increase of investment from period 1 to period

[11] In the first stage we can imagine, for instance, that both investment and wear and tear are very small in relation to equipment; thus the equipment changes only a little in the course of the process considered.

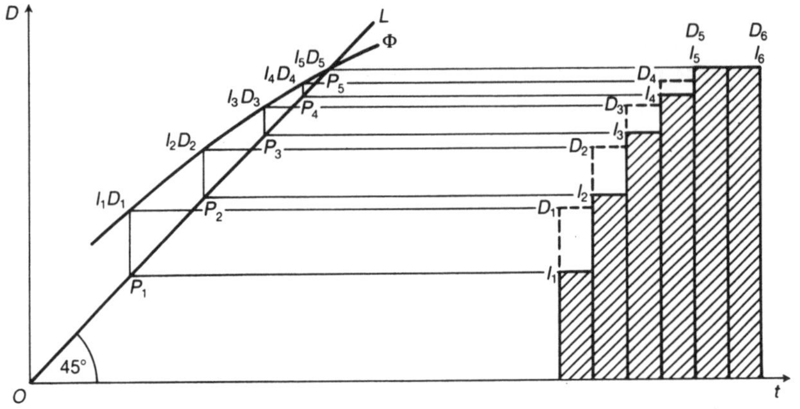

FIG. 41

2, and $I_2 - D_1$ is due to the corresponding rise of prices of investment goods.

Now, with the help of the curve ϕ, we can obtain again the level of investment decisions D_2, which is again greater than I_2 and which causes the increase of investment to the level I_3 in the third period, and so on.

In that way we reach, finally, in the fifth period the level of investment I_5, to which there corresponds on the curve ϕ the point of intersection of this curve with the straight line $0L$, i.e. we reach a position in which $D_5 = I_5$. Thus from this very moment the investment ceases to grow and in the sixth υ-period, the investment remains on the same level, and so also does the rate of investment decisions, which is equal to investment. All the process can be represented by the following scheme:

$$I_1 < D_1 < I_2 < D_2 < I_3 < D_3 < I_4 < D_4 < I_5 = D_5 = I_6 = D_6$$

We see here that the excess of investment decisions over investment in the first period causes a self-stimulating rise of investment, which in its essential nature is identical with the so-called Wicksellian cumulative process. This rise, however, leads to a position in which the investment ceases to grow, remaining afterwards at a constant level. (This maintenance of investment after period 5 takes place only on the assumption of constant equipment; we shall see in the next paragraph that it is precisely the increase of equipment, which disturbs this equilibrium.) It is easy to see that the equilibrium reached in period 5 is stable; if the investment is lowered beneath the level I_5 we shall have a rise represented above bringing it back to this level. But, also, if it rose above this value a fall of investment would take place and push it again back to the equilibrium level; for it is clear, in general, that if we start from a position in which $D < I$ we shall obtain a downward cumulative process in exactly the same way as we constructed the upward one above.

With a given curve ϕ, the time of adjustment leading to the state of equilibrium is proportional to the length of the υ-period. In general the time of change of investment from one given level to another with a given curve ϕ is proportionate to υ.

In the plane I, D the cumulative upward or downward process is always represented by the movement of point (I, D) along the curve ϕ towards its point of intersection with $0L$.

It is worth noting that these cumulative processes have nothing (at least directly) to do with the Keynesian multiplier. This last answers only the question of how much the national income will increase from a certain υ-period to the next υ-period as a result of the increase of investment; while the mechanism of the cumulative process determines this growth of investment as such. We can represent this by the following scheme:

$$I_1 < I_2 < I_3 < I_4 \ldots$$
$$Y_1 < Y_2 < Y_3 < Y_4 \ldots$$

where the first series represents the cumulative rise of investment and the second one the corresponding rise of national income. The multiplier is the ratio of the increment of income to the increment of investment.

2. We come to the second stage of our analysis of the dynamic process: we have now to consider the influence exerted on this process by changes in the capacity of equipment.

To every state of equipment there corresponds a certain level, W, of investment needed to maintain the equipment's capacity, which in the absence of this investment would shrink on account of wear and tear. If the investment I in a υ-period is equal to W, investment decisions in the next period are not affected by the changes in equipment. If $I > W$, the capacity of equipment increases in this period, which causes, *ceteris paribus*, a fall of investment decisions in the next one. Consequently, if we have an upward cumulative process and the investment is greater than the level needed for the maintenance of equipment capacity, this process is hampered by the increase of capacity; whilst when $I < W$ the opposite influence operates.

Thus, if the upward cumulative process described above starts from a position in which the investment is lower than the 'level of maintenance' W, the change of equipment stimulates it. But the situation alters when the investment begins to exceed the level of maintenance of capacity. The equipment capacity is expanding and this retards the cumulative process. Or, in other words, the curve ϕ along which the point (I, D) moves shifts upwards at the same time so long as $I < W$, but it begins to shift down when I becomes greater than W.

The influence of increasing capacity has, however, the greatest importance at the point at which investment decisions D become equal to investment I, and at which, consequently, the latter ceases to grow. For the expansion of equipment with constant investment greater than W causes a fall of investment decisions, which thus become in the next υ-period lower than the investment (see Fig. 42). In that way the downward cumulative process sets in.

So long as the investment is greater than the level of maintenance of the equipment capacity W, this capacity is further expanding, thus stimulating the downward cumulative process; but after the investment I becomes lower than W, the shrinkage of the equipment begins to retard it. When the point is reached in which $I = D$ and the investment ceases to decline, the further shrinkage of equipment causes

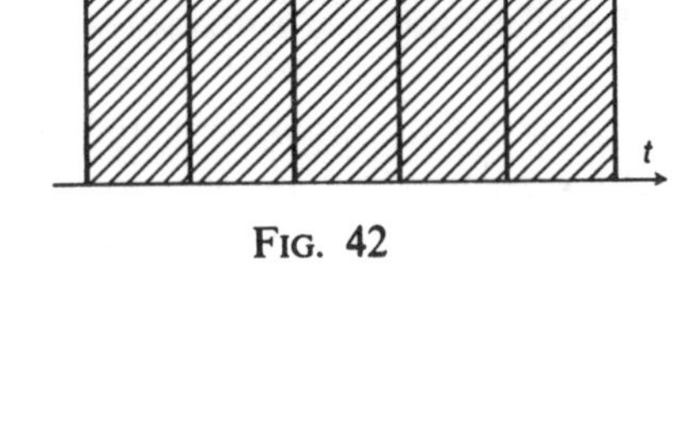

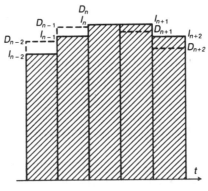

FIG. 42

an increase of investment decisions, and this will be the beginning of an upward cumulative process.

We have shown in section 1 above that a cumulative process with constant equipment leads to a state in which investment decisions are equal to investment and thus the latter remains in the following υ-periods at a constant level. Now we see that this equilibrium is disturbed by the change of capital equipment. After the upward cumulative process has come to an end, the rise of equipment capacity at the peak of prosperity causes a downward cumulative movement, which in turn is followed by an upward process started with the contraction of capacity at the bottom of the depression. The dynamic process consists thus of a series of upward and downward cumulative processes following each other. In other words, it forms a business cycle.

3. It is useful for the understanding of the nature of the business cycle to represent it as a movement of the point in the plane I, D. In Fig. 43 we have the curves ϕ representing the functional dependence of investment decisions D on investment I with various equipment capacities. The greater the equipment capacity, the lower the position of the corresponding curve ϕ.

We shall mark now on every curve the point whose abscissa is equal to the level W of investment needed for the maintenance of the capacity of equipment to which this curve ϕ corresponds. The locus of all these points is the curve *EG*.[12] For all points on that curve we have $I = W$, for all points on the left of it $I < W$, and for all points on the right $I > W$.

Now, if investment and investment decisions in a certain υ-period are represented by a point (I, D), this point will move along the curve ϕ towards the point of intersection with 0*L*, while this curve will shift upwards, downwards, or remain stationary according to whether the point (I, D) lies on the left of curve *EG* on the right of it, or on that curve.

Let us now assume that to investment and investment decisions in the first υ-period there corresponds the point *E*. At that point $I = W$, and thus the moving point (I, D), representing the variable investment and the rate of investment decisions in our dynamic process, moves along the curves *EA* towards *A* whilst this curve is stationary.

[12] This curve is descending because the lower the position of a curve ϕ the greater the corresponding equipment and the greater the level of investment W by which the capacity is maintained.

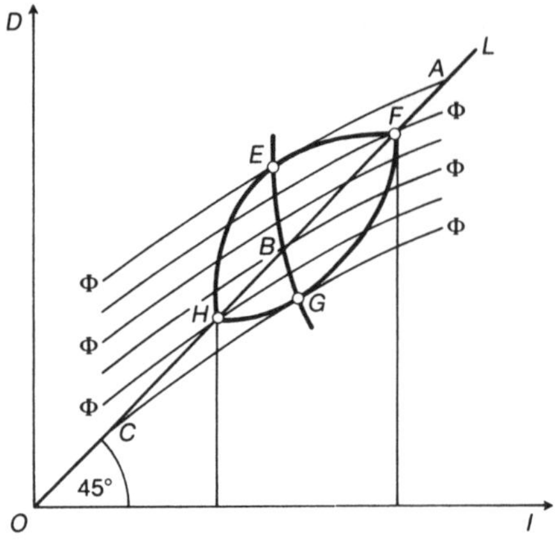

FIG. 43. The 'kinks' of the curve *EFGH* in *F* and *H* are due to discontinuity introduced by division of the process into τ-periods (cf. Fig. 42; point *F* corresponds to period *n*).

Investment *I* increases. Because of this, however, the investment in the next period is higher than the 'level of maintenance' *W*, and the curve ϕ begins to shift down. Consequently the moving point (*I*, *D*) has the trajectory *EF*, which is the resultant of the movement along ϕ and the downward shift of it. (In point *E* this trajectory is tangential to the curve ϕ.) At point *F* the investment *I* ceases to grow because $D = I$, whilst the curve ϕ shifts farther down; consequently the point (*I*, *D*) moves here vertically. In that way it falls below 0*L*; the investment decisions are now lower than investment and the latter begins to fall. The point (*I*, *D*) now moves along the curve ϕ to the left, whilst this curve shifts farther down because still $I > W$. In that way the moving points meets the curve *EG* in *G*. The curve ϕ now ceases to shift down, and the trajectory is here again tangential to *GC* as before to *EA*. But soon *I*, falling further, becomes lower than *W* and the curve ϕ begins to shift up, whilst the movement along the curve ϕ is further directed to the left because still $D < I$. At point *H* investment decisions become equal to investment, and the latter ceases to fall, while the curve shifts farther up. The point (*I*, *D*) moves here again vertically, but upwards. Thus *D* becomes greater than *I*, the movement along ϕ is directed to the right, while the curve ϕ shifts further up. In that way the moving point comes back to point *E* and the new cycle begins.

It is clear that the moving point cannot stop at any point of the trajectory. At *E* and *G* the investment is equal to the level of maintenance, but investment decisions are higher or lower respectively than the investment. In *F* and *H* the rate of investment decisions is equal to investment, and thus there is no tendency for a cumulative process, but investment is higher or lower respectively than the level of maintenance, and the equipment capacity expands or shrinks. The only point in the plane *I*, *D* from which there is no tendency to move is *B*, the point of intersection of *EG* and 0*L*. In that point $D = I = W$, or there is no tendency towards the cumulative process and no change of equipment capacity. It thus corresponds to long-run equilibrium. If the initial position of the moving point does not coincide with *B* it must move round it. In other words, if, in the first υ-period investment, investment decisions and equipment do not correspond to the point *B*, there must arise a business cycle.

Clearly it is an arbitrary assumption that the moving point comes back to its initial position *E*—the trajectory need not be a closed curve but may also be a spiral.

4. We see that the question, 'What causes the periodic crises?' could be answered briefly: the fact that the investment is not only produced but also producing. Investment considered as capitalist spending is the source of prosperity, and every increase of it improves business and stimulates a further rise of spending for investment. But at the same time investment is an addition to the capital equipment, and right from birth it competes with the older generation of this equipment. The tragedy of investment is that it calls forth the crisis because it is useful. I do not wonder that many people consider this theory paradoxical. But it is not the theory which is paradoxical but its subject—the capitalist economy.

Note

We shall try to make tenable that the average time of finishing investment orders υ varies only slowly within a narrow range. Let us define first υ for one kind of investment good with gestation period δ. In the formula $\upsilon(O/I) = \Sigma o_k / \Sigma(o_k/\upsilon_k)$ we can express o_k in terms of the investment good which we deal with, for it is clear that in the above expression the price of this good in the given moment is irrelevant for υ. On Fig. 44 we see the time curve *PQ* of the rate of investment decisions *y* (i.e. how much of our type of investment is ordered in a given moment per unit of time). All orders under construction at moment *M* were given in the time space *MN*, for all earlier orders are already

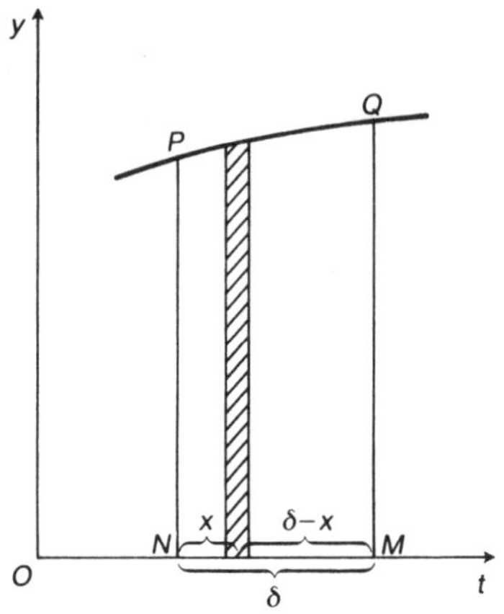

FIG. 44

completed, whilst none of these orders is finished. The order given at moment x (reckoned from N) is equal to $y\,.\,dx$; this order was under construction during time $\delta - x$ (because it was given $\delta - x$ time units ago) and thus the time needed to complete it is $\delta - (\delta - x) = x$ and its part to be completed equals $ydx\,.\,(x/\delta)$. Consequently, Σo_k expressed in terms of investment good considered is at moment M:

$$\omega = \frac{1}{\delta}\int_o^\delta yxdx$$

For $\Sigma(o_k/\upsilon_k)$ expressed in terms of investment goods—which is nothing else than the 'real' investment i at moment M—we get, if one takes into account that υ_k, the time needed to complete the order $ydx\,.(x/\delta)$, is here equal to x,

$$i = \frac{1}{\delta}\int_o^\delta ydx$$

It follows that

$$\upsilon = \frac{\omega}{i} = \frac{\int_o^\delta yxdx}{\int_o^\delta ydx}$$

Taking approximately that PQ is a straight line segment, this expression gives:

$$\upsilon = \frac{\delta}{2}\left(1 + \frac{a}{6}\right)$$

where a is the relation e/k of the increase of y in the time from N to M to the average of y at N and M. [See Fig. 45.] Now it is clear: (i) if the rate of increase (or decrease) of y during δ is not very great, υ differs slightly from $\partial/2$. (ii) If the rate of increase (or decrease) of y does not change much within a certain time, the change of υ in this time is small.

Let us now come back to our general expression $\upsilon = \Sigma o_k/\Sigma(o_k/\upsilon_k)$. We shall divide the uncompleted projects o_k into groups, each of them including all uncompleted investment orders of a certain type l with gestation period δ_l. The real value of these uncompleted orders of type l is ω_l and the corresponding υ_l-period is equal to $\delta_l/2\,[(1+(a_l/6)]$.

Denoting the price per investment unit at a given moment by p_l, we have now $\Sigma o_k = \Sigma \omega_l p_l$ and

$$I = \sum \frac{o_k}{\upsilon_k} = \sum i_l p_l$$

Thus we obtain:

$$\upsilon = \frac{\Sigma \omega_l p_l}{\Sigma \dfrac{\omega_l p_l}{\dfrac{\delta_l}{2}\left(1 + \dfrac{a_l}{6}\right)}}$$

Now it is clear that if: (i) the rates of increase a_l of a single type of investment do not change much within a certain time; (ii) the distribu-

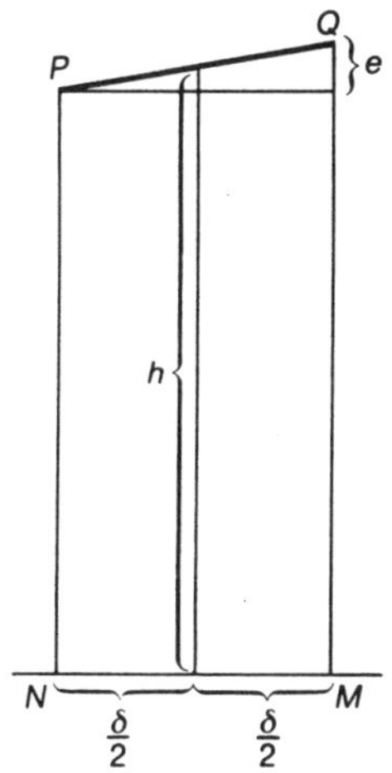

FIG. 45

tion of the value of uncompleted investment projects among single investment types does not change much, too—the change of υ during this time is small. It is also obvious that, if a_l are not very great, υ differs slightly from half of the average gestation period.

[5]

THE "BURDEN OF THE DEBT" AND THE NATIONAL INCOME[1]

By Evsey D. Domar*

I

"Full employment after the war" has now become the subject most frequently discussed by economists. When the war is over, the level of employment and income will be determined to a great extent by the speed and character of the reconversion process. After that, hopes of maintaining full employment are based, for good or for ill, on the various backlogs developed during the war. But when both periods are over, the old and so painfully familiar problem of the disposal of intended savings will again appear.

It is possible that private investment will be able to absorb all savings year in and year out, or that private investment will at least fluctuate around a sufficiently high average so that deficits which may be incurred by the government in some years will be offset by surpluses made in others. Whether or not this will actually happen is a matter of opinion; it is a problem not discussed here. Instead I propose to examine the less optimistic case, when private investment is insufficient to absorb intended savings over a relatively long period of time.

Public investment financed by borrowing, though perhaps the most direct and evident, is by no means the only method of dealing with the situation. The income-generating properties of various kinds of taxation still remain to be explored;[2] the possibilities of encouraging private investment by means of various tax devices have not been sufficiently worked out either; the same can be said about plans designed to reduce the propensity to save. It will be assumed here, however, either that all these measures cannot be tried, or that they have not proved sufficiently effective so that a continuous policy of deficit financing must still be pursued.[3]

* Mr. Domar is with the Board of Governors of the Federal Reserve System. The opinions expressed are those of the author and do not necessarily reflect the position of the Board.

[1] Thanks are due to Miss Mary Painter for her assistance in the preparation of this paper.

[2] See, however, P. A. Samuelson, "Full Employment After the War" in *Postwar Economic Problems* edited by S. E. Harris (New York, McGraw-Hill, 1943), p. 44; A. H. Hansen and H. S. Perloff, *State and Local Finance in the National Economy* (New York, Norton, 1944), pp. 245-46; L. A. Metzler, "Effects of Income Redistribution," *Rev. Econ. Stat.*, Vol. 25 (Feb., 1943), pp. 49-57; B. Ruml, *National Fiscal Policy and the Two Super Budgets*, an address delivered before the Institute of Public Affairs, University of Virginia, June 27, 1941.

[3] At this stage, "public investment financed by borrowing" and "deficit financing" are

The theory of the multiplier and our actual experience during this war have demonstrated, I believe, that money income can be raised to any desired level if the total volume of public expenditures is sufficiently high. This view will probably be accepted also by the opponents of deficit financing. Their objections to such a policy are based on several grounds, the most important being the belief that continuous government borrowing results in an ever-rising public debt, the servicing of which will require higher and higher taxes; and that the latter will eventually destroy our economy, or result in outright repudiation of the debt.

That continuous borrowing will result in an ever-growing public debt is evident; that, with a non-falling interest rate, the interest charges will grow is likewise true; and finally, assuming—as we shall in this paper—that all funds for payment of interest charges are to be raised by taxation,[4] there is no question that the absolute amount of taxes to be collected for that purpose will increase at the same rate. But all these *absolute* amounts do not mean much.

Whatever favorable or unfavorable effects the existence and growth of the debt may have, what matters is its relation to other economic variables, such as national income, resources of the banking system, volume of private securities outstanding, and so on, the particular relation to be studied depending on the character of the problem at hand. The phrase "burden of the debt," if it has any meaning, evidently refers to the tax rate (or rates) which must be imposed to finance the service charges, and that the *tax rate* will rise is far from evident.

The belief that government borrowing must necessarily result in rising tax rates is so widespread both in technical and popular writings that no quantitative analysis of it has, to my knowledge, ever been made. It has been pointed out, however, particularly by Professor Hansen, that the debt problem should be studied in its relation to national income, and that with a growing national income the "debt burden" is likely to be confined within manageable limits.[5] The proponents of deficit financing have also argued that the burden of a domestically-held debt depends to a great extent on the distribution

---

used synonymously. The essential fact is that government absorbs the savings and spends them. The nature of these expenditures will be discussed in Section IV.

[4] This assumption is made both to simplify the argument and to protect the reader from a shock. To many, government investment financed by borrowing sounds so bad that the thought of borrowing to pay interest charges also is simply unbearable.

[5] A. H. Hansen and Guy Greer, "The Federal Debt and the Future," *Harpers Magazine*, Apr., 1942, pp. 489-500; A. H. Hansen, *Fiscal Policy and Business Cycles* (New York, Norton, 1941), pp. 135-185; "Moulton's *The New Philosophy of Public Debt*" in Hansen and Perloff, *op. cit.*, pp. 285-298; and his other writings.

of the debt ownership;[6] that however large the debt may be, interest charges can still be collected because interest income constitutes a part of taxable income;[7] and finally, that a tax rate, however high, will not deter investment if losses can be offset against other income.[8]

No evaluation of these last three arguments will be made here. But the issues of the debt problem will appear clearer if we adopt the attitude of the opponents of deficit financing and treat this tax rate as a burden, as a price for the privilege of having a higher level of income (and employment) than would prevail without deficit financing. We shall therefore explore the behavior of the tax rate over time under several sets of assumption. In addition, it will be interesting to examine what the community gets for this payment, *i.e.*, the net income of the non-bondholders after the transfer of interest charges to the bondholders has taken place.

It is true that the existence and growth of the debt raise a number of other problems besides the behavior of the tax rate and of the net income of the non-bondholders. I hope it will be recognized, however, that these two variables are the most important ones, and that an analysis of their behavior will be of considerable help in the understanding of the whole problem of the debt.

The paper is based on several dynamic models which are developed mathematically. All mathematics, however, is concentrated in the Mathematical Appendix and only the final results are given in the text. As in most investigations of this character, certain simplifying assumptions will have to be made, but ways of modifying them will become apparent as the argument progresses.

II

The burden of the debt, or the average tax rate covering the interest charges, equals, roughly speaking, the ratio of the interest charges to income; or the ratio of the debt to income multiplied by the interest rate paid on bonds.[9] *It will be assumed that this interest rate is a given constant* (i). If we now want to find the effects of

[6] A. H. Hansen: sources given in footnote 5; A. P. Lerner, "Functional Finance and the Federal Debt," *Social Research,* Vol. 10 (Feb., 1943), pp. 38-51; Stuart Chase, *Where's the Money Coming From?* (New York, Twentieth Century Fund, 1943), pp. 97-110.

[7] Lerner, *op. cit.,* S. E. Harris, "Postwar Public Debt" in *Postwar Economic Problems* edited by him, pp. 169-186. Unfortunately both Lerner and Harris assumed perfectly arbitrary magnitudes of the debt and income without any analysis of their interrelationship.

[8] Lerner, *op. cit.* For a more elaborate analysis of the effects of loss offset, see E. D. Domar and R. A. Musgrave, "Proportional Income Taxation and Risk Taking," *Quart. Jour. Econ.,* Vol. 58 (May 1944), pp. 388-422.

[9] Though not quite correct, this statement will do for the time being. A more correct one will be given on pp. 802-03.

deficit financing on the tax rate, we should examine its effects on the magnitude of the debt and of the national income.

The effect of borrowing on the debt is somewhat complex and will be taken up in Section III. At this stage we can only record the obvious fact that continuous borrowing will of course result in an ever-increasing debt. Indeed, this point has never been overlooked in the numerous writings on the subject.

The other relevant fact—that deficit financing may have some effect on income—has received a different treatment. Opponents of deficit financing often disregard it completely, or imply, without any proof, that income will not rise as fast as the debt. On the other hand, we sometimes get the incorrect impression that it is sufficient for the government to spend, say $100, and the national income will *rise* by $300 or $400, depending on the magnitude of the multiplier. If this were really so, there would be no debt problem at all: it would certainly pay us to *raise* the national income by $300 at the expense of some $2.00 increase in interest charges.[10]

A clear distinction should be made between *levels* of investment expenditures and income and *increments* in investment expenditures and income. With a given average propensity to save, the level of national income will be a multiple of the level of investment expenditures (public or private). Similarly, with a given marginal propensity to save, an increment in national income will be a multiple of an increment in investment expenditures. But neither of these two statements tells anything about the relation between the *level* of investment expenditures and an *increment* in income.

It should be emphasized that the stimulating effects of a given increment in expenditures tend to disappear quite soon, unless, of course, one believes in pump-priming which does not at present find many proponents. Pump-priming aside, an increase in national income of, say, $300 produced by an increase in investment expenditures of, say, $100 will presently disappear and income will fall back to its former level. But the public debt (if investment expenditures are financed by government borrowing) has permanently increased (by $100), and so have interest charges (by $2.00). This is the source of the debt problem. If the national income is to be maintained at the new level, new amounts must be spent.[11]

In order to simplify the problem, *it will be assumed that the community's average and marginal propensities to save are equal and*

[10] That is, 2 per cent of the $100 borrowed.

[11] That this is so can be easily demonstrated by means of algebra, a numerical table or a chart. For a good example, see Hansen, *Fiscal Policy and Business Cycles*, Chart 16, p. 272. It was from this chart that the present paper originated.

constant.[12] Under this assumption, national income will be simply a multiple of investment expenditures, and the two series will behave in exactly the same manner.[13] To maintain a *constant* level of income it is sufficient to have a *constant* stream of investment expenditures, public and private, but to achieve a *rising* income, total investment expenditures must also be *rising*. Thus, if it is desired that income should rise at a constant absolute rate, total investment expenditures must also rise at a constant absolute rate; or if income is to rise at a constant percentage rate, investment expenditures must also rise at a constant percentage rate; and so on. In other words, by regulating the total investment expenditures, national income can be made to behave in any desired manner.

All this refers to *money* income. Nothing has been said so far about *real* income. Whether or not real income will follow the movements of money income depends on a number of circumstances which will be discussed briefly in Section IV. But it will greatly simplify our analysis if *we now assume that the price level remains constant* (whatever that means over long periods of time), *so that changes in money income and in real income are the same.*[14]

Before proceeding to the actual analysis of our problem, two other questions have to be settled. The first refers to the distinction between national income and taxable income. Without getting into current controversies, it will be sufficient to define *national income* as the sum of all wages, salaries, dividends, etc., paid out plus undistributed corporate profits, but excluding interest paid on the public debt. *Taxable income* will be defined as the national income *plus* interest receipts on the public debt, since interest receipts are also subject to taxation. It will be assumed that service charges are raised by means of a proportional income tax imposed on the total taxable income (without any exemptions), so that the tax rate will equal the ratio of interest

[12] This would be a bad assumption to make in any problem of cyclical character. It may be quite reasonable, however, in an analysis of a secular problem such as ours. More about it will be said in Section IV, pp. 821-22.

[13] This of course follows from the definition of the propensity to save. Using I for investment, Y for income and λ for propensity to save, we have $Y = I \cdot \frac{1}{\lambda}$ so that if $I = f(t)$ where t is time, $Y = f(t) \cdot \frac{1}{\lambda}$.

[14] It is well to recognize that the assumption of a constant price level considerably reduces the quality of the analysis. As a matter of fact, in three out of the four cases to be analyzed (1, 2 and 4), a constant price level is quite unlikely to be maintained. But the purpose of this paper is to study the debt problem in its bearing on deficit financing. It, therefore, appears worth while to sacrifice some theoretical completeness in order to bring out clearly the essence of the problem. I do not think that the validity of the final conclusions is thereby impaired.

charges to taxable income, it being understood that taxes levied for other purposes than to service the debt have already been subtracted in arriving at this definition of national income.[15]

Since no mathematical derivations are given in the text, it will be necessary to construct numerical tables to demonstrate the argument. It must be made perfectly clear that these tables are given as an illustration only and do not represent any attempt to forecast. They cover a period of 300 years not because I expect deficit financing, in the accepted sense of the terms, to last that long, but simply to convey the notion of a long period of time.

To construct the tables, the parameters used must be given numerical values. An effort to take reasonable magnitudes could as readily be made.

Let the debt at the beginning of the "experiment" = \$300 billion, the national income at the beginning of the "experiment" = \$130 billion, the interest rate on the debt, i, = 2 per cent.

In addition, a decision must be made with regard to the magnitude of government borrowing. To do this, we must have some idea about the community's propensity to save. The examination of Professor Kuznet's estimates shows that over the period 1879-1928 net capital formation constituted about 13 per cent of national income (in 1929 prices). This percentage appears to have been remarkably stable, with a slight downward trend; in the decade 1919-28 it was about 10.6 per cent.[16] There may be serious objections against this kind of approach to an estimate of a future secular propensity to save under conditions of full employment, but it is a question which cannot be discussed here. I shall assume that the propensity to save will be 12 per cent. How this 12 per cent will be divided between private and public investment is again a matter of guesswork. It can just as well be assumed that they share in it equally. In other words, the fraction of national income borrowed by the government, to be indicated by α, will be assumed to equal 6 per cent.[17]

[15] Disposable income after taxes will equal taxable income minus tax collections, *i.e.*, national income, since interest charges equal tax collections. It appears reasonable to apply the propensity to save to *disposable* income, and the fact that it equals national income considerably simplifies the mathematics of the problem.

[16] It may be well argued that non-deflated series should be used. Numerically, the difference is very small, and there is no need to elaborate this point any further here. Source: Simon Kuznets, an unpublished revision of Table 2 in *Uses of National Income in Peace and War*, Occasional Paper 6, March 1942, National Bureau of Economic Research (New York, 1942), p. 31.

[17] Some remarks about a rising propensity to save and a rising α will be made in Section IV, pp. 821-22. In addition, a variable percentage of national income borrowed by the government is discussed in Case 4 (The War Model), pp. 812-16.

By referring to the Mathematical Appendix, the reader can easily construct other tables based on different numerical magnitudes of the parameters.

III

All preliminaries having been disposed of, a direct attack on the problem can now be made, which is to find out what the tax rate and other variables will be when national income is made to behave in a given manner.[18] Theoretically, there is an infinite number of patterns which the national income may be assumed to follow, but only the simplest ones will be considered here. It is clear that, in a problem of this type, it is more meaningful to express the growth of income in percentage rather than absolute terms, and a function with a constant percentage rate of growth will occupy the center of the discussion (Case 3).[19] But it may be also interesting to examine the situations when income is held constant (Case 1), or is increasing at a constant absolute rate (Case 2). Finally, a variable percentage of income borrowed by the government is analyzed in the so-called "War Model" (Case 4).

Case 1. When National Income Remains Constant

Since the government keeps borrowing α per cent of national income, it is evident that the debt will increase at a constant absolute rate. The ratio of the debt to national income will therefore grow without limit and the tax rate will approach asymptotically 100 per cent.[20] The net income after taxes of the non-bondholders will approach zero. The picture is rather dismal.

Actually, it takes quite a long time before conditions become really bad, depending of course on the magnitude of the parameters. As shown in Table I, after 50 years the tax rate is only about 10 per cent, and it takes almost 250 years to bring it to 25 per cent. But there is something inherently odd about an economy with a continuous stream of investment expenditures and a stationary national income. There may exist at least two explanations:

(1) Investment expenditures do not result in a higher per manhour

[18] As stated on pp. 801-02, national income is made to behave in a given manner by regulating the volume of investment expenditures. Investment expenditures are the independent variable. This must be borne in mind, because the discussion in this section might give the misleading impression that national income is the independent variable.

[19] From a realistic point of view, a function with a slowly declining percentage rate of growth would probably be more significant. This paper being but a first step in an analysis of this type, I thought it better to make no use of the more complex functions. A declining percentage rate of growth is, however, discussed in Section IV.

[20] It may appear strange that the tax rate does not go beyond 100 per cent, in view of the fact that the ratio of the debt to income increases without limit. But the tax rate is the ratio of the interest charges to the *taxable* income, and as the debt and therefore the interest charges grow, taxable income increases as well. It is on this fact that Harris and Lerner based their defence of a large public debt, as already mentioned in footnote 7.

productivity, and there is no increase in the number of manhours worked. It is doubtful whether these expenditures should be called ***investment*** in the first place. But such a situation is not incompatible with full employment, if the level at which national income is kept is sufficiently high.

TABLE I.—THE TAX RATE AND THE RATIO OF THE DEBT TO NATIONAL INCOME WHEN NATIONAL INCOME REMAINS CONSTANT

Original debt =\$300 billion — α=6 per cent
Original income=\$130 billion — i=2 per cent

Years	Tax Rate Per Cent	Ratio of Debt to National Income
0	4.41	2.31
1	4.52	2.37
2	4.63	2.43
3	4.74	2.49
4	4.85	2.55
5	4.96	2.61
10	5.50	2.91
15	6.03	3.21
20	6.56	3.51
25	7.08	3.81
30	7.60	4.11
40	8.61	4.71
50	9.60	5.31
75	11.98	6.81
100	14.25	8.31
125	16.10	9.81
150	18.44	11.31
175	20.40	12.81
200	22.25	14.31
225	24.02	15.81
250	25.71	17.31
275	27.33	18.81
300	28.88	20.31
At the limit	100.00	Infinitely large

(2) As a result of the investment expenditures, productivity per manhour rises, but there is a continuously falling number of manhours worked. It may mean an ever shortening work-week. Under present institutional conditions, it is more likely to mean ever increasing unemployment. Together with the ever rising tax rate, it would combine the bleakest prophesies of both Karl Marx and the *Wall Street Journal*.[21]

[21] There is, of course, a third possibility, namely, that of a falling price level, so that the real income would be actually rising. Such a case would exclude neither increasing productivity nor full employment. It is worth further study. What really matters is the fact that an ever increasing share of the national income goes to the bondholders. This of course

To repeat, continuous government borrowing not accompanied by a rising national income results in an ever, though slowly, rising debt burden in addition to other possible economic dislocations already mentioned. How long such a policy can be pursued is a matter of conjecture. It will be shown in Cases 2 and 3, however, that the difficulty lies not in deficit financing as such, but in its failure to raise the national income. To have a rising income, investment expenditures (public and private) must not remain constant, but must increase.

Case 2. When National Income Increases at a Constant Absolute Rate

As the percentage of income borrowed (α) is constant, by assumption, and the income grows at a constant absolute rate, the annual deficits become larger and larger, so that the debt itself grows at an accelerated absolute rate.[22] Therefore the ratio of the debt to national income will rise without limit, and the tax rate will again approach 100 per cent.

It is of course evident that in the present case the absolute magnitude of the income is larger than it was in Case I. It is equally evident that a more rapidly growing income will, with our assumptions, result in a larger debt. We might therefore expect that the tax rate (and the ratio of the debt to income) will be the greater the more rapidly income rises. Actually, exactly the opposite holds true.

Table II compares the tax rates resulting from a constant income (as in Case I) and from income rising at 5 and 10 billion dollars per year, respectively. After 50 years, the tax rate equals 9.6 per cent when income is constant, 5.3 per cent when it rises at 5 billions per year, and only 4.4 per cent when the rate of growth equals 10 billions. It takes about 280 years to raise the tax rate to 15 per cent when income increases at 10 billions per year, and only 110 years when it remains constant. And in general, it can be easily shown,[23] that *the faster income rises the lower will be the tax rate,* even though a more rapidly rising income results in a larger absolute magnitude of the debt. This point will be taken up again in Case 3 and in Section IV.

It is still true, however, that we are confronted with an ever rising tax rate. It could therefore be expected that the net income after taxes of the non-bondholders would gradually approach zero as it did in

raises grave doubts as to the advisability of fiscal and price policies resulting in a constant money and a rising real national income.

[22] Mathematically speaking, this means that while national income is linear, the debt, being a function of the integral of income, is a quadratic. See Mathematical Appendix, p. 824.

[23] See Mathematical Appendix, p. 824.

Case 1. But this growth of the tax rate is more than offset by the ever rising national income, so that the net income of the non-bondholders after taxes approaches a very high asymptote.[24] It therefore follows that the non-bondholders will be much better off than they were at the beginning of the experiment, in spite of the rising tax rate.

TABLE II.—A COMPARISON OF TAX RATES WHEN NATIONAL INCOME REMAINS CONSTANT AND INCREASES AT $5 BILLION AND $10 BILLION PER YEAR (IN PERCENTAGES)

Original debt = $300 billion $\alpha=6$ per cent
Original income = $130 billion $i=2$ per cent

Years	Constant Income	Income Increasing at $5 Billion per Year	Income Increasing at $10 Billion per Year
0	4.41	4.41	4.41
1	4.52	4.36	4.22
2	4.63	4.32	4.06
3	4.74	4.29	3.92
4	4.85	4.26	3.80
5	4.96	4.24	3.71
10	5.50	4.18	3.43
15	6.03	4.22	3.35
20	6.56	4.29	3.37
25	7.08	4.42	3.47
30	7.60	4.56	3.61
40	8.61	4.91	3.96
50	9.60	5.31	4.37
75	11.98	6.41	5.52
100	14.25	7.57	6.74
125	16.40	8.75	7.95
150	18.44	9.92	9.16
175	20.40	11.08	10.35
200	22.25	12.21	11.54
225	24.02	13.33	12.33
250	25.71	14.42	13.77
275	27.33	15.49	14.86
300	28.88	16.53	15.92
At the limit	100.00	100.00	100.00

But it is doubtful, nevertheless, whether an economy with an ever rising tax rate levied for the sole purpose of paying interest on the debt will be able to escape serious economic and social difficulties which may possibly lead to a repudiation of the debt.

What is the nature of the economy described in this model? We see

[24] This asymptote is given by the expression $\frac{2b}{\alpha i}$ where b is the absolute rate of increase of the national income, and i is the interest rate paid on the debt.

that larger and larger absolute amounts are invested (publicly and privately), but in spite of this, national income rises only by the *same* amount. The explanation of this phenomenon is practically the same as in Case 1:

(1) Investment fails to raise productivity per manhour sufficiently to allow the national income to grow faster; neither is there a sufficient rise in the number of manhours worked. In other words, the result is a diminishing productivity of investment which may be due to the wasteful character of investment expenditures, or to a lack of new technological improvements.[25]

(2) Productivity per manhour rises sufficiently, but there is a continuous decline in the number of manhours worked. This may mean more voluntary leisure or more unemployment.

If it is unemployment that prevents national income from rising faster (*e.g.*, at a constant percentage rate), the remedy is simple (at least in theory): investment expenditures should proceed at a faster rate. But if productivity per manhour fails to advance sufficiently, the situation is more serious. This question will be taken up in Section IV.

Case 3. When National Income Increases at a Constant Percentage Rate

Since Case 3 is the most important model, the major part of the subsequent discussion refers to it. Use will be made here of three symbols, two of which have already been introduced:

α—percentage of national income borrowed,

i—interest rate paid on bonds,

and

r—percentage rate at which national income increases.

To understand the relationship between the debt and income in this case, it is necessary to make use of the following two propositions *on which the whole analysis rests*:

1. If a variable Q is the sum of q_1, q_2, q_3, q_4, . . . and so on, each of which is r per cent larger than the preceding one, then the addition of more and more q's makes Q itself increase at a rate approaching r per cent.

2. If any two variables increase at the same percentage rate, the ratio between them remains constant.

[25] Productivity of investment as used in this paper refers to an increment in *national income* due to a given investment, and not to return over cost received or expected by an investor, which forms the essence of Keynes's marginal efficiency of capital and allied concepts.

Mathematically, both propositions can be proved very simply.[26] The non-mathematical reader can construct numerical tables and plot the results on semi-logarithmic paper. He will find that as time goes on, his sum, whose components grow at a constant percentage rate, will look more and more like a straight line, *i.e.*, its rate of growth will approach a constant. If he plots two functions growing at the some constant rate, they will be represented by two *parallel* straight lines.

Now, according to our assumption national income grows at a constant percentage rate r. Since every year a constant α percentage of that income is being borrowed, it is clear that the deficits also grow at r per cent per year. The total debt is simply the sum of all the deficits. Therefore, according to the first proposition, the rate of growth of the debt itself will also approach r, and according to the second proposition, *the ratio between the debt and the national income will approach a constant.* This conclusion presents a striking contrast with the results obtained in Cases 1 and 2 where the ratio of the debt to income increased without limit.

It is shown in the Mathematical Appendix (pp. 824-25) that the

[26] *The first proposition:*

A proof not involving the use of calculus: as stated in the text, let

$$Q = a + a(1+r) + a(1+r)^2 + \dots\dots\dots a(1+r)^t$$

where a is the original value of Q, r is the percentage rate of increase, and t indicates the number of years. We have here a geometric progression in which $(1+r)$ is the common ratio. Its sum is

$$Q = \frac{a\,[(1+r)^{t+1} - 1]}{r}$$

As t increases, Q approaches the expression

$$\frac{a}{r}(1+r)^{t+1}$$

which increases at r per cent per year.

The reader familiar with calculus can use a continuous function. If

$$\frac{dQ}{dt} = ae^{rt}$$

over the interval from 0 to t, then

$$Q = a\int_0^t e^{rt}dt = \frac{a}{r}(e^{rt} - 1),$$

which increases at a rate approaching r as t becomes large.

The second proposition:

Any two variables increasing at the same rate r can be expressed as $a_1(1+r)^t$ and $a_2(1+r)^t$ (or a_1e^{rt} and a_2e^{rt}),

where a_1 and a_2 are constants. Their ratio equals $\frac{a_1}{a_2}$ which is also constant.

Gustav Cassel applied these principles to the relationship between capital and income. See his *On Quantitative Thinking in Economics* (Oxford, Clarendon Press, 1935), p. 24.

constant which the ratio of the debt to income approaches equals the simple expression

$$\frac{\alpha}{r}. \tag{1}$$

Similarly, the average tax rate approaches the limit expressed by

$$\frac{i}{\frac{r}{\alpha}+i}. \tag{2}$$

To obtain some idea of the magnitudes of these two expressions, numerical values must be given to r. We shall experiment with $r=2$ per cent and $r=3$ per cent.[27]

The ratio of the debt to national income will approach 3 when $r=2$ per cent, and 2 when $r=3$ per cent. The tax rate will approach 5.7 per cent and 3.9 per cent with $r=2$ and 3 per cent respectively. These figures and the examination of expressions (1) and (2) again show that *the greater is the rate of growth of income, the lower will be the*

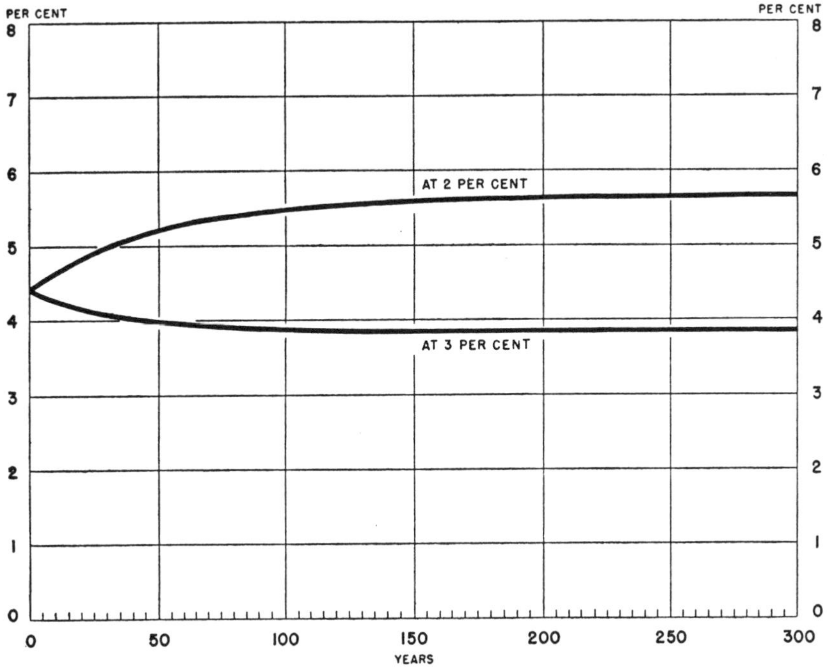

FIG. 1.—The Behavior of the Tax Rate When National Income Increases at a Constant Percentage Rate.

[27] A brief discussion of what r was in the past and may be expected to be in the future is presented in Section IV, pp. 817-20 and in Appendix B.

tax rate, even though a more rapidly rising income results in a larger absolute magnitude of the debt.

The net income of the non-bondholders after taxes will also grow at a rate approaching r per cent.

We thus see that, in spite of continuous government borrowing, the tax rate does not rise indefinitely but approaches a fairly reasonable limit. Even if private (net) investment disappears altogether, and the government has to borrow all the 12 per cent of income that the community desires to save, the tax rate will approach only 10.7 per cent and 7.4 per cent with r equal to 2 per cent and 3 per cent respectively.

TABLE III.—THE BEHAVIOR OF THE TAX RATE WHEN NATIONAL INCOME INCREASES AT A CONSTANT PERCENTAGE RATE (IN PERCENTAGES)

Original debt = \$300 billion; $\alpha = 6$ per cent
Original income = \$130 billion; $i = 2$ per cent

Years	$r = 2$ per cent	$r = 3$ per cent
0	4.41	4.41
1	4.44	4.40
2	4.46	4.38
3	4.49	4.36
4	4.51	4.35
5	4.53	4.33
10	4.64	4.27
15	4.74	4.21
20	4.82	4.16
25	4.91	4.11
30	4.98	4.08
40	5.10	4.02
50	5.21	3.97
75	5.39	3.91
100	5.49	3.87
125	5.56	3.86
150	5.60	3.85
175	5.62	3.85
200	5.64	3.85
225	5.65	3.85
250	5.65	3.85
275	5.66	3.85
300	5.66	3.85
At the limit	5.71	3.85

Table III and Figure 1 show the behavior of the tax rate over time with $r = 2$ and 3 per cent. It is interesting to note that when $r = 2$ per cent, the tax rate approaches its asymptote from below up; while with $r = 3$ per cent, the corresponding asymptote is reached by a downward movement.[28] This latter situation takes place because the ratio

[28] In general, the movement will be up or down depending on whether the original magnitude of the debt is smaller or larger than $Y \cdot \frac{\alpha}{r}$.

of the debt to income 300/130 = 2.3 assumed here to exist at the beginning of the experiment is larger than the final ratio which equals 2; some doubt is, therefore, thrown on the soundness of the assumption that α will equal only 6 per cent. Evidently, greater percentages of national income were borrowed in the past, especially in periods of war.[29] It is of course hoped that the future will be free of wars. Still, it may be interesting to inquire what will happen to the variables if wars or other similar emergencies occur. This brings us to Case 4.

Case 4. The War Model

The amount of guesswork involved in the preceding three cases will appear negligible compared with the degree of imagination required from here on. Probably the best thing to do is to present a very dark picture and then find relief in the thought that the future will not be as bad as that.

Accordingly, let us assume that the future will consist of alternating periods of 25 years of peace (p) and 5 years of war (w); let the percentages of income borrowed be 6 (α) in peacetime, and 50 (β) during the war; and finally let the national income continue to grow at 2 (r) per cent per year.[30]

It can be easily shown by means of a table or a semi-logarithmic chart that the debt will grow very fast during wartime and more slowly in peacetime, but that *its average rate of growth will still approach r. Therefore the average tax rate will again approach a constant.*[31]

[29] Strictly speaking this means that the ratio of the debt to income $\frac{300}{130}$ is inconsistent with the assumed magnitude of $\frac{\alpha}{r} = \frac{6 \text{ per cent}}{3 \text{ per cent}} = 2$. If we retain the $\frac{300}{130}$ ratio, we should change α, r or both. As will be shown in Section IV and Appendix B, 3 per cent is a reasonable estimate of the rate of growth of the (real) national income in the past. Therefore the magnitude of α should be raised.

[30] This statement represents a drastic simplification of the problem. In particular, objections can be raised against our assumption of a constant price level, which is unlikely to prevail during these alternating periods of war and peace. During the wars, money income will probably rise much faster than at the rate of 2 per cent per year. But we can treat the 2 per cent rate as representing a long-run trend, to which the parameters apply. A comparison of methods of financing the last and the present wars (both in this country and in Great Britain) would indicate a movement toward a smaller reliance on borrowing; hence, the 50 per cent of income assumed to be borrowed during future wars is probably too high. If, however, this percentage is applied to the trend rather than to the actual money income, it will appear more reasonable.

The reader may also wonder whether an economy engaged in such frequent wars can expect to have a steadily rising income. This remains an interesting question.

[31] This statement will become clearer if we assume that the government borrows β (*i.e.*, 50) per cent of the national income *every* year. Then the tax rate, as given by (2) p. 810, will approach $\frac{i}{\frac{r}{\beta}+i}$ which is a constant. Since the actual percentage of income

Actually the behavior of the tax rate is more complex. As shown in Table IV and Figure 2, it fluctuates between two curves, reaching a maximum at the end of each war period and then going down to its

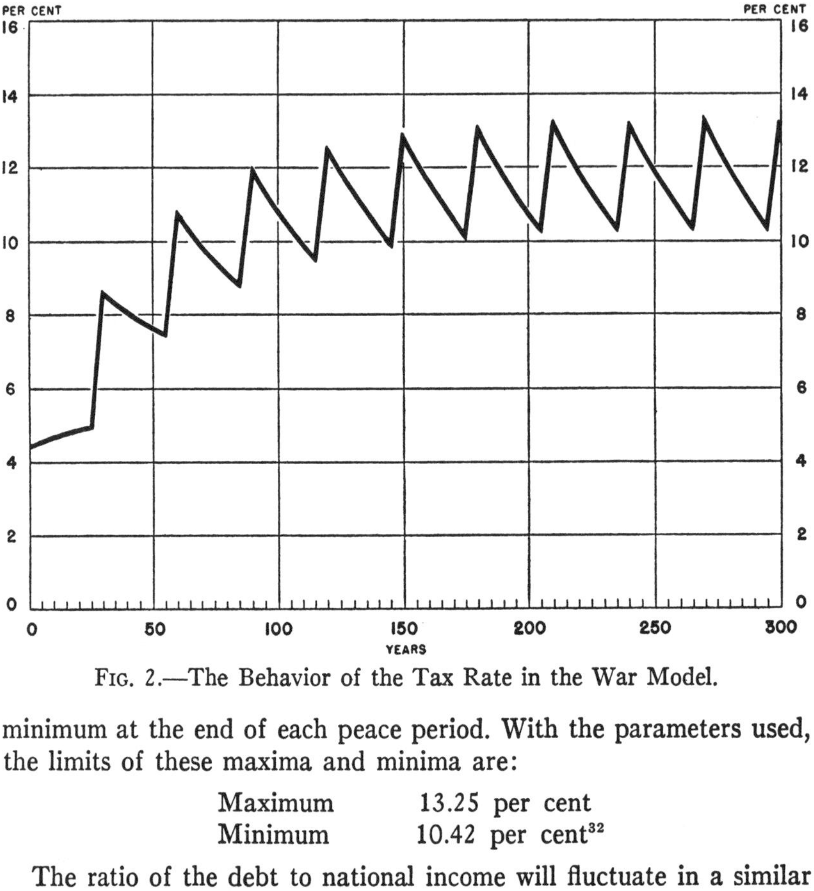

FIG. 2.—The Behavior of the Tax Rate in the War Model.

minimum at the end of each peace period. With the parameters used, the limits of these maxima and minima are:

Maximum	13.25 per cent
Minimum	10.42 per cent[32]

The ratio of the debt to national income will fluctuate in a similar manner, its maximum and minimum values approaching 7.64 and 5.82.

Since the tax rate and the ratio of the debt to income continue to fluctuate between their maximum and minimum values, it may be interesting to inquire what limits their *average* magnitudes approach.[33] The latter are given by the expressions:

---

borrowed is smaller than β the ratio of the debt to income must be below $\dfrac{i}{\dfrac{r}{\beta}+i}$.

[32] The formulas for these expressions are too complex to be reproduced here. See Mathematical Appendix, p. 825.

[33] I refer to simple arithmetic averages of actual tax rates (and ratios of debt to income) over the whole period of time.

$$\text{(3)} \qquad \text{Average ratio of debt to income} = \frac{\sigma}{r} = 6.67;$$

$$\text{(4)} \qquad \text{Average tax rate} = \frac{i}{\frac{r}{\sigma} + i} = 11.76 \text{ per cent;}$$[34]

where

$$\text{(5)} \quad \sigma = \frac{\alpha p + \beta w}{p + w} = \frac{.06 \times 25 + .50 \times 5}{25 + 5} = 13.33 \text{ per cent,}$$

i.e., σ is the weighted average of percentages of income borrowed.

TABLE IV.—THE BEHAVIOR OF THE TAX RATE IN THE WAR MODEL

Original debt = \$300 billion r = 2 per cent
Original income = \$130 billion i = 2 per cent

Years	Tax rate Per Cent
0	4.41
1 peace time	4.44
2 peace time	4.46
3 peace time	4.48
4 peace time	4.51
5 peace time	4.53
25 end of peace	4.91
30 end of war	8.61
55 end of peace	7.48
60 end of war	10.77
85 end of peace	8.83
90 end of war	11.91
115 end of peace	9.55
120 end of war	12.52
145 end of peace	9.94
150 end of war	12.85
175 end of peace	10.16
180 end of war	13.04
205 end of peace	10.28
210 end of war	13.13
235 end of peace	10.34
240 end of war	13.19
265 end of peace	10.37
270 end of war	13.22
295 end of peace	10.39
300 end of war	13.24
At the limit	
end of war	13.25
end of peace	10.42
average	11.76

It is evident that the expressions (3) and (4) are identical to (1) and (2) (see page 810), respectively, except that α is replaced by σ.

[34] For a minor qualification of this formula see Mathematical Appendix, p. 825.

This fact makes the results obtained in Case 3 much more general. *It is no longer necessary that a constant percentage of income be borrowed every year. Variable percentages can be borrowed, and the α of Case 3 can then be treated as their weighted average.*

Whether the average tax rate of 11.8 per cent can still be regarded as "reasonable" is a matter of opinion. Those who expect it to ruin the economy should remember that more than half of it is due to government borrowing to finance the wars; as shown in Case 3, peacetime deficit financing resulted in a tax rate of only 5.8 per cent. But it is a curious fact that those who have been most vociferous against government borrowing to achieve a high level of income and employment in peacetime have also opposed higher taxes during the present war!

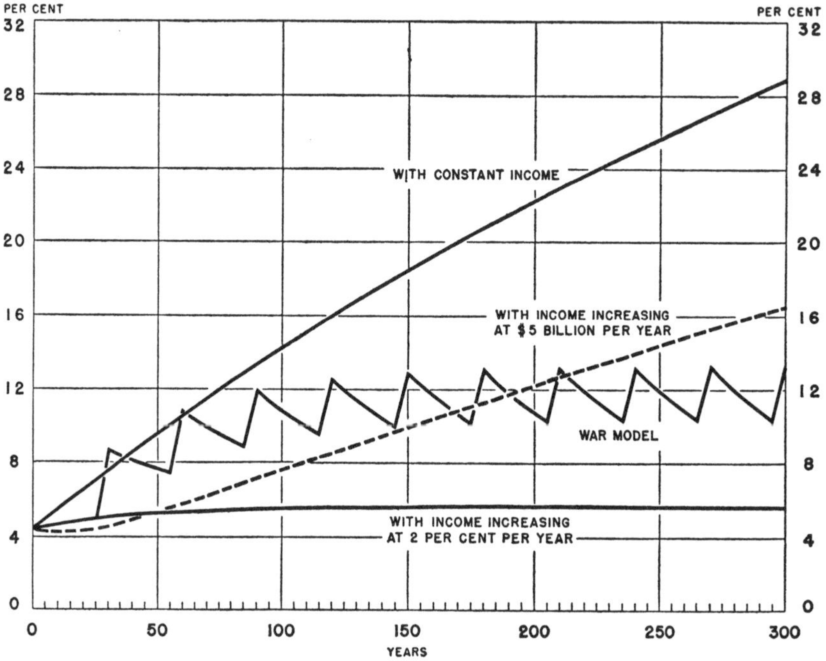

FIG. 3.—A Comparison of Tax Rates in Models 1-4.

Figure 2 has important implications for post-war fiscal policy. To repeat, the tax rate reaches its maximum at the end of the war, and then gradually declines during the peace period, *in spite of the fact that the government does not stop borrowing and the debt itself continues to rise.*[35] Now, some economic and political circles are burning with a desire to reduce the debt burden after the war. They recognize no other method of achieving their goal but by reducing the absolute size

[35] It is true, however, that the percentage of income borrowed does fall after the end of the war.

of the debt; that the government must stop borrowing is of course taken for granted. They should beware, however, lest the policies they advocate exert such a depressing effect on the national income as to result in an actually heavier debt burden, even though they succeed in paying off a part of the debt.

Finally, it may be worth while to compare the several tax rates obtained from the four cases discussed. In Case 2 it is assumed that income rises at 5 billion dollars per year; in Cases 3 and 4, at 2 per cent. Such a comparison is presented in Figure 3. It reveals the interesting fact that a constant percentage rate of growth of income is such a powerful force that we could engage in a 5-year war every thirty years and eventually come out with a lower tax rate than would be the case in continuous peace, but with the national income rising at a constant *absolute* rate!

IV

In Cases 3 and 4 of the preceding section, we have established that when national income grows at r per cent per year, the result at the limit is

$$\text{Ratio of debt to income} = \frac{\alpha}{r}, \tag{6}$$

and

$$\text{Tax rate} = \frac{i}{\frac{r}{\alpha} + i}, \tag{7}$$

where α can be interpreted either as a constant percentage of national income borrowed, or as a weighted average of variable percentages actually borrowed. As expression (7) for the tax rate looks rather complicated, it will be convenient—for purposes of exposition—to use an approximation to it, according to which

$$\text{Tax rate} = \frac{\alpha}{r}\, i. \tag{8}$$ [36]

The reader is reminded that a constant price level is assumed as before, so that movements of money income and real income are identical.

Expression (8) clearly shows that the burden of the debt is directly proportional to α and i and inversely to r. If the burden is to be light (with given α and i), there must be a rapidly rising income. *The prob-*

[36] This expression is derived from (7) by omitting i from the denominator, since i is apt to be quite small relative to $\frac{r}{\alpha}$. By this simplification, we are in fact assuming that interest on the debt is exempt from taxation. But numerically speaking, the mistake thus made is quite small and will be more than compensated for by convenience in exposition.

lem of the debt burden is a problem of an expanding national income.

How can a rapidly rising income be achieved?

If this question were asked in the pre-Keynesian era, the answer would be given in terms of manhours worked, productivity, and other *real* factors. Since the appearance of the *General Theory,* analysis has run in terms of investment expenditures, the multiplier, and other *monetary* considerations. Actually, there is no conflict in these two approaches: they simply state two sides of the same problem.

The real productive powers of economy establish the ceiling beyond which real national income, at any given time, cannot go, but whether or not it will reach this ceiling depends on the volume of expenditures actually made. If a rising income is desired, there must be both rising expenditures and rising productive capacity.

As explained in Section II, national income will grow at a constant percentage rate if and only if investment expenditures grow at the same rate (provided, of course, that the propensity to save remains constant). Since a stated fraction of these expenditures is made by the government out of borrowed funds, it follows that deficits must also grow at the same percentage rate. In absolute terms, the deficits must grow at an accelerated rate. It is horrifying to many to watch the public debt grow at an accelerated rate;[37] such a growth, however, is the only one which (with constant α and i) will *not* result in a rising burden of the debt.

From now on the heroic assumption is made that the stream of monetary expenditures will always be sufficient to maintain the national income at the maximum level established by the productive forces of the country. The growth of income will then be determined by the growth of these productive forces. Their behavior in the past and their expected rate of growth in the future represent an important and interesting subject which can be but briefly touched upon here. As a matter of fact, available past estimates refer to actually realized real income, and it can hardly be asserted that productive resources were always fully utilized even before the collapse of 1929.

Appendix B presents rates of growth of real national income for several countries, but the data are so fragmentary that not much reliance can be placed on them. For the United States, there are, fortunately, Professor Kuznets's estimates going back to 1879, which are presented in Table V. Over the whole period 1879-1928, total and per capita income grew at 3.3 and 1.5 per cent per year, respectively.[38]

[37] "Government spending tends to be like a drug, in that it takes larger and larger doses to get results, and all the time debt and taxes get higher and higher." National City Bank, *Economic Conditions* (Jan., 1944), p. 11.

[38] In regard to *money* income over the period 1879-1928, Professor Kuznets's estimates place the rates of growth of total and per capita income at 5.0 and 3.2 per cent, respectively. A comparison of these rates with the 3.3 and 1.5 per cent at which total and per

It is hard to form a definite opinion about their secular trend, because up to 1919 the estimates are presented only by (overlapping) decades, and the comparison between 1919 and 1929 is not very meaningful in view of the difficulty of measuring real output in a year like 1919. The general impression one gets from these figures is that there may have been some slackening of the rate of growth of total income, and

TABLE V.—PERCENTAGE RATES OF GROWTH OF REAL NATIONAL INCOME IN THE UNITED STATES, 1879–1929 (1929 PRICES)[a]

Period	Total	Per Capita
Annual averages by decades[b]		
1884–1894	2.8	0.7
1894–1909	4.2	2.4
1909–1914	3.1	1.5
1884–1914	3.6	1.7
1914–1919	1.8	0.4
1919–1924	2.9	1.5
1914–1924	2.4	0.9
1884–1924	3.3	1.5
Annual estimates		
1919–1923	5.4	3.7
1923–1929	3.5	2.1
1919–1929	4.2	2.7

Source: Simon Kuznets, an unpublished revision of Table 2 in *Uses of National Income in Peace and War*, Occasional Paper 6, March 1942 (New York, Nat. Bur. of Econ. Research, 1942), p. 31; and *National Income and Its Composition, 1919–1938* (New York, Nat. Bur. of Econ. Research, 1941), Vol. I, p. 147.

[a] All rates were computed exponentially by comparing the corresponding magnitudes at the beginning and end of each period.

[b] Each year represents the mid-point of a decade. For instance, 1884 indicates the average magnitude for the decade 1879–1888; 1924, the period 1919–1928; and so on.

possibly also of the per capita income, though the performance of both rates in the twenties appears to have been extremely encouraging. Not much can be said about the period after 1929, because real output during the thirties had certainly little to do with productive powers. Also, there has been so much controversy about the measurement of real income during the present war years that it is better to postpone judgment. Estimates obtained from the U. S. Commerce Department show that, in the thirteen years 1929-42, total and per capita real income increased at an average rate of 3.4 and 2.6 per cent, respec-

capita *real* income was growing indicates that the price level rose at an average rate of 1.7 per cent.

Since the burden of the debt depends on the rate of growth of money income, a secular rise in prices will lighten the burden. In this paper it was agreed, however, to maintain a constant price level.

tively. Finally, there are estimates by the National Industrial Conference Board going back to 1799; these are also given in Appendix B.

The rate at which real output can be expected to grow in the future is a question about which a present-day economist has amazingly little to say. The problem of making full use of available productive capacity (except for the last few years when the war offered a solution) has been so challenging that not much attention has been devoted to the problem of long-run expansion. Indeed, one hesitates to talk about the expansion of productive powers when unemployment still looms as the most pressing post-war problem.

In general it appears very unlikely that national income, or any economic series for that matter, can grow indefinitely at some constant percentage rate.[39] The rate of growth achieved in the United States in the period 1879-1928 was due to technological improvements, growth of the labor force, and the discovery of new resources. Whether much reliance can be placed on resources still to be discovered is hard to say. It is true, however, that improved technological methods find new applications for known resources and thus may have the same effect as an actual discovery of new ones. The rate of growth of the population has been slackening ever since about 1850, and the various estimates of future population growth predict a practically stationary if not declining population by 1980. Under these conditions, a 3 per cent rate of growth of real income may be too much to hope for, but a 2 per cent rate for the next 50 or even 100 years can probably be well defended.

We have to recognize that the main, and later on the only, propelling force in the economy will be technological improvements which should result in an ever-rising productivity per manhour. Only technological improvements can offset the diminishing productivity of investment which would be caused by the insufficient growth of the labor force and of natural resources. Whether new inventions will be forthcoming in sufficient numbers and whether they will be applied fast enough is hard to tell; one often gets the impression that the scientific age is just beginning, and that once monetary problems are solved, technological advance will proceed at a tremendous rate. On the other hand, one also cannot escape the impression that certain institutional developments, particularly the growth of huge corporations and monopolies, are not conducive to rapid technological change, and that the mere assurance of an adequate effective demand will not solve the whole problem. A thorough reform of the whole process of industrial research and particularly of the application of inventions may be needed as well.

[39] For instance, one cent invested at 2 per cent 1944 years ago would amount now to something like 768,000 billion dollars.

It thus follows that, if it is desired to have national income grow at a given rate, two conditions must be satisfied:

1. The total volume of monetary expenditures, public and private, must grow at the same rate;

2. Of the total volume of these expenditures, a sufficient amount should be directed toward increasing the efficiency of production, so as to allow the required volume of monetary expenditures to take place without a rise in prices.

Since government is absorbing a part of savings, it is of course desirable that its expenditures be productive. This productivity has nothing to do, however, with such questions as whether or not the assets constructed make a direct contribution to the federal treasury or are self-liquidating. As a matter of fact, the term "investment expenditures" may be misleading, because it is too closely associated with steel and concrete.[40] If healthier people are more productive, expenditures on public health satisfy these requirements. The same holds true for expenditures on education, research, flood control, resource development and so on. Finally, if institutional forces prevent the government from spending money on anything but leaf-raking, it should still absorb the savings unused by private enterprise and spend them on leaf-raking, relying on private investment to raise the efficiency of production, rather than do nothing at all and thus create a shortage of monetary expenditures and unemployment.[41] Of course, national income would be able to advance at a higher rate if governmental expenditures were productive in our sense. In 1940 total private and public expenditures on industrial and scientific research in the United States were less than 500 million dollars. What would be the result if this amount were doubled, tripled or multiplied ten times? Indeed, large-scale governmental participation in industrial and scientific research could become one of the major propelling forces in the economy.[42]

[40] A substantial part of efficiency-raising expenditures is usually treated as current costs, and does not appear under the heading of capital formation or investment.

[41] It is an interesting question whether private investment would be able to take place at all in an economy characterized by a chronic shortage of monetary expenditures.

[42] Expenditures on industrial research made by private business in 1940 amounted to about 300 million dollars. To this should be added some 50 millions spent by universities; the latter figure includes their expenditures on research in social sciences as well. The figures for federal expenditures on scientific and industrial research in 1940 are not available; in 1938, they amounted to some 52 millions, the largest share going to the Department of Agriculture. See U. S. National Resources Committee, *Research—A National Resource, Vol. I—Relation of the Federal Government to Research* (Washington, 1938), U. S. National Resources Planning Board, *Research—A National Resource, Vol. II—Industrial Research* (Washington, 1941).

Since the beginning of the war, federal expenditures on research, particularly in the fields connected with the war effort, have shown a marked increase. A bill recently introduced by Senator Kilgore would authorize an annual appropriation of 250 millions on

It is possible, or even likely, that, in spite of all these efforts, national income will grow at a *decreasing* percentage rate. Several possibilities should now be examined:

(a) The fall in the rate of growth is accompanied, or rather caused, by a declining propensity to save. The public prefers to consume a greater share of its income today; therefore, a smaller percentage is invested, and income cannot grow as fast as it otherwise would. If the decline in the propensity to save and therefore in α is proportional to that in r, the burden of the debt $\frac{\alpha}{r} i$ remains unchanged. If, however, r suffers a greater proportional decline than α, we have the next case (b).

(b) r declines while the propensity to save and α remain constant, or at least do not decline as fast (proportionally) as r. The result is a genuine diminishing productivity of investment: further investments of the same percentage of national income result in smaller and smaller percentage increases in income. Under these conditions, whether the investment be made by private enterprise or by the government, it is impossible to pay a constant percentage return on the investment without increasing indefinitely the relative share of the national income going to property owners. If such a course is regarded as impossible or undesirable, the rate of return on the amounts invested must go down as well. This would mean in the case under discussion here that the interest rate on bonds must be continuously reduced.[43]

All of this discussion, with the exception of the case (a) just considered, was based on the assumption that over a period of time α remained constant. It will be worth while to examine the not improbable case when α increases, *i.e.*, when the government borrows an increasing percentage of the national income. There are again several possibilities:

(c) α remains a constant fraction of the propensity to save, but the propensity to save itself rises. In other words, a larger percentage of national income is invested. If so, the rate of growth may also increase and thus leave the burden of the debt, $\frac{\alpha}{r} i$, unchanged. If, on the other hand, r does not rise—or at least does not rise as fast (proportionally) as α—the result is diminishing productivity of investment already discussed under (b).

(d) The propensity to save remains constant, but α increases. In other words, a larger fraction of total savings is absorbed by the gov-

subsidies to various research organizations and on direct research by the federal government. The amount is rather small, but may prove to be a good beginning.

[43] It is very amusing that those who appear most worried about the burden of the debt are usually least willing to advocate a lower interest rate on the debt!

ernment and a smaller one by private business. As the propensity to save remains constant, there is no reason to expect an increase in r. Therefore, the ratio $\frac{a}{r}i$ and, hence, the burden of the debt will increase.

On the face of it, such a development appears quite unfavorable, since it was agreed to regard the debt burden as an evil which should be minimized. It is presumably an evil because a part of the national income has to be taken from the public and given to the bondholders. But if interest charges on the public debt are treated in this manner, a question arises why other forms of property income should be treated differently. After all, in peacetime society has a choice (at least in theory) of having its investment undertaken by the government or by private business. In the first case, a fixed return is given to the bondholders, and presumably neither the interest nor the principal is subject to default. In the second case, society promises the investors nothing, but allows them, subject to certain rules, to get whatever they can. Which method will result in a more rapidly rising national income is a question on which many opinions have been expressed but few, if any, studies ever undertaken. Nor has any serious attempt been made (at least to my knowledge) to analyze the possible changes in the magnitude of property income produced by a replacement of private investment by government investment. Too often has it been implicitly assumed that interest on government bonds is necessarily a net *addition* to other property income, rather than a *substitution* for other forms of property income; or, in other words, that investment by government, rather than by private business, must increase the magnitude of income going to property owners. Since this may or may not be true, there is no ground as yet for asserting that government investment raises the "burden" of the total, public and private, debt, that it increases the concentration of wealth and income, that it accelerates the growth of the *rentier* class, or that it raises the community's propensity to save—thus creating new difficulties all of which would be absent if the investment were done solely by private business.

There is also the question whether the transfer of income to property owners by means of taxation is more or less "painful" to the public or disturbing to the economy than a transfer of an equal amount by means of higher prices or lower wages.

The whole problem needs further study.

It is hoped that this paper has shown that the problem of the debt burden is essentially a problem of achieving a growing national income. A rising income is of course desired on general grounds, but in addition to its many other advantages it also solves the most important aspects of the problem of the debt. The faster income grows, the lighter will be the burden of the debt.

In order to have a growing income there must be, first of all, a rising volume of monetary expenditures. Secondly, there must be an actual growth in productive powers in order to allow the increasing stream of expenditures to take place without a rise in prices.

When post-war fiscal policy is discussed, the public debt and its burden loom in the eyes of many economists and laymen as the greatest obstacle to all good things on earth. The remedy suggested is always the reduction of the absolute size of the debt or at least the prevention of its further growth. If all the people and organizations who work and study, write articles and make speeches, worry and spend sleepless nights—all because of fear of the debt—could forget about it for a while and spend even half their efforts trying to find ways of achieving a growing national income, their contribution to the benefit and welfare of humanity—and to the solution of the debt problem—would be immeasurable.

MATHEMATICAL APPENDIX

Y = national income; D = public debt; $U = Di$ = interest charges on the debt; $T = Y + U$ = taxable income; $\frac{U}{T}$ = tax rate; $Y' = Y\left(1 - \frac{U}{T}\right)$ = net income of the non-bondholders after the payment of taxes; a = national income at the beginning of the "experiment"; α = percentage of national income borrowed by the government; i = interest rate paid on the debt; b = absolute annual rate of growth of national income (in Case 2); r = percentage annual rate of growth of national income (in Cases 3 and 4); t = time (in years).

Case 1.

$$Y = a;$$

$$D = D_0 + \alpha a t;$$

(1)
$$\frac{D}{Y} = \frac{D_0}{a} + \alpha t;$$

(2)
$$\lim_{t \to \infty} \frac{D}{Y} = \infty;$$

$$\frac{U}{T} = \frac{Di}{Y + Di} = \frac{1}{\frac{Y}{Di} + 1};$$

$$\lim_{t\to\infty} \frac{U}{T} = 1 = 100 \text{ per cent}; \tag{3}$$

$$\lim_{t\to\infty} Y' = Y\left(1 - \lim_{t\to\infty} \frac{U}{T}\right) = 0. \tag{4}$$

Case 2.

$$Y = a + bt;$$

$$D = D_0 + \alpha \int_0^t (a + bt)dt$$

$$= D_0 + \alpha t\left(a + \frac{b}{2}t\right);$$

$$\frac{D}{Y} = \frac{D_0 + \alpha t\left(a + \frac{b}{2}t\right)}{a + bt}; \tag{5}$$

$$\lim_{t\to\infty} \frac{D}{Y} = \infty; \tag{6}$$

$$\lim_{t\to\infty} \frac{U}{T} = 1 = 100 \text{ per cent}; \tag{7}$$

$$Y' = Y\left(1 - \frac{U}{T}\right) = \frac{Y^2}{Y + U};$$

$$\lim_{t\to\infty} Y' = \frac{2b}{\alpha i}.$$

It can be readily shown from (5) that $\frac{D_1}{Y_1} < \frac{D_2}{Y_2}$ if $b_1 > b_2$, other parameters remaining the same. This also holds true for $\frac{U}{T}$.

Case 3.

$$Y = ae^{rt}$$

$$D = D_0 + \alpha a \int_0^t e^{rt}dt = D_0 + \frac{\alpha a}{r}(e^{rt} - 1);$$

$$\frac{D}{Y} = \frac{D_0}{ae^{rt}} + \frac{\alpha}{r}(1 - e^{-rt}); \tag{9}$$

$$\lim_{t\to\infty} \frac{D}{Y} = \frac{\alpha}{r}; \tag{10}$$

(11) $$\lim_{t\to\infty} \frac{U}{T} = \frac{i}{\frac{r}{\alpha} + i} \cdot$$

Case 4. The "War Model"

Additional Symbols:

p = length of the "peace" period; α = percentage of national income borrowed during the "peace" period; w = length of the "war" period; β = percentage of national income borrowed during the "war" period; $\sigma = \frac{\alpha p + \beta w}{p + w}$ = the average percentage of national income borrowed.

Only the final results are given here; the derivations are available.[44]

(12) Maximum $$\lim_{t\to\infty} \frac{D}{Y} = \frac{\alpha + Ke^{rp}}{r};$$

(13) Minimum $$\lim_{t\to\infty} \frac{D}{Y} = \frac{\alpha + K}{r};$$

(14) where $$K = \frac{(\beta - \alpha)(e^{rw} - 1)}{e^{(p+w)r} - 1};$$

(15) Average $$\lim_{t\to\infty} \frac{D}{Y} = \frac{\sigma}{r};$$

(16) Maximum $$\lim_{t\to\infty} \frac{U}{T} = \frac{(\alpha + Ke^{rp})i}{r + (\alpha + Ke^{rp})i};$$

(17) Minimum $$\lim_{t\to\infty} \frac{U}{T} = \frac{(\alpha + K)i}{r + (\alpha + K)i};$$

(18) Average $$\lim_{t\to\infty} \frac{U}{T} = \frac{i}{\frac{r}{\sigma} + i} \cdot$$

In expressions (15) and (18) a simple arithmetic average is used.

The expression (18) is actually an approximation of the true value of Aver. $\lim_{t\to\infty} \frac{U}{T} \cdot$ It can be shown that the difference between them is likely to be very small and that (18) always overstates the true magnitude of Aver. $\lim_{t\to\infty} \frac{U}{T} \cdot$

[44] Please write the author, c/o Board of Governors of the Federal Reserve System, Washington, D.C.

APPENDIX B

BY MARY PAINTER

Table VI is presented here merely as an illustration: the data are not sufficiently comparable and are too fragmentary to warrant a more serious use. Definitions and accuracy of measurement vary from country to country. In addition, some figures were deflated by a cost-of-living index, while an index of wholesale prices had to be used for others. The relatively low rates of growth

TABLE VI.—PERCENTAGE RATES OF GROWTH OF REAL INCOME, TOTAL AND PER CAPITA, IN VARIOUS COUNTRIES[a]

Country	Period	Rate of Increase of Total Real Income	Rate of Increase of Per Capita Real Income	Percentage of Income Invested (Current Prices)
Australia	1901–03–1928–29	3.0	1.1	
	1921–22–1928–29	4.6	3.6	
	1901–03–1937–38	2.6	1.0	
	1921–22–1937–38	2.8	1.9	8.8[b]
Canada	1919 –1929	3.6	1.7	
	1919 –1940	2.5	1.0	
Germany	1891 –1913	1.8	0.5	18.0
Great Britain	1880 –1891–95	3.4	2.6	
	1891–95–1913	1.5	0.6	11.1
Hungary	1925–26–1936–37	1.9	1.2	4.8
Japan	1919 –1936	3.9	2.5	
New Zealand	1926 –1940	3.0	2.0	
Sweden	1913 –1930	2.3	1.8	11.2
	1922 –1930	2.9	2.6	10.5
United States				
N.I.C.B.[c]	1799 –1859	3.6	0.6	
	1879 –1929	3.2	1.4	
	1799 –1929	3.3	0.8	
Kuznets[d]	1884 –1924	3.3	1.5	13.3
	1919 –1929	4.2	2.7	10.8
U.S. Dept of Commerce	1929 –1942	3.4	2.6	6.3

[a] All rates were computed exponentially by comparing the corresponding magnitudes at the beginning and at the end of each period.

[b] Average for years 1928–29 through 1937–38.

[c] National Industrial Conference Board.

[d] See Table V, p. 818.

obtained for Germany may be due to the fact that a wholesale price index was used as a deflator.[45]

Sources of the figures for each country and the deflator used to get real income are given below.

Australia—Income, deflated by an index of prices of consumption and investment goods: Colin Clark and J. G. Crawford, *The National Income of Australia* (Sydney and London, 1938), p. 65. Investment: Clark, *The Conditions of Economic Progress* (London, 1940), p. 406.

Canada—Income, deflated by index of cost-of-living: *Monthly Review of Business Statistics,* April, 1943. Population: *Canadian Yearbooks,* 1940 and 1942.

Germany—Income figures, deflated by wholesale price index: *Das Deutsche Volkseinkommen vor und nach dem Kriege,* bearbeitet im Statischen Reichsamt, 1931, p. 68. Savings, as a percentage of income: Leon Goldenberg, *Income and Savings in France 1871-1914* (unpublished), p. 139.

Great Britain—Income, deflated by cost-of-living index: A. L. Bowley, *Wages and Income Since 1860* (Cambridge, 1937), p. 94. Savings as percentage of income: Leon Goldenberg, *Income and Savings in France 1871-1914* (unpublished), p. 145.

Hungary—All figures: Matthias Matolcsy and Stephen Varga, *The National Income of Hungary* (London, 1938), pp. 68 *ff*. The deflator used was a comprehensive price index.

Japan—Income, in current prices: *Mitsubishi Economic Research Bureau Monthly Circular,* April, 1937, p. 12. Deflated by index of wholesale prices: the *Federal Reserve Bulletin.* Population: *Japan Yearbook,* 1937.

New Zealand—Income, in fiscal years: *New Zealand Official Yearbook,* 1937, 1938, and 1943, interpolated to calendar years and deflated by index of retail prices from same source. Population: *Official Yearbook.*

Sweden—All figures: E. Lindahl, E. Dahlgren, and K. Koch, *National Income of Sweden 1861-1930* (London, 1937). The deflator was a cost-of-living index.

United States—N.I.C.B. figures: Income, deflated by an index of the general price level: Robert F. Martin, *National Income in the United States, 1799-1938,* National Industrial Conference Board, Inc. (New York, 1939), p. 6.

Kuznet's figures: Income deflated by a comprehensive price index. See Table V, page 818.

U. S. Department of Commerce figures: Income, deflated by comprehensive price index: National Income Unit of the Bureau of Foreign and Domestic Commerce.

[45] The period 1891-1913 was one of rising prices, and wholesale prices were rising faster than the cost of living. For instance, during this period the wholesale price index in England rose by 26.6 per cent, while the rise in the cost-of-living index was only 17 per cent. It is very likely that if the national income in Germany were deflated by a cost-of-living index, it would show a higher rate of growth than given in the table. Such an index, however, was not available.

[6]

Studies in the theory of economic expansion[1])

By **R. F. Harrod,** Oxford

Dr. Lundberg has made an extremely important contribution to economic studies. His primary concern is with the proper method to be employed in the analysis of an expanding economy and of the trade cycle. With this in view, he engages in an elaborate criticism of the theories of a number of writers of leading importance, and he himself conducts some exercises, by way of example, in the method which he lays down.

In his introductory chapter he seeks, very properly, to show that the apparatus employed by writers seeking to determine conditions of static equilibrium are inappropriate for the matter in hand. In establishing the nature of a new equilibrium consequent upon a specific change, they use the method of partial analysis containing a ceteris paribus assumption. But the movement to the new equilibrium involves a process of adjustment and this may render the ceteris paribus assumption invalid. It is necessary to examine not only the conditions of a new equilibrium, but the process of adaptation, and this may require consideration of the reactions of the system as a whole to it.

Having made his initial point with considerable cogency, Dr. Lundberg proceeds to his critical sections. These contain a vast amount of interesting matter. He shows great fairness of mind in the treatment of his authors, and, while his main object is to demonstrate the limitations of their theories, for lack of an adequate method of attack, he often throws much light upon them and brings out merits which may have escaped the reader.

In such a wide survey it is not to be expected that Dr. Lundberg's exposition should be wholly exempt from misunderstanding. It may suffice to mention his treatment of the most recent work of Mr. Keynes. On p. 39 he makes an illegitimate use of a figure derived from Mr. Keynes' last volume. He implies (see also p. 42) that Mr. Keynes regards hoarding as an alternative way of using non-consumed income, so that the funds available in the capital market are equal to non-consumed income less hoarding. But this is precisely the opposite of Mr. Keynes' view, according to which the whole of non-consumed income is available in the capital market. The volume of hoarding, which takes place, is determined not by savers but by the banking system. If there is an increased propensity to hoard and the banks do not increase loans or purchases, no extra hoarding will take place; but the rate of interest will rise. If the banks make extra loans, an increase of hoarding will occur, but the deduction from current saving

---

[1]) **By Erik Lundberg, Stockholm Economic Studies published by writers connected with Institute for Social Sciences of Stockholm University, No. 6.**

available for the capital market due to the increased hoards will be exactly offset by the increased loans of the banks. Thus the hoarding causes no deflection of saving. But it may affect the rate of interest and so the level of activity. Dr. Lundberg may have intended, at this point, to give his own interpretation, rather than a faithful transcription, of the doctrines of Mr. Keynes; but he does not seem to be aware that his interpretation is in contradiction to Mr. Keynes' view.

Dr. Lundberg also suggests that it is reasonable to suppose that the ‚bear' motive only comes into play when the rate of interest is below a critical figure, say 3%. He infers that, for levels above this, the rate would, according to Mr. Keynes' argument, be indeterminate, and that the classical theory may be brought back into use for higher rates. But the ‚bear' motive, as Dr. Lundberg himself explains on p. 33, is not the only element in Mr. Keynes' ‚liquidity preference'. That part of it due to ‚time discrepancies' and ‚reserve holdings', will vary according to the level of activity. The rate of interest must be just high enough to keep activity down to the level at which the demand for liquid assets for these purposes does not exceed the supply available, which is determined by the banks. Thus liquidity preference may suffice to determine the rate of interest even above the alleged critical figure.

Dr. Lundberg's further criticism that the propensity to consume depends on income distribution and on the accrual of un-anticipated income, both of which vary in the course of the cycle, may easily be met, if we suppose these two to vary in a determinate manner. His criticism that the curve of the marginal efficiency of capital may be expected to shift during an ‚adaptation process' and that this matter is not analysed by Mr. Keynes is better founded.

As he studies the first 180 pages of this volume, the reader may come to feel that, with the exception of a brilliant interlude in Ch. IV, they are rather over-loaded with methodological matter. There is a certain amount of repetition; the language is not always perfectly clear; Dr. Lundberg seems to rely too much on the power of certain collocations of abstract terms to convey the meaning he requires. The reader will be wrong if he is disappointed; let him persevere. The story has a climax; the meat of the volume is contained in Ch. IX, which constitutes approximately the last third of it. Here Dr. Lundberg gives demonstrations of his own method. I am confident that if he had placed this earlier in the volume, his critical sections would have been much more telling.

He holds that the proper method of dynamic analysis is the construction of „model sequences". These are done with great care and ingenuity. Making plausible assumptions with regard to the values of certain determining factors, the proportion of income saved, the proportion of costs which do not generate incomes, etc., he constructs tables which demonstrate the manner in which expansion is followed by recession and examines the conditions governing the speed and amplitude of the movement. These tables are based on the division of production into that of consumption- and capital-goods, the application of the ‚acceleration principle' to part of the capital production, and, in a roundabout way, the operation of ‚the multiplier'.

For Dr. Lundberg's procedure it is necessary to assume that action in the period t_1 depends not only on the whole concatenation of circumstances and expectations in t_1 but in part at least upon the events of period t_0. This is essential to the ,sequence' method of analysis. As Dr. Lundberg ably demonstrates in an earlier passage (Ch. IV.), much depends on the length of the unit period, which constitutes a ,reaction time'.

The factor which Dr. Lundberg chooses for his link between successive periods is the decision of entrepreneurs with regard to their volume of production. He assumes that they base their estimate of what the market will bear in the present period by reference to their receipts in that immediately preceding. The assumption is not altogether unreasonable. He further particularises by assuming that they will produce so much as to equate the total cost of their output, including amortization and normal profit, to the receipts of the preceding period. The assumption is an arbitrary one, but the results obtained are interesting. In the real world it is possible that the actual volume of output is intermediate between that so determined and one based on correct anticipation.

The link required for this kind of sequence is, if I understand aright, necessarily of an arbitary character. At one point in the system at least it has to be supposed that decision is based not on the totality of surrounding circumstances but on some factor carried over from the past, which is strictly irrelevant. Dr. Lundberg presents his method as the alternative to the methods of static analysis. I am not convinced that it is the only alternative.

It is true that the equilibrium of static analysis does not allow for growth, that this analysis can only describe an expanding system in terms of successive states of equilibrium, with the intervening stages of transition left, and left with danger to the validity of the argument, unanalysed. The condition for equilibrium in the static analysis is that, given all preference schedules, individuals could not improve their position otherwise than by continuing to do as they are doing. They will continue to produce, to sell, to buy, to save so many units per unit of time. Now if a change occurs, the new equilibrium is not reached per saltum. In the interval it is necessary to make some assumption as to how the members of the system react; in the type of analysis recommended by Dr. Lundberg we suppose that in some respect their action is governed by conditions belonging to the previous state of affairs. This assumption provides the link required to explain what people do during the interregnum. And their action in the interregnum modifies the conditions governing the new equilibrium position.

Now, while it is doubtless true that sequence analysis of this kind has its own sphere of importance, since in the real world the past does no doubt modify present behaviour, I suggest that it may be possible to construct a method of dynamic analysis more closely analogous to the dynamics of mechanics. In place of the static question, what rate of production of eggs per day will be consistent with the maximization of the advantage of egg producers, we ask, what rate of increase in the production of eggs per day will lead to this result? This is a natural extension of the static theory, appropriate to an expanding economy. At what rates of increase (or decrease) must all members of the system pursue their operations so that, when they all do this, no one shall find it to his advantage to do otherwise than continue expanding at this rate? A system of equations in which these rates of increase (or decrease) are unknowns should be elaborated, on lines similar to those of traditional static systems, with sufficient equations to determine the values of the additional unknowns also. If a dynamic system of this kind could be established, the considerations introduced by reference to ‚sequences' could be superimposed as corrections. My complaint of the sequence analysis is that it seeks to introduce the corrections, before the dynamic principles themselves are established. It is true that Dr. Lundberg's tables are to some extent concerned with true dynamic principles. They embody the consequences of the acceleration principle, which is a true dynamic principle and is not a factor linking the present with the past. But the consequences of the acceleration principle are not disentangled from those of the assumption, which is a mere sequence assumption, by which the outlay of entrepreneurs is related to receipts in a past period.

Approach the matter in another way. The essence of Dr. Lundberg's sequence assumption, and, I take it, of any assumption of that kind, is that it introduces an irrational element. And irrationality is connected with ignorance. It is reasonable to assume that entrepreneurs base their action on the past rather than the present, which in itself is irrational, because it is reasonable to assume that they are not fully apprised of what the present has to offer. Now ignorance is connected not with expansion as such, but with the possibility of unforeseen change. Changes may occur in a system that is not expanding. The existence of change reduces pro tanto the applicability of the static analysis to the real world. It gives rise to problems of profit, which to some extent disrupt the traditional static system. It may be that a sequence analysis is the best method of coping with these problems. But they have no direct connexion with the problem of growth. Per contra the acceleration principle has no direct connexion with the problems of ignorance. All that it has in common with those problems is that it is not comprehended within the analysis of static equilibrium. I suggest that we shall make a methodological error of the first order if we do not rigidly distinguish between matters relating to ignorance and matters relating to growth. The former set of problems, because they involve arbitary decisions, may prove amenable to a sequence analysis. The latter should be solved by a system of equations relating to a given point of time but containing terms expressing rates of growth. In Dr. Lundberg's tables the two sets of problems are confounded.

A sequence analysis is especially attractive to students of the trade cycle, because it is not difficult to make reasonable assumptions which generate a cycle. None the less I incline to the view that the real secret of the cycle is to be found in a dynamic analysis, of the kind here contrasted with the sequence analysis.

The weakest part of the traditional static analysis is concerned with saving, since saving of its essence entails a growth of productive power, and growth is contradictory of static assumptions. The static analysis is only valid for saving = O. Dr. Lundberg in the course of his sequence analysis introduces a new method for determining the rate of interest, which appears open to serious criticism. He uses the tools of sequence analysis. This implies a most healthy scepticism with regard to the power of static analysis to determine the rate of interest. But it does not appear that his sequence method is successful.

He supposes that the rate of interest used in period t_1 for computing the profitability of projects and thus determining the volume of capital outlay in t_1 is the yield of bonds in t_0. This capital outlay will be financed contemporaneously by bank loans; but in period t_2 bonds will be issued at a nominal rate of interest equal to the yield to bonds in t_0, and the nominal capital value of the new bonds will be equal to the capital outlay in t_1. The demand for these bonds will be constituted by the ex ante saving of period t_2. The market value of the bonds when issued, f_{t_2}, will be determined by the equation.

$$f_{t_2} = \frac{S_{t_2}}{I_{t_1}}$$

where S is saving ex ante and I is capital outlay ex post. The yield of bonds or rate of interest, i, in period t_2 will be related to that in t_0, which is taken to fix the nominal rate at which the bonds in t_2 are issued, by the equation

$$i_{t_2} = \frac{i_{t_0}}{f_{t_2}}$$

This rate of interest, i_{t_2}, will serve to determine the nature of capital outlay in t_3. Thus the rate of interest in each period is determined not by the intersection of demand and supply curves, but by a sort of Quantitiy Theory. The aggregate nominal capital of the issue is determined by the amount of capital outlay ex post in the preceding period, and the aggregate funds devoted to their purchase is equal to the saving ex ante. Thus the market price of the bonds, which governs their yield, i. e. the rate of interest in the period, is determined by dividing one aggregate by the other. This determines the rate of interest used for planning purposes in the next period. And so on period by period. It is characteristic of the sequence method that it uses aggregate rather than marginal quantities. Without being concerned at the holy horror which traditionalists may be expected to show, one may retain the suspicion that marginal considerations play some part in the formation of interest rates. In order to criticise this theory it is not necessary to consider in detail the propriety of the sequence assumptions. It suffices to ask what happens to the difference between saving ex ante and saving ex post, which is outstanding at the end of each period.

Dr. Lundbergs book is one which all students of the Trade Cycle should study. It breaks new ground, and displays high qualities of intellectual insight and grasp.

[7]

AN ESSAY IN DYNAMIC THEORY

1. THE following pages constitute a tentative and preliminary attempt to give the outline of a "dynamic" theory. Static theory consists of a classification of terms with a view to systematic thinking, together with the extraction of such knowledge about the adjustments due to a change of circumstances as is yielded by the "laws of supply and demand." It has for some time appeared to me that it ought to be possible to develop a similar classification and system of axioms to meet the situation in which certain forces are operating steadily to increase or decrease certain magnitudes in the system. The consequent "theory" would not profess to determine the course of events in detail, but should provide a framework of concepts relevant to the study of change analogous to that provided by static theory for the study of rest.

The axiomatic basis of the theory which I propose to develop consists of three propositions—namely, (1) that the level of a community's income is the most important determinant of its supply of saving; (2) that the rate of increase of its income is an important determinant of its demand for saving, and (3) that demand is equal to supply. It thus consists in a marriage of the "acceleration principle" and the "multiplier" theory, and is a development and extension of certain arguments advanced in my *Essay on the Trade Cycle*.[1]

2. Attempts to construct a dynamic theory have recently been proceeding upon another line—namely, by the study of time lags between certain adjustments. By the introduction of an appropriate lag the tendency of a system to oscillate can be established. In these studies there is some doubt as to the nature of the trend on which the oscillation is superimposed. Supposing

[1] Especially in Ch. 2, secs. 4–5. The "Acceleration Principle" was there designated the "Relation." There is an objection to the use of the term acceleration in this connection. The study of the condition in which demand and supply are flowing at an unaltered rate has long been known as Static Theory: this implies that the equilibrium of prices and quantities resulting therefrom is regarded as analogous to a state of rest. By analogy, therefore, a steady rate of increase of demand, which is our first matter for consideration in dynamic theory, and a major effect of which is expressed by the "Relation," should be regarded as a velocity. Acceleration would be a rate of change in this.

However, the use of the expression Acceleration Principle in the sense of my relation is rapidly accelerating in current literature, and I reluctantly bow to the *force majeure* of usage.

damping measures could be introduced, to counteract the oscillation caused by the lag, would the system be stationary or advancing? And at what rate? Dynamic theory in my sense may throw some light upon this.

Moreover it is possible, and this the following argument seeks to establish, that the trend of growth may itself generate forces making for oscillation. This, if so, would not impair the importance of the study of the effect of lags. But it may be that the attempt to explain the trade cycle by *exclusive* reference to them is an unnecessary *tour de force*. The study of the operation of the forces maintaining a trend of increase and the study of lags should go together.

3. The significance of what follows should not be judged solely by reference to the validity or convenience of the particular equations set forth. It involves something wider: a method of thinking, a way of approach to certain problems. It is necessary to "think dynamically." The static system of equations is set forth not only for its own beauty, but also to enable the economist to train his mind upon special problems when they arise. For instance, an economist may pose to himself the question, What would be the effect on the system of an increase of exports or of a labour-saving invention? By reference to the static equations, he then proceeds to work out the new equilibrium position supposing the new higher level of exports to be maintained in perpetuity or the labour-saving invention to be incorporated in the productive technique once for all.

But let the question be: Suppose the level of exports begins and continues to increase steadily, or suppose its rate of increase to increase, or suppose labour-saving inventions begin to be made in a steady or growing stream; then the static method will not suffice. The static theorist may hope to reduce this supposed steady increase to a succession of steps up, each having the same effect. But if the following argument is correct, the effect on the moving equilibrium of advance may often be in the opposite direction to the effect on the static equilibrium produced by each of the steps considered singly. A new method of approach—indeed, a mental revolution—is needed.

Once the mind is accustomed to thinking in terms of trends of increase, the old static formulation of problems seems stale, flat and unprofitable. This is not to deny to static theory its own appropriate sphere. It will become apparent which kind of problem belongs to each branch of study.

4. I now propose to proceed directly to the Fundamental

Equation, constituting the marriage of the acceleration principle and the multiplier theory. This probably gives too much importance to the acceleration principle, and the necessary modification is introduced subsequently.

Let G stand for the geometric rate of growth of income or output in the system, the increment being expressed as a fraction of its existing level. G will vary directly with the time interval chosen —*e.g.*, 1 per cent. per annum = $\frac{1}{12}$ per cent. per month. Let G_w stand for the warranted rate of growth. The warranted rate of growth is taken to be that rate of growth which, if it occurs, will leave all parties satisfied that they have produced neither more nor less than the right amount. Or, to state the matter otherwise, it will put them into a frame of mind which will cause them to give such orders as will maintain the same rate of growth. I use the unprofessional term warranted instead of equilibrium, or moving equilibrium, because, although every point on the path of output described by G_w is an equilibrium point in the sense that producers, if they remain on it, will be satisfied, and be induced to keep the same rate of growth in being, the equilibrium is, for reasons to be explained, a highly unstable one.

If x_0 is output in period 0 and x_1 output in period 1, $G = \frac{x_1 - x_0}{x_0}$. Since we suppose the period to be short, x_0 or x_1 may alternatively stand in the denominator.

x_0 and x_1 are compounded of all individual outputs. I neglect questions of weighting. Even in a condition of growth, which generally speaking is steady, it is not to be supposed that all the component individuals are expanding at the same rate. Thus even in the most ideal circumstances conceivable, G, the actual rate of growth, would diverge from time to time from G_w, the warranted rate of growth, for random or seasonal causes.

Let s stand for the fraction of income which individuals and corporate bodies choose to save. s is total saving divided by x_0 or x_1. This may be expected to vary, with the size of income, the phase of the trade cycle, institutional changes, etc.

Let C stand for the value of the capital goods required for the production of a unit increment of output. The unit of value used to measure this magnitude is the value of the unit increment of output. Thus, if it is proposed in month 1 to raise the output of shoes, so that in month 1 and all subsequent months output is one pair higher than in month 0, and the machine required to do this—neglecting all other capital that may be required—has a value 48 times the value of a pair of shoes, C per month = 48.

The value of C is inversely proportional to the period chosen. C per annum $= 4$ in this case.[1] The value of C depends on the state of technology and the nature of the goods constituting the increment of output. It may be expected to vary as income grows and in different phases of the trade cycle; it may be somewhat dependent on the rate of interest.

Now, it is probably the case that in any period not the whole of the new capital is destined to look after the increment of output of consumers' goods. There may be long-range plans of capital development or a transformation of the method of producing the pre-existent level of output. These facts will be allowed for in due course. For the moment let it be assumed that all new capital goods are required for the sake of the increment of output of consumers' goods accruing.

Reserving proof for the next paragraph, we may now write the Fundamental Equation in its simplest form[2] :—

$$G_w = \frac{s}{C} \quad . \quad . \quad . \quad . \quad . \quad . \quad 1$$

It should be noticed that the warranted rate of growth of the system appears here as an unknown term, the value of which is determined by certain " fundamental conditions "—namely, the propensity to save and the state of technology, etc. Those who define dynamic as having a cross-reference to two points of time may not regard this equation as dynamic; that particular definition of dynamic has its own interest and field of reference. I prefer to define dynamic as referring to propositions in which a rate of growth appears as an unknown variable. This equation is clearly more fundamental than those expressing lags of adjustment.

5. The proof is as follows. Let C_p stand for the value of the increment of capital stock in the period divided by the increment of total output. C_p is the value of the increment of capital per

[1] If a month is the unit, the number of shoes added per period is 1, if a year 144. The value of G per annum is 12 times as great as that of G per month, since the numerator of G per annum is 144 times as great and the denominator 12 times as great as the numerator and denominator respectively of G per month. The number of machines added per month is $1 \equiv 48$ shoes $\equiv 48$ units of increment of output. C per month $= 48$. The number of machines added per year is $12 \equiv 48 \times 12$ shoes. Thus the value in shoes of the annual increment of capital required to produce an annual increment of 144 shoes is 48×12 units. Therefore C per annum $= \frac{48 \times 12}{144} = 4 = \frac{1}{12}$ of C per month.

[2] Since the value of G_w varies directly and that of C inversely with the unit period chosen, and the value of s is independent of the unit, the validity of the equation is independent of the unit period chosen.

unit increment of output actually produced. Circulating and fixed capital are lumped together.

$$G = \frac{S}{C_p} \quad . \quad . \quad . \quad . \quad . \quad . \quad 1(a)$$

is a truism, depending on the proposition that actual saving in a period (excess of the income in that period over consumption) is equal to the addition to the capital stock. Total saving is equal to sx_0. The addition to the capital stock is equal to $C_p(x_1 - x_0)$. This follows from the definition of C_p. And so,

$$sx_0 = C_p(x_1 - x_0)$$

$$\therefore \frac{s}{C_p} = \frac{x_1 - x_0}{x_0} = G$$

G is the rate of increase in total output which actually occurs; C_p is the increment in the stock of capital divided by the increment in total output which actually occurs. If the value of the increment of stock of capital per unit increment of output which actually occurs, C_p, is equal to C, the amount of capital per unit increment of output required by technological and other conditions (including the state of confidence, the rate of interest, etc.) then clearly the increase which actually occurs is equal to the increase which is justified by the circumstances. This means that, since C_p includes all goods (circulating and fixed capital), and is in fact production minus consumption per unit increment of output during the period, the sum of decisions to produce, to which G gives expression, are on balance justified—*i.e.*, if $C = C_p$, then $G = G_w$, and (from 1(*a*) above)

$$G_w = \frac{s}{C}$$

This is the fundamental equation, stated in paragraph 4, which determines the warranted rate of growth. To give numerical values to these symbols, which may be fairly representative of modern conditions: if 10 per cent. of income were saved and the capital coefficient per annum (C) were equal to 4, the warranted rate of growth would be $2\frac{1}{2}$ per cent. per annum.

It may be well to emphasise at this point that no distinction is drawn in this theory between capital goods and consumption goods. In measuring the increment of capital, the two are taken together; the increment consists of total production less total consumption. Some trade-cycle theorists concern themselves with a possible lack of balance between these two categories; no doubt that has its importance. The theory here considered is more fundamental or simple; it is logically prior to the considerations regarding lack of balance, and grasp of it is required as a preliminary to the study of them.

6. To use terminology recently employed by distinguished authorities, C_p is an *ex post* quantity. I am not clear if C should be regarded as its corresponding *ex ante*. C is rather that addition to capital goods in any period, which producers regard as ideally suited to the output which they are undertaking in that period. For convenience the term *ex ante* when employed in this article will be used in this sense.

The truism stated above, 1(*a*), gives expression to Mr. Keynes' proposition that saving is necessarily equal to investment—that is, to *ex post* investment. Saving is not necessarily equal to *ex ante* investment in this sense, since unwanted accretions or depletions of stocks may occur, or equipment may be found to have been produced in excess of, or short of, requirements.

If *ex post* investment is less than *ex ante* investment, this means that there has been an undesired reduction of stocks or insufficient provision of productive equipment, and there will be a stimulus to further expansion of output; conversely if *ex post* investment exceeds *ex ante* investment. If *ex post* investment is less than *ex ante* investment, saving is less than *ex ante* investment. In his *Treatise on Money* Mr. Keynes formulated a proposition, which has been widely felt to be enlightening, though experience has led him subsequently to condemn the definitions employed as more likely to be misconstrued than helpful. He said that if investment exceeded saving, the system would be stimulated to expand, and conversely. If for the definitions on which that proposition was based, we *substitute* the definition of *ex ante* investment given above, it is true that if *ex ante* investment exceeds saving, the system will be stimulated, and conversely. This truth may account for the feeling of satisfaction which Mr. Keynes' proposition originally evoked and the reluctance to abandon it at his behest. In many connections we are more interested in *ex ante* than in *ex post* investment, the latter including as it does unwanted accretions of stocks. Mr. Keynes' proposition of the *Treatise* may still be a useful aid to thinking, if we substitute for " Investment " in it *ex ante* investment as defined above.

7. Two minor points may be considered before we proceed with the main argument.

(i) It may be felt that there is something unreal in this analysis, since the increase in capital which producers will regard as right in period 1 is in the real world related not to the increase of total output in period 1, but to prospective increases in subsequent periods. This objection may be divided into two parts. (*a*) In view of the fact that much of the outlay of capital is connected with long-range planning, it may be held that the fundamental equation gives too much weight to the short-period effect of the acceleration principle. This objection is freely admitted and allowed for in the subsequent modification of the equation. (*b*) It may further be objected that even in the sphere in which the acceleration principle holds there must be some lag between the increased provision of equipment (and stocks?) and the increased flow of output which they are designed to support. There may be some force in this. But the point is deliberately neglected in this part of the argument, along with all questions of lags. The study of these lags is of undoubted importance, but a division of labour in analysis is indispensable, and in this case the neglect is necessary in order to get the clearest possible view of the forces determining the trend and its influence as such. Moreover, the lag referred to in this sub-heading (*b*) may properly be regarded as unimportant, since, in the event of a ***steady*** advance (G) being maintained, the difference between $x_1 - x_0$ and $x_2 - x_1$ will be of the second order of small quantities. In other words, it matters not whether we regard the increment of capital as required to support the increment of total output in the same period or in the one immediately succeeding it.

8. (ii) In the demonstration given above (paras. 6 and 7) reference was made to the distinction between the *ex post* and the *ex ante* increase of capital goods. No reference was made to the distinction between *ex post* and *ex ante* saving.[1] Suppose that G is not equal to G_w might not the discrepancy show itself on the other side of the equation, not in any divergence of C_p from C, but in *ex post* saving not being equal to *ex ante* saving?

I have no very clear view as to possible causes likely to operate in a systematic way to distort *ex post* from *ex ante* saving, or of the probable importance of such distortions. It is said, for instance, that in a time of rising prices, fixed-income classes will not adapt their modes of life simultaneously, and so may save less than they would be disposed to do had they clearly foreseen the impending rise. *Per contra* variable-income classes may not foresee their own rise of income, and so spend less than they would have been disposed to do.

[1] Be it noted that *ex ante* is here used of saving in a sense analogous to that defined in the expression *ex ante* investment; it is the saving which savers would choose to make in any period, were they able to adapt expenditure simultaneously with the changing circumstances of the period.

This question of the possible divergence of *ex post* from *ex ante* saving must be kept entirely distinct from that of the variations in s in the different phases of the trade cycle, which not only are admitted, but also play a part in the argument. s may vary because the level of income or of profit is abnormally swollen or depressed.

The neglect of these possible divergences has no importance for the argument, since they will have the same effect on growth as the divergences of C_p from C for which they may serve as substitute. Thus if G exceeds G_w, the right-hand side of the equation must exceed s/C. If the whole of this effect is found in C_p it will be *less* than C, and this is a stimulus to expansion.[1] Firms finding themselves short of stock or equipment will increase their orders. If, on the other hand, the whole of this effect is found in a divergence of *ex post s* from *ex ante s*, *ex post s* will be *greater* than *ex ante s*. Savers will find that they have saved more than they would have done had they foreseen their level of income or the level of prices correctly. Consequently they will be stimulated to expand purchases, and orders for goods will consequently be increased. Throughout the following pages the reader, whenever he finds a reference to the excess or deficiency of C_p compared with C, may substitute, if he prefers it, a supposed deficiency or excess of *ex post* saving compared with *ex ante* saving, without affecting the course of the argument.

9. We now come to a point of major importance, constituting the difference between the dynamic equilibrium (warranted rate of growth) and the static equilibrium. Normally the latter is stable and the former unstable. This gives a *prima facie* reason for regarding the dynamic analysis as a necessary propædeutic to trade-cycle study.

Some recent writers have been disposed to urge that the static equilibrium is not so stable as is sometimes claimed. Suppose that an increased output of a commodity, constituting a departure from equilibrium, is tried, so that its supply stands at a point at which the supply curve is above the demand curve. It is argued that, instead of a relapse at once occurring, reducing supply to the point of intersection of the supply and demand curves—this showing the stability of the old equilibrium—the upshot depends on how all parties now proceed. It is suggested that there may be a tendency to waltz round the point of intersection or, more broadly, that in the backward adjustment there may be

[1] The reader who is surprised that an excess of G over G_w is stimulating will find the explanation in the next paragraph.

wide repercussions disturbing the whole system. It is even held that the whole question of the stability of the static equilibrium, in the sense of the tendency of a relapse to it when a random departure occurs, is itself a dynamic problem, which cannot be looked after by the system of static equations. I have the impression that this type of criticism exaggerates the importance of this problem, and constitutes to some extent a failure to see the wood for the trees, and that on its own ground the theory of static equlibrium is well able to hold its own.

But when we look at the dynamic equilibrium, new vistas are opened. The line of output traced by the warranted ratė of growth is a moving equilibrium, in the sense that it represents the one level of output at which producers will feel in the upshot that they have done the right thing, and which will induce them to continue in the same line of advance. Stock in hand and equipment available will be exactly at the level which they would wish to have them. Of course what applies to the system in general may not apply to each individual separately. But if one feels he has over-produced or over-ordered, this will be counterbalanced by an opposite experience of an equal importance in some other part of the field.

But now suppose that there is a departure from the warranted rate of growth. Suppose an excessive output, so that G exceeds G_w. The consequence will be that C_p, the actual increase of capital goods per unit increment of output, falls below C, that which is desired. There will be, in fact, an undue depletion of stock or shortage of equipment, and the system will be stimulated to further expansion. G, instead of returning to G_w, will move farther from it in an upward direction, and the farther it diverges, the greater the stimulus to expansion will be. Similarly, if G falls below G_w, there will be a redundance of capital goods, and a depressing influence will be exerted; this will cause a further divergence and a still stronger depressing influence; and so on. Thus in the dynamic field we have a condition opposite to that which holds in the static field. A departure from equilibrium, instead of being self-righting, will be self-aggravating. G_w represents a moving equilibrium, but a highly unstable one. Of interest this for trade-cycle analysis !

Suppose an increase in the propensity to save, which means that the values of s are increased for all levels of income. This necessarily involves, *ceteris paribus*, a higher rate of warranted growth. But if the actual growth was previously equal to the warranted growth, the immediate effect is to raise the warranted rate above the actual rate. This state of affairs sets up a depressing influence which will drag the actual rate progressively farther below the warranted rate. In this as in other cases, the movement of a dynamic determinant has an opposite effect on the warranted path of growth to that which it has on its actual path. How different from the order of events in static theory !

The reader may have some difficulty in the expression " stimulus to expansion." What is the significance of this, in view of the fact that some growth is assumed as a basic condition ? It must be remembered that the value of G depends on aggregates x_0 and x_1. These are sums of numerous quantities for which individuals are responsible. It must be supposed that at all times some individuals are jogging on at a steady level, others are risking an increase of orders or output, others are willy-nilly curtailing. G is the resultant of their separate enterprises. Some are in any event likely to be disappointed. If G is equal to G_w, it is to be supposed that the general level of enterprise undertaken in period 0, including in sum a certain increase over that in the preceding period, is found to be satisfactory. Those running short of stock balance those with surpluses. This justifies further action on similar lines, though the individuals increasing orders for stock in trade or planning new equipment in period 1 may not be identical in person with those doing so in period 0. If an expansive force is in operation, more individuals, or individuals having greater weight, will be induced by their trading position to venture increases than did so in the preceding period. Conversely if a depressing force is in operation.

The dynamic theory so far stated may be summed up in two propositions. (i) A unique warranted line of growth is determined jointly by the propensity to save and the quantity of capital required by technological and other considerations per unit increment of total output. Only if producers keep to this line will they find that on balance their production in each period has been neither excessive nor deficient. (ii) On either side of this line is a " field " in which centrifugal forces operate, the magnitude of which varies directly as the distance of any point in it from the warranted line. Departure from the warranted line sets up an inducement to depart farther from it. The moving equilibrium of advance is thus a highly unstable one.

The essential point here may be further explained by reference to the expressions over-production and under-production. The distinction between particular over-production and general over-production is well known. In the event of particular over-production, there will normally be a tendency to reduce production of the particular line, and so equilibrium will be restored. We may define general over-production as a condition in which a majority of producers, or producers representing in sum the major part of production, find they have produced or ordered too much, in the sense that they or the distributors of their goods find themselves in possession of an unwanted volume of stocks or equipment. By reference to the fundamental equation it appears that this state of things can only occur when the actual growth has been *below* the warranted growth—*i.e.*, a condition of general over-production is the consequence of producers in sum producing too little. The only way in which this state of affairs could have been avoided would have been by producers in sum producing more than they did. Over-production is the consequence of production below the warranted level. Conversely, if producers find that they are continually running short of stocks and equipment, this means that they are producing above the warranted level.

But the condition of over-production, or, as we should perhaps call it, apparent over-production, will lead to a curtailment of production or orders, or a reduction in the rate of increase on balance, and consequently, so long as the fundamental conditions governing the warranted rate are unchanged, to a larger gap between actual and warranted growth, and so to an intensification of the evils which the contraction was intended to cure.

It must be noted that a rate of growth lying on either side of the warranted rate is regarded here as unwarranted. If the actual rate exceeds the warranted rate, producers on balance will not feel that they have produced or ordered too much; on the contrary, they will be running short of stocks and/or equipment. Thus they will not feel that they have produced the warranted amount plus something; on the contrary, they will feel that everything which they have produced has been warranted, and that they might warrantably have produced something more. None the less, we define their production as unwarrantably large, meaning by that that they have produced in excess of the unique amount which would leave them on balance satisfied with what they had done and prepared to go forward in the next period on similar lines.

10. The foregoing demonstration of the inherent instability of the moving equilibrium, or warranted line of advance, depends on the assumption that the values of s and C are independent of the value of G. This is formally correct. The analysis relates to a single point of time. s is regarded as likely to vary with a

change in the size of income, but a change in the rate of growth at a given point of time has no effect on its size. C may also be expected to vary with the size of income, *e.g.*, owing to the occurrence of surplus capital capacity from time to time, but the same argument for regarding it as independent of the rate of growth at a particular point of time applies.

It may be objected, however, that this method of analysis is too strict to be realistic, since the discovery that output is excessive or deficient, and the consequent emergence of a depressing or stimulating force, takes some time, and in the interval required for a reaction to be produced an appreciable change in s or C may have occurred.

Consider this with reference to an experimental increase in G above a warranted level. According to the theory of instability, any such experiment will be apparently over-justified, stocks or equipment running short in consequence of it. Is it possible that if resulting changes in the values of s or C are taken into account, this doctrine will have to be modified?

In order to justify modifying the doctrine, it would be necessary to show that, in consequence of the experimental increase, s was substantially increased or C reduced. It is unlikely that C would be reduced. The capital coefficient may often stand below the level appropriate to the technological conditions of the age, owing to the existence of surplus equipment. If this were so, the higher rate of output consequent upon the experimental increase would tend to raise C. A smaller proportion of firms would come to find their capacity redundant, and a larger proportion would have to support a greater turnover by ordering extra equipment.

With saving the case is different. An expansion of activity might increase the proportion of income saved. What increase of saving is required for a modification of the instability theory?

This can be shown simply. Let x_e be an experimental increase of output above the warranted level. Let s_m stand for the fraction of the consequential income saved. The instability principle requires that

$$Cx_e > s_m x_e$$

i.e., that

$$s_m < C$$

$$< \frac{s}{G_w}$$

This condition needs interpretation. Since C and G_w do not both appear in the equation, it is necessary to define the period by which G_w is measured. This should be done by reference to the reaction time mentioned above—namely, the time required for an undue accretion or depletion of capital goods to exert its influence upon the flow of orders. If this reaction time is six months, then G_w must be measured as growth per six months.

Thus the instability condition requires that the fraction of marginal income saved shall not be more than the fraction of total income saved multiplied by the total income and divided by the increment of warranted income per six months. Thus if the warranted growth is 2½ per cent. per annum, or 1¼ per cent. per six months, the instability principle requires that the fraction of marginal income saved must be less than eighty times the fraction of average income saved. Supposing that the high figure of 50 per cent. is taken as the fraction of marginal income saved, the fraction of total income saved must be greater than five-eighths of 1 per cent. Thus for any normal warranted rate of growth and level of saving, the instability principle seems quite secure.

The force of this argument, however, is somewhat weakened when long-range capital outlay is taken into account. It will then appear that the attainment of a neutral or stable equilibrium of advance may not be altogether improbable in certain phases of the cycle.

11. It should be noticed that the instability theory makes the empirical verification of the acceleration principle more arduous. For it leads to the expectation that in the upward phase of the cycle the actual rate will tend to run above the warranted rate, and the accretion of capital to be less than that required by the acceleration principle; and conversely in the downward phase. Thus a finding that the volume of investment fluctuates less than is required by direct computation from the acceleration principle is consistent with the theory here set forth, in which, none the less, the acceleration principle is presented as a leading dynamic determinant.

12. It is now expedient to introduce further terms into our equation to reduce the influence of the acceleration principle. Some outlays of capital have no direct relation to the current increase of output. They may be related to a prospective long-period increase of activity, and be but slightly influenced, if at all, by the current increase of trade. Or they may be induced by new inventions calculated to cheapen production or change consumers' modes of spending their income, so that they are not related to increments of output, but are designed to revolutionise the methods for producing some portion of already existing output or to substitute one line of goods for another in the consumers' budget. There are doubtless numerous factors, including the

state of confidence and the rate of interest affecting the volume of such outlay. It may suffice for the purpose in hand to divide it into two parts.

One part, K, is conceived to be quite independent both of the current level of income and its current rate of growth. The other, expressed as a fraction of income, k, is conceived to vary with the current level of income, as distinct from its rate of growth. This seems a reasonable assumption. Long-period anticipations are bound to be influenced by the present state of prosperity or adversity: even public authorities are apt to reduce the volume of public works in a slump. Companies may relate their expenditure on long-range plans to the current state of their profit account.

Having regard to the principle that the total increase of capital is equal to the total saving in the period, our fundamental equation may be modified as follows :—

$$G_w = \frac{s - k - \frac{K}{x}}{C} \quad . \quad . \quad . \quad . \quad (2)[1]$$

$$\therefore \frac{s - k - \frac{K}{x_0}}{C_p} = \frac{x_1 - x_0}{x_0} = G$$

$$\therefore G_w = \frac{s - k - \frac{K}{x_0}}{C}$$

It must be noticed that C and C_p now stand not for the total increase of capital (desired and actual, respectively) per unit increment of output, but only for the net increase of capital after the capital represented by k and K has been subtracted.

It may be noticed that the larger the volume of outlay which will be sustained independently of the current rate of growth, the *smaller* is the warranted rate of growth. A larger part of savings being absorbed in such outlay, there will be a smaller part to be looked after by the acceleration principle.

13. In the following pages the expression long-range capital outlay will be used for the magnitude denoted by $xk + K$. This must not be supposed to cover all investment in durable fixed equipment; for much of that is related to, and directly governed by, the current output of consumption goods. It refers only to that part of the output of fixed equipment the production of which is not governed by the current demand for consumption goods.

If long-range capital outlay were large by comparison with that required to support the current increase in turnover of consumable

[1] $sx_0 = C_p(x_1 - x_0) + kx_0 + K$

goods, the peculiar conditions defined in § 10 for the invalidity of the instability principle might in certain circumstances be realised. For the fraction of total income saved *and* devoted to the finance of the increase of current output might be very small compared with the fraction of marginal income saved. It is not, however, to be supposed that it would normally be small enough to invalidate the instability principle. For, with normal growth at 2½ per cent., saving at 10 per cent., marginal saving at 50 per cent. and the reaction time 6 months, this would mean that fifteen-sixteenths of capital would normally be devoted to long-range capital outlay and only one-sixteenth would be directly associated with the current increase of output (cf. § 10). But such a situation might well arise in certain phases of the trade cycle, especially when capital capacity was redundant and saving low. In that case a stable equilibrium of advance might for a time be achieved.

14. To complete the picture, foreign trade must be taken into account. It is reasonable to measure exports, including invisible exports and the earnings of foreign investments, in absolute terms. The value of income which may be earned in this way may be conceived to be independent both of the level of activity at home and of its growth (though in so far as the trade cycle is world-wide, its value will be *de facto* related to income). Let E stand for this value. Imports, on the other hand, are better taken as a fraction, i, of the current level of income. We then have, by parity of reasoning,

$$G_w = \frac{s + i - k - \frac{K}{x} - \frac{E}{x}}{C} \quad . \quad . \quad . \quad (3)$$ [1]

i need not be equal to $\frac{E}{x}$; the difference represents an international movement of capital. The influence of the various magnitudes on the warranted rate of growth is shown by the equation.

15. The fundamental dynamic equation has been used to demonstrate the inherent tendency of the system to instability. Space forbids an application of this method of analysis to the successive phases of the trade cycle. In the course of it the values expressed by the symbols on the right-hand side of the equation undergo considerable change. As actual growth departs

[1] The principle now is that saving plus income expended on imports must be equal to the increase of capital in the country plus income derived from abroad. This is deducible from the fact that income derived from the sale of home made goods to consumers at home is equal to the income devoted to their purchase. Thus :—

$$sx_0 + ix_0 = C_p(x_1 - x_0) + kx_0 + K + E$$

upwards or downwards from the warranted level, the warranted rate itself moves,[1] and may chase the actual rate in either direction. The maximum rates of advance or recession may be expected to occur at the moment when the chase is successful.

For the convenience of the reader who may be tempted to experiment with this tool, it must be observed that C is always positive. Being the total quantity of capital required in connection with increments (or decrements) of current output divided by the increment (or decrement) of that output, when the latter is negative the former is negative also, and the coefficient remains positive. C_p, on the other hand, may be negative; it is not negative whenever there is a depletion of capital goods, but only when the amount of capital goods outstanding is moving in the opposite direction to the level of total output.

The formula is not well adapted to dealing with the case of zero growth. But that matter is quite simple. Zero growth is only warranted when the amount of saving is equal to the amount required for long-range capital outlay. If the amount of saving exceeds this, there will be a tendency for output to decline, and conversely.

It may be well to make one point with regard to a downward departure from the warranted position of sufficient importance to outlive one reaction time and bring the system within the field where the centrifugal forces have substantial strength. The downward lapse will then continue until the warranted rate, determined by the values on the right-hand side of the equation, itself moves down. This will happen when the numerator falls or the denominator rises. But in a phase of declining rate of growth the capital coefficient is not in general likely to rise. And so long as there is still some positive growth, albeit at a declining rate, the fraction of income saved is not likely to fall. Therefore, once the rate of growth is driven downwards from the warranted level, the warranted level is not itself likely to fall, or the downward movement therefore to be checked until the rate of growth becomes negative and the level of income recedes. Now, if the actual rate is standing below the warranted rate, the centrifugal force will continue to operate, driving the actual rate progressively downwards, unless or until the warranted rate itself falls to a level as low as the actual rate. But, since the actual rate is now negative, this cannot happen until the numerator of the right-

[1] This idea is analogous to that propounded by Mr. D. H. Robertson that the "natural" rate of interest may be expected to vary in the different phases of the trade cycle. Cf. ECONOMIC JOURNAL, December 1934.

hand side of the equation becomes negative—that is, until saving falls below the level required for long-range capital outlay.

16. Alongside the concept of warranted rate of growth we may introduce another, to be called the natural rate of growth. This is the maximum rate of growth allowed by the increase of population, accumulation of capital, technological improvement and the work/leisure preference schedule, supposing that there is always full employment in some sense.

There is no inherent tendency for these two rates to coincide. Indeed, there is no unique warranted rate; the value of warranted rate depends upon the phase of the trade cycle and the level of activity.

Consideration may be given to that warranted rate which would obtain in conditions of full employment; this may be regarded as the warranted rate "proper" to the economy. *Prima facie* it might be supposed healthier to have the "proper" warranted rate above than below the natural rate. But this is very doubtful.

The system cannot advance more quickly than the natural rate allows. If the proper warranted rate is above this, there will be a chronic tendency to depression; the depressions drag down the warranted rate below its proper level, and so keep its average value over a term of years down to the natural rate. But this reduction of the warranted rate is only achieved by having chronic unemployment.

The warranted rate is dragged down by depression; it may be twisted upwards by an inflation of prices and profit. If the proper rate is below the natural rate, the average value of the warranted rate may be sustained above its proper level over a term of years by a succession of profit booms.

Thus each state of affairs has its appropriate evils. There is much to be said for the view that it is better that the proper warranted rate should be lower rather than higher than the natural rate.

17. In order fully to grasp the dynamic principle, it is necessary to bear in mind that changes in fundamental conditions have opposite effects on the actual rate and the warranted rate. An increased amount of long-range capital outlay, an increase in the capital coefficient, an increase in the propensity to consume, and an increase in the active balance on international account, or a decline in the passive balance, are all properly thought to have a stimulating effect on the system. But they all tend, as may

readily be seen from the equation, to reduce the warranted rate. This paradox may be readily explained.

Suppose that one of these stimulants begins to operate when the actual rate is equal to the warranted rate. By depressing the warranted rate, it drags that down below the actual rate, and so automatically brings the actual rate into the field of centrifugal forces, driving it away from the warranted rate—that is, in this case, upwards. Thus the stimulant causes the system to expand.

It must not be inferred that these stimulants are only of temporary benefit. For it may be healthy for an economy to have its proper warranted rate reduced. This is likely to be so when its proper warranted rate is tending to be above the natural rate.[1] The long-run value of the stimulant can only be assessed if it is known whether, in its absence, the proper warranted rate is running above or below the natural rate.

It is often felt that a high propensity to save should warrant a great increase in the output of wealth, and this induces an extreme aversion to accept Mr. Keynes' view that excessive saving in the modern age is hostile to prosperity. The feeling is justified to the extent that higher propensity to save does, in fact, *warrant* a higher rate of growth. Trouble arises if the rate of growth which it warrants is greater than that which the increase of population and the increase of technical capacity render permanently possible. And the fundamental paradox is that the more ambitious the rate *warranted* is, the greater the probability that the actual output will from time to time, and even persistently fall below that which the productive capacity of the population would allow.

18. Policy in this field is usually appraised by reference to its power to combat tendencies to oscillation. Our demonstration of the inherent instability of the dynamic equilibrium confirms the importance of this. But there are two points to be noticed in this connection. 1. The nature of the measures suitable for combating the tendency to oscillate may depend on whether the natural rate is above or below the proper warranted rate. 2. In addition to dealing with the tendency to oscillation when it occurs, it may be desirable to have a long-range policy designed to

[1] This may be the most fundamental rational explanation of the common view that it is dangerous for an old country to be a large importer of capital. For this involves a high warranted rate of growth, and it is dangerous to have a high warranted rate when the natural rate is low. *Per contra* for a young country, whose natural rate is high, it is considered healthy and proper to have a large import of capital.

influence the relation between the proper warranted rate of growth and the natural rate.

If, in the absence of interference, the proper warranted rate is substantially above the natural rate, the difficulties may be too great to be dealt with by a mere anti-cycle policy. In the first place, there is the probability of a slump occurring before full employment is reached, since during the revival the warranted rate may be dangerously near the actual rate, and liable at any time to overpass it, thus generating depression. Secondly, there is an acute problem if the actual rate reaches the ceiling of full employment and is depressed to the natural rate, and therefore below the warranted rate. An attempt may then be made to drag down the warranted rate below its normal level by increasing public works (K). But the difficulty of the proper warranted rate being above the natural rate will be chronic, and this means that only by keeping in being a large and growing volume of public works can the slump be prevented. In fine, the anti-cycle policy has to be converted into a permanent policy for keeping down the proper warranted rate.

19. The ideal policy would be to manipulate the proper warranted rate so that it should be equal to the natural rate. If this could be achieved—but in fact only a rough approximation would be possible—an anti-cycle policy would none the less be an indispensable supplement. For the warranted rate is bound to be disturbed by the varying incidence of inventions and fluctuations in the foreign account. An anti-cycle policy would be necessary to combat the run-away forces which come into being as soon as a substantial change occurs in the warranted rate.

20. A low rate of interest makes for a low warranted rate of increase, by encouraging high values of K and C and, possibly also, by having a depressing influence on s. Since the effects of changes in the rate of interest are probably slow-working, it may be wise to use the rate of interest as a long-range weapon for reducing the warranted rate of growth, and to reserve *suitable* public works for use against the cycle. It is not suggested, however, that a low rate of interest has sufficient power of its own to keep down the warranted rate without the assistance of a programme of public works to be kept permanently in operation.

If permanent public works activity and a low long-term rate availed to bring the proper warranted rate into line with the natural rate, variations in the short-term rate of interest might come into their own again as an ancillary method of dealing with oscillations.

21. This essay has only touched in the most tentative way on a small fraction of the problems, theoretical and practical, of which the enunciation of a dynamic theory suggests the formulation. In the last paragraph it was implicitly hinted that our present situation is one of a relatively high proper warranted rate. The evidence for this comes from inside and outside the dynamic theory itself. According to the dynamic theory, the tendency of a system to relapse into depression before full employment is reached in the boom suggests that its proper warranted rate exceeds its natural rate. Outside evidence includes the known decline in the growth of population, which involves a decline in the natural rate. More controversial points are the tendency of a more wealthy population to save a larger fraction of its income (high value of s involves high warranted rate), and the tendency of modern progress to depress rather than elevate the value of C (low value of C involves high warranted rate).

The main object of this article, however, is to present a tool of analysis, not to diagnose present conditions.

R. F. Harrod

Christ Church, Oxford.

ERRATA

We have to apologise for four misprints in the ECONOMIC JOURNAL of March, 1939. In a note under " Current Topics " (page 178) concerned with the varied spellings of " autarky," that word was made to derive from the root ἀαρκεῖν. We need hardly point out that that should have read ἀρκεῖν. In Mr. Harrod's review of *Political Economy* by Nassau Senior, page 148, line 23, "ability" should read " utility." The other two both appear in Mr. Harrod's article, *An Essay in Dynamic Theory*. On page 18, line 3, equation 1(a), large S should read small s. On page 27, lines 18 and 19, namely

$$\therefore \frac{s - k - \frac{K}{x_0}}{C_p} = \frac{x_1 - x_0}{x_0} = G$$

$$\therefore G_w = \frac{s - k - \frac{K}{x_0}}{C}$$

belong to the footnote at the bottom of the page and should follow the equation therein set out.

[8]

A Parable on Savings and Investment

By Joan Robinson

THE recent controversy between Mr. Keynes and Dr. Hayek has been extremely bewildering, but one important point of difference at least appears to have been clearly expressed by Mr. Keynes. In ECONOMICA, November 1931 (p. 391), he writes:

> " 'Voluntary' saving, according to Dr. Hayek, always finds its way into investment. This is so because (in his view) an increase of saving means (*cet. par.*) a net increase of purchasing power directed to buying what I call 'investment goods' but which Dr. Hayek calls 'intermediate products.' . . . In my view, saving and investment (as I define them) can get out of gear . . . merely as a result of the public changing their rate of saving or the entrepreneurs changing their rate of investment, there being no automatic mechanism in the economic system (as Dr. Hayek's view would imply that there must be) to keep the two rates equal, provided that the effective quantity of money is unchanged."

In his rejoinder, Dr. Hayek definitely declares himself to be unable to understand this view, and with misdirected charity attempts to impute to Mr. Keynes opinions which would seem to Dr. Hayek to be sensible, but which Mr. Keynes would hold to be totally erroneous. Dr. Hayek's last contribution (ECONOMICA, February 1932) seems to throw no new light on this central point of difference and perhaps a merely miscellaneous reader of the *Treatise on Money* may now step in with an attempt to elucidate the problem.

I do not presume to speak for Dr. Hayek. I speak for the ordinary muddle-headed reader of economics, brought up in the Quantity Theory school, who is suddenly presented with the argument of the *Treatise*. I wish to state what seems to me the fundamental difficulty of such a reader in the simplest possible terms, leaving on one side all the subtleties and complications both of Dr. Hayek's and Mr. Keynes' arguments.

It appears that no one finds any difficulty in accounting for a divergence between saving and investment when there is at the same time a continuous increase in " hoarding " of money, that is, a continuous decline in the velocity of circulation or increase in unspent balances. We must therefore study a simplified case in which all incomes are currently spent on something, either on consumption goods or on securities, and see whether it is still possible that savings should fail to be invested. Starting from a position of equilibrium in which savings and investment are equal, suppose that voluntary saving increases, everything else remaining the same. Since all incomes are being spent, this must mean that the demand for goods goes down, and the demand for securities goes up. Mr. Keynes tells us that this will lead to a decline in the price of consumption goods, but need not lead to a rise in the price of securities. He is admittedly a little vague about the connection between the price of securities and the value of new investment goods (the I of his equations), but it is clear that there must be a close relationship between them, and if old capital (securities) does not rise in price, there is no reason to expect an increase in the price of new capital, and so an increase in the value of investment.

At first the simple-minded reader finds this extremely odd. He immediately asks himself: " If the public take to spending more money on hats and less on boots, the price of hats goes up and the price of boots goes down, and after a short time the output of hats goes up and the output of boots goes down. Why is not the same thing true of capital goods and of consumption goods?" Mr. Keynes' opponents appear to have common sense on their side.

But a moment's reflection will show the simple-minded reader that he has been superficial. The price of goods is not directly affected by the amount being produced, but by the amount *coming on to the market*. Suppose he had thought, not of hats and boots, but of gold and green peas. The daily supply of green peas coming on to the market, and therefore the day-to-day price of peas, depends upon the current output, but the price of gold (in a country in which gold is not money) does not only, or even mainly, depend on the output of the mines, but upon the amount put on to the market by the owners of gold which was mined long ago. Now, when the demand for peas falls, their price is reduced and they are sold at a loss, but the rise in the demand for gold calls forth buried treasures, and the price of gold rises very little. Thus the price level of the two together falls. The simple-minded reader finds that the Quantity Theory of Money has led him to concentrate too much on Demand. He had been apt to forget Supply. He knew that a change in the flow of money directed on to the market will alter prices, but somehow or other he was always overlooking the fact that a change in the daily flow of goods coming on to the market is just as important, and just as likely to occur, even apart from changes in the volume of production.

He is not yet any nearer, however, to solving the main question. The stocks of gold are not inexhaustible, and sooner or later there must be some increase in the price of gold, and there will be some increase in new mining. In the long run the output of peas will fall and the output of gold go up, just like the outputs of boots and of hats. To illustrate Mr. Keynes' argument, we must suppose that it is not a rise in the price of gold, but the very same fall in the price of peas which caused them to be sold at a loss, that has caused an increase in the supply of gold coming on to the market. The market gardeners, finding that they have made a loss on peas, are obliged to dig up their buried gold to sell instead. The increase in the demand for gold is exactly matched by an increase in supply coming on to the market, and its price need not rise at all. At this point common sense objects that the market gardeners would not finance their losses entirely by selling gold. They would cut down their expenditure. But Mr. Keynes points out that this would merely be to pass on the loss (and, in our parable, the necessity to sell gold) to someone else. After a bewildered pause over the famous Widow's Cruse, the simple-minded reader realises that he is intended to suppose that the output of goods is unchanged in spite of the change in price, and that employment in the pea gardens will not be reduced by the fall in the price of peas. I shall return to this point later on. Mr. Keynes' unnatural assumption simplifies the argument without, I believe, destroying its general validity. For the moment we may let it pass, but it is important always to remember that this assumption has been made.

Having come so far, the simple-minded reader once more realises that he had been inclined to overlook Supply. It now seems perfectly possible that the increase in demand for gold should leave its price unchanged. He is now beginning to get the drift of the argument in the *Treatise*. If, in the parable, he substitutes for green peas all consumption goods; for gold, titles to capital; and for mining, new investment, he begins to see what Mr. Keynes is at. But he is still not satisfied. He has only shown that the price of securities (gold in the story) will not rise by assuming that it does not. With the same disregard for the rules of logic the opposite case can equally well be maintained. Assume that the price of gold rises to just such an extent that the profits of the gold-miners, on the new gold which they are currently selling, offset the losses of the market gardeners : then there are no net losses, and the demand for gold of the new savers is not met by a supply of buried treasures dug up and put on to the market, but by the enhanced value of the new gold coming from the mines. And equally, on any other assumption, the total supply of gold, coming from the mines and out of old accumulations, is equal to the total demand, coming from saving and from profits. Any change in the value of the newly mined gold produces compensating changes in losses and profits, and consequently compensating changes in the digging up of gold hoards or the accumulation of them. At any price of gold there is equilibrium between demand and the supply coming on to the market.

It now seems to the simple-minded reader that the price of gold may be anything it likes. But here his first false start comes to his aid. He at first supposed that some members of the community (neither the market gardeners nor the new savers) owned gold which they dug up when its price was tending to rise. He was evidently supposing that they "took a view" on the price of gold, and were prepared to sell as soon as the market price rose above their figure. The story can now be completed thus :—First saving increases, and the price of gold tends to rise. The gold-holders sell out, thus preventing the price from rising. Meanwhile the price of peas has fallen, and an amount of gold corresponding (at the existing price) to the total increase in saving is now coming on to the market. The tendency for a rise in the price of gold is checked, and a new equilibrium is established with the same volume of spending as before, no increase in the holding of unspent balances, and no change in the price of gold. The only change is the fall in the price of green peas, and the unhappy situation of the market gardeners. In Mr. Keynes' equations, S has increased, I′ remains the same, therefore P has fallen ; I remains the same, therefore π has fallen. At this point Mr. Robertson[1] steps in with a complicated argument about the sequence of events in time, but anyone who has followed the story so far

[1] *Economic Journal*, September, 1931, p. 402.

will easily be able to judge between him and Mr. Keynes. It is the first step which is difficult. The notion of a class of speculators (the gold-owners of the parable) separate from the other persons in the story is clearly a drastic simplification of real conditions, but if it were not the case that some such class of speculators existed, it would be impossible that any transactions should ever take place on the Stock Exchange. If everyone became a bull, or everyone a bear, at the same moment, the price of securities would be constantly fluctuating between infinity and zero. No one who wished to sell could find a buyer, and no one who wished to buy could find a seller, and no transactions would ever take place. These "speculators" need not be professionals. They are merely any owners of securities who will be prepared to sell out when the price rises sufficiently.

We have here, evidently, the clue to Mr. Keynes' somewhat mystifying references to a "state of bearishness." He describes it as a given demand curve for liquid assets in terms of the price of securities. It might equally well be represented as a kind of supply curve connecting the price of securities with the total amount of securities held by the speculators. At each price there is a certain volume of securities which the speculators will hold. The curve which shows this relationship may be called the speculative supply curve of securities. If this supply curve is given, the price of securities is determined by the amount in the hands of the speculators. For each amount of securities held by the speculators there is a certain price, and if the amount they are required to hold does not fall, the price of securities cannot rise. But if the demand for securities from new savers continued day by day without any additional securities coming from the makers of consumption goods (who are making losses), the stocks of the speculators would gradually decline and the price of securities would gradually rise. Actually, the makers of consumption goods are selling their commodities at a loss, and, on the assumption (admittedly unreal) that output remains unchanged, they are obliged to sell out securities to the full extent of their loss, that is to the full extent of the saving. It is the combination of the transactions of the speculators and the sales by loss-makers which keeps the price of securities from rising in spite of the increase in demand for them. Thus, if it were not for the sale of gold by the market gardeners, the price of gold would rise as soon as the stocks of the speculators ran low. And if it were not for the speculators the price of gold might be at any level. And at any level there would be equilibrium. It is the " view " of the speculators (which we assume to remain unchanged) that determines which of all possible prices shall be the actual price of gold. Of course, Mr. Keynes would be the first to admit that in any actual case the " state of bearishness " would not remain constant in this way. The speculators' supply curve is always shifting, the " view " that they take always altering. The change in savings, in fact, would be likely to lower it. As we all know, the price of securities is anything but stable, and a change in the price of consumption goods would never in fact leave the " view " of the speculators unchanged. We have supposed that a single speculative supply curve for securities remains in force throughout the story, merely to simplify the problem. The point of the argument is not to illustrate what is *likely* to happen, but to show that something in fact *may* happen which, if the view of Mr. Keynes' adversaries were correct, could never occur. By this means we are able to see the chain of causation which determines the price level of securities. The price of gold, in the parable, depends on the supply curve of the speculators. By altering their " view " they can make the price of gold whatever they please. In our story they kept it unchanged. They might have raised or lowered it. But, on our assumptions, all savings are spent on gold, and all losses are met by selling gold, so whatever the price of gold, the total value of the amount to be sold is equal to the total value of the amount to be bought. The price of gold is independent (upon these assumptions) of the volume of new savings. Thus we find that the price of securities depends on the speculative supply curve (assuming that the banking system does not alter their assets and so the amount of money). If this supply curve does not alter, the price of securities will not alter. Their price is determined by this supply curve, and will not rise merely because the demand for them (new savings) has increased.

Exactly the same argument would apply to consumption goods. As long as stocks of consumption goods are available, if speculators in consumption goods " take a view " on their price, the price of goods will be determined by the speculative supply curve of goods, and not by the current flow of new output. But since new production is a very high percentage of the total stock in the case of consumable goods, this influence upon their price level is relatively slight, while in the case of capital goods it is of preponderating importance. Thus even when we allow for the existence of speculation in consumption goods, the difference between consumption goods and capital goods, though only a matter of degree, is very great. Stocks of consumption goods available for speculation must be small, because they are perishable and awkward to hold. The current output cannot be held off the market for very long, and once they have passed out of the hands of professional dealers the public will not usually resell them. Some cannot be resold because (like green peas) they are eaten up at once. Others are not perishable, but they are less easy than capital goods to buy and sell at second hand. I might prefer to sell my grand piano when the price of pianos goes up, but then I could no longer play it, whereas cotton looms can be sold ten times a day, and go on weaving cotton, without anyone in the mill knowing who owns them. Stocks of consumption goods available for speculation are thus very small relatively to current output. The speculators cannot hold the price constant in the face of any considerable change in demand, even if their "view" on the price of consumption goods remains constant. A rise in demand rapidly exhausts stocks, and leads to a rise in price. A fall in demand quickly saturates the capacity of dealers to hold stocks and leads to a fall in price. The amount of capital goods in existence, on the other hand, is very large relatively to current new output, and any that are in existence are readily bought and sold. The day-to-day price of consumption goods thus depends mainly on current output, and the day-to-day price of capital goods depends mainly not on current output, but on dealings in titles to capital produced long ago.

To summarise the whole argument, if all incomes are currently spent, and there is no change in the effective amount of money, then, when there is a change in demand, more money being spent on securities, and less on consumption goods, the price of consumption goods will fall, but the price of securities need not rise; producers' losses will call forth a supply of securities, which, whatever their price may happen to be, is exactly equal to the demand for them. And their price will be determined, quite independently of this increase in demand, by the speculative supply curve of the holders of securities.

If my interpretation is correct, the simple-minded reader (along with Dr. Hayek) has a rightful grudge against Mr. Keynes. If what he meant was so simple, why must he have made it appear so hard? The distinction between consumption goods and capital goods, over which Mr. Keynes casts such an air of mystery, turns out to be merely one of degree, and, moreover, to be one which has always been well known. The difference between the forces determining the price level of consumption goods and the price level of new capital goods (P and P′ in the *Treatise*) was, after all, perfectly familiar from our general notions of supply and demand. There was no need for him to make us work so hard to find it out.

This account of the matter is a drastic simplification of the argument of the *Treatise,* still more of the conditions of the real world, but the simple-minded reader, with this clue in his hands, can return to the *Treatise* with more confidence, and may in the end hope to discover how it is that Mr. Keynes and his opponents have got at cross purposes.

Before we leave him to return to those distracting pages (140-146) in Book III of Volume I, we must say a word about his first difficulty—the Widow's Cruse. Mr. Keynes has now admitted that in that passage (p. 139) he was tacitly assuming that output was unchanged although the price level was falling. Evidently he, like the rest of us, had been misled by his upbringing into keeping his eye on Demand and forgetting Supply. In fact when P, the price level of consumption goods—in our parable the price of green peas—begins to fall, the market gardeners do not only economise by cutting down their consumption of peas, leaving the total sales of gold unchanged. They will dismiss men and produce fewer peas. Clearly if the current supply of peas is perfectly elastic, the price of peas *cannot* fall, even though there is no speculation in peas. The decline in demand for peas will show itself entirely in a reduction of output. Now neither the assumption of a perfectly elastic supply of current output of consumption goods nor Mr. Keynes' assumption of a perfectly inelastic supply is sufficiently realistic to be interesting. Actually the supply of goods in the short period is likely to be fairly inelastic, but not completely so. The difference in Mr. Keynes' argument, however, made by introducing more plausible assumptions, is far less than might be expected at first sight. When men become unemployed they do not live upon air. They must continue to spend money, although they are earning none. Then what they spend must either come from their past savings, or from their friends and relations, or from the dole. If their spending comes out of their own past accumulations, there will be dis-saving. If it comes out of the current savings of their friends, there is a reduction in the net amount of new savings, and the original excess of savings is reduced. If it comes out of a dole financed by selling Treasury Bills, new securities are forthcoming. And each of these methods of financing the unemployed will absorb the new savings just as effectively as the sale of securities due to the losses of the makers of consumption goods. It may be objected that the unemployed men will not spend as much as they spent when they were in work. But in so far as they spend less than before, the demand for consumption goods falls still further, and more unemployment is created. In so far as what they do spend is at the expense of consumption by someone else, the same effect is produced as if they curtail their own consumption. If their friends finance them at the expense of consumption, or if the dole is paid out of taxation which falls on consumption, unemployment will continue to grow. It will grow until it becomes impossible to curtail consumption any further, so that the expenditure of the unemployed must come in the end from a sale of securities or from a reduction in the excess of savings which first caused the trouble. Unemployment will continue to grow until in one way or the other the whole flow of new savings is being currently absorbed.

Thus the new savings are bound to find a home somewhere. Either they are matched by new investment, and do not upset equilibrium, or they are offset by a reduction in saving elsewhere, or they are matched by sales of securities coming either from losses on consumption goods, or from dis-saving, or from sales to finance the dole. If there is not enough new investment to match them, they will create losses and unemployment, and so create a demand for themselves. If we rule out *ex hypothesi* the possibility of savings accumulating in unspent money balances, it is clear that purchases of securities must be equal to the net amount of savings, but in so far as new investment is insufficient to provide securities on which the whole flow of savings can be spent, losses and unemployment will make up the difference. It does not follow that because the purchase of securities is equal to saving, the amount of investment must be equal to saving.

Mr. Keynes' assumption that the whole excess of saving over investment is accounted for by losses on consumption goods, and the consequent sale of securities, is thus only a simplification of the problem and does not falsify his argument. Once more the simple-minded reader may accuse Mr. Keynes of causing him a great deal of unnecessary trouble. It was naturally hard for him to realise when he first read on page 139 of the *Treatise* that he was expected to visualise an acute slump with full employment, and a trade boom without any increase in output, but once he has seen his way through this difficulty, it ceases to be very important.

My attempt to reconcile Mr. Keynes and the simple-minded reader of the *Treatise* has been only rudimentary; many important complications have been left on one side. But once the problem has been examined on the simplest possible assumptions, it becomes easier to deal with the intricacies of the argument of the *Treatise,* and the still greater intricacies of the problems presented by the real world.

[9]

The Theory of Money and the Analysis of Output

By JOAN ROBINSON

THE plain man has always found the Theory of Money a bewildering subject, but at the present time many academic economists are as much bewildered by it as the plain man. The reason for this state of affairs is that the Theory of Money has recently undergone a violent revolution. It has ceased to be the Theory of Money, and become the Analysis of Output.

The conclusions and methods of economic analysis are naturally much influenced by the technique of thought employed by the economists, and in almost every case where a divergence between "schools of thought" is to be found in economics the difference between one "school" and another arises from a difference in the mental tools which their members employ. Now the orthodox Theory of Money may be generally described as an attempt to apply the supply-and-demand tool to the analysis of the purchasing power of money. Just as, in the Theory of Value, the supply-and-demand mechanism is used to analyse the forces determining the value of a single commodity, so in the traditional Theory of Money the supply-and-demand mechanism, with some necessary modifications, is used to analyse the forces determining the value of money. The entity with which this analysis is mainly concerned is therefore the price level.

It has always been admitted that the chief justification for a study of the price level lies in the fact that changes in the price level may affect the volume of output, that is to say they may affect the amount of employment and the wealth of the community. But until recently no economist appears to have considered the possibility of tackling this problem directly, and setting the supply-and-demand apparatus to work on the question in which he was really interested—the forces determining the volume of output.

The apparatus used to analyse the determination of the price level were tautological statements known as Quantity Equations. The "Cambridge" equation was consciously designed to deal with the value of money in terms of supply and demand. In its simplest form the "Cambridge" equation was as follows:

$$\pi = \frac{kR}{M}$$

where π is the purchasing power of money, R the real national income, k the proportion of real income held in the form of money (cash and bank balances), and M the quantity of money. kR then represents the demand for money in terms of real wealth, and M the supply of money. The equation leads naturally to the simple argument that the greater the supply of money (M) the smaller is its value (π), and the greater the demand for money (kR) the greater is its value.

The Fisher equation was not cast in so definitely supply-and-demand a form, but it was essentially of the same nature. MV=PT or $P=\frac{MV}{T}$, where P is the price level, M the quantity of money, V its velocity of circulation (V varies roughly inversely with k), and T the volume of transaction. MV represents the effective supply of money, and PT the amount of work that money is required to do. The price level, P (which is roughly equivalent to $\frac{1}{\pi}$) is then regarded as the resultant of T, which without straining our terms too much may be regarded as the demand for money, and MV the supply of it. An increase in M or V is equivalent to an increase in the supply of money, and leads to a fall in its value, that is, to a rise in P; while an increase in T is equivalent to a rise in the demand for money, and leads to a rise in its value, that is, to a fall in P.

An imposing theoretical structure was built up on these simple tautologies. The exponents of the Theory of Money were never satisfied with their apparatus, and were always finding themselves led into paradoxical positions. The necessity to adapt the equations to the analysis of observed events led to greater and greater refinements and complications, but in essence the apparatus of thought remained the same.

The nature of the equations, the fact that they were tautologies, devoid of causal significance, was recognised by the experts. But in the hands of the inexpert they were very misleading. Any student of economics who was set the beginner's question—" Describe the manner in which the price level is determined upon an island in which the currency consists of shell picked up on the beach," would glibly reply, " The price level on this island is determined by the number of shells and their velocity of circulation," and nine times out of ten would omit to mention that it was equally true to say that the number of shells in circulation was determined by the price level. And economists who had ceased to be students were prone to say that the rise of prices in Germany in the great inflation was caused by the increase in the note issue and aggravated by the increase in the velocity of circulation due to the " flight into real values " induced by the rise of prices.

It was in protest against this naïve view of the theory of money that Mr. Kahn set out the Quantity Equation for hairpins. Let P be the proportion of women with long hair, and T the total number of women. Let $\frac{1}{V}$ be the daily loss of hairpins by each woman with long hair, and M the daily output of hairpins. Then $M=\frac{PT}{V}$, and MV=PT. Now suppose that the Pope, regarding bobbed hair as contrary to good morals, wishes to increase the proportion of long-haired women in the population, and asks a student of economics what he had best do. The student sets out Mr. Kahn's equation, and explains it to the Pope. " All you need do," he says, " is to increase M, the daily output of hairpins (for instance you might give a subsidy to the factories) and the number of long-haired women is bound to increase." The Pope is not quite convinced. " Or, of course," the student adds, " if you could persuade the long-haired women to be less careless, V would increase, and the effect would be the same as though the output of hairpins had increased."

Now the experts in the Theory of Money certainly avoided these crude errors, but when they recognised that their equations were tautologies without causal significance they were beset by an uneasy feeling that their theory only provided them with wisdom after the event. Anything that had happened could always be explained in terms of their truisms, but they were never very confident in predicting what would happen next. Moreover their methods condemned them to discuss the price level, when what they had really at heart was the volume of employment.

Now, once Mr. Keynes has shown us how to crack the egg, it appears the most natural thing in the world to attack the interesting part of the problem directly, instead of through the devious route of the Quantity Theory of Money. If we are interested in the volume of output, why should we not try what progress can be made by thinking in terms of the demand for output as a whole, and its cost of production, just as we have been taught to think of the demand and cost of a single commodity? But though the altered line of approach appears, once it has been seen, to be the obvious one to adopt, the sudden change of angle has caused a great deal of bewilderment. The new analysis still masquerades under the name of the Theory of Money; Mr. Keynes published his book on the subject under the title of a *Treatise on Money*. Moreover Mr. Keynes, when he published the *Treatise* had no very clear perception of the fact that the subject with which he was dealing was the Analysis of Output. This can be illustrated from several of the conceptions in the Treatise. For instance, consider the Widow's Cruse of profits.[1] Mr. Keynes' analysis may be summarised thus: When prices are in excess of costs windfall profits are earned by entrepreneurs, and however much of these profits the entrepreneurs spend the total of profits remains unchanged, since spending by one entrepreneur only serves to increase the windfall profits of others. This argument is valid upon the assumption that an increase in demand for consumption goods leads to no increase in their supply. Now to assume that the supply of goods is perfectly inelastic is a natural simplification to make, at the first step in the argument, if we are primarily interested in the price-level, but to make such an assumption when we are primarily interested in the volume of output is to assume away the whole point of the argument.

A second example of Mr. Keynes' failure to realise the nature of the revolution that he was carrying through is to be found in the emphasis which he lays upon relationship of the quantity of investment to the quantity of saving.[2] He points out that if savings exceed investment

[1] *Treatise on Money*, p. 139.

[2] Using " saving " as it is defined in the *Treatise on Money*.

consumption goods can only be sold at a loss. Their output will consequently decline until the real income of the population is reduced to such a low level that savings are perforce reduced to equality with investment.[3] But he completely overlooks the significance of this discovery, and throws it out in the most casual way without pausing to remark that he has proved that output may be in equilibrium at any number of different levels, and that while there is a natural tendency towards equilibrium between savings and investment (in a very long run) there is no natural tendency towards full employment of the factors of production. The mechanism of thought involved in the equations of saving and investment compels its exponent to talk only of short-period disequilibrium positions. And it was only with disequilibrium positions that Mr. Keynes was consciously concerned when he wrote the *Treatise*. He failed to notice that he had incidentally evolved a new theory of the long-period analysis of output.

Moreover, Mr. Keynes, like the exponents of the Quantity Theory of Money, was apt to fall into the hairpins fallacy, and attribute a causal significance to his tautologies. The price level will only be in equilibrium when savings are equal to investment. Well and good. But suppose that over a certain range the supply of goods is perfectly elastic? Then whatever happens prices cannot rise or fall. Since Mr. Keynes' truisms must be true, a rise or fall in demand for goods, which will be met by an increase or decrease of output without any change in prices, must necessarily be accompanied by changes in savings and investment which keep the two in equality. When an increase in output is brought about by an increase in investment, if prices do not alter, the increase in output must bring about an increase in savings (as defined by Mr. Keynes) equal to the initial increase in investment, for Mr. Keynes' truisms must be true. Or, as Mr. Hawtrey[4] points out, in face of a very-short-period decline in demand the supply of goods is perfectly elastic because shopkeepers do not immediately lower prices, but allow stocks to accumulate on their shelves. This also can be explained in terms of Mr. Keynes' equations. The demand for consumption goods falls off, say, because of an increase in savings. This leads to an accumulation of stocks, that is to say an increase in investment, exactly equal to the increase in saving, and prices do not fall. But to say that prices do not fall *because* investment has increased is merely to argue that women bob their hair because the output of the hairpin factories has fallen off.

The case of a perfectly elastic supply of output as a whole presents an interesting analogy with the traditional Theory of Value. Marshall's analysis is described by him as showing how the price of a commodity is determined by utility and by cost of production. He himself shows that when cost of production is constant for all amounts of output the price of a commodity will not be altered by a change in demand, but he complains that it is idle to argue that price is determined more by cost than by demand. This violent contradiction can be resolved by

[3] *Op. cit.*, p. 178.
[4] *Art of Central Banking*, p. 341.

substituting the word " output " for the word " price." It is true that the output of single commodities is determined by the interaction of supply and demand even when the price is uniquely determined by cost. It was this earlier misapprehension of the subject-matter of the so-called Theory of Value which misled the economists into supposing that the proper subject-matter of the so-called Theory of Money was the level of prices, and not the volume of output.

A further example of Mr. Keynes' initial failure to understand the significance of his new analysis is to be found in the emphasis which he lays upon profits as the " mainspring of action " determining output. Here again there is an analogy with the traditional Theory of Value. When profits are more than normal in a certain industry, we are taught, new firms will enter the industry, and output will expand. Now it is sufficiently obvious that entrepreneurs who are deciding whether to set up in a certain industry are not guided merely, or even mainly, by the level of profits being earned by existing firms. They will take a general view of the conditions in the market, and of future prospects, and make their choice accordingly. It is idle to say that the abnormal profits *cause* the new investment. At the same time, it is true that if the new entrepreneur decides to set up in the industry then (if he expects that his cost will be about the same as those of existing firms) it must be the case that abnormal profits are being earned by the existing firms, for unless the price of the commodity is greater than their costs (including normal profits) it will not be worth while for additional entrepreneurs to enter the trade. Thus the abnormal profits are a symptom of a situation in which new investment in the industry will take place. But to speak of them as a cause of new investment is only legitimate as an artificial device adopted to simplify the exposition of what is happening. In the same way profits as defined by Mr. Keynes are a symptom of a situation in which output will tend to increase. Output tends to increase when the price of commodities exceeds their cost of production because, in that situation, it is profitable for entrepreneurs to increase their sales. To regard the profits as a direct cause of the increase in output is apt to be misleading, and since in long-period equilibrium there are no profits in Mr. Keynes' sense, a theory which regards profits as the mainspring of action is incapable of dealing with long-period analysis.

When Mr. Keynes himself overlooked the fact that he was writing the analysis of output, as these examples show, it is small wonder that the change in the Theory of Money should have caused bewilderment. But once it becomes clear what has happened the confusion disappears. The Theory of Money, relieved of its too-heavy task, can be confined to its proper sphere, and become indeed a theory of money, while the Analysis of Output can continue to develop an analysis of output.

[10]

THE ECONOMIC JOURNAL

JUNE, 1931

THE RELATION OF HOME INVESTMENT TO UNEMPLOYMENT

I

THE case for "public works" has often been discussed, and there is a final plea that the advocate almost invariably appends to his argument. It is important, we are told, not to overlook the beneficial repercussions that will result from the expenditure of the newly-employed men's wages. But little is done to evaluate these repercussions in concrete terms. The main purpose, though not the only purpose, of this article is to outline the means by which this gap could be filled, and incidentally to suggest that the case for "public works" may be stronger than is always recognised.

The argument will apply to the effects of any net increase in the rate of home investment. The increased employment that is required in connection actually with the increased investment will be described as the "primary" employment. It includes the "direct" employment, and also, of course, the "indirect" employment that is set up in the production and transport of the raw materials required for making the new investment. To meet the increased expenditure of wages and profits that is associated with the primary employment, the production of consumption-goods is increased. Here again wages and profits are increased, and the effect will be passed on, though with diminished intensity. And so on *ad infinitum*. The total employment that is set up in this way in the production of consumption-goods will be termed the "secondary" employment. The ratio of secondary to primary employment is a measure of these "beneficial repercussions" that are so often referred to.

It will simplify the process of exposition if *expenditure by the Government on roads* is taken as a convenient instance of an increase in home investment. But this simplification must not be taken to imply either that there is anything in the argument that confines its application to investment taking place directly under the auspices of the Government, or that the building of more *roads* is a particularly desirable form of investment.

II

It is necessary, in the first place, to clear out of the way the objection that any reduction of unemployment that is effected by Government action will be at the expense of an equal increase of unemployment in some other quarter. If the Government were to raise the funds required to pay for the roads by means of taxation, it is obvious that unfavourable reactions would be probable. Of these the most important would be the "secondary unemployment" that would result if increased taxation were to reduce the taxpayers' expenditure on consumption-goods. The amount of this "secondary unemployment" would depend on the extent to which increased taxes are paid at the expense of consumption rather than of saving. But that is a matter for separate study; and throughout this article it will be supposed that the necessary funds are raised by means of borrowing.

It is sometimes claimed that if the Government borrows money for the purpose of building roads, this necessitates an equal reduction in the funds available for investment from other sources.[1] But it is clear that even if this claim has any force at all, it cannot have a universal application. For it is always within the power of the banking system to advance to the Government the cost of the roads without in any way affecting the flow of investment along the normal channels. If it assists the processes of thought, it may be imagined that the Government obtains its funds in this kind of way. But it will become clear in the sequel that no such hypothesis is really necessary. For it will be demonstrated later on [2] that, *pari passu* with the building of roads, funds are released from various sources at precisely the rate that is required to pay the cost of the roads.

It is, however, important to realise that the intelligent co-operation of the banking system is being taken for granted. It is supposed that the object of the Central Bank is to achieve the maximum of employment that is consistent with remaining on the gold standard. If the increased circulation of notes and

[1] How important is the influence that has been exerted upon British policy by this claim is forcibly demonstrated by the following information supplied in 1927 by the British Government to the International Labour Office: "While it is not possible to give any specific indications that competition arose with other enterprises owing to the raising by the State of moneys for the various State-assisted employment projects, the decision taken by the Government at the end of 1925 to restrict grants for relief schemes was based mainly on the view that, the supply of capital in the country being limited, it was undesirable to divert any appreciable proportion of this supply from normal trade channels." (*Unemployment and Public Works*, published by The International Labour Office, 1931, p. 30.)

[2] See p. 189.

the increased demand for working capital that may result from increased employment are made the occasion for a restriction of credit, then any attempt to increase employment—whether it is by way of road-building or by any other means, or, indeed, by awaiting the return of world prosperity—may be rendered nugatory.

III

It will be assumed throughout the greater part of this article that money-wages are not raised as a consequence of the reduction in unemployment or of any rise in prices with which the reduction in unemployment may be associated. Even if this assumption is not entirely reasonable, it is clear that it is essential if the analysis is to proceed at all. (But it *is* suggested, though with some hesitation, that over a limited, and not so very limited, range the assumption is not appreciably wide of reality.) To take into account the effects of a possible rise in wages would necessitate, not only an estimate of the amount of the rise, but, far more serious, an analysis of the effect of a rise in wages on the level of employment; and such an investigation must be ruled outside the scope of this article.

An attempt will, however, be made [1] to demonstrate that there is *some* increase in employment even though real-wages are maintained at their former level—or, in other words, if money-wages are raised so as to compensate for the rise in prices. But to the extent, on the other hand, that it is to the reduction in unemployment rather than to the rise in prices that wages respond, there is clearly no method whatever of increasing the volume of employment.

IV

Finally, no account will be taken, in assessing the effects on employment, of any increase in productive efficiency that may result from the Government's expenditure. That, perhaps, is why roads are a good illustration to adopt as an object of such expenditure.

For this reason, too, the argument of this article could, with suitable modifications, be applied to a discussion of the desirability of reducing the Sinking Fund or of the undesirability of reducing the dole.

V

Considerable use will be made in these pages of the expression "saving on the dole." It must be clearly understood that these

[1] In a subsequent number of the ECONOMIC JOURNAL.

words are not intended to imply any moral judgment on the system of unemployment insurance. The word "dole" is used, purely as a matter of convenience, to cover the whole of the expenditure of an unemployed man on consumption, whether it is derived from the Unemployment Insurance Fund, from local authorities, from charity, from borrowing, from his friends and relations or from his own accumulated savings.

For the purpose of developing the argument it will be assumed that when a man obtains work, the "saving on the dole" that results does not have the effect of increasing the consumption of other members of the community. Above all, this assumption presupposes that any change that occurs in the expenditure of the Unemployment Insurance Fund falls entirely on the rate at which the fund is increasing or diminishing its debt and on the amount of the budgetary Sinking Fund. Manifestly this assumption is a somewhat unreal one. Even if contributions to the Fund are not affected, a reduction in the cost of transitional benefit will almost certainly lead to some reduction of national taxation, and a reduction of the rate at which the Fund is getting into debt will lead to some scaling down of the Chancellor of the Exchequer's standards of respectability in regard to Sinking Funds—and so again to a reduction of taxation.

But, in relation to the amount of the saving on the dole, any reduction of taxation that occurs is likely to be small—this will be obvious if consideration is paid to the present level of the real Sinking Fund—and the consequent increase in expenditure on consumption will be still smaller. In so far, however, as it occurs, it adds an *a fortiori* force to the argument of the following pages. The secondary employment is increased if road-building results in less taxation and consequently in greater expenditure by taxpayers on consumption-goods.[1]

VI

I turn now to the often debated question of the effect of Government investment on the general level of prices. This question has been debated from various points of view. It has

[1] If this increase in expenditure were exactly equal to the saving on the dole, and if it were divided between home- and foreign-produced goods in the same proportions as the dole is divided, then the same consequences would ensue as would ensue on my assumption—that there is no such increase in expenditure—if the dole were zero, *i.e.* if the unemployed lived on air. If a greater amount were spent on home-produced goods than would have been spent on home-produced goods if the money had been spent by the unemployed, then the results can be gauged by supposing, on the basis of my assumption, that the dole is negative.

been debated with an eye on the expansion of bank credit that may accompany the building of roads. Somewhat more adapted, perhaps, to the end in view have been the discussions that have centred on the various alleviations that partially set off the increase in purchasing power caused by increased investment. Of these the most important are the saving on the dole and the increased imports of consumption-goods and of raw materials that take place when employment is increased.

But it is, I think, quite clear that a very important, though nevertheless extremely obvious, consideration is usually omitted in these discussions. It is, perhaps, its very obviousness that accounts for its being so persistently overlooked. For the line of approach that will now be taken up is the one that would be followed under the impulse of crude common-sense—there is no room here for analytical subtleties. No claims of originality are advanced for adopting it, but that does not mean that it is not very important.

The price-level and output of home-produced consumption-goods, just like the price and output of any single commodity, are determined by the conditions of supply and demand. If the conditions of supply can be regarded as fixed, both the price-level and the output are determined by the demand; and there is a unique correlation between price-level and output. For a given output of consumption-goods there corresponds a certain price-level of consumption-goods; and this is their price-level quite independently of the causes that are responsible for maintaining the given output. If there is a certain increase in employment on the production of consumption-goods, the change in their price-level is the same whether the increased employment is fostered by large advances from the Central Bank to the Government or whether it is the symptom of the return of prosperity by a more natural route. If this is to be true, it is only necessary that the change shall be actuated by a change in the conditions of demand and not by a change in the conditions of supply. Then the volume of employment engaged in producing consumption-goods and the price-level of home-produced consumption-goods are uniquely correlated. For a given increase in the output of consumption-goods the change in their price-level depends only on the supply curve of consumption-goods in general, the curve being drawn from the point of view of the particular period of time that is under consideration—long, short, or otherwise. If the supply curve rises steeply, there is a large rise in prices; if conditions of constant supply price prevail, there is no rise in prices; and if the supply curve were falling, there would be a fall in prices.

VII

The relief of unemployment by means of national development is often objected to on the grounds that it will cause a rise in the cost of living. The extraordinary fatuity of this objection is, of course, quite apparent. There is nothing unnatural about the rise in prices caused by the building of roads. It will occur equally if employment in the production of consumption-goods is stimulated to an equal extent by more natural means (other than a reduction of costs). Indeed, if it is an improvement in world economic conditions that is the cause of increased employment, the cost of living will rise by considerably *more* than if the cause is the building of roads. And this for two reasons. In the first place, not only the whole of the secondary employment but also part of the primary employment will in this case be engaged in producing consumption-goods. For part of the primary employment will be engaged in the production of commodities that are to be exported or that were previously imported, and some of these commodities will be identical with commodities that enter into consumption at home. It follows that, for a given volume of primary and secondary employment, the output of home-produced consumption-goods is greater, and therefore the cost of living is higher, if the cause of the change is an improvement in the conditions of world demand than if it is the building of such things as roads, whose production can be carried on without appreciably affecting the condition of supply of consumption-goods. But it is the second reason that is likely to be more important quantitatively. An increase in employment that is part of a general revival in world trade will be accompanied by a rise in the prices of imported consumption-goods (including the supremely important category of food) and of imported raw materials, while the rise in prices that is caused by a purely local policy of road-building will be almost entirely confined to that part of the national consumption that is produced at home. The effect on the cost of living is, therefore, far more serious in the former case than in the latter case.

Even more fantastic is it to argue at the same time that road-building causes a rise in prices and yet that it is not responsible for any *net* addition to the volume of employment. The rise in prices, if it occurs at all, is a natural concomitant of increased output, to a degree indicated by the slope of the supply curve.

It is impossible to maintain at the same time that prices will rise and that there will be no increase in output. If the result, owing to the operation of some mysterious cause, of the construction of roads by the Government is an equal reduction of investment in other channels, there is no secondary employment and no rise in prices. But if it is a fall in the output of *consumption*-goods that compensates for the employment provided on the roads (as might *conceivably* be the case if the Government raises the necessary funds by taxation rather than by borrowing), then the effect of road-building is to cause a *fall* in prices (on the assumption that production takes place under conditions of increasing supply price).

VIII

It should now be clear why it is hopeless to discuss the possibility of a rise in prices in terms merely of the saving on the dole and the increase in imports that result from increased employment. These indeed are two factors, as we shall see later, that determine the amount of the secondary employment. But before it is possible to deduce the magnitude of the change in prices, it is necessary to introduce the slope of the supply curve. Nor is it as simple as that. For the amount of secondary employment itself depends, as will be shown later, on the extent of the rise in prices by which it is accompanied. The two are uniquely correlated, but the amount of secondary employment is effect as well as cause. The amount of secondary employment must be such that, together with the primary employment, it gives rise to just so much alleviation to the original investment (in the shape of saving on the dole, increased imports, and so on) as will account for the rise in prices that is appropriate to that amount of secondary employment. If the supply of commodities in general is perfectly elastic, there can be no rise in prices and the secondary employment must be such as to make it so. If the supply of commodities in general is perfectly inelastic, there can be no secondary employment and the rise in prices must be so great that the net secondary employment is zero.

In general it can be said that, for a given supply curve, the secondary employment is smaller the greater are the saving on the dole, the increase in imports, and the other alleviations that accompany a unit increase in employment. It follows that it is perfectly true to state that the greater the extent of these alleviations, the smaller is the rise in prices that results from a given amount of road-building. But from such a view-point the problem is liable to assume a peculiarly distorted aspect. It is not merely that there would be a failure to recognise the predominant importance of the supply curve—the fact, for instance, that if supply is perfectly elastic, there *can* be no rise in prices. It might also appear that the claims of road-building as a national policy are stronger if the alleviations (saving on the dole, increase in imports, etc.) are great than if the alleviations are small, because it is when the alleviations are great that the rise in prices is small. But in fact it may just be if the alleviations are great that road-building is least justifiable, for it is then that the *secondary employment* is small—and the "beneficial repercussions" are weak. It is possible to imagine a case—it is very far removed from reality—where unemployed men who are set to work on making roads devote the whole of the net increase in their incomes to goods that have to be imported. There would then be no rise in prices—the alleviations are equivalent to the whole of the original investment. But road-making would be a far weaker economic proposition than it is in fact, for there would be no secondary employment.

IX

Perhaps it is not altogether inappropriate to pause at this point to consider the appearance of our line of approach in the light of Mr. Keynes' new equations. The building of roads represents an increase in investment. But before it is possible to assess the net effect on the difference between savings and investment, it is necessary to bring into the account those alleviations which have already been several times referred to. Payment of the dole represents negative saving, and the saving on the dole represents, therefore, an addition to total savings. An increase of imports, whether of consumption-goods or of raw materials, represents a diminution of the foreign balance and therefore of total investment. If entrepreneurs continue to spend the same amount of money on consumption-goods as before although output has increased, their savings, in Mr. Keynes' sense, have increased. On the other hand, to the extent that non-wage-earners (and wage-earners who were previously in employment) increase their expenditure on consumption-goods irrespective of any increase in total output—whether as a result of the fact that they have more to spend, because of increased profits, or of the fact that prices of consumption-goods have gone up—savings diminish: this is an *aggravation*. The new value of the difference between savings and investment, appropriate to

Mr. Keynes' equations, can only be deduced by subtracting the alleviations corresponding to the total new employment from the cost of the roads, and adding the aggravation.

If the supply of consumption-goods is perfectly inelastic, there is no secondary employment and the problem is considerably simplified. It is only necessary now to consider the alleviations associated with a *known* volume of primary employment—and to subtract the aggravation. Prices rise by an amount corresponding to the difference between the cost of the roads and the amount of these alleviations. If the aggravation can be neglected, the rise in the price-level of home-produced consumption-goods is equal to the increase in expenditure directed towards them by the roadmakers divided by their volume. This is the case when all productive resources available for the production of consumption-goods are already being utilised and, over a certain range of output and over a sufficiently short period of time, it is not possible to increase their output appreciably and there is no incentive for an appreciable reduction of output.

But simplest of all is the case where it is not the supply of consumption-goods that is completely inelastic but *total* employment that is fixed, so that if investment increases, the production of consumption-goods must diminish by an equal amount. Then there is no alleviation, since there is no change in employment, and if in addition the aggravation is negligible, the rise in the price-level of consumption-goods is simply equal to the cost of the new investment divided by their volume. This is the case to which Mr. Keynes' equations apply in their full simplicity. It occurs when the whole of the factors of production are employed, and continue to be employed, in producing either for consumption or for investment.

At the other end of the scale is the case, very much closer to the actual conditions that prevail to-day, where the supply of consumption-goods is perfectly elastic. The price-level of consumption-goods is then constant, and, however great may be the cost of the investment that is taking place in road-building, the secondary employment will be such that the total alleviation (*minus* the aggravation) keeps the difference between total savings and total investment at a constant amount (or, more accurately, at an amount that varies in direct proportion with the output of consumption-goods).

But this conclusion—that under certain circumstances employment can be increased without any significant alteration in the difference between savings and investment—does not in the slightest degree invalidate the causal force of Mr. Keynes' argument. The motive force that increases employment is an increase in investment or a reduction in savings. As a concomitant of this increase in employment occur other changes in savings and investment which, partially or wholly, neutralise the effect on the difference between savings and investment of the change that is the cause of the increased employment.

X

It should now be clear that the whole question ultimately turns on the nature of the supply curve of consumption-goods. At normal times, when productive resources are fully employed, the supply of consumption-goods in the short period is highly inelastic. The building of roads carries with it little secondary employment and causes a large rise in prices. But at times of intense depression, when nearly all industries have at their disposal a large surplus of unused plant and labour, the supply curve is likely to be very elastic. The amount of secondary employment is then large and the rise in prices is small.

If there is in existence a large stock of surplus resources that are not very inferior to the worst of those that are actually being employed,[1] the elasticity of supply is likely to be very large indeed up to the level of output at which this surplus would be becoming inappreciable. Provided that output is not carried above this level, an expansion of employment bears with it only a very small rise of prices. The greater the depth of the depression, the greater is the expansion of employment that is associated with a given rise in prices. And the greater the expansion of employment that has already been secured by a policy of road-building, the greater is the rise in prices that accompanies a given further expansion of employment; for the short-period supply curve is concave upwards. It is clear, then, that if there is ever any justification for expenditure on " public works " as a means of reducing unemployment, the justification is greatest when depression is most severe; and the scale on which it is desirable that such a policy should be carried on is also then most extensive.

XI

I turn now to a calculation of the ratio of secondary to primary employment, and I begin by assuming that the supply of con-

[1] As is, *par excellence*, the case when the " short-time " method of working plant is in operation over a wide field.

sumption-goods is perfectly elastic over the range that is in question. (The adoption at this point of such a sweeping assumption is to be regarded purely as a means of simplifying the treatment—it would be quite possible, on lines that will be indicated later, to begin with a perfectly general case.) An attempt will be made below [1] to assess the extent to which the results require modification in the light of the conditions that prevail in this country at the moment, and it will be suggested that the modification is not very large.

Let each man who is placed in employment receive a wage W, and let the increase in profits that is associated with the employment of each additional man be P. Let the value of the increase in imports of raw materials and unfinished goods that accompanies the employment of each additional man be R. For the sake of simplicity it will be assumed that W and P are the same for both primary and secondary employment.

Let the employment of each additional man involve a *net increase* in the rate of expenditure on home-produced consumption-goods of mW out of his wages and of nP out of the addition to profits with which his employment is associated. Then the total increase in the rate of expenditure on home-produced consumption-goods is

$$m\mathrm{W} + n\mathrm{P}.$$

The direct result is a further addition to the volume of employment [2] of amount

$$\frac{m\mathrm{W} + n\mathrm{P}}{\mathrm{W} + \mathrm{P} + \mathrm{R}} \text{ men}$$

$$= m\frac{\mathrm{W}}{\mathrm{W} + \mathrm{P} + \mathrm{R}} + n\frac{\mathrm{P}}{\mathrm{W} + \mathrm{P} + \mathrm{R}} = k \text{ (say) men.} \quad (1)$$

It follows that for each man placed in primary employment, the number who receive secondary employment is

$$k + k^2 + k^3 + \ldots$$

$$= \frac{k}{1 - k}.$$

And the ratio of secondary employment to primary employment is

$$\frac{k}{1 - k} \quad . \quad . \quad . \quad . \quad . \quad . \quad . \quad . \quad (2)$$

[1] See p. 186.

[2] I am here considering the position in the final position of equilibrium when everything has settled down. But some time will, of course, elapse between the point when the primary employment begins and the point when the secondary employment reaches its full dimensions, because wages and profits are not spent quite as soon as they are earned. I do not enter into the question of this time-lag.

Let the expenditure of an unemployed man (the " dole ") be U, and let a proportion m' of the increase that takes place in his income when he becomes employed be devoted to home-produced consumption-goods.

Then $$m'(W - U) = mW;$$

or $$m = m'\left(1 - \frac{U}{W}\right) \quad . \quad . \quad . \quad . \quad (3)$$

It can be seen that, for every man put to work on the roads, the volume of secondary employment is great to the extent that the dole forms only a small proportion of a full wage, to the extent that a man who becomes employed devotes a large proportion of the increase in his income to home-produced goods, to the extent that a large proportion of any addition to profits that accompanies increased output is spent on home-produced consumption-goods, and to the extent that increased production necessitates the import of only a small proportion of raw materials. The more a country approximates to a closed system and the smaller the dole in relation to a full wage, the greater is the ratio of secondary to primary employment. Now the United States constitute a better approximation to a closed system than do most countries and the ratio of the income of an unemployed American to that of an employed American is notoriously small. It may be expected, therefore, that the ratio of secondary to primary employment is a good deal larger in the United States than in most other countries.[1] A perfectly closed system, to go one step further, is the world as a whole. It follows, as is indeed quite obvious, that an international policy of " public works " would be far more efficacious from the point of view of each separate country than a purely local policy. Finally, as a limiting case, it may be instructive to contemplate a closed system in which there is no dole,[2] and in which any increase in profits that accompanies an increase of output is either negligible in amount or devoted entirely to consumption. One man put to work on the roads would then place all the remainder of the unemployed into secondary employment.[3]

[1] The argument, can, of course, be reversed to deal with the secondary unemployment that accompanies primary unemployment due to a *decrease* in the rate of investment. A slump in the rate of investment spread evenly all over the world would fall more heavily in those regions, like the United States, where the dole is relatively low than in those regions, like this country, where the dole is relatively high.

[2] Or in which any saving on the dole results in an equal increase of expenditure on consumption on the part of taxpayers, etc. (see p. 176).

[3] For a general statement of this possibility, to cover the case when supply is not perfectly elastic, see p. 189 below.

It is a matter of considerable difficulty to make exact, or even at all approximate, estimates of the various quantities contained in the above equations. But it is hoped that, until more precise investigation can be undertaken, the following figures [1] will help to convey some idea of the orders of magnitude that are concerned for the case of this country at the present time.

I shall assume in the first place that the cost of imported raw materials and unfinished goods entering into the *addition* to output that is associated with increased employment constitutes $\frac{1}{10}$ of the *retail* price of the extra product. In other words, $\frac{R}{W + P + R}$ is supposed to be $\frac{1}{10}$. I shall then assume that $\frac{W}{W + P + R}$ (the ratio of marginal wages cost to the price of the product) is $\frac{7}{10}$ and that $\frac{P}{W + P + R}$ is $\frac{1}{5}$.

It also seems reasonable to suppose that when a man becomes employed, $\frac{1}{6}$ of the *increase* in his income is devoted to imported *finished* goods (excluding the costs of transport and distribution, payment for which is to be regarded as expenditure on *home*-produced goods). In other words, I put m' equal to $\frac{5}{6}$.

The estimate of the ratio of the " dole " to a full wage involves some consideration of the type of man who will be drawn into employment by a policy of the kind that is under consideration. It seems probable that a moderate addition to the ranks of the employed would be recruited mainly from the younger of the unemployed, whose families are of less than the average size. It may perhaps be concluded that $\frac{U}{W}$ is rather *less* than $\frac{1}{2}$.

There remains only the quantity n, but here assessment is largely a matter of guess-work. The best that I can do is to suggest that it would be extremely unreasonable to suppose that as small a proportion as $\frac{1}{3}$ of any increase that took place in the rate of business men's earnings [2] would be devoted to home-produced consumption-goods.

The following table is intended to indicate how the value of the ratio of secondary to primary employment, given in

[1] They are based, for the most part, on statistical material that has been placed at my disposal by Mr. Colin G. Clark, to whom I should like to express my great gratitude. But the responsibility for the statistical conclusions that I have attempted to derive from this material rests entirely with me.

[2] The part played by the earnings of small shopkeepers, poor shareholders, etc. is not to be overlooked.

the last column, depends on the values that are adopted for $\frac{U}{W}$ and n.

$$\frac{W}{W+P+R} = \frac{7}{10}, \frac{P}{W+P+R} = \frac{1}{5}, m' = \frac{5}{6}.$$

$\frac{U}{W}$	n	$m = m'\left(1 - \frac{U}{W}\right)$	k (by equation (1))	$\frac{k}{1-k}$
$\frac{3}{7}$	$\frac{3}{4}$	$\frac{10}{21}$	$\frac{29}{60}$	$\frac{29}{31} = \cdot 94$
$\frac{3}{7}$	$\frac{2}{3}$	$\frac{10}{21}$	$\frac{7}{15}$	$\frac{7}{8} = \cdot 88$
$\frac{1}{2}$	$\frac{1}{2}$	$\frac{5}{12}$	$\frac{47}{120}$	$\frac{47}{73} = \cdot 64$
$\frac{1}{2}$	$\frac{1}{3}$	$\frac{5}{12}$	$\frac{43}{120}$	$\frac{43}{77} = \cdot 56$

The first row of figures is possibly on the liberal side, as supplying an estimate of the ratio of secondary to primary employment, but it seems very much more certain that the last row is on the conservative side. If we were to suppose that in actual fact the ratio is $\frac{3}{4}$, we might, it may perhaps be suggested, be erring in the direction of under-statement.

XII

The next step is to make an allowance for the fact that supply is not perfectly elastic. Under the conditions that prevail at the moment it seems reasonable to suppose that the short-period elasticity of supply is not less than 4, *i.e.* that a 4 per cent. increase in the domestic output of consumption-goods would be accompanied by a rise in prices to the *ultimate consumer* of less than 1 per cent. It is now necessary to make an estimate of the elasticity of demand for these goods. If people's expenditure on consumption-goods does not alter when their price-level is raised, the elasticity of demand for them is unity. But actually it seems probable that people would spend rather more on consumption, and save less, if prices were to rise. To the extent that they would do so, the elasticity of demand is less than unity. On the other hand, many classes of consumption-goods meet with foreign competition, either abroad, in the case of exports, or in the domestic market itself, and for them the demand may easily be elastic rather than inelastic.[1] Setting one consideration against the other and assessing each so far as it is possible to do so, I suggest that the demand for home-produced consumption-goods

[1] But the tendency of foreign competition to increase the aggregate elasticity of demand for our goods is offset to some small extent by the rise that takes place in the foreigners' demand curve as a result of the expansion in our imports.

is likely to be inelastic rather than elastic, provided that small changes are under consideration. Let us suppose that the elasticity is unity. A 1 per cent. rise in prices would then, taken by itself, be responsible for a 1 per cent. contraction of consumption, and consequently of output. But we are supposing that a 1 per cent. rise in prices would be accompanied by an increase in output of at least 4 per cent. It would appear then that when the output of consumption-goods expands by 4 per cent., the extra expansion that *would* have taken place if there had been no rise in prices would have been less than 1 per cent.—and the total expansion would then have been less than 5 per cent. It may be concluded, on the basis of the assumptions that have been made, that the fact that supply is not perfectly elastic necessitates a reduction of the estimate of secondary employment of the last section by less than $\frac{1}{5}$. Such a small alteration is, of course, negligible.

But even this conclusion is unduly conservative.[1] It completely overlooks the fact that a rise in prices is the cause of an increase in profits and that part of these increased profits is likely to be spent on home-produced consumption-goods. It can easily be seen that if the whole of the increase in profits that is the direct result of higher prices were spent on home-produced consumption-goods, then, on the basis of an elasticity of demand of unity, output would be precisely the same as though there were no rise in prices at all. And if the demand for consumption-goods has an elasticity less than unity, then the same assumption leads to the conclusion that the rise in prices actually causes the output to be greater than it would be if there were no rise in prices. The less elastic the supply, the *greater* would be the secondary employment! This last result is mentioned here mainly as a *curiosum*—it is unlikely in practice that a sufficient proportion of the increase in profits that results from a higher level of prices would be devoted to home-produced consumption-goods—but the theoretical possibility of its occurring is worth emphasising.

XIII

Let us return for a moment to the case, worked out in section XI, in which supply is supposed to be perfectly elastic. If N

[1] This section, and a considerable portion of the rest of the article, is largely the result of the co-operation that I have received from Mr. J. E. Meade of Hertford College, Oxford. I must content myself with a general acknowledgment, but it will, I hope, be clear that my treatment is fundamentally based on work of Mr. Meade's that is as yet unpublished.

men are placed in primary employment, the total increase in employment is, by equation (2),

$$N\left(1+\frac{k}{1-k}\right)=\frac{N}{1-k}.$$

For each man placed in employment the saving on the dole is U, the increase in imports of raw materials and unfinished goods is R in value, the increased imports of finished goods that result from the newly-employed man's expenditure are $(1-m')(W-U)$ in value, and the sum of the increase in unspent profits and of the increase in imports of finished goods to which the newly-accruing profits are devoted is $(1-n)P$. The total sum of these items is

$$\begin{aligned} & U+R+(1-m')(W-U)+(1-n)P \\ = {} & W+P+R-(mW+nP), \text{ by equation (3)} \\ = {} & (W+P+R)(1-k), \text{ by equation (1).} \end{aligned}$$

But we have seen that if N men are placed in primary employment, the total increase in employment is $\frac{N}{1-k}$. It follows that the sum of these items is $N(W+P+R)$, which is precisely the value of the product of the primary employment, *i.e.* the cost to the State of the roads.

We have then the following relation :—

Cost of investment = saving on dole + increase in imports + increase in unspent profits.

The last head comprises that part of the increase in profits that is devoted neither to home-produced consumption-goods nor to imported goods.

Now this relation, far from being the logical consequence of summing an infinite geometrical progression, is in reality self-evident in nature and is merely a particular case of a general relation, due to Mr. J. E. Meade, that covers the case when supply is not perfectly elastic, so that prices rise when employment increases. This general relation is a derivative form of Mr. Keynes' formula for profits.[1] In its most general form Mr. Meade's relation runs as follows :—

Cost of investment = saving on dole + increase in excess of imports over exports + increase in unspent profits − diminution in rate of saving due to rise in prices.

[1] It is to be noted that the word profits is here being employed in the ordinary sense of the difference between business men's receipts and their outgoings, and not in the sense in which Mr Keynes employs the word. But it is clear that Mr. Meade's relation is merely a special statement of Mr. Keynes' general proposition that " profits " are equal to the difference between investment and savings.

In this equation the second term on the right-hand side includes both the effect of increased employment in causing an increase in the volume of imports of consumption-goods and of raw materials and the effect of higher prices in causing an increase of imports and a reduction of exports. The third term comprises the unspent portion (*i.e.* spent neither on home-produced consumption-goods nor on imported goods) of the profits that emerge as a result both of greater output and of higher prices. And the fourth term allows for the increase in people's expenditure that may result when prices go up.

The relation can be deduced in an *a priori* kind of way by considering that money paid out by the Government to the builders of roads continues to be passed on from hand to hand until it reaches one of the *culs-de-sac* indicated by the various terms on the right-hand side of the equation. By utilising it as a basis, it should be possible to deduce a formula for the ratio of secondary to primary employment that is applicable whatever may be the elasticity of supply of consumption-goods.

This relation should bring immediate relief and consolation to those who are worried about the monetary sources that are available to meet the cost of the roads. The increase in the excess of imports over exports is equal, if gold is not flowing at an appreciable rate, to the reduction in foreign lending. So that if one is looking for sources *outside* the banking system, they are available to precisely the right extent. The cost of the roads is equal to the saving on the dole *plus* the reduction in foreign lending *plus* the increase in unspent profits *minus* the reduction in the rate of saving.[1]

In a closed system, such as the world as a whole, the second term of Mr. Meade's relation is *ex hypothesi* zero. If, in such a closed system, there were no dole (*i.e.* the unemployed lived on air) and the newly-accruing profits were devoted in their entirety to consumption,[2] the ratio of secondary to primary

[1] There are some who maintain that if a tariff causes an increase of foreign lending, lending at home must necessarily be contracted in an equal degree. Without entering at all into the question of the general validity of their point of view, it would appear possible to defeat them *on their own ground* by using an argument precisely analogous to the argument of the text. For if a tariff is successful in causing an increase in foreign investment, funds will be released, and will—if one likes to think of it in that kind of way—be available for foreign lending, to an extent exactly equal to the increase in foreign investment—just as the building of roads (home investment) releases funds exactly equal to their cost.

[2] Or, more accurately, if the newly-accruing profits remained unspent at a rate equal to or less than the rate at which savings are diminished as a result of the rise in prices.

employment would be infinite. No matter how small the elasticity of supply of consumption-goods, "one man put to work on the roads would then place all the remainder of the unemployed into secondary employment." Such a system would, of course, be unstable. A small decrease in the rate of investment would result in everybody becoming unemployed.[1]

XIV

I turn now to the question of the quantitative importance of the saving on the dole. Mr. Meade's relation tells us that it falls short of the total cost of the roads by an amount equal to the increase in the excess of imports over exports *plus* the increase in unspent profits *minus* the diminution in the rate of saving that may be brought about by the rise in prices. In a closed system there can be no change in exports or imports, and if only the increase in unspent profits were less than the diminution in the

[1] It may, finally, be of interest to notice how Mr. Meade's methods can be applied to deal with the controversy that is at present raging as to the effect on a country's exports of a reduction in its imports. If there is no change in the rate of home investment, either in this country or in the rest of the world, the effect of a tariff on this country's imports can be represented as follows. (For the sake of simplicity the effect of an alteration in prices on the rate of saving is omitted. It can easily be brought in if its presence is desired.) For this country:

Decrease in excess of imports over exports = saving on dole + increase in unspent profits.

For the rest of the world (considered as a single country):

Decrease in excess of exports over imports = loss on dole + diminution in unspent profits.

If it were supposed that in the rest of the world there is no "dole" (*i.e.* the unemployed live on air) and that business men reduce their expenditure on consumption to the full amount of any reduction in their profits, then it would be quite true that our tariff would cause such a large reduction in the foreigner's volume of output and employment that his purchases from us would fall by an amount precisely equal to the reduction of our imports. Exports then *would* pay for imports, even under those short-period conditions that underlie the argument. But this conclusion depends essentially on assumptions of an extraordinary degree of absurdity; and an examination of the actual conditions that prevail would, it may be supposed, lead to a result of an entirely different order of magnitude. Moreover, if we *are* to make absurd assumptions, it is hard to see why this country should not be allowed to participate. Let us therefore suppose that, in this country also, there is no dole and that business men devote to consumption the whole of any increase in their profits. Then it would follow from the above equation that the imposition of a tariff would cause such a large increase in the volume of our output and employment that (leaving on one side, as irrelevant to the present argument, the effect on our exports of a *rise in their price*, as opposed to that of a fall in the foreigner's demand curve) our imports would not contract at all in the aggregate. We might import less manufactured goods, but we should import more food and raw materials. Exports would pay for imports—yes, but a tariff would cause no net reduction in our imports.

rate of saving, the saving on the dole would more than cover the cost of the roads. Now the world is a closed system. It follows that an international policy of digging holes and filling them up again would result in a net gain to the united treasuries of the world, provided only that business men could be persuaded to be sufficiently spendthrift with the additions to their profits which such a policy would secure for them. Such a hope is almost certainly a vain one. But no account has been taken of the increase in the yield of taxation that would accompany an expansion of output and of employment. If the treasuries of the world were to gain as increased revenue an amount equal to the excess of the increase in unspent profits over the diminution in savings, the promotion, on an international scale, of perfectly useless "public works" would still be profitable, even from a narrow budgetary point of view. We are probably still a little way off reality—but can it be so very far?

To consider international action of this kind is perhaps a little premature. More interesting is the question of the cost that this country would be involved in if it were to act alone. Part of the benefit without any of the cost would then accrue to other countries. To the internationally minded this should not be an objection—indeed this is one of the main respects in which the stimulation of home investment is superior to the stimulation of foreign investment. Moreover, the adoption of a policy of this kind by this country would, by the force of example, induce other countries to adopt similar policies, in whose benefits we should then take a share. But I am content to consider the case where this country acts alone and where the benefits received by the rest of the world are left out of account. It follows from Mr. Meade's relation that under conditions in which in a closed system the building of roads would *just* be a sound proposition (from the narrow budgetary point of view), the national debt, if a single country acts alone, will be raised by the value of the increase in imports (and reduction in exports) which the building of roads will bring about.

XV

But let us consider the saving on the dole in the case of this country in concrete terms. Let it be supposed that expenditure on road-building and other forms of home investment increases by £50 million per annum. The primary employment can then be supposed to amount to 250,000 and, on the basis of a ratio of $\frac{3}{4}$, the secondary employment will be 187,500—to make quite certain let us call it 150,000,[1] so that the total employment will be 400,000. If the dole amounts on the average only to 25*s.* a week, the saving to the Unemployment Insurance Fund will be £25 million per annum, which is just half the total cost. This £25 million the Exchequer can then afford to contribute out of its own resources—that is to say, out of the Sinking Fund in so far as the saving on the dole diminishes the rate at which the Insurance Fund is getting into debt, and out of the ordinary budget to the extent that the saving is in respect to the cost of transitional benefit.

We still have to allow for the increase in the yield of taxation. For each man who is put into employment the money-income of the community increases by considerably more than £120 per annum (say in the form of profits £30 *plus* such increase in the value of output as a whole that takes place as the result of the rise in prices, and £90 as the difference between the wage and the dole). It seems reasonable to suppose that of this amount at least £15 will be paid to the Exchequer in the form of taxation. It follows that if employment is increased by 400,000, the revenue will expand by £6 million—and clearly this is an extremely conservative estimate.

At any rate it would appear safe to conclude that the Exchequer would actually reap a net gain if it were to subsidise capital investment to the extent of *one-half* the capital sum involved. A necessary condition is, of course, that the work would not be undertaken if no subsidy were forthcoming. This condition severely restricts the field over which subsidies to investment are applicable. But even if the Treasury were to confine itself to railway companies and local authorities, it might reasonably be expected that the payment of subsidies of one-half of the capital cost would induce a very substantial increase in the rate of investment.

Let us now take the case where the whole cost is borne by the State. Let us suppose that the Government, national and local, spends the £50 million per annum for three years, at the end of which time conditions may be imagined to have improved. Then if a saving of only one-half is allowed for, the addition to the national debt (including the debt of local authorities) will be £75 million, which, at an average rate of interest of $3\frac{1}{2}$ per cent., amounts to an annual charge in perpetuity of a little over £$2\frac{1}{2}$ million, or about $\frac{1}{15}$ per cent. of the present national income and

[1] This is what the secondary employment would be if the ratio of secondary to primary employment were only $\frac{3}{5}$.

¼ per cent. of the revenue raised by taxation. For this, 400,000 men are put into employment for three years and £150 million, equal in money-value to about ¾ per cent. of the national capital, are spent on capital works. To suppose that the consequent increase in efficiency could lead to an automatic expansion in the yield of taxation equal to the whole of this interest charge of £2½ million would be quite unjustifiable—particularly when account is taken of the reduction in foreign investment that is associated with this increase in home investment—but the increase of efficiency should certainly be taken into account if one wants to consider how a policy of public works at the present time would affect the budgetary problems of the future.

I turn now from the budgetary to the national standpoint. At first sight the natural line of approach might appear to be to regard the increase of £2½ million in the interest payable on the national debt as a burden on posterity and to measure against it the increase in their national income that would result from £150 million having been spent in the past on schemes of a greater or less degree of permanent utility and from 400,000 men having been given work to do for three years instead of having lived in idleness. If this view were correct, it would be sufficient to show that the national income of posterity would be increased by at least £2½ million as a result of this expenditure of £150 million, and then the policy would be fully justified without taking into account any of the benefits that it would confer on the present generation.

XVI

But this view is, of course, fallacious. The payment of interest on the internal debt is not a burden in the real sense of the term—it is a case of transfer expenditure. It is only if the policy results in a reduction of posterity's income that it can be said to inflict a real burden. The only respect in which such a burden can be inflicted is as a result of the reduction in foreign investment that results from the policy. The expenditure of £50 million per annum for three years might reduce our annual balance of trade by, say, £20 million per annum, resulting in a total diminution of our foreign investment of £60 million. The loss of interest from abroad on this £60 million represents, taken by itself, a real burden on posterity. But against it has to be set the benefits that will be permanently derived by increasing the national equipment at a cost of £150 million and by rescuing 400,000 men for three years from the deteriorating influences of involuntary idleness. It can scarcely be doubted that posterity would inherit an asset rather than a liability as a result of such a policy as we are considering.

But even if there *were* a nèt real burden on posterity, it would still remain to set against its discounted value the benefit that would be derived by the present generation. Here the problem is a simple one, at any rate so long as the community is regarded as a single entity. The aggregate consumption of the community is necessarily increased as a result of a policy of " road-building," for both the production and the importing of consumption-goods are stimulated. This increase in consumption is a measure of the benefit received by the present generation.

And so long as the building of roads does not involve any diversion of resources away from the production of consumption-goods, it will continue to add to the rate of aggregate consumption of the community. Provided then that it does not result in an actual decrease in the rate of accumulation of capital, material and immaterial, *i.e.* provided that the benefit conferred at home is greater than the loss in respect to foreign investment, as it almost certainly would be—there would appear to be no limit to the period of time during which it would be desirable to continue this policy of public works, except the very important one imposed by the condition that the factors of production employed in building the roads would, if the roads were not being built, remain unemployed.

But this conclusion reaches too far. The progressive increase in the rate of taxation that is necessitated when the national debt increases faster than the national income only fails to involve any real burden on the community as a whole if its " announcement " aspects can be neglected. As the rate of taxation becomes higher and higher, the " announcement " effects become more and more serious—and it is on these lines that one would have to assess the undesirability of progressively increasing the national debt or of permanently retarding its liquidation.

So far we have considered the community as a whole. It remains to say a word about the effect of road-building, while the roads are being built, on the real incomes of the various constituent classes of the community. There are two classes whose real incomes are certainly increased—the newly employed and the business class—and, to the extent that prices rise, there are two classes whose real incomes are diminished—those who were already *fully* employed and the *rentier* class. It has already been said that the real income of the community as a whole is increased. But of more interest is the effect on the real income of wage-earners as a whole, taking employed and unemployed together.

This involves the question of the rise in prices that would accompany an increase in employment. Under the conditions that rule at present it seems certain that if 400,000 were put into employment, primary and secondary, the real value of the aggregate income (wages *plus* dole) of the wage-earning class would increase. But under conditions in which the supply of consumption-goods were considerably less elastic than it is likely to be to-day it is quite possible that an increase of employment, brought about in this kind of way, would entail a reduction of the real value of wage-earners' aggregate income. But even then it would not necessarily follow that it would be contrary to the interests of wage-earners as a class for a policy of national investment to be adopted. It is too often forgotten that the main purpose of schemes of this kind is to *reduce unemployment*, and that unemployment does not fail to be an evil when its persistence involves a higher real income to the wage-earning class than would otherwise be obtainable. If this were not so, it might often be in the interests of wage-earners to advocate steps that would still further increase unemployment. But unemployment is an evil in itself, it is an evil on account of the *maldistribution* of the wage-earners' aggregate income that it usually causes, and it is an evil, together with the depression of the industrial system with which it is generally associated, on account of its effect in retarding the rate of economic progress.

XVII

It is necessary, finally, to turn to the effect on the foreign exchanges of an increase in the rate of home investment. Increased employment means increased imports of raw materials and finished goods and, to the extent that prices rise, there is a further increase of imports and a decrease of exports.

The result is that the net amount lent abroad by this country has to be reduced. It has been suggested above that the employment of 400,000 men might mean a reduction in the balance available for foreign lending of £20 million per annum. Unless other factors are brought into operation, this reduction in lending has to be effected by a rise in the various rates of interest. If other things remain equal, there ensues some decrease in the home investment that flows along normal channels, and this partially offsets the increase in investment that takes the form of road-building. It is important to assess the magnitude of this counteracting effect. Two factors are involved :—(*a*) the sensitivity of foreign lending to the rate of interest, and (*b*) the sensitivity of home investment to the rate of interest. It seems reasonable to suppose that, provided that the change that is under consideration is a fairly small one, the sensitivity of foreign lending to a rise in the rate of interest is considerably larger than the sensitivity of home investment. Moreover, under the conditions that prevail in this country at the present time, an increase in home investment, in the form of road-building, provided it is not undertaken on too large a scale, will result in a considerably smaller diminution in the amount available for lending abroad. It may therefore be concluded that it is not necessary to make any substantial deduction in respect to the effect of the rise in the rate of interest.

But if an attempt is made to increase home investment by a very considerable amount, the reduction in foreign lending is likely to be relatively greater—because a less elastic portion of the supply curve for consumption-goods will now come into operation and because the demand for goods that meet with foreign competition is likely to become more elastic as their price is raised.[1] It also seems likely that the sensitivity of home investment to a rise in the rate of interest becomes greater as the extent of the rise in the rate of interest is increased. It may, therefore, be concluded that the case of an extremely bold policy of road-building might necessitate more serious consideration of the effects of the rise in the rate of interest on home investment. But even then it must not be forgotten that the whole point of a policy of public works is that it enables an increase in the rate of home investment to take place without that *fall* in the rate of interest that would be necessary if we were relying on private enterprise. The fact that it necessitates some rise in the rate of interest is not in itself a valid objection.

But there are available, of course, methods for curtailing, partially or completely, the necessity for this rise in the rate of interest. In the first place, there are the various devices that could be employed with the object of restricting the freedom of foreign lending. Secondly, there is the possibility of combining

[1] On the other hand, the ratio of secondary to primary employment is likely to be less and, therefore, the ratio of the increase in employment (to which a portion of the increase in imports is directly proportional) to the cost of the roads is likely to be less. It follows that the reduction in foreign lending *may* be relatively less when many roads are being built than when only a few roads are being built.

a vigorous policy of home development with the imposition of a tariff. By combining the two measures in suitable proportions, it would be possible to maintain the value of imports at its present level. In this way each would be freed of one of the main objections that can be raised against it. The strain inflicted by road-building on the foreign exchanges would very largely disappear and the tariff would fail to impoverish our customers.

So far it has been supposed that a policy of national investment has no influence on the schedules of people's desire and ability to carry on investment at home and to lend abroad. This is a manifestly unwarranted supposition, but two opposing forces have to be reckoned with, and it is not at all clear where the issue lies.

An increase of output, and of the margin of profit that goes with it, cannot, taken by themselves, fail both to increase the attractiveness and to facilitate the process of investment at home. It is quite obvious that this effect is of great quantitative importance. If there were no opposing forces in operation, it might easily happen that, in spite of the rise in the rate of interest, the ordinary processes of home investment would be promoted rather than retarded by a policy of public works.

This supposes that the state of general confidence is not affected. There is strong justification for concluding on *a priori* grounds that the inauguration of an active economic policy would promote confidence rather than upset it. But this is not a valid reason for disbelieving the warning, so frequently put forward at the present time, that an extensive policy of public works would promote a feeling of distrust. For the state of confidence is a function of what people are thinking, even though their thinking may be completely irrational, and therefore only those who are in touch with the minds of the people are competent to pass judgment on this question.

A lowering of confidence may operate in two ways. It may, in the first place, reduce people's willingness or ability to carry on real investment at home. But also of great importance is its effect in increasing people's desire to hold their money abroad rather than at home. To the extent of the increased pressure to lend abroad, to which the phrase "flight from the pound" is often employed to give exaggerated prominence, the rise in the rate of interest that is necessary to protect the exchanges becomes greater, and its depressing influence on the rate of home investment also becomes greater.

But it is very difficult to believe that the dangers are as great as is often suggested. There can be no doubt that close contact with men of affairs must lead further towards a realisation of these dangers than can *a priori* reasoning. The only question is whether it may not lead too far. When a practical man declares that a policy of national development would result in a "flight from the pound," his judgment is really valuable only if he means that he himself would fly from the pound—and if he really would undertake the flight when the occasion arose. But too often the economic theory held by the business man bears little relation to his own practices—it is only if the practices of himself and of others like him were different from what they are that their theories could be correct. When a business man's theory involves a hypothesis about men's behaviour to which his own individual conduct fails to conform, he cannot be regarded as a very much sounder judge than the theoretical economist.

R. F. KAHN

King's College,
Cambridge.

[11]

THE
QUARTERLY JOURNAL
OF
ECONOMICS

FEBRUARY, 1937

THE GENERAL THEORY OF EMPLOYMENT

SUMMARY

I. Comments on the four discussions in the previous issue of points in the General Theory, 209. — II. Certain definite points on which the writer diverges from previous theories, 212. — The theory of interest restated, 215. — Uncertainties and fluctuations of investment, 217. — III. Demand and Supply for output as a whole, 219. — The output of capital goods and of consumption, 221.

I

I am much indebted to the Editors of the Quarterly Journal for the four contributions relating to my General Theory of Employment, Interest and Money which appeared in the issue for November, 1936. They contain detailed criticisms, much of which I accept and from which I hope to benefit. There is nothing in Professor Taussig's comment from which I disagree. Mr. Leontief is right, I think, in the distinction he draws between my attitude and that of the "orthodox" theory to what he calls the "homogeneity postulate." I should have thought, however, that there was abundant evidence from experience to contradict this postulate; and that, in any case, it is for those who make a highly special assumption to justify it, rather than for one who dispenses with it, to prove a general negative. I would also suggest that his idea might be applied more fruitfully and with greater theoretical precision in connection with the part played by the quantity of money in determining the rate of interest.[1] For it is here, I think, that the homogeneity postulate primarily enters into the orthodox theoretical scheme.

1. Cf. my paper on "The Theory of the Rate of Interest" to appear in the volume of Essays in honor of Irving Fisher.

My differences, such as they are, from Mr. Robertson chiefly arise out of my conviction that both he and I differ more fundamentally from our predecessors than his piety will allow. With many of his points I agree, without, however, being conscious in several instances of having said (or, anyhow, meant) anything different. I am surprised he should think that those who make sport with the velocity of the circulation of money have much in common with the theory of the multiplier. I fully agree with the important point he makes (pp. 180–183) that the increased demand for money resulting from an increase in activity has a backwash which tends to raise the rate of interest; and this is, indeed, a significant element in my theory of why booms carry within them the seeds of their own destruction. But this is, essentially, a part of the liquidity theory of the rate of interest, and not of the "orthodox" theory. Where he states (p. 183) that my theory must be regarded "not as a refutation of a common-sense account of events in terms of supply and demand for loanable funds, but as an alternative version of it," I must ask, before agreeing, for at least one reference to where this common-sense account is to be found.

There remains the most important of the four comments, namely, Professor Viner's. In regard to his criticisms of my definition and treatment of involuntary unemployment, I am ready to agree that this part of my book is particularly open to criticism. I already feel myself in a position to make improvements, and I hope that, when I do so, Professor Viner will feel more content, especially as I do not think that there is anything fundamental between us here. In the case of his second section, however, entitled "The Propensity to Hoard" I am prepared to debate his points. There are passages which suggest that Professor Viner is thinking too much in the more familiar terms of the quantity of money actually hoarded, and that he overlooks the emphasis I seek to place on the rate of interest as being the inducement *not* to hoard. It is precisely because the facilities for hoarding are strictly limited that liquidity preference mainly operates by increasing the rate of interest. I cannot agree that "in modern monetary theory the propensity to hoard is generally dealt with, with results which in kind are substantially identical with Keynes', as a factor operating to reduce the 'velocity' of money." On the contrary, I am convinced that the monetary theorists who try to deal with it in this way are altogether on the wrong track.[2] Again, when Professor Viner points out that most people invest their savings at the best rate of interest they can get and asks for statistics to justify the importance I attach to liquidity-preference, he is overlooking the point that it is the *marginal* potential hoarder who has to be satisfied by the rate of interest, so as to bring the desire for actual hoards within the narrow limits of the cash available for hoarding. When, as happens in a crisis, liquidity-preferences are sharply raised, this shows itself not so much in increased hoards — for there is little, if any, more cash which is hoardable than there was before — as in a sharp rise in the rate of interest, *i.e.* securities fall in price until those, who would now like to get liquid if they could do so at the previous price, are persuaded to give up the idea as being no longer practicable on reasonable terms. A rise in the rate of interest is a means *alternative* to an increase of hoards for satisfying an increased liquidity-preference. Nor is my argument affected by the admitted fact that different types of assets satisfy the desire for liquidity in different degrees. The mischief is done when the rate of interest corresponding to the degree of liquidity of a given asset leads to a market-capitalization of that asset which is less than its cost of production.

There are other criticisms also which I should be ready to debate. But tho I might be able to justify my own language, I am anxious not to be led, through doing so in too much detail, to overlook the substantial points which may, nevertheless, underlie the reactions which my treatment has produced in the minds of my critics. I am more attached to the comparatively simple fundamental ideas which underlie my theory than to the particular forms in which I have embodied them, and I have no desire that the latter should be crystal-

2. See below.

lized at the present stage of the debate. If the simple basic ideas can become familiar and acceptable, time and experience and the collaboration of a number of minds will discover the best way of expressing them. I would, therefore, prefer to occupy such further space, as the Editor of this Journal can allow me, in trying to reëxpress some of these ideas, than in detailed controversy which might prove barren. And I believe that I shall effect this best, even tho this may seem to some as plunging straight off into the controversial mood from which I purport to seek escape, if I put what I have to say in the shape of a discussion as to certain definite points where I seem to myself to be most clearly departing from previous theories.

II

It is generally recognized that the Ricardian analysis was concerned with what we now call long-period equilibrium. Marshall's contribution mainly consisted in grafting on to this the marginal principle and the principle of substitution, together with some discussion of the passage from one position of long-period equilibrium to another. But he assumed, as Ricardo did, that the amounts of the factors of production in use were given and that the problem was to determine the way in which they would be used and their relative rewards. Edgeworth and Professor Pigou and other later and contemporary writers have embroidered and improved this theory by considering how different peculiarities in the shapes of the supply functions of the factors of production would affect matters, what will happen in conditions of monopoly and imperfect competition, how far social and individual advantage coincide, what are the special problems of exchange in an open system and the like. But these more recent writers like their predecessors were still dealing with a system in which the amount of the factors employed was given and the other relevant facts were known more or less for certain. This does not mean that they were dealing with a system in which change was ruled out, or even one in which the disappointment of expectation was ruled out. But at any given time facts and expectations were assumed to be given in a definite and calculable form; and risks, of which, tho admitted, not much notice was taken, were supposed to be capable of an exact actuarial computation. The calculus of probability, tho mention of it was kept in the background, was supposed to be capable of reducing uncertainty to the same calculable status as that of certainty itself; just as in the Benthamite calculus of pains and pleasures or of advantage and disadvantage, by which the Benthamite philosophy assumed men to be influenced in their general ethical behavior.

Actually, however, we have, as a rule, only the vaguest idea of any but the most direct consequences of our acts. Sometimes we are not much concerned with their remoter consequences, even tho time and chance may make much of them. But sometimes we are intensely concerned with them, more so, occasionally, than with the immediate consequences. Now of all human activities which are affected by this remoter preoccupation, it happens that one of the most important is economic in character, namely, Wealth. The whole object of the accumulation of Wealth is to produce results, or potential results, at a comparatively distant, and sometimes at an *indefinitely* distant, date. Thus the fact that our knowledge of the future is fluctuating, vague and uncertain, renders Wealth a peculiarly unsuitable subject for the methods of the classical economic theory. This theory might work very well in a world in which economic goods were necessarily consumed within a short interval of their being produced. But it requires, I suggest, considerable amendment if it is to be applied to a world in which the accumulation of wealth for an indefinitely postponed future is an important factor; and the greater the proportionate part played by such wealth-accumulation the more essential does such amendment become.

By "uncertain" knowledge, let me explain, I do not mean merely to distinguish what is known for certain from what is only probable. The game of roulette is not subject, in this sense, to uncertainty; nor is the prospect of a Victory bond being drawn. Or, again, the expectation of life is only slightly uncertain. Even the weather is only moderately uncertain. The sense in which I am using the term is that in which the prospect of a European war is uncertain, or the price of copper and the rate of interest twenty years hence, or the obsolescence of a new invention, or the position of private wealth-owners in the social system in 1970. About these matters there is no scientific basis on which to form any calculable probability whatever. We simply do not know. Nevertheless, the necessity for action and for decision compels us as practical men to do our best to overlook this awkward fact and to behave exactly as we should if we had behind us a good Benthamite calculation of a series of prospective advantages and disadvantages, each multiplied by its appropriate probability, waiting to be summed.

How do we manage in such circumstances to behave in a manner which saves our faces as rational, economic men? We have devised for the purpose a variety of techniques, of which much the most important are the three following:

(1) We assume that the present is a much more serviceable guide to the future than a candid examination of past experience would show it to have been hitherto. In other words we largely ignore the prospect of future changes about the actual character of which we know nothing.

(2) We assume that the *existing* state of opinion as expressed in prices and the character of existing output is based on a *correct* summing up of future prospects, so that we can accept it as such unless and until something new and relevant comes into the picture.

(3) Knowing that our own individual judgment is worthless, we endeavor to fall back on the judgment of the rest of the world which is perhaps better informed. That is, we endeavor to conform with the behavior of the majority or the average. The psychology of a society of individuals each of whom is endeavoring to copy the others leads to what we may strictly term a *conventional* judgment.

Now a practical theory of the future based on these three principles has certain marked characteristics. In particular, being based on so flimsy a foundation, it is subject to sudden and violent changes. The practice of calmness and immobility, of certainty and security, suddenly breaks down. New fears and hopes will, without warning, take charge of human conduct. The forces of disillusion may suddenly impose a new conventional basis of valuation. All these pretty, polite techniques, made for a well-panelled Board Room and a nicely regulated market, are liable to collapse. At all times the vague panic fears and equally vague and unreasoned hopes are not really lulled, and lie but a little way below the surface.

Perhaps the reader feels that this general, philosophical disquisition on the behavior of mankind is somewhat remote from the economic theory under discussion. But I think not. Tho this is how we behave in the market place, the theory we devise in the study of how we behave in the market place should not itself submit to market-place idols. I accuse the classical economic theory of being itself one of these pretty, polite techniques which tries to deal with the present by abstracting from the fact that we know very little about the future.

I daresay that a classical economist would readily admit this. But, even so, I think he has overlooked the precise nature of the difference which his abstraction makes between theory and practice, and the character of the fallacies into which he is likely to be led.

This is particularly the case in his treatment of Money and Interest. And our first step must be to elucidate more clearly the functions of Money.

Money, it is well known, serves two principal purposes. By acting as a money of account it facilitates exchanges without its being necessary that it should ever itself come into the picture as a substantive object. In this respect it is a convenience which is devoid of significance or real influence. In the second place, it is a store of wealth. So we are told, without a smile on the face. But in the world of the classical economy, what an insane use to which to put it! For it is a recognized characteristic of money as a store of wealth that it is barren; whereas practically every other form of storing wealth yields some interest or profit. Why should anyone outside a lunatic asylum wish to use money as a store of wealth?

Because, partly on reasonable and partly on instinctive grounds, our desire to hold Money as a store of wealth is a barometer of the degree of our distrust of our own calculations and conventions concerning the future. Even tho this feeling about Money is itself conventional or instinctive, it operates, so to speak, at a deeper level of our motivation. It takes charge at the moments when the higher, more precarious conventions have weakened. The possession of actual money lulls our disquietude; and the premium which we require to make us part with money is the measure of the degree of our disquietude.

The significance of this characteristic of money has usually been overlooked; and in so far as it has been noticed, the essential nature of the phenomenon has been misdescribed. For what has attracted attention has been the *quantity* of money which has been hoarded; and importance has been attached to this because it has been supposed to have a direct proportionate effect on the price-level through affecting the velocity of circulation. But the *quantity* of hoards can only be altered either if the total quantity of money is changed or if the quantity of current money-income (I speak broadly) is changed; whereas fluctuations in the degree of confidence are capable of having quite a different effect, namely, in modifying not the amount that is actually hoarded, but the amount of the premium which has to be offered to induce people not to hoard. And changes in the propensity to hoard, or in the state of liquidity-preference as I have called it, primarily affect, not prices, but the rate of interest; any effect on prices being produced by repercussion as an ultimate consequence of a change in the rate of interest.

This, expressed in a very general way, is my theory of the rate of interest. The rate of interest obviously measures — just as the books on arithmetic say it does — the premium which has to be offered to induce people to hold their wealth in some form other than hoarded money. The quantity of money and the amount of it required in the active circulation for the transaction of current business (mainly depending on the level of money-income) determine how much is available for inactive balances, *i.e.* for hoards. The rate of interest is the factor which adjusts at the margin the demand for hoards to the supply of hoards.

Now let us proceed to the next stage of the argument. The owner of wealth, who has been induced not to hold his wealth in the shape of hoarded money, still has two alternatives between which to choose. He can lend his money at the current rate of money-interest or he can purchase some kind of capital-asset. Clearly in equilibrium these two alternatives must offer an equal advantage to the marginal investor in each of them. This is brought about by shifts in the money-prices of capital-assets relative to the prices of money-loans. The prices of capital-assets move until, having regard to their prospective yields and account being taken of all those elements of doubt and uncertainty, interested and disinterested advice, fashion, convention and what else you will which affect the mind of the investor, they offer an equal apparent advantage to the marginal investor who is wavering between one kind of investment and another.

This, then, is the first repercussion of the rate of interest, as fixed by the quantity of money and the propensity to hoard, namely, on the prices of capital-assets. This does not mean, of course, that the rate of interest is the only fluctuating influence on these prices. Opinions as to their prospective yield are themselves subject to sharp fluctuations, precisely for the reason already given, namely, the flimsiness of the basis of knowledge on which they depend. It is these opinions taken in conjunction with the rate of interest which fix their price.

Now for stage three. Capital-assets are capable, in general, of being newly produced. The scale on which they are produced depends, of course, on the relation between their costs of production and the prices which they are expected to realize in the market. Thus if the level of the rate of interest taken in conjunction with opinions about their prospective yield raise the prices of capital-assets, the volume of current investment (meaning by this the value of the output of newly produced capital-assets) will be increased; while if, on the other hand, these influences reduce the prices of capital-assets, the volume of current investment will be diminished.

It is not surprising that the volume of investment, thus determined, should fluctuate widely from time to time. For it depends on two sets of judgments about the future, neither of which rests on an adequate or secure foundation — on the propensity to hoard and on opinions of the future yield of capital-assets. Nor is there any reason to suppose that the fluctuations in one of these factors will tend to offset the fluctuations in the other. When a more pessimistic view is taken about future yields, that is no reason why there should be a diminished propensity to hoard. Indeed, the conditions which aggravate the one factor tend, as a rule, to aggravate the other. For the same circumstances which lead to pessimistic views about future yields are apt to increase the propensity to hoard. The only element of self-righting in the system arises at a much later stage and in an uncertain degree. If a decline in investment leads to a decline in output as a whole, this may result (for more reasons than one) in a reduction of the amount of money required for the active circulation, which will release a larger quantity of money for the inactive circulation, which will satisfy the propensity to hoard at a lower level of the rate of interest, which will raise the prices of capital-assets, which will increase the scale of investment, which will restore in some measure the level of output as a whole.

This completes the first chapter of the argument, namely, the liability of the scale of investment to fluctuate for reasons quite distinct (*a*) from those which determine the propensity of the individual to *save* out of a given income and (*b*) from those physical conditions of technical capacity to aid production which have usually been supposed hitherto to be the chief influence governing the marginal efficiency of capital.

If, on the other hand, our knowledge of the future was calculable and not subject to sudden changes, it might be justifiable to assume that the liquidity-preference curve was both stable and very inelastic. In this case a small decline in money-income would lead to a large fall in the rate of interest, probably sufficient to raise output and employment to the full.[3] In these conditions we might reasonably suppose that the whole of the available resources would normally be employed; and the conditions required by the orthodox theory would be satisfied.

III

My next difference from the traditional theory concerns its apparent conviction that there is no necessity to work out a theory of the demand and supply of output *as a whole*. Will a fluctuation in investment, arising for the reasons just described, have any effect on the demand for output as a whole, and consequently on the scale of output and employment? What answer can the traditional theory make to this question? I believe that it makes no answer at all, never having given the matter a single thought; the theory of effective demand, that is the demand for output as a whole, having been entirely neglected for more than a hundred years.

My own answer to this question involves fresh considerations. I say that effective demand is made up of two items — investment-expenditure determined in the manner just explained and consumption-expenditure. Now what governs the amount of consumption-expenditure? It depends mainly on the level of income. People's propensity to spend (as I call it) is influenced by many factors such as the distribution of income, their normal attitude to the future and — tho probably in a minor degree — by the rate of interest. But in the main the prevailing psychological law seems to be that when aggregate income increases, consumption-expenditure will also increase but to a somewhat lesser extent. This is a very obvious conclusion. It simply amounts to saying that

3. When Professor Viner charges me with assigning to liquidity-preference "a grossly exaggerated importance," he must mean that I exaggerate its instability and its elasticity. But if he is right, a small decline in money-income would lead, as stated above, to a large fall in the rate of interest. I claim that experience indicates the contrary.

an increase in income will be divided in some proportion or another between spending and saving, and that when our income is increased it is extremely unlikely that this will have the effect of making us either spend less or save less than before. This psychological law was of the utmost importance in the development of my own thought, and it is, I think, absolutely fundamental to the theory of effective demand as set forth in my book. But few critics or commentators so far have paid particular attention to it.

There follows from this extremely obvious principle an important, yet unfamiliar, conclusion. Incomes are created partly by entrepreneurs producing for investment and partly by their producing for consumption. The amount that is consumed depends on the amount of income thus made up. Hence the amount of consumption-goods which it will pay entrepreneurs to produce depends on the amount of investment-goods which they are producing. If, for example, the public are in the habit of spending nine-tenths of their income on consumption-goods, it follows that if entrepreneurs were to produce consumption-goods at a cost more than nine times the cost of the investment-goods they are producing, some part of their output could not be sold at a price which would cover its cost of production. For the consumption-goods on the market would have cost more than nine-tenths of the aggregate income of the public and would therefore be in excess of the demand for consumption-goods, which by hypothesis is only the nine-tenths. Thus entrepreneurs will make a loss until they contract their output of consumption-goods down to an amount at which it no longer exceeds nine times their current output of investment goods.

The formula is not, of course, quite so simple as in this illustration. The proportion of their incomes which the public will choose to consume will not be a constant one, and in the most general case other factors are also relevant. But there is always a formula, more or less of this kind, relating the output of consumption-goods which it pays to produce to the output of investment-goods; and I have given attention to it in my book under the name of the *Multiplier*. The fact that an increase in consumption is apt in itself to stimulate this further investment merely fortifies the argument.

That the level of output of consumption-goods, which is profitable to the entrepreneur, should be related by a formula of this kind to the output of investment-goods depends on assumptions of a simple and obvious character. The conclusion appears to me to be quite beyond dispute. Yet the consequences which follow from it are at the same time unfamiliar and of the greatest possible importance.

The theory can be summed up by saying that, given the psychology of the public, the level of output and employment as a whole depends on the amount of investment. I put it in this way, not because this is the only factor on which aggregate output depends, but because it is usual in a complex system to regard as the *causa causans* that factor which is most prone to sudden and wide fluctuation. More comprehensively, aggregate output depends on the propensity to hoard, on the policy of the monetary authority as it affects the quantity of money, on the state of confidence concerning the prospective yield of capital-assets, on the propensity to spend and on the social factors which influence the level of the money-wage. But of these several factors it is those which determine the rate of investment which are most unreliable, since it is they which are influenced by our views of the future about which we know so little.

This that I offer is, therefore, a theory of why output and employment are so liable to fluctuation. It does not offer a ready-made remedy as to how to avoid these fluctuations and to maintain output at a steady optimum level. But it is, properly speaking, a Theory of Employment because it explains *why*, in any given circumstances, employment is what it is. Naturally I am interested not only in the diagnosis, but also in the cure; and many pages of my book are devoted to the latter. But I consider that my suggestions for a cure, which, avowedly, are not worked out completely, are on a different plane from the diagnosis. They are not meant to be definitive; they are subject to all sorts of special assumptions and are necessarily related to the particular conditions of the time. But my main reasons for departing from the traditional theory go much deeper than this. They are of a highly general character and are meant to be definitive.

I sum up, therefore, the main grounds of my departure as follows:

(1) The orthodox theory assumes that we have a knowledge of the future of a kind quite different from that which we actually possess. This false rationalization follows the lines of the Benthamite calculus. The hypothesis of a calculable future leads to a wrong interpretation of the principles of behavior which the need for action compels us to adopt, and to an underestimation of the concealed factors of utter doubt, precariousness, hope and fear. The result has been a mistaken theory of the rate of interest. It is true that the necessity of equalizing the advantages of the choice between owning loans and assets requires that the rate of interest should be *equal* to the marginal efficiency of capital. But this does not tell us at what *level* the equality will be effective. The orthodox theory regards the marginal efficiency of capital as setting the pace. But the marginal efficiency of capital depends on the price of capital-assets; and since this price determines the rate of new investment, it is consistent in equilibrium with only one given level of money-income. Thus the marginal efficiency of capital is not determined, unless the level of money-income is given. In a system in which the level of money-income is capable of fluctuating, the orthodox theory is one equation short of what is required to give a solution. Undoubtedly the reason why the orthodox system has failed to discover this discrepancy is because it has always tacitly assumed that income *is* given, namely, at the level corresponding to the employment of all the available resources. In other words it is tacitly assuming that the monetary policy is such as to maintain the rate of interest at that level which is compatible with full employment. It is, therefore, incapable of dealing with the general case where employment is liable to fluctuate. Thus, instead of the marginal efficiency of capital determin-

ing the rate of interest, it is truer (tho not a full statement of the case) to say that it is the rate of interest which determines the marginal efficiency of capital.

(2) The orthodox theory would by now have discovered the above defect, if it had not ignored the need for a theory of the supply and demand of output as a whole. I doubt if many modern economists really accept Say's Law that supply creates its own demand. But they have not been aware that they were tacitly assuming it. Thus the psychological law underlying the Multiplier has escaped notice. It has not been observed that the amount of consumption-goods which it pays entrepreneurs to produce is a function of the amount of investment-goods which it pays them to produce. The explanation is to be found, I suppose, in the tacit assumption that every individual spends the whole of his income either on consumption or on buying, directly or indirectly, newly produced capital goods. But, here again, whilst the older economists expressly believed this, I doubt if many contemporary economists really do believe it. They have discarded these older ideas without becoming aware of the consequences.

J. M. Keynes.

King's College, Cambridge

[12]

A NON-LINEAR THEORY OF THE CYCLE

R. M. Goodwin

WHEN a leading theorist has his attention diverted to business cycle analysis, the result is usually a happy one, as witness the examples provided by Schumpeter, Pigou, Frisch, J. M. Clark, Harrod, and Haberler. The most recent of Professor Hicks' works continues this impressive record.[1] It is a book that no one interested in the cycle — and what economist is not? — can afford to miss reading. The following bare enumeration of its accomplishments should suffice to make this clear: (1) an elegant restatement of the *General Theory* on dynamic lines, (2) a basic elaboration of Mr. Harrod's multiplier-accelerator version of Keynes, (3) an alteration of accelerator theory which removes its major flaw (as distinguished from numerous lesser ones), (4) the use of this alteration to suggest a solution to a central, unsolved problem, i.e., the persistence of cycles, (5) a reaffirmation and restatement of the role of money in the cycle in such a way as to give it an ancillary, though important, role. Such a theoretical offering, so well written, in such narrow compass (168 pages), for so little ($2.25), is most welcome, especially if we compare it with the ponderous, uninspired, expensive texts which are continually being hurled at us. It will speak most directly to the professional economist, for it is essentially an experimental effort, a true "model," but my guess is that it was also aimed at the better undergraduate and graduate students as well. A preliminary trial has convinced me that, while it has to be taught, the book's central thesis can be understood by honors undergraduates.

Professor Hicks launches his model with a humility rare amongst economists: "I do believe that the argument which I am going to set out is quite likely to be the main part of the answer to the great question with which I am concerned. . . . I am not by any means positive that the answer which I have found is the right answer; one cannot begin to be sure of that until one has tested one's theory against the facts, and I am well aware that any testing which I have been able to do has been extremely superficial. If the theory which is here offered stands up to theoretical criticism, the next stage will be the concern of statisticians, econometrists, and (most of all) economic historians, . . ." (Preface.) In this short note, I propose to restrict myself to the theoretical issues and to leave — with some misgivings — the empirical aspects to others better equipped for carrying out the arduous task of testing.

With an engaging frankness, the author spells out in detail his trinitarian sources — Keynes for the multiplier, Clark for the accelerator, and Harrod for growth phenomena — so clearly that one might almost miss the element of originality involved in erecting a quite new building out of old and familiar building blocks. He then proceeds to lay out the nature of the dynamical multiplier in such a way as to undo the damage done by Keynes in telescoping the Kahn process. If only this lucid exposition had been available fifteen years ago, what mountains of confusion and quibbling we might have been spared. The chief new element is contained in his careful discussion of the difficult problem of distributed lags and in his demonstration that they do not alter fundamentally the conclusions derived from a simple lag hypothesis.

In Chapter IV is the second pillar of the edifice, for "The theory of the multiplier and the theory of the accelerator are the two sides of the theory of fluctuations, just as the theory of demand and the theory of supply are the two sides of the thory of value" (p. 38). Here appears one of the two non-linearities which distinguish Hicks' theory from its predecessors: "The expansion in investment, induced by a rise in output, can be as large as it likes, provided that the necessary resources are available; but the corresponding contraction is slowed up by the condition that Gross Investment in fixed capital cannot be negative" (p. 66). There is also a discussion of the acceleration theory of liquid and working capital

[1] J. R. Hicks, *A Contribution to the Theory of the Trade Cycle* (London, 1950).

where the asymmetry is not necessarily present. The simple income-expenditure lag is here (p. 52 ff.) reinterpreted in terms of stocks of goods and entrepreneurial reactions. While this step seems desirable, it does involve non-clock time, which presents treacherous problems and leaves a certain vagueness in the length of the cycle. There is in my mind some doubt as to whether Professor Hicks has really succeeded in side-stepping the difficulties of a full-dress, dynamical treatment along the lines of the Frisch carry-on function (an integral rather than a difference equation).

Mr. Harrod's Regularly Progressive Economy is accepted as possible but not probable, for the reason that it is an unstable equilibrium motion, so that a small deviation does not set up a tendency to return to the steady motion. After the rejection of smooth growth, Professor Hicks quite naturally turns to cyclical theory, for which he chooses a variant of the Hansen-Samuelson formulation of the multiplier-accelerator interaction. Since he utilizes income and not consumption for the acceleration effect, he loses the second difference in his equation (and hence the possibility of oscillation). This second lag he unobtrusively, and without much attempt at justification, reinserts as a single period lag in investment outlays, although subsequently he considers the more realistic and immensely more difficult case of distributed lags. From this, purely linear, model we get the familar four behavior types — exponential (compound interest) growth, exponential decay, explosive oscillation (complex exponential), and attenuated oscillation. Beyond this there are murky waters, with the result that the real argument is transferred to the mathematical appendix, the text being used to report a few, rather tentative, conclusions. The reason is that even this very simple model is too rich in possibilities to allow one to take explicit account of the complications of introducing the realistic assumption of distributed lags in both consumption and investment outlays. While it is not possible to be rigorous or precise, Professor Hicks does make a pretty convincing argument that these complications are indeed complications and not matters of basic importance, so that they may be substantially ignored in analyzing the major cycle. This very useful result is typical of the many subsidiary pieces which adorn the book.

Finally, the central point of the book is reached: how do cycles persist? For all linear models there are three possibilities, the first of which — explosive oscillations — may be summarily rejected. Secondly, we know that an acceleration coefficient of one *exactly* will lead to a persisting, undamped cycle. Professor Frisch long ago argued quite conclusively, against the early models of Tinbergen and Kalecki, that this will not do.[2] Since that time, it has been fashionable to assume a damped system with renewal of amplitude through erratic shocks. Professor Hicks rejects this solution in an elegant, but rather too compact, passage (pp. 90–91), for the full understanding of which the conscientious reader will have to wrestle with paragraph 27 on pages 193–95 in the appendix. The gist of the argument is that since random shocks will work both with and against the cycle, the *net* effect is too small to be relied on to keep the cycle going with any appreciable amplitude.

Having disposed, correctly I think, of the existing hypotheses that will explain the persistence of the cycle, he is then free to develop a new one. Since the basic importance of the problem, and its difficulties, are not likely to be familiar to the economist (indeed, it is not clear that they are even to the author), I should like to indicate briefly something of its history and present situation. The simple linearized pendulum theory, which we all learn, fails to explain most observed oscillations, i.e., the ones that neither die away nor explode as in the cases of clocks, steam engines, electric bells and buzzers, wind and string instruments, vacuum tube oscillators, the human heart, and a great variety of other similar phenomena. The first reasonably successful assault on the analysis of the problem was made late in the nineteenth century in acoustic theory (a tuning fork oscillator) by Lord Rayleigh. At about the same time the great mathematician Henri Poincaré succeeded in blocking out a large part of the basic theory and applied it to certain

[2] It is interesting to note that radio engineers originally made essentially the same assumption and have been gradually forced to give it up as an unsatisfactory way to explain the maintenance of oscillation.

problems in celestial mechanics. Neither effort had much effect on the general theory of cycles, however, until the advent of vacuum tube circuits made a non-linear oscillator theory imperative. About two decades ago B. van der Pol gave a satisfactory account of what he called relaxation oscillations, and this work has been extended by Ph. Le Corbeiller and others. Research is being actively pursued in many places, especially the United States and Soviet Russia, where notable results have been achieved. A superior account of the whole field is to be found in the *Theory of Oscillations*, by A. A. Andronow and C. E. Chaikin.[3] As a result of all this we have a reasonably all-embracing and much profounder theory of oscillations. It has become abundantly clear that self-maintaining cycles occur because of essential non-linearities in the structure of the system.

Since Professor Hicks proposes a theory which will explain the maintenance of oscillation, we can be sure, on formal grounds, that this implies a non-linearity. In fact, he assumes two — the lower limit of zero in gross investment and the upper limit of full employment in real income. From the point of view of systematic vibration theory, his model is probably best regarded as an over-energetic clock. The ordinary clock maintains its oscillation by delivering to its pendulum in each swing a blow which is timed by the escapement. The economy seems to have a strong tendency to instability, and hence would swing in ever greater arcs were it not for the inevitable limit of full employment, which thus provides an essential non-linearity. By analogy, we may visualize a clock placed next to a wall; it is so constructed that each swing of the pendulum is greater until it begins to hit the wall; thereafter it will oscillate perpetually with this uniquely determined amplitude. Even if it is slowed down or speeded up or nearly stopped, it will always work back to its proper limit cycle.

Actually Professor Hicks considers two quite distinct "constraints."[4] It is evident that full employment constitutes a barrier because in order to get there we must have a rate of expansion, and hence a level of investment, of real income which cannot be maintained when once we have attained it. Hence induced investment must fall with consequent drops in income and employment.[5] This one barrier would suffice to maintain a steady oscillation, but in fact there is a second barrier of a quite different sort from the first. There is no effective lower limit to income short of zero, but there is one to investment. Net investment cannot drop below a negative value equal to depreciation. The economy cannot, however, remain permanently at this depressed level, because replacement outlays will have eventually to be undertaken and then income increases, positive investment takes place, and the boom is on again. Between the floor and the ceiling the economy bounces back and forth. Indeed the economy need have no tendency to oscillate at all, apart from the two thresholds, but need only be explosive in both upward and downward directions.

Abstracting from trend and autonomous investment, we may state the theory as follows: today's income is greater than yesterday's income by the difference between today's investment and the saving, $s(y)$, out of yesterday's income. If to this we add the accelerator as sole determinant of investment we have a complete theory. Today's investment is determined as some multiple, say two, of the difference

[3] English translation published by the Princeton University Press, 1949.

[4] His choice of word "constraint" to describe a non-linearity seems most unfortunate. It has in dynamics a well-defined meaning which has nothing to do with non-linearities. A much better word would have been threshold, for threshold oscillators are a clearly-defined class, e.g., household heating systems with thermostatic controls.

[5] This point has not, of course, by any means gone unnoticed before. For example in *Monetary Theory and Fiscal Policy*, Professor Hansen writes on page 199, "In the first place, when the *rate of increase* of output has begun to decline, as it must as full employment is approached, the *induced* investment in inventories and in fixed plant and equipment will fall." It is in this form that the Hansen-Frisch-Clark controversy (*Journal of Political Economy*, October 1931 and subsequent issues) should have been posed. Then it would have been clear that Professor Clark was really right, although formally Professor Frisch (and Mr. Harrod and Professor Domar after him) was right in saying that a smooth exponential growth will always satisfy a first order differential equation. The point is that if by induced investment we rise from unemployment to full employment, there must at that point occur an impasse and the smooth development breaks down. Even if the structural parameters were such as to permit a steady 3 per cent growth rate — which seems to me quite unrealistic — once unemployment existed it would never be reduced and hence we would never reach boom and full employment.

between yesterday's income and day-before-yesterday's income. Calling the acceleration coefficient v, we have symbolically

$$\Delta y_t = i_t - s(y_{t-1}),$$
$$= v\Delta y_{t-1} - s(y_{t-1}),$$

which becomes Hicks' equation if $s(y)$ is linear. It is reasonable to assume that the system is unstable since any v, the ratio of capital to output, greater than one implies it.

The whole theory is susceptible of a quite simple graphical development which Professor Hicks neglects to present.[6] As shown in Chart I, given any two, arbitrary, initial values such

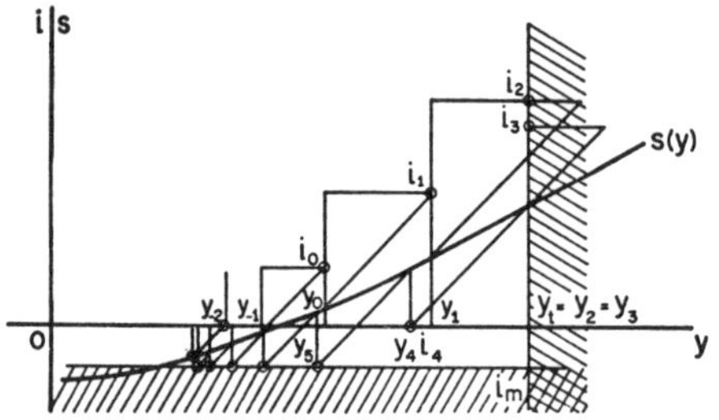

CHART I

as y_{-2} and y_{-1}, we find i_0 as twice their difference. Then y_0 will be greater than y_{-1} by the difference between i_0 and $s(y_{-1})$. As is indicated, this is conveniently carried out by projecting a 45° line from the $s(y_{-1})$ until it cuts the horizontal i_0 line. The horizontal coordinate of this point is y_0. Next the difference between y_{-1} and y_0 determines i_1 and from this and $s(y_0)$, we locate y_1, and continuing thus we finally reach the full employment threshold, y_t. If, as is almost certain to be the case, the last step carries us beyond the threshold, this means that an inflationary situation has arisen — a condition analyzed with much insight in the last two chapters of the book. Neglecting these complications we may say, simply, that real income becomes constant, $y_2 = y_3$ in our example, and hence i_4 drops to zero. Therefore income must drop sharply to y_4, which in turn would entail an enormous further drop in investment. But here the second threshold (this time in investment) becomes operative and i cannot fall below a certain minimum i_m. In this way, income falls at a decreasing rate until that rate becomes less than one half of i_m, at which point some replacement is required. If, as in Chart I, this raises investment to the level of saving, income no longer falls. Hence investment is further increased to zero, but this means an increase in income, investment becomes positive, and the upswing commences.[7] This model possesses at once simplicity and great analytic power. It will oscillate for a wide variety of different savings functions and of acceleration coefficients. It tends to a *limit cycle* of a typical sort independently of how it commences or how it is disturbed. There is no assumption that the supply of capital is perfectly adjusted to the demand for it (as with the simple accelerator). The cycle will not die away, nor will it explode, but rather the conditions for its *maintenance* are built into it. Either the "ceiling" or the "floor" will suffice to check and hence perpetuate it. Thus the boom may die before hitting full employment, but then it will be checked on the downswing by the limit on disinvestment. Or again it may, indeed it ordinarily does, start up again before eliminating the excess capital as a result of autonomous outlays by business or government.

The way in which Professor Hicks introduces a trend, following Mr. Harrod, seems to me highly doubtful. He assumes a *steady* growth

[6] Possibly the reason is that he wished to include the trend, which is not so easily done in the graph. Yet it surely is a good thing to separate trend and cycle analytically. On the other hand, in his defense, it can be said that trend makes much more difference in non-linear than in linear systems. It is even possible to cite systems which will oscillate about a trend but would remain in equilibrium if left alone (although Hicks' system would oscillate indefinitely in the absence of trend, it would do so in a peculiar and unrealistic way). Another questionable feature of the book is that in a book on a non-linear cycle we are presented with nothing but *linear* theory, even in the mathematical appendix. It is, however, much easier to cavil than to suggest what might have been done, for non-linear difference equations represent virgin territory mathematically — except for that extraordinary, but deceptively simple, performance of Professor Leontief in "Verzögerte Angebotsanpassung und partielles Gleichgewicht", *Zeitschrift für Nationalökonomie*, 1934. Combining the difficulties of difference equations with those of non-linear theory, we get an animal of a ferocious character and it is wise not to place too much confidence in our conclusions as to behavior.

[7] It should be said that the complexity of reality escapes this form of diagram, for in the course of the slump excess capacity is accumulated, so that a cessation of decline alone is not enough to ensure replacement investment. Some autonomous investment, or failing that ultimately the mere lapse of time with continuing output, is necessary.

in autonomous investment and in the full employment ceiling, quite independently of the cycle. Significantly enough Schumpeter's name is never mentioned, and yet surely some form of his innovational theory is essential to the description of the contours of capitalistic evolution, particularly in relating trend to cycle. This leads into another problem, peculiar to Keynesian theory, on which Professor Hicks is less than adequate. Even if we include secular progress in the form of the accumulation of capital and labor, whether steadily or in spurts, we are still left with an awkward question about the savings function. If $s(y)$ is as drawn in Chart 1, it is adequate for cycle analysis, but we get into trouble over the long run, for we would always return to the same trough level, e.g., a depression in 1920 would carry us down to an 1820 level and back up again but only with fantastically high levels of savings and investments. We escape this difficulty (by drawing a flatter $s(y)$ curve passing through the origin) only to fall into another (income would go to zero or lower in each cycle).

This dilemma may be resolved by a resolute application of Professor Duesenberry's "ratchet effect," whereby savings depend not only on income but on the previous highest income.[8] As a result of secular progress the full employment limit moves to the right, and once we pass the previous highest income we proceed along the secular savings function as distinguished from the cyclical one. Yet the threshold does exist and, being encountered, reverses the boom. But now we descend along a new cyclical savings function, which is simply the old one translated to the right by the difference between the old peak and the new. In this way, without too great a strain on our geometrical intuition, we can fuse trend and cycle in a more satisfactory manner that is strongly reminiscent of, and parallel to, the Schumpeterian innovations theory. An example is given in Chart 2, with no particular attention to accuracy or realism, of such a cyclical-secular process. By joining together with a solid line the points representing successive combinations of investment and income, we get a vivid picture of how the economy may slip and slide along. Each forward lurch along the secular savings function (the straight line) generates consumption habits

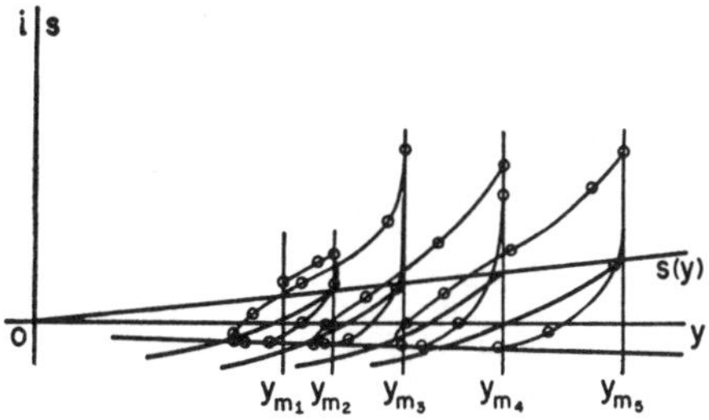

CHART 2

which produce a new cyclical curve, which we follow down and back up again. No account has been taken of autonomous investment, but it is easily inserted by simply adding it to induced investment, and, since it is likely never to be of the same magnitude, it imparts to each cycle an historical individuality.

In this short compass I have tried only to suggest to the reader the main outlines of a most impressive performance. My purpose will have been served if I have sent him hurrying to the original, to which he must repair for a proper view of the rich embroidery of theoretical detail. There he will find illuminating discussions of inflation and the monetary theory of the cycle, of a hitherto unnoticed cobweb in the Keynesian theory (but surely not as a result of disuse!), of distributed lags, of difference equations (the mathematical appendix provides perhaps the best available introduction to that important subject), of the dynamics of the pure theory of investment and of the distinction between its fixed and liquid forms, of the theory of the secular steady state, and finally of the many problems of saving and investment in a dynamical multiplier process.

[8] James Duesenberry, *Income, Saving and the Theory of Consumer Behavior* (1949), Chapter VII. Unfortunately, the important results obtained by Professors Duesenberry and Modigliani appeared too late for incorporation in the book (cf. page vi of the Preface).

[13]

ECONOMETRICA

VOLUME 19 JANUARY, 1951 NUMBER 1

THE NONLINEAR ACCELERATOR AND THE PERSISTENCE OF BUSINESS CYCLES[1]

BY R. M. GOODWIN

By taking account of obvious and inescapable limitations on the functioning of the accelerator, we explain some of the chief characteristics of the cycle, notably its failure to die away, along with the fact that capital stock is usually either in excess or in short supply. By a succession of increasingly complex models, the nature and methods of analyzing nonlinear cycle models is developed. The roles of lags and of secular evolution are illustrated. In each case the system's equilibrium position is unstable, but there exists a stable limit cycle toward which all motions tend.

INTRODUCTION

ALMOST without exception economists have entertained the hypothesis of linear structural relations as a basis for cycle theory. As such it is an oversimplified special case and, for this reason, is the easiest to handle, the most readily available. Yet it is not well adapted for directing attention to the basic elements in oscillations—for these we must turn to nonlinear types. With them we are enabled to analyze a much wider range of phenomena, and in a manner at once more advanced and more elementary.

By dropping the highly restrictive assumptions of linearity we neatly escape the rather embarrassing special conclusions which follow. Thus, whether we are dealing with difference or differential equations, so long as they are linear, they either explode or die away with the consequent disappearance of the cycle or the society.[2] One may hope to avoid this unpleasant dilemma by choosing that case (as with the frictionless pendulum) just in between. Such a way out is helpful in the classroom, but it is nothing more than a mathematical abstraction. Therefore,

[1] This paper, with the exception of a few modifications in the last section, was presented at the 1948 meeting of the Econometric Society in Cleveland, and it was summarized in ECONOMETRICA for April, 1949 (Vol. 17, pp. 184–185). In its various metamorphoses it was followed with great interest and many helpful comments by the late J. A. Schumpeter. His influence on the whole of it is so pervasive, and I hope so evident, that particular acknowledgment would be inadequate.

[2] Cf. any good book on mechanics, e.g., A. A. Andronow and C. E. Chaikin, *Theory of Oscillations* (English translation by S. Lefschetz), Princeton: Princeton University Press, 1949, Chapter I.

economists will be led, as natural scientists have been led, to seek in nonlinearities an explanation of the maintenance of oscillation. Advice to this effect, given by Professor Le Corbeiller in one of the earliest issues of this journal, has gone largely unheeded.[3]

Mention should also be made of the fact that there exists an alternative way out of the dilemma—that of an impulse-excited mechanism. There are two basically different classes of such mechanisms to be distinguished. (a) There are the synchronized systems of which the most familiar is the ordinary pendulum clock. Here the pendulum executes damped motion, but its own motion is used to time regular shocks so that it settles down to a steady routine in which the energy which is dissipated in friction during each cycle is exactly replaced. The wider system, including the feedback mechanism (the escapement) for delivering the shocks, is a particular type of nonlinear oscillator since it is autonomous and maintains a uniform cycle independently of initial conditions. (b) Significantly different is a system subject to random shocks. Here the mechanism itself is damped, but an outside, unexplained source keeps it going, and in this sense it is not a complete theory, for the source of maintenance lies outside the theory. Also, since the shocks are not synchronized with the cycle, they work both with and against

[3] Ph. Le Corbeiller, "Les systèmes autoentretenus et les oscillations de relaxation," ECONOMETRICA, Vol. 1, July, 1933, pp. 328–332. "If statistical data lead us to believe that a given magnitude varies periodically, and if we look for the cause of these oscillations, we may suppose that that magnitude executes either (a) forced oscillations, or (b) maintained oscillations, which may be either (bα) sine-like, or (bβ) relaxation type." My debt to Professor Le Corbeiller is very great, not only for the original stimulation to search for the essential nonlinearities, but also for his patient insistence, in the face of the many difficulties which turned up, that this type of analysis *must* somehow be worked out.

Since the statement in the text was written, I have discovered that there has been an increasing amount of work on nonlinear theories, culminating in Professor Hicks's admirable book, *A Contribution to the Theory of the Trade Cycle* (Oxford: Clarendon Press, 1950, 199 pp.), which appeared while I was making final revisions on this paper. Professor Tinbergen has also attacked the subject in his article, "Ligevægtstyper Og Konjunkturbevægelse" (*Nordisk Tidsskrift for Teknisk Økonomie*, Vol. 32, Nos. 2–4, 1943, pp. 45–63). This development corroborates the position of Professor Le Corbeiller and promises much good for economics. In Hicks's book the reader will find reference to other investigations as well as a much more complete statement of why nonlinear cycle theory is necessary. I find most impressive the extent to which he and I have hit on the same problems and, substantially, the same answers, although his techniques appear, on the surface, to be quite different since he deals with difference equations and since he does not approach the subject in terms of formal, nonlinear theory. The similarities are not purely accidental, partly because we have both started from the unsatisfactory, but profoundly stimulating, dynamical closure of the Keynesian system put forth by Mr. Harrod in his book, *The Trade Cycle* (Oxford: Clarendon Press, 1936, 234 pp.).

it so that their effects largely cancel out. That they do not entirely cancel out can be seen by the fact that, if the system were to come to rest, the next shock would excite it and the motion would be cyclical, so that there will always be a small tendency to cyclical motion. The shocks, however, would have to be large to produce much of a continuing cycle, which would make it desirable to analyze the individual causes and consequences of each shock rather than to treat them as a random element collectively. It also raises the question of whether or not the cycle would be more swamped in the random motions than is actually the case. Somewhere in between these two types lies the theory which might be called the Schumpeter clock (although it would be a chronometrically bad clock). The steady evolution of ideas leads to intermittent, irregular, but not random, bursts of expenditure. If these large and variable outlays impinge on a damped cycle, they may seriously alter its character and keep it from dying away. Professor Frisch has provided the basic analysis of this range of problems, and I shall attempt to indicate its relevance to nonlinear theories below.[4] The difficult question remains as to what extent the explanation lies entirely with the innovation, giving forced oscillations, and to what extent there is mutual conditioning, leading to an erratic clockwork (and hence nonlinear) theory.

Along with explaining the maintenance of oscillation, nonlinear theory does away with the necessity for "initial conditions." No matter how the mechanism is started, it tends to a certain type of cycle. Otherwise we are involved in believing that the magnitude and turning points, for example, of a cycle now are completely determined by events which took place many years ago. The absurdity of such an assumption is obvious.

Another advantage lies in the possible treatment of the acceleration principle. Because statistical studies (e.g., Tinbergen's "Statistical Evidence on the Acceleration Principle")[5] have shown that it does not correspond to the facts, many economists favor dropping it entirely. Yet this would surely be mistaken since it is merely the statement of a simple consequence of the one omnipresent, incontestable dynamic fact in economics—the necessity to have both stocks and flows of goods. In any case, it is worth while to try assumptions which take account of this fact but do not require any rigid proportionality. In doing this we

[4] Cf. Frisch, "Propagation Problems and Impulse Problems in Dynamic Economics," in *Economic Essays in Honour of Gustav Cassel*, London: George Allen and Unwin Ltd., 1933, pp. 171–205, and also my own "Innovations and the Irregularity of Economic Cycles," *Review of Economic Statistics*, Vol. 28, May, 1946, pp. 95–104.

[5] *Economica*, Vol. 5 (New Series), May, 1938, pp. 164–176.

may avoid another shortcoming of linear theory—the requirement that the upswing be essentially the same type of thing as the downswing. With nonlinear theory we may make the depression as different from the boom as we wish; in fact this is one way of assessing the degree of nonlinearity.

I shall proceed in order of increasing difficulty, taking up a series of models which are all variants of the simple multiplier and accelerator principles. The first is a threshold oscillator in which the economy once started up continues until it removes the capital deficiency which started it, and then it goes down until it removes the excess capacity with which it started downward. The second model introduces a simple linear trend (which is more important to nonlinear systems than to linear) which makes it unnecessary to await the wearing out of all the capital from the preceding boom before beginning the coming one. A third model consists of a combination of a dynamical accelerator and a less crude form of the nonlinear accelerator. This gives a more complicated evolution, but it still contains sudden shifts from declining to rising income and the reverse. This unreality is eliminated in the final model by taking account of the lag between investment decisions and the resulting outlays.

THE SIMPLEST MODEL

The central difficulty with the acceleration principle is that it assumes that actual, realized capital stock is maintained at the desired relation with output. We know in reality that it is seldom so, there being now too much and now too little capital stock. For this there are two good reasons. The rate of investment is limited by the capacity of the investment goods industry. Furthermore, entrepreneurial expectations are such that, even if it were possible to expand plant in the boom, there would be a great resistance to it. At the other extreme there is an even more inescapable and effective limit. Machines, once made, cannot be unmade, so that negative investment is limited to attrition from wear, from time, and from innovations. Therefore, capital stock cannot be increased fast enough in the upswing, nor decreased fast enough in the downswing, so that at one time we have shortages and rationing of orders and at the other excess capacity with idle plants and machines.

Call k capital stock, ξ the desired capital stock (proportional to income or output), c consumption, y income, and α, β, and κ constants. Then, with a linear consumption function,

$$(1) \qquad \xi = \kappa y,$$

$$(2) \qquad c = \alpha y + \beta,$$

$$(3) \qquad y = c + \dot{k},$$

where $\dot{k}$ is dk/dt, the rate of change in capital stock and, hence, net investment. I shall assume that the economy seeks the perfect adjustment of capital to output and that it does so in either of two extreme ways, capacity output of investment goods or zero gross investment. If actual capital equals desired capital, no adjustment is necessary and capital is simply maintained with zero net investment. When the stock of capital, k, is insufficient, the rate of investment, $\dot{k}$, proceeds at capac-

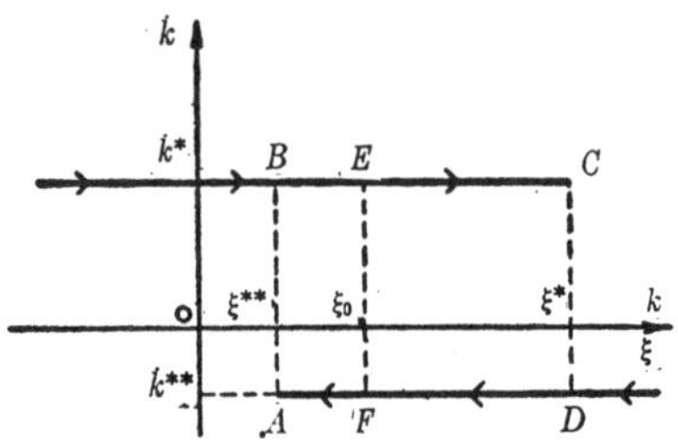

FIGURE 1—Simplest limit cycle in phase space.

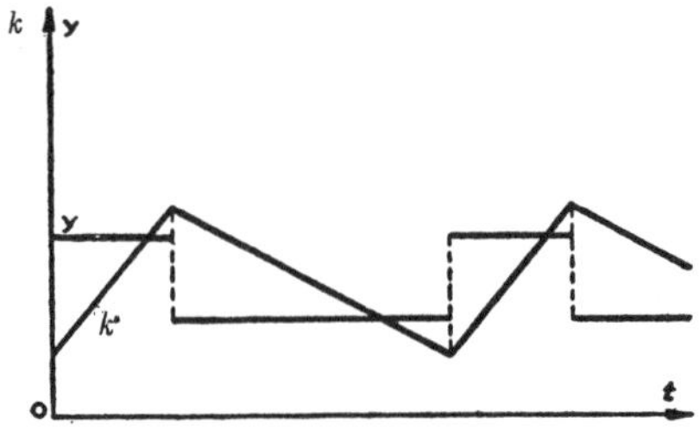

FIGURE 2—Time series for simplest model.

ity, $\dot{k}^*$, and when it is in excess, it is retired by scrapping at a rate, $\dot{k}^{**}$, so that

$$\dot{k} = \begin{cases} \dot{k}^*, & \xi > k, \\ 0, & \xi = k, \\ \dot{k}^{**}, & \xi < k. \end{cases} \tag{4}$$

Combining (1), (2), (3), and (4) we have

$$\xi = \frac{\kappa}{1-\alpha}\dot{k} + \frac{\kappa\beta}{1-\alpha},$$

which gives ξ^*, ξ_0, ξ^{**} upon substitution of the corresponding values for $\dot{k}$. ξ has therefore only three possible values because it is linearly related to $\dot{k}$, which has only three by hypothesis.

If we plot this system in phase space we get the picture given in Figure 1. By contrast, a linear system would be a single straight line sloping upward to the right. The arrows indicate the direction of movement. The point ξ_0 is an equilibrium point ($k = \xi$ and consequently $\dot{k} = 0$) and satisfies the relationships defining the system. It is, however, an unstable equilibrium, since a small displacement in the phase plane leads to a large displacement from which it never returns. For example, if to ξ_0 we add $\Delta\xi$, then $\dot{k}$ changes from zero to $\dot{k}^*$ and ξ becomes ξ^*, and hence we are transferred to a point near E in the phase diagram. From there we travel continuously to C, at which point the system exhibits discontinuous change in $\dot{k}$. At C, $k = \xi$, which means $\dot{k}$ drops to zero, but that makes $\xi = \xi_0 < k$; hence $\dot{k} = 0$ is not a possible value and $\dot{k}^{**}$ is required. Thus the representative point in the phase plane jumps discontinuously from C to D and then travels continuously at a much slower pace, to A, where it jumps, for the opposite reasons, to B and thence to C, and so on indefinitely. Therefore we arrive at the limit cycle $ABCD$, and it is always the same cycle no matter where we start. The time series of k and y corresponding to the limit cycle are shown in Figure 2. For any initial stock of capital we get a determinate path for all subsequent time. To the left of B we travel on the top line, to the right of D on the bottom one. Between these two limits we have to specify not only the stock of capital but also whether it is increasing or decreasing since, as in any oscillation, the same quantity position must be traversed twice, once going up and once coming down. It is to be noted that very rapid changes are possible in investment but are quite impossible in the stock of capital. Hence, whenever the system reaches an impasse of any sort, the necessary discontinuity (which may be taken as an idealization of a very rapid change) must occur in $\dot{k}$, not in k.

It would be difficult to imagine a cruder or more oversimplified model of the business cycle, but it does serve to illustrate clearly the general characteristics of nonlinear oscillators:

A. The final result is independent of the initial conditions.

B. The oscillation maintains itself without the need of any outside "factors" to help in the explanation. In this sense it is a complete, self-contained theory.

C. The equilibrium is unstable and therefore the mechanism starts itself given even the smallest disturbance. Yet in spite of this instability it is a usable theory because the mechanism does not explode or break down but is kept within limits by the nonlinearity.

D. No questionable lags are introduced. The mechanism operates by its own structure.

While such a crude model cannot claim to be a representation of actual cycles, it does have many of the basic characteristics (as opposed to the refinements) of the picture of cycles that economists have agreed on. In particular, its nature is such that when there is heavy investment, businessmen desire more capital than they have and when there is no investment, they have too much capital. Yet neither of these apparently circular and hence self-sustaining conditions can persist indefinitely because of an *inherent* dynamical contradiction. The boom generates its own ruin by fulfilling its purpose, and the depression brings about its own cure by removing the source of its being. One striking shortcoming of the mechanism is its tendency to spend much more of its time in depression than in boom, since capital can be built much more rapidly than it is worn out. Our mechanism gets rid, during depression, of all the capital created during the boom. Clearly, any account of growth will change this and remove the shortcoming.

TECHNOLOGICAL PROGRESS

To make a crude allowance for technological progress, we may assume a steady growth in the desired amount of capital. Altering (1) accordingly, we get

(1a) $$\xi = at + \kappa y; \qquad \dot{\xi} = a,$$

where t is time and a the constant growth rate in the capital requirements. Keeping the other relations (2), (3), (4), we find that, as might be expected, no equilibrium exists, since $\dot{k} = 0$ means that k is constant

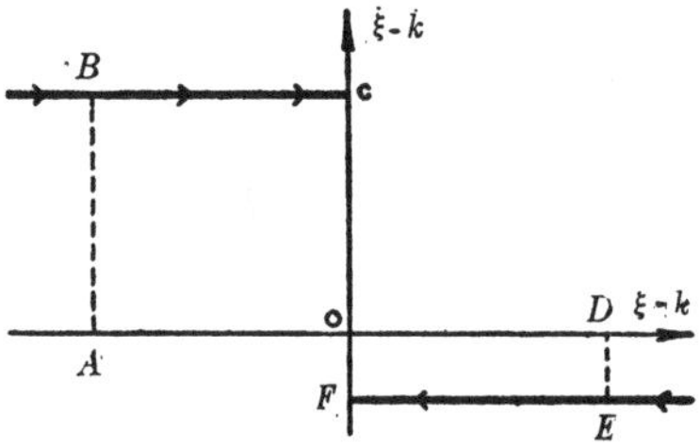

FIGURE 3—Phase diagram with steady growth.

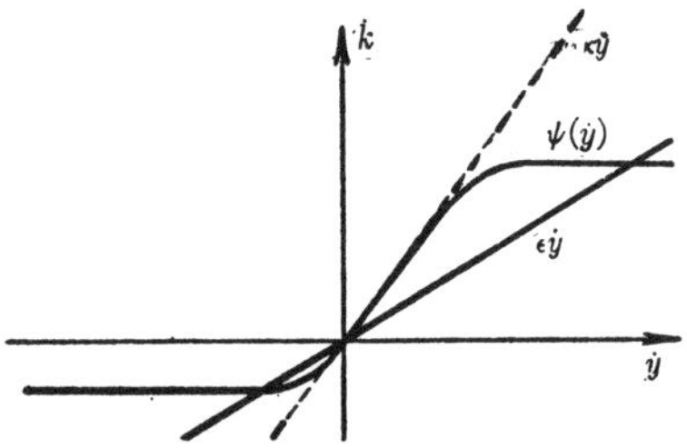

FIGURE 4—The nonlinear accelerator-multiplier.

and hence that ξ would become greater than k and hence that $\dot{k}$ would cease to be zero.

Desired capital, ξ, depends on time and on the level of income, and hence

$$\xi = \begin{cases} at + \xi^*, & \xi - k > 0; \\ at + \xi^{**}, & \xi - k < 0. \end{cases}$$

It is more convenient to plot $\dot{\xi} - \dot{k}$ against $\xi - k$, as is done in Figure 3. $\dot{\xi}$ is always equal to a except at the points of discontinuity, whereas $\dot{k}$ has two values, $\dot{k}^*$ and $\dot{k}^{**}$. If a is greater than $\dot{k}^*$, the economy can never catch up with its capital needs. Excluding this unrealistic case, we find that in boom the economy proceeds slowly along the path EF, gradually catching up with its requirements (desired capital, ξ, is greater than actual capital stock, k). When enough capital has been accumulated ($\xi = k$), investment ceases, but this means a great fall in income and hence capital requirements, so that decumulation begins. Hence we *add* to $\dot{\xi} = a$ the *negative* net investment $\dot{k}^{**}$, and hence (with $k > \xi$)

we proceed rapidly along the line *BC*—rapidly because excess capacity is being eliminated both through failure to replace and the steady occurrence of capital-using innovations. The distance *AO* is equal to *OD* since in each case the distance from the origin represents the jump in the value of ξ consequent upon a shift from $\dot{k}^*$ to $\dot{k}^{**}$ or vice versa. But while ξ shifts by the difference between ξ^* and ξ^{**}, k does not alter at the time of shift. Given any initial value of $\xi - k$, the path of the system is uniquely determined. If the mechanism was not already oscillating, it will, in the course of one motion, commence to vibrate on the closed cycle *BCEFBC*, and so on indefinitely in the absence of a change from "outside."

In addition to the characteristics of the first example, this one has certain other important aspects:

A. So long as there is technological progress, it has no equilibrium point; it can never settle down, even for a moment. It strains to get to its equilibrium point, but once there it relaxes, and that relaxation means that so much capital is no longer needed. Then it strains to slough off the excess capital, which, once eliminated, changes the situation again.

B. The depression is almost certain to be shorter than the boom and in any case is not symmetrical with it. The relative length of the two phases depends entirely on the rate of secular progress.

C. There is secular progress with capital accumulation.

D. The mode of action of this progress has considerable affinity with the Schumpeterian theory of innovations. New ideas requiring investment occur regularly, but nonetheless investment goes by spurts. Thus one of the most fundamental aspects of nonlinear oscillators is demonstrated: they are frequency converters. A steady change (zero frequency) is converted into a fluctuating motion with a positive frequency, or period.

E. In the simplest possible way, autonomous and induced investments are combined.

By virtue of its simplicity, this model has great flexibility. We may consider any variable rate of progress that we wish by taking short periods of constant rates of progress but allowing the rate to be different in each short space of time. In this manner we may easily introduce an historical element, prolonging or shortening the boom or depression according to the actually realized rate of progress.

THE DYNAMICAL MULTIPLIER AND THE NONLINEAR ACCELERATOR

There are two directions in which we may soften the crudities of the theory. The first is by considering the dynamical operation of the multiplier and the second by doing the same for investment decisions and outlays (to be taken up only in the next section). The use of the instantaneous multiplier introduces a quite unreal and unnecessary awkwardness, while clarifying and simplifying the problem. It is certain that the process of multiplication takes time, and in any dynamical situation it is important to take this into account. I propose to do this by replacing equations (2) and (3) by

$$y = \alpha y + \beta + \dot{k} - \epsilon \dot{y}. \tag{5}$$

This is a multiplier, with a lag introduced by $\epsilon\dot{y}$, where ϵ is analogous to the lag in the usual time period analysis.[6] If we rewrite (5) in the form,

$$y = \frac{1}{1 - \alpha} (\beta + \dot{k} - \epsilon \dot{y}),$$

we see that it states that income is the multiplier value of investment plus consumer injections less a kind of saving or disinvestment (it can be interpreted as either) resulting from a changing level of income.

The investment, $\dot{k}$, consists of an autonomous part, $l(t)$, and an induced part, φ. About induced investment we may make the less crude (than the previous one) assumption that the acceleration principle ($\xi = \kappa y$) holds over some middle range but passes to complete inflexibility at either extreme, as is shown in Figure 4. The upper limit is the $\dot{k}^*$ of the previous models and the lower limit the $\dot{k}^{**}$. $d\varphi(\dot{y})/d\dot{y}$ is equal to the acceleration coefficient, κ, in its middle range and zero (or some quite small value) at either extremity. If we let

$$\psi(\dot{y}) = \varphi(\dot{y}) - \epsilon \dot{y}, \tag{6}$$

it will have the shape shown in Figure 5 when it is merely "multiplied" by $1/(1 - \alpha)$. It is assumed that $d\varphi(0)/d\dot{y}$ is greater than ϵ. If, for the moment, we measure y in deviations from its (dis-) equilibrium value, we may ignore β and l. Thus we get the result shown in Figure 5 which represents the equation

$$y = \frac{1}{1 - \alpha} \psi(\dot{y}). \tag{5a}$$

Thus for every value of y we can find whether it is increasing or decreasing and by how much. Therefore, once we specify an initial income, its whole subsequent evolution is determined.

We find that there is an equilibrium point, E, at the origin, but that it is unstable, as indicated by the arrows. Therefore, a small change in outside conditions leads, for example, to explosive growth to A, where

[6] Cf. my paper, "Secular and Cyclical Aspects of the Multiplier and the Accelerator," in *Employment, Income, and Public Policy*, Essays in Honor of Alvin H. Hansen, New York: W. W. Norton and Co., 1948, pp. 108–132.

the development becomes untenable with a discontinuous change in $\dot{y}$ to point B. And thence to C to D to A, and so forth, so that we have a closed path constituting a self-sustaining cycle.

The points A and C are critical points and there one of the variables suffers a discontinuous jump. Which variable can only be decided in terms of knowledge about the variables involved. In our case it is clearly $\dot{y}$ and not y, which is analogous to the jump from $\dot{k}^*$ to $\dot{k}^{**}$. The discontinuity should be considered as an approximation to a rapid change. That there must be a jump can be deduced from the two facts that (a) the point, representative of the economy, must be on the curve, and (b) it must follow the direction of the arrows.

The model abstracts from secular progress, and by taking account of it we escape the peculiarity that the model spends more of its time in

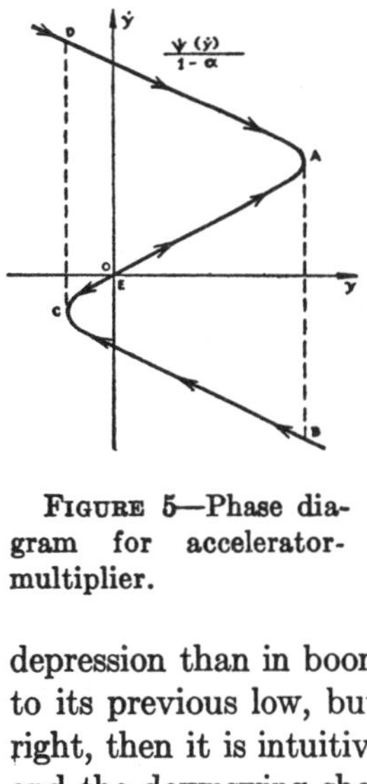

FIGURE 5—Phase diagram for accelerator-multiplier.

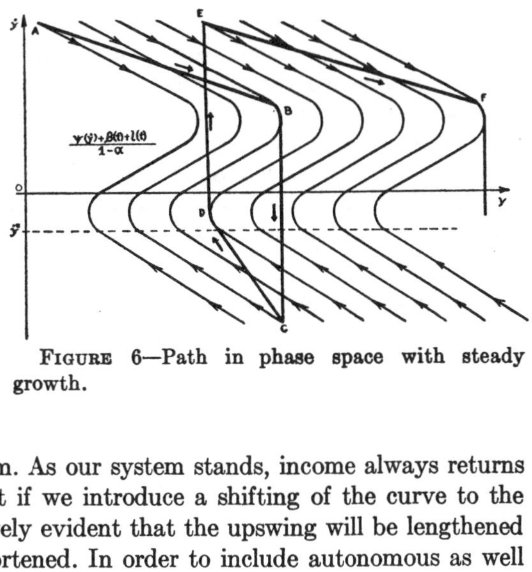

FIGURE 6—Path in phase space with steady growth.

depression than in boom. As our system stands, income always returns to its previous low, but if we introduce a shifting of the curve to the right, then it is intuitively evident that the upswing will be lengthened and the downswing shortened. In order to include autonomous as well as induced investment we must rewrite (5a) as

$$y = \frac{\psi(\dot{y})}{1-\alpha} + \frac{\beta(t)}{1-\alpha} + \frac{l(t)}{1-\alpha}, \tag{5b}$$

where $l(t)$ is the historically given investment outlay, which does not depend on output and which may be roughly associated with innovations and governmental injections of purchasing power. As an interesting, though not essential, refinement, we may say that $l(t)$ is identically zero whenever $\dot{y}$ is below some negative threshold value, indicated as $\dot{y}^*$ in Figure 6. $\beta(t)$ is the historically given upward drift of the consumption function. This may be associated with rising population (because a given level of output means ever greater numbers of unemployed, all of whom consume without income) and with the accumulation of capital leading to greater *fixed*, short-run outlays of business. It is also possible to regard the long-run consumption function (with β as zero) as basic and the short-run one as a deviation from it depending on the previous high income.[7] The graphical technique is somewhat more complicated (the ψ curve is elongated in the upper phases of the boom) but the results are otherwise much the same. For simplicity of exposition only, I shall take the simple case of a steady increase in $\beta(t)$ and an $l(t)$ irregularly positive in boom and zero in deep depression. The effect of any increase in β and l is to translate the $\psi(\dot{y})$ curve to the right by the multiplier value of the current rates of outlay which they represent.

The resulting trajectory is no longer a closed curve, which merely expresses the fact that it is an evolutionary and not a stationary economy. It goes from A to B to C to D to E to F, and so on. The most important formal result is that the boom is lengthened and the depression shortened, thus avoiding the unrealistic behavior that the depression would otherwise have to last long enough to wear out all the capital constructed in the boom. It is possible to construct a good approximation to the trajectory in this phase space for any arbitrary $l(t)$. Thus every cycle may be (and certainly will be) different in shape and duration. Large innovational outlays lengthen the boom and carry it further. On the other hand, if there is only induced investment the upswing will not last so long. If innovational outlays commence early in the depression they will shorten it but not (unless very large) stop it. But, coming late in the depression, they may well reverse the downward motion of income; it is this case which is shown in Figure 6. Should no innovational outlays occur, the depression may drag out for a long time.

By graphical integration from Figure 6, we may determine the behavior of national income over time. The rate of growth of income is greatest at the beginning of the boom and then declines somewhat but not to zero. It changes at the peak to a decline, first great and then ever milder. The kind of behavior implied is shown roughly in Figure 7

EXPANDED MODEL WITH INVESTMENT LAG

The second lag that must be considered in order to come closer to reality is the lag between decisions to invest and the corresponding outlays. We may say that outlays will tend to lag behind decisions by

[7] Cf. James S. Duesenberry, *Income, Saving, and the Theory of Consumer Behavior*, Cambridge, Mass.: Harvard University Press, 1949, 128 pp.; and Franco Modigliani, "Fluctuations in the Savings-Income Ratio: A Problem in Economic Forecasting," in *Studies of Income and Wealth*, Vol. XI, New York: National Bureau of Economic Research, 1949, pp. 371–438.

approximately one half the length of time required for fabrication, which is longer than the time required for consumption goods. Therefore we may say

$$O_I(t + \theta) \approx O_D(t) = \varphi[\dot{y}(t)],$$

where O_I equals investment outlays, O_D investment decisions, and θ is one half the construction time of new equipment. Hence equation (5) is more correctly written as

$$\epsilon\dot{y}(t + \theta) + (1 - \alpha)y(t + \theta) = O_A(t + \theta) + \varphi[\dot{y}(t)], \tag{5c}$$

where O_A stands for the sum of the autonomous outlays β and l. Expanding the two leading terms in a Taylor series and dropping all but the fist two terms in each, we get

$$\epsilon\dot{y} + \epsilon\theta\ddot{y} + (1 - \alpha)y + (1 - \alpha)\theta\dot{y} - \varphi(\dot{y}) = O_A(t + \theta), \tag{5d}$$

where $\dot{y} = dy/dt$ and $\ddot{y} = d^2y/dt^2$. Or, shifting our autonomous injections by θ time units and calling it O^*, we get

$$\epsilon\theta\ddot{y} + [\epsilon + (1 - \alpha)\theta]\dot{y} - \varphi(\dot{y}) + (1 - \alpha)y = O^*(t). \tag{5e}$$

For the moment we may take $O^*(t)$ to be a constant, O^*. Then we may study deviations from the equilibrium income $O^*/(1 - \alpha)$ by substituting

$$z = y - O^*/(1 - \alpha),$$

which gives us

$$\epsilon\theta\ddot{z} + [\epsilon + (1 - \alpha)\theta]\dot{z} - \varphi(\dot{z}) + (1 - \alpha)z = 0. \tag{5f}$$

If $d\varphi(0)/d\dot{z} < \epsilon + (1 - \alpha)\theta$, we get damped oscillations, and if it is considerably less, we get nonoscillatory stable motion. In these cases we may write a linear approximation by taking $d\varphi(0)/d\dot{z}$ as a constant, and thus we will get a valid representation for small motions around the equilibrium point. But if $d\varphi(0)/d\dot{z} > \epsilon + (1 - \alpha)\theta$, which there is good reason to suppose to be the case, the system explodes beyond the limited region of valid linear approximation. Then we must resort to the Poincaré-Liénard method of graphical integration.[8] First, however, (5f) must be reduced to a dimensionless form. Let

$$\psi(\dot{z}) = [\epsilon + (1 - \alpha)\theta]\dot{z} - \varphi(\dot{z}),$$

[8] A particularly lucid and illuminating account of the entire subject, as well as of the Liénard construction, may be found in Ph. Le Corbeiller, "The Non-Linear Theory of the Maintenance of Oscillations," *Journal of the Institution of Electrical Engineers*, London, Vol. 79, September, 1936, pp. 361–378. A good account of the general methods employed in this, as well as of a much wider range of topics, will be found in the English translation, already referred to, of the important work of the two Russian scientists, Andronow and Chaikin.

$$x = \sqrt{(1-\alpha)/\epsilon\theta}\, z/\dot{z}_0,$$
$$\dot{x} = dx/dt_1 = \dot{z}/\dot{z}_0,$$
$$\ddot{x} = d^2x/dt_1^2,$$
$$t_1 = \sqrt{(1-\alpha)/\epsilon\theta}\, t.$$

$\dot{z}_0$ is any convenient unit in which to measure velocity. Noting that

$$\ddot{z} = \dot{z}_0 \frac{d^2x}{dt_1\, dt} = \dot{z}_0 \sqrt{\frac{1-\alpha}{\epsilon\theta}} \frac{d^2x}{dt_1^2},$$

we may substitute these new variables in (5f), which becomes, after simplification,

(7) $$\ddot{x} + \frac{\psi(\dot{z}_0\dot{x})}{\dot{z}_0\sqrt{\epsilon\theta(1-\alpha)}} + x = 0.$$

Letting

(7a) $$\mathrm{X}(\dot{x}) = \frac{\psi(\dot{z}_0\dot{x})}{\dot{z}_0\sqrt{\epsilon\theta(1-\alpha)}},$$

we get

(7b) $$\ddot{x} + \mathrm{X}(\dot{x}) + x = 0.$$

An illuminating way to regard this is to write it as

(7c) $$\ddot{x} + [\mathrm{X}(\dot{x})/\dot{x}]\dot{x} + x = 0,$$

where the expression in square brackets may be regarded as a variable damping coefficient. As is well known, a positive coefficient leads to an attenuating cycle and a negative one to an exploding cycle. $\mathrm{X}(\dot{x})$ differs only in scale from $\psi(\dot{y})$, and therefore $\mathrm{X}(\dot{x})/\dot{x}$ has the general form shown in Figure 8. Consequently the system oscillates with increasing violence in the central region, but as it expands into the outer regions, it enters more and more into an area of positive damping with a growing tendency to attenuation. It is intuitively clear that it will settle down to such a motion as will just balance the two tendencies, although proof requires the rigorous methods developed by Poincaré. It is interesting to note that this is how the problem of the maintenance of oscillation was originally conceived by Lord Rayleigh and that our equation is of the Rayleigh, rather than the van der Pol, type. The result is that we get, instead of a stable equilibrium, a stable motion. This concept is the more general one, for a stable equilibrium point may be considered as a stable motion so small that it degenerates into a point. Perfectly general conditions for the stability of motion are complicated and difficult to formulate, but what we can say is that any curve of the general shape of $X(\dot{x})$ [or $\psi(\dot{y})$] will give rise to a *single*, *stable* limit cycle. Of another equation mathematically equivalent to ours, Andronow and Chaikin say: "Thus while there is no convenient method for solving van der Pol's equation, it is known that: (a) there is a unique periodic solution and it is stable; (b) every solution tends asymptotically to the periodic solution. These two properties manifestly provide most valuable practical information."[9] Therefore, making only assumptions acceptable to most business cycle theorists, along with two simple approximations, we have been able to arrive at a stable, cyclical motion which is self-generating and self-perpetuating.

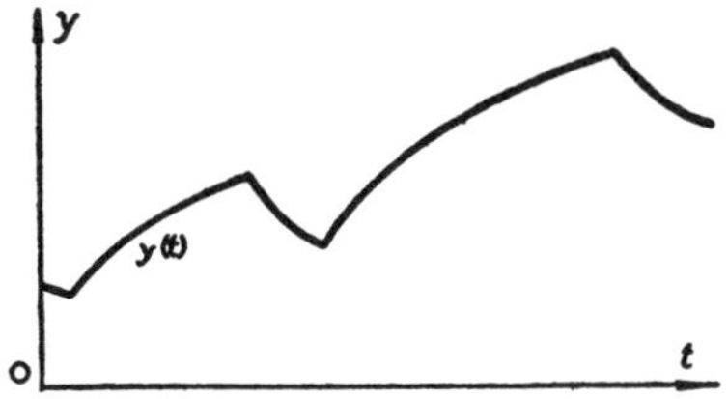

FIGURE 7—Time series with steady growth.

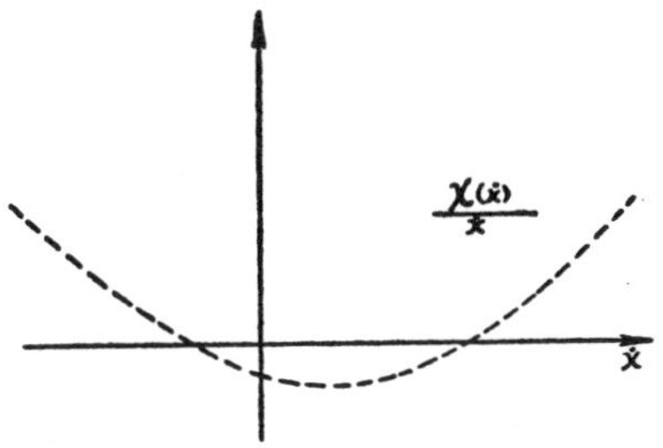

FIGURE 8—The variable damping coefficient.

For performing the graphical integration it is convenient, letting $v = \dot{x}$, to rewrite (7b) as

$$v \frac{dv}{dx} + X(v) + x = 0. \tag{7d}$$

Thus we have an extremely simple, nonlinear, first order, differential equation, which may easily (the Liénard method makes it truly easy) be integrated graphically, provided we have an empirically given $X(v)$ curve. $X(v)$ need not be expressible in any simple mathematical form, although some approximation, say by a cubic expression, does facilitate qualitative discussion of the type of system. In our case we have only a very rough idea of the X function, which we may derive from the structural parameters, ϵ, θ, α, and the acceleration coefficient operative when there is no excess capacity. Regarding these parameters we have but a crude idea of their order of magnitude, nothing more. In estimating the fabrication period (twice the time lag) of consumption goods we must remember that it includes not only the time required to make any one article but also the raw materials that go to make it, and those that go to make the raw materials, and so on. If we replace all this by a single hypothetical firm producing consumption goods, we

[9] Andronow and Chaikin, *op. cit.*, pp. 4 and 302 ff.

must make the assumption of a fairly long fabrication time, say one-half to one and one-half years. Taking the mean of this range, we might put the time at one and hence ϵ at 0.5. Professor Frisch estimated the fabrication time for capital goods on the average at three years, and I shall take it to be two, which makes θ equal to 1.0. There is good evidence that in the course of the cycle α is around 0.6.[10] The acceleration coefficient is the ratio of national capital to national income, which was around 4.0 for Britain in the 1930's and was undoubtedly of this

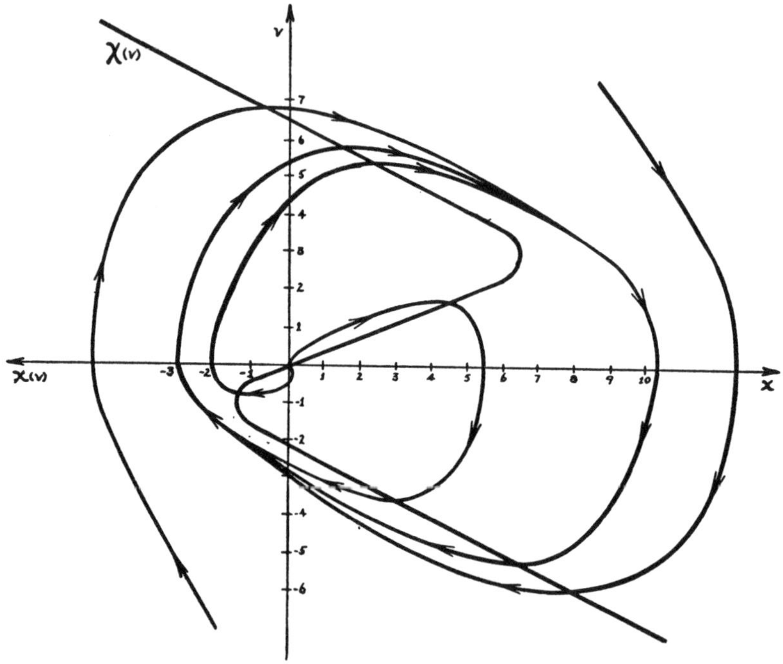

FIGURE 9—Phase portrait of the accelerator-multiplier with investment lag.

order of magnitude for the United States, although accurate statistics are still lacking. There is no doubt, however, that the marginal coefficient operative in a boom is much smaller. I shall assume that the slope of $\varphi(\dot{y})$ (the acceleration coefficient, κ) is 2.0 in the middle range and zero at either end. There remains only to determine the possible

[10] For simplicity I choose to ignore the thesis of Professors Duesenberry and Modigliani that the marginal propensity to consume has different values according to the recent past levels of income. But it is interesting to note that such hereditary effects (level dependent on path) have few terrors here since analytic solutions are impossible and graphical or arithmetical methods are used in any case.

limits of net annual investment. From Kuznets' data for the great boom and depression, these might be placed at -3.0 and $+9.0$ billions of dollars per year.

In Figure 9 is given the Poincaré limit cycle for the foregoing values of parameters. Also represented are four possible phase trajectories, starting from arbitrary initial conditions and approaching asymptotically the unique limit cycle. All points in the phase plane represent pairs of initial conditions, the vertical axis giving the initial velocities and the horizontal axis the initial levels of income (in deviations from some steady level). Through every point in the phase plane passes a single trajectory, which leads ultimately to the one limiting motion. In Figure 9 we have velocity as a function of income, and hence, by a second graphical integration, we can get income as a function of time for the undisturbed or limiting cyclical form. The range of fluctuation

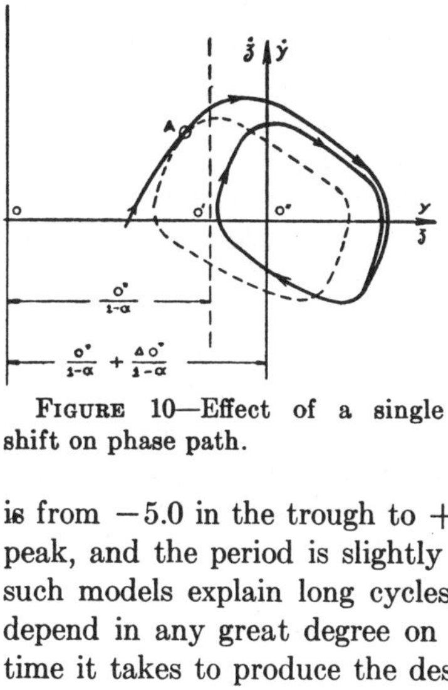

FIGURE 10—Effect of a single shift on phase path.

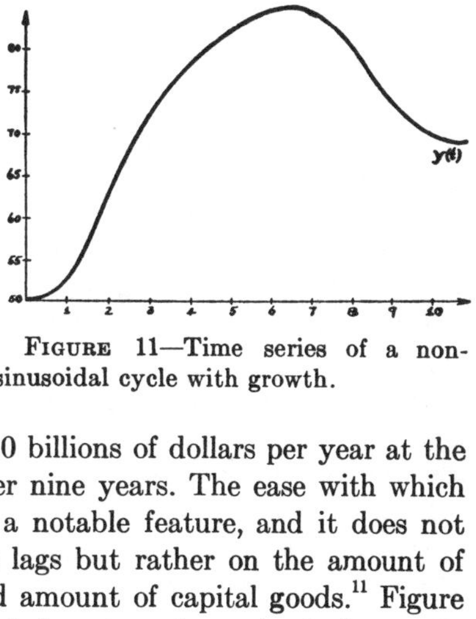

FIGURE 11—Time series of a non-sinusoidal cycle with growth.

is from -5.0 in the trough to $+19.0$ billions of dollars per year at the peak, and the period is slightly over nine years. The ease with which such models explain long cycles is a notable feature, and it does not depend in any great degree on the lags but rather on the amount of time it takes to produce the desired amount of capital goods.[11] Figure 9 also gives an idea of the extent of departure from simple harmonic motion as represented by a sine curve. The closed phase diagram for a sine curve is a circle, whereas this phase diagram is very uncircular. The upswing gets under way more quickly and the high level of activity is held longer than with a sine curve. The upper turning point is followed by a rapid decline and a tendency to remain longer at a depressed

[11] This can be seen perhaps more clearly in the model without time lags which I have presented in Chapter XXI of *Business Cycles and National Income* (New York: W. W. Norton and Co., 1950) by Alvin H. Hansen. There I have also indicated how we may take general full employment rather than full employment in the investment goods trades as our upward limiting factor.

level. In spite of the obvious asymmetry of $X(v)$, the two phases have approximately the same duration, a little more than four years being spent in the region of increasing income and a little more than four and one-half years with decreasing income. Our model is, however, of an unprogressive economy in which income and capital always return to their previous lows. In a progressive society the limit cycle would shift irregularly to the right and the representative point would pursue it in a complicated spiral to the right. We can see this by considering a single shift to the right brought about by an increase in O^* to $O^* + \Delta O^*$, as shown in Figure 10. The origin for y is O and the origin for z is O'; the previous steady regime is given by the broken contour and the new one by the solid one. The representative point will be at some point, say A, on the broken contour at the moment of the shift. This then specifies the initial conditions (level and rate of change) for a transient motion towards the new regime. We may consider a continual, regular or irregular, shifting to the right so long as it is not too rapid as compared with the undisturbed motion (i.e., adiabatic change).

Plotted roughly in Figure 11 is the resulting time series of income from a steady shifting (about 3% per year) to the right of the limit cycle. We see that the upswing is prolonged to 6.5 years and the downswing shortened to 4.2 years. The whole cycle is moderately lengthened to 10.7 years. Income rises from 50 to 85 billions of dollars and falls back to 69. The introduction of historically given innovational outlays would make each cycle different.

Finally, it should be noted that, while I have assumed a particular shape for $\varphi(\dot{y})$, the power of the Liénard construction is shown by the fact that an equation containing any given curve may be easily integrated. Therefore, whatever sort of investment function is found actually to hold, that type may be completely analyzed in its cyclical functioning. If we look closely into this problem, we find that what is really necessary is to take individual account of many different industries because, while one industry may still have excess capacity, another may be short of fixed capital. Therefore, the combined operation may depend as much on the points at which different industries fire into investment activity as on the actual shape of the X function for each industry or any conceivable aggregation of all of them. Thus we will have a kind of propagation of an impulse through an industry space with the (possibly quite slow) staggered responses of the various industries, with a resultant sluggishly cumulative boom.

Harvard University

[14]

THE SUMMATION OF RANDOM CAUSES AS THE SOURCE OF CYCLIC PROCESSES*

By Eugen Slutzky

I. SCOPE OF THE INVESTIGATION

Almost all of the phenomena of economic life, like many other processes, social, meteorological, and others, occur in sequences of rising and falling movements, like waves. Just as waves following each other on the sea do not repeat each other perfectly, so economic cycles never repeat earlier ones exactly either in duration or in amplitude. Nevertheless, in both cases, it is almost always possible to detect, even in the multitude of individual peculiarities of the phenomena, marks of certain approximate uniformities and regularities. The eye of the observer instinctively discovers on waves of a certain order other smaller waves, so that the idea of harmonic analysis, viz., that of the possibility of expressing the irregularities of the form and the spacing of the waves by means of the summation of regular sinusoidal fluctuations, presents itself to the mind almost spontaneously. If the results of the analysis happen sometimes not to be completely satisfactory, the discrepancies usually will be interpreted as casual deviations superposed on the regular waves. If the analyses of the first and of the second halves of a series give considerably divergent results (such as, for example, were found by Schuster while analyzing sunspot periodicity),[1] it is, even then, possible to find the solution without giving up the basic concept. Such a discrepancy may be the result of the interference of certain factors checking the continuous movement of the process and substituting for the former regularity a new one which sometimes may

* Professor Eugen Slutzky's paper of 1927, "The Summation of Random Causes as the Source of Cyclic Processes," *Problems of Economic Conditions*, ed. by The Conjuncture Institute, Moskva (Moscow), Vol. 3, No. 1, 1927, has in a sense become classic in the field of time-series analysis. While it does not give a complete theory of the time shape that is to be expected when a given linear operator is applied to a random (auto-non-correlated) series, it has given us a number of penetrating and suggestive ideas on this question. It has been, and will no doubt continue to be, highly stimulating for further research on this vast and—not least for business-cycle analysis—most important problem. Unfortunately Professor Slutzky's paper so far has been available only in Russian (with a brief English summary). Some years ago Professor Henry Schultz had the original article translated into English by Mr. Eugene Prostov, and suggested that it be published in Econometrica. At the request of the Editor Professor Slutzky has prepared for our Journal a revised English version with which he has incorporated also a number of important results obtained after 1927.—Editor.

[1] Arthur Schuster, "On the Periodicities of Sunspots," *Phil. Trans.*, Series A, Vol. 206, 1906, p. 76.

even happen to be of the same type as the former one. Empirical series are, unfortunately, seldom long enough to enable one definitely to prove or to refute such an hypothesis. Without dwelling on the history of complicated disputes concerning the above-mentioned problem, I will mention only two circumstances as the starting points for the present investigation—one, so to speak, in the field of chance, the other in the field of strict regularity.

One usually takes the analysis of the periodogram of the series as the basis for the discovery of hidden periodicities. Having obtained from the periodogram the values of the squares of the amplitudes of the sinusoids, calculated by the method of least squares for waves of varying length, we ask whether there is a method of determining those waves which do not arise from chance. Schuster apparently has discovered a suitable method;[2] but we must give up his criterion when we remember that among his assumptions is that of independence of the successive observations. As a general rule we find that the terms of an empirical series are not independent but correlated and at times correlated very closely. This circumstance, as is known, may very perceptibly heighten the oscillation of the derived characteristics of the series, and it is quite conceivable that waves satisfying Schuster's criterion would in fact be casual—just simulating the presence of a strict regularity.[3] Thus we are led to our basic problem: is it possible that a definite structure of a connection between random fluctuations could form them into a system of more or less regular waves? Many laws of physics and biology are based on chance, among them such laws as the second law of thermodynamics and Mendel's laws. But heretofore we have known how regularities could be derived from a chaos of disconnected elements because of the very disconnectedness. In our case we wish to consider the rise of regularity from series of chaotically-random elements because of certain connections imposed upon them.

Suppose we are inclined to believe in the reality of the strict periodicity of a business cycle, such, for example, as the eight-year period postulated by Moore.[4] Then we should encounter another difficulty. Wherein lies the source of the regularity? What is the mechanism of

[2] A. Schuster, "On the Investigation of Hidden Periodicities, etc.," *Terrestrial Magnetism*, Vol. 3, 1898.

[3] The further development of Schuster's methods, which we find in his extremely valuable paper, "The Periodogram of the Magnetic Declination as Obtained from the Records of the Greenwich Observatory during the Years 1871–1895," *Trans. of the Cambridge Philos. Soc.*, Vol. 18, 1900, p. 107, seems to overcome this difficulty. Because it is rather unfinished in mathematical respects, however, the influence of this paper seems not to have been comparable to its importance.

[4] H. L. Moore, *Generating Economic Cycles*, New York, 1923.

causality which, decade after decade, reproduces the same sinusoidal wave which rises and falls on the surface of the social ocean with the regularity of day and night. It is natural that even now, as centuries ago, the eyes of the investigators are raised to the celestial luminaries searching in them for an explanation of human affairs. One can dauntlessly admit one's right to make bold hypotheses, but still should not one try to find out other ways?[5] What means of explanation, however, would be left to us if we decided to give up the hypothesis of the superposition of regular waves complicated only by purely random components? The presence of waves of definite orders, the long waves embracing decades, shorter cycles from approximately five to ten years in length, and finally the very short waves, will always remain a fact begging for explanation. The approximate regularity of the periods is sometimes so distinctly apparent that it, also, cannot be passed by without notice. Thus, in short, *the undulatory character of the processes and the approximate regularity of the waves* are the two facts for which we shall try to find a possible source in random causes combining themselves in their common effect.

The method of the work is a combination of induction and deduction. It was possible to investigate by the deductive method only a few aspects of the problem. Generally speaking, the theory of chance waves is almost entirely a matter of the future. For the sake of this future theory one cannot be too lavish with experiments: it is experiment that shows us totally unexpected facts, thus pointing out problems which otherwise would hardly fall within the field of the investigator.[6]

II. COHERENT SERIES OF CONSEQUENCES OF RANDOM CAUSES AND THEIR MODELS

There are two kinds of chance series: (1) those in which the probability of the appearance, in a given place in the series, of a certain value of the variable, depends on previous or subsequent values of the variable, and (2) those in which it does not. In this way we distinguish

[5] A similar viewpoint is found in the remarkable work of G. U. Yule, "Why Do We Sometimes Get Nonsense-Correlations between Time Series?" *Journal of the Royal Statistical Society*, Vol. 89, 1926. This work approaches our theme rather closely.

[6] The following exposition is based on a large amount of calculation. The author expresses special gratitude to his long-time collaborator, E. N. Pomeranzeva-Ilyinskaya and also to O. V. Gordon, N. F. Rein, M. A. Smirnova and E. V. Luneyeva. The calculations were carefully checked, almost all work having been independently performed by two individuals. It is very unlikely that undetected errors are sufficiently significant to affect to any perceptible degree our final conclusions. A few errors, detected in the course of time in Tables I, III, and IX of the original paper, are noted at the end of this paper, and an error in Figure 7, B_4, has been corrected when it was re-drawn.

between *coherent*[7] and *incoherent* (or random) series. The terms of the series of this second kind are not correlated. In series in which there is correlation between terms, one of the most important characteristics is the value of the coefficient of correlation between terms, considered as a function of the distance between the terms correlated. We shall call it the *correlational function* of the corresponding series and shall limit our investigation to those cases in which the distribution of probabilities remains constant. The coefficient of correlation, then, is exclusively determined by the distance between the terms and not by their place in the series. The coefficient of correlation of each member with itself (r_0) will equal unity, and its coefficient of correlation (r_t) with the tth member following will necessarily equal its coefficient (r_{-t}) with the tth member preceding.

Any concrete instance of an experimentally obtained chance series we shall regard as a *model* of empirical processes which are structurally similar to it. As the basis of the present investigation we take three models of purely random series and call them the first, second, and third basic series. These series are based on the results obtained by the People's Commissariate of Finance in drawing the numbers of a government lottery loan. For the first basic series, we used the last digits of the numbers drawn; for the second basic series, we substituted 0 for each even digit and 1 for each odd digit; the third basic series was obtained in the same way as the second, but from another set of numbers drawn.[8]

Let us pass to the coherent series. Their origin may be extremely varied, but it seems probable that an especially prominent role is played in nature by the process of *moving summation* with weights of one kind or another; by this process coherent series are obtained from other coherent series or from incoherent series. For example, let causes $\cdots x_{i-2}, x_{i-1}, x_i, \cdots$ produce the consequences $\cdots y_{i-2}, y_{i-1}, y_i, \cdots$, where the magnitude of each consequence is determined by the influence, not of one, but of a number of the preceding causes, as for instance, the size of a crop is determined, not by one day's rainfall, but by many. If the influence of causes in retrospective order is expressed by the weights $A_0, A_1, A_2, \cdots A_{n-1}$, then we shall have

$$(1)\qquad \begin{cases} y_i = A_0x_i + A_1x_{i-1} + \cdots + A_{n-1}x_{i-(n-1)}, \\ y_{i-1} = \qquad\quad A_0x_{i-1} + \cdots + A_{n-2}x_{i-(n-1)} + A_{n-1}x_{i-n}, \\ \cdots\cdots\cdots\cdots\cdots\cdots\cdots\cdots\cdots\cdots\cdots . \end{cases}$$

[7] I venture to propose this name because it seems to me that it truly expresses what is intended, namely, the existence of some connection between the elements or parts of a thing (for example, of a series), but not a connection between this thing as a whole and another.

[8] The tables giving these series and seven others derived from them will be found in the original paper (*loc. cit.*, pp. 57–64) and are not repeated here.

Each of two adjacent consequences has one particular cause of its own, and $(n-1)$ causes in common with the other consequence. Because the consequences possess causes in common there appears between them a correlation even though the series of causes are incoherent. When all the weights are equal (*simple* moving summation) the coefficient of correlation expresses the share of the common causes in the total number of independent causes on which the consequences

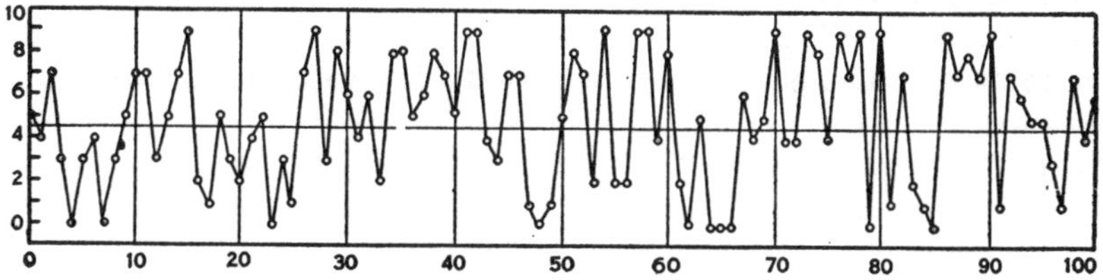

FIGURE 1.—The first 100 terms of the first basic series.

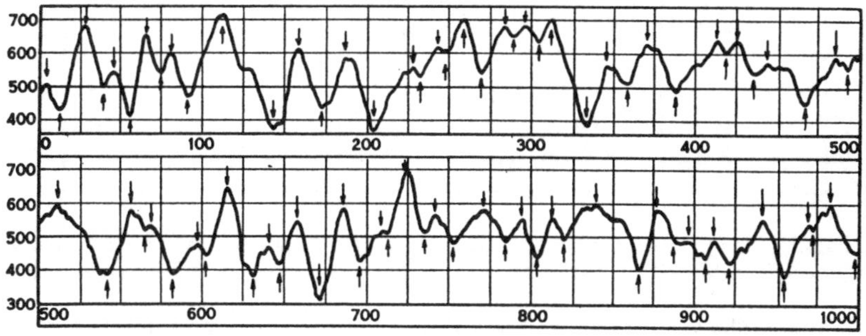

FIGURE 2.—The first 1000 terms of Model II.

depend (as has long been known from the theory of the experiment of Darbishire); then

$$r_0 = 1, r_1 = r_{-1} = \frac{n-1}{n}, r_2 = r_{-2} = \frac{n-2}{n}, \quad \cdots, r_{n-1} = r_{-(n-1)} = \frac{1}{n},$$

further coefficients being equal to zero. By taking a ten-item moving summation of the first basic series, Model I was obtained.[9] A small section of Model I is plotted in Figure 3 with an index[10] of the English

[9] In addition, 5 was added to each sum. This does not change the properties of the series. Neither does it make any difference as to the method of numbering consequences in comparison with the scheme used in formula (1). At the outset of the work, it seemed to be technically more convenient to give the consequence the same number as the earliest cause and not the latest. Thus, for example, for Model I,

$$y_0 = x_0 + x_1 + x_2 + \cdots + x^9 + 5.$$

[10] Dr. Dorothy S. Thomas, "Quarterly Index of British Cycles," in W. L. Thorp, *Business Annals*, New York, 1926, p. 28.

business cycles for 1855–1877 in juxtaposition—an initial graphic demonstration of the possible effects of the summation of unconnected causes.

In turn the consequences become causes. Taking a ten-item moving summation of Model I, we obtained the 1000 numbers of Model II. Performing a two-item moving summation twelve times in succession on the third basic series,[11] we obtained the 1000 numbers of Model IVa. First and second differences of Model IVa give Models IVb and IVc respectively (See Figure 4). Furthermore, the application of scheme (1) to the second basic series gives[12] Model III if the weights used are

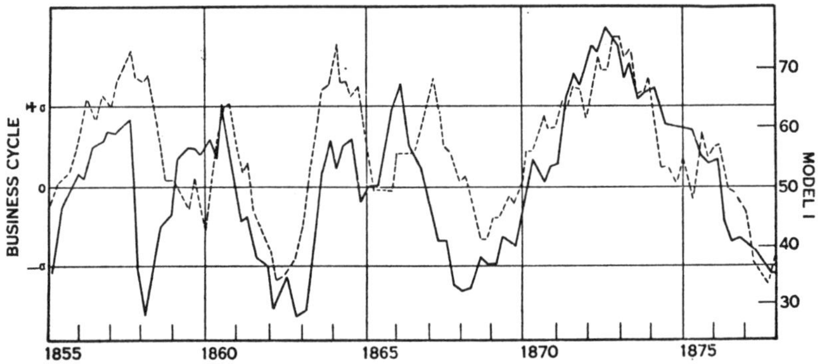

FIGURE 3.———An index of English business cycles from 1855 to 1877; scale on the left side. ------Terms 20 to 145 of Model I; scale on the right side.

10^4 times the ordinates of the Gaussian curve taken at intervals of 0.1σ. Because this model was very smooth it appeared sufficient to use only the 180 even members out of the 360 items (see Figure 11 under the numbers 0, 2, 4, $\cdots$ 358). Model IIIa—the last one—is 10^4

[11] It actually was computed by applying the scheme (1) to the third basic series with the weights 1, 12, 66, 220, 495, 792, 924, 792, $\cdots$, 12, 1, because s-fold simple summation of two items is equivalent, as can be shown easily, to direct summation with the weights $C_0^s, C_1^s, C_2^s, \cdots, C_s^s$, (where C_k^s is the number of combinations of s things taken k at a time.

[12] The exact values of Model III could be obtained by multiplying the corresponding items of the basic series by the exact values of the function $10^4 \exp\{-\frac{1}{2}(0.1t)^2\}/\sqrt{2\pi}$, for integral values of t. This function was the basis of obtaining the 4th differences of Model III. Approximate values of Model III were found by using a set of weights composed of 95 numbers corresponding to the values of the above function for integral values of t from -47 to $+47$, with the numbers less than 1 rounded off to the nearest tenth and numbers greater than 1 to whole units. The numbers of the basic series were written on a ribbon which we slid along the column of weights. Inasmuch as the basic series consisted of zeros and ones, all of the computations were plain additions. For Model IVa, a ribbon with holes in the place of unities was constructed.

times the 4th differences of the numbers of Model III from the 7th to the 97th.[13]

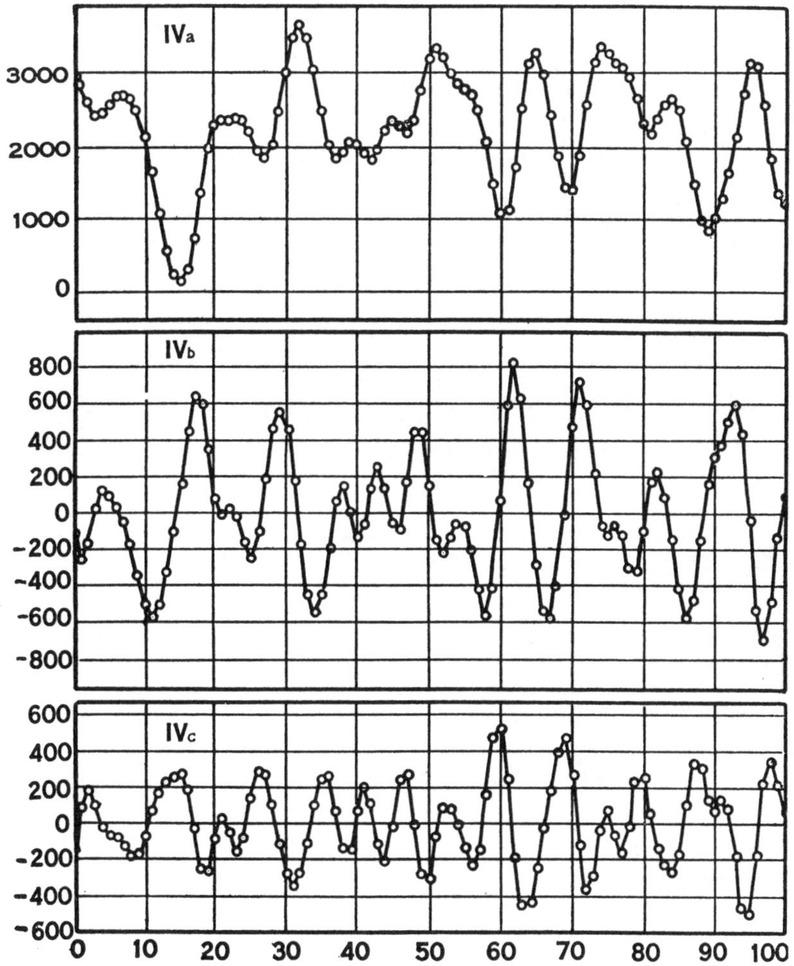

FIGURE 4.—The first 100 terms of Models IVa, IVb, and IVc.

We could not be satisfied by a smaller number of models because it was necessary to observe their various properties and to have illustra-

[13] For the calculation of these differences the accuracy with which we determined the items of Model III was not sufficient, so the following method was used: It is easy to see that the *n*th order differences of the items of the series obtained by scheme (1) are equivalent to those computed by the same scheme but applying weights equal to the differences of the original weights (keeping in mind that the series of original weights is extended at both ends with zeros).

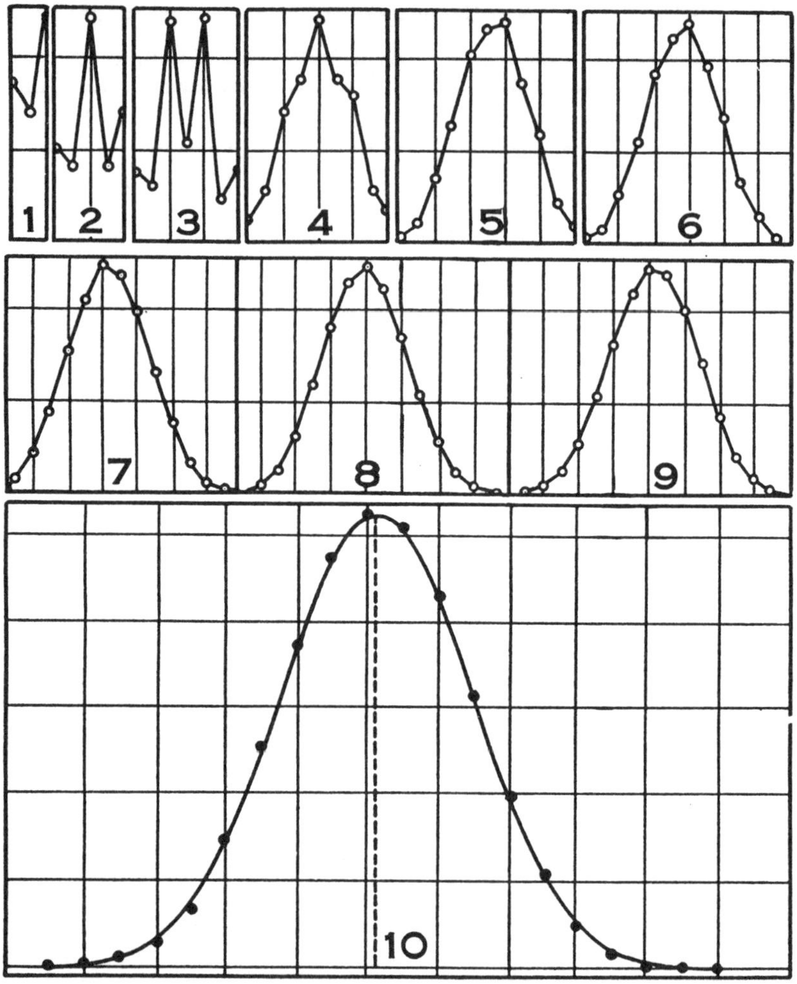

FIGURE 5.—An example of the crossing of random weights. The weights of the causes for each of 10 successive summations are shown, i.e., $A_k'^{(1)}$, $A_k'^{(2)}$, $\cdots$, $A_k'^{(10)}$. See Appendix, Section 1.

With the help of S. Pineto's *Tables de logarithmes vulgaires a dix decimales*, St. Petersburg, 1871, the values of the function

$$\exp\left\{-\tfrac{1}{2}(0.1t)^2\right\}/\sqrt{2\pi}$$

were obtained to ten decimal places for integral values of t from 0 to 44; this series was completed by using Sheppard's tables, and the differences of the entire series up to and including the 4th differences were taken. Multiplying the latter by 10^8 and expressing the result in integers, we obtained weights with the help of which—and by using scheme (1)—the values of $10^4\,\Delta^4 y_{III}$ were obtained from the second basic series.

tions for the elucidation of the different aspects of the problem. We could not aspire to imitate nature in forming a set of weights; still, in the course of the work, we have come across an exceptionally curious circumstance. First, each multifold simple summation of n items at a time gives a set of weights which approaches the Gaussian curve as a limit. In the Appendix, Section 1, there is given the instance of a tenfold summation of three items at a time with the weights chosen absolutely at random for each successive summation. The ten con-

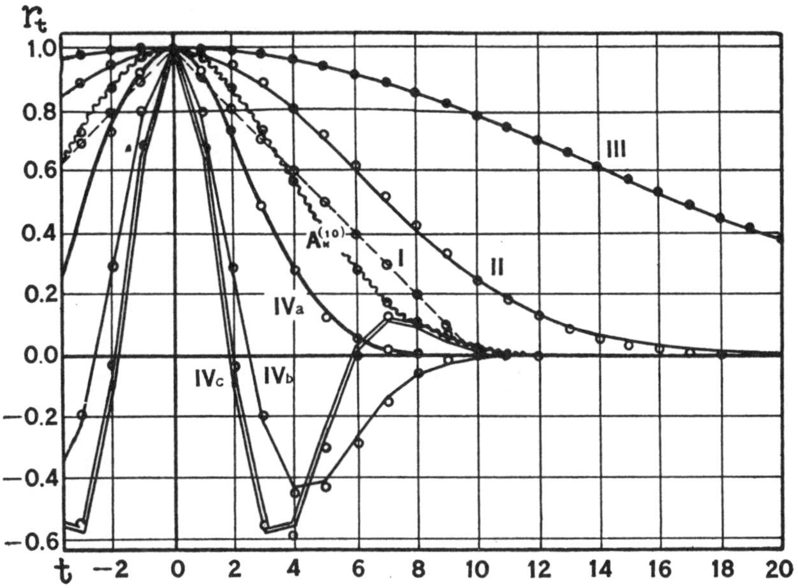

FIGURE 6.—oooo The correlational functions of Models I–IVc, and of the scheme of the crossing of the chance weights ($A_k'^{(10)}$).

} Corresponding Gaussian curves and the reduced differences of the ordinates of the Gaussian curve.

secutive sets of weights are depicted in Figure 5. It is easily seen how they gradually become more and more like the Gaussian curve, and for the tenth summation the weights approach the Gaussian curve very closely.

This is far from being a chance result. From further considerations (Appendix, Section 1) we find that we have here actually encountered a law which, under certain conditions, must necessarily realize itself in the chaos of random entanglements and crossings of endless numbers of series of causes and consequences. The problem is specially important for the reason that the correlational function of a derived series is defined entirely by the respective weights-function. It is possible to prove (see Appendix, Sections 1, 2, and 3) that if the series of weights follows the Gaussian curve, the correlational function of the resulting consequence series is capable of being expressed by a similar curve with a greater or smaller degree of approximation. For the series of consequences proportionate to the increments of the cause—that is, the differences of order k of the series of causes—the correlational function can be represented by the series of the differences (of order $2k$) of the ordinates of the Gaussian curve. It could not be by chance that the correlational function of all of our models, with the exception of the most elementary one (Model I), belong to one of the two types mentioned (see Figure 6). No exception is found in the correlational

TABLE 1

Distance between terms	Correlation coefficients with random weights	Ordinates of Gaussian curve	Differences
t	r_t	R_t	$r_t - R_t$
0	1.000	1.000	0.000
1	0.965	0.965	0.000
2	0.868	0.866	+0.002
3	0.727	0.723	+0.004
4	0.567	0.562	+0.005
5	0.410	0.407	+0.003
6	0.275	0.274	+0.001
7	0.171	0.171	0.000
8	0.097	0.100	−0.003
9	0.051	0.054	−0.003
10	0.024	0.027	−0.003
11	0.011	0.013	−0.002
12	0.004	0.006	−0.002
13	0.001	0.002	−0.001
14	0.000	0.001	−0.001

function for the series of consequences of the 10th order obtained in the course of the crossing of the random weights in the example mentioned above. The values of these correlation coefficients (r_t), together with the ordinates of the corresponding Gaussian curve (R_t), are given in Table 1 (for the calculation see Appendix, Section 2).

III. THE UNDULATORY CHARACTER OF CHANCE SERIES; GRADUALITY AND FLUENCY AS TENDENCIES

Our models, representing several sets of experiments, give an inductive proof of our first thesis, namely, *that the summation of random causes may be the source of cyclic, or undulatory processes.*[14] It is, however

[14] The definition of the business cycle as being a process (not necessarily periodic) characterized by successive rises and falls, is given by *W. C. Mitchell* in Introduction to *W. L. Thorp, Business Annals*, New York, 1926, pp. 32–33.

not difficult to determine the reason why it must be so inevitably. We shall first observe a series of independent values of a random variable. If, for the sake of simplicity, we assume that the distribution of probabilities does not change, then, for the entire series, there will exist a certain horizontal level such that the probabilities of obtaining a value either above or below it would be equal. The probability that a value, which has just passed from the positive deviation region to the negative, will remain below at the subsequent trial is $\frac{1}{2}$; the probability that it will remain below two times in succession is $\frac{1}{4}$; three times $\frac{1}{8}$; and so on. Thus the probability that the values will remain for a long time above the level or below the level is quite negligible. It is, therefore, practically certain that, for a somewhat long series, the values will pass many times from the positive deviations to the negative and vice versa. Let us designate as a *half-wave* a portion of the series in which the deviation does not change sign. Thus, for 1000 numbers of the third basic series we find 540 half-waves (instead of the theoretically expected 500). Taking from this number the first 512 half-waves we find among them a number of half-waves of the length 1,2, etc. In Table 2 the actual (n_i') and theoretical[15] (n_i) frequencies for half-waves of various lengths are shown. That the observed series is consistent with the theoretical series can be found by the câlculation of the χ^2 criterion of goodness of fit.[16]

TABLE 2

Length of half-wave	Actual frequency	Theoretical frequency
i	n'_i	n_i
1	261	256
2	137	128
3	65	64
4	29	32
5	14	16
6	4	8
7	1	4
8 and more	1	4
Total	512	512

If a variable can have more than two values and if, in a certain interval of a more or less considerable length, it happens to remain above

[15] L. von Bortkiewicz, *Die Iterationen*, 1917, Formel 75, p. 99.

[16] We find, indeed,

$$\chi^2 = \sum \frac{(n_i' - n_i)^2}{n_i} = 7.78,$$

the corresponding probability being $P = 0.35$; see *Tables for Statisticians and Biometricians*, ed. by K. Pearson, Part I, Table XII.

(or below) its general level, then in that interval it will have a temporary level about which it almost certainly will oscillate. Thus on the waves of one order there appear superimposed waves of another order.

The unconnected random waves are usually called irregular zigzags. A correlation between the items of a series deprives the waves of this characteristic and introduces into their rising and falling movements an element of *graduality*. In order to make the reasoning more concrete, let us consider a series obtained from an incoherent series by means of a ten-item moving summation. Our Model I will be used as the example. Any items of this model separated from each other by more than 9 intervals (as, for example, the values $y_0, y_{10}, y_{20}, \cdots$) are not correlated with each other and consequently form waves of the above considered type, i.e., irregular zigzags. But if we consider the entire series, we shall certainly find gradual transitions from the maximum point of a wave to its minimum and vice versa, since the correlation between neighboring items of the series makes small differences between them more probable than large ones. This we find to be true for all of our models.

We must distinguish between the *graduality* of the transitions and their *fluency*. We could speak about the absence of the latter property if a state of things existed where there would be an equal probability for either a rise or a fall after a rise as well as after a fall. If fluency were missing we should obtain waves covered by zigzags such as we find in Model I (see Figure 3).

For example, we have for Model I,

$$\begin{aligned} y_0 &= 5 + x_0 + x_1 + x_2 + \cdots + x_9, \\ y_1 &= 5 \qquad\; + x_1 + x_2 + \cdots + x_9 + x_{10}, \\ y_2 &= 5 \qquad\qquad\;\; + x_2 + \cdots + x_9 + x_{10} + x_{11}, \\ &\cdots\cdots\cdots\cdots\cdots\cdots\cdots\cdots \end{aligned}$$

from which we obtain

$$\begin{aligned} \Delta y_0 &= y_1 - y_0 = x_{10} - x_0, \\ \Delta y_1 &= y_2 - y_1 = x_{11} - x_1, \\ &\cdots\cdots\cdots\cdots \end{aligned}$$

Thus we see that the adjacent first differences do not have any causes in common, and hence are not correlated. The same applies to differences which are further apart, with the exception of such as $y_1 - y_0 = x_{10} - x_0$ and $y_{11} - y_{10} = x_{20} - x_{10}$. The series of differences is almost incoherent and hence the waves will be covered by chaotically irregular zigzags such as we find in Model I.

Let us assume further that adjacent differences are positively correlated. Then, in all probability, after a rise another rise will occur, after a fall a further fall; a steep rise will have the *tendency* to continue with the same steepness, a moderate one with the same moderateness. So small sections of a wave will tend to be straight lines; and the greater the coefficient of correlation between adjacent differences the closer the sections approximate straight lines.[17]

Correlation between second differences plays an analogous role. The greater this correlation coefficient, the greater the tendency toward the preservation of the constancy of the second differences. Over more or less considerably long intervals a series with approximately constant second differences will tend to approximate a second-degree parabola as all "good" curves do. In Table 3 are given, for Models, I, II, and III, the values of the correlation coefficients between the adjacent items of the series (r_1), between the adjacent first differences ($r_1^{(1,1)}$), and between the adjacent second differences ($r_1^{(2,2)}$). The coefficients were calculated by the formulas of the Appendix, Section 1. As we go from the first basic series to Model I and then to Models II and III, we find progressive changes in their graphic appearance (see Figures, 3, 2, 8, and 11 respectively). These changes are produced at first by the introduction and then by the growth of graduality and of fluency in the movements of the respective chance waves. The growth of the degree of correlation between items (or between their differences) as we go from the first basic series to Model I, etc. (see Table 3) corresponds to the changes in the graphic appearance of our series.

TABLE 3

Model	Coefficient of correlation between:		
	Terms	First differences	Second differences
	r_1	$r_1^{(1,1)}$	$r_1^{(2,2)}$
I	0.9	0.0	−0.5
II	0.985	0.85	0.0
III	0.9975	0.9925	0.9876

IV. EMPIRICAL EVIDENCE OF THE APPROXIMATE REGULARITY OF CHANCE WAVES

Our first thesis, that is, the demonstration of the possibility of the appearance of undulatory processes of a more or less fluent character as the result of the summation of random causes, may be considered

[17] The term *tendency* is used here in a strict sense. To each equation of regression (giving the value of the conditional mathematical expectation of a variable as a function of some other variable) there corresponds an approximate equation between the variables themselves. The closer to unity the absolute value of the coefficient of correlation lies, the greater is the probability that this functional relationship will be maintained within the limits of the desired accuracy; i.e., the stronger will be the *tendency*.

as practically proved. However, our second thesis, that is, the demonstration of *the approximate regularity of the waves,* offers considerably greater difficulties. Again we shall begin with the inductive method.

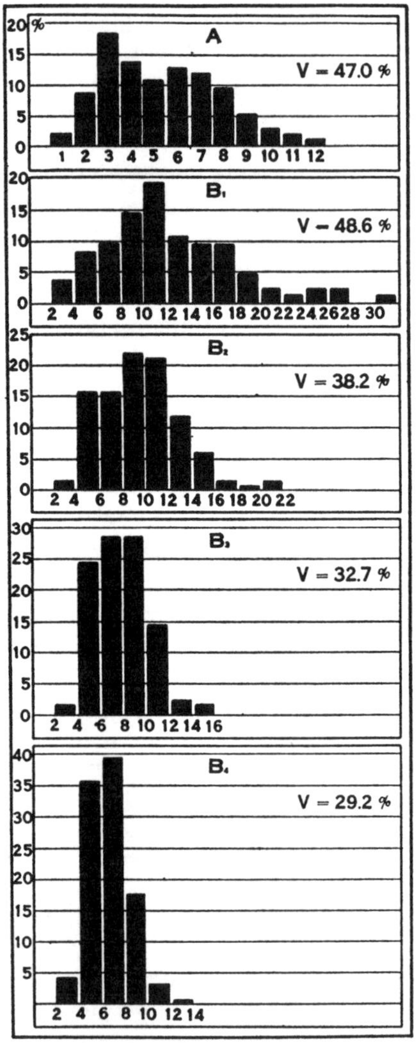

FIGURE 7.—The frequency distributions of the lengths of waves and half-waves: A, Business cycles of 12 countries, not including England (Mitchell); B_1 to B_4, Models II, IVa, IVb, and IVc respectively.

In Figure 2 are plotted 1000 points of Model II; a continuous line has been passed through them, which, because of the small scale, seems to be a comparatively fluent curve. One can distinguish on the curve waves of different orders—even down to insignificant zigzags, of which a number are not apparent on the graph because of their minuteness. The maxima and minima having been listed, together with the length of their half-waves and amplitudes, we have found that, since an empirically descriptive point of view, in its very nature, permits only approximate solutions,[18] it was legitimate to draw a boundary between waves and *ripples:* maxima and minima with amplitudes of ten units or less being discarded as ripples. The remaining maxima and minima are indicated by arrows in Figure 2. The distribution of the lengths of the 83 half-waves for Model II is given graphically in Figure 7 (B_1). Figure 7 includes the distribution (A) of the lengths of 93 cycles of economic life for 12 countries outside of England, as given by Mitchell.[19] The coefficient of variation for the latter is 47.0%[20] as compared to 48.6% for Model II. Thus we find variation of the same degree in the two distributions. The distributions for Models IVa, IVb, and IVc are also shown in Figure 7. The average lengths of waves are 9.23, 7.36 and 6.15, while the coefficients of variation are 38.2%, 32.7% and 29.2% respectively. In general appearance these last three distributions are similar to the first two, although the last three have less variation, in spite of the fact that for Models IV, a, b, and c, the data are taken without discarding the ripples. Our models being based on some a priori schemes, it appears quite likely that some day it will be possible to calculate the mathematical expectation and variability of the distances between maxima and minima. In this respect, therefore, the chance waves in coherent series must be subject to some kind of regularity, the regularity of this type being observed even in the chaotic zigzags of purely random series.[21]

We are interested, however, in a different aspect of the problem. The attempt of Mitchell to deny the periodicity of business cycles is a result of his tendency to stick to a purely descriptive point of view. The means of description which he uses and which we tried to imitate for our models are far too crude. If we try to apply the same method to a sum of two or three sinusoids the result would be approximately the same. Those investigators of economic life are right who believe in their acumen and instinct and subscribe to at least an approximate correctness in the concept of the periodicity of business cycles. Let us

[18] Cf. E. Husserl, *Ideen zu einer reinen Phänomenologie und phänomenologischen Philosophie*, Halle a.d.S., 1922, § 74: *Deskriptive und exakte Wissenschaften*, p. 138–139.

[19] W. L. Thorp, *Business Annals*, Introduction by W. C. Mitchell, p. 58.

[20] *Ibid.*

[21] Cf. L. von. Bortkiewicz, *Die Iterationen*, 1917.

again examine Model II (Figure 2). In many places there are, apparently, large waves with massive outlines as well as smaller waves lying, as it were, over them; sometimes these are detached from them, sometimes they are almost completely merged into them. For example, at the beginning of Figure 2, three waves of nearly equal length are apparent, that is, from the first to the third minimum, from the third to the fifth, and from the fifth to the sixth. Upon these waves smaller

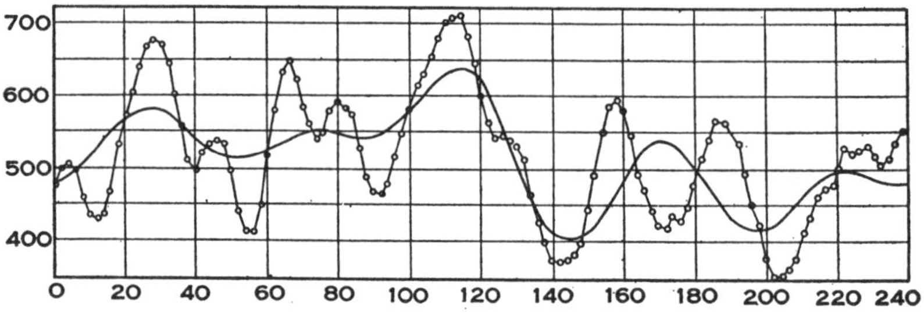

FIGURE 8.—o-o-o The first 120 even terms of Model II. ——— Sum of the first five harmonics of Fourier series: $y=518.14-20.98\cos(2\pi t/240)+50.02\sin(2\pi t/240)+17.30\cos(2\pi t/120)-3.16\sin(2\pi t/120)-10.93\cos(2\pi t/80)+35.66\sin(2\pi t/80)+17.18\cos(2\pi t/60)-21.92\sin(2\pi t/60)-38.53\cos(2\pi t/48)-3.65\sin(2\pi t/48)$.

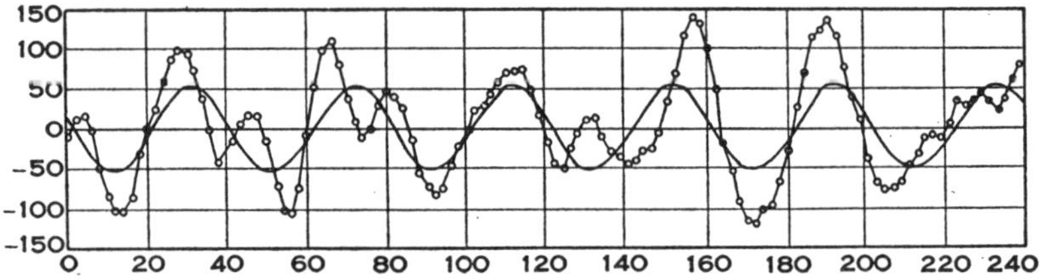

FIGURE 9.—o-o-o The deviations of Model II from the sum of the first five harmonics of Fourier series. ——— 6th sinusoid: $y=12.98\cos(2\pi t/40)-51.50\sin(2\pi t/40)$.

ones can be seen having also approximately equal dimensions. A careful examination of the graphs of our models will disclose to the reader a number of places where the approximate equality of the length of the waves is readily apparent. If we had a much shorter series, such as a series offered by the ordinary statistics of economic life with its small number of waves, we should be tempted to consider the sequence as strictly periodic, that is, as composed of a few regular harmonic fluctuations complicated by some insignificant casual fluctuations. For instance, let us consider two sections of Model II, lying one directly above the other in Figure 2, namely, the section from item 100 to item 250 and the one from 600 to 750. The similarity between the waves in these sections is apparent.

The accuracy of the above deduction is limited by the imperfection of a visual impression. To eliminate this shortcoming, let us analyze one or two sections of our models harmonically by means of Fourier's analysis. This has been done for a section of 240 points of Model II and the 360 points of Model III. Because of the great fluency of these series it was sufficient to use only the even-numbered ordinates (i.e., 0, 2, · · · 238, and 0, 2, · · · 358, respectively), thus saving some computation. The results for the 120 points of Model II are shown in Figures 8, 9 and 10, those for the 180 points of Model III in Figures 11 and 12.

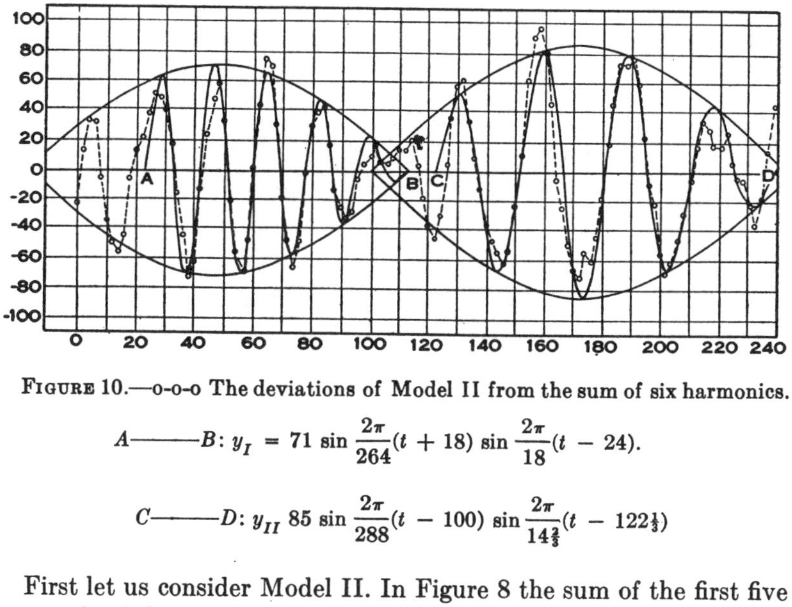

FIGURE 10.—o-o-o The deviations of Model II from the sum of six harmonics.

$$A \text{———} B: y_I = 71 \sin \frac{2\pi}{264}(t + 18) \sin \frac{2\pi}{18}(t - 24).$$

$$C \text{———} D: y_{II}\ 85 \sin \frac{2\pi}{288}(t - 100) \sin \frac{2\pi}{14\frac{2}{3}}(t - 122\tfrac{1}{3})$$

First let us consider Model II. In Figure 8 the sum of the first five sinusoids of the Fourier series are shown, while in Figure 9 the deviations from that sum are shown together with the sixth sinusoid. It is known, of course, that practically any given curve can be represented by a sum of a series of sinusoids provided a large enough number of terms is taken. It is not for every empirical series, however, that we can obtain such a significant correspondence and such a sharply expressed periodicity with a comparatively small number of harmonics. The approximately regular waves which were apparent even in the crude series are much more distinct now when they are isolated by deducting the sum of the first five harmonics. Of course, we cannot assert that the rest of Model II would follow the same periodicity, but, for our purposes, it is sufficient that successive waves should maintain an approximate equality of length for six periods. This hardly can be considered to be a chance occurrence; the explanation of such an effect must be found in the mechanism of the connection of the random values.

The deviations from the sum of six harmonics are plotted in Figure 10 together with the corresponding fluent curves. These curves are obtained as interference waves of two sinusoids with equal amplitudes and approximately equal periods. In other words, such a curve can be represented as the product of two sinusoids or as a sinusoid with an amplitude also changing along a sinusoid. These *bending sinusoids*

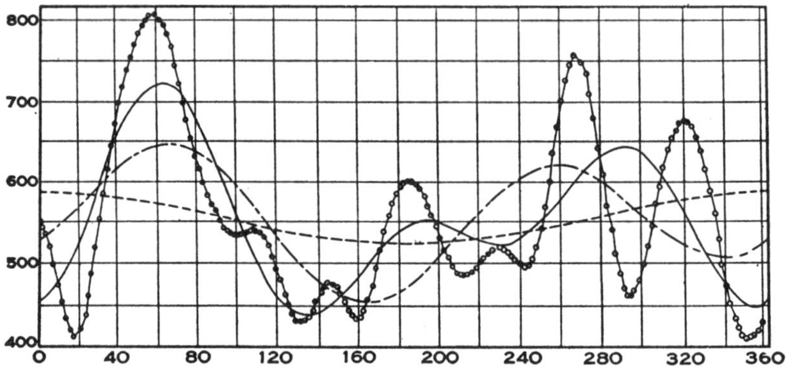

FIGURE 11.—o-o-o The first 180 even terms of Model III. —$y_I = 554.8 + 31.79 \cos(2\pi t/360) + 3.40 \sin(2\pi t/360)$. ----- $y_{II} = y_I - 58.82 \cos(2\pi t/180) + 46.63 \sin(2\pi t/180)$. ——— $y_{III} = y_{II} - 75.36 \cos(2\pi t/120) + 0.61 \sin(2\pi t/120)$.

separate on the graph the regions which place our empirical series in a definite *regime*.[22] Over a large part of the first region the regime is maintained for three or four periods with a correspondence that is much greater than could reasonably be expected between an analytical curve and a random series. At the beginning and end of a region the regime is broken. The point where a bending sinusoid cuts the axis of abscissas is the *critical point*. After this point a regime is replaced by another regime of the same type, but having different parameters. Throughout the greater part of the second region, as in the first, the regime is quite well sustained.[23]

[22] The term *regime* has been borrowed for the purposes of theoretical statistics from hydrography by N. S. Tchetverikov. See his work: "Relation of the Price of Wheat to the Size of the Crop," *The Problems of Economic Conditions*, Vol. 1, Issue 1, Moscow, 1925, p. 83.

[23] The parameters of a regime,

$$y = A \sin [(360°/L)(x - a)] \sin [(360°/l)(x - b)]$$

are easy to determine by means of graphical construction after a few trials. It is also possible to make corrections, using the method of least squares, but in our case we did not think it necessary.

If a result like the foregoing is not due to chance, a much better proof could be expected from an analysis of Model III for which the correlation between the elements is greater than for Model II. In Figure 11 the even-numbered points from 0 to 358 of Model III are plotted together with the first harmonic of the Fourier series, the sum of the first two, and the sum of the first three sinusoids. Instead of the six sinusoids needed for Model II, only three are here necessary for our purposes. The deviations from these are shown in Figure 12. Three regions are apparent with a change of regimes at the critical

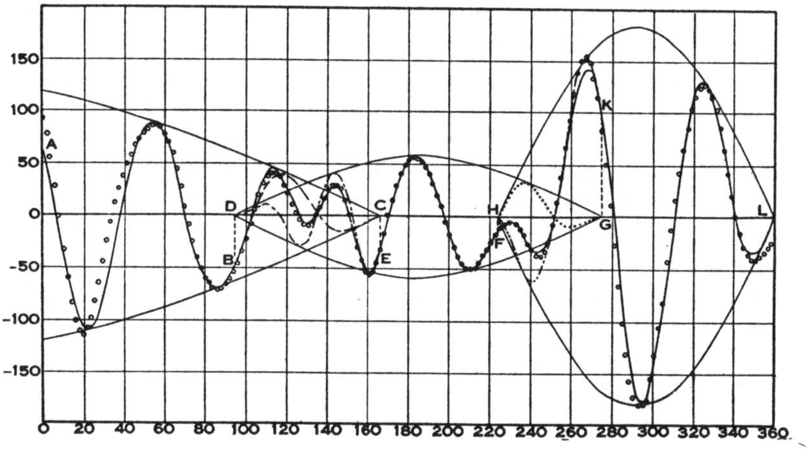

FIGURE 12.—oooo Deviations of Model III from the sum of the first three harmonics. *A*——*B*—*C*, Regime I: $y_I = 136 \sin [2\pi(t-167)/960] \sin [2\pi(t-39)/64]$. D—·—·—*E*, Regime II′: $y_{II}' = 58 \sin [2\pi(t-94)/360] \sin [2\pi(t-98)/36]$. *E*——*F*····*G*, Regime II″: $y_{II}'' = 58 \sin [2\pi(t-94)/360] \sin [2\pi(t-170)/54.4]$. *H*—··—··—*K*——*L*, Regime III: $y_{III} = 182 \sin [2\pi(t-222)/276] \sin [2\pi(t-250.6)/59.6]$. *B*——*E*; $y = y_I + y_{II}'$. *F*——*K*: $y = y_{II}'' + y_{III}$.

points. In addition we find one more regularity: to the overlapping parts of the said regions corresponds every time the partial superposition of the regimes, i.e., the algebraical addition of the respective curves.

Let us try now to summarize our observations in the following tentative and hypothetical manner:

The summation of random causes generates a cyclical series which tends to imitate for a number of cycles a harmonic series of a relatively small number of sine curves. After a more or less considerable number of periods every regime becomes disarranged, the transition to another regime occurring sometimes rather gradually, sometimes more or less abruptly, around certain critical points.

V. THE TENDENCY TO SINUSOIDAL FORM

In addition to the tendencies towards graduality and fluency (that is towards linear and parabolic forms for small sections) we find a third tendency, namely, the tendency toward a sinusoidal form.

Let $y_i, y_{i+1}, y_{i+2}, \cdots$ be the ordinates of a sinusoid. Then it is always true that

$$(2) \qquad \Delta^2 y_i = -a y_{i+1},$$

where $\Delta^2 y_i = (y_{i+2} - y_{i+1}) - (y_{i+1} - y_i)$, that is, the ith second difference of the series.

Conversely, it can easily be proved that the function defined by an equation of the form (2) in case $0 < a < 4$ must be a sinusoid.[24] Now, if there is a high correlation between the second differences ($\Delta^2 y_i$) and the ordinates (y_{i+1}) of a series, then equation (2) will be approximately true and there will exist a tendency toward a sinusoidal form in the series. The closer the correlation coefficient between $\Delta^2 y_i$ and y_{i+1}, denoted by us by $r_1^{(2,0)}$, is to -1, the more pronounced (or strong) is the tendency to a sinusoidal form.

A tendency toward either linear or parabolic forms cannot appear in a very large section of a coherent series because it would disrupt its cyclic character. The accumulation of deviations necessarily destroys every linear or parabolic regime even though the respective correlations are very high. After a regime is disrupted the new section will have a new, let us say a parabolic, regime (i.e., a regime of parabolas with different parameters). This process continues throughout the entire series, so that each coherent series of the type considered here is patched together out of a number of parabolas with variable parameters whose variations generally cannot be foreseen.

A sinusoidal regime is also bound to disrupt gradually, this being a property which distinguishes every tendency from an exact law. But under favorable conditions the sinusoidal tendency can be maintained over a number of waves without contradicting the basic property of a coherent series. In order to obtain a result of this kind it is necessary that the respective correlations be sufficiently high. But, as a matter of fact, $r_1^{(2,0)}$ for Model II is approximately the same as for Model I (-0.315 and -0.316), while Model III with its great smoothness has an $r_1^{(2,0)}$ less than that of Model IVa (-0.578 as compared to -0.599). It seems, however, to be very probable that this criterion is insufficient just because we have to deal here not with one sinusoid but with a whole series of sinusoids having different periods. Equation (2), of

[24] The condition $0 < a < 4$ is always satisfied in our case since $a = 2\ (1 - r_1)$ where r_1 is a correlation coefficient between the adjacent terms of the series (between y_i and y_{i+1}). See Appendix, Section 4.

course, is true only for a single sinusoid and cannot be applied to a sum of sinusoids.

To find an instance more apt to illustrate the tendency in question, let us consider the differences of various orders for Model III, the series best adapted for such purposes. If a curve is represented by a sum of sinusoids, then the differences of all orders are sums of sinusoids having waves of the same periods as the curve. The higher the order of the difference, the more pronounced are the shorter periods, since the differencing process weights the shorter periods as against the longer ones. Thus, by applying the formulas of the Appendix, Section 1, we find

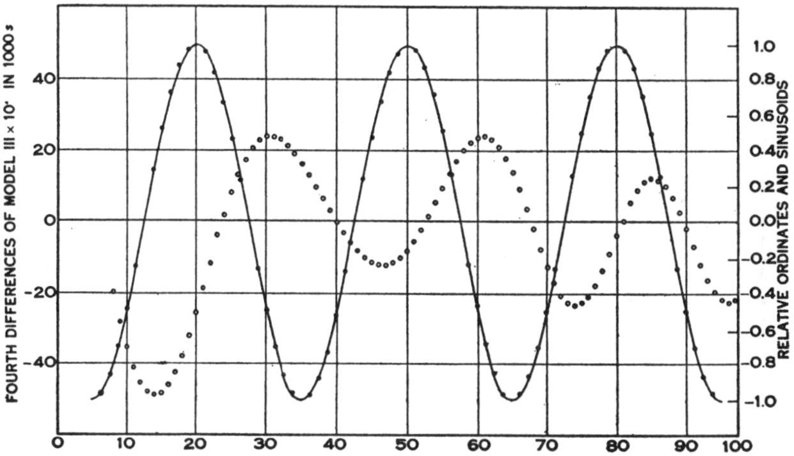

FIGURE 13.—oooo The fourth differences of Model III$\times 10^4$. –·–·– Their relative ordinates, together with the sinusoid.

that the coefficients of correlation, $r_1^{(2,0)}$, for Model III itself, and for its first, second, third, and fourth differences, are -0.5781, -0.7756, -0.8462, -0.8830, and -0.9057, respectively. The following considerations will show us to what extent the simple sinusoidal regime is maintained at least over small portions of the last series.

Let us determine the highest (or lowest) point of a typical wave (*A* or *B*, respectively, in Figure 14) as the apex of a second-degree parabola which passes through the three highest (or the three lowest) points of the wave. Then, let us draw a horizontal line bisecting the distance between the highest and lowest points of the wave. Further, let us denote the point where this horizontal line crosses the straight line joining the two points between which the horizontal line passes as *C*. This point divides *AB* into two quarter-waves, *AC* and *BC*. For each of these, let us make the following construction: Dividing the base line *DC* (*D* having the same abscissa as *A*) into six equal parts, we obtain seven points corresponding to 0°, 15°, 30°, 45°, 60°, 75°, and 90°. At the five central points construct perpendiculars and extend them to the parabola fitted to the three empirical points (interpolated according to Newton's formula). These perpendiculars are the ordinates of an empirical half-wave and, if we divide through by the maximum ordinate AD, we obtain the relative ordinates y_{15}, y_{30}, y_{45}, y_{60}, and y_{75}. If our wave is a sinusoid, these relative ordinates will equal the sines of 15°, 30°, 45°, 60°, and 75°, respectively. The empirical relative ordinates for the 12 quarter-waves of Δ^4_{VIII} are shown by black dots around the regular sinusoid of Figure 13, while the relative ordinates of the first, second, etc., quarters of every empirical wave are shown on the first,

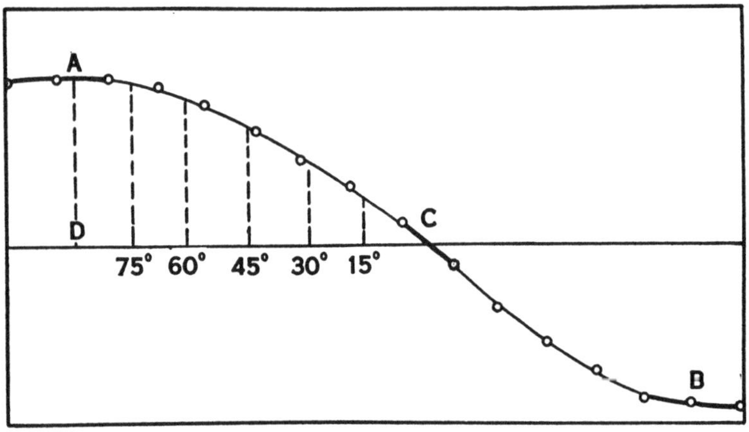

FIGURE 14.—A Scheme for Calculation of the Relative Ordinates.

second, etc., quarters of the sinusoid. The points can hardly be distinguished from the curve. Thus the tendency to a sinusoidal form is shown rather distinctly. If we compute the arithmetic averages of the relative ordinates having the same abscissa (e.g., $\bar{y}_{15} = 1/12(y_{15}^{(1)} + y_{15}^{(2)} + \cdots + y_{15}^{(12)})$ and compare them with the corresponding sines (e.g., sin 15°), we shall see that the deviations are less than $\frac{1}{2}$ in the second decimal place (see Table 4). The agreement is, therefore, close enough

TABLE 4

Phase-angle (α)	15°	30°	45°	60°	75°
$\bar{y}_\alpha$	0.258	0.496	0.703	0.863	0.964
Sin α	0.259	0.500	0.707	0.866	0.966
Deviations	−0.001	−0.004	−0.004	−0.003	−0.002

to be considered as the clear manifestation of the tendency toward a sinusoidal form, and thus displays once more the ability of chance waves to simulate regular harmonic oscillations.

VI. ON THE PSEUDO-PERIODIC CHARACTER OF THE EMPIRICAL CORRELATIONAL FUNCTION[25]

As a further illustration of the sinusoidal tendency, I shall consider here a chance series satisfying, to a rather high degree of approximation, the equation

$$\Delta^4 z_i - p\Delta^2 z_{i+1} - qz_{i+2} = 0, \tag{3}$$

corresponding, if treated as a precise one, to the sum of two sinusoids.

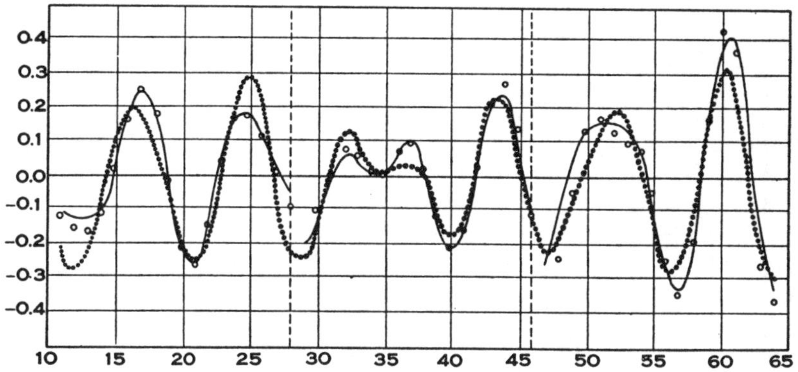

FIGURE 15.— o o o o The reduced empirical correlation function of Model IVc. ——— Sum of two sinusoids, separately for each of three intervals. ..... Sum of three sinusoids.

Let us denote the series in question by the symbols

$$\rho'_{11}, \rho'_{12}, \cdots, \rho'_{64},$$

the values of ρ'_t (see Figure 15) being given by the equation

$$\rho'_t = \sqrt{\frac{128 - t}{128}}\,\rho_t, \tag{4}$$

where ρ_t is the empirical correlation coefficient between the terms (y_i, y_{i+t}) of the series made up by 128 items of Model IVc. As the values of ρ_t have been calculated from very different numbers of items varying from 117 (that is, $128-11$) to 64 (that is, $128-64$), the reduction

[25] Eugen Slutzky, "On the Standard Error of the Correlation Coefficient in the Case of Homogenous Coherent Chance Series" (in Russian, with English summary). Transactions of the Conjuncture Institute, Vol. 2, 1929, pp. 94–98, 154.

by (4) has been thought useful in order to bring the respective standard deviations to approximate equality.

Before going further, the following remarks will be made. Let y_0, $y_1, \cdots$ be a stationary chance series. This implies that the mathematical expectation, $E(y_i)$, is a constant, that the standard deviation, σ, is a constant, and that the correlation coefficient, r_t, between y_i and y_{i+t}, is a function of t only. Then, putting, without loss of generality, $E(y_i)=0$, we shall have $\sigma^2=E(y_i^2)$ and $r_t=E(y_iy_{i+t})/\sigma^2$. This being the *theoretical* correlation coefficient, let us suppose that $r_t=0$ if $t>\omega$. Then the correlation coefficient, r'_u, between the empirical correlation coefficients, ρ_t and ρ_{t+u}, will be given by the equation

$$(5) \qquad r'_u = r(\rho_t, \rho_{t+u}) = \frac{\sum_{-\omega}^{\omega} r_t r_{t+u}}{\sum_{-\omega}^{\omega} r_t^2},$$

this formula being approximately correct if it be supposed (1) that ρ_t and ρ_{t+u} are calculated from the same number of values, n; (2) that n is sufficiently large; and (3) that $t>2\omega$, $n-t>\omega$, and $u>0$.[26]

Let us suppose now that the values of r'_u calculated from (5) may be held to be approximately true for the series of the reduced correlation coefficients ($\rho'_{11}, \rho'_{12}, \cdots \rho'_{64}$) defined above. Then we have to consider the following problem:

The series given (ρ'_t) being a chance series, there can exist no periodicity in the strict sense of the word. Its cyclical character being, however, obvious (see Figure 15), it may be asked whether the law of its composition from simple harmonics cannot be detected when its correlational function is known.

Let us try to solve this problem to the first approximation by supposing that our series can be duly approximated by the sum of two sinusoids with constant periods and varying amplitudes and phases. To this end, let us find the parameters of the regression equation which can be written in the form

$$(6) \qquad \Delta^4\rho'_u = p\Delta^2\rho'_{u+1} + q\rho'_{u+2} + \epsilon,$$

ϵ being the "error," and p and q being determined by the method of least squares. If we denote the correlation coefficients between the pairs of values

$$(\Delta^4\rho'_u, \Delta^2\rho'_{u+1}), (\Delta^4\rho'_u, \rho'_{u+2}), (\Delta^2\rho'_{u+1}, \rho'_{u+2}),$$

by r_{12}, r_{13}, r_{23} respectively, then, using the formulae (43)–(44) (Appendix, Section 1), we obtain

[26] Cf. Slutzky, *loc. cit.* in note 25, pp. 91–94.

$$(7) \qquad r_{12} = \frac{\Delta^6 r'_{-3}}{\sqrt{\Delta^8 r'_{-4} \Delta^4 r'_{-2}}}; \quad r_{13} = \frac{\Delta^4 r'_{-2}}{\sqrt{\Delta^8 r'_{-4}}}; \quad r_{23} = \frac{\Delta^2 r'_{-1}}{\sqrt{\Delta^4 r'_{-2}}},$$

where r'_{-u} $(= r'_u)$ is the correlation coefficient defined by the equation (5). These values are

$$r'_{-4} = r'_4 = -0.761{,}874{,}30,$$
$$r'_{-3} = r'_3 = -0.618{,}465{,}96,$$
$$r'_{-2} = r'_2 = -0.013{,}793{,}10,$$
$$r'_{-1} = r'_1 = -0.689{,}655{,}17,$$

whence, using (7),

$$r_{12} = 0.945{,}847, \quad r_{13} = 0.760{,}844, \quad r_{23} = -0.919{,}999.$$

Then, by the well-known formula of linear regression, we obtain

$$p = -1.419{,}386, \quad q = -0.425{,}828,$$

the multiple correlation coefficient, between $\Delta^4\rho_u$ on the one hand, and $\Delta^2\rho_{u+1}$ and ρ_{u+2} on the other, being $r_{1.23} = 0.986$. The correlation is thus very high and so it is quite reasonable to omit ϵ in (6) and to treat the resulting approximate equation according to the rules of the calculus of finite differences. We find thus that the solution of this equation is the sum of two sinusoids with the periods

$$L_1 = 9.40, \quad L_2 = 6.04.$$

Let us, then, divide our series $(\rho'_{11}, \rho'_{12}, \cdots \rho'_{64})$ into three parts, of 18 items each, and let us find, for each part separately, two sinusoids with the periods $L_1 = 9, L_2 = 6$, these being the whole numbers nearest to the theoretical values just obtained. We find the results given in Table 5.

TABLE 5

	Part I		Part II		Part III	
	$L_1 = 9$	$L_2 = 6$	$L_1 = 9$	$L_2 = 6$	$L_1 = 9$	$L_2 = 6$
Amplitude	0.19790	0.07820	0.12614	0.12527	0.29123	0.13340
Phase	231°37′	52°39′	218°2′	295°2′	270°52′	2°33′

A glance at Fig. 15 shows that the theoretical curves fit the empirical points very satisfactorily and it seems fairly certain that, if we had included one or two sinusoids more, we could have obtained a quite satisfactory fit, even if treating our empirical series as a whole. This can be proved by the fact that the sum of three sinusoids

$$z = 0.1893 \sin\left[(360°/8.80)t - 47°3'\right]$$
$$+ 0.1000 \sin\left[(360°/7.14)t + 168°24'\right]$$
$$+ 0.0794 \sin\left[(360°/5.87)t - 76°3'\right],$$

though found by rather a rough graphical estimate, fits our empirical curve in a fairly satisfactory manner.[27]

VII. THE LAW OF THE SINUSOIDAL LIMIT

Many tendencies dealt with rather empirically in the preceding discussion will be more clearly understood, and their significance more fully appreciated, if we take into consideration the following propositions.[28]

THEOREM A: (*The Law of the Sinusoidal Limit*)

Let $y_1, y_2, \cdots$ *be a chance series fulfilling the conditions,*

$$E(y_i) = 0, \quad E(y_i^2) = \sigma^2 = f(n),$$

$$\frac{E(y_i y_{i+t})}{E(y_i^2)} = r_t = \phi(t, n),$$

where n is a parameter specifying the series as a whole, and $f(n)$ and $\phi(t, n)$ are independent of i. If, furthermore, the correlation coefficient, r_1, between y_i and y_{i+1}, satisfies the condition

$$|r_1| \leqq c < 1, \qquad (n \to \infty),$$

and the correlation coefficient between $\Delta^2 y_i$ and y_{i+1}, that is, ρ_1, is such that

$$\lim \rho_1 = -1, \qquad (n \to \infty),$$

then (1) ϵ and η being taken arbitrarily small and s arbitrarily large, there will exist a number, n_0, such that for every $n > n_0$, the probability, that the absolute values of the deviations of $y_i, y_{i+1}, \cdots y_{i+s}$ from a certain sinusoid will not exceed $\epsilon\sigma$, will be $>1-\eta$; (2) the period of this sinusoid will be determined by the equation

$$\cos(2\pi/L) = r_1;$$

(3) the number of the periods in the interval $(i, i+s)$ will be arbitrarily large provided s and n be taken large enough.

This proposition (for its proof see Appendix, Section 4) would be of no interest could we not give at least a single instance of a chance series satisfying the conditions of Theorem *A*. This is done by

[27] The above illustration seems to throw some light on the difficulties connected with the idea of a correlation periodogram. Cf. Dinsmore Alter, "A Group or Correlation Periodogram," etc., *Monthly Weather Review*, Vol. 55, No. 6, June, 1927, pp. 263–266; Sir Gilbert Walker, "On Periodicity in Series of Related Terms," *Proc. Royal Soc.*, Ser. A, Vol. 131, No. A 818, 1931, pp. 518–532.

[28] E. Slutsky, "Sur un théorème limite relatif aux séries des quantités éventuelles," *Comptes Rendus*, Paris, t. 185, seance du 4 Juli, 1927, p. 169.

THEOREM B: Let $x_1, x_2, \cdots$ be a random series fulfilling the conditions

$$E(x_i) = 0, E(x_i^2) = \sigma_x^2 = \text{const.}, E(x_i x_j) = 0, \qquad (i \neq j).$$

Now, if we put

$$x_i^{(1)} = x_i + x_{i-1}, x_i^{(2)} = x_i^{(1)} + x_{i-1}^{(1)}, \cdots,$$

$$x_i^{(n)} = x_i^{(n-1)} + x_{i-1}^{(n-1)},$$

and

$$y_i = \Delta^m x_i^{(n)},$$

then the series $y_1, y_2, \cdots$ will tend to obey the law of the sinusoidal limit, provided m and n be increasing indefinitely and m/n = constant (for the proof see Appendix, Section 4).

Both propositions can be generalized to the case of a chance series practically coinciding, not with one sinusoid, but with the sum of a certain number of sinusoids.[29] In every case, however, the practical coincidence (and it is a very essential character of the series under consideration) does not extend itself to the series as a whole, the respective sinusoids of closest fit being different for different partial series. This is plainly evident for the chance series of Theorem *B*, for, s being arbitrarily large and n and m being sufficiently large, the values y_i and y_{i+t} will be wholly independent of each other as soon as $t>m+n+1$, whence it follows that the phases and the amplitudes of the sinusoids practically coincident with the partial series, $y_i, y_{i+1}, \cdots y_{i+s}$, and $y_{i+t+s}, y_{i+t+s+1}, \cdots y_{i+t+2s}$, respectively, will also be independent of each other provided $t>m+n+1$.

The following considerations will show us the same problem from a somewhat different standpoint. Let us suppose a certain mechanism is being subjected to damped vibrations of a periodic character and to casual disturbances accumulating energy just sufficient to counterbalance the damping.[30] Then the movement of the system could be regarded as consisting of the two parts: of the vibrations determined by the initial conditions at some given moment, and of the vibrations generated by the disturbances that have occurred since. As soon as the first part has been nearly extinguished by the damping process after due lapse of time, the actual vibrations will be reduced practically to the second part, that is, to the accumulated consequences of the chance

[29] V. Romanovsky, "Sur la loi sinusoidale limite," *Rend. d. Circ. mat. di Palermo*, Vol. 56, Fasc. 1, 1932, pp. 82–111; V. Romanovsky, "Sur une generalisation de la loi sinusoidal limite," *Rend d. Circ. mat. di Palermo*, Vol. 57, Fasc. 1, pp. 130–136; cf. Sir Gilbert Walker, *op. cit.*, in note 27.

[30] Cf. G. Udney Yule, "On a Method of Investigating Periodicities in Disturbed Series with Special Reference to Wolfer's Sunspot Numbers," *Phil. Trans. Roy. Soc. of London*, Ser. A. Vol. 226, 1927, pp. 267–298.

causes. The latter, after a due time, being again reduced to a value not different practically from zero, the vibrations will consist of the disturbances accumulated during the second interval of time and so on. It is evident that the vibrations ultimately will have the character of a chance function, the described process being a particular instance of the summation of random causes. Should the disturbances be small enough, there would exist an arbitrarily large, but finite, number, L_0, such that the resulting process would be practically coincident, in every interval of the length, $L \leq L_0$, with a certain periodic (or nearly periodic) function, obeying thus the law of the sinusoidal limit.

Analogous considerations may be applied to the motion of planetary, or star systems, the innumerable cosmic influences being considered as casual disturbances. The paths of the planets, if regarded during billions of years, should be considered, therefore, as chance functions, but if we do not wish to go beyond thousands of years their approximate representation must be taken as not casual.

The chance functions of the type just considered appearing on the one end of the scale, and the random functions on the other, there evidently must exist all possible intermediate gradations between these extremes. The ability of the coherent chance series to simulate the periodic, or the nearly periodic, functions, seems thus to be definitely demonstrated.

It remains for us to try to clear up theoretically the remarkable property of some specimens of chance series, which do not belong to the extreme classes of their type, of being approximately representable by a small number of sinusoids, over a shorter or longer interval.

It is well known that every empirical series consisting of a finite number of terms ($N=2n$ or $2n+1$) can be represented precisely by a finite Fourier series, that is by the sum of a finite number (n) of sinusoids. Further, it is plainly evident, the series under consideration being chance series and the coefficients of the Fourier expansion,

$$y_t = A_0 + \sum_1^n A_k \cos(2\pi kt/N) + \sum_1^n B_k \sin(2\pi kt/N),$$

that is, the values $A_0, A_1, \cdots A_n$, and $B_0, B_1, \cdots B_n$, being linear functions of $y_1, y_2, \cdots y_n$, that the variables A_k and B_k will also be chance variables. Their mathematical expectations, standard deviations, and the correlation coefficients between them can be easily obtained.[31] Denoting by R_k^2 the intensity of the kth harmonic, that is,

[31] E. Slutsky, "Alcuni applicazioni di coefficienti di Fourier al analizo di sequenze eventuali coherenti stazionarii," *Giorn. d. Istituto Italiano degli Attuari*, Vol. 5, No. 4, 1934; see also E. Slutsky, "Sur l'extension de la theorie de periodogrammes aux suites des quantités dependentes." *Compte Rendus*, t. 189, seance du 4 novembre, 1929, p. 722.

the square of its amplitude, we shall have

$$R_k^2 = A_k^2 + B_k^2,$$

and

$$(8)\quad E(R_k^2) = (4\sigma_y^2/N)\left[1 + 2\sum_1^{N-1} r_t \cos(2\pi kt/N)\right] - (8\sigma_y^2/N^2)\sum_1^{N-1} tr_t \cos(2\pi kt/N),$$

whence, for the case of a random series, we obtain at once the formula of Schuster,

$$(9)\quad E(R_k^2) = 4\sigma_y^2/N,$$

the probability distribution being the same in both cases,

$$(10)\quad P(R_k^2 > Z^2) = \exp\left[-Z^2/E(R_k^2)\right].$$

Let us suppose the m intensities happening to have the largest values in some given case are those with the indices: $\alpha, \beta, \cdots \mu$ and let

$$\tfrac{1}{2}(R_\alpha^2 + R_\beta^2 + \cdots + R_\mu^2) = ps^2,$$

s^2 being the square of the empirical standard deviation and p the coefficient measuring the degree of approximation reached in the given case by means of m harmonics. By taking account of (8), (9), and (10), we see at once that, in the case of a random series, the indices $\alpha, \beta, \cdots \mu$ are able to assume any values with equal probability but that in the case of a coherent series those having the largest values of $E(R_k^2)$ will be the most probable. As half of the sum of the intensities is equal to the square of the empirical standard deviation (Parceval's theorem), it is but natural that the coherent chance series, in many cases at least, may be represented—the degree of approximation being the same—by a smaller number of harmonics than the random series.

It can be proved further (under suppositions of a not very restrictive character) that the correlation coefficients between the intensities belonging to the same interval, as well as between those belonging to the adjacent intervals, are quantities of the order $1/N^2$, and that the standard deviation of the intensity, σ_{R^2}, tends to be equal to its probable value, $E(R_k^2)$. Whence it is evident that the indices of the harmonics which happen to be the most suited for the representation of the series in a certain interval must also be practically independent of the indices of the "best" harmonics in adjacent intervals, the length of these intervals being sufficiently large. The larger the probable value of the intensity the larger also must be the extent of its casual variation. These are properties quite consistent with a considerable degree of regularity—as well as with the abrupt changes of the "regimes" determined by studying the empirical series dealt with in the foregoing pages.

Appendix

MATHEMATICAL NOTES OF THE THEORY OF RANDOM WAVES

1. Let $x_0, x_1, \cdots x_i, \cdots$ be a random series, that is, a series of chance values independent of each other. Let this be our basic series and let it be considered as a model of incoherent series of random causes. Denoting by the symbol E the mathematical expectation, let us suppose that

$$(1) \qquad E(x_i) = 0,\ E(x_i^2) = \sigma_x^2 = \text{const.};\ E(x_i x_j) = 0, \qquad (i \neq j).$$

From the basic incoherent series of causes let us construct a coherent series of "consequences," $\cdots y_{i-2}, y_{i-1}, y_i, \cdots$, by the scheme

$$(2) \qquad y_i = \sum_{k=0}^{n-1} A_k x_{i-k},$$

where the quantities A_k are constants.[32] Then, by using (1) and (2), it can easily be shown that

$$(3) \qquad E(y_i) = 0,$$

$$(4) \qquad E(y_i^2) = \sigma_y^2 = \sigma_x^2 \sum_{k=0}^{n-1} A_k^2,$$

$$(5) \qquad E(y_i y_{i+t}) = \sigma_x^2 \sum_{k=0}^{(n-1)-t} A_k A_{k+t}.$$

Since equations (4) and (5) do not depend on i, the coefficient of correlation between y_i and y_{i-t}, that is, r_t, is also independent of i, and we have

$$(6) \qquad r_t = \frac{\sum_{k=0}^{(n-1)-t} A_k A_{k+t}}{\sum_{k=0}^{n-1} A_k^2},$$

from which it immediately follows that

$$(7) \qquad r_0 = 1;\ r_t = r_{-t};\ r_t = 0,\ (t \geqq n).$$

The process of moving summation can be repeated. As before, let us take $\cdots x_{i-2}, x_{i-1}, x_i, \cdots$ as the basic series underlying the conditions

[32] Cf. Prof. Birger Meidell's valuable investigation of the analogous cumulative processes in his paper, "Über periodische und angenäherte Beharrungszustände," *Skandinavisk Aktuarietidskrift*, 1926, p. 172.

(1). Then on performing an s-fold moving summation we obtain the following successive consequence series:

$$x_i^{(1)} = \sum_{k=0}^{n-1} \alpha_k^{(1)} x_{i-k}; \quad x_i^{(2)} = \sum_{k=0}^{n-1} \alpha_k^{(2)} x_{i-k}^{(1)}; \cdots \tag{8}$$
$$x_i^{(s)} = \sum_{k=0}^{n-1} \alpha_k^{(s)} x_{i-k}^{(s-1)}.$$

After the s-fold summation we have an expression of type (2) with $y_i = x_i^{(s)}$. Hence, if we take $n=2$ and $\alpha_k^{(j)}=1$, it can easily be shown that

$$y_i = x_i^{(s)} = \sum_{k=0}^{s} C_k^s x_{i-k}. \tag{9}$$

If we put

$$\phi(t) = \frac{1}{\sqrt{2\pi}} \exp\left(-\tfrac{1}{2}t^2\right), \tag{10}$$

we can, by the use of well-known transformations, obtain the approximate expression (which we write for an *even* s)

$$y_i = D \sum_{k=0}^{s} x_{i-k} \phi\left(\frac{k - s/2}{\sqrt{s/4}}\right), \tag{11}$$

D being a coefficient, the value of which need not concern us here.

It is very remarkable that a similar result will always be obtained for s sufficiently great, whatever be the weights used, provided it is supposed (1) that the weights are not negative, (2) that they remain constant at every given stage of the process, and (3) that the summation does not tend to degenerate into a mere repetition of the same values, which would be the case should all $\alpha_k^{(s)}$ but one tend to approach 0; (the sum of the weights is supposed, without loss of generality, to be constant).

To prove this, let us remark first that the result of the s-fold summation given by (8) can evidently be obtained by a similar s-fold summation with the weights

$$p_0^{(j)}, p_1^{(j)}, \cdots, p_{n-1}^{(j)}, \qquad (j = 1, 2, \cdots, s),$$

where

$$p_k^{(j)} = \frac{\alpha_k^{(j)}}{m_j}, \quad m_j = \sum_{k=0}^{n-1} \alpha_k^{(j)},$$

if we multiply the resulting weights by the proportionality factor $m_1 \cdot m_2 \cdot \cdots \cdot m_s$.

Now to prove our proposition we shall use the following analogy (kindly suggested to the author by Prof. A. Khinchin).

Let $z_1, z_2, \cdots z_s$ be a set of random variables whose possible values are $0, 1, 2, \cdots, n-1$, the respective probabilities being $p_0^{(j)}$, $p_1^{(j)}$, $\cdots p_{n-1}^{(j)}$, $(j=1, 2, \cdots s)$. Then it is easy to see that the probability of the equation

$$k = z_1 + z_2 + \cdots + z_s \tag{12}$$

must be equal to the coefficient of x^k in the expansion of

$$\prod_{j=1}^{s} (p_0^{(j)} + p_1^{(j)}x + p_2^{(j)}x^2 + \cdots + p_{n-1}^{(j)}x^{n-1}). \tag{13}$$

On the other hand, it can be proved that the same coefficient, multiplied by $m_1 \cdot m_2 \cdot \cdots \cdot m_s$, will be equal to the coefficient A_k in the equation (2) obtained by an s-fold summation according to the scheme (8) with the weights

$$m_jp_0^{(j)},\ m_jp_1^{(j)},\ \cdots,\ m_jp_{n-1}^{(j)}, \qquad (j = 1, 2, \cdots, s).$$

This is easily seen for $s=2$ and the result can be generalized by mathematical induction from s to $s+1$.

This analogy leads us to the following considerations. Let us put

$$\begin{cases} a_j = E(z_j) = \sum_{k=0}^{n-1} kp_k^{(j)}, \\ b_j = E[(z_j - a_j)^2] = \sum_{k=0}^{n-1} (k - a_j)^2 p_k^{(j)}, \\ c_j = E[|z_j - a_j|^g] = \sum_{k=0}^{n-1} |k - a_j|^g p_k^{(j)}, \qquad (g > 2). \end{cases} \tag{14}$$

It is evident that $b_j=0$ only if every $(k-a_j)^2p_k^{(j)}=0$ for $k=0, 1, 2, \cdots (n-1)$, and that this is possible only when every $p_k^{(j)}$ but one is equal to zero, the exceptional p being 1, in which case the values $x_k^{(j)}$ are merely repetitions of the values $x_k^{(j-1)}$.

This case being excluded, we shall have, on the average at least,

$$(1/s)\sum_1^s b_i > \epsilon > 0; \tag{15}$$

whence

$$\frac{\left[\sum_1^s c_i\right]^2}{\left[\sum_1^s b_i\right]^g} < \frac{\left[(1/s)\sum_1^s c_i\right]^2}{s^{g-2}\epsilon^g} \to 0. \tag{16}$$

But this is the well known Liapounoff's condition, under which the probability distribution of the sum $z_1+z_2+\cdots+z_s$, that is, the distribution of the coefficients A_k, tends to the normal law.[33]

Let us put, for instance,

$$\alpha_0^{(j)} = \alpha_1^{(j)} = \cdots = \alpha_{n-1}^{(j)} = 1, \qquad (j = 1, 2, \cdots, s).$$

Then we obtain

$$\begin{aligned} m_j &= \sum_{k=0}^{n-1} \alpha_k^{(j)} = n, \\ m_1 m_2 \cdots m_s &= n^s, \\ p_k^{(j)} &= 1/n, \end{aligned} \tag{17}$$

for

$$j = 1, 2, \cdots, s, \quad \text{and} \quad k = 0, 1, \cdots, n-1;$$

and

$$\begin{aligned} a_j &= E(z_j) = \sum_{k=0}^{n-1} k p_k^{(j)} = (n-1)/2, \\ b_j &= E[(z_j - a_j)^2] = (1/n)\left\{\sum_{k=0}^{n-1} k^2 - n a_j^2\right\} = (n^2-1)/12. \end{aligned} \tag{18}$$

Whence

$$k_0 = E(k) = E\left[\sum_1^s z_j\right] = s(n-1)/2, \tag{19}$$

and

$$\sigma_k = \sqrt{s b_j} = \sqrt{s(n^2-1)/12}. \tag{20}$$

As s tends towards ∞, the value of A_k will thus approach a limit, which enables us to write, for s large but finite, the following approximate equations:[34]

[33] It is evident that, since Liapounoff's theorem is a proposition about the limit properties of certain integrals and not of the individual ordinates, the above demonstration must be interpreted also in the same sense. For many cases, however, for example, in the case of the illustration below, the additional conditions are satisfied under which the values of the variables A_k themselves are tending toward the ordinates of the Gaussian curve.

Cf. Liapounoff, "Nouvelle forme du théorème sur la limite de probabilité," *Memoires de l'Academie de science de St.-Petersbourg,* serie 8, Vol. 12, No. 5.

R. von Mises, *Vorlesungen aus dem Gebiete der Angewandten Mathematik,* Bd. I—*Wahrscheinlichkeitsrechnung und ihre Anwendungen,* 1931, p. 200–212.

R. von Mises, "Generalizzazione di un teorema sulla probabilità della somma di un numero illimitato di variabili casuali," *Giornale dell'Istituto Italiano degli Attuari,* Anno 5, N4, p. 483–495.

[34] This result coincides with that given in the first edition of this memoir in 1927; it was supplied to the author by the courtesy of Prof. A. Khinchin who derived it by the application of the well-known Cauchy theorem to the evaluation of the coefficient of x^k in the expansion of

$$(1 + x + x^2 + \cdots + x^{n-1})^s.$$

I am sorry that the calculations are too long to be reproduced here.

(21) $A_k \overset{a}{=} n^s\sqrt{6/\pi s(n^2-1)}\ \exp\{-6(k-k_0)^2/s(n^2-1)\}.$

For the general case, we shall give here the following illustration Let the weights for a set of successive summations be certain random numbers. For this purpose, let us choose consecutive groups of three numbers from the first basic series (Column 2, Table I, Appendix II). For the first moving summation the weights will be $\alpha_0^{(1)}=5$, $\alpha_1^{(1)}=4$, $\alpha_2^{(1)}=7$; for the second $\alpha_0^{(2)}=3$, $\alpha_1^{(2)}=0$, $\alpha_2^{(2)}=3$, etc. Performing the substitutions indicated by formula (8) we obtain the resulting weights corresponding to A_k of formula (2), $A_k^{(1)}=\alpha_k^{(1)}$, $A_k^{(2)}$, $A_k^{(3)}$, $\cdots$ $A_k^{(10)}$. For each given s, we divide the weights by the largest $A_k^{(s)}$ to obtain the relative weights, $A'^{(s)}_k$ (see Table VIII, Appendix II, of the original paper, and Figure 5). The series of quantities $A'^{(10)}_k$ does not differ greatly from the Gaussian curve obtained by putting[35]

(22) $B'^{(10)}_k = 1004 \exp\{-\tfrac{1}{2}[(k-9.26)/2.67]^2\}.$

2. The coefficients of correlation between the terms of a coherent series are, in many cases, easy to obtain by using formula (6). For a simple moving summation of n equally weighted items at a time, we have $A_0=A_1=\cdots=A_{n-1}=1$. It is easy to see that

$$(23)\qquad \begin{cases} r_t = (n-|t|)/n, & (|t| \leqq n) \\ r_t = 0, & (|t| \geqq n). \end{cases}$$

From formulas (4), (5), (9) and the properties of $\overset{s}{C_k}$, we find for the s-fold moving summation of two terms, that is, $(n=2)$, that

$$(24)\qquad \sigma_y^2 = \sigma_x^2[1 + (\overset{s}{C_1})^2 + (\overset{s}{C_2})^2 + \cdots + (\overset{s}{C}_{s-1})^2 + 1] = \sigma_x^2 \overset{2s}{C_s},$$

and

$$(25)\qquad E(y_i y_{i+t}) = \sigma_x^2[\overset{s}{C_0}\overset{s}{C_t} + \overset{s}{C_1}\overset{s}{C}_{t+1} + \cdots + \overset{s}{C}_{s-t}\overset{s}{C_s}] = \sigma_x^2 \overset{2s}{C}_{s-t}.$$

Hence

$$(26)\qquad r_t = \overset{2s}{C}_{s-t}/\overset{2s}{C_s} = \frac{s(s-1)\cdots(s-t+1)}{(s+1)(s+2)\cdots(s+t)}.$$

Consider another case. Let us form, from a basic series, a coherent series by the scheme:

[35] Let us pass a second degree parabola through $A_0'^{(10)}$, $A_1'^{(10)}$, $A_2'^{(10)}$; another through $A_2'^{(10)}$, $A_3'^{(10)}$, $A_4'^{(10)}$; etc. Denote the area of this figure by S, its maximum ordinate by y_0, and the abscissa bisecting the area by k_0. Then, in the Gaussian equation

$$B'^{(10)}_k = [S/\sigma\sqrt{2\pi}]\exp\{-\tfrac{1}{2}[(k-k_0)/\sigma]^2\},$$

all of the parameters are known, since

$$k_0 = 9.26,\ y_0 = S/\sigma\sqrt{2\pi} = 1004,$$

and hence

$$\sigma = S/y_0\sqrt{2\pi} = 2.67$$

$$y_i = D\sum_{k=0}^{2k_0} x_{i-k}\phi[(k-k_0)/\sigma], \tag{27}$$

where $\phi(t)$ is given by formula (10), D is a constant, and k_0 is a number large enough so that $\phi(t)$ can be neglected for $|t| > k_0/\sigma$. Then, from (6), the coefficient of correlation is

$$r_t = \frac{\sum_{k=0}^{2k_0-t} \phi[(k-k_0)/\sigma]\phi[(k-k_0+t)/\sigma]}{\sum_{k=0}^{2k_0} \{\phi[(k-k_0)/\sigma]\}^2}. \tag{28}$$

If σ is sufficiently large we can substitute integrals for the summations in (28). Inserting $z=k-k_0$, we then obtain the approximation formula

$$r_t = \frac{\int_{-\infty}^{+\infty} \exp\left[-\tfrac{1}{2}\frac{z^2+(z+t)^2}{\sigma^2}\right]dz}{\int_{-\infty}^{+\infty} \exp\left[-\frac{z^2}{\sigma^2}\right]dz} \tag{29}$$

$$= \exp(-t^2/4\sigma^2) = \frac{\phi(t/\sigma\sqrt{2})}{\phi(0)}.$$

Inasmuch as Model III is formed by the scheme of formula (27), with $D=10^4$, $k_0=48$, and $\sigma=10$, we can calculate the correlation function by formula (29). The values for $[\phi(t/\sqrt{200})]/\phi(0)$, $(t=0, 1, 2, \cdots)$, were calculated with the aid of Sheppard's tables.[36] The symbol $R_{t(III)}$, instead of $r_{t(III)}$, indicates that an approximate, and not an exact, formula was used in the calculation.

Model IVa was obtained by a 12-fold moving summation of two items; therefore, its correlation function, $r_{t(IVa)}$, is obtained by using formula (26), which, if we consider (11), gives $R_{t(IVa)}=\phi(t/\sqrt{6})/\phi(0)$. The discrepancies between the two results are rather small. The correspondence between $r_{t(IVb)}$ and $R_{t(IVb)}$ is somewhat less, as is also that between $r_{t(IVc)}$ and $R_{t(IVc)}$. Both sets were computed by formula (45) (see next paragraph), but for the calculation of $r_{t(IVb)}$ and $r_{t(IVc)}$ the actual values of $r_{t(IVa)}$ were used as the base, while for $R_{t(IVb)}$ and $R_{t(IVc)}$ the approximate values of $R_{t(IVa)}$, obtained by the Gaussian formula, were used. Even here the discrepancies are not very great when regarded from the same point of view (see Figure 6).

[36] *Tables for Statisticians and Biometricians*, ed. by K. Pearson, Cambridge, 1914, Table II.

Finally, for Model II, corresponding to the scheme

$$y_i = x_i^{(2)} = \sum_{k=0}^{18} A_k^{(2)} x_{i+k} + 50, \tag{30}$$

$$(A_k^{(2)} = 1, 2, \cdots, 9, 10, 9, \cdots, 2, 1),$$

the coefficients of correlation can be obtained directly from formula (6). It is worth noting that, even in this case, a good approximation, $R_{t(II)}$, can be obtained by the use of the Gaussian curve, the equation being

$$R_{t(II)} = \exp\left[-\tfrac{1}{2}(t/5.954)^2\right], \tag{31}$$

where $\sigma = 5.954$ was obtained by equating the areas of the Gaussian curve and of the empirical curve, and the computations were carried through with the help of Simpson's rule (see Figure 6).

A few more words may be said about the correlational function for the weights, $A'_k{}^{(10)}$, of our example of the crossing of random weights (see Section 2 of the text, Appendix, Section 1, and Figure 6). The exact values of the coefficients of correlation (r_t) were found by formula (6), while approximate values (R_t) were obtained from the equation

$$R_t = \exp\left[-\tfrac{1}{2}(t/3.727)^2\right], \tag{32}$$

which was obtained in the same manner as was equation (31). Both the exact and approximate values are given in Table 1 (see also Figure 6). Also, let us note that, from the equation of the Gaussian curve which approximates the weights, $A'_k{}^{(10)}$ (see formula (22) above), it is possible to find an approximate expression for the coefficients of correlation by using formula (29). An expression analogous to (32) would be obtained, but instead of $\sigma = 3.727$, we would have $\sigma = 3.776$. The correlation coefficients are only slightly less accurate than those found from formula (32), the deviations are all of one sign, and none is greater than 0.009.

Let us make one more observation. If a chance variable $y_i = u_i + v_i$, where u_i is a coherent series and v_i is a random series, it is easy to show that

$$E(y_i y_{i+t}) = E(u_i u_{i+t}), \tag{33}$$

$$(E y_i^2) = \sigma_u^2 + \sigma_v^2, \tag{34}$$

$$r_{y_i, y_{i+t}} = \frac{r_{u_i, u_{i+t}}}{1 + (\sigma_v^2/\sigma_u^2)}, \tag{35}$$

where $E(u_i)$ and $E(v_i)$ are taken equal to zero.

If $r_{u_i, u_{i+t}}$ lies along the Gaussian curve, then $r_{y_i, y_{i+t}}$ will lie along a similar curve with ordinates proportionally reduced, except that r_0 will, as formerly, equal unity; the *chapeau de gendarme* has taken on the spike of the *budenovka* (a Soviet military cap). It is to be expected that this figure and the analogous figures for the correlation function of the differences (formula (45) of the following paragraph) will be encountered in the investigation of empirical series.[37]

3. Let us now investigate the differences of various orders of the series y_i, i.e., $\Delta^\alpha y_i$, $\Delta^\beta y_i$, and their coefficients of correlation.[38] As before, let

$$(36)\qquad E(y_i) = 0;\ E(y_i^2) = \sigma_y^2 = \text{constant};\ E(y_i y_{i+t})/\sigma_y^2 = r_t,$$

where r_t is supposed to be independent of i. Let us introduce the notation

$$(37)\qquad r_t^{(\alpha,\beta)} = r_{\Delta^\alpha y_i \Delta^\beta y_{i+t}}, \qquad (\alpha \geqq \beta);$$

and, in particular,

$$(38)\qquad r_t^{(\alpha,\alpha)} = r_{\Delta^\alpha y_i \Delta^\alpha y_{i+t}} \qquad r_t^{(\alpha,0)} = r_{\Delta^\alpha y_i, y_{i+t}}.$$

By using the equality

$$(39)\qquad C_k^{2\alpha} = C_{\alpha-k}^{\alpha} C_0^{\alpha} + C_{\alpha-(k-1)}^{\alpha} C_1^{\alpha} + \cdots + C_{\alpha-1}^{\alpha} C_{k-1}^{\alpha} + C_\alpha^{\alpha} C_k^{\alpha},$$

it can be shown that

$$(40)\qquad \begin{aligned} \sigma_{\Delta^\alpha y_i}^2 = E[(\Delta^\alpha y_i)^2] &= E[(C_\alpha^\alpha y_{i+\alpha} - C_{\alpha-1}^\alpha y_{i+\alpha-1} + C_{\alpha-2}^\alpha y_{i+\alpha-2} \\ &\quad - \cdots + (-1)^\alpha C_0^\alpha y_i)^2] = (-1)^\alpha \Delta^{2\alpha} r_{-\alpha} \sigma_y^2. \end{aligned}$$

From (40), by using the equality,

$$(41)\qquad C_k^{\alpha+\beta} = C_{\alpha-k}^{\alpha} C_0^{\beta} + C_{\alpha-k+1}^{\alpha} C_1^{\beta} + \cdots + C_{\alpha-1}^{\alpha} C_{k-1}^{\beta} + C_k^{\beta},$$

we obtain

$$(42)\qquad E[\Delta^\alpha y_i \Delta^\beta y_{i+t}] = (-)^\alpha \Delta^{\alpha+\beta} r_{t-\alpha} \sigma_y^2, \qquad (\alpha \geqq \beta),$$

and from this we have

$$(43)\qquad r_t^{(\alpha,\beta)} = \frac{(-1)^\alpha \Delta^{\alpha+\beta} r_{t-\alpha}}{\sqrt{(-1)^{\alpha+\beta} \Delta^{2\alpha} r_{-\alpha} \Delta^{2\beta} r_{-\beta}}}.$$

In the same manner we obtain

$$(44)\qquad r_t^{(\alpha,0)} = \frac{(-1)^\alpha \Delta^\alpha r_{t-\alpha}}{\sqrt{(-1)^\alpha \Delta^{2\alpha} r_{-\alpha}}},$$

[37] Cf. Figure 19 of Yule, "Why Do We Sometimes Get Nonsense-Correlations · · · ," *loc. cit.*, p. 43.

[38] Cf. O. Anderson, "Über ein neues Verfahren bei Anwendung der 'Variate-Difference' Methode," *Biometrika*, Vol. 15, 1923, pp. 142 ff.

and, as a special case of formula (43), we have

$$r_t^{(\alpha,\alpha)} = \frac{\Delta^{2\alpha} r_{t-\alpha}}{\Delta^{2\alpha} r_{-\alpha}}. \tag{45}$$

By this formula and by (26) the correlation coefficients for Models IV*b* and IV*c* have been computed.

4. Let us now prove Theorem A (see Section VII above). The regression coefficient of $\Delta^2 y_i$ on y_{i+1} being

$$E(\Delta^2 y_i \cdot y_{i+1})/\sigma_y^2 = -2(1 - r_1),$$

we obtain the approximate equation

$$\Delta^2 y_i \overset{a}{=} -2(1 - r_1) y_{i+1}.$$

Whence

$$y_{i+2} \overset{a}{=} 2 r_1 y_{i+1} - y_i, \tag{46}$$

the errors of both equations being evidently identical. If we denote this error by α_2 and put $\beta_2 = \alpha_2/\sigma_y$, we may apply the well-known formula of correlation theory and thus obtain

$$E(\beta_2^2) = E(\Delta^2 y_i)(1 - \rho_1^2)/\sigma_y^2 = (1 - \rho_1^2)(6 - 8r_1 + 2r_2). \tag{47}$$

Now, under the suppositions of Theorem A,

$$\lim_{n \to \infty} \beta_2^2 = 0;$$

whence, applying Tchebycheff's theorem, we see that β_2 has the stochastical limit $E(\beta_2) = 0$, $(n \to \infty)$; that is, ϵ and η being arbitrarily small, the probability

$$P\{ |\beta_2| > \epsilon \} < \eta,$$

provided n is sufficiently large.

On the other hand, if we put

$$\begin{aligned}
y_{i+2} &= 2 r_1 y_{i+1} - y_i + \alpha_2, \\
y_{i+3} &= 2 r_1 y_{i+2} - y_{i+1} + \alpha_3, \\
&\cdots\cdots\cdots\cdots \\
y_{i+s} &= 2 r_1 y_{i+s-1} - y_{i+s-2} + \alpha_s;
\end{aligned}$$

and if we insert y_{i+2} in the second equation of this system, y_{i+3} in the third, and so on, we obtain, after reduction,

$$y_{i+s} = C_1 y_{i+1} + C_2 y_i + \lambda_s \sigma_y, \tag{48}$$

where

$$\lambda_s = a_0\beta_s + a_1\beta_{s-1} + \cdots + a_{s-2}\beta_2, \tag{49}$$

the values $a_0, a_1, \cdots a_{s+2}$, being determined by the conditions

$$\begin{cases} a_0 = 1, \quad a_1 = 2r_1, \\ a_{k+2} = 2r_1 a_{k+1} - a_k. \end{cases} \tag{50}$$

This equation is identical with

$$y_{i+2} = 2r_1 y_{i+1} - y_i, \tag{51}$$

that is, with (46) considered as a precise equation. The solution of (51) or (50) can be obtained easily. We find

$$y_t = A \cos (2\pi t/L) + B \sin (2\pi t/L), \tag{52}$$

and

$$a_k = C \cos (2\pi k/L) + D \sin (2\pi k/L), \tag{53}$$

where we have put

$$\cos (2\pi/L) = r_1, \tag{54}$$

L being the period of the respective sinusoid. It is evident that, under the assumptions of Theorem A, ($|r_1| \leqq \lambda < 1$), we shall have

$$L \leqq 2\pi/\text{arc} \cos \lambda = H = \text{constant}. \tag{55}$$

Two sinusoids must now be considered. The first, which will be denoted by S_1, is determined by (51), or (52), and the initial points y_i, y_{i+1}. It is evident that $C_1 y_{i+1} + C_2 y_i$ in (48) is the ordinate of S_1 which could be obtained in this form from (51) by successive substitutions. The deviation of the actual value of y_{i+s} from S_1 is $\lambda_s \sigma_y$ as given by (48) and (49), the coefficients a_k being the ordinates of the second sinusoid (S_2) determined by (50) or (53), and the initial values $a_0 = 1$, $a_1 = 2r_1$. But, if we put, in (53), $k = 0$, and then $k = 1$, we obtain

$$C = 1, \quad D = r_1/\sqrt{1 - r_1^2}.$$

Hence the amplitude of S_2 is

$$\sqrt{C^2 + D^2} = 1/\sqrt{1 - r_1^2} \leqq 1/\sqrt{1 - \lambda^2} = K = \text{constant}.$$

$$C = 1, \quad D = r_1/\sqrt{1 - r_1^2}.$$

Thus, taking into account that every a_k in (49) has an upper limit $\leqq\sqrt{C^2+D^2}$, $(n\to\infty)$ and remembering the theorems of my *Metron* memoir[39] we conclude that λ_s has the stochastical limit $=0$ and that, ϵ and η being arbitrarily small and s arbitrarily large, the probability that the conditions

$$\lambda_2 < \epsilon,\ \lambda_3 < \epsilon,\ \cdots,\ \lambda_s < \epsilon,$$

are simultaneously satisfied will be $>1-\eta$ provided n is sufficiently large. The formulas (54) and (55) complete the proof.

To prove theorem B, we may proceed here as follows: It is seen by (43) and (45) that the correlation coefficient between y_i and y_{i+1} is

$$r_1 = r_1^{(m,m)} = \frac{\Delta^{2m}r_{-m+1}}{\Delta^{2m}r_{-m}}, \tag{56}$$

and the correlation coefficient between $\Delta^2 y_i$ and y_{i+1} is given by

$$\rho_1 = r_1^{(m+2,m)} = \frac{(-1)^m\Delta^{2m+m}r_{-(m+1)}}{\sqrt{\Delta^{2(m+2)}r_{-(m+2)}\Delta^{2m}r_{-m}}}, \tag{57}$$

where, using (26) we must put

$$r_t = \frac{C^{2n}_{n-t}}{C^{2n}_{n}}.$$

On the other hand, r_{-t} being equal to r_t, it can easily be seen that

$$C^{2n}_n\,\Delta^{2m}r_{-m} = \sum_{k=0}^{2m}(-1)^k C^{2m}_k C^{2n}_{n-m+k} = A_{n+m}, \tag{58}$$

where A_{n+m} is the coefficient of x^{n+m} in the expansion of $(1+x)^{2n}(1-x)^{2m}$. Applying Cauchy's theorem we have

$$A_{n+m}\frac{1}{2\pi i}\int_{|1|}\frac{(1+x)^{2n}(1-x)^{2m}}{x^{n+m+1}}\,dx.$$

If we put $x=e^{i\phi}$, we obtain, after reduction,

$$A_{n+m} = [(-1)^m 2^{2(n+m)}/\pi]\int_0^\pi \cos^{2n}\phi\,\sin^{2m}\phi\,d\phi.$$

[39] E. Slutzky, "Über Stochastische Asymptoten und Grenzwerte," *Metron*, Vol. 5, N. 3, 1925, pp. 61–64.

Hence

$$(59)\quad A_{n+m} = \frac{(-1)^m 2^{n+m} 1\cdot 3 \cdots (2n-1)\cdot 1\cdot 3 \cdots (2m-1)}{1\cdot 2\cdot 3 \cdots (n+m)}.$$

Thus we obtain, by (58),

$$(60)\qquad \Delta^{2m} r_{-m} = \frac{(-1)^m 2^m 1\cdot 3 \cdots (2m-1)}{(n+1)(n+2)\cdots(n+m)}.$$

If we notice that

$$\Delta^{2m+2} r_{-(m+1)} = \Delta^{2m} r_{-(m+1)} - 2\Delta^{2m} r_{-m} + \Delta^{2m} r_{-(m-1)},$$

where, evidently,

$$\Delta^{2m} r_{-(m+1)} = \Delta^{2m} r_{-(m-1)},$$

we get

$$(61)\qquad \begin{aligned} \Delta^{2m} r_{-m+1} &= \tfrac{1}{2}\Delta^{2(m+1)} r_{-(m+1)} + \Delta^{2m} r_{-m} \\ &= \frac{(-1)^m 2^m 1\cdot 3 \cdots (2m-1)(n-m)}{(n+1)(n+2)\cdots(n+m+1)}, \end{aligned}$$

so that, by (56), (57), (60), and (61), we obtain

$$(62)\qquad r_1 = (n-m)/(n+m+1)$$

and[40]

$$(63)\qquad \rho_1 = -\sqrt{\frac{(2m+1)(n+m+2)}{(2m+3)(n+m+1)}}.$$

Now, it is evident that, n/m being constant,

$$r_1 < \frac{n/m - 1}{n/m + 1} < 1$$

and

$$\rho_1 \to -1, \qquad (n \to \infty),$$

which proves Theorem B.

CORRECTIONS OF BASIC DATA

The tables of figures which contain the series used in the present investigation are to be found in the original paper (*loc. cit.*, pp. 57–64). As the preparation of them has involved a great deal of time and labor

[40] To apply this formula in the case of No. V, we should notice that Model III is approximately equivalent to the series (y_1) of Theorem B, with $n=400$.

and as it may be expected that someone will make use of them for the purpose of analogous studies, we give here correct readings for the *errata* found after the figures had been published. (Those relating to Table VI are immaterial and are omitted here.)

Table	Column					
	1	2	6	7	8	10
I	300				−453	
	418			−361		
	637				332	
	638			− 10	461	
	639		1367	451	295	
	807			255		
	819				211	
	820			496	−252	
	821		2290	244	−488	
	971				− 99	
	972			263	− 98	
	973		2134	165	−186	
III	23	− 4551				
	72	−20219				
IX	9		0.0007			
	11					0.0059
	13					0.0001
	14					0.0000

EUGEN SLUTZKY

Mathematical Institute of the Moscow State University
Moscow, U.S.S.R.

[15]

Capital accumulation and efficient allocation of resources*†

EDMOND MALINVAUD

1. *Introduction.* Among the many questions concerning the accumulation of capital the following has been said to be the most important [31]. According to which rules should choices between direct and indirect processes of production be determined; that is, when can we say that it is efficient to save today in order to increase future consumption? The present paper is devoted to this problem, which is clearly relevant for both the theory of capital and for welfare economics. The results given below are not essentially new. The author thinks, however, that his approach is likely to show in a more vivid light a few facts which, although obscurely felt, are not yet generally accepted in economic science.

The reader acquainted with welfare economics and the theory of efficient allocation of resources knows how some appropriate price system is associated with an efficient state. Loosely speaking, such a state would be an equilibrium position for a competitive economy using the given set of prices. The model introduced to prove this result does not allow explicitly for investment and capital accumulation. Thus one may wonder whether it can be extended to the case of capitalistci production. Admittedly, this is very likely. The introduction of time does not seem to imply any new principle. Choices between commodities available at different times raise essentially the same problem as choices between different commodities available at the same time. How can

* *Econometrica*, 21(1953): pp. 233–68. The proof of Theorem 1 was then incorrect, as was pointed out to the author by several readers, notably H. Uzawa. A corrigendum was published in *Econometrica*, 30(1962), pp. 570–73. The necessary changes are inserted in the present text. Reprinted by courtesy of the author and *Econometrica*.

† Based on Cowles Commission Discussion Paper, Economics, No. 2026 (hectographed), and a paper presented at the Minneapolis meeting of the Econometric Society in September, 1951. Acknowledgment is due staff members and guests of the Cowles Commission and those attending econometrics seminars in Paris. Their interest in the subject greatly helped me to bring the study to its present formulation. I am particularly indebted to M. Allais, T. C. Koopmans, and G. Debreu. Anyone acquainted with their work will discern their influence in this paper. But the reader might not know how much I owe to their personal encouragement and friendly criticism. I am also indebted to Mrs. Jane Novick who read my manuscript carefully and made many stylistic improvements.

Reprinted from READINGS IN WELFARE ECONOMICS, Kenneth J. Arrow and Tibor Scitovsky (eds.), Vol. XII (1969), Richard D. Irwin consumers' needs best be satisfied when the production of goods involves strong relations of interdependence?

However, one thing may not be clear: in a competitive economy there is a rate of interest that is used to discount future values both on the loan market and in business accounting. Is this rate a part of the price system associated with an efficient economic process? In particular, should prices of the same commodity available at different times stand in some definite ratio depending only on the time lag and not on the specific commodity considered?

In order to deal with this and related questions this paper is divided into four parts. In the first, the process of capitalistic production is analyzed. A general model is defined that may be given two equivalent presentations. An "extensive form" generalizes current capital-theory models, while a "reduced form" makes it possible to apply the usual welfare reasoning.

The second part is purely mathematical, the main result of the paper being proved there. It provides a somewhat straightforward generalization of what was already known for the timeless case, the only difficulty arising when the future is assumed not bounded by some given horizon. The economic meaning and implications of the main theorem are examined in Part III. As most of the previous work on the theory of capital was based on statonary economies, it is worth studying them carefully. This is attempted in Part IV.

Because this study is mainly concerned with formal results, heuristic comments are reduced as much as the subject permits. It is supposed that the reader is well acquainted with welfare economics.

2. *Notation.* The mathematical tools used here are primarily vectors and sets in finite-dimensional Euclidean spaces. A vector in m-dimensional Euclidean space is denoted by a Latin letter (x_t, for instance), with an index specifying the time considered. The components of x_t are denoted by x_{it}, the distinction between vectors and their components being shown by the placement of the index t.

The symbol $\{x_t\}$ represents a sequence of vectors $x_1, x_2, \ldots, x_t, \ldots$, where t takes all positive integral values. This sequence is also written more simply as $\mathbf{x}$, where the index is removed and the symbol is printed in boldface type.

The inequality $x_t \leqq y_t$ (as well as $\mathbf{x} \leqq \mathbf{y}$) applied to vectors x_t and y_t (or to sequences $\mathbf{x}$ and $\mathbf{y}$) means that no component x_{it} of x_t (or x_{it} of $\mathbf{x}$) is greater than the corresponding components of y_t (or of $\mathbf{y}$). The inequality $x_t \leq y_t$ (as well as $\mathbf{x} \leqq \mathbf{y}$) means $x_t \leqq y_t$ and $x_t \neq y_t$ (or $\mathbf{x} \leqq \mathbf{y}$ and $\mathbf{x} \neq \mathbf{y}$).

A vector x_t (as well as a sequence $\mathbf{x}$) is said to be nonnegative if $x_t \geqq 0$ (or if $\mathbf{x} \geqq 0$).

Sets are denoted by bold faced capitals. The addition of sets is defined as follows:

$\mathbf{V} = \mathbf{U}_1 + \mathbf{U}_2$ means: v is an element of $\mathbf{V}$ if and only if it can be written as $v = u_1 + u_2$, where u_1 and u_2 are elements of $\mathbf{U}_1$ and $\mathbf{U}_2$ respectively; that is, $u_1 \in \mathbf{U}_1$, $u_2 \in \mathbf{U}_2$. u_0 is said to be a minimal element of $\mathbf{U}$ if there is no $u \in \mathbf{U}$ with $u \leqq u_0$.

I. GENERAL MODEL OF CAPITALISTIC PRODUCTION

3. *Time, commodities, and capital goods.* Although time is usually considered as some continuous variable taking any value from minus infinity to plus infinity, it is given here as a succession of periods beginning at the present and going to infinity in the future. Indeed, since the past cannot be changed by any present economic decision, we may disregard it; moreover, there is little harm in assuming a decomposition in periods since their length may be made as short as one wishes.

Formally time appears as an index t that can take any positive integral value; $t = 1$ refers to the present moment, which is the beginning of the coming period, called period 1; $t + 1$ refers to the end of period t, or to the beginning of period $t + 1$.

The description of all economic activity proceeds in terms of commodities. Commodities, therefore, must be understood in a very general sense, and so as to cover in particular all services. The total number of commodities is supposed to be finite and equal to m.[1]

Formally, a set of given quantities of commodities is represented by a vector x_t in the m-dimensional Euclidean space. The component x_{it} of x_t defines which quantity of commodity i is included in x_t.

The concept of capital does not appear explicitly in our treatment and it is not needed. But for the interpretation of the following parts it may be better to define at least capital goods. Capital goods at time t include everything that has been made in preceding periods and is transferred to period t for further use in production. This definition is the old "produced means of production."[2] It stems from the essential character of capital. Indeed, it is made in order to make possible the use in future periods of goods or services that do not exist as natural resources or are not available in sufficient quantity.

4. "*Chronics*"—*extensive form.* We shall mean by a "chronic"[3] a quantitative description of the economic activity occurring during all future periods. It is one of all possible courses of events. A chronic is completely determined when the quantities produced, traded, and consumed are known, i.e., it does not require the definition of any standard of value. Two different chronics, C^1 and C^2, are distinguished by their upper indexes; any vector written with an upper index 1, x_t^1 for instance, represents the value taken by the corresponding vector, x_t, in the chronic C^1.

---

[1] This assumption is not strictly necessary. All that follows remains true as long as there is only a finite number of commodities inside each period.

[2] This might be thought of as too inclusive. Indeed, there is little in our modern world that is not the result of previous economic activity. But the origin of existing wealth does not concern us here. The distinction between natural resources and produced means of production is not important as far as past activity is concerned. The only condition we need to keep in mind is the following: the available natural resources during all future periods must be independent of any present or future economic decision.

[3] This neologism was introduced by G. Th. Guilbaud in his study on time series [11] (Added for the 1967 reprint: The word "chronic" was not used in later writings but replaced by "program," which is now the appropriate technical term.)

More precisely, a chronic *C* provides the following picture. At the present time certain commodities are available and are represented by a vector $\bar{b}_1$. Parts of them are devoted to consumption during period 1, the rest being kept for further consumption or used in production. Let us call x_1^+ and c_1 these two parts:

$$\bar{b}_1 = x_1^+ + c_1.$$

For production during the first period c_1 is used, together with natural resources z_1 and services x_1^- obtained from consumer (labor). If a_1 represents the aggregate vector of productive factors, then

$$a_1 = x_1^- + z_1 + c_1,$$

which is reminiscent of the familiar trilogy: labor, land, and capital.[4]

Productive activity transforms a_1 into some other vector, b_2, available at time 2.

The description of the second period will be similar to that of the first, with vectors b_2, x_2^+, c_2, x_2^-, z_2, a_2, b_3, and so on, for all periods. This defines the "extensive form" of chronics *C*.

The following equations hold:

$$b_t = x_t^+ + c_t \qquad \text{(for all } t\text{)}, \tag{1}$$

and

$$a_t = x_t^- + z_t + c_t \qquad \text{(for all } t\text{)}. \tag{2}$$

If we define

$$x_t = x_t^+ - x_t^-, \tag{3}$$

then, we also have

$$a_t = b_t - x_t + z_t. \tag{4}$$

C may be represented as in Figure 1.

Such a chronic is possible if and only if the transformation from a_t to b_{t+1} is technically possible and if the resources used, z_t, never exceed the resources available, given by a vector $\bar{z}_t$. The second condition is formally expressed as

$$z_t \leqq \bar{z}_t. \tag{5}$$

The condition that the transformation from a_t to b_{t+1} be technically possible may be translated into formal language by saying that the pair (a_t, b_{t+1}) must be in some set $\mathbf{T}_t$, given a priori from the state of technological knowledge at time *t*, or

$$(a_t, b_{t+1}) \in \mathbf{T}_t. \tag{6}$$

[4] The question of whether there are two or three primary factors of production has been much debated. However, the answer seems to be fairly clear. Considering any one period there are indeed three factors. But if economic development as a whole, past, present, and future, is considered, capital cannot be considered a primary factor.

Figure 1

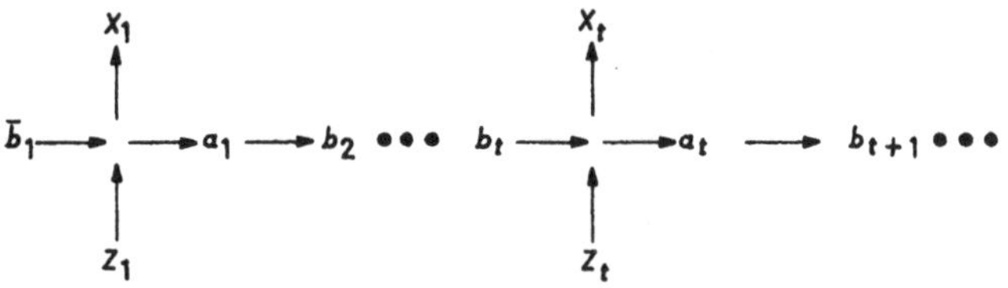

From this definition, $\mathbf{T}_t$ is clearly a set in the $2m$-dimensional Euclidean space.

5. *Assumptions concerning the sets of technological possibilities.* The theoretical results of the following sections make extensive use of some assumptions concerning the sets $\mathbf{T}_t$ of technological possibilities. The first assumption can hardly be objected to if one remembers that the limitation of resources is independently represented in the model.

ASSUMPTION 1 (additivity): *If from a_t^1 it is possible to obtain b_{t+1}^1 in period t, and from a_t^2 to obtain b_{t+1}^2 in the same period, then from $a_t^1 + a_t^2$ it is possible to obtain $b_{t+1}^1 + b_{t+1}^2$.*

Or, formally, if $(a_t^1, b_{t+1}^1) \in \mathbf{T}_t$ and $(a_t^2, b_{t+1}^2) \in \mathbf{T}_t$, then

$$(a_t^1 + a_t^2, b_{t+1}^1 + b_{t+1}^2) \in \mathbf{T}_t.$$

The second assumption is not so immediate and could be challenged by many readers. But it is taken as a crude first approximation to reality. Moreover, it is necessary in the proofs of the following sections. So it is justified in some way by its usefulness.

ASSUMPTION 2 (divisibility): *If from a_t it is possible to obtain b_{t+1}, then from αa_t it is possible to obtain αb_{t+1}, where α is any positive number less than* 1.

Or, formally, if $(a_t, b_{t+1}) \in \mathbf{T}_t$ and $0 < \alpha < 1$, then

$$(\alpha a_t, \alpha b_{t+1}) \in \mathbf{T}_t.$$

When Assumptions 1 and 2 are made, $\mathbf{T}_t$, considered as a set in the $2m$-dimensional Euclidean space, is a convex cone with vertex at the origin.

In most of the demonstrations given below, only convexity of $\mathbf{T}_t$ plays an essential role. For the sake of clarity, it is better to assume convexity alone, although in practice such an assumption is probably as restrictive as Assumptions 1 and 2 together.

ASSUMPTION 3 (convexity): *If from a_t^1 it is possible to obtain b_{t+1}^1 and from a_t^2 to obtain b_{t+1}^2, then from any combination $\alpha a_t^1 + \beta a_t^2$ it is possible to obtain the corresponding $\alpha b_{t+1}^1 + \beta b_{t+1}^2$, where α is any positive number less than* 1 *and $\beta = 1 - \alpha$.*

Or, formally, if $(a_t^1, b_{t+1}^1) \in \mathbf{T}_t$ and $(a_t^2, b_{t+1}^2) \in \mathbf{T}_t$, with $0 < \alpha < 1$ and $\alpha + \beta = 1$, then

$$(\alpha a_t^1 + \beta a_t^2, \alpha b_{t+1}^1 + \beta b_{t+1}^2) \in \mathbf{T}_t.$$

The next and last assumption is trivial; it amounts to saying that production is not restricted if more of each good is available.

ASSUMPTION 4 (free disposal): *If from a_t^1 it is possible to obtain b_{t+1}^1, then it is also possible to obtain it from any vector a_t such that $a_t \geqq a_t^1$.*

Or, formally, if $(a_t^1, b_{t+1}^1) \in \mathbf{T}_t$ and $a_t \geqq a_t^1$, then

$$(a_t, b_{t+1}^1) \in \mathbf{T}_t.$$

6. *Decentralization of production.* In an actual economy production is not planned by a central bureau but is accomplished by many different firms, each having its own technology. The activity of the kth production unit during period t consists in a transformation of the vector a_{tk} into the vector $b_{t+1,k}$.[5] This transformation can be performed if and only if $(a_{tk}, b_{t+1,k})$ is an element of some set of technological possibilities, $\mathbf{T}_{tk}$, or if

$$(a_{tk}, b_{t+1,k}) \in T_{tk}. \tag{7}$$

For the economy as a whole the simultaneous operation of all production units, n in number,[6] results in a transformation of a_t into b_{t+1}, with

$$a_t = \sum_{k=1}^{n} a_{tk}, \qquad b_t = \sum_{k=1}^{n} b_{tk}. \tag{8}$$

Since (a_t, b_{t+1}) is in $\mathbf{T}_t$, it is clear that in all cases

$$\sum_{k=1}^{n} \mathbf{T}_{tk} \subset \mathbf{T}_t,$$

which only means that, if some transformation is possible within the framework of given production units, it is also possible a priori for society as a whole. However, the decomposition into production units could be inefficient, in the sense that it would make impossible some transformations that we know to be

[5] The vectors a_{tk} and b_{tk} may be decomposed as follows:

$$a_{tk} = c_{tk} + q_{tk}, \qquad b_{tk} + g_{tk} = s_{tk} + c_{tk},$$

with c_{tk} representing capital equipment of firm k at time t; q_{tk}, current purchases of firm k at time t; g_{tk}, Purchases of equipment of firm k at time t; and s_{tk}, sales of firm k at time t.

The following relations hold:

$$c_t = \sum_{k=1}^{n} c_{tk}, \qquad z_t + \sum_{k=1}^{n} s_{tk} = x_t + \sum_{k=1}^{n} q_{tk} + \sum_{k=1}^{n} g_{tk}.$$

[6] The reader might object that the decomposition into production units need not remain unchanged as time goes on. This is quite true. We do not want, however, to make the model too involved. From the treatment given below for consumption units the reader will see that our results hold true with little change as long as there is only a finite number of firms during each period.

possible a priori. In the following pages it is supposed that some decentralization of production has been found that is efficient, or, in other words, that

$$\sum_{k=1}^{n} \mathbf{T}_{tk} = \mathbf{T}_t . \tag{9}$$

The technological possibilities for the kth firm are given by a sequence of sets, $\{\mathbf{T}_{tk}\}$. The assumptions on each $\mathbf{T}_{tk}$ are the same as those made on $\mathbf{T}_t$.

The decomposition of $\mathbf{T}_t$ may also be used to overcome the following difficulty. The inequality $z_t \leqq \bar{z}_t$ would introduce in the following Part II some complications that can be avoided by supposing the equality sign to hold, i.e., the utilized resources to be always equal to the available resources. This can easily be done by assuming the existence of some $(n + 1)$th activity which uses $\bar{z}_t - z_t$ but does not produce anything.

Formally, there is an activity characterized by the vectors

$$\left.\begin{aligned} a_{t,n+1} &= \bar{z}_t - z_t \\ b_{t,n+1} &= 0 \end{aligned}\right\}. \tag{10}$$

The set associated with this activity is defined by

$$(a_{t,n+1}, b_{t+1,n+1}) \in \mathbf{T}_{t,n+1} \qquad \text{if} \quad a_{t,n+1} \geqq 0, \quad b_{t+1,\,n+1} = 0. \tag{11}$$

From Assumption 4, the following is obvious:

$$\mathbf{T}_t + \mathbf{T}_{t,n+1} = \mathbf{T}_t . \tag{12}$$

Throughout the following pages we shall write

$$z_t = \bar{z}_t \qquad \text{(for all } t\text{)}. \tag{13}$$

The fictitious activity will be removed from the picture only when the final result is reached.

7. *Chronics—reduced form.* Let us now define the "input vector" y_t for time t as

$$y_t = a_t - b_t . \tag{14}$$

From equalities (4) and (13), it follows that

$$x_t + y_t = \bar{z}_t . \tag{15}$$

The "reduced form" of the chronic C is defined when the two sequences $\mathbf{x}$ and $\mathbf{y}$ are given, with the following necessary condition:

$$\mathbf{x} + \mathbf{y} = \bar{\mathbf{z}}. \tag{16}$$

From the limitation on technological knowledge, $\mathbf{y}$ is a possible sequence of input vectors if and only if

$$\mathbf{y} \in \mathbf{Y}, \tag{17}$$

where $\mathbf{Y}$ may be defined from $\{\mathbf{T}_t\}$ in the following way:

$\mathbf{y} \in \mathbf{Y}$ *if and only if there are two sequences* $\mathbf{a}$ *and* $\mathbf{b}$ *such that*[7]

$$\left.\begin{aligned} b_1 &= \bar{b}_1 \\ y_t &= a_t - b_t \\ (a_t, b_{t+1}) &\in \mathbf{T}_t \end{aligned}\right\} \quad \text{(for all } t\text{).} \tag{18}$$

From the convexity of $\mathbf{T}_t$, $\mathbf{Y}$ is convex. If $\mathbf{y}^1$ and $\mathbf{y}^2$ are in $\mathbf{Y}$, then there are $\mathbf{a}^1$, $\mathbf{b}^1$ and $\mathbf{a}^2$, $\mathbf{b}^2$ satisfying (18). Now, if $0 < \alpha < 1$ and $\alpha + \beta = 1$, then $\{\alpha a_t^1 + \beta a_t^2\}$, $\{\alpha b_t^1 + \beta b_t^2\}$ satisfies (18). Hence, $\alpha\mathbf{y}^1 + \beta\mathbf{y}^2$ is in $\mathbf{Y}$.

To the decomposition of $\mathbf{T}_t$ into convex sets $\mathbf{T}_{tk}$ corresponds a decomposition of $\mathbf{Y}$ into convex sets $\mathbf{Y}_k$. Each $\mathbf{y}$ in $\mathbf{Y}$ can be written as[8]

$$\mathbf{y} = \sum_{k=1}^{n+1} \mathbf{y}_k$$

with $\mathbf{y}_k \in \mathbf{Y}_k$ and $y_{tk} = a_{tk} - b_{tk}$.

8. *Social choice among chronics.* According to principles first made clear by Pareto, it is sometimes possible to say that a chronic C^2 is "better" than some other chronic C^1. The exact definition of this preference may vary, but in all cases comparison is made only on the consumption vectors x_t. Indeed, economic organization aims at satisfying consumers' needs; hence, the technical process by which this is done is irrelevant to social choice.

The simplest possible criterion is undoubtedly the following: C^2 is said to be better than C^1 if the consumption sequences $\mathbf{x}^2$ and $\mathbf{x}^1$ fulfill the condition $\mathbf{x}^2 \geq \mathbf{x}^1$.

Loosely speaking, this means that there is at least as much of everything to consume in C^2 as in C^1 and that no more labor is required. This leads us to the concept of efficiency:[9]

Definition 1: *A chronic C^1 is efficient if there is no possible chronic C leading to a consumption sequence* $\mathbf{x}$ *such that* $\mathbf{x} \geq \mathbf{x}^1$.

More generally, if there are any social preferences, then, attached to any given chronic C^1, there exists a set $\mathbf{X}$ of all $\mathbf{x}$ corresponding to chronics C that are preferred to C^1. The following assumption on $\mathbf{X}$ will be made:

Assumption 5: $\mathbf{X}$ *is convex and, if it contains* $\mathbf{x}^2$, *it also contains any* $\mathbf{x}$ *such that* $\mathbf{x} \geqq \mathbf{x}^2$.

---

[7] The reader might find that the constraint $b_1 = \bar{b}_1$ does not pertain to technology and should not enter the definition of $\mathbf{Y}$. Nothing is changed in the following mathematical treatment and little in the economic interpretation if $\bar{z}_1$ is defined so as to include the services of natural resources *and* all existing commodities at time 1. As was pointed out in footnote 2, the exact content of initial capital has no real significance here; thus we are free to assume $\bar{b}_1 = 0$. If this is done, the first formula in (18) must be changed accordingly and the reasoning may proceed without any alteration.

[8] Using the definitions introduced in footnote 5, we may write $y_{tk} = q_{tk} + g_{tk} - s_{tk}$, so that the input vector for firm k at time t is the difference between purchases and sales.

[9] Because of its simplicity, this definition is not fully satisfactory. In particular, it does not provide for the existence of commodities that are not wanted for consumption. However, since we shall also deal with the most general criterion for social preferences, it is advisable to choose here the simplest possible definition of efficiency so as to make the treatment of this case easily understandable.

C^1 may be said to be optimal if there is no possible C with $\mathbf{x} \in \mathbf{X}$. In the following pages we shall, however, restrict the meaning of optimality and deal only with the usual welfare criterion. According to this criterion social choices are determined from individual preferences in the following way:

There are present and future consumers,[10] each of whom is characterized by an index j (a positive number). His activity is represented by a consumption sequence $\mathbf{x}_j$, which may also be written $\mathbf{x}_j = \mathbf{x}_j^+ - \mathbf{x}_j^-$.

Since the life of any consumer j is limited,[11] then necessarily $x_{tj} = 0$, except for a finite number of values of t. More precisely, let us suppose that the indexes j are so chosen that, for a given t, $x_{tj} = 0$, except for $j_t^0 \leqq j \leqq j_t^1$. (There is only a finite number of consumers living at any time.) For a given j we also have $x_{tj} = 0$, except for $t_j^0 \leqq t \leqq t_j^1$ and, for any j, $t_j^1 - t_j^0 \leqq \theta$.

With these assumptions we may write

$$\mathbf{x} = \sum_j \mathbf{x}_j. \tag{19}$$

Now, for each consumer j, there is a set X_j of all sequences $\mathbf{x}_j$ that are at least equivalent to $\mathbf{x}_j^1$, and a set $\mathbf{X}_j$ of all sequences $\mathbf{x}_j$ that are preferred to $\mathbf{x}_j^1$. According to the Pareto principle[12] we say that $\mathbf{x}$ is preferred to $\mathbf{x}^1$ (or $\mathbf{x} \in \mathbf{X}$) if it may be written as a sum of sequences $\mathbf{x}_j$ with

$$\mathbf{x}_j \in X_j \quad \text{for all } j, \text{ and}$$
$$\mathbf{x}_j \in \mathbf{X}_j \quad \text{for at least one } j.$$

In the following we shall suppose that X_j and $\mathbf{X}_j$ fulfill Assumption 5. We may now give the following definition.

DEFINITION 2: *A chronic C^1 is "optimal" if there is no possible chronic C such that $\mathbf{x} \in \mathbf{X}$, where $\mathbf{X}$ is defined according to the Pareto principle.*

It is not necessary to insist here on the meaning of such concepts as efficiency and optimality for practical economic policy. This has been done elsewhere.

---

[10] It might seem strange to introduce those consumers who do not yet exist. But if we consider all the consequences of our present economic decisions, however distant they might be, we have to take account of future generations, at least in a crude fashion. If they are not taken into consideration, production of certain very durable equipment would never be profitable.

[11] It would also be possible to introduce consumption units with infinite life, such as a national army. This would not create much difficulty.

[12] One might think the Pareto principle is still too restrictive as soon as choices involving time are concerned. Old people often say they would have planned their lives differently "if they had known." Clearly, only present individual preferences are considered in this paper. Each consumer is supposed fully to appreciate the relative urgency of his present and future needs. However, should this hypothesis be rejected, it would still be possible to introduce a weaker principle for social choices. One may say C is better than C^1 if it is preferred by all consumers now, and will still be preferred by them given all their future preference patterns. The latter concept has been used extensively by M. Allais [3, Chapter VI].

II. PROPERTIES OF EFFICIENT AND OPTIMAL CHRONICS

In this part, general properties of efficient and optimal chronics are studied. Nothing is assumed regarding the rhythm of expansion in the economy. In particular, some chronics may be efficient although they include periods with low levels of consumption and high investment followed by periods of disinvestment and high consumption. As usual in welfare economics and the theory of efficient allocation of resources, the final theorem introduces a price vector and rules of decentralization very similar to those which would hold in a competitive economy.

In order to make the main proof easier to understand, it is given in full detail for efficient chronics. The generalization to optimal chronics is merely sketched in the last paragraph. The reader will probably better understand the process of deduction if we first consider the case in which there is an economic horizon.

9. *Case of a finite horizon.* A chronic C^1 is efficient if there is no chronic C fulfilling[13]

$$\left.\begin{array}{l}\mathbf{x} \geq \mathbf{x}^1, \\ \mathbf{x} + \mathbf{y} = \bar{\mathbf{z}} \text{ and} \\ \mathbf{y} \in Y\end{array}\right\}. \tag{20}$$

Suppose now that there is some finite economic horizon h; in other words suppose that the result of economic activity is no longer an infinite sequence of consumption vectors but that there are only consumption vectors x_t for the $h - 1$ coming periods and the final stock of commodities b_h for the last period. Thus, the economic output is given by the finite set

$$\mathbf{x} = \{x_1, x_2, \ldots, x_t, \ldots, x_{h-1}, b_h\}.$$

$\mathbf{x}$ is a vector in the mh-dimensional Euclidean space. In the same way,

$$\mathbf{y} = \{y_1, y_2, \ldots, y_t, \ldots, y_{h-1}, \bar{z}_h - b_h\},$$

and Y becomes a convex set in the mh-dimensional Euclidean space.

In this form the problem is mathematically the same as in the static case. From previous works it is known that an efficient state is associated with some price vector,

$$\mathbf{p} = \{p_1, p_2, \ldots, p_t, \ldots, p_h\}.$$

The reader will find, for instance, a complete treatment of this finite case in Debreu's paper [8]. The price vector $\mathbf{p}$ is introduced, and its meaning when several periods are considered is indicated. See, in particular [**8**, p. 282, lines 10 to 14].

---

[13] Hence, we look for minimal elements in **Y**. From a mathematical viewpoint, Theorem 1 provides a characterization of a minimal element in a convex set embedded in the linear space obtained by the Cartesian product of an infinite sequence of m-dimensional Euclidean spaces.

The existence of a price sequence will also be the essential result of the next section. But, as it stands now, it is somewhat unsatisfactory because nothing implies that the final stock of commodities is economically efficient in any sense.

In order to remove this limitation the efficiency of a chronic C^1 will be determined by successive steps. First C^1 will be compared to all C that are analogous to if after some given period h. Then h will be moved farther and farther into the future. If in this process there is never found any C better than C^1, then C^1 is efficient. This is indeed, the only way in which the problem can be handled in practice; hence, one may expect that it is also the only way in which economically meaningful results can be reached.

10. *Existence of a price vector.* To justify this procedure we need, however, to establish the following lemma:

LEMMA 1: *Under Assumption* 4, C^1 *is efficient if and only if, for all* h, *there is no possible* C *with*

$$\begin{cases} \mathbf{x} \geq \mathbf{x}^1, \\ x_t = x_t^1 \qquad (\text{for } t > h). \end{cases} \tag{21}$$

PROOF: If C^1 is efficient, there is clearly no C fulfilling (21). Conversely, suppose there is some possible C fulfilling $\mathbf{x} \geq \mathbf{x}^1$. Then, for at least one h, $x_h \geq x_h^1$. Given such an h, consider $\mathbf{x}^2$ defined by

$$x_t^2 = x_t \qquad (\text{for all } t \leqq h), \text{ and}$$

$$x_t^2 = x_t^1 \qquad (\text{for all } t > h).$$

Clearly $\mathbf{x}^2 \leqq \mathbf{x}$, so that, by Assumption 4, there is associated with $\mathbf{x}^2$ some possible chronic C^2. C^2 satisfies (21), which completes the proof.

Given a chronic C^1, suppose we now restrict our attention to the possible chronic C fulfilling

$$\left.\begin{matrix} \mathbf{y} \in \mathbf{T} \\ x_t = x_t^1 \end{matrix}\right\} \qquad (\text{for } t > h). \tag{22}$$

This leads to the following lemma:

LEMMA 2: *Under Assumptions* 3 *and* 4, *if* C^1 *is efficient among all* C *satisfying* (22), *then there are* h *nonnegative vectors* p_t, *not all zero, such that*

$$\sum_{t-1}^{h} p_t y_t$$

is minimum for C^1 *among all* C *satisfying* (22).

PROOF: For all possible C satisfying (22) the following holds:

$$\begin{cases} \mathbf{y} \in \mathbf{T} \\ y_t = \bar{z}_t - x_t^1 \qquad (\text{for all } t > h). \end{cases} \tag{23}$$

Thus, if C^1 is efficient among all C satisfying (22), $\mathbf{y}^1$ is minimal among all $\mathbf{y}$ satisfying (23).

Now, consider the following vector in the mh-dimensional Euclidean space: $\mathbf{y}_h = \{y_1, \ldots, y_t, \ldots, y_h\}$. $\mathbf{y}$ fulfills (23) only if the vector $\mathbf{y}_h$ obtained from it is in some set $\mathbf{Y}_h$ depending on C^1 and h. From the convexity of $\mathbf{Y}$ it follows that $\mathbf{Y}_h$ is convex. Thus, $\mathbf{y}_h^1$ has to be a minimal element in the convex set $\mathbf{Y}_h$. This implies the existence in $\mathbf{y}_h^1$ of a support plane to $\mathbf{Y}_h$ whose normal vector $\mathbf{p}_h$ is nonnegative;[14] or the existence of a nonnegative linear form

$$\sum_{t=1}^{h} p_t y_t$$

which is minimal for $\mathbf{y}_h^1$. Lemma 2 follows from this.

More precisely, if there are several support planes, the normal vectors generate a convex closed cone in the mh-dimensional Euclidean space.[15]

Going back to the extensive form of the chronics, we may write

$$\sum_{t=1}^{h} p_t y_t = -p_1 \bar{b}_1 + \sum_{t=1}^{h-1} (p_t a_t - p_{t+1} b_{t+1}) + p_h a_h. \tag{24}$$

Since the sets $\mathbf{T}_t$ are defined independently of the values taken by the y_t,

$$\sum_{t=1}^{h} p_t y_t$$

is minimal for C^1 among all C satisfying (22) if and only if:

---

[14] The following mathematical theorem is applicable here:

THEOREM: *In finite-dimensional Euclidean space, given a convex set* A *with a nonempty interior and a point x not interior to* A, *there is a plane* P *containing x and such that* A *is entirely contained in one of the closed half-spaces limited by* P.

For proof of this one may, for instance, transpose a proof by Banach [4, p. 28]. The reader may notice that A need not be closed.

y_h^1, being minimal, is necessarily a boundary point of $\mathbf{Y}_h$. So there is a nonzero vector p_h fulfilling the conditions of Lemma 2. The fact that $p_h \geqq 0$ follows directly from Assumption 4.

[15] If

$$\sum_{t=1}^{h} p_t(y_t - y_t^1) \geqq 0 \quad \text{and} \quad \sum_{t=1}^{h} p_t'(y_t - y_t^1) \geqq 0,$$

then, clearly

$$\sum_{t=1}^{h} (\alpha p_t + \beta p_t')(y_t - y_t^1) \geqq 0$$

for any $\alpha \geqq 0$ and $\beta \geqq 0$.

Also, if p_h^n is a sequence of vectors converging to $\mathbf{p}_h$, and if

$$\sum_{t=1}^{h} p_t^n(y_t - y_t^1) \geqq 0 \quad \text{for all } n,$$

then

$$\sum_{t=1}^{h} p_t(y_t - y_t^1) \geqq 0.$$

Figure 2

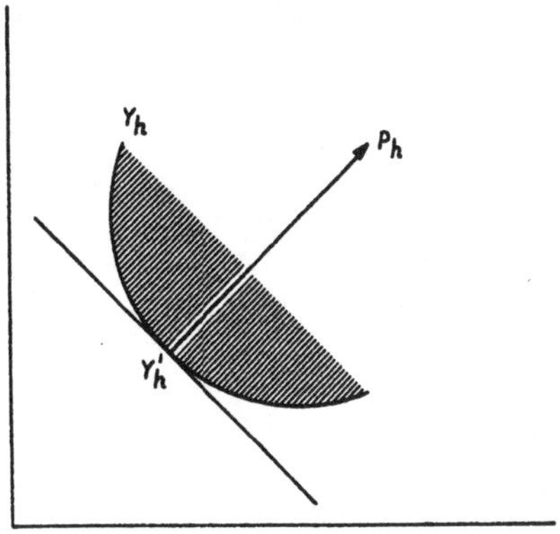

i) For all $t < h, p_t a_t - p_{t+1} b_{t+1}$ is minimal at (a_t^1, b_{t+1}^1) among all $(a_t, b_{t+1}) \in \mathbf{T}_t$;

ii) $p_h a_h$ is minimal at a_h^1 among all a_h that make possible $y_t = \bar{z}_t - x_t^1$ for all $t > h$.

If p_t is interpreted as a vector of discounted prices, $p_{t+1}b_{t+1} - p_t a_t$ will be the discounted profit from production during period t (see sections 14 and 15 below). Property (i) asserts that this profit should be maximized over the set of feasible productions. Property (ii) states that the value of capital at time h should be minimal over the set of chronics that permit the same consumption after time h as C^1 does.

We should now prove the existence of an infinite sequence $\mathbf{p}$ such that, for all h,

$$\sum_t p_t y_t$$

is minimal for C^1 among all C satisfying (22). But, in order to do so, we shall make a new assumption, which will be economically acceptable if we distinguish those commodities that cannot be produced or stored, essentially the various services of labor. Let us suppose they are the last n_2 commodities, and partition the vectors of inputs, outputs, and prices as follows:

$$a_t = \begin{bmatrix} d_t \\ e_t \end{bmatrix}, \qquad b_t = \begin{bmatrix} f_t \\ 0 \end{bmatrix}, \qquad p_t = \begin{bmatrix} q_t \\ s_t \end{bmatrix}, \tag{25}$$

where d_t, f_t, and q_t will be vectors of $n_1 = n - n_2$ components; e_t and s_t vectors of n_2 components, and 0 a vector of n_2 zeros.

Let us now make the following hypothesis about the optimum program C^1 and the technological sets $\mathbf{T}_t$.

ASSUMPTION 6. In any period t, it would be technically possible to produce outputs f_{t+1} larger than f^1_{t+1} by using inputs of labor services e_t smaller than e^1_t and some conveniently chosen inputs d_t of the other commodities.[16]

Formally, for any t, there is some $(a_t, b_{t+1}) \in \mathbf{T}_t$ such that $f_{t+1} > f^1_{t+1}$ and $e_t < e^1_t$.

Since no restriction is placed on d_t, this assumption seems to be quite acceptable. A sufficiently large increase of the inputs of nonlabor commodities should permit reducing the inputs of labor services while increasing outputs. The assumption would, however, fail to hold if no input of some particular kind of labor service appeared in the optimum program, or if technology would imply strict proportionality between total labor inputs and total outputs.

We are now able to prove the following natural generalization of the efficiency theorem:

THEOREM 1: *Under Assumptions* 3, 4, *and* 6, *associated with an efficient chronic* C^1, *there is a nonnegative nonnull sequence* $\mathbf{p}$ *such that, for all h,*

$$\sum_{t=1}^{h} p_t y_t$$

is minimal for C^1 *among all C satisfying* (22).

PROOF: Let us define the following norm on the nonnegative prices:

$$|q_t| = \sum_{i=1}^{n_1} q_{it}, \qquad |s_t| = \sum_{i=n_1+1}^{n_2} s_{it}. \tag{26}$$

Assumption 6 implies the existence of numbers α_t such that, in any nh-dimensional nonnegative and nonzero vector $(p_1, p_2, \ldots, p_h)$ fulfilling conditions (i) and (ii):

$$q_1 \geq 0, \qquad |q_{t+1}| \leqq \alpha_t |q_t|, \qquad |s_t| \leqq \alpha_t |q_t|, \qquad \text{for all } t < h. \tag{27}$$

Indeed, write condition (i) for the input-output combination whose existence is asserted by Assumption 6:

$$q_{t+1}(f_{t+1} - f^1_{t+1}) - q_t(d_t - d^1_t) - s_t(e_t - e^1_t) \leqq 0 \tag{28}$$

with

$$\left.\begin{array}{lll} q_{t+1} \geqq 0; & q_t \geqq 0; & s_t \geqq 0; \\ f_{t+1} - f^1_{t+1} > 0; & & e_t - e^1_t < 0. \end{array}\right\} \tag{29}$$

[16] Assumption 6 is now known in the technical literature as the "non tightness assumption". The proof also holds if all commodities can be produced ($ne = 0$). The condition on e_t may then obviously be deleted.

Suppose now $q_t = 0$; then (28) and (29) imply $q_{t+1} = 0$ and $s_t = 0$. Since $(p_1, p_2, \ldots, p_h)$ is nonzero, q_1 must then necessarily be nonzero and the first inequality in (27) is established. [17]

Let now φ_t and δ_t be any positive numbers such that

$$\begin{aligned} f_{i,t+1} - f^1_{i,t+1} &\geqq \varphi_t && \text{for all } i = 1, 2, \ldots, n_1, \\ e_{i,t} - e^1_{i,t} &\leqq -\varphi_t && \text{for all } i = n_1 + 1, \ldots, n_2, \\ d_{it} - d^1_{it} &\leqq \delta_t && \text{for all } i = 1, 2, \ldots, n_1. \end{aligned}$$

Then the left-hand side of (28) is not smaller than $|q_{t+1}|\varphi_t - |q_t|\delta_t + |s_t|\varphi_t$ which must therefore be nonpositive. Taking $\alpha_t = \delta_t/\varphi_t$, the last two inequalities in (27) follow directly.

After these preliminaries, it is possible to show how an infinite sequence of prices can be obtained. Suppose one nh-dimensional vector fulfilling condition (i) and (ii) has been found for each h ($h = 1, 2, \ldots$ ad infinitum). Let this vector be $(p^h_1, p^h_2, \ldots, p^h_t, \ldots, p^h_h)$. The first inequality in (27) shows that $q^h_1 \geq 0$. We may therefore assume that the nh-dimensional vector has been normalized in such a way that $|q^h_1| = 1$. It then follows from the second and third inequalities in (27) that, for any t, p^h_t is bounded, uniformly in h.

The sequence $\{p^h_1\}$, for $h = 1, 2, \ldots$ ad infinitum, being bounded has a converging subsequence. Let $h^1_{\tau_1}$, with $\tau_1 = 1, 2, \ldots$ ad infinitum, be the indices of this subsequence and p_1 its limit point. Since q^h_1 has been normalized p_1 is non-null.

The sequence $\{p^h_2\}$, for $h = h^1_{\tau_1}$ with $\tau_1 = 1, 2, \ldots$ ad infinitum, is bounded and has a converging subsequence. Let $h^2_{\tau_2}$, with $\tau_2 = 1, 2, \ldots$ ad infinitum, be the indices of this subsequence and p_2 its limit point.

By induction, we can find for any t a converging subsequence $\{p^h_t\}$ with $h = h^t_{\tau_t}$ and $\tau_t = 1, 2, \ldots$ ad infinitum. We may designate by p_t the limit point of this subsequence.

The $p_1, p_2, \ldots, p_t, \ldots$ so defined provide us with the sequence whose existence is asserted by Theorem 1. Indeed, for all h and in particular for $h = h^t_{\tau_t}$, $(a_{t-1}, b_t) \in T_{t-1}$ implies:

$$p^h_{t-1}(a_{t-1} - a^1_{t-1}) - p^h_t(b_t - b^1_t) \geqq 0; \tag{30}$$

hence also, taking the limit for increasing τ_t,

$$p_{t-1}(a_{t-1} - a^1_{t-1}) - p_t(b_t - b^1_t) \geqq 0. \tag{31}$$

Similarly, as soon as a_h makes possible $y_t = \bar{z}_t - x^1_t$ for all $t > h$:

$$p^{h'}_h(a_h - a^1_h) \geqq 0 \tag{32}$$

---

[17] The reader might object that this argument does not exclude the case $p_t = 0$ for all $t < h$; $q_h = 0$, but $s_h \geqq 0$. In fact, with the partitioning of the commodities into two groups, the n_2 last components should not appear in the last period. Instead of considering the nh-dimensional vector $(p_1, p_2, \ldots, p_h)$, we should consider the $(nh - n_2)$-dimensional vector $(p_1, p_2, \ldots, p_{h-1}, q_h)$ in Lemma 2 and in all the subsequent argument. For simplicity, I preferred not to introduce this complication here.

for all h' and in particular for $h' = h^h_{\tau_h}$; hence also, taking the limit for increasing τ_h,

$$p_h(a_h - a_h^1) \geqq 0. \tag{33}$$

Therefore, the sequence $p_1, p_2, \ldots, p_t, \ldots$, in which p_1 is nonnull, fulfills the two conditions (i) and (ii), and therefore

$$\sum_t p_t y_t$$

is minimal for C^1 among all C satisfying (22), as was to be proved.

The following lemma will give the converse of Theorem 1:

LEMMA 3: *Under Assumption* 4, *a sufficient condition for the efficiency of a chronic* C^1 *is the existence of a positive*[18] *sequence* $\mathbf{p}$ *such that, for all h,*

$$\sum_{t=1}^{h} p_t y_t$$

is minimum for C^1 *among all* C *satisfying* (22).

PROOF: Suppose C^1 is not efficient. Then, by Lemma 1, there exists an h and a C satisfying (22) such that $\mathbf{x} \geq \mathbf{x}^1$; hence $\mathbf{y} \leq \mathbf{y}^1$. Since $p_t > 0$, then

$$\sum_{t=1}^{h} p_t(y_t - y_t^1) < 0,$$

contradicting the hypothesis.

11. *Decentralization rule.* The preceding section provides a generalization of the first part of the efficiency theorem which was obtained in the static case. The second part of the same theorem specifies a rule of decentralization; more explicitly, it says that $\mathbf{py}$ is minimal for the society as a whole if and only if $\mathbf{py}_k$ is minimal for each firm. This will be the subject of Lemmas 4 and 5.

LEMMA 4: *Under Assumptions* 3, 4 *and* 6, *if* C^1 *is efficient there is a nonnegative sequence* $\mathbf{p}$ *such that, for all h and k,*

$$\sum_{t=1}^{h} p_t y_{tk}$$

is minimal at C^1 *among all* C *satisfying*

$$\left.\begin{array}{l} \mathbf{y}_k \in \mathbf{Y}_k, \text{ and} \\ y_{tk} = y_{tk}^1 \end{array}\right\} \quad (\text{for } t > h). \tag{34}$$

[18] The reader may notice we have $\mathbf{p} \geq 0$ in Theorem 1 and $\mathbf{p} > 0$ in Lemma 3, so that the lemma is not exactly the converse of the theorem. However, it does not seem to be worth extending our investigations here in order to reduce the gap. This would lead us into a rather long study. It was done for the static case in Koopmans' work. Moreover, in dealing with optimality we shall presently give a more satisfactory treatment of the difficulty.

PROOF: This follows directly from Theorem 1 because, if there were any C satisfying (34) such that

$$\sum_{t=1}^{h} p_t(y_{tk} - y_{tk}^1) < 0$$

for some k, then we could find a chronic C^2 identical with C^1 except for the input vectors of firm k. For the latter we would choose $y_{kt}^2 = y_{tk}$. Hence, C^2 would satisfy (22) and

$$\sum_{t=1}^{h} p_t(y_t^2 - y_t^1) < 0,$$

contradicting Theorem 1.

Let us first note as a consequence of Lemma 4 that C^1 is not efficient unless there is complete use of those resources which have a nonzero price. Indeed, for the $(n + 1)$th production unit we should have

$$\sum_{t=1}^{h} p_t(\bar{z}_t - z_t)$$

at a minimum. Since p_t and $\bar{z}_t - z_t$ are nonnegative, the minimum is reached when $p_t(\bar{z}_t - z_t) = 0$ for all t.

Even if $\mathbf{p} > 0$, the converse of Lemma 4 does not necessarily hold.[19] The difficulty lies in the possibility of having some C^2 such that

$$\begin{cases} y_t^2 = y_t^1 & \text{(for } t > h\text{), but not necessarily } y_{tk}^2 = y_{tk}^1, \\ \sum_{t=1}^{h} p_t(y_t^2 - y_t^1) < 0 & \end{cases}$$

[19] The following counterexample illustrates the point. Suppose there are two commodities and two firms with the same technological set:

$$(a_{tk}, b_{t+1,k}) \in \mathbf{T}_{tk} \text{ if } \begin{cases} a_{itk} \geqq 0, \ b_{i,t+1,k} \geqq 0; \text{ and} \\ a_{1tk} + a_{2tk} - b_{1,t+1,k} - b_{2,t+1,k} \geqq 0. \end{cases}$$

Consider C^1 defined by

$$C^1 \begin{cases} a_{1t} = 1, & a_{2t} = 2, & b_{1t} = 2, & b_{2t} = 1, & y_{1t} = -1, & y_{2t} = 1, \\ a_{1t1} = 0, & a_{2t1} = 2, & b_{1t1} = 2, & b_{2t1} = 0, & y_{1t1} = -2, & y_{2t1} = 2, \\ a_{1t2} = 1, & a_{2t2} = 0, & b_{1t2} = 0, & b_{2t2} = 1, & y_{1t2} = 1, & y_{2t2} = -1. \end{cases}$$

C^1 fulfills the condition of Lemma 4, with the price vector $p_t = (1, 1)$, but it is not efficient, as can be seen by comparison with the following

$$C \begin{cases} a_{1t} = a_{1t1} = 0, & a_{2t} = a_{2t1} = 1, & a_{it2} = b_{it2} = 0 & \text{(for all } t\text{)}, \\ b_{2t} = b_{2t1} = 0, & b_{1t} = b_{1t1} = 1, & & \text{(for all } t > 1\text{)}, \\ y_{t2} = 0, & y_{1t1} = -1, \ y_{2t1} = 1 & & \text{(for all } t > 1\text{)}. \end{cases}$$

Indeed, C provides us with the same net output for all periods after the first one: $x_t = x_t^1 = \bar{z}_t + (1, -1)$ for $t > 1$. And it makes possible an increase in the first consumption vector $x_1 = \bar{z}_1 + (2, 0)$, $x_1^1 = \bar{z}_1 + (1, -1)$.

although there is no C such that

$$\begin{cases} y_{tk} = y_{tk}^1 \\ \sum_{t=1}^{h} p_t(y_t - y_t^1) < 0 \quad \text{(for } t > h, \text{ and all } k). \end{cases}$$

Such a case corresponds to an inadequate distribution of capital among firms, which cannot be detected when comparisons are limited to any finite horizon.

However, the possibility of this can be ruled out if $p_h a_h$ tends to zero when h tends to infinity, i.e., if the present value of capital for period h decreases to zero when h tends to infinity. This is the meaning of the following lemma.

LEMMA 5: *Under Assumption* 4, *a sufficient condition for the efficiency of* C^1 *is that there is a positive sequence* $\mathbf{p}$ *such that*:

i) *for all h and k,*

$$\sum_{t=1}^{h} p_t y_{tk}$$

is minimal at C^1 *among all C satisfying* (34);

ii) $p_t a_t^1$ *tends to zero when t tends to infinity.*

PROOF: Suppose C^1 is not efficient. There is some h and some C^2 such that

$$\sum_{t=1}^{h} p_t(y_t^2 + y_t^1) < 0, \tag{35}$$

$$y_t^2 = y_t^1 \quad \text{or } a_t^2 - b_t^2 = a_t^1 - b_t^1 \qquad \text{(for all } t > h). \tag{36}$$

From Condition (i) it follows that $p_t a_{tk} - p_{t+1} b_{t+1,k}$ is minimal at $(a_{tk}^1, b_{t+1,k}^1)$ for all t and all $(a_{tk}, b_{t+1,k}) \in \mathrm{T}_{tk}$. Hence, for all t,

$$p_t(a_t^2 - a_t^1) \geqq p_{t+1}(b_{t+1}^2 - b_{t+1}^1). \tag{37}$$

(35) and (37) imply

$$p_h(a_h^2 - a_h^1) < 0. \tag{38}$$

Now, (36), (37), and (38) imply that the following is a nonincreasing sequence of negative vectors:

$$0 > p_h(a_h^2 - a_h^1) \geqq p_{h+1}(b_{h+1}^2 - b_{h+1}^1) = p_{h+1}(a_{h+1}^2 - a_{h+1}^1) \geqq \cdots.$$

But such a sequence cannot exist because $p_t a_t^2$ is nonnegative and, from condition (ii), $p_t a_t^1$ can be made smaller than any positive number, so that $p_h(a_h^2 - a_h^1)$ would have to be greater than any negative number.

12. *Properties of optimal chronics.* In dealing with optimal chronics the mathematical technique will be essentially the same as in the two preceding sections. Detailed demonstrations will therefore be omitted and only the main steps given.

Let us recall Definition 2: C^1 is optimal if there is no possible chronic C such that $\mathbf{x} \in \mathbf{X}$; i.e., if there is no $\mathbf{x} \in \mathbf{X}$ and $\mathbf{y} \in \mathbf{Y}$ such that $\bar{\mathbf{z}} = \mathbf{x} + \mathbf{y}$.

Let us define the set $\mathbf{Z} = \mathbf{X} + \mathbf{Y}$.

C^1 is optimal if and only if $\bar{\mathbf{z}}$ is not in $\mathbf{Z}$. From Assumptions 3, 4, and 5, $\mathbf{Z}$ is convex, and if it contains $\mathbf{z}^2$ it also contains any $\mathbf{z} \geqq \mathbf{z}^2$. Hence, the following may be proved:[20]

THEOREM 1′: *Under Assumptions* 3, 4, 5, *and* 6, *if* C^1 *is optimal, there is a nonnegative sequence* $\mathbf{p}$ *such that*

$$\sum_{t=1}^{h} p_t(z_t - \bar{z}_t) \geqq 0$$

for all h and all $\mathbf{z}$ *satisfying*

$$\left.\begin{aligned} \mathbf{z} &\in \mathbf{Z}, \\ z_t &= \bar{z}_t \end{aligned}\right\} \quad (\text{for } t > h). \tag{39}$$

The following trivial lemma goes in the opposite direction:

LEMMA 3′: *Under the Assumptions* 4 *and* 5, *a sufficient condition for optimality of* C^1 *is the existence of a nonnegative sequence* $\mathbf{p}$ *such that*

$$\sum_{t=1}^{h} p_t(z_t - \bar{z}_t) > 0$$

for all h and $\mathbf{z}$ *fulfilling* (39).

Theorem 1′ and Lemma 3′ may be summed up into a single theorem if the following weak assumption on $\mathbf{X}$ is made:

ASSUMPTION 7: *If* $\mathbf{x} \in \mathbf{X}$, *then there is* $\epsilon > 0$ *such that if* $|x_{it}^2 - x_{it}| < \epsilon$ *for all i and t, it is implied that* $\mathbf{x}^2 \in \mathbf{X}$.

This says that, if $\mathbf{x}$ is preferred to $\mathbf{x}^1$, then any sequence $\mathbf{x}^2$ sufficiently close to $\mathbf{x}$ is also preferred to $\mathbf{x}^1$.[21]

We may now formulate

THEOREM 2. *Under Assumptions* 3, 4, 5, 6, *and* 7, C^1 *is optimal if and only if there is a nonnegative sequence* $\mathbf{p}$ *such that*

$$\sum_{t=1}^{h} p_t(z_t - \bar{z}_t) > 0$$

for all h and all $\mathbf{z}$ *satisfying* (39).

---

[20] As in Section 10, one would define finite sequences $\mathbf{z}_h$ and the sets $\mathbf{Z}_h$ of all $\mathbf{z}_h$ such that $\mathbf{z}^2 \in \mathbf{Z}$ if $\mathbf{z}_t^2 = \mathbf{z}_t$ for $t \leqq h$, and $z_t^2 = \bar{z}_t$ for $t > h$. C^1 is optimal if and only if $\bar{\mathbf{z}}_h \notin \mathbf{Z}_h$ for all h. Hence, the existence of finite nonnegative sequences $\mathbf{p}_h$ such that $\mathbf{z}_h \in \mathbf{Z}_h$ implies

$$\sum_{t=1}^{h} p_t(z_t - \bar{z}_t) \geqq 0$$

(cf. footnote 14), and hence, finally, the existence of an infinite nonnegative sequence $\mathbf{p}$.

[21] Although it is not satisfied by the efficiency concept, this assumption does not seem to be restrictive. It is clearly fulfilled if the individual preferences may be represented by continuous utility functions.

Along with the existence of a price vector, a scheme of decentralization may be introduced. This is included in Lemmas 4′ and 5′.

LEMMA 4′: *Under Assumptions* 3, 4, 5, *and* 6, *if* C^1 *is optimal, there is a nonnegative* **p** *such that, for all h, k, and j,*

i) $\sum_{t=1}^{h} p_t y_{tk}$ *is minimal at* C^1 *among all C satisfying* (34);

ii) $\sum_t p_t(x_{tj} - x_{tj}^1) \geqq 0$ *for all* $\mathbf{x}_j \in \mathbf{X}_j$.

Since the vectors of the sequence $\mathbf{x}_j$ are null except for a finite number, the sum in Condition (ii) does make sense. Also, Condition (ii) may be written with the strict sign if Assumption 7 holds for the individual preference sets $\mathbf{X}_j$.

For the converse of Lemma 4′ one more assumption is needed:

ASSUMPTION 8: *For all t and j, there exist vectors* $\bar{u}_{tj}$ *such that* $\mathbf{x}_j \in \mathbf{X}_j$ *implies* $\mathbf{x}_{tj} \geqq \bar{u}_{tj}$.

Since $x_{tj}^+ \geqq 0$, Assumption 8 means essentially that there is some upper limit to the amount of labor x_{tj}^- that can be required from consumer *j*. For society as a whole we shall write

$$\bar{u}_t = \sum_j \bar{u}_{tj}.$$

Hence we have the following lemma:

LEMMA 5′: *Under Assumptions* 3, 4, 5, 7, *and* 8, *a sufficient condition for the optimality of* C^1 *is the existence of a nonnegative sequence* **p** *such that, for all h, j, and k,*

i) $\sum_{t=1}^{h} p_t y_{tk}$ *is minimal for* C^1 *among all C satisfying* (34);

ii) $\sum_t p_t(x_{tj} - x_{tj}^1) \geqq 0$ *for all* $\mathbf{x}_j \in \mathbf{X}_j$;

iii) $p_t a_t^1$ *and* $p_t(x_t^1 - \bar{u}_t)$ *tend to zero when t tends to infinity.*

As in the efficiency case, Condition (iii) means that the present values of future capital and future consumption tend to zero when we consider periods that are farther and farther away in the future. Conditions (ii) in Lemmas 3′ and 4′ are not exactly the same. But they are equivalent if X_j is contained in the closure of $\mathbf{X}_j$, or if, for any $\mathbf{x}_j^2 \in X_j$ and any positive sequence **u**, there is some $\mathbf{x}_j \in \mathbf{X}_j$ such that $\mathbf{x}_j - \mathbf{x}_j^2 \leqq \mathbf{u}$. This amounts to saying that there does not exist any complete saturation of all consumers' needs. By increasing the quantity of some conveniently chosen commodity, the consumer may be made better off, however small the increase might be.

III. EFFICIENCY AND THE RATE OF INTEREST

13. *Efficiency in actual societies.* The results of the last part were concerned mainly with the general properties of efficient and optimal chronics. They merely extended what was already known about the static case. It is, however, of paramount interest to study the extent to which these requirements are fulfilled in a real society. This is the purpose of the present part, in which we shall try to move closer to reality, introducing some institutional rules together with the general scheme of production and consumption. This inquiry aims at showing which restrictions are necessary in order to interpret the preceding formal lemmas as a justification of a competitive economic system.

We shall first rule out uncertainty in its two-fold aspect. Any firm will be supposed to know exactly which technical transformations are, and will be, possible; that is, firm k knows perfectly the sets $\mathbf{T}_{tk}$ for all values of t. In addition every economic unit, whether firm or consumer, also knows the present and future conditions of the market, i.e., prices and interest rates.

A second hypothesis concerns money. We shall suppose that firms and consumers do not hold money, either because they are not allowed to or because they do not want to. Once uncertainty is removed, this amounts to supposing that interest rates are positive and services of the banking system free (by which we mean only the fixed costs for any transfer from one account to another—not the normal interest discounts, which are, indeed, retained in the model). Thus, money will be a value unit only.

With these hypotheses we shall proceed to show, first, how interest rates do appear in the price system and, second, how the usual profit-maximizing principles coincide with the preceding decentralization rules. Then we shall be able to exhibit very simply some relations between private and national accounting. Finally, we shall deal with the question of why interest rates should be positive.

14. *Interest rates in actual economies.* As in Sections 11 and 12, the price system $\mathbf{p}$ apparently does not include a rate of interest. This may seem strange since, in society as we know it, interest rates are used on the loan market and in business accounting for discounting future values. The point may be made clearer by the following remark.

In the static case the efficiency theorem leads to a set of prices that are determined up to some common multiplicative scalar. Thus only a set of relative prices is given. Absolute prices may be fixed at any level in accordance with monetary conditions. Our result in the dynamic case is formally similar but entails a different interpretation: The whole set of present and future prices is still determined up to a multiplicative scalar; this, however, determines not only the relative prices for each period but also all future prices, given the present ones. If, as is usually the case, the institutional structure is such that that the absolute prices must satisfy some normalization condition within each period, then our lemmas must be modified.

A normalization rule states which multiple of p_t should be taken as the absolute price vector for period t. To avoid confusion, let us denote by p'_t the normalized price vector associated with p_t:

$$p_t = \beta_t p'_t, \tag{41}$$

where β_t is some convenient positive scalar.[22] Let us call it the discount coefficient for period t. Since the sequence $\mathbf{p}$ is determined up to a multiplicative constant, we shall suppose $\beta_1 = 1$.

In the following, the sequence $\mathbf{p}$ will be replaced by two sequences, one of nonnegative normalized price vectors $\mathbf{p}'$ and the other of the positive discount coefficients β_t. However, it should be clear that neither, taken alone, has any intrinsic meaning.

Let us define

$$1 + \rho_t = \beta_t / \beta_{t+1}. \tag{42}$$

ρ_t will appear as a rate of interest in the next section and later on in the treatment of stationary cases.

15. *Rules of behavior for consumers and firms.* As we have seen, the firm k should maximize in each period $p_{t+1} b_{t+1,k} - p_t a_{tk}$ subject to $(a_{tk}, b_{t+1,k}) \in \mathrm{T}_{tk}$. This is equivalent to maximizing

$$B_{tk} = p'_{t+1}(b_{t+1,k} - a_{tk}) + (p'_{t+1} - p'_t)a_{tk} - \rho_t p'_t a_{tk}. \tag{43}$$

B_{tk} is the usual net profit concept[23] for period t. It is computed as the sum of

+ value of net production,	$p'_{t+1}(b_{t+1,k} - a_{tk})$
+ capital gains,	$(p'_{t+1} - p'_t)a_{tk}$
− interest costs,	$\rho_t p'_t a_{tk}$.

One may also note that if $a^1_{tk} = b^1_{tk} = 0$ after some horizon h, maximizing

$$\sum_{t=1}^{h} p_t y_{tk}$$

is equivalent to maximizing

$$F_{1k} - p'_1 c_{1k} = \sum_t \beta_{t+1} B_{tk}. \tag{45}$$

F_{1k}, so defined, may be interpreted as being the present value of the firm.

Formulas (42), (43), and (45) show that the theory of allocation of resources justifies the usual accounting procedures. The interest rates here introduced play the same role as they do in business accounting.

Let us also remark that, if additivity of the technical processes holds, together with divisibility, then necessarily

$$B_{tk} = 0 \quad \text{and} \quad F_{1k} = p'_1 c_{1k}. \tag{46}$$

---

[22] For the sake of simplicity, it is supposed that $p_t \neq 0$.

[23] It has not always been clear in economic literature which quantity the entrepreneur ought to maximize. (See, for instance, Boulding [7], Samuelson [28], Lutz [21], Rottier [27].) In any case, maximization of B_{tk} is a necessary but not a sufficient condition.

Indeed, if Assumptions 1 and 2 hold for firm k (i.e. if $\mathbf{T}_{tk}$ are convex cones), then Lemma 4 implies

$$-\beta_{t+1}B_{tk} = p_t a_{tk}^1 - p_{t+1}b_{t+1,k}^1 = 0.$$

Suppose for instance this quantity to be negative. Then, with

$$a_{tk} = \alpha a_{tk}^1 \quad \text{and} \quad b_{t+1,k} = \alpha b_{t+1,k}^1,$$

we would have

$$p_t a_{tk} - p_{t+1}b_{t+1,k} < p_t a_{tk}^1 - p_{t+1}b_{t+1,k}^1$$

for any α greater than 1, which would contradict the fact that $(a_{tk}^1, b_{t+1,k}^1)$ maximizes $(a_{tk}, b_{t+1,k})$ in $\mathbf{T}_{tk}$.

In interpreting the rule of behavior for consumers, suppose that they can receive or make loans. An account of their assets and liabilities is kept at some bank, and the net assets at the beginning of period t for consumer j is equal to A_{tj}. The consumer will be paid interest on it equal to

$$K_{tj} = \rho_{t-1}A_{t-1,j}. \tag{47}$$

K_{tj} may be called the consumer's capitalist income. During period t he will save

$$S_{tj} = A_{tj} - A_{t-1,j}.$$

If we write

$$C_{tj} = p_t' x_{tj}^+ \quad \text{and} \quad W_{tj} = p_t' x_{tj}^-,$$

the budget equation for j will be

$$C_{tj} + S_{tj} = Y_{tj} = W_{tj} + K_{tj}, \tag{48}$$

which may be read as *consumption + saving = income*. Formally it may be written

$$p_t x_{tj} = \beta_{t-1}A_{t-1,j} - \beta_t A_{tj}. \tag{49}$$

Minimizing

$$\sum_t p_t x_{tj}$$

subject to $\mathbf{x}_j \in \mathbf{X}_j$ amounts to maximizing the final assets $A_{tj,j}^1$ under the constraints $\mathbf{x}_j \in \mathbf{X}_j$, and $p_t x_{tj} = \beta_{t-1}A_{t-1,j} - \beta_t A_{tj}$.

Thus, roughly speaking, the rule advises us to choose C^1 if, among all chronics that are at least as good, it is associated with the greatest final assets.[24]

---

[24] This is clearly only one among many possible rules which would bring about a minimum of

$$\sum_t p_t x_{tj}$$

subject to $\mathbf{x}_j \in \mathbf{X}_j$.

The budget equation, together with this last rule, shows how the interest rates we have introduced play the usual role on the loan market.[25]

In fact, we shall introduce a somewhat different definition, which is a little more involved but makes the following section simpler. We shall suppose wages to be paid at the end of the period and to include conveniently the interest earned thereon. Thus the budget equation becomes

$$Y_{tj} = K_{tj} + (1 + \rho_{t-1})W_{t-1,j} = C_{tj} + S_{tj}. \tag{50}$$

Accordingly, formula (49) becomes

$$p_t x_{tj} = \beta_{t-1}(A_{t-1,j} + W_{t-1,j}) - \beta_t(A_{tj} + W_{tj}). \tag{51}$$

Since consumer j disposes of initial assets $A^0_{tj,j}$ but does not get any wage before the end of period t^0_j, the intuitive meaning of the behavior rule is still to maximize the final assets while enjoying a given level of utility.

16. *Real capital and assets; private and national accounting.* As was shown by Fetter [9], there are essentially two concepts of capital given in the economic literature. According to the first, capital includes all "owned sources of income"; thus, it may be defined as the totality of assets:

$$A_t = \sum_j A_{tj}.$$

According to the other definition it is a "stock of physical goods used as means of production." The latter concept is sometimes called "real capital" and could be written $p'_t c_t$.

But assets and real capital are not independent of each other. Indeed, if any net assets exist, they represent some "real" values. If, to simplify, we deal directly with aggregates and write

$$B_t = \sum_k B_{tk},$$

we may define:

$$A_t = L_t + F_t, \tag{52}$$

where L_t and F_t are the values of natural resources (land) and of firms, respectively.

$$L_t = \frac{1}{\beta_t} \sum_{\theta=t}^{\infty} \beta_\theta p'_\theta z_\theta, \tag{53}$$

$$F_t = p'_t c_t + \frac{1}{\beta_t} \sum_{\theta=t}^{\infty} \beta_{\theta+1} B_\theta, \tag{54}$$

supposing that the infinite sums are meaningful.

---

[25] Thus here, as in classical economics, interest rates appear in their two-fold aspect—as a marginal rate of return and as a price for loans.

From these definitions it is possible to give an expression for capitalist income:

$$K_{t+1} = \rho_t A_t = B_t + \rho_t p_t' c_t + (1 + \rho_t) p_t' z_t + G_t', \tag{55}$$

where $G_t' = G_t - (p_{t+1}' - p_t')c_t$, $G_t = (L_{t+1} - L_t) + (F_{t+1} - F_t)$. Formula (55) shows that capitalist income is the sum of

+ *profits of firms*	B_t
+ *interest from real capital,*	$\rho_t p_t' c_t$
+ *rents from land,*	$(1 + \rho_t) p_t' z_t$
+ *capital gains,*	G_t'.

The capital gains on real capital, which are not included in G_t', are part of profits.[26]

It is now possible to show very simply how national production is related to national income. Let us define the latter by

$$Y_t = \sum_j Y_{tj}, \tag{56}$$

and net national production by

$$P_t = p_{t+1}'(b_{t+1} - c_t). \tag{57}$$

Let us also define net national investment as

$$I_t = p_{t+1}'(c_{t+1} - c_t). \tag{58}$$

The reader may check that the following relations hold:

$$P_t = C_{t+1} + I_t, \tag{59}$$

$$Y_t = C_t + S_t, \tag{60}$$

$$S_{t+1} = I_t + G_t, \qquad Y_{t+1} = P_t + G_t. \tag{61}$$

These relations bear a strong resemblance to the usual national accounting equations. However, the matter of capital gains seems to introduce some

[26] We considered firms and consumers as different units and found some behavior rules for them separately. But actually many consumers do perform productive activities; there is no such sharp distinction in reality between production and consumption units. It is therefore important to notice here that the two behavior rules are consistent. Nobody is faced with the difficult problem of choosing between a maximum of B_t and a maximum of A_t.

difficulty.[27] Needless to say, our relations are not directly transposable to actual societies because money and international trade have been deliberately excluded.

17. *Why should interest rates be nonnegative?* Interest theory, if not capital theory, has often been thought of as dealing only with one question: Why does competition not bring the rate of interest down to zero? The emphasis on this point seems to have been a little misplaced. Once it is understood that two equal quantities of the same thing available at two different moments are not economically equivalent, there is no a priori reason for the interest rate to be zero. However, we do observe in fact that interest rates have always been positive; thus, we may wonder why this is so. The following remarks are intended to reformulate a few reasons that seem to be important in this respect.

First, in a monetary economy, consumers may always hold money, so that there would not be any loans unless the interest rate were positive. This reason, however important as it is, does not provide a complete answer. It has been argued that not only monetary but also real interest rates[28] are always positive. We also want to see if positive interest rates in a nonmonetary economy can be explained.

Note that in such an economy interest rates alone do not have any intrinsic meaning, so that the question does not make sense unless one specifies the normalization rule on the price vector p_t'. This must be kept in mind to understand the following remarks.

1. Suppose first that the prices p_t' are such that

$$p_t'\bar{z}_t = p_{t+1}'\bar{z}_{t+1} \qquad \text{(for all } t\text{)}$$

[27] Of course, this difficulty could be avoided by changing our definitions. But there are good reasons for our choice. If income did not include capital gains, the behavior rules could no longer be interpreted in the frame of a competitive economy. If capital gains were included in national production and investment, these aggregates would no longer be evaluated from real physical net output and investment by using a unique set of prices. Concepts like the investment schedule would also be much more difficult to define.

The above equations should not, however, lead the reader to think that the whole of the present national accounting analysis is not well founded. If one considers what would happen in times of inflation, he will find that net national production is the very concept people have in mind when they speak of national income. As we have defined the latter it would include large capital gains which should be saved and invested on the loan market if capitalists wanted to keep constant the *real* value of their assets. Thus, both income and savings might seem to be largely overrated by our definitions.

One should also notice that the equation $S = I + G$ is not an equilibrium relation on any market but rather a necessary identity as soon as net assets are supposed to equate the value of firms and natural resources.

[28] Real interest rates are defined once the effect of changes in the general level of prices is removed. Here, the real interest rate associated with chronic C^1 appears if the normalization rule is such as to make invariant the value of some representative bundle of goods. Usually this concept is defined as follows: Let r be the monetary interest rate and P the general level of prices. The real interest rate is then given by the formula: $\rho = r - (1/P) \cdot (dP/dt)$.

so that ρ_t may be computed by

$$1 + \rho_t = \frac{p_t \bar{z}_t}{p_{t+1}\bar{z}_{t+1}}.$$

If the natural resources are privately owned, they must have some value. Formula (53) defining L_t must have meaning. This implies that

$$\lim_{h\to\infty} \sum_{\theta=t+1}^{h} \beta_\theta$$

exists for all t. This cannot be so unless

$$\lim_{t\to\infty} (\beta_t/\beta_{t+1}) \geqq 1,$$

or, equivalently, unless $\lim_{t\to\infty} \rho_t \geqq 0$. Such was the idea behind Turgot's theory of fructification.

2. Suppose now that the price of some commodity i_θ is kept constant: $p'_{i_0 t} = p'_{i_0 \cdot t+1}$ for all t, so that ρ_t may be computed by

$$1 + \rho_t = \frac{p_{i_0 t}}{p_{i_0, t+1}}.$$

If commodity i_0 may be stored without any cost, we may write $(a_t^2, b_{t+1}^2) \in \mathbf{T}_t$ with $a_{it}^2 = a_{it}^1$, $b_{i,t+1}^2 = b_{i,t+1}^1$, for $i \neq i_0$; $a_{i_0 t}^2 = a_{i_0 t}^1 + \alpha_t$ and $b_{i_0,t+1}^2 = b_{i_0,t+1}^1 + \alpha_t$, with $\alpha_t > 0$. If $\mathrm{p}_t a_t - p_{t+1} b_{t+1}$ is minimum for C^1, then necessarily $(p_{i_0 t} - p_{i_0,t+1})\alpha_t \geqq 0$; hence $\rho_t \geqq 0$.

3. With the same normalization rule as in 2, we may suppose $\mathbf{x}^2 \in \mathbf{X}$ when $\mathbf{x}^2$ is defined by $x_t^2 = x_t^1$ for $t > 2$; $x_1^2 = x_1^1 + a$; and $x_2^2 = x_2^1 - \beta a$, with $a_i = 0$ for $i \neq i_0$ and with $a_{i_0} > 0$ and $\beta > 1$. Thus, $\mathbf{x}^2$ is analogous to $\mathbf{x}^1$ except that it allows for a greater consumption of i_0 in the first period and a smaller consumption of i_0 in the second period, the total quantity of i_0 for both periods being smaller than in $\mathbf{x}^1$. And it is supposed that C^2 is preferred to C^1.

If C^1 is optimal, then $p_1(x_1^2 - x_1^1) + p_2(x_2^2 - x_2^1) \geqq 0$. Hence

$$\rho_1 \geqq \beta - 1 > 0.$$

This is the usual theory of preference for present commodities.

4. It is sometimes said that the rate of interest is, or should be, equal to the rate of expansion of the economy. More precisely, suppose that the rate of interest is computed from nonnormalized prices by

$$1 + \rho_t = \frac{p_t c_t}{p_{t+1} c_t},$$

or, equivalently, that the normalization rule specifies $p'_{t+1} c_t = p'_t c_t$. Let us define the rate of capital accumulation δ_t as

$$1 + \delta_t = \frac{p'_{t+1} c_{t+1}}{p'_{t+1} c_t}.$$

Then $\rho_t - \delta_t$ is of the same sign as $-p'_{t+1}(c_{t+1} - c_t) + \rho_t p'_t c_t$. In particular, if the $\mathbf{T}_t$ are cones, this is also the sign of

$$p'_{t+1}x^+_{t+1} - (1 + \rho_t)p'_t(x^-_t + z_t).$$

There does not seem to be, in general, any definite sign for this expression. However, if we suppose $x^+_{t+1} = x^-_t = z_t = 0$, then, clearly, $\rho_t = \delta_t$. Such was the case in von Neumann's model of 1937 [24].

IV. STATIONARY ECONOMICS

Usually in capital theory "production is defined in relation to economic equilibrium ... in the form of a stationary economy."[29] Indeed, if such an assumption is made, the interest rate appears quite naturally in the requirements for efficiency, along with the "marginal productivity of capital." In this part we shall deal first with the properties of efficient stationary chronics,[30] second with the marginal productivity of capital, and third with the concept of the optimum amount of capital. A last section will be devoted to some historical comments.

18. *Properties of efficient stationary chronics.* We shall now assume the set of technological possibilities and the available resource vector to be identical to a set $\mathbf{T}$ and to a vector $\bar{z}$ independent of time. The chronic C^1 is said to be stationary if the vectors characterizing the economic activity remain unchanged from one period to another. Thus, C^1 is fully described by the four m-dimensional vectors, a, b, z, and x, with the conditions

$$\left.\begin{array}{l} a = b + z - x, \\ (a, b) \in \mathbf{T}, \\ z \leqq \bar{z} \end{array}\right\} \tag{62}$$

According to Theorem 1, if the stationary chronic C^1 is efficient, there is some nonnegative sequence $\mathbf{p}$ such that, for all t,

i) $p_t a - p_{t+1} b$ is minimal at (a^1, b^1) among all $(a, b) \in \mathbf{T}$;

ii) $p_t a$ is minimal at (a^1, b^1) among all $(a, b) \in \mathbf{T}$ such that $a - b = a^1 - b^1$.

Conversely, if there is a positive sequence $\mathbf{p}$ such that C^1 fulfills conditions (i) and (ii), then C^1 is efficient. More precisely, we state

LEMMA 7: *Under Assumptions* 3, 4, *and* 6, *if a stationary chronic* C^1 *is efficient, there exists a nonnegative vector p and a scalar* $\rho > -1$ *such that*

i) *$p(b - a) - \rho pa$ is maximal at (a^1, b^1) among all $(a, b) \in \mathbf{T}$;*

ii) *pa is minimal at (a^1, b^1) among all $(a, b) \in \mathbf{T}$ such that $a - b = a^1 - b^1$.*

Conversely, if there is a positive vector p and a scalar $\rho > -1$ such that the stationary chronic C^1 fulfills conditions (i) and (ii), then C^1 is efficient.

---

[29] Knight [15].

[30] Throughout this part we shall study efficiency alone. The introduction of consumers' preferences would make the whole treatment unnecessarily involved.

PROOF: The second statement of the lemma follows directly from Lemma 3 if we define the sequence **p** by $p_t = p/(1+\rho)^{t-1}$.

Conversely, if C^1 is efficient, there is, by Theorem 1, a nonnegative sequence **p** such that $(p_t, -p_{t+1})$ is in the closed convex cone of normals to **T** at (a^1, b^1). This implies that this cone contains some vector of the form $(p, -\beta p)$ with $\beta > 0$.[31] Lemma 7 follows, with $1+\rho = 1/\beta$.

Thus, associated with any efficient stationary chronic, there is some set of relative prices and some rate of interest. This seems to contradict the preceding result, according to which interest rates appear only when some monetary rule is given. But this last condition is in fact implicitly included in Lemma 7.

---

[31] This is obvious if the cone of normals is just a half line. In general, the proof is somewhat more difficult. It is given here for completeness. We want to prove

LEMMA: *Given a sequence* **p** *of vectors in the m-dimensional Euclidean space, with* $p_t \geqq 0$ and the convex closed cone $\mathbf{\Gamma}$ *generated by* $(p_t, -p_{t+1})$ *in the 2m-dimensional space, there is some vector* $p \geq 0$ *and some positive* β *such that* $(p, -\beta p) \in \mathbf{\Gamma}$.

PROOF: Define

$$p_t^{(1)} = p_t, \; p_t^{(h)} = p_t^{(h-1)} + p_{t+1}^{(h-1)} \qquad (\text{for } h > 1).$$

Let $\mathbf{C}^{(h)}$ be the convex closed cone generated by the $p_t^{(h)}$ in m-dimensional space ($t = 1, 2, \ldots,$ *ad infinitum*).

$$\mathbf{C}^{(h)} \subset \mathbf{C}^{(h-1)}.$$

Define

$$\mathbf{C}^{\infty} = \bigcap_{h=1}^{\infty} \mathbf{C}^{(h)}.$$

$\mathbf{C}^{\infty}$ is a nonempty closed convex cone.

By definition of $\mathbf{C}^{(h)}$, for any $u \in \mathbf{C}^{(h)}$ there is a sequence $\{u_n\}$ of vectors fulfilling the following:

$$\lim_{n\to\infty} u_n = u, \tag{a}$$

$$u_n = \sum_t \alpha_{tn} p_t^{(h)}, \tag{b}$$

with scalars $\alpha_{tn} \geqq 0$, all zero except for a finite number.

Define

$$v_n = \sum_t \alpha_{tn} p_t^{(h-1)}, \qquad w_n = \sum_t \alpha_{tn} p_{t+1}^{(h-1)}.$$

Clearly, $u_n = v_n + w_n$. $\{v_n\}$ and $\{w_n\}$ are two bounded nondecreasing sequences of vectors in $\mathbf{C}^{(h-1)}$. They have limits v and w in $\mathbf{C}^{(h-1)}$, with $u = v + w$. It is trivial to note that $(v, -w) \in \mathbf{\Gamma}$.

Hence, for any $u \in \mathbf{C}^{(h)}$, there are two v and $w \in \mathbf{C}^{(h-1)}$, with

$$u = v + w, \tag{a}$$

$$(v, -w) \in \mathbf{\Gamma}. \tag{b}$$

It follows that, for any $u \in \mathbf{C}^{\infty}$, there are two v and $w \in \mathbf{C}^{\infty}$ such that (*a*) and (*b*) above are satisfied. [Indeed, for all h, $u \in \mathbf{C}^{(h+1)}$. Hence, there are $v^{(h)}$ and $w^{(h)}$ in $\mathbf{C}^{(h)}$ with $u = v^{(h)} + w^{(h)}$ and $(v^{(h)}, -w^{(h)}), \in \mathbf{\Gamma}$. $\{v^{(h)}\}$ is a sequence of positive bounded vectors; it has a limit point v which is in all $\mathbf{C}^{(h)}$. $w = u - v$ is a limit point of $\{w^{(h)}\}$; it is in all $\mathbf{C}^{(h)}$; and $(v, -w) \in \mathbf{\Gamma}$.]

Now, there is in $\mathbf{C}^{\infty}$ an extreme element, i.e., an element u such that $u = v + w$ with v and w in $\mathbf{C}^{\infty}$ implies $w = \alpha u = \beta v$ with positive scalars α and β.

Hence, for this element u, $(v, -w) = (v, -\beta v) \in \mathbf{\Gamma}$, which completes the proof.

Indeed, when prices are used in the computation of $p(b - a) - \rho pa$, it is supposed that absolute prices remain the same in all periods; or, in other words, that the normalization rule does not change.[32]

19. *Marginal productivity of capital.* It is a much debated question to know whether the interest rate is, or ought to be, equal to the marginal productivity of capital. As we shall see, the whole controversy boils down to the definition given to marginal productivity. Following Knight [15], we shall adopt here the most usual concept.

Given the efficient stationary chronic C^1, let us consider the class $\mathscr{C}$ of all possible stationary chronics for which the inputs x^- and z take the same values as in C^1. These chronics differ by their capital vector c and their consumption vector x^+. Let p^1 be an efficient price vector associated with C^1. The marginal productivity of capital for C^1 is defined as

$$\mu = \operatorname*{Sup}_{C \in \mathscr{C}} \frac{p^1(x - x^1)}{p^1(c - c^1)}. \tag{63}$$

This formula relates the gain in consumption, $p^1(x - x^1)$, to the corresponding increase of social capital, $p^1(c - c^1)$, both being evaluated from the set of prices p^1; μ is the maximum value taken by this ratio.

Now, from Lemma 7 it directly follows that

$$\rho^1 \geqq \mu, \tag{64}$$

where ρ^1 is the efficient interest rate associated with C^1. One might, moreover see that the equality holds if T is bounded by a differentiable surface.

On the other hand, a long line of economists[33] define marginal productivity of capital as the ratio between the increase in value of consumption, $px - p^1x^1$, to the increase in value of real capital, $pc - p^1c^1$. Or, in our present terminology,

$$\mu' = \operatorname*{Sup}_{C \in \mathscr{C}} \frac{px - p^1x^1}{pc - p^1c^1}. \tag{65}$$

Clearly, μ' is not related by any definite formula to ρ^1. Thus there is no reason why they should be equal.

There remains the question which of the two definitions should be adopted in economic theory. There seem to be at least three resaons for choosing

---

[32] Similar results may be obtained by an approach more in accordance with the usual technique in capital theory. One can say that a stationary chronic is not efficient if it is possible, without any present loss, to pass to some other stationary chronic allowing for a higher consumption.

Or, formally, C^1 is not efficient if there is some possible C such that:

i) $x \geq x^1$; and

ii) there are some b^2 and z^2 such that $(a^1, b^2) \in \mathrm{T}$, $z^2 \leqq \bar{z}$, $a = b^2 - x^1 + z^2$.

Condition (ii) says that it is possible to go from C^1 to C in one period with a consumption vector equal to x^1.

[33] Cf., for instance, Wicksell [33]. For more detailed references the reader may consult Metzler [23].

formula (63). First, it makes the marginal productivity of capital just equal to the interest rate. Second, it is the right measure for the ratio between the permanent future increase in national consumption and the necessary present savings, as one might easily see from our model. From this viewpoint, it provides welfare economics with a concept that has a much more profound meaning than the alternative, μ'. Finally, the definition of μ coincides with the general definition of marginal productivity, while formula (65) does not. Indeed, marginal productivity is always computed with a single set of prices. This may be made clearer if we suppose that $C - C^1$ is null except for its first component γ_1, a given quantity of commodity 1, while the corresponding increase in the consumption vector $x - x^1$ is null except for commodity 2, the component then being ξ_2. Formula (63) gives $\mu p_1^1/p_2^1 \geqq \xi_2/\gamma_1$, so that the ratio on the left-hand side is directly related to physical conditions of production, like any other substitution ratio in an efficient position. A similar result does not hold with formula (65).

μ is also equal to the marginal productivity of capital such as it is sometimes defined by considering a lengthening of a production or investment period. Indeed, let us compare C^1 with a stationary chronic C absolutely similar except for a one-unit increase of the investment period of commodity 1. If the invested quantity of commodity 1 in C^1 equal to γ, $c - c^1$ is null except for its first component, which is equal to γ, then $\mu \geqq p^1(x - x^1)/p_1^1 \gamma$. Thus, μ is also at least equal to the ratio between the increase in the product from a one-unit lengthening of the investment period of some commodity to the value of the quantity annually invested of the same commodity, or equivalently, to the value which is to be saved on consumption during the present period in order to realize the given lengthening of the investment period. Such was the essential idea behind the Jevonian analysis.

20. *Optimum amount of capital.* The concept of an optimum amount of capital is given in a few places in economic literature.[34] It appears in such situations as the following. The government thinks some sacrifice should be made in order to accumulate enough capital to raise consumption above its present level. The rate of accumulation is not required to be in accordance with present consumers' preferences; these could be neglected if necessary in order to ensure a better future for the community. Is it always profitable for this purpose to increase the quantity of capital? Or is there any optimum beyond which one should rather disinvest than invest?

Indeed, as long as some increase in a_t leads to some increase in b_{t+1}, consumption may be made larger during the next period if it is reduced during the present one. However, it would not be reasonable to impose any given decrease in x_t if the corresponding increase in b_{t+1} becomes too small. This may be better formulated for stationary chronics. For these an increase of the capital vector will be said to be advantageous if it results in a permanent

[34] Cf., for instance, Wicksell [33, p. 209], Ramsey [25], Meade [22], Knight [16, p. 402], Allais [3].

improvement in the future or, in other words, if the stationary chronic associated with the new capital vector is preferable to that associated with the former one. It may seem likely a priori that the greater the capital vector, the higher the consumption level. This is not necessarily true because in stationary chronics provision must be made for capital replacement. The latter may become so heavy as to exceed the increase in production.

We shall adopt the following formal definition:

DEFINITION: *The efficient stationary chronic C^1 is associated with an optimal capital vector if there is no possible stationary chronic C such that $x \geqq x^1$, whatever the value taken by the capital vector.*[35]

We shall show that if some optimal capital vector exists, it is associated with a zero interest rate. By comparison with Lemma 7 this is the result of the following:

LEMMA 8: *Under Assumptions* 3 *and* 4, *if C^1 is an efficient stationary chronic associated with an optimal capital vector, then there is a nonnegative price vector p such that $p(b - a)$ is maximum at (a^1, b^1) among all $(a, b) \in$ T.*

PROOF: If C^1 is an efficient stationary chronic associated with an optimal capital vector, there is no $(a, b) \in \mathrm{T}$ with $b - a \geqq b^1 - a^1$. Indeed, suppose there is such an (a, b); there would exist a possible stationary chronic C such that

$$x = b - a + \bar{z} \geqq b^1 - a^1 + z^1 = x^1.$$

Consider now the set U of all $u = b - a$ where $(a, b) \in \mathrm{T}$. U is convex and has u^1 as a maximal element; hence, there is a nonnegative vector p such that pu is maximum at u^1 among all $u \in \mathrm{U}$.

As we noticed earlier, the rate of interest in a stationary chronic provides a measure of the marginal productivity of capital. It is therefore not surprising to find that it is equal to zero when the capital vector is optimal.

Finally, we must insist on the very restricted meaning of the concept of the optimal amount of capital and, hence, on the restricted applicability of Lemma 8.

---

[35] The objection that an optimal capital vector could not conceivably exist has frequently been raised against this concept, i.e., that a complete saturation of all capital needs can never occur, even under ideal conditions. Cf., for instance, Knight [16]. In the author's view this is not correct. It is indeed true that we shall probably never reach a state of complete saturation of all capital needs, but the reason is psychological or institutional and not technological.

The question of the existence of a stationary chronic C^1 associated with an optimal capital vector would be worth studying. Our present formulation, however, is not suitable for dealing with existence problems in a sufficiently precise way. The reader might find it interesting to consider the following example:

Suppose an economy with three commodities, the available resources vector $\bar{z} = (\bar{z}_1, \bar{z}_2, 0)$, and the technological set defined by $(a, b) \in \mathrm{T}$ if $b_1 = 0$, $(b_2)^2 + (b_3)^2 \leqq 8a_1a_2$. The following stationary chronic is associated with an optimal capital vector:

$$a = (\bar{z}_1, 2\bar{z}_1 + \bar{z}_2, 0) \qquad b = (0, 4\bar{z}_1, \sqrt{8\bar{z}_1\bar{z}_2}), \qquad x = (0, 2\bar{z}_1, \sqrt{8\bar{z}_1\bar{z}_2}).$$

Indeed, as we have seen, optimal capital vectors cannot be defined except for stationary chronics whose practical significance could be disputed.

21. *Historical note on the theory of capital.*[36] Throughout the preceding pages the traditional theory of capital has been related to welfare economics. But this attempt is now new. In economic literature, any sound approach to the analysis of capital formation stemmed from the theory of value whose connection with welfare economics is obvious. Thus, it may be worthwhile to compare the main expositions of the theory of capital and interest with the model presented here.

For this purpose we need not consider whether the authors were concerned with problems of equilibrium or with welfare, nor whether they took account consumers' preferences. Moreover, we need not consider production or distribution theories that take capital as given; indeed, from our viewpoint they miss the essential problem, which is how choices are, or should be, made between direct and indirect processes of production.

We shall examine the principal theories of capital according to two criteria: first, the descriptive scheme of the productive process and, second, the author's solution.

Broadly speaking, the models describing capitalistic production may be classified under four main headings:

First, some theories start from a law, given a priori, of substitution between present and future commodities. This is made quite clear, for instance, in Irving Fisher's theory of interest [10]. In this approach the real nature of the substitution is not explored except for some heuristic comments. Thus, the theory is bound either to consider only a particular aspect of production (as, for instance, the growing of trees) or to assume the prices for each period to be independently determined. In this way, the substitution law must be interpreted as relating present to future income. This procedure, used extensively by Fisher, will be examined below.

Second, most theories of capital describe production as the result of the simultaneous operation of numerous elementary processes,[37] each of them specialized in the production of a particular commodity from labor and natural resources. Most often, roundabout methods are introduced so that the final product may be obtained after a very long time. But, in any case, labor and natural resources are considered as the only inputs in the process. Capital goods do not exist as such; they are expressed in terms of the original services invested in them at the time of their production. These services are said to "mature" when the final product is delivered for consumption. Such is the scheme underlying the theories of John Rae [26], Jevons [14], Böhm-Bawerk [5, 6], Wicksell [33], Åkerman [1], Lindahl [19], and

[36] We shall not consider the theories dealing with welfare economics or efficient allocation of resources. For a short analysis of these subjects and references, see Debreu [8].

[37] Usually the models were not as general as they could have been. Many unnecessary restrictions, which were intended to simplify the theoretical exposition, in fact often resulted in making the subject more abstruse.

Hayek [12, 13]. Sometimes it is also supposed that present and future prices are determined independently, so that somewhat less care is required in setting the problem.

To these theories is often attached the concept of the production or investment period. But, although it might be very helpful from an expository viewpoint, it is not at all necessary and could be deleted altogether. Furthermore, as has been shown repeatedly, the definition of these periods raises innumerable difficulties.

In fact, the fundamental shortcoming of this approach follows from the assumption that it is possible to impute the service of capital goods to the original factors, land and labor. This is surely not the case except in some particular instances. Thus, the whole theoretical construction is dangerously weakened.

As a third alternative one may consider the services used in production as originating either from original sources or from existing equipment. Accordingly, the commodities produced include new durable equipment as well as consumption goods. This approach was used first by Walras [22] and more recently by Allais [2]. In order to arrive at manageable equations, both supposed that any capital good, once produced, provides a series of services that cannot be altered by more or less intensive utilization. Even so, this third approach seems to provide a good approximation to the conditions of the real world, as was rightly pointed out by Lindahl [19] in his penetrating essay.

It is apparent that the theory we have built throughout this paper proceeded from an attempt to give to Walras' model a more general content and to explain how a substitution law may be obtained from it.

Finally, it is also possible to give a simple and completely general description of production if the economy is assumed to be stationary. In this case there is a law relating capital equipment to the permanent consumption which it makes possible. This is the idea underlying most of Knight's writings [16]. One may wonder, however, whether his analysis can provide an answer to the question: Why should the study of stationary, and therefore artificial, economies enable us to understand the conditions of production in our changing world? Moreover, as we have seen, the efficiency of any stationary chronic cannot be determined except by comparison with other chronics that are not stationary.

It may be noted also that a stationary economy has often been assumed in theories classified under the second heading (such as those of Jevons and Wicksell), but it does not play there the essential part it does in Knight's treatment.

What sort of answers do the theories give? Here again we may group them under three headings.[38]

[38] To do full justice to earlier theories, we should mention that they also wanted at times to study the effects of capital increments on wages, or similar questions related to distribution theory. But this does not concern us here.

First, a few of them try to determine which relations must hold for a firm in a competitive economy. They more or less implicitly assume that these also hold for the whole economy. This is particularly clear in papers by Åkerman [1], Leontief [20], Schneider [30], and Boulding [7]. The approach is, indeed, quite successful because it provides a simple answer to a difficult problem. However, a doubt may remain as to the generality of the results. Clearly, also, it is not suitable for dealing with efficiency or welfare.

Second, most theories aim at determining the interest rates, assuming the prices for all periods given a priori.[39] Although this method may bring sound results, there are strong objections to it. In the first place, prices are determined at the same time as interest rates; it is just in the philosophy of capitalistic production that no simple dichotomy exists between the markets for present and future goods. One may wonder, moreover, whether it has always been realized that interest rates to be associated with chronics do not exist independently of the monetary conditions ruling the economy. If any misunderstanding arose on that point, it should surely be attributed to those writers who studied interest formation independently of price formation.

Finally, a few writers did show how prices and interest rates were simultaneously determined. They made quite clear the connection between interest and the general theory of value. To the author's knowledge, Böhm-Bawerk [5], Wicksell [33], Landry [18], Lindahl [19], and Allais [2] provided us with valuable theories of capital. Unfortunately, their writings were largely misunderstood, if not unknown. The diffusion of their main ideas was greatly hampered by endless discussions on details in their exposition. It was the purpose of the present paper to make the analysis more general, and it is hoped in this way to help avoid in the future such lengthy debates as have occurred on the theory of capital in the past.

REFERENCES[40]

1. ÅKERMAN, GUSTAV. *Realkapital und Kapitalzins*, Stockholm, Centraltrycheriet, 1923.
2. ALLAIS, MAURICE. *A la recherche d'une discipline économique*, Tome I, Paris: Ateliers Industria, 1943; reprinted as *Traité d'économie pure*, Paris 1953.
3. ALLAIS, MAURICE. *Economie et intérêt*, Paris, Imprimerie Nationale, 1947.
4. *BANACH, STEFAN. *Théorie des opérations linéaires*, Warsaw: Subwencju Funduszu kultury narodowej, 1932, and New York: Hafner Publishing Co., 1949.
5. BÖHM-BAWERK, EUGEN VON. *Geschichte und Kritik der Kapitalzins Theorien*, 1884.

[39] Here again, simplicity of exposition was often thought necessary but such misplaced simplifications were needed because all deductions had to be made on two-dimensional diagrams.

[40] This bibliography contains writings on capital theory only, except for references marked with an asterisk, which do not deal with this theory but were specifically mentioned in this paper. For references on welfare economics, see Debreu [8].

6. BÖHM-BAWERK, EUGEN VON. *Positive Theorie des Kapitales*, first published 1888, dritte Auflage, Innsbrück: Wagner'schen Universitäts-Buchhandlung, 1912.

7. BOULDING, KENNETH. "The Theory of a Single Investment," *Quarterly Journal of Economics*, Vol. 49, May, 1935, pp. 475–94.

8. *DEBREU, GÉRARD. "The Coefficient of Resource Utilization," *Econometrica*, Vol. 19, July, 1951, pp. 273–92.

9. FETTER, FRANK A. "Capital," in Seligman and Johnson, eds., *Encyclopedia of the Social Sciences*, New York: Macmillan Co., 1932, pp. 187–90.

10. FISHER, IRVING. *The Theory of Interest*, New York: Macmillan Co., 1930

11. *GUILBAUD, GEORGES TH. "L'étude statistique des oscillations économiques," *Cahiers du Séminaire d'Econométrie*, N° 1, Paris: Librairie de Médicis, 1951, pp. 5–41.

12. HAYEK, F. A. VON. "The Mythology of Capital," *Quarterly Journal of Economics*, Vol. 50, February, 1936, and *Readings in the Theory of Income Distribution*, London: Allen and Unwin, 1950, pp. 355–83.

13. HAYEK, F. A. VON. *The Pure Theory of Capital*, London: Macmillan and Co., 1941.

14. JEVONS, WILLIAM STANLEY. *The Theory of Political Economy*, London, 1871.

15. KNIGHT, FRANK H. "The Theory of Investment Once More: Mr. Boulding and the Austrians," *Quarterly Journal of Economics*, Vol. 50, November, 1935, pp. 36–67.

16. KNIGHT, FRANK H. "Capital and Interest," *Encyclopedia Brittanica*, Chicago: University of Chicago Press, 1946, pp. 799–800, and *Readings in the Theory of Income Distribution*, London: Allen and Unwin, 1950, pp. 384–417.

17. *KOOPMANS, TJALLING C., ed. *Activity Analysis of Production and Allocation*, Cowles Commission Monograph 13, New York: Wiley and Sons, 1951.

18. LANDRY, ADOLPHE. *L'intérêt du capital*, Paris: V. Giard et E. Brière, 1904.

19. LINDAHL, ERIK ROBERT. *The Place of Capital in the Theory of Prices*, 1929, reprinted in *Studies in the Theory of Money and Capital*, London: G. Allen and Unwin, 1939.

20. LEONTIEF, WASSILY. "Interest on Capital and Distribution: A Problem in the Theory of Marginal Productivity," *Quarterly Journal of Economics*, Vol. 49, November, 1934, pp. 147–61.

21. LUTZ, FRIEDRICH A. "Théorie du capital et théorie de la production," *Economie appliquée*, Janvier, 1948.

22. MEADE, JAMES EDWARD. *An Introduction to Economic Analysis and Policy*, 2d ed., London, Oxford University Press, 1937.

23. METZLER, LLOYD A. "The Rate of Interest and the Marginal Product of Capital," *Journal of Political Economy*, Vol. 58, August, 1950, pp. 289–306, and "The Rate of Interest and the Marginal Product of Capital: A Correction," *Journal of Political Economy*, Vol. 59, February, 1951, pp. 67–68.

24. NEUMANN, JOHN VON. **"A Model of General Economic Equilibrium," *Review of Economic Studies*, Vol. 13, No. 1, 1945–46.

25. RAMSEY, FRANK P. **"A Mathematical Theory of Savings," *Economic Journal*, Vol. 38, December, 1928, pp. 543–59.

26. RAE, JOHN. *Statement of Some New Principles on the Subject of Political Economy*, Boston: Hilliard, Gray and Co., 1834.

27. ROTTIER, GEORGES. "Notes sur la maximation du profit," *Economie Appliquée*, Janvier-Mars, 1951, pp. 67–84.

28. SAMUELSON, PAUL A. "Some Aspects of the Pure Theory of Capital," *Quarterly Journal of Economics*, Vol. 51, May, 1937, pp. 469–96.

29. SAMUELSON, PAUL A. "The Rate of Interest under Ideal Conditions," *Quarterly Journal of Economics*, Vol. 53. February, 1939, pp. 286–97.

30. SCHNEIDER, ERICH. "Das Zeitmoment in der Theorie der Produktion," *Jahrbücher für Nationalökonomie und Statistik*, January, 1936, pp. 45–67.

31. SCHNEIDER, ERICH. "Bemerkung zum Hauptproblem der Kapitaltheorie," *Jahrbücher für Nationalökonomie Statistik*, February, 1938, pp. 183–88.

32. WALRAS, LÉON. *Eléments d'économie pure*, Lausanne, 1877.

33. WICKSELL, KNUTT. *Lectures on Political Economy*, London: Routledge and Kegan Paul, 1934.

[16]

Journal of Public Economics 1 (1972) 1–24.

ON THE OPTIMAL USE OF FORECASTS IN ECONOMIC POLICY DECISIONS

Leif JOHANSEN

Institute of Economics, University of Oslo, Norway

Received November 1971

1. Introduction

Some 20 years ago Milton Friedman warned economists and politicians that government anticyclical actions may be destabilizing, not only when they are plainly wrong or overly strong, but "even though they are more often in the right than in the wrong direction and even though they are smaller in magnitude than the fluctuations they are designed to offset". He brought the point out clearly by means of a simple formal model (Friedman, 1953).

Both as a convenient starting point for the following discussion and for the purpose of comparisons and references I shall very briefly review Friedman's model and theorems. The symbols which I use here are dictated more by comparability with the following more general models than by Friedman's own notations.

The central variable of stabilization policy is national income, x. This is conceived by Friedman as consisting of two components, z and v, so that

$$x = z + v \,, \qquad (1.1)$$

where z is the value which would obtain in the absence of a conscious stabilization policy and v is *the effect* on national income of countercyclical actions.

The variables x, z and v refer to the same period or point of time, but v is a result of actions decided upon at one or more points of time prior to this.

Now Friedman measures the magnitude of fluctuations by considering the variance of national income, σ_x^2. (This can, I think, be interpreted in various ways, for instance as a measure of uncertainty about a specific period or as a measure of variations over a sequence of periods.) This is the same as

$$\sigma_x^2 = \sigma_z^2 + \sigma_v^2 + 2r_{zv}\sigma_z\sigma_v , \tag{1.2}$$

where σ_z and σ_v are the standard deviations of z and v and r_{zv} is the correlation coefficient between them. σ_z indicates the magnitude of the fluctuations which we want to counteract, σ_v measures the scale of the effects of our actions and r_{zv} measures the degree of precision of our actions. Clearly with $r_{zv} = -1$ and $\sigma_z = \sigma_v$ we would have a perfectly successful countercyclical policy.

Now it is easy to see that, in other cases, the countercyclical policy does not necessarily help to stabilize even if we have *some* precision, i.e. even if $r_{zv} < 0$. We achieve some stabilizing effect, i.e. $\sigma_x^2 < \sigma_z^2$, if and only if

$$\sigma_v < -2r_{zv}\sigma_z \tag{1.3}$$

assuming $r_{zv} < 0$.

If we consider r_{zv} as representing given facts, i.e. such things as lags in decisions and actions and our ability to foresee the relevant future variables and events, then it is natural to seek an optimization of the results of our actions by scaling the actions so that σ_x^2 is minimized for the given value of r_{zv}. This is obtained by minimizing (1.2) with respect to σ_v. This yields

$$\sigma_v = -r_{zv}\sigma_z \tag{1.4}$$

The degree of reduction of the fluctuations may be measured by the proportion of σ_x^2 to σ_z^2, i.e. the proportion of the size of fluctuations in national income under the optimal countercyclical policy to the size of the fluctuations in the absence of such policy:

$$\frac{\sigma_x^2}{\sigma_z^2} = 1 - r_{zv}^2 \qquad \text{(when } \sigma_v = -r_{zv}\sigma_z\text{)}. \tag{1.5}$$

This means that with some degree of precision in the policy decisions we can always obtain some stabilization effect if the actions are appropriately scaled. The actions taken should clearly be of a more moderate scale the smaller is the expected precision indicated by r_{zv}.

The formulas above give the main formal results of Friedman's analysis. I think they are very suggestive and the ideas are worth pursuing in a more explicit and general framework. It is natural then to bring them into the framework of a target-instrument approach to fiscal policy or more general economic policy analysis. [1] But we must clearly supplement the traditional target-instrument model by explicit recognition of uncertainty or limited ability to predict the future. We shall do this by introducing exogenous variables which are not known when decisions about the use of instruments have to be taken, but for which more or less precise forecasts are available. The question analysed by Friedman will then be reformulated as a question about how the use of the instruments should be influenced by such less than perfect forecasts. By this procedure we decompose the factors behind Friedman's variable v which measures *the effect* of countercyclical policy into more operational components. It is then also natural that the correlations between forecasts and realized values of exogenous variables will appear as important elements describing our ability to predict the future and accordingly play a part corresponding to r_{zv} in Friedman's analysis.

We shall proceed by first considering the case of an equal number of target variables and instruments, which is the simpler and more transparent case, and next considering the case of more target variables than instruments.

2. The case of an equal number of target variables and instruments

Let there be n target variables $x_1, ..., x_n$ and n instrument variables $t_1, ..., t_n$ and furthermore q exogenous variables $z_1, ..., z_q$ which are connected by the following equations:

[1] For expositions of the target-instrument approach, see e.g. Tinbergen (1952), Hansen (1958) or Johansen (1965).

$$x_i = \sum_{j=1}^{n} a_{ij} t_j + \sum_{j=1}^{q} b_{ij} z_j \qquad (i = 1, ..., n)\,, \tag{2.1}$$

or in matrix notation,

$$X = AT + BZ\,, \tag{2.2}$$

where X is the column vector of $x_1, ..., x_n$, T is the column vector of $t_1, ..., t_n$, Z is the column vector of $z_1, ..., z_q$, A is the $n \times n$ matrix of the constant coefficients a_{ij} and B is the $n \times q$ matrix of the constant coefficients b_{ij}. This system is in the nature of a reduced form system which may be derived from a larger system after endogenous variables which are not target variables have been eliminated and the system has been solved so as to express target variables in terms of instruments and exogenous variables.

As a preparatory operation, let us put down what we would do if the exogenous variables Z were known. With target values given by $\bar{X} = (\bar{x}_1, ..., \bar{x}_n)'$ we would then solve for the values of the instrument variables to obtain

$$T = A^{-1}(\bar{X} - BZ) = A^{-1}\bar{X} - A^{-1}BZ \tag{2.3}$$

where A^{-1} is the inverse of A, which we shall assume to exist. [2]

Now we recognize the fact that Z is not known when the decision about T is to be taken, but we have a set of forecasts $Z^* = (z_1^*, ..., z_q^*)'$. A straight-forward procedure would then be simply to use these as if they represented sure knowledge and determine the instrument values by analogy with (2.3), i.e. to set

$$T = A^{-1}\bar{X} - A^{-1}BZ^* \tag{2.4}$$

The actual vector of target variables realized would then be

[2] We shall comment on the assumption about the rank of A in connection with the more general case treated in section 3.

$$X = A(A^{-1}\bar{X} - A^{-1}BZ^*) + BZ = \bar{X} + B(Z - Z^*) . \qquad (2.5)$$

It is clear that if the forecasts Z^* are wide of the mark a policy which uses these forecasts in this way may do more harm than good. On the other hand, if the forecasts are relevant in the sense that they are correlated with the realized values, then they do contain information which we ought to be able to utilize in such a way as to benefit from them.

In order to discuss how to use the forecasts in a meaningful way we must be willing to say something about how good they are. The most natural way of formulating ideas about the reliability of the forecasts is to cast them in a stochastic framework. We accordingly introduce the joint probability distribution of $z_1, ..., z_q, z_1^*, ..., z_q^*$. This distribution describes the situation before the forecasts are given to us in an actual situation. The joint probability distribution may be a purely subjective affair, or we may know how the forecasts will be produced and perhaps also have experience from earlier periods so that we have some firmer basis for formulating an idea about how good the forecasts are "on average". On the basis of this joint probability distribution of Z and Z^* we want to formulate a strategy, i.e. a decision rule which tells us how to calculate the optimal values of the instruments once we have received the forecasts.

Before proceeding further we should perhaps comment a little bit more on the joint probability distribution of Z and Z^*.

We shall assume that the forecasts are unbiased in the sense that

$$Ez_j^* = Ez_j \qquad (j = 1, ..., q) , \qquad (2.6)$$

where E means the expected value of the variable in question. If this were not so, we could have corrected the forecasts first so as to make them satisfy (2.6).

For the variances and covariances we shall introduce the notations

$$\sigma_{ij} = E[(z_i - Ez_i)(z_j - Ez_j)] ,$$
$$\sigma_{ij}^* = E[(z_i - Ez_i)(z_j^* - Ez_j^*)] ,$$
$$\sigma_{ij}^{**} = E[(z_i^* - Ez_i^*)(z_j^* - Ez_j^*)] \qquad (i, j = 1, ..., q) \qquad (2.7)$$

We shall not assume that $\sigma_{ij} = \sigma_{ij}^{**}$. For $i = j$ we might have assumed $\sigma_{ii} = \sigma_{ii}^{**}$, i.e. equal variances. This might have been obtained by appropriate scaling of the forecasts, but there is not much of simplifications to gain by this and for some purposes it is better to permit σ_{ii} and σ_{ii}^{**} to be different.

In special cases we might have independent exogenous variables so that $\sigma_{ij} = 0$, and also $\sigma_{ij}^{**} = 0$, for $i \neq j$. However σ_{ij}^{*} ought to be positive so that there is positive correlation between forecasts and realized values. We introduce the symbol r_i for the correlation coefficient, i.e.

$$r_i = \frac{\sigma_{ii}^{*}}{\sqrt{\sigma_{ii}\sigma_{ii}^{**}}}. \tag{2.8}$$

It will be convenient to introduce the following notations for the matrices of the variances and covariances defined by (2.7):

$$\begin{aligned} \Sigma \ &= \text{the matrix of } \sigma_{ij} \ ; \\ \Sigma_{*} &= \text{the matrix of } \sigma_{ij}^{*} \ ; \\ \Sigma_{**} &= \text{the matrix of } \sigma_{ij}^{**}. \end{aligned} \tag{2.9}$$

We now formulate the strategy. We do this by letting the instrument values be linear functions of the forecast values, i.e.

$$t_j = \sum_{h=1}^{q} k_{jh} z_h^{*} + k_{j0} \qquad (j = 1, ..., n), \tag{2.10}$$

where k_{jh} and k_{j0} ($j = 1, ..., n; h = 1, ..., q$) are constants to be determined. By larger or smaller values of k_{jh} we let the forecasts influence policy to a larger or smaller extent.

In (2.10) the target values $\bar{x}_1, ..., \bar{x}_n$ will influence the decision with regard to the instruments $t_1, ..., t_n$ through the k_{j0} terms.

In matrix notation we write (2.10) as

$$T = KZ^{*} + K_0 \ , \tag{2.11}$$

where K is the $n \times q$ matrix of k_{jh} and K_0 is the column vector of $k_{10}, ..., k_{n0}$.

The decision rule (2.4), which pretends that Z^* represents perfect forecasts, corresponds to

$$K = -A^{-1}B, \; K_0 = A^{-1}\bar{X} . \tag{2.12}$$

In general this is however not the optimal strategy.

If we use the strategy (2.11), then the realized values of the target variables will be

$$X = AKZ^* + AK_0 + BZ . \tag{2.13}$$

When Z and Z^* are considered as stochastic variables, then clearly T and X will be stochastic. A decision about the coefficients of K and K_0 which characterize the strategy can only be taken by evaluating uncertain prospects. We introduce the simple idea of minimizing the expected value of a weighted sum of squared deviations from target values, i.e. we seek to minimize

$$E\Phi = E\left[\sum_{i=1}^{n} w_i(x_i - \bar{x}_i)^2 \right] = E\left[(X - \bar{X})' W (X - \bar{X})\right] , \tag{2.14}$$

where w_i are positive weights and W is the diagonal matrix formed by $w_1, ..., w_n$. This idea is most thoroughly developed and used in Theil (1964). Theil uses the more general formulation of a quadratic form where also non-diagonal terms $(x_i - \bar{x}_i)(x_j - \bar{x}_j)$ for $i \neq j$ enter. This could be done also in the following context and most of the results could easily be shown to hold also in this more general case. For simplicity we shall however retain the formulation in (2.14). Furthermore Theil lets the instrument variables enter the objective function. This is reasonable for instance in the case of some government expenditures. This can however be accommodated in the present formulation by letting such variables be represented both as x variables and as t variables and introducing the equality between them among the equations in (2.2).

The problem now is to minimize $E\Phi$ given by (2.14) with respect to K and K_0 where X is determined by (2.13) and Z and Z^* are vectors of stochastic variables.

It is convenient to introduce

$$y_i = x_i - Ex_i\,, \qquad \text{or} \qquad Y = X - EX \tag{2.15}$$

For the expectation EX we have from (2.13)

$$EX = (AK + B)EZ + AK_0\,, \tag{2.16}$$

where we have used assumption (2.6). By means of (2.15) $E\Phi$ can be written as

$$E\Phi = \sum_{i=1}^{n} w_i E y_i^2 + \sum_{i=1}^{n} w_i (Ex_i - \bar{x}_i)^2 \tag{2.17}$$

Considering now the two sums in the expression (2.17) it is clear that minimization of $E\Phi$ requires $EX = \bar{X}$, i.e.

$$EX = (AK + B)EZ + AK_0 = \bar{X} \tag{2.18}$$

This follows from the fact that fulfillment of (2.18) can be achieved by a suitable choice of K_0 for any choice of K (when A^{-1} exists), and K_0 does itself not affect the term $\Sigma\, w_i E y_i^2$. Thus we can use K to minimize $\Sigma\, w_i E y_i^2$ and afterwards adjust K_0 so as to satisfy (2.18).

Now let us develop the expression for Y further. We have, using (2.13) and (2.18),

$$Y = AKZ^* + AK_0 + BZ - \bar{X} = AKZ^* + [\bar{X} - (AK + B)EZ]$$

$$+ BZ - \bar{X} = AK(Z^* - EZ) + B(Z - EZ) \tag{2.19}$$

For convenience we introduce the matrix C with elements c_{ih} given by

$$C = AK, \quad c_{ih} = \sum_{g=1}^{n} a_{ig} k_{gh} \tag{2.20}$$

Instead of seeking the optimal matrix K we now first seek the matrix C. Then K is found afterwards as $K = A^{-1}C$.

Furthermore we introduce

$$U^* = Z^* - EZ^* = Z^* - EZ, \quad U = Z - EZ\,, \tag{2.21}$$

with elements u_j^* and u_j respectively. Then (2.19) can be written as

$$Y = CU^* + BU\,. \tag{2.22}$$

On this basis we can write the individual term y_i^2 as

$$y_i^2 = \left(\sum_{j=1}^{q} c_{ij}u_j^* + \sum_{j=1}^{q} b_{ij}u_j\right)^2$$

$$= \sum_{g,h} c_{ig}c_{ih}u_g^*u_h^* + 2\sum_{g,h} b_{ig}c_{ih}u_g u_h^*$$

$$+ \sum_{g,h} b_{ig}b_{ih}u_g u_h\,.$$

Taking the expectation and using (2.7) we have

$$Ey_i^2 = \sum_{g,h} c_{ig}c_{ih}\sigma_{gh}^{**} + 2\sum_{g,h} b_{ig}c_{ih}\sigma_{gh}^* + \sum_{g,h} b_{ig}b_{ih}\sigma_{gh}\,. \tag{2.23}$$

It is seen that Ey_i^2 depends only upon the elements of row no. i of the matrix C. Since we are free to choose each element of C independently of the others, we can clearly minimize the sum $\Sigma\, w_i Ey_i^2$ by minimizing each term Ey_i^2 independently of the others. The weights $w_1, ..., w_n$ thus do not influence the solution (as long as they are all positive).

We minimize Ey_i^2 with respect to $c_{i1}, ..., c_{ij}, ..., c_{iq}$ by setting the partial derivatives equal to zero:

$$\frac{\partial Ey_i^2}{\partial c_{ij}} = 2\left(\sum_{h=1}^{q} c_{ih}\sigma_{hj}^{**} + \sum_{h=1}^{q} b_{ih}\sigma_{hj}^*\right) = 0\,. \tag{2.24}$$

Such equations should now hold for $j = 1, ..., q$, and furthermore for $i = 1, ..., q$. We then have q^2 equations to determine the q^2 elements c_{ih} of C. Since $\Sigma_h c_{ih} \sigma_{hj}^{**}$ is the typical element of the matrix $C\Sigma_{**}$ and $\Sigma_h b_{ih} \sigma_{hj}^{*}$ is the typical element of the matrix $B\Sigma_*$ – see the notation introduced by (2.9) – this complete set of equations can be written as

$$C\Sigma_{**} + B\Sigma_* = 0 , \qquad (2.25)$$

(where the 0 signifies a matrix of zeroes).

Σ_{**} is the variance–covariance matrix of $z_1^*, ..., z_q^*$. If the joint distribution of $z_1^*, ..., z_q^*$ is not degenerate, then this matrix is non-singular so that the inverse Σ_{**}^{-1} exists. We then have the solution:

$$C = -B\Sigma_*\Sigma_{**}^{-1} , \; K = -A^{-1}B\Sigma_*\Sigma_{**}^{-1}. \qquad (2.26)$$

When K is thus determined K_0 is to be determined by (2.18). We get

$$K_0 = A^{-1}[\bar{X} - B(I - \Sigma_*\Sigma_{**}^{-1})EZ] \qquad (2.27)$$

where I is the unit matrix.

Inserting now in (2.11) we get the decision about the instruments determined as

$$T = A^{-1}\bar{X} - A^{-1}B[\Sigma_*\Sigma_{**}^{-1}Z^* + (I - \Sigma_*\Sigma_{**}^{-1})EZ] \, . \qquad (2.28)$$

From (2.28) it appears that

$$ET = A^{-1}\bar{X} - A^{-1}B(EZ)$$

in analogy with (2.3) which would hold if Z were known with certainty.

In general (2.28) can be written as

$$T = A^{-1}\bar{X} - A^{-1}B\tilde{Z} , \qquad (2.29)$$

where $\tilde{Z}$ is given by

$$\tilde{Z} = \Sigma_*\Sigma_{**}^{-1}Z^* + (I - \Sigma_*\Sigma_{**}^{-1})EZ \, . \qquad (2.30)$$

This means that the instruments are to be used as in the case of certainty, only modified by using the values $\tilde{Z} = (\tilde{z}_1, ..., \tilde{z}_q)'$ in the calculations instead of $Z = (z_1, ..., z_q)'$. Thus we have a kind of certainty equivalence result.

Let us take a further look at the construction of $\tilde{Z}$. From the formulation in (2.30) we can interpret $\tilde{Z}$ as an average between the forecast vector Z^* and the expectation vector EZ, with weight matrices $\Sigma_* \Sigma_{**}^{-1}$ and $(I - \Sigma_* \Sigma_{**}^{-1})$ adding up to the unit matrix I. If each forecast z_i^* is correlated only with the corresponding z_i, then the matrices Σ_* and Σ_{**} are diagonal matrices. If we introduce the correlation coefficients from (2.8) a row in (2.30) would then appear as

$$\tilde{z}_i = r_i \frac{\sqrt{\sigma_{ii}}}{\sqrt{\sigma_{ii}^{**}}} z_i^* + \left(1 - r_i \frac{\sqrt{\sigma_{ii}}}{\sqrt{\sigma_{ii}^{**}}}\right) Ez_i \, . \tag{2.31}$$

In this case $\tilde{z}_i$ is a simple average of z_i^* and Ez_i. If the forecasts are scaled so that $\sigma_{ii}^{**} = \sigma_{ii}$ it is seen that the weight on the forecast is simply the correlation coefficient between the forecast and the realized value z_i. A perfect forecast means $r_i = 1$ and all weight should be attached to such a forecast, while an irrelevant forecast means $r_i = 0$ and should not be taken account of at all.

In the general case (2.30) more correlations enter the formulation of a $\tilde{z}_i$, but the direct correlations illustrated by (2.31) would perhaps in most cases represent the most dominant influences.

The formulations (2.30–31) above were used because they bring out clearly the nature of $\tilde{Z}$ as being an average between Z^* and EZ, giving more weight to Z^* the more reliable are the forecasts. They can, however, be rewritten in another form which is easy to recognize and which provides an obvious interpretation, viz.

$$\tilde{Z} = EZ + \Sigma_* \Sigma_{**}^{-1} (Z^* - EZ^*) \, , \tag{2.32}$$

$$\tilde{z}_i = Ez_i + r_i \frac{\sqrt{\sigma_{ii}}}{\sqrt{\sigma_{ii}^{**}}} (z_i^* - Ez_i^*) \, . \tag{2.33}$$

Formula (2.33) gives the simple regression of z_i with respect to z_i^*. In the same way (2.32) represents the set of regression equations for all $z_1, ..., z_q$; row no. i in the vector equality represents the regression of z_i on $z_1^*, ..., z_q^*$. Thus the certainty equivalent which should replace z_i in the calculation of the optimal policy decision is simply the regression value, in the joint probability distribution of Z and Z^*, of z_i on all forecasts $z_1^*, ..., z_q^*$. This appears natural in view of the fact that this under linearity is the same as $E[z_i | z_1^*, ..., z_q^*]$, i.e. the conditional expectation of the exogenous variable z_i for given values of the forecasts $z_1^*, ..., z_q^*$. Our strategy then simply amounts to establishing these regression equations, and then when the forecasts $z_1^*, ..., z_q^*$ are supplied, inserting these so as to obtain $\tilde{z}_1, ..., \tilde{z}_q$ which are finally used as if they represent sure information about the exogenous variables. It is crucial in this connection that we use the regressions of Z on Z^* and not the other way round as would perhaps be equally natural if we were only interested in studying the relation between forecasts and realizations and not in taking decisions. The regressions in the direction of Z on Z^*, which come out of the optimization above, have the property that they get "flatter" in the $z_1^*, ..., z_q^*$-directions the more uncertain is the information which these forecasts provide. It is this property that leads to the reasonable result that less reliable information should be allowed to influence the decisions to a lesser degree.

Having arrived thus far it is tempting to quote Professor Friedman, in his paper referred to in the introduction: "In writing this note, I feel at one and the same time as if I were preaching in the wilderness and belaboring the obvious. For the major conclusions ... are important and widely neglected, yet they seem distressingly obvious." I shall return to the question of whether the conclusions are widely neglected *in practice* with a few remarks towards the end of this paper. In the more theoretical literature on how to use models in formulating economic policy I think the problem of how to use uncertain information has not been faced sufficiently explicitly. However, once the point is raised, the answer seems to be pretty obvious within the framework of the model used here. I prefer not to consider this as a "distressing" fact, however; I rather find it reassuring that a somewhat deeper justification can be given for what would in any case appear as a very natural thing to do.

Before closing this section let me briefly point out more explicitly the connection between our results and Friedman's results reviewed in the introduction. It is then natural to consider z in (1.1), the value of national product which would obtain in the absence of stabilization policy, as an exogenous variable. For the comparison we may also consider v, the effect of policy, as if it were itself an instrument. Comparing (1.1) and (2.1–2) we then see that Friedman's case is simply the case where the matrix A reduces to one element 1 and B does the same.

If we now have a forecast z^* of z, then the adjusted value $\tilde{z}$ which corresponds to (2.33) would be

$$\tilde{z} = Ez + r \frac{\sigma_z}{\sigma_{z^*}} (z^* - Ez^*) , \tag{2.34}$$

where σ_z and σ_{z^*} are the standard deviations of z and z^* respectively and r is the correlation coefficient between them. The optimal policy – with v considered as an intrument – is then according to (2.29) :

$$v = \bar{x} - \tilde{z} = (\bar{x} - Ez) - r \frac{\sigma_z}{\sigma_{z^*}} (z^* - Ez) . \tag{2.35}$$

In this case we might consider $(\bar{x} - Ez)$ to be the value we should fix for v if we did not want to pursue an active policy, whereas the term $-r(\sigma_z/\sigma_{z^*})(z^* - Ez)$ represents the active policy which takes into account the specific information which is given to us in the form of the forecast z^*.

For comparison with Friedman's formulas we consider the standard deviation of v as a measure of the scale at which we pursue the active policy. This yields, on the basis of (2.35),

$$\sigma_v = r\sigma_z . \tag{2.36}$$

This is in perfect agreement with Friedman's prescription (1.4) of an optimal scaling of countercyclical policy. The symbol r in (2.36) is the correlation coefficient between the forecast value z^* and the realized value of the exogenous element z, while r_{vz} in (1.4) is the correlation coefficient between the policy variable v and z. However, under the strategy (2.35) it is clear that the correlation coefficient between v and z will be the same as between z^* and z since v is made a linear function of z^*, only with opposite sign because the relation between v and z^* in (2.35) is negative.

In this case the objective function (2.14) reduces to the variance of x around $\bar{x}$. We have under the optimal strategy

$$x = z + v = z + (\bar{x} - Ez) - r \frac{\sigma_z}{\sigma_{z^*}} (z^* - Ez) , \tag{2.37}$$

from which follows

$$\sigma_x^2 = (1 - r^2)\sigma_z^2 \tag{2.38}$$

which conforms with Friedman's formula (1.5) for the relative gain in stabilization by an optimally scaled policy.

As an alternative interpretation of Friedman's analysis as compared with ours we might consider the effect of stabilization policy, v, not as an instrument in itself, but rather as being composed of two elements: one component known with certainty, and a stochastic "disturbance". The first could then be treated as an instrument while the latter could be transferred to the realm of exogenous, stochastic elements. The main point here is however not to discuss possible interpretations in detail, but only to show that our results are of the same nature as Friedman's.

3. The case of more target variables than instruments

We now proceed to consider the case where we have more target variables than instruments. Otherwise we shall make the same assumptions as in section 2.

We now have

$$x_i = \sum_{j=1}^{m} a_{ij} t_j + \sum_{j=1}^{q} b_{ij} z_j , \qquad (i = 1, ..., n) , \tag{3.1}$$

$$X = AT + BZ , \tag{3.2}$$

which are the same as (2.1–2) apart from the fact that we now have $m < n$ where m is the number of instruments and n (as before) the number of target variables, and accordingly A is an $n \times m$ matrix.

As will be seen below the treatment which follows is valid also for $m = n$, so that we may put $m \leqq n$. But for $m = n$ the results will of course reduce to the same as in the preceding section.

The fact that a variable x_i is given the distinction of being a "target variable" now only means that we attach preferences to it. It does not mean that we can put up a fixed target $\bar{x}_i$ for this variable and request it to be precisely adhered to. Even under perfectly forecasted values of the exogenous variables, i.e. even when $Z = (z_1, ..., z_q)'$ is known, a preference function is now needed. Let this be, as before

$$\Phi = \sum_{i=1}^{n} w_i (x_i - \bar{x}_i)^2 , \tag{3.3}$$

where $\bar{x}_1, ..., \bar{x}_n$ designate some sort of most desired values of $x_1, ..., x_n$. Alternatively we may simply consider (3.3) as an approximation to a non-linear preference function in a certain relevant region without attaching any special significance to the values $\bar{x}_1, ..., \bar{x}_n$, these values themselves not being attainable under the restrictions of the model.

Before introducing uncertainty again we shall put down the solution for the case of Z being known with certainty.

Combining (3.1) and (3.3) we have

$$\Phi = \sum_{i=1}^{n} w_i \left(\sum_{j=1}^{m} a_{ij} t_j + \sum_{j=1}^{q} b_{ij} z_j - \bar{x}_i \right)^2 . \tag{3.4}$$

Setting the partial derivative of Φ with respect to t_k equal to zero we have

$$\sum_{i=1}^{n} w_i \left(\sum_{j=1}^{m} a_{ij} t_j + \sum_{j=1}^{q} b_{ij} z_j - \bar{x}_i \right) a_{ik} = 0 . \tag{3.5}$$

This is the same as

$$\sum_{j=1}^{m}\left[\sum_{i=1}^{n} a'_{ki} w_i a_{ij}\right] t_j + \sum_{j=1}^{q}\left[\sum_{i=1}^{n} a'_{ki} w_i b_{ij}\right] z_j = \sum_{i=1}^{n} a'_{ki} w_i \bar{x}_i \,, \tag{3.6}$$

where we have introduced $a'_{ki} = a_{ik}$ as the element in the kth row and ith column of the transposed matrix A'. With this notation equations (3.6) for $k = 1, ..., m$ can be written as

$$A'WAT + A'WBZ = A'W\bar{X} \,. \tag{3.7}$$

Here $A'WA$ is now an $m \times m$ matrix, $A'WB$ an $m \times q$ matrix and $A'W\bar{X}$ is a column vector of m elements.

If the inverse of $(A'WA)$ exists, then we have the solution

$$T = (A'WA)^{-1}A'W(\bar{X} - BZ) \,. \tag{3.8}$$

If $m = n$ and A is non-singular, then $(A'WA)^{-1}A'W = A^{-1}W^{-1}A'^{-1}A'W = A^{-1}$ (3.8) is the same as (2.3).

If $m < n$ this does not hold. Let us then consider the existence of $(A'WA)^{-1}$ a little bit further.

First it is well known that $(A'WA)^{-1}$ exists if the rank of A is m and W is positive definite. [3]

The assumption about W is not problematic in our case with all $w_i > 0$. The meaning of the assumption about the rank of A can be understood by the following consideration. Suppose that the rank of A is ρ, where $\rho \leq m$. Then A can be written as a product of two matrices, the first one being an $n \times \rho$ and the second one a $\rho \times m$ matrix, [4] i.e. as

$$A = PQ = \begin{pmatrix} p_{11} & p_{12} & \cdots & p_{1\rho} \\ p_{21} & p_{22} & \cdots & p_{2\rho} \\ \vdots & \vdots & & \vdots \\ p_{n1} & p_{n2} & \cdots & p_{n\rho} \end{pmatrix} \begin{pmatrix} q_{11} & q_{12} & \cdots & q_{1m} \\ q_{21} & q_{22} & \cdots & q_{2m} \\ \vdots & \vdots & & \vdots \\ q_{\rho 1} & q_{\rho 2} & \cdots & q_{\rho m} \end{pmatrix} \tag{3.9}$$

[3] See e.g. Goldberger (1964), p. 35.
[4] See e.g. Hohn (1964), p. 179.

(There is of course more than one way of doing this.) The equation system (3.2) can then be written as

$$X = PQT + BZ = PS + BZ\ , \tag{3.10}$$

where

$$S = QT\ , \quad \text{i.e.} \quad s_i = \sum_{j=1}^{m} q_{ij} t_j \qquad \text{for} \quad i = 1, ..., \rho. \tag{3.11}$$

This means that if $\rho < m$, then we can define ρ new variables $s_1, ..., s_\rho$ on the basis of $t_1, ..., t_m$ and replace the original system $X = AT + BZ$ by a new system $X = PS + BZ$, and think of the ρ vector S as the instrument vector. Thus the influences of the original instruments $t_1, ..., t_m$ on the endogenous variables of the system are passed on through a smaller number of variables $s_1, ..., s_\rho$. One might say that there are in fact only ρ independent instruments when the instrument variables have been economically defined. (As an example, if two instrument variables t_1 and t_2 in the T vector always appear combined as a sum in the system, then they would, in the S vector, be represented by only one element, say $s_1 = t_1 + t_2$.)

On this basis it is clear that nothing is lost by assuming that A has rank m. If it were not in this form from the beginning we could have obtained this by a suitable redefinition of the instruments; thus there is no need to operate with a matrix A with a smaller rank than the number of columns.

In the following we therefore assume that $(A'WA)^{-1}$ exists so that the solution (3.8) applies.

This solution has a form which is well known from statistics and econometrics. If we try to insert $X = \bar{X}$ in (3.2), then we can in general not expect equality to hold. But we could try to select the vector T so that AT fits the values $(\bar{X}-BZ)$ as closely as possible. This is a regression problem with $(\bar{X}-BZ)$ as a vector of "observations" of the "dependent variable", A as a matrix of "observations" of m "explanatory variables" and T as a vector of "regression coefficients" to be determined. By this analogy it is not surprising that the solution (3.8) is formally the same as the formula for a vector of regression coefficients, in particular for

Aitken's generalized least squares regression coefficients when W is not the unit matrix.[5]

As in the preceding section we now assume that we will have access to forecasts $Z^* = (z_1^*, ..., z_q^*)'$ for the exogenous elements and introduce a strategy

$$T = KZ^* + K_0 ,$$

which has the same meaning as (2.10–11), only that there are now m instruments instead of n and K and K_0 are accordingly of orders $m \times q$ and $m \times 1$.

We now want to determine the elements of K and K_0 in such a way that $E\Phi$ is minimized where Φ is given by (3.3). In the present case we cannot obtain $Ex_i = \bar{x}_i$ by help of K_0 only. The solution does therefore not come out as simply as it did by (2.14–27).

Let us write

$$\xi_i = x_i - \bar{x}_i = \sum_{j=1}^{m} a_{ij} t_j + \sum_{j=1}^{q} b_{ij} z_j - \bar{x}_i , \tag{3.12}$$

so that $E\Phi$ can be written as

$$E\Phi = \sum_{i=1}^{n} w_i E\xi_i^2 = \sum_{i=1}^{n} w_i [\text{var}\,\xi_i + (E\xi_i)^2] \tag{3.13}$$

where $\text{var}\,\xi_i = E[(\xi_i - E\xi_i)^2]$ = the variance of ξ_i.

Inserting for t_j in (3.12) we have

$$\xi_i = \sum_{h=1}^{q} \left(\sum_{j=1}^{m} a_{ij} k_{jh} \right) z_h^* + \sum_{j=1}^{m} a_{ij} k_{j0} + \sum_{j=1}^{q} b_{ij} z_j - \bar{x}_i . \tag{3.14}$$

[5] See e.g. Goldberger (1964), pp. 231–235 or Theil (1971), pp. 236–239.

From this follows

$$E\xi_i = \sum_{h=1}^{q}\left(\sum_{j=1}^{m} a_{ij}k_{jh}\right) Ez_h^* + \sum_{j=1}^{m} a_{ij}k_{j0} + \sum_{j=1}^{q} b_{ij}Ez_j - \bar{x}_i \,, \tag{3.15}$$

$$\text{var}\,\xi_i = \sum_{g=1}^{q}\sum_{h=1}^{q}\left(\sum_{j=1}^{m} a_{ij}k_{jg}\right)\left(\sum_{j=1}^{m} a_{ij}k_{jh}\right)\sigma_{gh}^{**} + 2\sum_{g=1}^{q}\sum_{h=1}^{q} b_{ig}\left(\sum_{j=1}^{m} a_{ij}k_{jh}\right)\sigma_{gh}^{*} + \sum_{g=1}^{q}\sum_{h=1}^{q} b_{ig}b_{ih}\sigma_{gh} \,. \tag{3.16}$$

Minimization of $E\Phi$ requires that all partial derivatives of (3.13) with respect to $k_{\alpha\beta}$ ($\alpha = 1, ..., m; \beta = 1, ..., q$) vanish. We have

$$\frac{\partial E\Phi}{\partial k_{\alpha\beta}} = \sum_{i=1}^{n} w_i \left[\frac{\partial \text{var}\,\xi_i}{\partial k_{\alpha\beta}} + 2E\xi_i \frac{\partial E\xi_i}{\partial k_{\alpha\beta}}\right] . \tag{3.17}$$

Using this and working out the derivatives involved on the basis of (3.15–16) we get a set of conditions which can be written as

$$A'WAK\Sigma_{**} + A'WB\Sigma_{*} + A'WAK(EZ)(EZ)' + A'WAK_0(EZ)' + A'WB(EZ)(EZ)' = A'W\bar{X}(EZ)', \tag{3.18}$$

where EX is the column vector of $Ez_1, ..., Ez_q$ and $(EZ)'$ the corresponding row vector. (3.18) is an equality between $m \times q$ matrices.

Setting in a similar way the derivatives of $E\Phi$ with respect to the elements of K_0 equal to zero we get

$$A'WAK(EZ) + A'WAK_0 + A'WB(EZ) = A'W\bar{X} \,, \tag{3.19}$$

which is an equality between column vectors of m elements.

It is seen that both K and K_0 are now involved both in (3.18) and (3.19). However, if we post-multiply (3.19) by $(EZ)'$ and combine the result with (3.18), then we get a simpler equation in K alone, viz.

$$A'WAK\Sigma_{**} + A'WB\Sigma_{*} = 0\,, \tag{3.20}$$

where 0 is a matrix of zeroes. This can be solved for K to yield

$$K = -(A'WA)^{-1}(A'WB)\Sigma_{*}\Sigma_{**}^{-1}\,. \tag{3.21}$$

Next K_0 is determined by (3.19):

$$K_0 = (A'WA)^{-1}A'W[\bar{X} - B(I - \Sigma_{*}\Sigma_{**}^{-1})EZ]\,. \tag{3.22}$$

The solutions (3.21) and (3.22) correspond to the solutions (2.26) and (2.27) in the preceding section and are seen to reduce to the same when we have an equal number of target variables and instruments so that A is a square matrix having an inverse. Then W drops out of the expressions and ceases to have an influence on the solution.

The full solution for the instrument vector is

$$T = (A'WA)^{-1}A'W(\bar{X} - B\tilde{Z})\,, \tag{3.23}$$

where $\tilde{Z}$ is as given by (2.32). Comparing with (3.8), which was valid when Z was considered as known with certainty, we see that we have a solution which is perfectly parallel with the simpler case studied in the preceding section: in the solution for the case of certainty we shall simply replace Z by its regression value $\tilde{Z}$, which is the same as its expected value conditional upon the forecasts $z_1^*, ..., z_q^*$. This conclusion is a natural extension of the certainty equivalence results of Theil and others for the case of a quadratic preference function and linear constraints with additive errors as presented most thoroughly in Theil (1964).

Before closing this section I will briefly comment on three points.

(1) A unified treatment of problems where there may be more target variables than instruments, equal numbers, or fewer target variables than instruments can be given in terms of so-called generalized inverses

or pseudo universes of matrices that are not necessarily square.[6] For a matrix A with full column rank the generalized inverse is $(A'A)^{-1}A'$, which if $W = I$ is the same as the matrix in front of $(\bar{X}-B\tilde{Z})$ in (3.23), i.e. the matrix which replaces A^{-1} in the solution (2.29) for the case of a square A when we go on to consider the case of fewer instruments than target variables. In order to utilize the theory of generalized inverses we could have redefined the units of measurement of $x_1, ..., x_n$ so that our preferences could have been expressed by $w_1 = ... = w_n = 1$ in the preference function Φ, thus permitting $W = I$.

For a further discussion and illustration of the use of generalized inverses in connection with economic policy models, see Spivey and Tamura (1970).

(2) Above we have all the time thought of $z_1^*, ..., z_q^*$ as a set of forecasts for the exogenous variables $z_1, ..., z_q$ which enter the equations determining $x_1, ..., x_n$. Essentially the same analysis would be valid if we think of $z_1^*, z_2^*, ...,$ no longer necessarily q in number, as a set of variables which contain information about $z_1, ..., z_q$ in the sense that they are correlated with $z_1, ..., z_q$ in the joint distribution. The simplifications due to assumption (2.6) would of course no longer hold; in particular we could no longer interpret $\tilde{Z}$ as an average of Z^* and EZ as we did in connection with (2.30–31). But it would be a simple matter to make the necessary amendments.

(3) A problem similar to the one treated in this section has been treated in a recent paper by Tisdell (1971). Tisdell makes the observation that "both for macroeconomic and microeconomic policy decisions, the question of whether it is optimal to pursue a sensitive zig-zag policy based upon ones changing forecasts or a steady course based on long-term forecasts is one of perennial importance", and he refers to recent discussions about monetary and fiscal policy in the United States. Tisdell points out that "in many circumstances, values of policy instruments should not be promptly altered as estimates of the non-controlled variables change, but an inflexible policy should be followed which ignores short-term estimates. This essay aims to show that even if the policy-maker has some (positive) ability to predict it may never-

[6] For definitions and important properties, see e.g. Theil (1971), pp. 268–271 and Ijiri (1965), appendix A.

theless be optimal for him to follow an inflexible policy." This is clearly very much in the same spirit as Friedman's analysis (1953). Tisdell's analysis is similar to the one of this paper in that he introduces forecasts of the exogenous variables and considers the correlations between forecasts and realized values, and furthermore similar to the analysis of this section in that he seeks an extremum of the expected value of a quadratic preference function. Tisdell compares the policy of using the forecasts as if there were no uncertainty attached to them and the policy of replacing the exogenous variables by their (unconditional) expected values, and arrives at conclusions similar to Friedman's and restated above in connection with formula (1.3). Now Tisdell is concerned with showing that there may be many inflexible policies (i.e. policies which do not use the forecasts) which are superior a policy based on the forecasts. However, he fails to raise the question of whether there are better ways of utilizing forecasts than simply to replace the exogenous variables by their forecasts as if they were certain. Therefore his conclusions to the effect that "an inflexible policy should be followed", and more explicitly that "ability to predict does not imply that discretionary policies are best", seem to me to be unwarranted. Both Friedman's analysis – see (1.4–5) above – and the more general analysis of this paper rather suggest the conclusion that ability to predict implies that discretionary policies are best, but there are degrees or scales of operation of discretionary policies, and these should be more modest the more modest is our ability to predict.

4. Suggestion for an empirical test

When Friedman wrote his paper he clearly felt that there was a tendency for an excessively active countercyclical policy. The analysis of the present paper, by bringing in explicitly the forecasts of the exogenous variables, suggests the possibility of an empirical approach to the problem of whether there is such a tendency.

The most direct approach would of course be to inquire with the ministries or other decision-making bodies whether they use forecasts in the way indicated by the analysis in sections 2 and 3 above. The answer would probably in most cases be rather vague. This is partly due to the fact that so many different kinds of information are drawn upon in the process before one settles for definitive forecasts which are used in connection with the final decision. It is very rare that well-defined forecasts are used without being modified and adjusted more or less according to judgement. My own impression is that such adjustments tend to scale down the variations in the forecasts. Intuition tells that one should not take the "full consequences" of large variations in forecasts of exogenous variables when one knows that the forecasts are not perfect. Thus intuition and practice may to some extent perform the function which is in our model executed by the replacement of the regression values $\tilde{z}_l, ..., \tilde{z}_q$ for given $z_l^*, ..., z_q^*$ for the original, unadjusted forecasts $z_1^*, ..., z_q^*$. However, we do not know if this is done to an optimal degree.

Now suppose that the government publishes forecasts of exogenous variables in connection with annual National Budgets or similar policy documents, as is done for instance in Norway, the Netherlands and other countries. If these are the forecasts actually used in the calculation of the plan or policy decision, then they should correspond to our magnitudes $\tilde{z}_1, ..., \tilde{z}_q$ if the procedure is optimally designed.

Let the published forecasts be $z_1^0, ..., z_q^0$. We could now treat these in the same way as any other forecasts generally denoted by $z_1^*, ..., z_q^*$ above, i.e. we could calculate the regressions of actually realized values of $z_1, ..., z_q$ on $z_1^0, ..., z_q^0$. If $z_1^0, ..., z_q^0$ are already correctly adjusted we should then come back to $z_1^0, ..., z_q^0$ so that no further adjustments should be made, i.e. we should (assuming linearity) obtain

$$E(z_i | z_1^0, ..., z_q^0) \equiv z_i^0 \qquad (i = 1, ..., q) , \tag{4.1}$$

or in vector notations,

$$Z^0 \equiv EZ + \Sigma_0 \Sigma_{00}^{-1} (Z^0 - EZ^0) , \tag{4.2}$$

which corresponds to (2.32) with Σ_0 and Σ_{00} as variance-covariances involving $Z^0 = (z_1^0, ..., z_q^0)'$ and Z in the same way as Σ_* and Σ_{**} are defined for Z^* and Z by (2.7) and (2.9). Assuming $EZ^0 = EZ$ this holds if and only if we have

$$\Sigma_0 \Sigma_{00}^{-1} = I , \qquad \text{or} \qquad \Sigma_0 = \Sigma_{00} . \tag{4.3}$$

Thus the question of whether $z_1^0, ..., z_q^0$ represent a set of optimality adjusted forecasts for decision purposes can be investigated by testing whether the condition (4.3) is fulfilled.

The facts which make this a simple and attractive test are that it does not require any information of what is behind the forecasts $z_1^0, ..., z_q^0$, and that it can clearly be carried out for any subset of exogenous variables if forecasts are not published for all of them.

Now the joint probability distribution of the various variables and forecasts are of course not known in practice. We can therefore only check (4.3) on the basis of a sample of observations. There are many problems involved in such a test on the basis of actual observations. One problem refers to trends in variables. It seems reasonable in the present context that trends should be taken account of through the expected values EZ, EZ^* and EZ^0 or, equivalently, be eliminated both from the time series of the various exogenous variables themselves and from the corresponding forecasts so that we have all unconditional expectations equal to zero. Another problem refers to stochastic aspects when we have a sample of limited size. What should be considered as a satisfactory approximation to the fulfillment of (4.3)? In spite of these problems I think the reasoning above suggests an interesting possibility for an empirical test of the degree to which actual policy behaves according to the prescriptions implied by the analysis of sections 2 and 3.

References

Friedman, M., 1953, The effects of a full-employment policy on economic stability: a formal analysis, in: Essays in positive economics (The University of Chicago Press). (Originally published in French in Economie Appliquée, 1951).

Goldberger, A.S., 1964, Econometric theory (John Wiley & Sons, Inc., New York).

Hansen, B., 1958, The economic theory of fiscal policy (George Allen & Unwin Ltd., London).

Hohn, F.E., 1964, Elementary matrix algebra, 2nd ed. (Collier-MacMillan Ltd., London).

Ijiri, Y., 1965, Management goals and accounting for control (North-Holland Publishing Company, Amsterdam).

Johansen, L., 1965, Public economics (North-Holland Publishing Company, Amsterdam).

Spivey, W.A. and H. Tamura, 1970, Generalized simultaneous equation models, International Economic Review, 2, 216–225.

Theil, H., 1964, Optimal decision rules for government and industry (North-Holland Publishing Company, Amsterdam).

Theil, H., 1971, Principles of econometrics (North-Holland Publishing Company, Amsterdam).

Tinbergen, J., 1952, On the theory of economic policy (North-Holland Publishing Company, Amsterdam).

Tisdell, C., 1971, Economic policy, forecasting and flexibility, in: Weltwirtschaftliches Archiv.

[17]

UNCERTAINTY AND THE EFFECTIVENESS OF POLICY*

By WILLIAM BRAINARD
Yale University

Economists concerned with aggregative policy spend a great deal of their time discussing the implications of various structural changes for the effectiveness of economic policy. In recent years, for example, monetary economists have debated at great length whether the rapid growth of nonbank financial intermediaries has lessened the effectiveness of conventional instruments of monetary control. Similarly, in discussions of the desirability of the addition or removal of specific financial regulations the consequences for the effectiveness of policy play an important role. One of the striking features of many of these discussions is the absence of any clear notion of what "effectiveness" is. At times it appears to be simply "bang per buck"—how large a change in some crucial variable (e.g., the long-term bond rate) results from a given change in a policy variable (e.g., open market operation). A natural question to ask is why a halving of effectiveness in this sense should not be met simply by doubling the dose of policy, with equivalent results.

It seems reasonable to suppose that the consequences of a structural change for the effectiveness of policy should be related to how it affects the policy-maker's performance in meeting his objectives. Suppose, for example, that the policy-maker wants to maximize a utility function which depends on the values of "target" variables. If, after some structural change, the policy-maker finds he is able to score higher on his utility function, then presumably the structural change has improved the effectiveness of policy and vice versa. One of the implications of the "theory of policy" in a world of certainty [6] or "certainty equivalence" [1] [3] [4] [5] is that structural changes which simply alter the magnitude of the response to policy do not alter the attainable utility level.[1] Hence such structural changes do not alter effectiveness in the above sense. Another feature of the theory of policy in a world of certainty is that a policy-maker with more instruments than targets is free to discard the excess instruments, and it makes no difference to his performance which ones he discards. These results are crucially dependent on the assumption that the response of target variables to policy in-

* I am indebted to Samuel Chase, Jr., Arthur Okun and James Tobin for many useful suggestions. A version of Parts I and II of this paper was presented at the Conference on Targets and Indicators of Monetary Policy held at U.C.L.A. in April, 1966.

[1] Assuming that the levels of instruments do not enter directly into the utility function.

struments is known for certain. Since it is difficult to imagine a real world policy-maker in such an enviable position, it would seem worthwhile to explore the implications of relaxing that assumption. The first two sections of this paper discuss the implications of uncertainty in the response to policy actions for the selection of optimal policy. Optimal policy in the presence of this type of uncertainty is found to differ significantly from optimal policy in a world of certainty. For example, in general all instruments are used, even if there is only one target variable. Analysis of the optimality question also provides some insight into what constitutes effectiveness.

In the third section it is shown that, not surprisingly, the way a structural change alters the effectiveness of policy depends on how it affects both the expected magnitude and the predictability of response to policy actions. The third section goes on to discuss briefly some of the problems involved in assessing the consequences of structural change for the effectiveness of policy when there are several instruments and several targets, and where the structural change affects the response of the system to disturbances as well as policy instruments.

I. *One Target—One Instrument*

It is instructive to discuss the complications uncertainty creates in a world of one target and one instrument before discussing the problem of optimal use of policy instruments when there are many instruments and targets. Suppose that the policy-maker is concerned with one target variable (y). Assume that y depends linearly on a policy instrument (P)—for example, government expenditures—and various exogenous variables—for example, autonomous investment demand. For our present purposes the impact of exogenous variables may be summarized in a single variable (u).

$$y = aP + u \tag{1}$$

where a determines the response of y to policy action.

The policy-maker faces two kinds of uncertainty. First, at the time he must make a policy decision he is uncertain about the impact of the exogenous variables (u) which affect y. This may reflect his inability to forecast perfectly either the value of exogenous variables or the response of y to them. Second, the policy-maker is uncertain about the response of y to any given policy action. He may have an estimate $\bar{a}$ of the expected value of the response coefficient a in (1) above, but he is aware that the actual response of y to policy action may differ substantially from the expected value. At the time of the 1964 tax cut, for example, there was considerable uncertainty over the magnitude of the tax multiplier.

Both types of uncertainty imply that the policy-maker cannot guarantee that y will assume its target value (y^*). But they have quite different implications for policy action. The first type of uncertainty, if present by itself, has nothing to do with the actions of the policy-maker; it is "in the system" independent of any action he takes. The assumption that all of the uncertainties are of this type is one of the reasons Theil and others [1] [3] [4] [5] are able to prescribe "certainty equivalence" behavior; that is, that the policy-maker should act on the basis of expected values as if he were certain they would actually occur. Since in this case the variance and higher moments of the distribution of y do not depend on the policy action taken, the policy-maker's actions only shift the location of y's distribution.

In the presence of uncertainty about the response of y to policy actions, however, the shape as well as the location of the distribution of y depends on the policy action. In this case the policy-maker should take into account his influence on the variability of y.[2]

We will assume that the policy-maker chooses policy on the basis of "expected utility." In particular, we will follow Theil in assuming that the policy-maker maximizes the expected value of a quadratic utility function. In the one-target case this is simply:

$$U = -(y - y^*)^2 \tag{2}$$

where y^* is the target value of y.

The assumption of the quadratic enables us to restrict our attention to the mean and variance of y and to compare our findings directly with the familiar certainty equivalence results. The assumption of a quadratic is, of course, subject to the objection that it treats positive and negative deviations from target as equally important. The use of a fancier utility function would provide additional reasons for departing from certainty equivalence.

The precise relationship between policy actions and the variance of y is not obvious. In (1) above, for example, the policy-maker may believe that the response coefficient a is a random variable depending on some unobserved variables, and that it is correlated with u. In that case the y is a random variable with a variance given by:

$$\sigma_y^2 = \sigma_a^2 P^2 + \sigma_u^2 + 2\rho\sigma_a\sigma_u P \tag{3}$$

where σ_u^2 and σ_a^2 are the variances of u and a, respectively, and ρ is the correlation coefficient between u and a.

On the other hand, it is possible to conceive of part of the uncertainty of y as the consequence of estimation error. Even if the policy-maker

[2] Theil is of course aware that certainty equivalence behavior is not optimal in this case. In fact, he suggests that the sampling errors in the response coefficients are the most "dangerous" ones for a policy-maker who acts as if all random coefficient matrices coincide with their expectations [4, p. 74].

regards the "true" population response coefficient a as nonrandom, he may have to base his actions on an estimate of it obtained by fitting equation (1) to sample data. The estimate he uses will be a random variable, and its variance will affect the "variance" of y around its forecast value.[3]

As in the case where the population response coefficient is random, the magnitude of the policy action affects the contribution of this type of uncertainty to the variance of y. In this case, however, the contribution depends on the difference between the policy taken in the forecast period and the average level of policy pursued in the sample period used in estimating a. Assuming the u's are independent over time, a will be uncorrelated with the u for the forecast period and equation (3) may be rewritten:

$$\sigma_y^2 = \sigma_a^2(P - \bar{P})^2 + \sigma_u^2 \tag{3'}$$

where $\bar{P}$ is the average P for the sample period on which the estimate of a is based. Although we will use the first formulation to illustrate the significance of uncertainty in the response of y to policy actions, our results can be translated easily for use in the forecast error case.

Assuming the response coefficient is a random variable, we may find the expected utility associated with a given policy action by substituting (1) in (2):

$$\begin{aligned} E(U) &= -\left[(\bar{y} - y^*)^2 + \sigma_y^2\right] \\ &= -\left[(\bar{a}P + \bar{u} - y^*)^2 + \sigma_a^2 P^2 + \sigma_u^2 + 2\rho\sigma_a\sigma_u P\right] \end{aligned} \tag{4}$$

where $\bar{y}$ and $\bar{u}$ are the expected values of y and u, respectively. There is no reason to suppose that $\bar{u}$ equals zero.

By differentiating (4) with respect to P and setting the derivative equal to zero, the optimal value of P is easily found to be:

$$P^* = \frac{\bar{a}(y^* - \bar{u}) - \rho\sigma_a\sigma_u}{\bar{a}^2 + \sigma_a^2} \tag{5}$$

The optimal policy indicated by equation (5) clearly differs from the policy which would be pursued in a world of certainty or of certainty equivalence. The policy-maker should make use of more information than the expected value of the exogenous variables and of the response coefficient of a. Even when a and u are independently distributed, he

[3] Hooper and Zellner [2] provide a discussion of the error of forecast for multivariate regression models. In general the variance of the forecast error is $\sigma_F^2 = \sigma^2(xX1^u)[1 + x_F'^{-1}x_F]$ where x is the matrix of sample observations on the independent variables, and x_F is the vector of deviations of the independent variables from their sample means for the forecast period.

should make use of information about the variance of a as well as its mean. If a and u are not independent, he also needs to know their correlation. The assumption of a quadratic utility function does not lead to certainty equivalence except when the policy-maker is certain about the effects of his actions. Another interesting implication of (5) is that it does not in general pay to aim directly at the target. If a and u are independent, for example, equation (5) can be rewritten to show that the fraction of the expected "gap" between $\bar{u}$ and y^* which should be filled by policy action depends only on the coefficient of variation of a:

$$P^* = g/(1 + V^2) \tag{5'}$$

where $g=(y^*-\bar{u})/\bar{a}$, the expected gap, and V equals $\sigma_a/\bar{a}$, the coefficient of variation of a.[4] Only if the policy-maker is absolutely certain about a ($V=0$) will he close the entire gap; so long as V is finite, he will partially fill the gap.

Some care must be used in interpreting this result. The gap in this context is not the difference between what policy was "last period" and what would be required to make the expected value of y equal to y^*. In the example we have used, the gap is the difference between P equal to zero—the point where the variance of y is least—and the P required to give an expected value of y equal to y^*. If the expected value of a and u and the standard deviation of a remained unchanged for several periods, the optimal policy would also remain unchanged—the policy-maker would not reduce the gap in successive periods. In the case of "forecasting error" the gap is the difference between the average value of policy in the sample used to estimate a and the P which gives $\bar{y}$ equal to y^*. In this case, if the parameter a were reestimated each period and the expected value of u remained the same, policy would be continually revised, making the expected value of y closer and closer to y^* in successive periods.

A natural question to ask is to what extent uncertainty about a affects optimal behavior. Equation (5) indicates that "moderate" uncertainty about a may have a substantial effect. Suppose, for illustrative purposes, that the monetary authority believes that the equation $Y=aM+u$ correctly specifies the relationship between the stock of money (M), an exogenous variable (u), and money income (Y). It puts its staff to work estimating the relationship and obtains an estimate of 5 for the value of a, significant at a "t" level of 2. Further suppose that for the sample of observations on Y and M used to estimate a, the average level of M was \$100. Now suppose that for the next period the desired level of Y is \$650 and the expected value of u is taken to be \$50. In a

[4] (5′) can be used for the estimation error case if P^* is interpreted as the deviation of optimal policy from the mean of P during the sample period, and u is defined to include $\bar{a}$ times that mean.

world of certainty M would simply be set at \$600/5 or \$120. Optimal policy in the uncertain situation confronting the policy-maker is most easily found by consulting equation (5′). If M were set at its average value during the sample period the expected value of Y would be \$550, leaving a gap of \$20 (\$100/5).

According to (5′), however, only 80 percent of this gap should be closed with a coefficient of variation of a equal to one-half. Hence it is optimal to set M at \$116 (=\$100+.8×\$20).

When a and u are not independent, the results are slightly more complicated. The policy-maker must now take into account the covariation

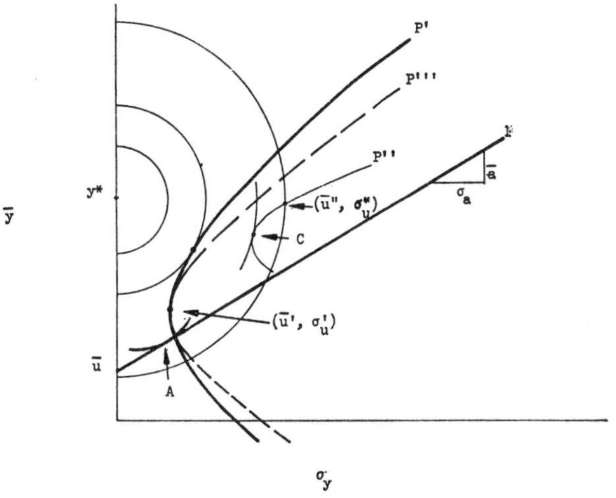

FIGURE 1

between the impact of his policy action and exogenous variables. If there is a positive correlation, it will pay him to shoot for a lower value of $\bar{y}$ than otherwise; if negative, higher. One interesting implication of this is that the fraction of the gap that the policy-maker should close will depend on which side of the target he is on. Perhaps more surprising, if a and u have sufficiently large positive correlation and there is a positive gap or sufficiently large negative correlation and there is a negative gap, it may actually pay for the policy-maker to go the "wrong" way! That is, at the initial point it may actually pay to reduce the variance of y at the expense of increasing the difference between expected y and y^*.

These results can be seen diagrammatically by consulting Figure 1 which shows the expected value of y on the vertical axis and the standard deviation of y on the horizontal axis. Indifference curves, showing various combinations of $\bar{y}$ and σ_y, which have the same expected utility, are drawn "around" y^*, the target value of y. These curves have the form $(y^*-\bar{y})^2+\sigma_y^2=\text{constant}$; i.e., they are concentric circles drawn around y^*.

In order to focus on the effects of uncertainty concerning the impact of policy, let us assume for the moment that σ_u is zero. Referring to Figure 1, suppose that in the absence of policy action, y is certain to be $\bar{u}$, which is well below y^*. By increasing P by "1 unit," the policy-maker may close the expected gap between y and $\bar{y}$ by an amount $\bar{a}$, but in so doing he also increases the standard deviation of y by σ_a.[5] The line P shows the possibilities open to the policy-maker. Optimal policy corresponds to point A. Because the indifference curves are horizontal where they leave $\bar{y}$ axis, and vertical at a value of $\bar{y}=y^*$, while the slope of the line P is $\bar{a}/\sigma_a$, it always pays to do something, but it never pays to aim for y^*. It is also apparent that reductions in σ_a for a given $\bar{a}$ increase the optimal amount of policy.

These results are not altered for σ_u not equal to zero, so long as the correlation between u and a is 0. In Figure 1 the point $(\bar{u}', \sigma_{u'})$ indicates the expected value and variance of y in the absence of policy action and the line drawn through that point labeled P' indicates the opportunities available to the policy-maker. This "opportunity locus" is curved, reflecting the absence of perfect correlation between a and u. This independence guarantees that unless $\bar{u}=y^*$ it will be optimal to pursue some policy action, for the opportunity locus is vertical at the point $(\bar{u}', \sigma_{u'})$ indicating that the first little bit of policy can be undertaken without increasing the variance of y.[6]

In Figure 1 the line P'' shows the way correlation between a and u alters the opportunity locus available to the policy-maker. In the example shown, a zero level of policy would leave the economy at the point $(\bar{u}'', \sigma_{u''})$. The positive correlation between a and u tilts the locus clockwise through that point so that a small decrease in P will decrease the variance of Y. Optimal policy involves choosing point C, which in this case involves going the "wrong" way. If by chance $\bar{a}(y^*-\bar{u})=\rho\sigma_u\sigma_a$, the policy-maker should do nothing.

Figure 2 shows the way in which the appropriate level of policy action depends on the size of the gap. For given values of $\bar{a}$, ρ, σ_a, σ_u, the larger the gap, the more the policy-maker should do. With independence of a and u this relationship is linear-homogeneous. When a and u are correlated the relationship is linear, but a zero level of policy is optimal for some nonzero gap.

[5] As a convention, the sign of policy is always chosen so that "positive" policy increases $\bar{y}$.

[6] For correlation between u and a equal to 0,

$$\frac{\partial\sigma_y}{\partial P}=\frac{\partial\left[(\sigma_u^2+P^2\sigma_a^2)^{1/2}\right]}{\partial P}=\left.\frac{P\sigma_a^2}{(\sigma_u^2+P^2\sigma_a^2)^{1/2}}\right|_{P=0}=0$$

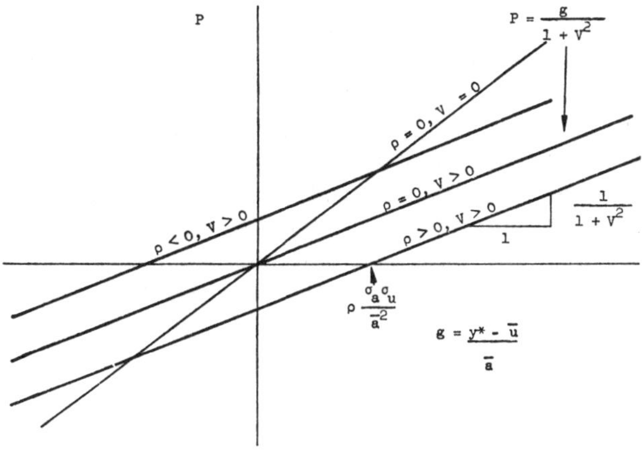

FIGURE 2

II. *Multiple Instruments*

One of the lessons of the theory of policy under certainty is that, in general, the attainment of n targets requires n instruments. If more than n instruments are available, the policy-maker is free to choose n arbitrarily in order to achieve his objectives. It should already be obvious that this rule breaks down under uncertainty. We will first show that with one target and two instruments it will generally be optimal to use some combination of both instruments.[7] It can similarly be shown that in general all instruments available should be used in pursuing one target. It follows that the addition of an objective requires some sacrifice in performance vis-à-vis objectives already being considered.

Suppose that:

$$y = a_1 P_1 + a_2 P_2 + u \tag{6}$$

where again it is desired to maximize the expected value of the utility function given in (2). It will be convenient to define units of policy such that the $\bar{a}_i$ associated with each policy instrument is exactly 1. For simplicity let us assume that correlation between each a_i and u is 0. Then by differentiating the expected value of (2) with respect to P_1 and P_2 we find the conditions for optimal policy to be:

$$0 = (P_1 + P_2 + \bar{u} - y^*) + P_1 \sigma_{a_1}^2 + \rho_{12} \sigma_{a_1} \sigma_{a_2} P_2 \tag{7a}$$

$$0 = (P_1 + P_2 + \bar{u} - y^*) + P_2 \sigma_{a_2}^2 + \rho_{12} \sigma_{a_1} \sigma_{a_2} P_1 \tag{7b}$$

where ρ_{12} is the correlation between a_1 and a_2.

[7] The idea of looking at the problem of optimal policy behavior in an uncertain world as essentially a problem of portfolio choice arose in discussions with Arthur Okun around 1962.

Solving for the ratio of P_1 to total policy impact (P_1+P_2) we obtain:

$$P_1/(P_1 + P_2) = \frac{\sigma_{a_2}^2 - \rho_{12}\sigma_{a_1}\sigma_{a_2}}{(\sigma_{a_2}^2 - 2\rho_{12}\sigma_{a_1}\sigma_{a_2} + \sigma_{a_1}^2)} \quad (8)$$ [8]

Equation (8) indicates the proportions in which the policy-maker should use the two policy instruments. The optimal policy portfolio as shown in (8) combines the instruments so as to minimize the coefficient of variation of their combined impact. Under the assumption of independence between the a_i's and the u, this policy portfolio can be treated as a single instrument and its optimal level determined as in Section I.

16.a

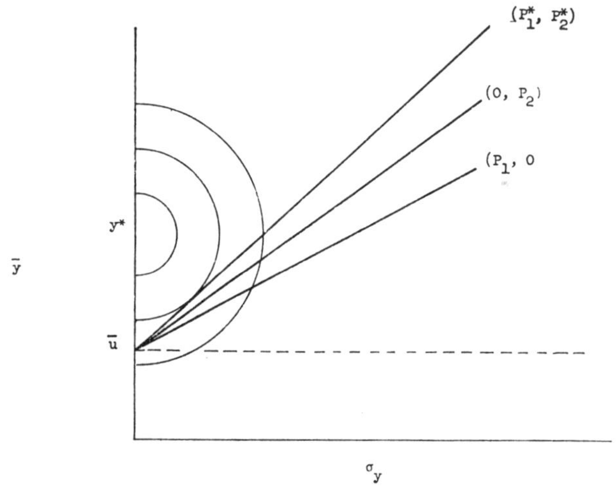

FIGURE 3

The coefficient of variation of the optimal policy package is, of course, less than or equal to the coefficient of variation of any single instrument. Figure 3 shows, for the special case where σ_u and ρ equal zero and where the ratio of the coefficient of variation of a_2 to that of a_1 is .8, the locus for the optimal combination of two policies compared to the loci available for each of the instruments used separately. Figure 3 assumes that the correlation between the impacts of the two instruments is zero. The presence of correlation between the a's complicates the computation of the optimal policy portfolio but does not alter the basic conclusion that several instruments are better than one in the pursuit of one goal.

The optimal amount of P_1 per "unit" of combined policy action

[8] By virtue of the normalization of a_i, of course, the standard deviations are coefficients of variation.

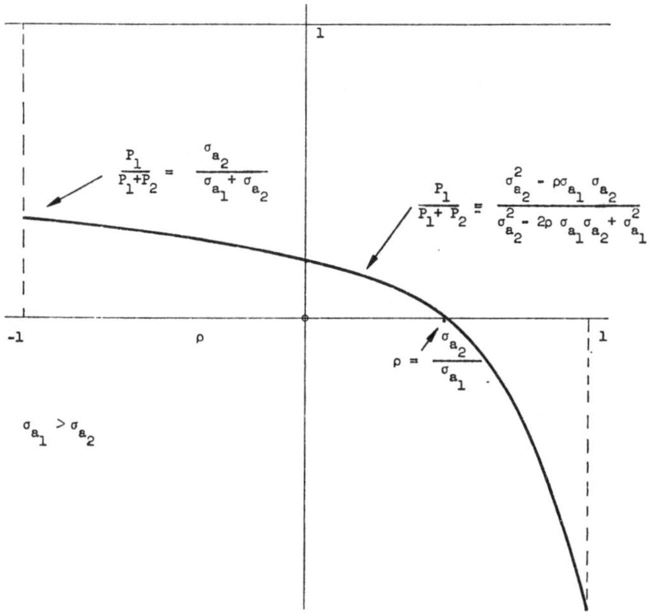

FIGURE 4

P_1+P_2 is shown in Figure 4 as a function of the correlation between a_1 and a_2. In the example shown it is assumed that the coefficient of variation of a_1 is greater than that of a_2. From Figure 4 it can be seen that for sufficiently high positive correlation it is optimal to use P_1 (the "less efficient" instrument) in the "wrong" direction.

Table 1 shows the coefficients of variation for the optimal policy

TABLE 1

COEFFICIENT OF VARIATION FOR ρ_{12} OPTIMAL POLICY PACKAGE

$\sigma_{a_1}/\sigma_{a_2}$	−9/10	−3/4	−1/2	−1/4	0	1/4	1/2	3/4	9/10	1
1.0	.22	.35	.50	.61	.71	.79	.87	.94	.97	1.0
1.1	.23	.37	.52	.64	.74	.83	.90	.97	1.00	0
1.2	.24	.39	.54	.67	.77	.86	.93	.99	.99	0
1.6	.27	.43	.61	.74	.85	.93	.99	.98	.85	0
2.0	.30	.47	.65	.79	.89	.97	1.00	.94	.74	0
2.4	.31	.49	.69	.82	.92	.99	1.00	.89	.67	0
2.8	.33	.51	.71	.85	.94	.99	.99	.86	.63	0
3.2	.34	.53	.73	.86	.95	1.00	.98	.83	.60	0
4.0	.35	.55	.76	.89	.97	1.00	.96	.80	.56	0
8.0	.39	.60	.81	.93	.99	.99	.92	.73	.49	0

$\sigma_{a_2}=1$.

package for various values of ρ_{12}, σ_{a_1}, σ_{a_2}. The table is constructed with the variance of a_2 normalized at one and with $\sigma a_2 < \sigma a_1$. Hence the lowest coefficient of variation of policy impact that would be obtained by using a single policy is one. The improvement realized by using both instruments rather than P_2 alone is indicated by the difference between one and the appropriate entry.

The gain from diversification of policy instruments is not a simple function of the correlation coefficient; it also depends on the ratio of coefficients of variation of the two policy instruments. As can be seen from Table 1, negative correlation between a_1 and a_2 greatly assists in reducing the variance in the impact of the policy package, the reduction being greatest for cases where the variances of the two instruments are equal. As the correlation increases, the gain from using two instruments decreases, until at some level of positive correlation none of policy P_1 is used. For correlation greater than that amount, P_1 will be used in the "wrong" direction and some reduction in variance will be realized. In the extreme cases of perfect positive or perfect negative correlation between the a's there exists a policy package with zero variance.

If there is correlation between the disturbance and the impact of either of the policy instruments, it should also be taken into account in the selection of a policy package. Other things being equal, increasing the correlation between the impact of a particular instrument and the disturbance will decrease its use relative to other instruments. The importance of such correlation depends on the size of the gap: the larger the gap, the less the relative contribution of the disturbance to the variance of y after policy action and the less important the correlation of the disturbance and instruments.

The optimal use of n instruments follows the principles illustrated with two; if the error term is independent of the policy response coefficients, the portfolio of instruments which has the lowest coefficient of variation should be chosen. In general this will involve using all of the instruments, and it may involve using some instruments the "wrong" way.

Generalization to many targets is conceptually simple but algebraically tedious. Solution of a multiple-goal problem requires specification of a multidimensional utility function which, if it is quadratic, implicitly provides weights for trading off expected values, variances, and covariances of the policy objectives. The particular solution obviously depends on the weights imbedded in the utility function. One feature of the results is perhaps worth noting: since all policy instruments would be used in pursuit of a single target, improvement in performance vis-à-vis one objective requires sacrificing other objectives—even when the number of instruments exceeds the number of objectives.

III. *Structural Change and the Effectiveness of Policy*

The evaluation of the impact of any particular structural change on the effectiveness of policy is extremely difficult.[9] For our purposes a structural change is described by the way it changes the joint distribution of the parameters a_i and u. The task of determining how the imposition of some new regulation or the emergence of some new financial market alters that distribution is obviously a major one and beyond the scope of this paper. Our relatively modest objective here is to indicate the empirical questions which the above analysis suggests are of importance.

A Single Instrument. First let us consider structural changes which affect only the impact of policy actions; i.e., which do not affect either the expected value or dispersion of the disturbance term. In addition, let us assume that the structural change in question does not alter the correlations among the policy impact coefficients and the disturbance. The effect of such a change on expected utility can be found directly by substituting the value of optimal policy (expressed in terms of $\bar{a}$, σ_a, ρ, $\bar{u}$, etc.) in the equation for expected utility (4). Alternatively, the consequences of structural change can be seen by noting how the "opportunity locus" in Figures 1 and 3 are affected. By substituting $(\bar{y}-\bar{u})/\bar{a}$ for P in equation (3) we find:

$$\sigma_y = \left(\frac{\sigma_a^2}{\bar{a}^2}(\bar{y}-\bar{u})^2 + 2\rho\frac{\sigma_a}{\bar{a}}\sigma_u(\bar{y}-\bar{u}) + \sigma_u^2\right)^{1/2} \tag{9}$$

It is immediately clear that a structural change which does not affect the coefficient of variation of a (nor ρ, $\bar{u}$, and σ_u) does not alter the opportunity locus and hence does not alter the expected utility derived from optimal policy. It is also clear that increasing the coefficient of variation, for ρ equal zero, results in an opportunity locus which has a larger variance for every value of $\bar{y}$ (except for zero policy). Hence increasing the coefficient of variation leads to a reduction in the effectiveness of policy. Such a shift is illustrated in Figure 1 by a movement of the opportunity locus labeled P' to the location indicated by the dotted locus labeled P'''.

One of the simplest illustrations of this result is the argument that increasing the legal reserve requirement, thereby reducing the expected response to a given sized change in reserve base, actually increases the effectiveness of monetary control. Suppose one believes that the money

[9] What is classified as a structural change obviously depends on the specific problem under discussion. The removal of the ceiling rate on time deposits, for example, would change the response of financial markets to open market operations; that is, it would change the structure within which the Federal Reserve conducts day-to-day policy. At the same time, however, the ceiling rate itself could be used as a policy instrument to influence target variables. While some changes in the "structure" are the direct consequence of actions by the monetary authority, others may be exogenous from their point of view.

stock is all that matters and, further, that the money stock (M) is related to the reserve base (R) by the following equation:

$$M = \frac{1}{k + \epsilon} R \tag{10}$$

where k is the legal reserve requirement and ϵ is banks' demand for free reserves (expressed as a fraction of their deposit liabilities). Suppose further that, from the viewpoint of the monetary authority, ϵ is a random variable with a known distribution. Then it is easy to see that, for reasonable distributions of ϵ, increases in k will reduce the expected response of M to R but can reduce the standard deviation of that response more than proportionately, thereby reducing its coefficient of variation. One of the appeals of the 100 percent reserve proposal, of course, is the fact that as k approaches one, the coefficient of variation of the response of M to R goes to zero.

If the correlation between the impact of the policy instrument and u is not zero, matters are slightly more complicated. From (9) it is apparent that increases in σ_a shift the opportunity locus to the right for some values of $(\bar{y}-\bar{u})$ and to the left for others. This is illustrated for a positive ρ in Figure 5 below where the dotted locus corresponds to a higher σ_a. As indicated in Figure 5, the minimum risk that can be obtained is independent of the value of σ_a, and depends only on the value of σ_u and ρ. Hence, it is possible to get the paradoxical result that an increase in the dispersion of response can make policy more "effective" for some set

22a

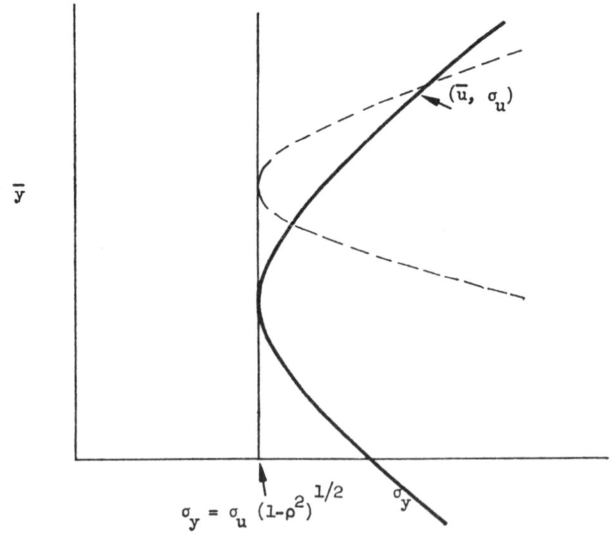

FIGURE 5

of values of $\bar{u}$ and σ_u. This peculiar result is a consequence of the fact that it is possible to reduce the variance of y below σ_u whenever μ and a are correlated. Consider, for example, the case where a and u are positively correlated, and where $\bar{\mu}$ is less than y^*. In this case a reduction in risk can be obtained for "negative" values of P; i.e., by setting $\bar{y}$ even further from y^* than $\bar{u}$. Suppose that the optimal policy initially involves going in the counterintuitive direction in order to take advantage of such risk reduction. With a larger σ_a the same reduction in risk can be obtained without pushing $\bar{y}$ as far away from y^*; hence it will result in a higher expected utility.

Multiple Instruments. The consequence of structural change when there are a number of instruments is closely analogous to the single instrument case. If the structural change does not affect the coefficient of variation for the individual instruments, their correlations, or the distribution of the disturbance, the opportunity locus is unaltered. If the coefficient of variation of an individual instrument is increased, the consequences can be analyzed in two steps.[10] First, the effect of the change on the coefficient of variation of the optimal policy package can be found. Once this is determined, its consequences for the performance of the policy-maker can be analyzed exactly as in the single instrument case.

The consequences of increasing the coefficient of variation of one instrument are illustrated in Table 1.[11] Two points illustrated in Table 1 are worthy of comment. First, so long as both instruments are used in the same direction (see Figure 4), increasing the coefficient of variation of one instrument increases the coefficient of variation of the optimal policy package. If an instrument is used in the counterintuitive direction, however, increasing its coefficient of variation improves the optimal policy package. Second, the table illustrates the obvious fact that decreasing the effectiveness of one instrument which is being used together with others has much less effect than if the instrument were being used by itself. For example, even with a correlation of $-9/10$, the consequence of increasing σ_{a_1} from 1 to 2 is to increase the coefficient of variation of the optimal policy package by less than 40 percent.

Multiple Targets. The presence of a number of target variables in the utility function greatly complicates the task of evaluating the consequences of a given structural change. It is quite unlikely that a change will affect the opportunity locus for different targets in the same way. Hence the desirability of the change will depend on the relative weights placed on the different targets in the utility function. For example, it is commonly argued that the development of the Euro-dollar market and

[10] Assuming the correlations between the a_i's and u are zero.

[11] Table 1 shows the effect of increasing the coefficient of variation for the less effective of the two instruments.

the general increase in international capital mobility in recent years has made monetary policy a more effective tool in stabilizing the balance of payments, while at the same time reducing its usefulness for controlling domestic economic disturbances.

Disturbances. The discussion thus far has focused on the consequences of structural change for the performance of the policy-maker when confronted with a given distribution of disturbances. A structural change which alters the response to policy actions is also likely to alter the magnitude of the problems with which he must cope. In the above example, greater capital mobility presumably increases the responsiveness of the U. S. balance of payments to disturbances; e.g., in this case to changes in the interest rates in other countries. Thus a structural change which gives the U. S. a more effective tool may also have given it a more difficult task to perform. If this is the case it is not clear that such a structural change is desirable. This can be illustrated by reference to the single instrument case with ρ equal to zero. Suppose for the moment that a structural change doubles $\bar{a}$ and σ_a, but also doubles σ_u, without altering $\bar{u}$. From Figure 1 it is clear that such a change leaves the policy-maker with a worse opportunity locus.[12] If, in addition, there is an increase in the variation of $\bar{u}$ from period to period, still greater losses result.

In the real world, evaluating the desirability of a given structural change is further complicated by the fact that a change which decreases the response of the system to one type of disturbance is likely to increase its response to another. Consider, for example, the consequences of a permanent fixed ceiling rate on time deposits. It can be argued that such a restriction on banks' competition for deposits reduces the response of the system to shifts in the demand of bank borrowers for loans. At the same time, the existence of such a ceiling may increase the destabilizing effect of shifts in depositors' preferences between the liabilities of banks and other financial intermediaries. In general, then, evaluation of some particular structural change requires an empirical judgment as to the relative importance of various kinds of disturbances.

[12] Again, when $\rho \neq 0$, it is possible to have the paradoxical result that increasing σ_u is advantageous.

REFERENCES

1. C. C. Holt, F. Modigliani, J. F. Muth and H. A. Simon, *Planning Production, Inventories, and Work Force* (Prentice-Hall, 1960).
2. John W. Hooper and Arnold Zellner, "The Error of Forecast for Multivariate Regression Models," Cowles Foundation Paper No. 171 (Cowles Found. for Res. in Econ., Yale Univ., 1962).
3. Henri Theil, *Economic Forecasts and Policy*, 2nd ed., Vol. XV of Contributions to Economic Analysis (North-Holland Pub. Co., Amsterdam, 1961).
4. ———, *Optimal Decision Rules for Government and Industry* (Rand McNally, 1964).
5. ———, "Linear Decision Rules for Macrodynamic Policy Problems," *Quantitative Planning of Economic Policy*, Bert G. Hickman, ed. (Brookings Institution, 1965), pp. 18–37.
6. J. Tinbergen, *On the Theory of Economic Policy*, 2nd ed., Vol. I of Contributions to Economic Analysis (North-Holland Pub. Co., Amsterdam, 1952).

[18]

STOCHASTIC MODELS OF ECONOMIC FLUCTUATIONS*

By LEONID HURWICZ

I. THE PROBLEM

1. DYNAMICAL systems serving as models for explanation of economic fluctuations are often described by sets of linear difference equations with constant coefficients. These equations are usually of the stochastic type: that is, they are nonhomogeneous and the nonhomogeneous term (the "disturbance") is a random variable.[1]

Since the economist's interest is frequently focused on one of the variates of the system, e.g., the level of employment, and also because some of the variates cannot be observed with the desired degree of accuracy, it is common practice to reduce the original system of equations to an equivalent single equation in one of the variates.[2]

* The problem discussed in this paper arose in interpreting the results of two business-cycle studies: one under a Babson Fund grant at the Economics Department of the Massachusetts Institute of Technology and one under a Social Science Research Committee grant at the University of Chicago. The writer wishes to acknowledge the assistance from both these sources, and to thank Professor Paul A. Samuelson of the Massachusetts Institute of Technology for valuable suggestions.

[1] One example would be Haavelmo's model (ECONOMETRICA, Vol. 11, January, 1943, p. 4):

$$\text{(f1.1)} \qquad \begin{cases} u_t = \alpha r_t + \beta + x_t, \\ r_t - u_t = \kappa(u_t - u_{t-1}) + y_t, \end{cases}$$

where u is consumption, r is income, and x and y are random variables.

Koopmans' model (*Annals of Mathematical Statistics*, Vol. 13, March, 1942, p. 14) has similar formal properties, although it refers to only one sector of the economy:

$$\text{(f1.2)} \qquad \begin{cases} x_t = \alpha - \beta y_t + z_t', \\ y_t = \gamma + \delta x_{t-1} + z_t'', \end{cases}$$

where x and y are respectively the price and supply of hogs and the z's are again random variables.

Samuelson's system (*Review of Economic Statistics*, Vol. 21, May, 1939, p. 76) belongs to the same class, although the effects of random variables have not been shown explicitly:

$$\text{(f1.3)} \qquad \begin{cases} Y_t = C_t I_t + g_t, \\ C_t = \alpha Y_{t-1}, \\ I_t = \beta(C_t - C_{t-1}), \end{cases}$$

where Y is national income, C consumption expenditure, I private investment, and g governmental expenditure.

The references are selected without consideration for historical sequence. Earlier papers, e.g., that of Frisch ("Propagation Problems and Impulse Problems in Dynamic Economics," *Economic Essays in Honor of Gustav Cassel*, 1933, pp. 171–205), are not always explicit enough for the purposes of our discussion.

The process of reduction yields, in general, a higher-order difference equation, to be called the "reduced equation," which is also nonhomogeneous.[3] The nonhomogeneous term will contain, possibly in addition to other terms, a linear combination of the "disturbances" of the initial system of equations. This "composite disturbance"[4] of the "reduced equation" differs in its properties from the original disturbances. In particular, it may be autocorrelated even though the disturbances of the original system were nonautocorrelated.[5]

2. Before proceeding to more general investigation of the properties of the reduced equation, it appears advisable to consider a simple example. Let there be given the system

$$\begin{cases} X_t = aX_{t-1} + b_1Y_{t-1} + b_2Y_{t-2} + \epsilon_t', \\ Y_t = cX_{t-1} + \epsilon_t'', \end{cases} \tag{1.2.1}$$

where the ϵ's are the "disturbances." By substituting Y from the second equation into the first equation we obtain the "reduced equation"

$$X_t = aX_{t-1} + b_1cX_{t-2} + b_2cX_{t-3} + \epsilon_t' + b_1\epsilon_{t-1}'' + b_2\epsilon_{t-2}'', \tag{1.2.2}$$

which can be rewritten as

$$X_t + \alpha_1X_{t-1} + \alpha_2X_{t-2} + \alpha_3X_{t-3} = \eta_t, \tag{1.2.3}$$

where

$$\eta_t \equiv \epsilon_t' + b_1\epsilon_{t-1}'' + b_2\epsilon_{t-2}'' \tag{1.2.4}$$

is the "composite disturbance."

---

[2] Thus Koopmans eliminates y from his system (*supra*, footnote 1) and obtains the equation

$$x_t = \epsilon - \zeta x_{t-1} + z_t, \tag{f2.1}$$

where ϵ and ζ are functions of α, β, γ, δ, while

$$z_t = z_t' - \beta z_t''. \tag{f2.2}$$

Similarly, Samuelson obtains

$$Y_t = g_t + \alpha(1 + \beta)Y_{t-1} - \alpha\beta Y_{t-2}, \tag{f2.3}$$

where, again, the disturbance is not introduced explicitly.

[3] In Koopmans' model, equation (f2.1).

[4] In Koopmans' model, $z_t \equiv z_t' - \beta z_t''$.

[5] A random variable is said to be nonautocorrelated when all of its autocorrelation coefficients r_k (except for $k=0$) are zero. r_k for a random variable x_t is defined as follows:

$$r_k = \frac{\mathcal{E}(x_tx_{t+k}) - [\mathcal{E}(x_t)]^2}{\mathcal{E}(x_t^2) - [\mathcal{E}(x_t)]^2}, \tag{f5.1}$$

where $\mathcal{E}$ is the symbol of mathematical expectation. (Cf. Herman Wold, *A Study in the Analysis of Stationary Time Series*, Uppsala 1938, p. 12.)

Now if the ϵ's are nonautocorrelated random variables with zero means and a finite covariance matrix $\|\sigma_{ij}\|$, we find that the lag product moment

$$\begin{aligned}\mathcal{E}(\eta_t\eta_{t+1}) &= \mathcal{E}[(\epsilon_t'+b_1\epsilon_{t-1}''+b_2\epsilon_{t-2}'')(\epsilon_{t+1}'+b_1\epsilon_t''+b_2\epsilon_{t-1}'')] \\ &= b_1\sigma_{12}+b_1b_2\sigma_{22}+R\neq 0,\end{aligned} \tag{1.2.5}$$

where R is due to correlation among the ϵ's. Hence η_t may be autocorrelated even though the ϵ's were nonautocorrelated. It is of interest to note that the autocorrelation properties of η are partly due to correlations between ϵ_t' and ϵ_t''. However, even if we had $\sigma_{ij}=0$ for all $i\neq j$ and all lags, η would still remain autocorrelated because it has the nature of a "moving average"[6] and pairs of its lagged values contain common elements, provided the lag does not exceed a certain integer. [For instance, it is easily seen that in case of η_t defined by (1.2.4) we should have

$$r_k = 0 \quad \text{for} \quad k \geqq 3.] \tag{1.2.6}$$

In economic investigations the interest centers as a rule on the variate itself [(X in Eq. (1.2.3)] rather than the "disturbance" (η). In particular we may want to examine the autocorrelation properties of X, say its "periodicity," and also obtain a "forecast equation" (or "forecast curve"):

$$\mathcal{E}(X_{t+k} \mid X_t, X_{t-1}, \cdots) = f(X_t, X_{t-1}, \cdots) \quad (k = 1, 2, \cdots), \tag{1.2.7}$$

where $\mathcal{E}(\mid)$ is the customary symbol for conditional expectations. Now if η_t in (1.2.3) were nonautocorrelated, as it is assumed to be in Wold's treatment of stochastic difference equations, the autocorrelation properties of X would depend on the ("structural") coefficients α_1, α_2, α_3, and, similarly, the forecast equation would involve the values of α_1, α_2, α_3 only. For instance, we should have

$$\mathcal{E}(X_{t+1} \mid X_t, X_{t-1}, X_{t-2}) = -\alpha_1X_t - \alpha_2X_{t-1} - \alpha_3X_{t-2}+\mathcal{E}. \tag{1.2.8}$$

As soon, however, as η_t is assumed to be autocorrelated we must consider the conditional expectations of future disturbances, since the latter are stochastically dependent on their predecessors. Thus instead of (1.2.8) we should have

$$\begin{aligned}\mathcal{E}(X_{t+1} \mid X_t, X_{t-1}, X_{t-2}) = &- \alpha_1X_t - \alpha_2X_{t-1} - \alpha_3X_{t-2} \\ &+ \mathcal{E}(\eta_t \mid X_t, X_{t-1}, X_{t-2}),\end{aligned} \tag{1.2.81}$$

where the last term depends on the autocorrelation properties of η and need not vanish if η is autocorrelated.

[6] Cf. Wold, *op. cit.*, p. 121.

3. Another important point is that in a stochastic difference equation with an autocorrelated "disturbance," of which (1.2.3) is an example, the autocorrelation pattern (the "correlogram") of the observed variate depends not only on the "structural coefficients" [the α's in (1.2.3)] but also on the correlogram of the "disturbance."

This can easily be shown in the simple case $[\mathcal{E}(\eta_t)=0]$

$$X_1 = \eta_1, \tag{1.3.11}$$

$$X_t - \alpha X_{t-1} = \eta_t \qquad (t = 2, 3, \cdots), \tag{1.3.12}$$

where $|\alpha| < 1$ and the autocorrelation coefficients of η_t, to be denoted by ρ_k, are given by

$$\begin{cases} \rho_1 \neq 0, \\ \rho_k = 0 \qquad (\text{for } k = 2, 3, \cdots). \end{cases} \tag{1.3.2}$$

From (1.3.11) and (1.3.12) it follows that X_t can be expressed as a linear combination of the η's:

$$X_\tau = \sum_{j=0}^{\tau-1} \alpha^j \eta_{\tau-j} \qquad (\tau = 1, 2, 3, \cdots). \tag{1.3.3}$$

Hence by multiplying together the respective members of (1.3.12) and (1.3.3) and taking the expectation of the products we obtain

$$\mathcal{E}(X_t X_\tau) - \alpha \mathcal{E}(X_{t-1} X_\tau) = \sum_{j=0}^{\tau-1} \alpha^j \mathcal{E}(\eta_t \eta_{\tau-j}). \tag{1.3.4}$$

Now if η were nonautocorrelated, we could choose $\tau = t-1$, and, by dividing by $\mathcal{E}(X^2)$, obtain the autocorrelation coefficient r_1 of X from

$$r_1 - \alpha = 0, \tag{1.3.5}$$

since all the expectations on the right-hand side would vanish. Then by setting

$$\tau = t-2, t-3, \cdots$$

we should obtain

$$r_k - \alpha r_{k-1} = 0 \qquad (k = 2, 3, \cdots), \tag{1.3.6}$$

which is the difference equation satisfied by the correlogram of X.

Since, however, we have assumed that the first autocorrelation coefficient (ρ_1) of η does not vanish, (1.3.5) no longer holds though (1.3.6) still does. For in this case we have, again setting $\tau = t-1$,

$$r_1 - \alpha = \sum_{j=0}^{t-2} \alpha^j \frac{\mathcal{E}(\eta_t \eta_{\tau-j})}{\mathcal{E}(X^2)}, \tag{1.3.7}$$

where

$$\mathcal{E}(X_\tau^2) = \mathcal{E}\left(\sum_{j=0}^{\tau-1} \alpha^j \eta_{\tau-j}\right)^2$$

(1.3.8)

$$= (1 + \alpha^2 + \cdots + \alpha^{2(\tau-1)})\mathcal{E}(\eta^2) + 2(\alpha + \alpha^3 + \cdots + \alpha^{2(\tau-1)-1})\mathcal{E}(\eta^2)\rho_1.$$

Hence

(1.3.9)

$$r_1 - \alpha = \frac{\rho_1 \mathcal{E}(\eta^2)}{\mathcal{E}(\eta^2)\left[\sum_{j=0}^{\tau-1} \alpha^{2j} + 2\rho_1 \sum_{j=0}^{\tau-2} \alpha^{2j+1}\right]} = \frac{\rho_1}{\sum_{j=0}^{\tau-1} \alpha^{2j} + 2\rho_1 \sum_{j=0}^{\tau-2} \alpha^{2j+1}}$$

and r_1 depends on both α and ρ_1.

4. The examples given in Sections 2 and 3 of this paper served to show (a) that the "reduced equation" may have an autocorrelated "disturbance" and (b) that in a stochastic difference equation with an autocorrelated "disturbance" the correlogram of the observed variate is partly determined by the correlogram of the "disturbance." That this phenomenon has not been given enough attention is probably due to the fact that the original set of difference equations is usually treated as a homogeneous one and the "disturbance" is introduced as a *deus ex machina* only after the reduction process has been completed.[7] When this deficiency is remedied, certain implications for the theory of economic fluctuations become apparent. The "forecast curve" for one variate, based on its own correlogram, is still a combination of superimposed harmonics, but with entirely different initial values. The important point is that the forecasts must be based not only on the coefficients of lagged values of the variate ("structural coefficients") but also on the autocorrelation properties of the "disturbance." It might well be that some of the distrust with which the "literary" economists have viewed the "mathematical" business-cycle theory has arisen from their opposition to the unrealistic postulate of nonautocorrelated "disturbances."

[7] This procedure may in some cases prove to be quite harmless. For example, in the case of Koopmans' system the "composite disturbance" $z_t \equiv z_t' - \beta z_t''$ is nonautocorrelated if z' and z'' are nonautocorrelated. This is a general property of "composite disturbances" consisting of simultaneous values of the original "disturbances."

II. NOTATION

In order to facilitate mathematical operations it will be found convenient to adopt the following notation.

The Boolean operator E will be equivalent to translation by one time unit:

$$\mathsf{E}X_t \equiv X_{t+1}, \tag{2.1}$$

and the subscript t will be omitted.

Thus

$$X_{1,t+1} = aX_{1,t} + bX_{2,t} + \epsilon_{1,t} \tag{2.2}$$

will be written as

$$\mathsf{E}X_1 = aX_1 + bX_2 + \epsilon_1. \tag{2.3}$$

Also, for the sake of brevity, we shall write

$$\begin{aligned} \mathsf{E}X &= X', \\ &\cdots\cdots \\ \mathsf{E}^N X &\equiv X^{(N)}, \end{aligned} \tag{2.4}$$

so that (2.3) could also be written as

$$X_1' = aX_1 + bX_2 + \epsilon_1 \tag{2.5}$$

(since no differential operations are used, there should be no danger of confusion).

III. TRANSFORMATION TO A FIRST-ORDER SYSTEM

1. Now consider the nth-order system

$$\mathsf{E}^h X^{(0)} + A_1^{(0)}\mathsf{E}^{h-1}X^{(0)} + \cdots + A_h^{(0)}X^{(0)} = \mathsf{E}\epsilon^{(0)}, \tag{3.1.1}$$

where

$$X^{(0)} \equiv \left\{x_1^{(0)}, x_2^{(0)}, \cdots, x_N^{(0)}\right\}, \tag{3.1.2}$$

$$\epsilon^{(0)} \equiv \left\{\epsilon_1^{(0)}, \epsilon_2^{(0)}, \cdots, \epsilon_N^{(0)}\right\}, \tag{3.1.3}$$

$$A_s^{(0)} \equiv \left\|a_{ijs}^{(0)}\right\| \qquad (i, j = 1, 2, \cdots, N) \tag{3.1.4}$$

and $\{\ \}$ denotes a column vector. As in differential equations,[8] this

[8] Cf. Frazer, Duncan, and Collar, *Elementary Matrices*, pp. 162 ff.

can be transformed into a first-order system

$$X' + AX = \epsilon', \tag{3.1.5}$$

where

$$A \equiv \|a_{ij}\| \qquad (i, j = 1, 2, \cdots, N, \cdots, Nh), \tag{3.1.6}$$

by defining a set of variables

$$x_{(p.N)+q} = \mathsf{E}^p x_q^{(0)} = \mathsf{E}^p x_x \qquad (q = 1, 2, \cdots, N;\ p = 0, 1, \cdots, h-1) \tag{3.1.7}$$

so that

$$X \equiv \{x_1, x_2, \cdots, x_{Nh}\} \equiv \{X^{(0)}, \mathsf{E}X^{(0)}, \cdots, \mathsf{E}^h X^{(0)}\}, \tag{3.1.8}$$

and adjoining the defining equations as a part of the "normal system."

It must be observed, however, that the new vector ϵ will acquire a set of zero components:[9]

$$\epsilon \equiv \{0, 0, \cdots, 0, \epsilon_1^{(0)}, \epsilon_2^{(0)}, \cdots\}. \tag{3.1.9}$$

This will imply special properties of "normal" first-order system derived by the above process from a higher-order system. Otherwise, in what follows the "normal" system

$$X' + AX = \epsilon' \tag{3.1.10}$$

will be discussed because the higher-order systems can be regarded as its special cases.

2. As an example, consider the system (1.2.1) discussed above. In order to conform with the new notation we shall rewrite it as

$$\begin{cases} \mathsf{E}^2 x_1^{(0)} = a_{111}^{(0)}\mathsf{E}x_1^{(0)} + a_{121}^{(0)}\mathsf{E}x_2^{(0)} + a_{112}^{(0)}x_1^{(0)} \\ \qquad + a_{122}^{(0)}x_2 + \mathsf{E}\epsilon_1^{(0)}, \\ \mathsf{E}^2 x_2^{(0)} = a_{211}^{(0)}\mathsf{E}x_1^{(0)} + a_{211}^{(0)}\mathsf{E}x_2^{(0)} + a_{212}^{(0)}x_1^{(0)} \\ \qquad + a_{222}^{(0)}x_2 + \epsilon_2\mathsf{E}^{(0)}, \end{cases} \tag{3.2.1}$$

or, in matrix form,

$$\begin{aligned} \mathsf{E}^2 \begin{Vmatrix} x_1^{(0)} \\ x_2^{(0)} \end{Vmatrix} &= \begin{Vmatrix} a_{111}^{(0)} & a_{121}^{(0)} \\ a_{211}^{(0)} & a_{221}^{(0)} \end{Vmatrix} \cdot \mathsf{E} \begin{Vmatrix} x_1^{(0)} \\ x_2^{(0)} \end{Vmatrix} \\ &+ \begin{Vmatrix} a_{112}^{(0)} & a_{122}^{(0)} \\ a_{212}^{(0)} & a_{222}^{(0)} \end{Vmatrix} \cdot \begin{Vmatrix} x_1^{(0)} \\ x_2^{(0)} \end{Vmatrix} + \mathsf{E} \begin{Vmatrix} \epsilon_1^{(0)} \\ \epsilon_2^{(0)} \end{Vmatrix}. \end{aligned} \tag{3.2.2}$$

[9] The example in Section III-2 contains such a "partly empty" random vector [cf. eq. (3.2.10)].

The relationships between the old and new symbols are as follows:

$$
(3.2.3)\qquad \begin{cases} X = x_1{}^{(0)}, \\ Y = x_2{}^{(0)}, \\ \epsilon' = \mathsf{E}\epsilon_1{}^{(0)}, \\ \epsilon'' = \mathsf{E}\epsilon_2{}^{(0)}, \\ a = a_{111}{}^{(0)}, \\ b_1 = a_{121}{}^{(0)}, \\ c = a_{211}{}^{(0)}, \\ b_2 = a_{122}{}^{(0)}, \\ 0 = a_{221}{}^{(0)} = a_{112}{}^{(0)} = a_{212}{}^{(0)} = a_{222}{}^{(0)}. \end{cases}
$$

Now we redefine our system as follows:

$$
(3.2.4)\qquad \begin{cases} x_1 = x_1{}^{(0)}, \\ x_2 = x_2{}^{(0)}, \\ x_3 = \mathsf{E}x_1{}^{(0)} = \mathsf{E}x_1, \\ x_4 = \mathsf{E}x_2{}^{(0)} = \mathsf{E}x_2. \end{cases}
$$

Then we can rewrite (3.1.1) in terms of x_1, x_2, x_3, x_4 and so avoid the E^2 operator. Thus we obtain a first-order system with 4 unknowns:

$$
(3.2.5)\qquad \begin{cases} \mathsf{E}x_1 = x_3, \\ \mathsf{E}x_2 = x_4, \\ \mathsf{E}x_3 = a^{(0)}\ x_1 + a^{(0)}\ x_2 + a^{(0)}\ x_3 + a^{(0)}\ x_4 + \mathsf{E}\epsilon_1{}^{(0)}, \\ \mathsf{E}x_4 = a_{212}{}^{(0)}x_1 + a_{222}{}^{(0)}x_2 + a_{211}{}^{(0)}x_3 + a_{221}{}^{(0)}x_4 + \mathsf{E}\epsilon_2{}^{(0)}. \end{cases}
$$

This, written in matrix form, becomes

$$
(3.2.6)\qquad \mathsf{E}X = AX + \mathsf{E}\epsilon
$$

or

$$
(3.2.7)\qquad X' = AX + \epsilon',
$$

where

$$
(3.2.8)\qquad X \equiv \{x_1, x_2, x_3, x_4\},
$$

$$
(3.2.9)\qquad A \equiv \|a_{ij}\| \equiv \begin{Vmatrix} 0 & 0 & 1 & 0 \\ 0 & 0 & 0 & 1 \\ a_{112}{}^{(0)} & a_{122}{}^{(0)} & a_{111}{}^{(0)} & a_{121}{}^{(0)} \\ a_{212}{}^{(0)} & a_{222}{}^{(0)} & a_{211}{}^{(0)} & a_{221}{}^{(0)} \end{Vmatrix},
$$

and

$$
(3.2.10)\qquad \epsilon \equiv \{0, 0, \epsilon_1{}^{(0)}, \epsilon_2{}^{(0)}\}.
$$

IV. "REDUCTION" TO AN EQUATION IN ONE VARIABLE

After having shown how any system of equations of order h in N variates can be reduced to a system of first order in Nh variates, we shall now show how any system of first order in N variates can be reduced to one equation of higher order (the "reduced equation") in one of the variates. Thus, it will have been shown that any system of order h in N variables can be reduced to one equation in one variate.

In order to investigate the properties of the "reduced equation" in one of the variates of the normal system, it will suffice to show how the process of reduction is performed.[10] In order to be able to eliminate all but one variate (say x_1), the operator E must be applied N times to the matrix difference equation

$$X' + AX = \epsilon' \tag{4.1}$$

so that the following system of N matrix equations is obtained:

$$\mathsf{E}^{j+1}X + A^j\mathsf{E}X = \mathsf{E}^{j+1}\epsilon \qquad (j = 0, 1, 2, \cdots, N-1). \tag{4.2}$$

As pointed out by Samuelson,[11] this is a system in $(N-1)(N+1) = N^2-1$ unknowns

$$\left\{\begin{matrix} x_2, & x_3, & \cdots, x_N \\ x_2', & x_3', & \cdots, x_N' \\ \cdot & \cdot \;\cdot \;\cdot & \cdot \;\cdot \;\cdot \\ x_2^{(N)}, & x_3^{(N)}, & \cdots, x_N^{(N)} \end{matrix}\right\} \tag{4.3}$$

since $(x_1, x_1', \cdots, x_1^{(N)})$ are treated as known. Now the number of equations available is N^2 since A is an N-rowed matrix and $j=0, 1, 2, \cdots, N-1$. Hence it is possible to eliminate all the unknowns listed in (4.3) and in this manner to obtain an Nth-order[12] difference equation in x_1, say

$$\mathsf{E}^N x_1 + a_1\mathsf{E}^{N-1}x_1 + \cdots + a_{N-1}\mathsf{E}x_1 + a_N x_1 = \mathsf{E}^N\eta \tag{4.4}$$

where $\mathsf{E}^N\eta_t$ is a linear combination of the components of the matrix[13,14]

[10] Moulton, *Differential Equations*, pp. 6 ff.; Paul A. Samuelson, "A Method of Determining Explicitly the Coefficients of the Characteristic Equation," *The Annals of Mathematical Statistics*, Vol. 13, December, 1942, pp. 424–429, esp. p. 425.

[11] See reference in footnote 10.

[12] If the resulting matrix is singular, (4.4) might turn out to be of lower order.

[13] If the system was obtained by a transformation of the type (3.1.7) then some columns of this matrix would be zero vectors.

$$(4.5) \qquad \begin{bmatrix} \epsilon_1', & \epsilon_2', & \cdots, & \epsilon_N' \\ \epsilon_1'', & \epsilon_2'', & \cdots, & \epsilon_N'' \\ \cdot & \cdot & \cdot & \cdot \\ \epsilon_1^{(N)}, & \epsilon_2^{(N)}, & \cdots, & \epsilon_N^{(N)} \end{bmatrix},$$

say

$$(4.6) \qquad \mathrm{E}^N \eta_t = \sum_{i,j=1}^{N} c_{ij} \epsilon_i^{(j)}.$$

This is a sum of the "moving average" type of variables with a correlogram characterized by zero autocorrelation coefficients for lags of N or more units provided the ϵ's are nonautocorrelated.

In this special case, discussed by A. Wald and H. B. Mann[15] where the ϵ's are nonautocorrelated, a part of the correlogram of x_1 will depend on the elements of the matrix A as well as the covariance matrix of the ϵ's.

V. AUTOCORRELATION PATTERN IN "REDUCED EQUATIONS"

It has been shown that the system

$$(5.1) \qquad X' + AX = \epsilon'$$

is in general equivalent to a single equation in one variable (we now drop the subscript "1" and revert to customary notation), say

$$(5.2) \qquad x_t + a_1 x_{t-1} + \cdots + a_N x_{t-N} = \eta_t,$$

where η_t is a sum of moving averages of order $N-1$. In order to obtain the autocorrelation coefficients of x (denoted by r_k, k being the lag) in terms of a's and of the autocorrelation coefficients of η (denoted by ρ_k), we follow the procedure of H. Wold,[16] writing

$$(5.3) \qquad x_\tau = \eta_\tau + b_1 \eta_{\tau-1} + \cdots + b_{\tau-1} \eta_1,$$

where b's are functions of the a's.[17]

---

[14] The explicit values of a's in the reduced equation (4.4) and of the c's in (4.6) can be obtained easily, but they are not needed in this context.

[15] "On the Statistical Treatment of Linear Stochastic Difference Equations," ECONOMETRICA, Vol. 11, July–October, 1943, pp. 173–220.

[16] *Op. cit.*, pp. 100 ff.

[17] A simple example of this method was given in Section I-3 of this paper.

By multiplying the respective numbers of (5.2) and (5.3) and by taking the expectations we obtain the lag moments

$$\mathcal{E}(x_t x_\tau) + a_1 \mathcal{E}(x_{t-1}, x_\tau) + \cdots + a_N \mathcal{E}(x_{t-N} x_\tau) = \mathcal{E}(\eta_t \eta_\tau) + b_1 \mathcal{E}(\eta_t \eta_{\tau-1}) + \cdots + b_{\tau-1} \mathcal{E}(\eta_\tau \eta_1). \tag{5.4}$$

It is immediately clear that if

$$\tau \leqq t - N \tag{5.5}$$

the right-hand member of (5.4) vanishes and we obtain

$$r_k + a_1 r_{k-1} + \cdots + a_N r_{k-N} = 0 \text{ provided } k \geqq N. \tag{5.6}$$

Thus the correlogram still satisfies the difference equation corresponding to (5.2) (as in the case of nonautocorrelated η_t), but the set $(r_1, r_2, \cdots, r_N)$ is affected by the autocorrelation properties of η. The same is true of the forecast curve for x: the initial values are affected by the ρ's but the later ones only by a's.[18]

Cowles Commission for Research in Economics
The University of Chicago

[18] The problems of interpreting an empirical correlogram of the observed variate in cases where the "disturbances" are autocorrelated will be treated in a later paper.

[19]

THEORY OF THE FIRM AND OF INVESTMENT*

By Leonid Hurwicz

OUTLINE

INTRODUCTION

A. Formulation of the Problem

A-1. Some of the most fundamental controversies in the theory of economic fluctuations are due to the lack of a well-integrated theory of the entrepreneur's investment policies. There exists a tendency, though not without important exceptions, to separate the financial from the technical and commercial aspects of the firm's operations. Moreover, there is no agreement on the fundamental maximizing principle to serve as basis for a general theory of entrepreneurial behavior.

* Cowles Commission Papers, New Series, No. 16. This paper is part of a study being carried out by the author on a Guggenheim Memorial Fellowship while on leave of absence from Iowa State College.

The author wishes to acknowledge his indebtedness to Professor Jacob Marschak, Dr. Tjalling Koopmans, Dr. Lawrence R. Klein, Dr. Theodore W. Anderson, Jr., Mr. Sami Tekiner, and other members of the staff of the Cowles Commission for valuable suggestions and criticism.

The traditional principle of (money) *profit maximization* is subject to attack from several quarters. First, of course, it is the expected profits that are being maximized. Second, when risk and uncertainty are present (the case of "stochastic expectations"), not only the most probable value of profits is of relevance, but also the degree of uncertainty: a cautious entrepreneur will choose a course of action promising one bird in the hand rather than two in the bush.

Thus the entrepreneur's psychological make-up (somewhat belatedly) enters the picture, and, at least implicitly, profit maximization is replaced by utility maximization. Upon insertion of appropriate specializing assumptions, the utility maximization principle will yield most, but not all, existing theories of the firm and of investment behavior.

Among approaches inconsistent with this principle, a very important one is based on an analysis of the prevailing accounting practices and their implications. For instance, some of these practices seem to imply that businessmen follow a principle of profit-*rate* maximization.[1]

It is not a priori inconceivable that business is run more by routine than by rationality, and, if such were the case, theorizing based on the utility- (or profit-) maximization principle would be little more than idle pastime. Whether the "rational" or the "routine" approach is more realistic can only be decided by appeal to empirical evidence (interviewing, a study of firm histories, statistical analysis). But for such evidence to be conclusive, the implications of the "rational" approach must be analyzed more rigorously than has as yet been done. Many phenomena may appear irrational and "routine" from the viewpoint of a purely static theory devoid of the uncertainty elements, but turn out to be quite "rational" when elements of uncertainty and long-run effects are taken into account.

A-2. The present paper is an attempt to develop the theory of the entrepreneur's behavior, especially those aspects of it which are of importance for investment policies, starting with the postulate of utility maximization. Thus it is an exploration in the possibilities of "rationalizing" the entrepreneur's behavior. It is not the author's intention to belittle the importance of studying the routine practices prevalent in business, but rather to sharpen the tools of analysis so that fruitful empirical work can be carried out. It would be hardly surprising if reality turned out to be a mixture of "rationality" and "routine."

The theory, as here developed, is more general than previous contributions in some respects, but less so in others. Generality was espe-

[1] Cf. Lutz [14], also [15], especially p. 817. [Numbers in square brackets refer to items in the list of References at the end of this article.] "Profit rate" is here defined as the ratio of net revenue to the cost of equipment.

cially sought with regard to those aspects of the firm's structure which are likely to affect its investment policies, credit operations, and liquidity. We shall try to construct a model explaining not only the entrepreneur's behavior with regard to purchases of equipment or utilization of labor and other factors of production, but also with regard to his financial operations (demand for loan funds, securities, cash) and inventories.

Simplifying assumptions are made when it is felt that this does not deprive the model of its essential features. But in many respects the level of generality is still too high; detailed study of special cases of interest cannot be undertaken here. Only occasionally will it be indicated how various theories in this field are related to our model. It should be made clear, however, that our interest is primarily centered on the logical relationships; the references to other theories, therefore, are highly incomplete and no attempt is made to establish priorities or to trace the origin of the ideas under consideration.

B. Some Limitations of the Treatment

B-1. While perfect competition in product, factor, or credit markets is not assumed, we do postulate *subjective predictability*, i.e., we assume that the entrepreneur is able to form some, possibly incorrect, expectations (with or without uncertainty), with regard to the behavior of those from whom he buys the factors of production, as well as the behavior of his customers and competitors. That this postulate breaks down completely in cases such as that of duopoly has been known to the economists for a considerable period of time. The duopolist A cannot form the "reaction curve" of the duopolist B, since B's response to A's reaction depends on B's expectations of A's response to B's reaction, etc. That it may not hold even in the more "ordinary" economic situations has only recently been emphasized.[2] We shall nevertheless assume the postulate to hold, since the analytical techniques for dealing with the cases where it does not apply are not yet sufficiently developed. Thus the assumption of subjective predictability certainly makes our model inapplicable to oligopolistic or cartel situations[3] and probably only approximately correct otherwise.

B-2. Another limitation is due to our identification of the interests of the firm with those of the entrepreneur as an individual. This may be realistic for a privately owned firm, but it certainly requires modification in the case of corporate enterprise with its conflicting interest groups (stockholders, directors, managers). A separate study is needed

[2] Cf. von Neumann and Morgenstern [21], Hurwicz [8], Marschak [18].

[3] In this respect Lange's treatment is of greater generality: [13], especially pp. 39 ff., 69–70, 75 ff.

to evaluate the seriousness of error committed in applying the theory of investment by a privately owned firm to the case of corporate enterprise.

B-3. Our model is also deficient in that it ignores business and other taxes of great practical importance but it is hoped that this shortcoming will be remedied in a later paper.

B-4. A continuous model (i.e., with time as a continuous variable) would be more realistic, more elegant, and in many ways easier to handle mathematically than a discrete one. We have chosen the latter, however, because it facilitates the use of certain tools of stochastic theory that are still undeveloped for the continuous case. A discrete model is also easier to compare with traditional economic theory most of which is formulated in terms of discrete time processes.

The paper is divided into two parts. In Part I the entrepreneur's expectations will be assumed to be free of risk and uncertainty elements; the latter will be introduced in Part II. This division appears justified since it makes possible some simplification in the exposition.

I. THE CASE OF NONSTOCHASTIC[4] EXPECTATIONS

C. The Principle of Utility Maximization

C-1. We picture the entrepreneur as making periodic[5] money withdrawals (usually positive, but sometimes zero or negative) from the firm's stock of cash. These withdrawals will be denoted by d_t.[6]

At the time t_0 (when decisions are being made) the entrepreneur considers the stream of *prospective*[7] withdrawals, i.e., the vector

[4] I.e., free of subjective uncertainty or risk; stochastic expectations imply the presence of subjective uncertainty or risk or both.

[5] The frequency of withdrawals need not of course be equal to the frequency of decision-making; moreover, frequency of decision-making may be different for different aspects of the firm's activities: say once a month for amount of labor used, but only once a year for major purchases of equipment; nevertheless, for the sake of simplicity of exposition we shall assume all these frequencies to be equal to the unit of time measurement and shall refer to this unit as a month; this in no way restricts the generality of the model. It is always possible during maximization to add a constant requiring that, say, every other month's withdrawals should be zero and that investment decisions should *be final* for 12 months ahead but decisions with regard to inventories only one month ahead.

[6] d is a "flow variable" (i.e., measured per unit of time); its subscript refers to the beginning of the time interval covered; d_t are withdrawals during the time interval $(t, t+1)$; the same principle of notation is applied throughout the paper to all other flow variables.

[7] $\bar{d}$ is a symbol for the expected values of d; all expectations, as well as decisions, are made at the time t_0; thus $\bar{d}_{t_0+1}$ are withdrawals expected at t_0 for the time interval (t_0+1, t_0+2); the same principle of notation is applied to all other expected variables.

We use as synonyms the terms "expected," "prospective," "imagined," and

$$\overline{D}_{t_0} = (\bar{d}_{t_0}, \bar{d}_{t_0+1}, \bar{d}_{t_0+2}, \cdots). \tag{1}$$

$\overline{D}_t$ is of (denumerably) infinite dimensionality, although its more remote components may have little effect on current decisions.

$\overline{D}_t$ depends on three types of factors: (a) those *known* at the time of decision making, e.g., the firm's assets; (b) some unknown ones that can only be *expected*, for instance the future market conditions; and (c) some that depend on the entrepreneur's *decisions*, for instance, purchases of equipment, borrowing, inventory policies.

Given the knowledge of expectations of the factors beyond the firm's control at the time of decision-making, the entrepreneur will decide on those matters where he does have a certain amount of choice.

These decisions will determine $\overline{D}_{t_0}$. The entrepreneur is thus able, within limits, to choose the time pattern of the prospective withdrawals stream, as well as its size. What considerations will affect his choice?

In answering this question we shall start by making two highly restrictive assumptions: 1. that the entrepreneur's utility depends only on the prospective real consumption stream, and 2. that the entrepreneur does not save within his household, i.e., that his money consumption within a given period equals the cash withdrawals from the firm for the same period. Then we have

$$u_{t_0} = u_{t_0}(\overline{C}_{t_0}), \qquad \overline{C}_{t_0} = \{\bar{c}_{t_0}, \bar{c}_{t_0+1}, \cdots\}, \tag{2}$$

where c is real consumption, and also

$$\bar{p}_t^c \bar{c}_t \equiv \bar{d}_t, \tag{3}$$

where p^c represents the prices of consumer goods purchased by the entrepreneur. Substituting (3) into (2) we obtain

$$u_{t_0} = u_{t_0}\left(\frac{\bar{d}_{t_0}}{\bar{p}_{t_0}{}^c}, \frac{\bar{d}_{t_0+1}}{\bar{p}_{t_0+1}{}^c}, \cdots\right). \tag{4}$$

Of course, if private income tax exists it should be deducted from the withdrawals.

In this highly simplified model the entrepreneur's decisions are determined[8] by 1. his preferences as given by the utility function, and 2. his opportunities (as they exist in his mind) given by the limits within which he can vary $\overline{D}_{t_0}$ and by the expected (consumer-goods) prices and tax rates. The entrepreneur's decision in favor of earlier, as against later, withdrawals might be due to his "impatience" or to expected rises in consumer-goods prices or tax rates.

"estimated"; all these terms have been used in the literature of the subject. "Anticipated" has also been used, but it is apt to be interpreted in the sense of preventive speculative measures and has, therefore, been avoided.

[8] Cf. Fisher [1].

A more general model can be obtained by relaxing both (2) and (3). First, we may introduce variables other than consumption influencing the entrepreneur's utility: the assets whose mere possession brings the entrepreneur to a higher utility level, effort connected with running the firm, amount of leisure,[9] or the level of the firm's activity, if this affects the entrepreneur's sense of self-importance and the pleasure he gets out of running his business. Second, we may allow for savings, as well as private sources of income, such as private lending by the entrepreneur. In this generalized model there are more decisions to be made; in order to see what determines decisions with regard to $\overline{D}_{t_0}$, we must consider the structure of the entrepreneur's preferences with regard to variables other than consumption, and also his opportunities as a private individual. A decision in favor of earlier withdrawals may be due to a number of causes in addition to those previously mentioned; for instance, it may be due to the fact that the entrepreneur does not want to assume the burden of running too big a business and that he expects the earlier withdrawals to arrest the growth of the firm; or he may have unusual opportunities of lending out privately and thus earning additional income, etc.

The decisions to be made within the entrepreneur's household and the dependence of utility on the various factors mentioned are thus of relevance for the theory of the firm. But they do not constitute a part of that theory. Their study is a proper branch of the theory of individual economic behavior and transcends the scope of this paper which is primarily concerned with the entrepreneur's activities as entrepreneur. In what follows, therefore, we shall write

$$u_{t_0} = \phi_{t_0}(\overline{D}_{t_0}), \tag{5}$$

which, formally, may be regarded as a special case of (4), *viz.*, where stationary expectations with regard to prices of consumer goods prevail. However, factors not included in (5) must be kept in mind since they are of importance for theory, prediction, and public policy.

ϕ_{t_0} in (5) is usually assumed to be such that

$$\frac{\partial \phi_{t_0}}{\partial \bar{d}_{t'}} > \frac{\partial \phi_{t_0}}{\partial \bar{d}_{t''}} \quad \text{for} \quad t' < t'', \tag{6}$$

which implies "impatience" on the part of the entrepreneur. (This may be stated in terms of marginal substitution rates if we wish to avoid the use of marginal utilities.)

The problem now consists in expressing $\overline{D}_{t_0}$ in terms of variables controlled by the entrepreneur, and then performing the maximization of u_{t_0} with regard to those variables.

[9] Cf. de Scitovsky [23].

C-2. The approach of the preceding section is based on the postulate that the entrepreneur is simply an individual attempting to maximize his utility. This does not mean that the traits which distinguish him from other members of the community (e.g., workers, bankers) are ignored. He differs from them with regard to 1. initial assets (plant, market connections, patents, good will): 2. organizational and productive skill; 3. character of expectations as to market phenomena and technology; 4. structure of preferences (this is particularly important when risk and uncertainty are introduced).

These are the factors making it possible and desirable for him to become (or remain) an entrepreneur; these same factors also explain why firms behave differently under similar circumstances.

The fact that the emphasis is placed on the cash withdrawals $\overline{D}_{t_0}$ makes the model more realistic for, say, a modern manufacturing firm than for a small farmer.

C-3. Our model, because it is based on utility maximization, has greater generality than the more usual one[10] which postulates that the entrepreneur maximizes the sum of discounted expected profits with a discount factor determined by the market rate of interest.

The need for explicit introduction of utility maximization as the appropriate criterion becomes especially apparent when risk and uncertainty are introduced into the picture, since the risk-preference pattern obviously determines the choice. No wonder, therefore, that those who have studied the cases of stochastic expectations[11] were led to the utility-maximization principle. However, even in the absence of risk or uncertainty we are forced to start with utility considerations,[12] once it becomes clear that the market rates of interest should *not* be used to determine the discount factors. For, as has been indicated by Mosak,[13] such treatment is permissible only in evaluating the anticipated profits at the point of equilibrium (where in general the marginal rates of substitution equal the corresponding price ratios), but not in deriving the location of this point.[14]

[10] Cf., e.g., Hicks [6], Tintner [24].

[11] Mosak [20], Tintner [24], Hart [3].

[12] Marschak [17].

[13] [20], p. 145.

[14] The discounting procedure *is* valid when *suitable* type of credit market for private borrowing exists. In such a case the nature of ϕ in (5) will not affect decisions with regard to $\overline{D}_{t_0}$. Similarly, in the stochastic case the "risk preference pattern" [ϕ in (51) below] may also be without influence on decisions with regard to $\overline{D}_{t_0}$ if suitable market exchange possibilities exist. In such a case market rates of exchange between various types of risk, etc., could be used to form a discounted value.

In both stochastic and nonstochastic cases the discount factors must be

D. *The Variables*

D-1. Classification of the variables. As has been stated above, Section C-1, the stream of prospective withdrawals $\overline{D}_{t_0}$ depends on three types of factors:

1. those known to the entrepreneur at the time of decision-making t_0; it is these factors that form the basis for anticipations and decisions; they will be called *initial conditions* and denoted by η;

2. those which are being expected; they will be called *predictands* and denoted by ω;

3. those over which the entrepreneur has control, subject, of course, to certain restrictions (transformation equations, etc.); they will be called *decision variables* and denoted by ζ.

The remainder of Section D is devoted to a description of the more important components of η, ω, and ζ.

D-2. The initial conditions. The initial conditions are important for two reasons. First, they impose certain restrictions on the future. Debts incurred in the past must be repaid in the future, past inputs may partly determine future outputs, etc. Second, the initial conditions affect the expectations. Thus expected prices may be the extrapolated values of the past prices, and so forth. This suggests a classification of the initial-conditions variables into two groups:

1. those which describe the state of the firm and whose values impose constraints on the entrepreneur's decisions, to be called *assets* and denoted by η';

2. those whose values serve as basis for the formation of expectations, to be called *predictors*, and denoted by η''.

These two groups overlap somewhat, especially under conditions of imperfect competition; for instance, inventories will be obviously among assets, but their size may, in an imperfect market, affect the entrepreneur's prediction of future market conditions.

D-2a. Assets. There are three kinds of assets: i. "real" assets, including α. inventories, β. plant, and γ. semi-finished products; ii. "financial" assets, including α. cash, β. securities, and γ. debts; and iii. "intangible" assets.

i-α. *Inventories.*[15] Stocks of the firm's μth product held at time t will be denoted by k_t^μ; we write

$$K_{t_0} = \{k_{t_0}^\mu\} = \{k_{t_0}^1, \cdots, k_{t_0}^\mu, \cdots\}$$

---

entered at their expected values and, in imperfect markets, may vary from one entrepreneur to another even if their "prediction equations" (cf. E below) are identical.

[15] Cf. Hawtrey [5].

where μ runs over all products. Factors of production other than equipment are treated as products with negative prices.

i-β. *Plant.* The quantity of σth type of equipment, installed during $(t', t'+1)$ and still in use at t'' will be denoted by $z_{t',t''}{}^{\sigma}$; we define investment $v_{t't''}{}^{\sigma}$ as

$$v_{t',t''}{}^{\sigma} = z_{t',t''+1}{}^{\sigma} - z_{t',t''}{}^{\sigma} = \Delta z_{t',t''}{}^{\sigma},$$

and also write

$$Z_{t_0} = \left\| z_{t,t_0}{}^{\sigma} \right\|,$$

where σ runs over all types of equipment and $t < t_0$.

i-γ. *Semi-finished Products.* These may be expressed in terms of past inputs and outputs; output of the μth product during $(t, t+1)$ is denoted by $x_t{}^{\mu}$. We write

$$X_{t_0} = \left\| x_t{}^{\mu} \right\| = \left\| \begin{matrix} x_{t_0-1}{}^{1}, & x_{t_0-1}{}^{2}, & \cdots, & x_{t_0-1}{}^{\mu}, & \cdots \\ x_{t_0-2}{}^{1}, & x_{t_0-2}{}^{2}, & \cdots, & x_{t_0-2}{}^{\mu}, & \cdots \\ \cdots & \cdots & \cdots & \cdots & \cdots \end{matrix} \right\|.$$

ii-α. *Cash.* Cash (including bank deposits) held at t is denoted by m_t.

ii-β. *Securities.* For simplicity's sake we consider only consols;[16] other types may easily be introduced; $s_{t',t''}{}^{*}$ denotes the market value, $s_{t',t''}{}^{**}$ the par value of securities purchased during $(t', t'+1)$ and still held at time t''; forward dealings are excluded; we write

$$\begin{cases} s_{t',t''+1}{}^{*} - s_{t',t''}{}^{*} = \Delta s_{t',t''}{}^{*} \\ \sum_{t'} \Delta s_{t',t''}{}^{*} = \Delta s_{t''}{}^{*} \end{cases} \qquad (t' \leqq t'').$$

The rate of interest payable during $(t'', t''+1)$ on $s_{t',t''+1}{}^{**}$ is denoted by $r_{t',t''}{}''$ and the prospective returns counted among the firm's assets. We write

$$S_{t_0} = \left\| \begin{matrix} s_{t_0-1,t_0}{}^{*} & s_{t_0-2,t_0}{}^{*} & \cdots \\ s_{t_0-1,t_0}{}^{**} & s_{t_0-2,t_0}{}^{**} & \cdots \end{matrix} \right\|$$

to represent both the resale value and the interest aspects of the securities held at time t_0.

ii-γ. *Debts* owed by the firm. The amount borrowed by the firm during $(t', t'+1)$ to be repaid during $(t'', t''+1)$ will be denoted by $e_{t',t''}{}^{+}$.

The amount repaid during $(t'', t''+1)$ on a loan incurred during $(t', t'+1)$ will be denoted by $e_{t'',t'}{}^{-}$; hence (if the firm is assumed to pay its obligations on time) we have

$$e_{t',t''}{}^{+} \equiv e_{t'',t'}{}^{-}. \tag{7}$$

[16] Perpetual (nonredeemable) bonds.

The symbol $e_{t',t''}$ will be used for the proceeds (positive or negative) from borrowing (or repayment of debt) thus

$$(8) \qquad \begin{aligned} e_{t',t''} &= e_{t',t''}{}^{+} && \text{for } t' < t'', \\ e_{t',t''} &= -\, e_{t',t''}{}^{-} && \text{for } t' > t''. \end{aligned}$$

The total amount of debt outstanding at t, no matter when incurred, and payable during $(t'', t''+1)$ will be denoted by $b_{t',t''}$; we have

$$(9) \qquad \begin{cases} b_{t,t''} = \sum e_{t,'t''}{}^{+} & (t' < t < t''), \\ b_t = \sum b_{t,t''} & (t < t''), \\ \Delta b_t = b_{t+1} - b_t. \end{cases}$$

The rate of interest payable during $(t''', t'''+1)$ on a loan $c_{t',t''}{}^{+}$ $(t' < t''' < t'')$ will be denoted by $r_{t',t'',t'''}{}'$ and the prospective interest payments counted among the (negative) assets. We write

$$B_{t_0} = \{b_{t_0,t'}\} \qquad (t' > t_0)$$

to represent the firm's commitments with regard to both the principal and interest charges on debts outstanding at t.

iii. *"Intangible" assets.* In addition to the above and other tangible assets, there exist some very important ones which cannot be represented in terms of quantities of goods or written documents: the firm's connections and clientele, its reputation for honesty and fairness, its past price and labor policies, etc. Those intangible assets affect other people's attitude toward the firm and hence influence its earning capacity.

When the entrepreneur's behavior is such as seemingly to contradict the utility- (or profit-) maximization postulate, the economist will do well to examine the phenomenon from the viewpoint of the intangible assets; it may well be that the entrepreneur's "irrationality" is actually due to his (highly rational) concern for the long-run standing of his firm; to this end he may be willing to sacrifice more immediate monetary advantages.[17]

We may now define the array

$$(10) \qquad \eta_{t_0}{}' = \{K_{t_0}, Z_{t_0}, X_{t_0}, m_{t_0}, S_{t_0}, B_{t_0}, \mathfrak{J}_{t_0}, \cdots\},$$

where $\mathfrak{J}_{t_0}$ represents the intangible assets at t_0. The leaders ($\cdots$) in (10) indicate that not all conceivable types of assets have been listed explicitly.

D-2b. Predictors. These are any variables that affect the entrepre-

[17] Thus, for instance, Lutz's remarks [15], pp. 813–814, imply such considerations rather than lack of profit-maximization motive.

neur's expectations. There are two important groups among them: the past values of the predictand variables (e.g., past prices of firm's product, wages) and "barometer" type variables which presage developments for the firm's environment. How these predictors are used in the formation of expectations is indicated in Section E.

D-3. Predictands and decision variables. There is a certain amount of arbitrariness in deciding which variables are to be regarded as predictands and which ones as decision variables.[18] Consider, for instance, the firm's expected revenue py (where p is the price and y the quantity sold) from the sale of its (say single) product. It would not be correct to regard the expected revenue as a predictand since it depends on the firm's action; but it is not a pure decision variable either, for it partly depends on demand conditions that the entrepreneur can only expect but not control. Thus it is natural and customary to split py into its two factors p and y and regard one of them as a predictand, the other as a decision variable. Under conditions of perfect competition we would be justified in regarding p as the predictand since the individual firm has no control over it; y would then be the decision variable.

But under imperfect competition the firm is free to fix either p or y, though of course not both. The language often used (references to "pricing policies") implies that prices are commonly thought of as the decision variables while quantity sold becomes the predictand.

In this paper we have adopted the principle of regarding the expectations as applying to market variables (prices, wages, interest rates, etc.) while the quantities are regarded as decision variables.

In the case of perfect competition, therefore, prices are the predictands; in imperfect markets it is the parameters of the (imagined) demand and supply curves (e.g., their elasticities) that are the predictands. This approach makes it possible to treat simultaneously the case of perfect and imperfect competition; this could not be accomplished by making prices into decision variables. Our approach also has the advantage of yielding the solutions for quantity variables as the unknowns in terms of anticipated prices, wages, etc. Since the volume of investment is our unknown it is convenient to have it among decision variables.

However, it is clear that a more symmetrical method of treatment may in some cases be desirable. This can be accomplished by a transformation from the space of, say, p and y (in the above example) to another space, say, of α and σ in the following manner.

[18] This arbitrariness is due to the fact that, as will be seen later, the correct distinction applies to *events* or *actions* rather than *variables;* events or actions independent of the entrepreneur are the predictands, those subject to his control are decision "actions."

Let the expected ("imagined") demand function be written in the symmetrical form

$$g(p, y; \bar{\alpha}) = 0, \tag{11}$$

where g is a given function and $\bar{\alpha}$ its parameter entered at its expected value.

Let the decision of the entrepreneur with regard to his future selling policy be formulated in an equally symmetrical form as the "policy equation"

$$h(p, y; \sigma) = 0, \tag{12}$$

where h is a known function and σ the parameter to be decided upon by the entrepreneur in such a way as to maximize (say) the revenue py.

Then clearly the last two equations can be solved for p and y in terms of $\bar{\alpha}$ and σ so that py becomes a function of these two parameters; in order to maximize an expression involving py we shall now differentiate it with regard to σ, keeping $\bar{\alpha}$ constant. Thus, effectively, $\bar{\alpha}$ has become the predictand and σ is the decision variable.[19]

The artificiality of the above treatment consists in regarding the functions g and h as given and only their parameters as expected or being decided. More generally, let the expected demand function be written as

$$\bar{g}(p, y) = 0 \tag{13}$$

and the "policy equation" as

$$h(p, y) = 0, \tag{14}$$

where now the function h itself is regarded as the unknown to be decided upon, depending on the nature of $\bar{g}$. If we now repeat the procedure followed in the parametric case, we shall have expressed py in terms of an unknown function h and a given function $\bar{g}$, and can then carry out the maximization with regard to the unknown function h, as in the calculus of variations.

E. Formation of Expectations

Just how expectations are actually formed is one of the most important questions and it can be answered by appeal to empirical evidence.

[19] The approach adopted in this paper of regarding y (or any other quantity variables) as the decision variable is equivalent to assuming

$$h(p, y; \sigma) \equiv y - \sigma = 0, \tag{14'}$$

which, of course, is a very special case.

Reference to "pricing policies" imply the opposite type of "policy equations" viz.,

$$h(p, y; \sigma) \equiv p - \sigma = 0. \tag{14''}$$

But a model that would not indicate at least the general nature of the expectation process cannot be regarded as complete.[20]

In fact, most theoretical work is based on exceedingly simple theories of expectation formation. For instance, Hicks's use of the elasticity of (say) price expectations,[21]

$$\epsilon = \frac{p_{t_0-1}}{\bar{p}_t} \frac{d\bar{p}_t}{dp_{t_0-1}} \qquad (t \geqq t_0), \tag{15}$$

would seem to be based on a "forecast equation" of the type

$$\bar{p}_t = \psi_t(p_{t_0-1}) \qquad (t \geqq t_0). \tag{16}$$

A special case of interest is obtained when (16) becomes

$$\bar{p}_t = p_{t_0-1}{}^{\epsilon}\phi(t); \tag{17}$$

in this case the elasticity of expectations is constant in time. Specializing still further we get

$$\bar{p}_t = p_{t_0-1}{}^{\epsilon}\gamma^{t-t_0+1}, \tag{18}$$

which implies

$$\begin{cases} \bar{p}_t = \gamma\bar{p}_{t-1} & (t = t_0 + 1, t_0 + 2, \cdots), \\ \bar{p}_{t_0} = \gamma p_{t_0-1}{}^{\epsilon}. \end{cases} \tag{19}$$

The difference-equation form of the "forecast equation" is of interest in connection with the case of stochastic expectations where the exact difference equation (19) is replaced by a stochastic one.[22]

A "forecast equation" of type (16) has the great advantage of combining simplicity with relatively great wealth of possible types of solutions. But they can hardly be regarded as possessing an adequate degree of realism.

First, they treat the different components of the predictand as independent: thus the forecast of wage trends is separate from the forecast of price trends. Second, they are too restrictive with regard to the types of predictors used. Actually it seems that, apart from cases of direct knowledge, businessmen's expectations of all the variables involved may often be expressed in terms of relatively few common "barometer" indices. For instance, certain types of governmental policies may be regarded as leading to a narrowing down of the ratio of prices to wages, while other policies may induce expectations of constancy of the average of these two variables. Then the structure of the expectations may be formalized as follows:

[20] Cf. Schumpeter [22], pp. 140 ff., Tintner [25], pp. 106 ff., Hart [3], pp. 75 ff.

[21] Cf. Lange [13], p. 20, note 2.

[22] Cf. (57) below.

$$(20) \qquad \begin{aligned} f_1(\bar{p}_t, \bar{w}_t; G_{t-1}', G_{t-2}'') &= 0, \\ f_2(\bar{p}_t, \bar{w}_t; G_{t-1}', G_{t-2}'') &= 0, \end{aligned}$$

where the G's represent the two policy variables; in our example f_1 contains $\bar{p}/\bar{w}$ and is independent of G'', while f_2 contains some weighted sum of $\bar{p}$ and $\bar{w}$ and is independent of G'.

It should be noted that while (20) happens to have as many predictors as it has predictands, this need not in general be the case. On the one hand, the two policy variables might have been functionally related, so that effectively there would have been only one predictor; on the other hand, any number of additional policy variables might have been introduced in (20).

In (20) governmental policy variables have been chosen as the "barometer" type predictors. But there are many other such predictors. One of them deserves mention, since it seems to be implicit in a number of models: it is the *past profit rate* for the market as a whole, possibly with an appropriately chosen distributed lag.[23] (It would be of interest to see to what extent the implications of regarding the profit rate as an important "barometer" type predictor are similar to the consequences of the assumption that the entrepreneur is maximizing profit *rates* rather than profits, or, more generally, utility.)

The above treatment is still inadequate in one important respect: the expectations are, in general, of a *conditional* nature. An extremely simple example of this has already been given in Section D-3. When the market for the product is imperfect and the price is regarded as the predictand, we may write

$$(21) \qquad \bar{p}_t = \bar{p}_t(y_t),$$

where the parenthesis, in addition to the decision variable y, may also include various predictors. Here, properly speaking, the entrepreneur is expecting not the price itself, but rather the shape of the demand function. Similarly the expected rate of interest may, *inter alia*, depend on the degrees of commitment and also on the amount to be borrowed at any given time. Thus we have a case where the firm's assets assume the role of predictors. (Cf. Section D-2.)

This situation may be expressed by

$$(22) \qquad \bar{\omega}_{t_0} = \bar{\omega}_{t_0}(\zeta_{t_0}, \eta_{t_0}''),$$

where the function $\bar{\omega}_{t_0}$ is the true object of expectations. ζ in (22) must satisfy certain constraints (cf. *F-2*).

F. Formation of Decisions

F-1. "Budget equation" and "surplus." We shall now relate the en-

[23] Marschak, in an unpublished note.

trepreneurial withdrawals d_t to changes in the firm's financial assets and its "surplus." This is accomplished through the *budget* (balance) *equation*

$$\Delta m_t = \pi_t + \Delta b_t - \Delta s_t - d_t, \tag{23}$$

where Δs_t is the current value of the securities purchased (or sold), and π_t is the *surplus*, defined below in equation (25).

Equation (23) may now be rewritten

$$d_t = \pi_t + \Delta b_t - \Delta s_t - \Delta m_t, \tag{24}$$

since it is the d_t's that enter the expression that is being maximized. The surplus π_t is given by[24]

$$\pi_t \equiv \sum_{\mu} p_t^{\mu} y_t^{\mu} - \sum_{\sigma} \sum_{t'} q_{t't}^{\mu} v_{t't}^{\sigma} - \sum_{\mu} g_t^{\mu} k_{t+1}^{\mu} - l_t^{(e)} + l_t^{(s)}, \tag{25}$$

where[25]

$$\begin{aligned} l_t^{(e)} &\equiv \sum_{t',t''} r_{t',t'',t}' e_{t',t''}^{+} + i_t' e_{t,t''}^{+} \qquad (t' < t < t''), \\ l_t^{(s)} &\equiv \sum_{t'} r_{t',t}'' s_{t',t+1}^{**} - i_t'' |\Delta s_t| \qquad (t' < t). \end{aligned} \tag{26}$$

Taxes, as noted before, are excluded from consideration. The *market variables* (p, q, g, r', r'') are assumed to be determined in *imperfect* markets. Thus p may be a function, say $p(y)$, of the volume of sales. In the case of advertising we have the quantity of advertising x^{μ} among the negative inputs, so that an additional term $p^{\mu}x^{\mu}$ appears in π and the demand function for the firm's νth product becomes say $p^{\nu}(y^{\nu}, x^{\mu})$.[26]

Some of the imperfections may be of a *frictional* character, i.e., dependent on the rate of change of the relevant variables.[27] For instance we may find that the (per unit) cost of storage g depends not only on the quantity k stored, but also on the rate of change Δk of the stocks.

It is important to note that the values of the market variables that enter the entrepreneur's calculations are the *expected* ones; similarly the demand curves [e.g., $p(y)$] are those *imagined* (i.e., *expected*) by the entrepreneur. They may or may not be near the true ones.

[24] y is quantity of product sold, p its price; q is the price of equipment, g unit storage cost; the other symbols have already been defined.

[25] i are brokerage charges; they are introduced to justify holding of cash under nonstochastic expectations.

[26] These imperfections may be of a discriminatory nature (objectively or subjectively) so that two otherwise identical firms may be facing entirely different markets.

[27] In the economic literature the term "friction" is often applied to market imperfections or to the dynamic nature of economic phenomena, i.e., absence of instantaneous adjustments. In this paper the term will be used only as defined in the text.

When imperfections are present, they may be among the important factors in limiting the firm's scale of operations or its size. In particular, the imperfections of the credit market have attracted a good deal of attention.[28] Thus

$$r_{t',t'',t}' = r_{t',t'',t}'(\delta_{t'}), \qquad \frac{\partial r'}{\partial \delta} > 0, \tag{27}$$

where

$$\delta = \frac{b}{m + s + \sum qv} \tag{28}$$

is the "degree of commitment." [Equation (28) is merely an example of a possible definition of δ.][29]

The market for securities is thought of as perfect, but this assumption is in no way essential.

The *expected withdrawals* are given by a system of equations exactly equivalent to the above except for the expectation symbol $^-$ placed over all the predictands. Thus in (25) we write $\bar{p}$, $\bar{w}$, instead of p, w, etc.

F-2. Constraints. In choosing the optimal values of decision variables the entrepreneur is limited by several types of constraints.

(*1*) *Stock-flow identities.* The most obvious ones are those relating the stock variables to the flow variables. For instance the inventories are related to output and volume of sales by the identity

$$k_{t+1} \equiv x_t - y_t + k_t. \tag{29}$$

Thus either x or y could be completely eliminated, but the use of Lagrange multipliers makes this unnecessary and permits a more symmetrical treatment of all the variables involved.

(*2*) *Effects of financial operations.* It will be assumed that debts incurred necessitate repayment so that [cf. (7)]

$$e_{t',t''}^{+} = e_{t'',t'}^{-}. \tag{30}$$

Also the interest charges at any time [given by (26)] depend on the volume of past borrowing. Similarly purchase of securities implies revenue in the future, their sale a corresponding loss.

The above two types of constraints are of a somewhat trivial nature; although only the first one is implied by the definitions of the variables used, neither one involves any unknown relationships or parameters.

[28] Kalecki [9].

[29] In the case of stochastic expectations fear of bankruptcy (i.e., the entrepreneur's utility function) will also discourage the firm from reaching too high a degree of commitment, but in the nonstochastic case "increasing risk" is a market phenomenon due to the lender's fears and his desire for protection in case of insolvency.

In the third and most important type of constraint, this is not the case.

(3) *Transformation functions.* A system of transformation functions may be written as

$$F^{(j)}(X_t, Z_t; E_t) = 0, \qquad t = \cdots, t_0 - 1, t_0, t_0 + 1, \quad j = 1, 2, \cdots, J, \tag{31}$$

(The significance of E_t will be explained below.) X_t, N_t, and Z_t are matrices (or vectors) covering a specified span of time, thus implying a great variety of lag relationships among factors, among products, and between the two. The reason for there being J such relationships is that, for instance, there may be fixed technical relationships ("fixed coefficients," etc.) between, say, two factors.

It is important to see that even if $J=1$, we are still left with a *system* of constraints and not a single one. This is indicated by the domain of variability of the subscript t.[30]

It is worth noting that Z_t does not become a scalar even if there is only one type of equipment, since equipment is differentiated according to the time of installation. This is of importance, because at the time of installation the entrepreneur has a considerable amount of freedom with regard to the most efficient arrangement of equipment within the plant; therefore, even apart from wear and tear, newly installed equipment may play a different role in the plant's output from that of equipment installed previously.

The variable E_t represents the various factors that influence technology: inventions, social and cultural phenomena. In the first approximation it may be represented as a trend function.

Since the transformation function that is of relevance is the one in the entrepreneur's mind (rather than the true one), its parameters are (like the parameters of the imagined demand functions) in the nature of expected variables. Ordinarily, we would assume that the entrepreneur knows his production function well enough so that there would be little justification for distinguishing between its subjective and ob-

[30] A simple example may be helpful at this point. Let $J=1$ and the transformation function be

$$x_t^1 = f(x_{t-1}^2, x_{t-2}^2), \qquad t = t_0, t_0 + 1, \cdots. \tag{31'}$$

This implies that (1) the entrepreneur is no longer free to choose $x_{t_0}^1$ since $x_{t_0}^1$ is predetermined by $x_{t_0-1}^2$ and $x_{t_0-2}^2$; (2) while $x_{t_0+1}^1$ is not absolutely fixed, it is only partly free since it depends on $x_{t_0-1}^2$; and, (3) if all the future x^2's were chosen there would be no more choice with regard to the x^1's.

A common error seems to be due to the use of only one of the values of t in systems like (31) or (31′). Hicks [6] for instance, has only a single Lagrange multiplier in his appendix, Section 23, instead of a whole set of them. Tintner may have had this in mind in regarding certain initial values as known in advance [24], p. 307.

jective version. But this is not always the case. With regard to untried innovations there is a great deal of difference between the two: it takes a certain amount of imagination to visualize possibilities of new productive processes, etc. The role played by these considerations in Schumpeter's model is well known.[31]

(*4*) *Restrictions on the frequency and timing of withdrawals and decision-making.* These are dictated partly by custom, partly by considerations of economy. As noted before frequency of decisions need not be the same for all variables.

(*5*) *Inequalities.* Assets are so defined that they cannot assume negative values. In order to take this into account we may proceed as follows:[32]

First find the optimal point disregarding the inequalities. In this manner the absolute maximum of utility is located. If this maximum is in a region where all assets have positive values, the optimum point is the correct one, since we can do no better than the absolute maximum. Suppose, however, that the optimal point is found in a region where some of the assets, say cash and securities, are negative. In that case the optimal level for these two assets will be zero; these zero values should be substituted in the function to be maximized and the maximization carried out with regard to other variables in the usual manner.[33]

F-3. Summary. The results so far obtained may now be summarized. The starting point is the requirement that utility, as a function of the prospective stream of withdrawals, be maximized subject to existing constraints:

$$u_{t_0} = \phi_{t_0}(\overline{D}_{t_0}) = \text{maximum}, \tag{32}$$

subject to

$$\begin{cases} \mathcal{J}_{t_0}{}^{(i)}(\eta_{t_0}', \zeta_{t_0}) = 0, & i = 1, 2, 3, 4, \\ \mathcal{J}_{t_0}{}^{(5)}(\eta_{t_0}', \zeta_{t_0}) \geqq 0. \end{cases} \tag{33}$$

The relation (33) represents all the existing constraints and by its form indicates the variables entering the constraints. (The superscript of $\mathcal{J}$ refers to the classification of constraints in *F-2*.)

The second stage consists in expressing the prospective stream of withdrawals in terms of assets, decision variables, and predictands, and,

[31] Cf. Schumpeter, [22]; also Lange [13], pp. 71 ff. It is worth noting that similar type of vision may be required to estimate correctly the market conditions for various products and factors.

[32] Cf. Koopmans and Rubin [11].

[33] When secondary maxima exist, complications may arise; cf. footnote 35 below.

in turn, the predictands in terms of the decision variables and the predictors.

Thus we have

$$\overline{D}_{t_0} = \overline{D}_{t_0}(\bar{\omega}_{t_0}, \zeta_{t_0}, \eta_{t_0}'), \tag{34}$$

and

$$\bar{\omega}_{t_0} = \bar{\omega}_{t_0}(\zeta_{t_0}, \eta_{t_0}''). \tag{35}$$

Finally, substituting (34) and (35) into (32) we have

$$u_{t_0} = \psi_{t_0}(\zeta_{t_0}; \eta_{t_0}) = \text{maximum subject to (33)}. \tag{36}$$

ψ in (5) depends on ϕ as well as on $\bar{\omega}$. Thus the outcome of maximization, which is, of course, carried out with regard to ζ_{t_0} (with η_{t_0} as given), depends on the preference pattern, the structure of expectations, and the nature of the transformation functions.

F-4. Maximization. The process of maximization is straightforward; cf. Lange [12]. Its results may be written implicitly as[34]

$$\chi_{t_0}(\hat{\zeta}_{t_0}; \eta_{t_0}) = 0, \tag{37}$$

which is a system of equations each of which indicates maximization with regard to one particular decision variable.[35] When the system is solved for the decision variables we obtain

$$\hat{\zeta}_{t_0} = \rho_{t_0}(\eta_{t_0}) \tag{38}$$

thus giving the optimal value $\hat{\zeta}_{t_0}$ of ζ_{t_0} as a function of the initial conditions η_{t_0}. The nature of the system of functional relationships ρ depends, as implied by the remarks in the preceding section, on ϕ, $\bar{\omega}$, and $\mathcal{J}$.

Now $\hat{\zeta}_{t_0}$ consists of two types of values of decision variables. There are those referring to the period (more or less) immediately following t_0 which will no longer be revised; these form the basis for the entrepreneur's *final decisions* and will be denoted by $\hat{\zeta}_{t_0}^{(0)}$. The remaining components of ζ_{t_0}, to be denoted by $\hat{\zeta}_{t_0}^{(1)}$ are in the nature of *tentative decisions*[36] and are of a purely auxiliary nature. We thus obtain, as a subset of (38), the system

$$\hat{\zeta}_{t_0}^{(0)} = \rho_{t_0}^{(0)}(\eta_{t_0}), \tag{39}$$

[34] The Lagrange multipliers are not shown explicitly. They can always be eliminated with the help of the constraints.

[35] Provided appropriate substitutions of the type $u = v^2$ are made for nonnegative variables and absolute value terms, (37) is simply $\partial\psi_{t_0}/\partial\zeta_{t_0} = 0$. Cf. [16]. However, the existence of *indivisibilities* will modify the nature of solutions. They may, for instance, reduce to zero some variables (e.g., investment) that would otherwise be nonzero.

[36] Cf. Hart [4].

which may be rewritten in the implicit form as

(40) $$\chi_{t_0}^{(0)}(\hat{\zeta}_{t_0}^{(0)};\ \eta_{t_0}) = 0.$$

The latter is obtained as follows. Rewrite (37) as

(41.1) $$\chi_{t_0}^{*}(\hat{\zeta}_{t_0}^{(0)},\ \hat{\zeta}_{t_0}^{(1)};\ \eta_{t_0}) = 0,$$

(41.2) $$\chi_{t_0}^{**}(\hat{\zeta}_{t_0}^{(0)},\ \hat{\zeta}_{t_0}^{(1)};\ \eta_{t_0}) = 0,$$

where the equations in (41.1) perform maximization with regard to $\hat{\zeta}_{t_0}^{(0)}$ while (41.2) do it with regard to $\hat{\zeta}_{t_0}^{(1)}$. Then solve (41.2) for $\hat{\zeta}_t^{(1)}$ in terms of $\hat{\zeta}_{t'_0}^{(0)}$ and η_{t_0} and obtain, say,

(42) $$\hat{\zeta}_{t_0}^{(1)} = \hat{\zeta}_{t_0}^{(1)}(\hat{\zeta}_{t_0}^{(0)};\ \eta_{t_0}).$$

Then, substituting this result in (41.1), we get

(43) $$\chi_{t_0}^{*}[\hat{\zeta}_{t_0}^{(0)},\ \hat{\zeta}_{t_0}^{(1)}(\hat{\zeta}_{t_0}^{(0)};\ \eta_{t_0});\ \eta_{t_0}] = 0,$$

which may be simplified into (40). The equations of which (40) consists formulate the laws of the entrepreneur's optimal behavior. One of these equations, for instance, carries out maximization with regard to, say, factor x_t^{μ} and is what would usually be referred to as the demand function of the entrepreneur for x^{μ} to be used at the time t, provided decision at time t_0 with regard to x_t^{μ} is final. (In practice, these equations are written after the constraints have been used to eliminate the Lagrange multipliers. This procedure introduces a certain amount of arbitrariness as well as lack of symmetry.)

Thus the firm's demand (or supply) functions for equipment, labor, other factors (e.g., raw materials, advertising space, etc.), inventories, products, cash, loans of various duration, and securities are obtained.

G. Aggregation and Market Phenomena

We shall now indicate, in a very formal manner and only for the sake of logical completeness, how the results of the preceding section are to be incorporated into macrodynamic economic models.

As a starting point, we shall take equation (39). We shall write it, however, in a somewhat modified form:

(44) $$\hat{\zeta}_{t_0}^{(0)E,\epsilon} = \rho_{t_0}^{(0)E,\epsilon}(\eta_{t_0}^{E,\epsilon}).$$

Here the superscript E stands for the entrepreneurial group as a whole,[37] while ϵ denotes the individual entrepreneur. The demand (or supply)

[37] E here is not related to the variable E_t in (26).

functions (1) of the individual entrepreneurs may now be aggregated[38] for all entrepreneurs thus giving

(45) $$\hat{\zeta}_{t_0}{}^{(0)E} \equiv \sum_{\epsilon} \hat{\rho}_{t_0}{}^{(0)E,\epsilon}(\eta_{t_0}{}^{E,\epsilon}) = \hat{\rho}_{t_0}{}^{(0)E}(\eta_{t_0}{}^{E}),$$

where

(46) $$\rho^E = \{\rho^{E,\epsilon}\}, \quad \eta^E = \{\eta^{E,\epsilon}\}.$$

Now suppose similar models have been developed for groups other than entrepreneurs, say workers, bankers, etc. We then obtain a system of equations like (45), one for each group:

(47) $$\hat{\zeta}_{t_0}{}^{(0)G} = \hat{\rho}_{t_0}{}^{(0)G}(\eta_{t_0}{}^{G}),$$

where G runs over all groups. We then perform aggregation over groups thus obtaining

(48) $$\hat{\zeta}_{t_0}{}^{(0)} \equiv \sum_{G} \hat{\rho}_{t_0}{}^{(0)G}(\eta_{t_0}{}^{G}) = \hat{\rho}_{t_0}{}^{(0)}(\eta_{t_0}),$$

where

(49) $$\rho = \{\rho^G\}, \quad \eta = \{\eta^G\}.$$

Now it would be desirable to throw (48) into the implicit form and also to scalarize[39] the variables it contains. But the theory of such a process still remains to be worked out.[40,41]

We shall therefore leave (48) as the final result. It is in a form that does not lend itself readily to immediate applications. But, in principle, it does enable us to predict the developments when the initial conditions η_{t_0} and the nature of the function $\hat{\rho}_{t_0}{}^{(0)}$ are known.

H. Special Problems

H-1. Motivation of investment. It may be useful to give a brief explicit description of the functioning of the model from the viewpoint of investment decisions. It should be noted that this is still the case of nonstochastic anticipations and many interesting aspects of the problem are thus left out of consideration.

[38] Under conditions approaching full employment decisions of individual entrepreneurs may be inconsistent and cannot always be aggregated. It may then be helpful to regard prices rather than quantities as decision variables.

[39] I.e., to represent vectors by means of scalar functions of their components; e.g., total national income is such a function of all individual incomes; price index is such a function of prices of individual goods; etc.

[40] Cf. Hicks [6], Marschak [17], Mosak [20].

[41] It is possible to obtain the implicit form when the distribution of firms according to various criteria is known. This is related to the concept of a "representative firm."

Suppose the entrepreneur considers the desirability of purchasing during (t_0, t_0+1) an additional piece of new equipment. Assume that the production plan is otherwise left unchanged. Then this implies a diminution of π_{t_0} by $q_{t_0}v_{t_0}$. On the other hand, through the transformation function, it also implies increases in some future outputs or decreases in some inputs. This may become apparent during (t_0, t_0+1), or it may only become apparent at some later time. Thus there will be a tendency for π_t to drop in the near future with a compensating rise at some later time; however, this tendency may be partly offset by other operations, say inventory variations.

Let us, for the sake of definiteness, say that π_{t_0} drops while π_{t_0+1} goes up. Then one thing the entrepreneur may do is to let d_{t_0} drop and d_{t_0+1} go up in parallel with the movements of the surplus; on the other hand, he may prefer to avoid such fluctuations in the level of his withdrawals by means of compensatory financial operations. This he can do by incurring debts (i.e., financing investment by borrowing), sale of securities, or diminishing his stock of cash (loss of liquidity). Higher debts will impose interest burdens on future surpluses, sale of securities previously held will also lower future surpluses by eliminating a part of the interest revenue. Loss of liquidity also implies certain additional future expenditures, but in the case of nonstochastic expectations this is of little consequence.

It is easy to see what types of price expectations would make the entrepreneur favor lower inventories, what interest-rate expectations would make him go into debt, sell securities, etc.

Clearly the entrepreneur's "impatience," his private financial condition, opportunities, etc. will also affect the decision.

Now it may turn out that even the optimal method of financing the investment (coupled with the best possible adjustments in the product plan) will leave the entrepreneur worse off in terms of the utility of prospective withdrawals than he would be without making the investment. Then, of course, the decision will be against purchase; in fact under extreme conditions it may be in favor of selling some equipment already in his possession or even dismantling the whole plant.

On the other hand, if the investment expenditure $q_{t_0}v_{t_0}$ is found advantageous (again in utility terms) it will be carried out, and the advisability of additional purchases of equipment may then be considered. It will be noted that a special case of this situation is the problem of entering the industry. This is simply the question of desirability of a certain volume of investment where the initial values of certain assets, e.g., the plant, are zero. The reasoning that applies is the same as before, but various market imperfections (borrowing difficulties, patent restrictions, discrimination on the part of suppliers of factors, attachment of consumers to known brands, etc.) may be of particularly great importance.

H-2. Size and rate of growth of the firm. The above considerations implicitly contain a (very general) theory of the size of the firm. (Since the size of the firm is usually regarded as determined by the size of its plant, a theory of investment is at the same time a theory of the firm's size. But even if other assets are included in the measure of the firm's size, our initial statement still holds.)

Among the factors limiting the firm's size we may list the more important ones:

1. initial assets,
2. market imperfections,
3. nature of the transformation functions,
4. the entrepreneur's lack of vision with regard to existing possibilities (markets, technology),
5. the entrepreneur's utility function.

The factors limiting the rate of growth of the firm are also of interest. The frictional imperfections of the markets are among the most important ones; the nature of transformation functions may also be slowing down the firm's growth.

With regard to both the firm's size and to the rate of growth, some of the most powerful limiting factors may be due to existence of uncertainty.

H-3. Inventories. In the absence of the stochastic element in expectations it is impossible to account for the "transaction" inventories. But the *speculative* inventories are present. Hawtrey's trader[42] is a special case of an entrepreneur whose production function is such that the optimum level of output (but not sales) is zero, and the materials purchased are physically identical with those sold.

H-4. Acceleration principle. This principle can be written, in a generalized form, as

$$\hat{v}_t \propto \Delta\bar{\alpha}_{t-1}, \tag{50}$$

where α is a shift parameter in the demand function for the firm's product. The foregoing theory indicates how the importance of factors neglected in (50) can be estimated.

II. THE CASE OF STOCHASTIC EXPECTATIONS

I. Preference Pattern, Expectations, Decisions

The discussion of this subject, stimulated by Knight's *Risk, Uncer-*

[42] Cf. Hawtrey [5]; also von Haberler [2], p. 18.

tainty, and Profit,[43] has led to considerable progress in economic thought.[44]

First, it has served to give a more realistic theory of the demand for cash, inventories, and the like.

Secondly, it has led to a realization that the entrepreneur is facing a problem different from that of a gambler or insurance company.

The common element in the various possible ways of approaching the problem is that the object of maximization (i.e., utility) depends on the probability distributions of the economic variables. In the terminology of this paper the predictands become stochastic variables and their probability-distribution functions determine for a given value of the initial values and decision variables the joint-multivariate-probability distribution of the elements of the prospective-withdrawals vector. The optimum choice of decision-variable is the one yielding a distribution of the prospective withdrawals that is more to the entrepreneur's liking than any alternative distribution. Clearly the psychological make-up of the entrepreneur plays a decisive role.

It may be helpful to summarize this, retaining the earlier notation.

We have the entrepreneur's utility as a functional on the probability distribution $\mathcal{G}_{\overline{D}_{t_0}}$ of the prospective vector withdrawals

$$u_{t_0} = \phi_{t_0}\{\mathcal{G}_{\overline{D}_{t_0}}\}, \tag{51}$$

subject to appropriate constraints. In turn

$$\overline{D}_{t_0} = \overline{D}_{t_0}(\bar{\omega}_{t_0}, \zeta_{t_0}, \eta_{t_0}'), \tag{52}$$

and $\bar{\omega}_{t_0}$ itself is stochastic with a distribution

$$\mathcal{H}_{t_0}(\bar{\omega}_{t_0} | \zeta_{t_0}, \eta_{t_0}''). \tag{53}$$

Hence when proper transformations are carried out we find

$$\mathcal{G}_{t_0}(\overline{D}_{t_0} | \zeta_{t_0}, \eta_{t_0}). \tag{54}$$

Moreover, there are again restrictions on ζ_{t_0}, as before. Some of these are of a nonstochastic character and create no problem, but the important point is that the transformation functions do become stochastic.

It appears convenient to adopt here a method that is less symmetrical than that used in the nonstochastic case: with the help of constraints (stochastic and nonstochastic) we eliminate some of the decision variables and also modify the distribution function in (54). Let the remaining *free decision variables* be denoted by ξ_{t_0}.

Then we have that $\overline{D}_{t_0}$ is distributed according to

$$\mathcal{K}_{t_0}(\overline{D}_{t_0} | \xi_{t_0}, \eta_{t_0}), \tag{55}$$

[43] [10].

[44] Marschak [17]; Tintner [24], [25]; Hart [3], [4].

and hence we have from (46)

$$u_{t_0} = \psi_{t_0}(\xi_{t_0}, \eta_{t_0}), \tag{56}$$

which is a function, *not* a functional and, formally, the problem is no different from that obtained in the case of nonstochastic expectations.

J. Risk, Uncertainty, Rational Expectations

At this point reference must be made to the two aspects of the stochastic nature of the expectations, customarily associated in the economic literature with the terms *risk* and *uncertainty*.

Consider, as an example, the (true) demand function for the firm's product[45]

$$p_t = \alpha_1 y_t + \alpha_2 p_{t-1} + \alpha_0 + u_t, \tag{57}$$

where u_t is a stochastic variable with a mean zero and variance σ^2. Here the variance of u is a measure of variability in the buyers' behavior. Even if the entrepreneur knew the true values of the α's and of σ^2, he still would not be able to predict the exact future price p_t corresponding to some given y_t and p_{t-1}, but he could determine the probability distribution of p_t. The dispersion of the distribution of $\overline{D}_{t_0}$ (due to the dispersion of p_t) may be called the entrepreneur's *risk* (this definition is somewhat narrow, but sufficient for our purpose).

Actually, however, the entrepreneur realizes that he does not know the true values of the α's and of σ^2. This lack of knowledge is referred to as *uncertainty* and it can be treated in two ways.

One approach, that of Tintner, is to postulate that in the entrepreneur's mind there exist some a priori known distributions of the α's and of σ^2; these parameters are now thought of as stochastic variables.

Another approach, that of Marschak, is to assume that the entrepreneur will estimate the α's and σ^2 by some (optimal) statistical methods; this, of course, does not imply the neglect of any a priori information the entrepreneur may possess, but it does not require that such information should be available. (Actually, Marschak treats estimation as an integral part of the decision-making rather than separate the two.)

Since in practice we are not always justified in assuming a priori distributions, it is obvious that procedures of statistical inference should be introduced whenever possible. But the question arises whether they will always be sufficient.

This problem is equivalent to that investigated by Wald,[46] viz., of the conditions under which optimal estimates exist ("optimal" in the

[45] Cf. equations (19) and (21).

[46] Wald [26].

sense of minimizing the maximum average loss[47]). Since our model has not been shown to fulfill all of Wald's assumptions, his theorem (stating that in certain circumstances optimal estimates can be found) need not follow. This question deserves more study, but we shall confine ourselves here to a general description of certain important cases.

Case A. The entrepreneur expects the structure of the economy to remain what it had been during the period prior to the time of decision-making. This implies, *inter alia*, that the demand curve for his product remains unchanged. It can be shown[48] that in this case ordinary least-squares procedures will give the entrepreneur the conditional distribution of p_t given y_t and p_{t-1} which is all that is needed; it is then not necessary to estimate the "structural coefficients" α and σ^2.

Case B. The entrepreneur does expect some structural changes, say a change in α_1. The new value of α_1 (say α_1') is a function of the old one. This means that either α_1' is given directly or, at least it can be found if the old value α_1 is known. Now it is here that the ordinary regression methods will usually fail and there is need for the "simultaneous equation" approach. It is then, in general, necessary to know the structural parameters.[49] Unfortunately, however, the structural parameters cannot always be found. We may now distinguish two cases.

Case B1. Parameters to be estimated are *identifiable*, i.e., it is possible to estimate them. Then it is still possible for the entrepreneur to find a basis for his decisions, provided he uses the correct estimation procedures.[50]

Case B2. Parameters to be estimated are *not* (or, at least, not completely) *identifiable*. This means that no matter how large a sample of past observations the entrepreneur has, he will not be able completely to determine the probability distribution of future prices.

It might then so happen that any decision on the part of the entrepreneur would imply the possibility of an infinite average loss. When this is the case, maximum average loss cannot be minimized and there is no rational basis for decision.

But this lack of identifiability of the parameters of the demand function will not always have such extreme consequences. The minimization of maximum average loss may lead to a policy of following certain routine procedures, or else the entrepreneur may not realize how deep his ignorance is. This may lead him to wrong decisions, but at least it does not paralyze him, as the knowledge of his ignorance would. Other-

[47] Wald uses the term "risk" instead of "average loss"; the use of the latter term was suggested by Professor Marschak to avoid confusion with "risk" in the sense defined above.

[48] Hurwicz [7].

[49] Marschak [19].

[50] Koopmans and Rubin [11].

wise, we must again resort to Tintner's approach if we believe that the entrepreneurs always do make some decisions.

K. Special Problems

There is need for explicit construction of preference functionals (or functions) and of the stochastic expectation equations. With these it would be possible to show how, for instance, "transaction demand" for cash or inventories is implied by the utility-maximization postulate. But the detailed study of these phenomena, especially of their impact on investment decisions is beyond the scope of this paper.[51]

It should be mentioned that in practice maximization is not performed accurately; that is, the values of decision variables chosen are not exactly those which would maximize u_{t_0}; also, the entrepreneur's preferences (i.e., ϕ) and ways of forming expectations (i.e., the function $\bar{\omega}$) fluctuate in time. If these fluctuations are *given* functions of time they are covered by the foregoing treatment (since all the relevant functions have a time subscript). But when these fluctuations are of a stochastic nature, our equations acquire an additional component, the "disturbance." It is worth noting that the presence or absence of the disturbance is unrelated to the presence of a stochastic element in the expectations.

Cowles Commission for Research in Economics
The University of Chicago

REFERENCES

[1] Irving Fisher, *The Theory of Interest*, New York, Macmillan, 1930, 566 pp.

[2] Gottfried von Haberler, *Prosperity and Depression*, New revised and enlarged edition, Geneva, League of Nations, 1939, 473 pp.

[3] Albert Gailord Hart, *Anticipations, Uncertainty, and Dynamic Planning*, Studies in Business Administration, Vol. 11, No. 1; also in *Journal of Business*, University of Chicago, Vol. 13, No. 4, October, 1940, Part 2, 98 pp.

[4] Albert Gailord Hart, "Risk, Uncertainty, and the Unprofitability of Compounding Probabilities," in Lange, McIntyre, Yntema, editors, *Studies in Mathematical Economics and Econometrics, In Memory of Henry Schultz*, Chicago, The University of Chicago Press, 1942, pp. 110–118.

[5] R. G. Hawtrey, *Capital and Employment*, London, Longmans, 1937, 348 pp.; *The Art of Central Banking*, London, Longmans, 1932, 464 pp., esp. p. 167.

[6] J. R. Hicks, *Value and Capital*, Oxford, Clarendon Press, 1939, 331 pp.

[7] Leonid Hurwicz, "Prediction and Least Squares," in *Statistical Inference in Dynamic Economic Systems*, to be published as Cowles Commission Monograph No. 10.

[51] Cf. Marschak [17], pp. 321 ff.

[8] LEONID HURWICZ, "The Theory of Economic Behavior," *American Economic Review*, Vol. 35, December, 1945, pp. 909–925.
[9] MICHAL KALECKI, *Essays in the Theory of Economic Fluctuations*, London, Allen and Unwin, 1939, 154 pp., esp. pp. 95 ff., "The Principle of Increasing Risk."
[10] FRANK H. KNIGHT, *Risk, Uncertainty and Profit*, Boston, Houghton Mifflin, 1921, 381 pp., esp. Chap. VII, "The Meaning of Risk and Uncertainty," pp. 197–232, esp. pp. 199, 216; Chap. VIII, "Structures and Methods for Meeting Uncertainty," pp. 233–263, "a priori" vs. "statistical judgment."
[11] TJALLING KOOPMANS and HERMAN RUBIN, "Measuring the Equation Systems of Dynamic Economics," in *Statistical Inference in Dynamic Economic Systems*, to be published as Cowles Commission Monograph No. 10.
[12] OSCAR LANGE, "The Foundations of Welfare Economics," ECONOMETRICA, Vol. 10, July–October, 1942, pp. 215–228, esp. Appendix, pp. 224 and 227.
[13] OSCAR LANGE, *Price Flexibility and Employment*, Cowles Commission Monograph No. 8, Bloomington, Principia Press, 1944, 114 pp.
[14] FRIEDRICH A. LUTZ, "The Criterion of Maximum Profits in the Theory of Investment," *Quarterly Journal of Economics*, Vol. 60, November, 1945, pp. 56–77.
[15] FRIEDRICH A. LUTZ, "The Interest Rate and Investment in a Dynamic Economy," *American Economic Review*, Vol. 35, December, 1945, pp. 811–830.
[16] JACOB MARSCHAK and WILLIAM H. ANDREWS, JR., "Random Simultaneous Equations and the Theory of Production," ECONOMETRICA, Vol. 12, July–October, 1944, pp. 143–205, esp. H. Rubin's note 46 on pp. 201–202.
[17] J. MARSCHAK, "Money and the Theory of Assets," ECONOMETRICA, Vol. 6, October, 1938, pp. 311–325.
[18] J. MARSCHAK, "Neumann's and Morgenstern's New Approach to Static Economics," *Journal of Political Economy*, Vol. 54, April, 1946, p. 97–115, especially Section 3.
[19] JACOB MARSCHAK, Abstract of paper presented at Cleveland meeting of Econometric Society, January, 1946, p. 165 of this issue of ECONOMETRICA.
[20] JACOB L. MOSAK, *General-Equilibrium Theory in International Trade*, Cowles Commission Monograph No. 7, Bloomington, Principia Press, 1944, 187 pp.
[21] JOHN VON NEUMANN and OSKAR MORGENSTERN, *Theory of Games and Economic Behavior*, Princeton University Press, 1944, 625 pp.
[22] JOSEPH A. SCHUMPETER, *Business Cycles*, Vol. I, New York, McGraw-Hill, 1939, 448 pp.
[23] T. DE SCITOVSKY, "A Note on Profit Maximisation and its Implications," *Review of Economic Studies*, Vol. 11, Winter, 1943, pp. 57–60.
[24] GERHARD TINTNER, "The Pure Theory of Production under Technological Risk and Uncertainty," ECONOMETRICA, Vol. 9, July–October, 1941, pp. 305–312.
[25] GERHARD TINTNER, "A Contribution to the Nonstatic Theory of Production," in Lange, McIntyre, Yntema, editors, *Studies in Dynamic Economics and Econometrics, In Memory of Henry Schultz*, Chicago, The University of Chicago Press, 1942, pp. 92–109.
[26] A. WALD, "Statistical Decision Functions which Minimize the Maximum Risk," *Annals of Mathematics*, Vol. 46, April, 1945, pp. 265–280.

[20]

A Model of General Economic Equilibrium[1]

The subject of this paper is the solution of a typical economic equation system. The system has the following properties:

(1) Goods are produced not only from "natural factors of production," but in the first place from each other. These processes of production may be circular, i.e. good G_1 is produced with the aid of good G_2, and G_2 with the aid of G_1.

(2) There may be more technically possible processes of production than goods and for this reason "counting of equations" is of no avail. The problem is rather to establish which processes will actually be used and which not (being "unprofitable").

In order to be able to discuss (1), (2) quite freely we shall idealise other elements of the situation (see paragraphs 1 and 2). Most of these idealisations are irrelevant, but this question will not be discussed here.

The way in which our questions are put leads of necessity to a system of inequalities (3)—(8′) in paragraph 3 the possibility of a solution of which is not evident, i.e. *it cannot be proved by any qualitative argument.* The mathematical proof is possible only by means of a generalisation of Brouwer's Fix-Point Theorem, i.e. by the use of very fundamental *topological* facts. This generalised fix-point theorem (the "lemma" of paragraph 7) is also interesting in itself.

The connection with topology may be very surprising at first, but the author thinks that it is natural in problems of this kind. The immediate reason for this is the occurrence of a certain "minimum-maximum" problem, familiar from the calculus of variations. In our present question, the minimum-maximum problem has been formulated in paragraph 5. It is closely related to another problem occurring in the theory of games (see footnote 1 in paragraph 6).

A direct interpretation of the function $\phi(X, Y)$ would be highly desirable. Its rôle appears to be similar to that of thermodynamic potentials in phenomenological thermodynamics; it can be surmised that the similarity will persist in its full phenomenological generality (independently of our restrictive idealisations).

Another feature of our theory, so far without interpretation, is the remarkable duality (symmetry) of the monetary variables (prices y_j, interest factor β) and the technical variables (intensities of production x_i, coefficient of expansion of the economy α). This is brought out very clearly in paragraph 3 (3)—(8′) as well as in the minimum-maximum formulation of paragraph 5 (7**)—(8**).

Lastly, attention is drawn to the results of paragraph 11 from which follows, among other things, that the normal price mechanism brings about—if our assumptions are valid—the technically most efficient intensities of production. This seems not unreasonable since we have eliminated all monetary complications.

The present paper was read for the first time in the winter of 1932 at the mathematical seminar of Princeton University. The reason for its publication was an invitation from Mr. K. Menger, to whom the author wishes to express his thanks.

1. Consider the following problem: there are n goods $G_1, \ldots, G_n$ which can be produced by m processes $P_1, \ldots, P_m$. Which processes will be used (as "profitable") and what prices of the goods will obtain? The problem is evidently

[1] This paper was first published in German, under the title *Über ein Ökonomisches Gleichungssystem und eine Verallgemeinerung des Brouwerschen Fixpunktsatzes* in the volume entitled *Ergebuisse eines Mathematischen Seminars*, edited by K. Menger (Vienna, 1938). It was translated into English by G. Morgenstern. A commentary note on this article, by D. G. Champernowne, is printed below.

non-trivial since either of its parts can be answered only after the other one has been answered, i.e. its solution is implicit. We observe in particular :

(*a*) Since it is possible that $m > n$ it cannot be solved through the usual counting of equations.

In order to avoid further complications we assume :

(*b*) That there are constant returns (to scale) ;

(*c*) That the natural factors of production, including labour, can be expanded in unlimited quantities.

The essential phenomenon that we wish to grasp is this : goods are produced from each other (see equation (7) below) and we want to determine (*i*) which processes will be used ; (*ii*) what the relative velocity will be with which the total quantity of goods increases ; (*iii*) what prices will obtain ; (*iv*) what the rate of interest will be. In order to isolate this phenomenon completely we assume furthermore :

(*d*) Consumption of goods takes place only through the processes of production which include necessities of life consumed by workers and employees.

In other words we assume that all income in excess of necessities of life will be reinvested.

It is obvious to what kind of theoretical models the above assumptions correspond.

2. In each process P_i ($i = 1, \ldots, m$) quantities a_{ij} (expressed in some units) are used up, and quantities b_{ij} are produced, of the respective goods G_j ($j = 1, \ldots, n$). The process can be symbolised in the following way :

$$P_i : \sum_{j=1}^{n} a_{ij} G_j \rightarrow \sum_{j=1}^{n} b_{ij} G_j \qquad (1)$$

It is to be noted :

(*e*) Capital goods are to be inserted on both sides of (1) ; wear and tear of capital goods are to be described by introducing different stages of wear as different goods, using a separate P_i for each of these.

(*f*) Each process to be of unit time duration. Processes of longer duration to be broken down into single processes of unit duration introducing if necessary intermediate products as additional goods.

(*g*) (1) can describe the special case where good G_j can be produced only jointly with certain others, viz. its permanent joint products.

In the actual economy, these processes P_i, $i = 1, \ldots, m$, will be used with certain *intensities* x_i, $i = 1, \ldots, m$. That means that for the total production the quantities of equations (1) must be multiplied by x_i. We write symbolically :

$$E = \sum_{i=1}^{m} x_i P_i \qquad (2)$$

$x_i = 0$ means that process P_i is not used.

We are interested in those states where the whole economy expands without change of structure, i.e. where the ratios of the intensities $x_1 : \ldots : x_m$ remain unchanged, although $x_1, \ldots x_m$ themselves may change. In such a case they are multiplied by a common factor α per unit of time. This factor is the *coefficient of expansion of the whole economy*.

3. The numerical unknowns of our problem are : (*i*) the *intensities* $x_1, \ldots, x_m$ of the processes $P_1, \ldots, P_m$; (*ii*) the *coefficient of expansion* of the whole economy α ; (*iii*) the *prices* $y_1, \ldots, y_n$ of goods $G_1, \ldots, G_n$; (*iv*) the interest factor β ($= 1 + \frac{z}{100}$, z being the rate of interest in % per unit of time. Obviously :

$$x_i \geqq 0, \qquad (3) \qquad\qquad y_j \geqq 0, \qquad (4)$$

and since a solution with $x_1 = \ldots = x_m = 0$, or $y_1 = \ldots = y_n = 0$ would be meaningless:

$$\sum_{i=1}^{m} x_i > 0, \qquad (5) \qquad\qquad \sum_{j=1}^{n} y_j > 0, \qquad (6)$$

The economic equations are now:

$$\alpha \sum_{i=1}^{m} a_{ij}\, x_i \leqq \sum_{i=1}^{m} b_{ij}\, x_i, \qquad (7)$$

and if in (7) $<$ applies, $y_j = 0$ .... (7′)

$$\beta \sum_{j=1}^{n} a_{ij}\, y_j \geqq \sum_{j=1}^{n} b_{ij}\, y_j, \qquad (8)$$

and if in (8) $>$ applies, $x_i = 0$.................................... (8′)

The meaning of (7), (7′) is: it is impossible to consume more of a good G_j in the total process (2) than is being produced. If, however, less is consumed, i.e. if there is excess production of G_j, G_j becomes a free good and its price $y_j = 0$.

The meaning of (8), (8′) is: in equilibrium no profit can be made on any process P_i (or else prices or the rate of interest would rise—it is clear how this abstraction is to be understood). If there is a loss, however, i.e. if P_i is unprofitable, then P_i will not be used and its intensity $x_i = 0$.

The quantities a_{ij}, b_{ij} are to be taken as given, whereas the x_i, y_j, α, β are unknown. There are, then, $m + n + 2$ unknowns, but since in the case of x_i, y_j only the ratios $x_1 : \ldots : x_m$, $y_1 : \ldots : y_n$ are essential, they are reduced to $m + n$. Against this, there are $m + n$ conditions (7) + (7′) and (8) + (8′). As these, however, are not equations, but rather complicated inequalities, the fact that the number of conditions is equal to the number of unknowns does not constitute a guarantee that the system can be solved.

The dual symmetry of equations (3), (5), (7), (7′) of the variables x_i, α and of the concept "unused process" on the one hand, and of equations (4), (6), (8),)8′) of the variables y_j, β and of the concept "free good" on the other hand seems remarkable.

4. Our task is to solve (3)—(8′). We shall proceed to show:

Solutions of (3)—(8′) ***always exist***, although there may be several solutions with different $x_1 : \ldots : x_m$ or with different $y_1 : \ldots : y_n$. The first is possible since we have not even excluded the case where several P_i describe the same process or where several P_i combine to form another. The second is possible since some goods G_j may enter into each process P_i only in a fixed ratio with some others. But even apart from these trivial possibilities there may exist—for less obvious reasons—several solutions $x_1 : \ldots : x_m$, $y_1 : \ldots : y_m$. Against this it is of importance that α, β should have the same value for all solutions; i.e. α, β ***are uniquely determined***.

We shall even find that α and β can be directly characterised in a simple manner (see paragraphs 10 and 11).

To simplify our considerations we shall assume that always:

$$a_{ij} + b_{ij} > 0 \qquad (9)$$

(a_{ij}, b_{ij} are clearly always $\geqq 0$). Since the a_{ij}, b_{ij} may be arbitrarily small this restriction is not very far-reaching, although it must be imposed in order to assure uniqueness of α, β as otherwise W might break up into disconnected parts.

Consider now a hypothetical solution x_i, α, y_j, β of (3)—(8′). If we had in (7) always $<$, then we should have always $y_j = 0$ (because of (7′)) in contradiction to (6).

If we had in (8) always $>$ we should have always $x_i = 0$ (because of (8′)) in contradiction to (5). Therefore, in (7) $\leqq$ always applies, but $=$ at least once; in (8) $\geqq$ always applies, but $=$ at least once.

In consequence :

$$\alpha = \underset{j=1,\ldots,n}{\text{Min.}} \left[\frac{\sum_{i=1}^{m} b_{ij} \, x_i}{\sum_{i=1}^{m} a_{ij} \, x_i} \right] \quad \ldots\ldots\ldots\ldots\ldots\ldots\ldots\ldots \text{(10)},$$

$$\beta = \underset{i=1,\ldots,m}{\text{Max.}} \frac{\sum_{j=1}^{n} b_{ij} \, y_j}{\sum_{j=1}^{n} a_{ij} \, y_j} \quad \ldots\ldots\ldots\ldots\ldots\ldots\ldots\ldots \text{(11)}.$$

Therefore the x_i, y_j determine uniquely α, β. (The right-hand side of (10), (11) can never assume the meaningless form $\frac{0}{0}$ because of (3)—(6) and (9)). We can therefore state (7) + (7′) and (8) + (8′) as conditions for x_i, y_j only :

$y_j = 0$ for each $j = 1, \ldots, n$, for which :

$$\frac{\sum_{i=1}^{m} b_{ij} \, x_i}{\sum_{i=1}^{m} a_{ij} \, x_i}$$

does not assume its minimum value (for all $j = 1, \ldots, n$) . . . (7*).

$x_i = 0$ for each $i = 1, \ldots, m$, for which :

$$\frac{\sum_{j=1}^{n} b_{ij} \, y_i}{\sum_{j=1}^{n} a_{ij} \, y_i}$$

does not assume its maximum value (for all $i = 1, \ldots, m$) . . . (8*).

The $x_1, \ldots, x_m$ in (7*) and the $y_1, \ldots, y_n$ in (8*) are to be considered as given. We have, therefore, to solve (3)—(6), (7) and (8) for x_i, y_j.

5. Let X' be a set of variables $(x'_1, \ldots, x'_m)$ fulfilling the analoga of (3), (5) :

$$x'_i \geqq 0, \ldots\ldots\ldots\ldots \text{(3′)} \qquad \sum_{i=1}^{m} x'_i > 0, \ldots\ldots\ldots\ldots \text{(5′)}$$

and let Y' be a series of variables $(y'_i, \ldots, y'_n)$ fulfilling the analoga of (4), (6) :

$$y'_j \geqq 0, \ldots\ldots\ldots\ldots \text{(4′)} \qquad \sum_{j=1}^{n} y'_j > 0, \ldots\ldots\ldots\ldots \text{(6′)}$$

Let, furthermore,

$$\phi(X'_i, Y'_i) = \frac{\sum_{i=1}^{m} \sum_{j=1}^{n} b_{ij} \, x'_i \, y'_j}{\sum_{i=1}^{m} \sum_{j=1}^{n} a_{ij} \, x'_i \, y'_j} \quad \ldots\ldots\ldots\ldots\ldots\ldots \text{(12)}$$

Let $X = (x_1, \ldots, x_m)$, $Y = (y_1, \ldots, y_n)$ the (hypothetical) solution, $X' = (x'_i, \ldots, x'_m)$, $Y' = (y'_1, \ldots, y'_n)$ to be freely variable, but in such a way that (3)—(6) and (3')—(6') respectively are fulfilled; then it is easy to verify that (7*) and (8*) can be formulated as follows:

$\phi(X, Y')$ assumes its minimum value for Y' if $Y' = Y$......(7**).

$\phi(X', Y)$ assumes its maximum value for X' if $X' = X$......(8**).

The question of a solution of (3)—(8') becomes a question of a solution of (7**), (8**) and can be formulated as follows:

(*) *Consider* (X', Y') *in the domain bounded by* (3')—(6'). *To find a saddle point* $X' = X$, $Y' = Y$, *i.e. where* (X, Y') *assumes its minimum value for* Y', *and at the same time* (X', Y) *its maximum value for* Y'.

From (7), (7*), (10) and (8), (8*), (11) respectively, follows:

$$a = \frac{\sum_{j=1}^{n}\left[\sum_{i=1}^{m} b_{ij}\, x_i\right] y_j}{\sum_{j=1}^{n}\left[\sum_{i=1}^{m} a_{ij}\, x_i\right] y_j} = \phi(x, y) \text{ and } \beta = \frac{\sum_{i=1}^{m}\left[\sum_{j=1}^{n} b_{ij}\, y_j\right] x_i}{\sum_{i=1}^{m}\left[\sum_{j=1}^{n} a_{ij}\, y_j\right] x_i} = \phi(x, y)$$

respectively.

Therefore:

(**) *If our problem can be solved, i.e. if* $\phi(X', Y')$ *has a saddle point* $X' = X$, $Y' = Y$ *(see above), then*:

$a = \beta = \phi(X,Y) =$ *the value at the saddle point*............(13)

6. Because of the homogeneity of $\phi(X', Y')$ (in X', Y', i.e. in $x', \ldots, x_m'$ and $y_1', \ldots y_m'$) our problem remains unaffected if we substitute the normalisations

$$\sum_{i=1}^{m} x_i = 1, \ldots\ldots\ldots\ldots (5^*) \qquad \sum_{j=1}^{n} y_j = 1, \ldots\ldots\ldots\ldots (6^*)$$

for (5'), (6') and correspondingly for (5), (6). Let S be the X' set described by:

$$x_i' \geqq 0, \ldots\ldots\ldots\ldots (3') \qquad \sum_{i=1}^{m} x_i' = 1, \ldots\ldots\ldots\ldots (5^*)$$

and let T be the Y' set described by:

$$y_j' \geqq 0, \ldots\ldots\ldots\ldots (4') \qquad \sum_{j=1}^{n} y_j' = 1, \ldots\ldots\ldots\ldots (6^*)$$

(S, T are simplices of, respectively, $m - 1$ and $n - 1$ dimensions).

In order to solve[1] we make use of the simpler formulation (7*), (8*) and combine these with (3), (4), (5*), (6*) expressing the fact that $X = (x_1, \ldots, x_m)$ is in S and $Y = (y_1, \ldots, y_n)$ in T.

7. We shall prove a slightly more general lemma: Let R_m be the m-dimensional

[1] The question whether our problem has a solution is oddly connected with that of a problem occurring in the Theory of Games dealt with elsewhere. (Math. Annalen, 100, 1928, pp. 295–320, particularly pp. 305 and 307–311). The problem there is a special case of (*) and is solved here in a new way through our solution of (*) (see below). In fact, if $a_{ij} \equiv 1$, then $\sum_{i=1}^{m} \sum_{j=1}^{n} a_{ij}\, x'_i\, y'_j = 1$ because of (5*), (6*). Therefore $\phi(X', Y') = \sum_{i=1}^{m} \sum_{j=1}^{n} b_{ij}\, x'_i\, y'_j$, and thus our (*) coincides with loc. cit., p. 307. (Our $\phi(X', Y')$, b_{ij}, x'_i, y'_j, m, n here correspond to $h(\xi, \eta)$, a_{pq}, ξ_p, η_q, $M + 1$, $N + 1$ there).

It is, incidentally, remarkable that (*) does not lead—as usual—to a simple maximum or minimum problem, the possibility of a solution of which would be evident, but to a problem of the saddle point or minimum-maximum type, where the question of a possible solution is far more profound.

space of all points $X = (x_1, \ldots, x_m)$, R_n the n-dimensional space of all points $Y = (y_1, \ldots, y_n)$, R_{m+n} the $m + n$ dimensional space of all points $(X, Y) = (x_1, \ldots x_m, y_1, \ldots, y_n)$.

A set (in R_m or R_n or R_{m+n}) which is *not empty, convex closed and bounded* we call a set C.

Let S°, T° be sets C in R_m and R_n respectively and let $S^\circ \times T^\circ$ be the set of all (X, Y) (in R_{m+n}) where the range of X is S° and the range of Y is T°. Let V, W be two closed subsets of $S^\circ \times T^\circ$. For every X in S° let the set $Q(X)$ of all Y with (X, Y) in V be a set C; for each Y in T° let the set $P(Y)$ of all X with (X, Y) in W be a set C. Then the following lemma applies.

Under the above assumptions, V, W have (at least) one point in common.

Our problem follows by putting $S^\circ = S$, $T^\circ = T$ and $V =$ the set of all $(X, Y) = (x_1, \ldots, x_m, y_1, \ldots, y_n)$ fulfilling (7*), $W =$ the set of all $(X, Y) = (x_1, \ldots, x_m, y_1, \ldots, y_n)$ fulfilling (8*). It can be easily seen that V. W are closed and that the sets $S^\circ = S$, $T^\circ = T$, $Q(X)$, $P(Y)$ are all simplices, i.e. sets C. The common points of these V, W are, of course, our required solutions $(X, Y) = (x_1, \ldots, x_m, y_1, \ldots, y_m)$.

8. To prove the above lemma let S°, T°, V, W be as described before the lemma.

First, consider V. For each X of S° we choose a point $Y^\circ(X)$ out of $Q(X)$ (e.g. the centre of gravity of this set). It will not be possible, generally, to choose $Y^\circ(X)$ as a continuous function of X. Let $\epsilon > 0$; we define:

$$w^\epsilon(X, X') = \text{Max.}\left(0, 1 - \frac{1}{\epsilon}\text{ distance }(X, X')\right) \quad \ldots\ldots\ldots\ldots \quad (14)$$

Now let $Y^\epsilon(X)$ be the centre of gravity of the $Y^\circ(X')$ with (relative) weight function $w^\epsilon(X, X')$ where the range of X' is S°. I.e. if $Y^\circ(X) = (y_1^\circ(x), \ldots, y_n^\circ(x))$, $Y^\epsilon(X) = (y_1^\epsilon(x), \ldots, y_n^\epsilon(x))$, then:

$$y_j^\epsilon(X) = \int_{S^\circ} w^\epsilon(X, X')\, y_j^\circ(X')\, dX' \Big/ \int_{S^\circ} w^\epsilon(X, X')\, dX', \ldots. \quad (15)$$

We derive now a number of properties of $Y^\epsilon(X)$ (valid for all $\epsilon > 0$):

(*i*) $Y^\epsilon(X)$ is in T°. Proof: $Y^\circ(X')$ is in $Q(X')$ and therefore in T°, and since $Y^\epsilon(X)$ is a centre of gravity of points $Y^\circ(X')$ and T° is convex, $Y^\epsilon(X)$ also is in T°.

(*ii*) $Y^\epsilon(X)$ is a continuous function of X (for the whole range of S°). Proof: it is sufficient to prove this for each $y_j^\epsilon(X)$. Now $w^\epsilon(X, X')$ is a continuous function of X, X' throughout; $\int_{S^\circ} w^\epsilon(X, X')\, dX'$ is always > 0, and all $y_j^\circ(X)$ are bounded (being co-ordinates of the bounded set S°). The continuity of the $y_j^\epsilon(X)$ follows, therefore, from (15).

(*iii*) For each $\delta > 0$ there exists an $\epsilon_0 = \epsilon_0(\delta) > 0$ such that the distance of each point $(X, Y^{\epsilon_0}(X))$ from V is $< \delta$. Proof: assume the contrary. Then there must exist a $\delta > 0$ and a sequence of $\epsilon_\nu > 0$ with $\lim_{\nu \to \infty} \epsilon_\nu = 0$ such that for every $\nu = 1, 2, \ldots$ there exists a X_ν in S° for which the distance $(X_\nu, Y^{\epsilon_\nu}(X_\nu))$ would be $\geq \delta$. A fortiori $Y^{\epsilon_\nu}(X_\nu)$ is at a distance $\geq \frac{\delta}{2}$ from every $Q(X')$, with a distance $(X_\nu, X') \leq \frac{\delta}{2}$.

All X_ν, $\nu = 1, 2, \ldots$, are in S° and have therefore a point of accumulation X^* in S°; from which follows that there exists a subsequence of X_ν, $\nu = 1, 2, \ldots$, converging towards X^* for which distance $(X_\nu, X^*) \leq \frac{\delta}{2}$ always applies. Substituting this subsequence for the ϵ_ν, X_ν, we see that we are justified in assuming: $\lim X_\nu = X^*$, distance $(X_\nu, X^*) \leqq \frac{\delta}{2}$. Therefore we may put $X' = X^*$ for every $\nu = 1, 2, \ldots$, and in consequence we have always $Y^{\epsilon_\nu}(X_\nu)$ at a distance $\geqq \frac{\delta}{2}$ from $Q(X^*)$.

$Q(X^*)$ being convex, the set of all points with a distance $< \frac{\delta}{2}$ from $(Q(X^*)$ is also convex. Since $Y^{\epsilon_\nu}(X_\nu)$ does not belong to this set, and since it is a centre of gravity of points $Y^\circ(X')$ with distance $(X_\nu, X') \leqq \epsilon_\nu$ (because for distance $(X_\nu, X') > \epsilon_\nu$, $w^{\epsilon_\nu}(X_\nu, X') = 0$ according to (14)), not all of these points belong to the set under discussion. Therefore: there exists a $X' = X_\nu$ for which the distance $(X_\nu, X'_\nu) \leqq \epsilon_\nu$ and where the distance between $Y^\circ(X'_\nu)$ and $Q(X^*)$ is $\geqq \frac{\delta}{2}$.

Lim $X_\nu = X^*$, lim distance $(X_\nu, X'_\nu) = 0$, and therefore lim $X'_\nu = X^*$. All $Y^\circ(Y_\nu)$ belong to T° and have therefore a point of accumulation Y^*. In consequence, (X^*, Y^*) is a point of accumulation of the $(X_\nu, Y^\circ(X_\nu))$ and since they all belong to V, (X^*, Y^*) belongs to V too. Y^* is therefore in $Q(X^*)$. Now the distance of every $Y^\circ(Y_\nu)$ including from $Q(X^*)$ is $\geqq \frac{\delta}{2}$. This is a contradiction, and the proof is complete.

(*i*)—(*iii*) together assert: for every $\delta > 0$ there exists a continuous mapping $Y_\delta(X)$ of S° on to a subset of T° where the distance of every point $(X, Y_\delta(X))$ from V is $< \delta$. (Put $Y_\delta(X) = Y^\epsilon(X)$ with $\epsilon = \epsilon_0 = \epsilon_0(\delta)$).

9. Interchanging S° and T°, and V and W we obtain now: for every $\delta > 0$ there exists a continuous mapping $X_\delta(Y)$ of T° on to a subset of S° where the distance of every point $(X_\delta(Y), Y)$ from W is $< \delta$.

On putting $f_\delta(X) = X_\delta(Y_\delta(X))$, $f_\delta(X)$ is a continuous mapping of S° on to a subset of S°. Since S° is a set C, and therefore topologically a simplex[1] we can use L. E. J. Brouwer's Fix-point Theorem[2]; $f_\delta(X)$ has a fix-point. I.e., there exists a X^δ in S° for which $X^\delta = f_\delta(X^\delta) = X_\delta(Y_\delta(X^\delta))$. Let $Y^\delta = Y_\delta(X^\delta)$, then we have $X^\delta = X_\delta(Y^\delta)$. Consequently, the distances of the point (X^δ, Y^δ) in R_{m+n} both from V and from W are $< \delta$. The distance of V from W is therefore $< 2\delta$. Since this is valid for every $\delta > 0$, the distance between V and W is $= 0$. Since V, W are closed and bounded, they must have at least one common point. This proves our lemma completely.

10. We have solved (7^*), (8^*) of paragraph 4 as well as the equivalent problem $(^*)$ of paragraph 5 and the original task of paragraph 3: the solution of (3)—(8'). If the x_i, y_j (which were called X, Y in paragraphs 7—9) are determined, α, β follow from (13) in $(^{**})$ of paragraph 5. In particular, $\alpha = \beta$.

We have emphasised in paragraph 4 already that there may be several solutions x_i, y_j (i.e. X, Y); we shall proceed to show that there exists only one value of α (i.e. of β). In fact, let X_1, Y_1, α_1, β_1 and X_2, Y_2, α_2, β_2 be two solutions. From (7^{**}), (8^{**}) and (13) follows:

$$\alpha_1 = \beta_1 = \phi(X_1, Y_1) \leqq \phi(X_1, Y_2),$$
$$\alpha_2 = \beta_2 = \phi(X_2, Y_2) \geqq \phi(X_1, Y_2),$$

therefore $\alpha_1 = \beta_1 \leqq \alpha_2 = \beta_2$. For reasons of symmetry $\alpha_2 = \beta_2 \leqq \alpha_1 = \beta_1$, therefore $\alpha_1 = \beta_1 = \alpha_2 = \beta_2$.

[1] Regarding these as well as other properties of convex sets used in this paper, c.f., e.g. Alexandroff and H. Hopf, *Topologie*, vol. I, J. Springer, Berlin, 1935, pp. 598–609.

[2] Cf., e.g. 1 c, footnote 1, p. 480.

We have shown:

At least one solution X, Y, α, β exists. For all solutions:

$$\alpha = \beta = \phi\ (X,\ Y) \qquad (13)$$

and these have the same numerical value for all solutions, in other words: The interest factor and the coefficient of expansion of the economy are equal and uniquely determined by the technically possible processes $P_1, \ldots, P_m$.

Because of (13), $\alpha > 0$, but may be $\gtreqless 1$. One would expect $\alpha > 1$, but $\alpha \leqq 1$ cannot be excluded in view of the generality of our formulation: processes $P_1, \ldots, P_m$ may really be *unproductive.*

11. In addition, we shall characterise α in two independent ways.

Firstly, let us consider a state of the economy possible on purely technical considerations, expanding with factor α' per unit of time. I.e., for the intensities $x_1, \ldots, x_m$ applies:

$$x_i \geqq 0 \qquad (3') \qquad\qquad \sum_{i=1}^{m} x_i' > 0 \qquad (5') \text{ and}$$

$$\alpha' \sum_{i=1}^{m} a_{ij}\ x_i' \leqq \sum_{i=1}^{m} b_{ij}\ x_i' \qquad (7'')$$

We are neglecting prices here altogether. Let x_i, y_j, $\alpha = \beta$ be a solution of our original problem (3)—(8′) in paragraph 3. Multiplying (7″) by y_j and adding $\sum_{j=1}^{n}$ we obtain:

$$\alpha' \sum_{i=1}^{m} \sum_{j=1}^{n} a_{ij}\ x_i'\ y_j \leqq \sum_{i=1}^{m} \sum_{j=1}^{n} b_{ij}\ x_i'\ y_j,$$

and therefore $\alpha' \leqq \phi\ (X',\ Y)$. Because of (8**) and (13) in paragraph 5, we have:

$$\alpha' \leqq \phi\ (X',\ Y) \leqq \phi\ (X,\ Y) = \alpha = \beta \qquad (15).$$

Secondly, let us consider a system of prices where the interest factor β' allows of no more profits. I.e. for prices $y_1', \ldots y'_n$ applies:

$$y'_j \geqq 0, \qquad (4') \qquad\qquad \sum_{j=1}^{n} y'_j > 0, \qquad (6') \text{ and}$$

$$\beta' \sum_{j=1}^{n} a_{ij}\ y'_j \geqq \sum_{j=1}^{n} b_{ij}\ y'_j \qquad (8'')$$

Hereby we are neglecting intensities of production altogether. Let x_i, y_j, $\alpha = \beta$ as above. Multiplying (8″) by x_i and adding $\sum_{i=1}^{m}$ we obtain:

$$\beta' \sum_{i=1}^{m} \sum_{j=1}^{n} a_{ij}\ x_i\ y'_j \leqq \sum_{i=1}^{m} \sum_{j=1}^{n} b_{ij}\ x_i\ y'_j$$

and therefore $\beta' \geqq \phi\ (X,\ Y')$. Because of (7**) and (13) in paragraph 5, we have:

$$\beta' \geqq \phi\ (X,\ Y') \geqq \phi\ (X,\ Y) = \alpha = \beta \qquad (16)$$

These two results can be expressed as follows:

The greatest (purely technically possible) factor of expansion α' of the whole economy is $\alpha' = \alpha = \beta$, neglecting prices.

The lowest interest factor β' at which a profitless system of prices is possible is $\beta' = \alpha = \beta$, neglecting intensities of production.

Note that these characterisations are possible only on the basis of our knowledge that solutions of our original problem exist—without themselves directly referring to this problem. Furthermore, the equality of the maximum in the first form and the minimum in the second can be proved only on the basis of the existence of this solution.

Princeton, N.J. J. v. NEUMANN.

[21]

ECONOMIC STRUCTURE, PATH, POLICY, AND PREDICTION

By JACOB MARSCHAK
Cowles Commission for Research in Economics

I. *Policy and Prediction*

1. Knowledge is called useful if it helps to choose the *best policy* (action).

2. Best policy depends on (a) the things which one values as goals (e.g., for a firm, profit; for a government, national income, or budget surplus, etc.); (b) noncontrolled conditions (e.g., for a firm, weather and government policy; for a government, weather). The best policy is an action that maximizes *a*, given *b*.

3. To choose the best policy, it is necessary to predict (a) the effect of alternative policies under any given noncontrolled conditions; (b) the future noncontrolled conditions.

4. Thus, all useful knowledge implies prediction; and knowledge useless at one time may become useful later when new goals and conditions present themselves.

5. In human affairs (but also in large parts of technology), to predict is, in general, to estimate, for given conditions and for a given probability level, a probable range of the results of a given policy. This range is wide if the observations are few or subject to large errors, or if structural relations (see II) are subject to large random disturbances.

II. *Stochastic Economic Structure and Path*

6. The probabilistic character of economic prediction is due to the chance ("stochastic") character of economic *structural relations*.

7. Each of the structural relations describes either (a) human behavior (of a specified group of people), e.g., consumers' demand depends on their current and past income, assets, prices and on a "random disturbance," the latter being the aggregate effect of numerous, separately insignificant factors; or (b) technology, e.g., crops depend on acreage, labor, fertilizers, humidity, and a random disturbance; or (c) legal rules, e.g., price ceilings, tax laws, bank reserve regulations. Economic structure is fully described by these relations provided the character of the random disturbances (their variances, covariances) is given.

8. The number of structural relations must equal the number of economic (or nonautonomous) variables. In addition, structural relations contain noneconomic (or autonomous) variables. At any time, the

probable range of values which an economic variable can take depends on the following conditions: (a) the economic structure; (b) the values of noneconomic variables.

9. Conditions can be noncontrolled (see 2 and 3 above) or controlled. Policies and controlled conditions are identical. Thus a policy fixes either some of the structural relations, or some of the noneconomic variables. However, certain government actions may lie outside of government control. For example, certain parts of the budget (interest on national debt) are determined by past values of certain variables; and tax rates may reflect political shifts which, in turn, are partly determined by economic conditions at or before election time. Such nonautonomous government actions will not be classified as policies; and relations stating what determines such actions may have to be included among structural relations (possibly using information gathered by political scientists). On the other hand, government policy may consist in deliberately invalidating such relations of the past and in fixing autonomously variables that were previously governed by structure.

The deliberate introduction of "automatisms" into the economic structure is a particular kind of policy; for example, adopting the legal rule that a change of level of employment or prices by given amounts should be followed by a certain change (stated in advance) in tax rates or public expenditures, with the object of stabilizing employment or prices; or the Bank of England's old rule to raise discount rate when gold flows out.

10. The path which an economic variable follows through time depends therefore on (a) economic structure and (b) on noneconomic variables.

Depending on the character of random disturbances the probable range of deviations from the most probable path will be larger or smaller; the most probable path may show *oscillations* if some of the structural relations are dynamic, e.g., if they contain time-lags or rates of change or acceleration—as in the case of "cobwebs."

III. *The Need for Structural Estimation*

11. Predictions for a future period, based on observations during a past period, are of different kinds according to whether both or one or none of the types of conditions 8 *a, b* changes within and between the two periods.

12. In particular, if structure is known to remain in the future what it was in the past, and if the noneconomic variables have constant values through both periods, the path of each variable would be predictable from the past, apart from random disturbances. In the pres-

ence of random disturbances, the problem is analogous to that of weather prediction.

13. If structure is known to be retained but the noneconomic variables have assumed and are going to assume changing though known values, it is possible to estimate for each current economic variable its dependence ("regression") on all noneconomic ones and on the past ("lagged") economic ones, and to apply this relation to the future. One can thus estimate the effect of policies that consist in controlling certain variables (tax rates, bank reserve ratios).

14. Finally, if structure is known to change in a given way, the prediction of the effect of this change requires the estimation of the original structure. In this case the study of past relations 7 *a, b, c,* is necessary.

15. Case 14 applies also with regard to the particular policy of introducing "automatisms" (see 9 above) of the most effective kind. For example, to fix in advance the best possible schedule relating tax rates to the unemployment and prices of the previous month, it is necessary to know the lags and elasticities in the consumption equation and in other structural relations at a time when no such legal schedules were in operation. Only when such new device has operated long enough can structural estimation be replaced by the more "mechanical" type of predictions described in 12 and 13.

IV. *Economic Theory, Statistics, and Mathematics*

16. The statistical estimation of the structural relations 7 *a, b, c* is the "filling of empty boxes of economic theory." The theory is a set of hypotheses. Most of these hypotheses state which variables enter which structural equations, or state certain inequalities (e.g., regarding the signs or relative sizes of certain elasticities). They are based, essentially, on experience independent of the material which is to be used in estimation. This experience includes statements on rational (i.e., utility-maximizing) behavior and on deviations from it, on a plausible psychology of anticipations, on technological data, etc.

17. Economic theory is useful in the case 14 and useless in the cases 12 and 13. It can be presumed, however, that cases 12 and 13 seldom occur in practice. In particular, any policy that changes one or more of the structural relations of the past, gives rise to case 14, and necessitates structural estimation for prediction purposes. Structural estimation may seem useless until a structural change is expected or intended: it comes in very useful then. Thus practice requires theory.

18. All the foregoing statements are concerned with the logic of economic knowledge and its uses. This logic is the same whether or not mathematical symbols are used. However, mathematical presentation is of great help in testing the internal consistency of a theory (see 8 on

the number of relations and variables); and it is hardly avoidable when the appropriate estimation methods are to be chosen and applied.

19. After stating the hypotheses about the structure, one may find that a certain collection of data will permit prediction only in the form of such a wide range of values as to make it useless for policy choice (since a wide range of policies will appear to yield equally good results). For this, mathematics cannot be blamed; it will merely reveal what otherwise might remain concealed. Mathematics does not suppress any information available for other methods; and it makes clearer when and how additional information must be used (e.g., extending time series, supplementing them by cross-section data including attitude surveys, etc.).

[22]

A MODEL OF THE TRADE CYCLE

1. THE following pages do not attempt to put forward any "new" theory of the Trade Cycle. The theory here presented is essentially similar to all those theories which explain the Trade Cycle as a result of the combined operation of the so-called "multiplier" and the investment demand function as, *e.g.*, the theories put forward in recent years by Mr. Harrod and Mr. Kalecki.[1] The purpose of the present paper is to show, by means of a simple diagrammatic apparatus, what are the necessary and sufficient assumptions under which the combined operation of these two forces inevitably gives rise to a cycle.

2. The basic principle underlying all these theories may be sought in the proposition—a proposition that is really derived from Mr. Keynes' *General Theory*, although not stated there in this form—that economic activity always *tends* towards a level where Savings and Investment are equal. Here the terms Savings and Investment are used, of course, in a sense different from the one according to which they are always and necessarily equal—in the *ex-ante*, and not the *ex-post* sense. Investment *ex-ante* is the value of the *designed* increments of stocks of all kinds (*i.e.*, the value of the net addition to stocks plus the value of the aggregate output of fixed equipment), which differs from Investment *ex-post* by the value of the undesigned accretion (or decumulation) of stocks. Savings *ex-ante* is the amount people intend to save—*i.e.*, the amount they actually *would* save if they correctly forecast their incomes. Hence *ex-ante* and *ex-post* Saving can differ only in so far as there is an unexpected change in the amount of income earned.

If *ex-ante* Investment exceeds *ex-ante* Saving, *either ex-post* Investment will fall short of *ex-ante* Investment, *or ex-post* Saving will exceed *ex-ante* Saving; and both these discrepancies will induce an expansion in the level of activity. If *ex-ante* Investment falls short of *ex-ante* Saving *either ex-post* Investment will exceed *ex-ante* Investment, *or ex-post* Saving will fall short of *ex-ante* Saving, and both these discrepancies will induce a contraction. This must be so, because a reduction in *ex-post* Saving as compared with *ex-ante* Saving will make consumers spend less on consumers' goods, an excess of *ex-post* Investment over *ex-ante*

[1] Harrod, *The Trade Cycle;* Kalecki, "A Theory of the Business Cycle," *Review of Economic Studies*, February 1937, reprinted in *Essays in Theory of Economic Fluctuations.*

Investment (implying as it does the accretion of unwanted stocks) will cause entrepreneurs to spend less on entrepreneurial goods; while the total of activity is always determined by the sum of consumers' expenditures and entrepreneurs' expenditures. Thus a discrepancy between *ex-ante* Saving and *ex-ante* Investment must induce a change in the level of activity which proceeds until the discrepancy is removed.

3. The magnitudes of both *ex-ante* Saving and *ex-ante* Investment are themselves functions of the level of activity, and both vary positively with the level of activity. Thus if we denote the level of activity (measured in terms of employment) by x, both S and I (*ex-ante* Savings and Investment) will be single-valued functions of x [1] and both $\frac{dS}{dx}$ and $\frac{dI}{dx}$ will be positive. The first of these expresses the basic principle of the "multiplier" (that the marginal propensity to consume is less than unity),[2] and the second denotes the assumption that the demand for capital goods will be greater the greater the level of production.[3]

If we regard the $S(x)$ and $I(x)$ functions as *linear*, as in the absence of further information one is inclined to do, we have two possibilities :—

(i) $\frac{dI}{dx}$ exceeds $\frac{dS}{dx}$, in which case, as shown by Fig. 1,[4] there can be only a single position of unstable equilibrium, since above

[1] S and I are, of course, both functions of the rate of interest in addition to the level of activity. But the rate of interest, at any rate in the first approximation, could itself be regarded as a single valued function of the level of activity, and thus its influence incorporated in the $S(x)$ and $I(x)$ functions. (It is not necessary to assume, in order that $\frac{dI}{dx}$ should be positive, that the rates of interest —short and long term—are *constant*. We can allow for *some* variation as the rates of interest, to be associated with a change in investment and incomes, provided this variation is not large enough to prevent the change in incomes altogether. All that we are excluding here is a banking policy which so regulates interest rates as to keep the level of incomes constant.)

[2] $\frac{dS}{dx}$ is, of course, the reciprocal of Mr. Keynes' investment multiplier, which is defined as $\frac{1}{1-\frac{dC}{dx}}$, where $\frac{dC}{dx} = 1 - \frac{dS}{dx}$.

[3] This assumption should not be confused with the "acceleration principle" (of Prof. J. M. Clark and others), which asserts that the demand for capital goods is a function of the *rate of change* of the level of activity, and not of the level of activity itself. The theory put forward below is thus not based on this "acceleration principle" (the general validity of which is questionable), but on a much simpler assumption—*i.e.*, that an increase in the current level of profits increases investment demand.

[4] In Fig. 1, as in all subsequent diagrams, the level of activity is measured along Ox and the corresponding value of *ex-ante* Investment and Saving along Oy.

the equilibrium point $I > S$, and thus activity tends to expand, below it $S > I$, and hence it tends to contract. If the S and I functions were of this character, the economic system would always be rushing either towards a state of hyper-inflation with full employment, or towards a state of complete collapse with zero employment, with no resting-place in between. Since recorded experience does not bear out such dangerous instabilities, this possibility can be dismissed.

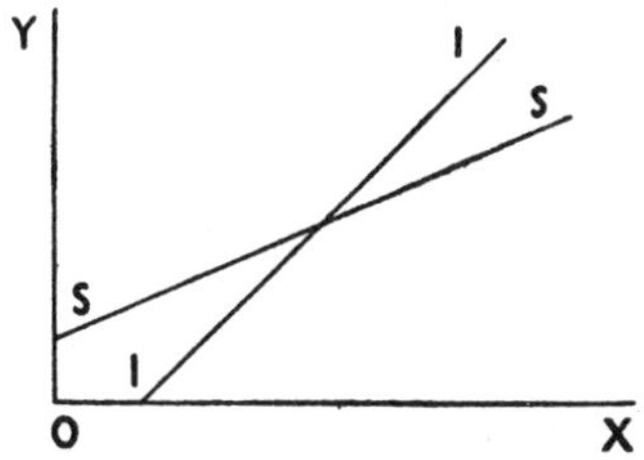

FIG. 1.

(ii) $\frac{dS}{dx}$ exceeds $\frac{dI}{dx}$, in which case, as shown in Fig. 2, there will be a single position of stable equilibrium. (This, I believe, is the assumption implied in Mr. Keynes' theory of employment.) If the economic system were of this nature, any disturbance, originating either on the investment side or on the savings side,

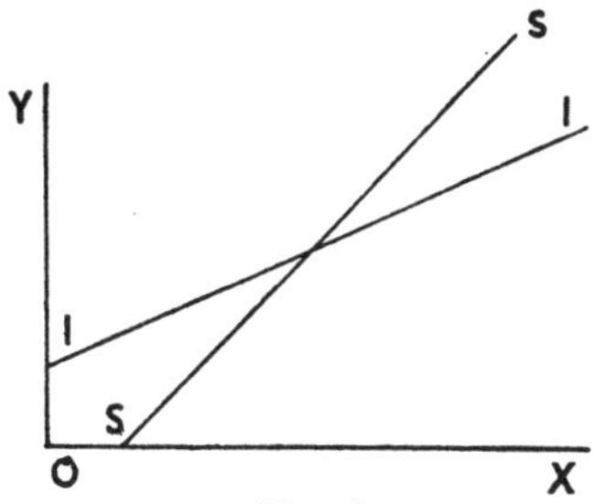

FIG. 2.

would be followed by the re-establishment of a new equilibrium, with a stable level of activity.[1] Hence this assumption fails in the opposite direction: it assumes *more* stability than the real world appears, in fact, to possess. Also, if there is any justification in the contention of the "accelerationists," the possibility of $\frac{dI}{dx}$

[1] Except in so far as the existence of time-lags of adjustment might prevent, on certain assumptions, the new equilibrium from being reached. Cf. Appendix below.

being greater than $\frac{dS}{dx}$, at any rate for certain values of x, cannot be excluded. For $\frac{dI}{dx}$ could be many times greater than dx, while $\frac{dS}{dx}$ can never be more than a fraction of dx.

4. Since thus neither of these two assumptions can be justified, we are left with the conclusion that the $I(x)$ and $S(x)$ functions cannot both be linear, at any rate over the entire range. And, in fact, on closer examination, there are good reasons for supposing that neither of them is linear.

(*a*) In the case of the investment function it is probable that $\frac{dI}{dx}$ will be *small*, both for low and for high levels of x, relatively to its " normal " level. It will be small for low levels of activity

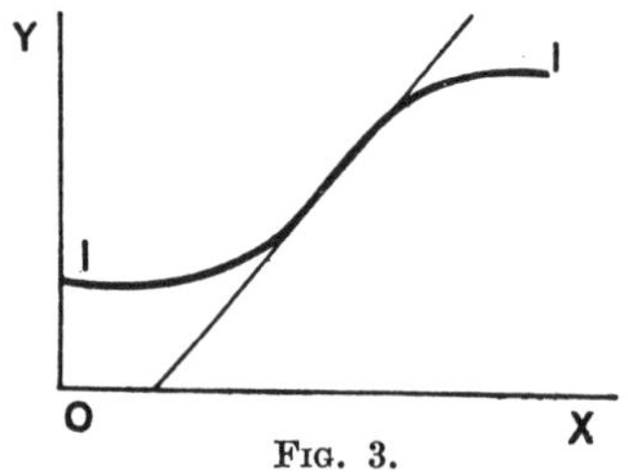

FIG. 3.

because when there is a great deal of surplus capacity, an increase in activity will not induce entrepreneurs to undertake additional construction : the rise in profits will not stimulate investment. (At the same time, the level of investment will not be zero, for there is always some investment undertaken for long-period development purposes which is independent of current activity.) But it will also be small for unusually high levels of activity, because rising costs of construction, increasing costs and increasing difficulty of borrowing will dissuade entrepreneurs from expanding still faster—at a time when they already have large commitments. Hence, given some " normal " value of $\frac{dI}{dx}$, appropriate for " normal " levels of activity, the $I(x)$ function will deviate from linearity in the manner suggested in Fig. 3.

(*b*) In the case of the savings function, the situation appears to be exactly the other way round : $\frac{dS}{dx}$ is likely to be relatively *large*, both for low and high levels of activity, as compared with its normal level. When incomes are unusually low, savings are cut drastically, and below a certain level of income they will be negative. When incomes are unusually high, people are likely to save not only a higher amount, but also a larger proportion of their income.[1] These tendencies, for society as a whole, are likely to be reinforced by the fact that when activity is at a low level, an increasing proportion of workers' earnings are paid out of capital funds (in the form of unemployment benefits); while when activity is at a high level, prices will tend to rise relatively to wages, there will be a shift in the distribution of incomes in favour of profits, and thus an increase in the aggregate propensity to save. Hence $\frac{dS}{dx}$ will deviate from its normal level in the manner suggested in Fig. 4.

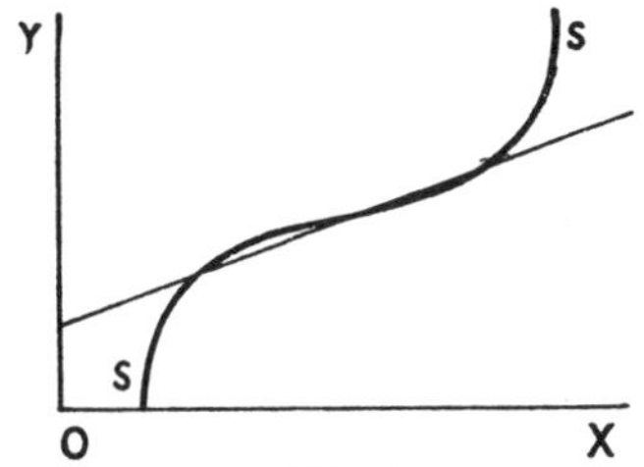

FIG. 4.

In what follows it will be assumed that the two functions conform to these criteria. But, as the reader will note, our analysis would remain valid even if only *one of the two* functions behaved in the manner suggested, while the other was linear.

5. Given these assumptions about the behaviour of the savings and investment functions, and assuming further that the *normal value* of $\frac{dI}{dx}$ is greater than the normal value of $\frac{dS}{dx}$, the situation will be one of multiple equilibria, as shown in Fig. 5. A and B (in the diagram) are both stable positions, for at points below A or B, $I > S$, hence activity tends to expand; above it $S > I$, hence activity tends to contract. C is an unstable position in both directions, and hence not a possible position of equilibrium. The significance of point C is simply that if activity happens to be above C, there will be a process of expansion which will come to a halt at B; if it happens to be below C, there will be a process of contraction until equilibrium is reached at A.

[1] Thus there is something like a "customary standard of living" based on the "normal level" of incomes, and, corresponding to it, there is a certain normal rate of savings. If incomes are much below it, individuals will attempt to maintain their standard of living by consuming capital; if incomes are much above it, they will tend to save a disproportionate amount.

Hence the economic system can reach stability either at a certain high rate of activity or at a certain low rate of activity. There will be a certain depression level and a certain prosperity level at which it offers resistance to further changes in either direction. The key to the explanation of the Trade Cycle is to be found in the fact that each of these two positions is stable only *in the short period*: that as activity continues at either one of these levels, forces gradually accumulate which sooner or later will render that particular position unstable. It is to an explanation of the nature of these forces that we must now turn.

6. Both $S(x)$ and $I(x)$ are "*short-period*" functions—*i.e.*, they assume the total amount of fixed equipment in existence, and hence the amount of real income at any particular level of

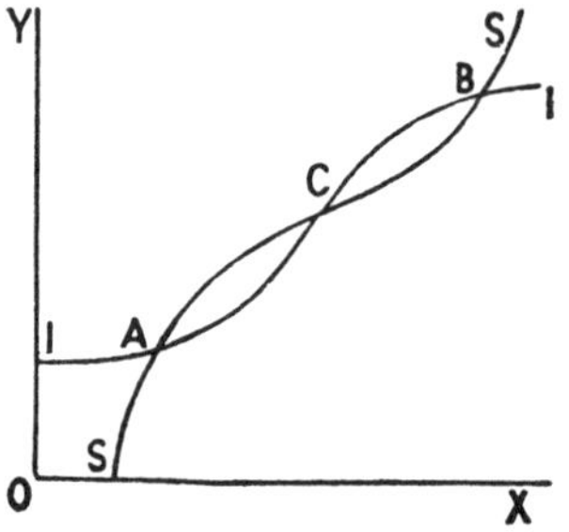

Fig. 5.

activity, as given. As these factors change in time, the S and I curves will shift their position; but according as activity is high or low (equilibrium is at B or at A) they will shift in different ways.

(i) When activity is high (equilibrium at B), the level of investment is high, the total amount of equipment gradually increases, and so, in consequence, the amount of consumers' goods produced at a given level of activity. As a result the S curve gradually shifts upwards (for there will be more consumption, and hence more saving, for any given activity); for the same reason the I curve gradually falls. (The accumulation of capital, by restricting the range of available investment opportunities, will tend to make it fall, while new inventions tend, on the whole, to make it rise. But the first of these factors is bound to be more powerful after a time.) As a result, the position of B is gradually shifted to the left and that of C to the right, thus reducing the level of activity somewhat and bringing B and C nearer to each other (see Fig. 6, "Stage II").

The critical point is reached when, on account of these movements, the *I* and *S* curves become tangential and the points *B* and *C* fall together (" Stage III "). At that point equilibrium becomes unstable in a downward direction, since in the neighbourhood of the point $S > I$ in both directions. The level of activity will now fall rapidly, on account of the excess of *ex-ante* Savings over *ex-ante* Investment, until a new equilibrium is reached at *A* where the position is again stable.[1, 2]

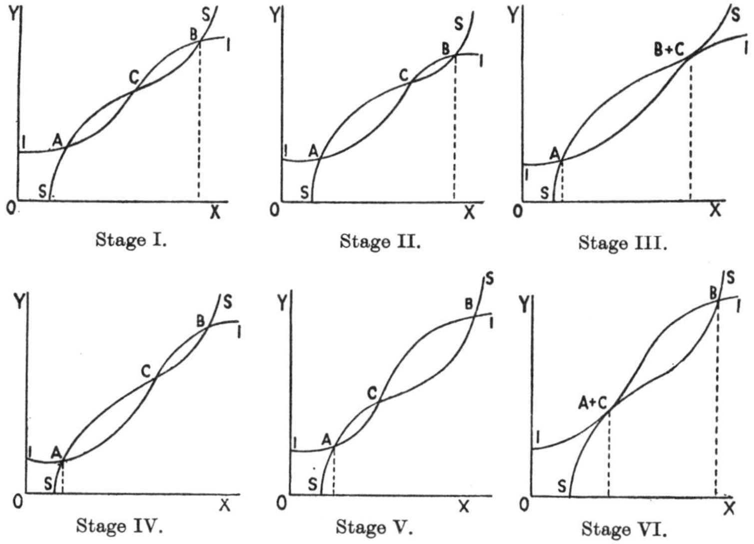

FIG. 6.—THE TRADE CYCLE.

(ii) When activity is low, the movement of the *I* and *S* curves will tend to be in the opposite direction. For if at the level of investment corresponding to *A* investment is not sufficient to cover replacement, so that *net* investment in industrial plant and equipment is negative,[3] investment opportunities gradually

[1] The route followed in the transition from *B* to *A* might be either along the *I* curve or the *S* curve, according to whether *ex-post* Saving is adjusted to *ex-ante* Investment, or *ex-post* Investment to *ex-ante* Saving—*i.e.*, according as the disappointment of expectations occurs on the side of incomes, or in the level of entrepreneurial stocks.

[2] The fall in the rate of activity during the transition need not be very rapid, and may even take some years. This is because both entrepreneurs and consumers take some time to adjust their scale of purchases to their changed rate of earnings. If the process is at all prolonged, the two curves will be back at their " normal " position (as shown in Fig. 5 or " Stage IV " in Fig. 6) by the time point *A* is reached.

[3] It is not necessary, of course, that *total* net investment should be negative, since investment can take forms (such as armaments, etc.) whose construction does not reduce the available opportunities for the future.

accumulate and the I curve will shift upwards; and this tendency is likely to be reinforced by new inventions. For the same reason, the gradual decumulation of capital, in so far as it causes real income per unit of activity to fall, will lower the S curve.[1] These movements cause the position of A to shift to the right and that of C to shift to the left (thus separating B and C and bringing A and C nearer to each other), involving a gradual improvement in the level of activity (Stages IV and V). This will proceed until A and C fall together (the two curves again become tangential), when a new critical situation is reached; the position becomes unstable in an upward direction, since $I > S$ on either side of the equilibrium point; an upward cumulative movement will follow which can only come to rest when position B is reached (Stage VI). Thereafter the curves gradually return to the position shown in Stage I, and the cyclical movement is repeated.

7. The necessary and sufficient assumptions under which the combined operation of the saving and investment functions inevitably generate a cyclical movement which nowhere tends to come to rest, can therefore be set out as follows :—

(1) The "normal value" of $\frac{dI}{dx}$, valid for normal levels of activity, must be *greater* than the corresponding value of $\frac{dS}{dx}$.

(2) The "extreme values" of $\frac{dI}{dx}$, valid for abnormally high or abnormally low levels of activity, must be *smaller* than the corresponding values of $\frac{dS}{dx}$.

(3) The level of investment at the upper equilibrium point must be sufficiently large for the $I(x)$ function to *fall* (in time) relatively to the $S(x)$ function; and at the lower equilibrium point it must be sufficiently small for the $I(x)$ function to *rise* (in time) relatively to the $S(x)$ function. In other words, the position of zero net investment must fall within the limits set by the levels of investment ruling at $B + C$ and $A + C$, in Stage III and Stage VI, respectively.

If condition (1) did not obtain, equilibrium at C (which is in fact the "normal" equilibrium position) would be stable, instead

[1] It is possible that even if net investment is negative, real output per head should gradually rise in time (on account of the introduction of superior or more "capitalistic" processes of production during the depression), as a result of which S would tend to rise rather than fall. But this makes no difference so long as the I curve rises faster than the S curve.

of unstable; equilibrium would tend to get established there, and, once established, the shifts in the I and S curves, due to capital accumulation or decumulation, would merely lead to gradual changes in the level of activity until a position of stationariness is reached; they would not generate cyclical movements. If condition (2) was not satisfied (at any rate as regards *low* levels of activity)[1] the system, as we have seen, would be so unstable that capitalism could not function at all. Finally, if condition (3) did not obtain, the cyclical movements would come to a halt at some stage, owing to a cessation of the movements of the $S(x)$ and $I(x)$ functions.

This is not to suggest that in the absence of these three conditions cyclical phenomena would be altogether impossible. Only they would have to be explained with the aid of different principles; they could not be accounted for by the savings and investment functions alone.

8. In fact, conditions (1) and (2) are almost certain to be satisfied in the real world; doubt could only arise in connection with condition (3). It can be taken for granted, of course, that net investment will be *positive* while equilibrium is at position B; but it is by no means so certain that net investment will be *negative* while equilibrium is at position A.[2] It is quite possible, for example, that savings should fall rapidly at a relatively early stage of the downward movement, so that position A is reached while net investment is still positive. In that case the S and I curves will still move in the same direction as at B, with the result that the position A is gradually shifted to the left, until net investment becomes zero. At that point the movements of the I and S curves will cease; the forces making for expansion or contraction come to a standstill. Alternatively, we might assume that net investment at A is initially negative, but in the course of the gradual improvement, the position of zero net investment is reached before the forces of cumulative expansion could come into operation—*i.e.*, somewhere during Stages IV and V, and *before* the cycle reaches Stage VI. In this case, too, the cyclical movement will get into a deadlock.

[1] It is possible that the point B should be situated *beyond* the position of full employment—*i.e.*, that in the course of the upward movement the state of full employment should be reached before *ex-ante* Savings and Investment reach equality. In that case the upward movement would end in a state of cumulative inflation, which in turn would, sooner or later, be brought to a halt by a rise in interest rates sufficient to push the point B inside the full-employment barrier. From then onwards the cyclical movement would proceed in exactly the same manner as described.

[2] The term " net investment " here is used in the sense defined in § 6 (ii).

Hence the forces making for expansion when we start from a state of depression are not so certain in their operation as the forces making for a down-turn when we start from prosperity; the danger of chronic stagnation is greater than the danger of a chronic boom. A boom, if left to itself, is certain to come to an end; but the depression might get into a position of stationariness, and remain there until external changes (the discovery of new inventions or the opening up of new markets) come to the rescue.

9. The preceding analysis offers also certain indications regarding the determination of the period and the amplitude of the Cycle. The period of the Cycle seems to depend on two time-lags, or rather time-rates of movement: (i) on the rate at which the S and I curves shift at any particular level of investment (this, of course, will vary with the level of investment, and will be faster when investment is high or low, than in the middle); (ii) on the time taken to complete a "cumulative movement"—*i.e.*, the time required for the system to travel from $B + C$ to A or from $A + C$ to B (Stages III and VI).

The second of these factors obviously depends on the velocity with which entrepreneurs and consumers adjust their expectations and thus their buying-plans to unexpected changes in the situation. The first factor, on the other hand, seems to depend on technical data, on the construction period and durability of capital goods. The shorter the construction period, the greater will be the output of capital goods, per unit period, at a given rate of investment; the shorter the life-time of capital goods, the larger will be the percentage addition to total equipment represented by a given output of capital goods. Hence the shorter the construction-period, and the lower the durability, the faster will be the rate of shift of the S and I curves at any given rate of investment; the shorter the length of the Trade Cycle.[1]

As regards the amplitude, this depends on the *shapes* of the I and S curves, which determine the distance between A and B, at their "normal" position (*i.e.*, at Stages I and IV). The amplitude will be all the smaller the shorter the range of activity over which the "normal values" of $\frac{dI}{dx}$ and $\frac{dS}{dx}$ are operative.

[1] If the "capital intensity" of investments varies in the different phases of the Cycle in an *inverse relation* to the rate of investment (*i.e.*, is less in boom periods than in depression periods), this will tend to reduce the period of the Cycle, as compared with a situation where the capital intensity is constant, since it will increase the rate of shift of the S and I curves. Conversely, if capital intensity varied *in direct relation* with the rate of investment, this would lengthen the period. Finally, if capital intensity showed a *steady increase* throughout the Cycle, this would lengthen the boom periods and shorten the depression periods.

Variations in the amplitude of successive cycles, on the other hand, seem to depend entirely on extraneous factors, such as new inventions or secular changes in habits of saving. There appears to be no necessary reason why, in the absence of such factors, the amplitude should be gradually decreasing or vice-versa.[1]

10. Our model should also enable us to throw some light on problems of economic policy. Here I confine myself to two points. (i) It appears that measures taken to combat the depression (through public investment) have much more chance of success if taken at a relatively early stage, or at a relatively late stage, than at the bottom of the depression. If taken early, the problem is merely to prevent that gradual fall in the investment function relatively to the saving function which carries the cycle from Stage II to Stage III. But, once Stage III is passed, nothing can prevent the switch-over from the B-equilibrium to the A-equilibrium, and then the problem becomes one of raising the investment demand schedule sufficiently to lift the position to Stage VI (at which the forces of expansion come into operation). The amount of public investment required to achieve this is obviously much greater in the early phase of the depression (at Stage IV) than in the later phase (at Stage V). Thus just when the depression is at its worst the difficulty of overcoming it is the greatest. (ii) The chances of "evening out" fluctuations by "anti-cyclical" public investment appear to be remote. For if the policy is successful in preventing the downward cumulative movement, it will also succeed in keeping the level of private investment high; and for this very reason the forces making for a down-turn will continue to accumulate, thus making the need for continued public investment greater. Thus, if, on the basis of past experience, the Government Authority contemplates a four years public investment plan, in the belief that thereby it can bridge the gap between one prosperity-period and the next, it is more likely that it might succeed in *postponing* the onset of the

[1] At first sight one might think that this question also depends on *endogenous* factors: that the cycle will be "damped" (amplitude of successive cycles decreasing) if the point of zero net investment is so situated that there will be net capital accumulation over the cycle as a whole, and vice versa. But this is not so. If there is net accumulation over the cycle as a whole (*i.e.*, the accumulation over the boom period exceeds the decumulation during the depression), then, in the absence of extraneous changes, the position B at the corresponding stages of successive cycles will be situated more and more to the left; but the position A will also be situated more to the left, with the result that, though there will be a gradual fall in the average level of activity, there need be no decrease in the deviations around the average. The same holds, *mutatis mutandis*, if there is net decumulation over the cycle as a whole.

depression for four years than that it will prevent its occurrence altogether.[1] If the Trade Cycle is really governed by the forces analysed in this paper, the policy of internal stabilisation must be conceived along different lines.

NICHOLAS KALDOR

London School of Economics.

APPENDIX

It may be interesting to examine the relations of the model here presented to other models of the Trade Cycle based on similar principles. The one nearest to it, I think, is Mr. Kalecki's theory, given in Chap. 6 of his *Essays in the Theory of Economic Fluctuations*. The differences can best be shown by employing the same type of diagram and the same denotation as used by Mr. Kalecki. Let income be measured along OY, and the rate of investment decisions along OD. Let $D_t = \Phi e(Y_t)$ represent the rate of invest-

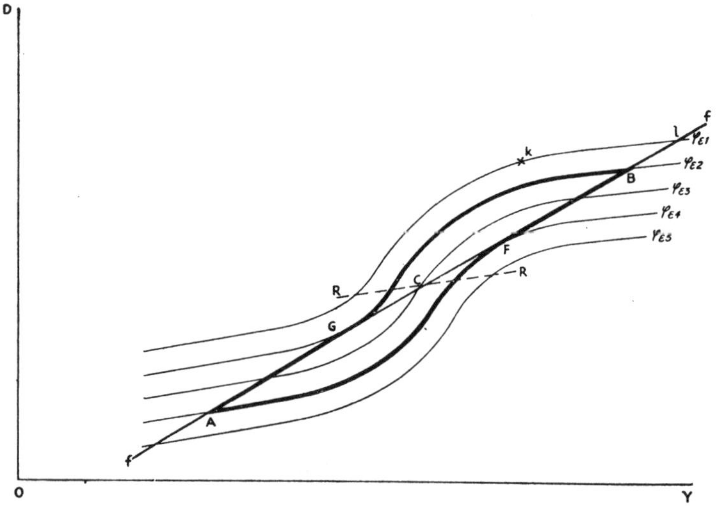

ment decisions at time t, given the quantity of equipment available. Let the family of curves Φe_1 . . . etc., represent this function for different quantities of available equipment, where e_1 represents a *smaller* quantity of equipment than e_2, and so on. Let $Y_t + \tau =$

[1] This argument is strictly valid only for a closed system; it is not valid in the case of a country which receives its cyclical impulses from abroad. For in that case the cyclical variations in the demand for exports can be taken as given irrespective of what the Government is doing; the chronological order of the "lean years" will not be altered by the attempt at suppressing them. Thus a policy of this type is much more likely to be successful in a small country, like Sweden, than in large countries, such as Britain or the United States, which themselves generate the cyclical forces and transmit them to others.

$f(D_t)$ be the level of income at time $t + \tau$ as a function of investment decisions at the time t. This is the same as our savings-function, which, for simplicity, and following Mr. Kalecki, we regard here as a straight line, independent of the amount of equipment. (τ represents the time lag between investment decisions and the corresponding income, which, as Mr. Kalecki has shown, depends partly on the construction-period of capital goods, and partly on the lag between income and consumption.) The meeting-points of Φe curves and the f curve are positions of short-period equilibrium, where Savings=Investment; the equilibrium is stable when the Φe curve cuts the f function from above, it is unstable when it cuts it from below. Let RR represent the locus of points on the Φe curves where the level of investment decisions corresponds to replacement so that *net* investment is zero. This curve is slightly *rising*, from left to right, since the higher the amount of equipment in existence, the greater the amount of investment needed for replacement. The point C represents the position of long period or stationary equilibrium, where Savings=Investment *and* net investment is zero.

Under our assumptions, where $\frac{d\Phi}{dY}$ exceeds $\frac{1}{\frac{df}{dD}}$ for certain values of Y, there must be certain levels of equipment at which the Φ curves cut the f function not once, but three times. In our diagram this will be the case if equipment is greater than e_2 and less than e_4. Given this assumption, and assuming further that the replacement level, *for the critical amounts of equipment*, falls between the limits of stability—*i.e.*, between points F and G in the diagram—the system can never settle down to a stationary equilibrium, but moves around it in a cycle. If we assume that the time-lag τ is small relatively to the time needed to reach successive Φ curves (*i.e.*, relatively to the rate at which the total quantity of equipment is increasing), so that a position of short-period equilibrium can be reached *before* significant changes occur in the amount of equipment in existence, the cyclical movement of the system will be indicated by the trajectory $AGBF$. For if we start from any arbitrary point, such as k, the cumulative forces will increase income and investment decisions until the system reaches l, and thereafter activity will move downwards (owing to the gradual accumulation of equipment) along the f line until it reaches F. At that point equilibrium becomes unstable, and a downward moving cumulative process is set up which lands the system at A. Here investment is less than replacement, and the gradual reduction in available equipment will increase activity until the system reaches G, at which the situation again becomes unstable, an upward cumulative movement follows which lands the system at B. Thus if we start from any point outside the trajectory, the system will move on to it, and the same follows if we start from any point inside. Hence, even if we started from the position of stationary long-period equilibrium (C), the un-stability of the situation there must generate forces which set up a cycle.

It follows, further, that if all the fundamental data which determine the Φ and f functions—*i.e.*, tastes, technique, population, monetary policy, the elasticity of expectations, etc.—remain unchanged, the cycle would continue indefinitely with constant amplitude and period and the trend (the accumulation of capital between successive cycles) would be zero. Hence changes in the nature of successive cycles would have to be explained by dynamic changes.

In Mr. Kalecki's model $\frac{d\Phi}{dY}$ is supposed to be smaller than $\frac{1}{\frac{df}{dD}}$ throughout, hence all his positions of short-period equilibrium are *stable* positions. In this case, on our assumptions, no cycle would be generated at all; the system would gradually approach stationary equilibrium. He assumes, however, that the time-lag between investment decisions and the corresponding income is large relatively to the rate at which the amount of equipment is increasing—*i.e.*, the movements *along* a Φ curve and the movement *between* Φ curves are of comparable speed—in which case the movement toward a stationary equilibrium may " overshoot the mark "—*i.e.*, the rate of investment decisions can continue to fall, even after it is less than what corresponds to replacement, simply because the fall in income lags behind. Thus the introduction of the time-lag between investment decisions and the corresponding income could explain a cyclical movement even if the underlying situation is a stable one; though, in order that this cycle should not be highly damped (*i.e.*, that it should not peter out quickly in the absence of new disturbing factors), it is necessary to suppose (i) that the effect of current investment on total equipment should be relatively large, so that the equipment added during the period of the time-lag has a considerable influence on the rate or profit, and hence on investment decisions; (ii) that the angle enclosed by the f and ϕ functions should be small—*i.e.*, that $\frac{1}{\frac{df}{dD}}$ should but slightly exceed $\frac{d\phi}{dy}$.[1]

Previous attempts at constructing models of the Trade Cycle —such as Mr. Kalecki's or Professor Tinbergen's—have thus mostly been based on the assumption of statically stable situations, where equilibrium would persist if once reached; the existence of the cycle was explained as a result of the operation of certain time-lags which prevented the new equilibrium from being reached, once the old equilibrium, for some external cause, had been disturbed. In this sense all these theories may be regarded as being derived from the " cobweb theorem." The drawback of such explanations is that the existence of an undamped cycle can

[1] Hence the positions of equilibrium in Mr. Kalecki's model, though formally stable, possess only a *low* degree of stability.

be shown only as a result of a happy coincidence, of a particular constellation of the various time-lags and parameters assumed. The introduction of the assumption of unstable positions of equilibrium at and around the replacement level provides, however, as we have seen, an explanation for a cycle of *constant amplitude* irrespective of the particular values of the time-lags and parameters involved. The time-lags are only important here in determining the *period* of the cycle, they have no significance in explaining its existence.

Moreover, with the theories of the Tinbergen–Kalecki type, the amplitude of the cycle depends on the size of the initial shock. Here the amplitude is determined by endogeneous factors and the assumption of " initial shocks " is itself unnecessary.

[23]

Rationing and the Cost of Living Index

1. In the last number of the REVIEW Mr. Rothbarth discussed the problems created by the existence of rationing on index numbers.[1] In this note an alternative method is suggested by which the effect of rationing on the cost of living index might be measured.

2. The problem can be stated as follows. The usual index numbers assume that the goods entering into the index are freely obtainable at the given prices, so that the satisfactions derived from a given income, at the given price system, are maximised. If this is not the case, and expenditure is diverted through rationing, there is an *additional* change in the cost of living (additional to the one indicated by price changes) due to the fact that a given money expenditure on unrationed goods cannot give the same satisfaction as the same expenditure on rationed goods. To obtain the same satisfaction the money expenditure on unrationed goods would therefore have to be higher. In the accompanying diagram rationed goods are measured along OX and unrationed goods along OY. In the absence of rationing, out of the given money income, y would be spent on unrationed goods, and x on rationed goods. Let us suppose that through rationing, the consumption of rationed goods is reduced to x'—prices remaining the same—which involves an expansion of consumption of unrationed goods to y'. Clearly the individual will be worse off than he was before; to be equally well off, the consumption of unrationed goods would have to increase to y''. The difference $y''—y'$ measures, in terms of unrationed goods—or money, if prices are given—the rise in the cost of living due to rationing.

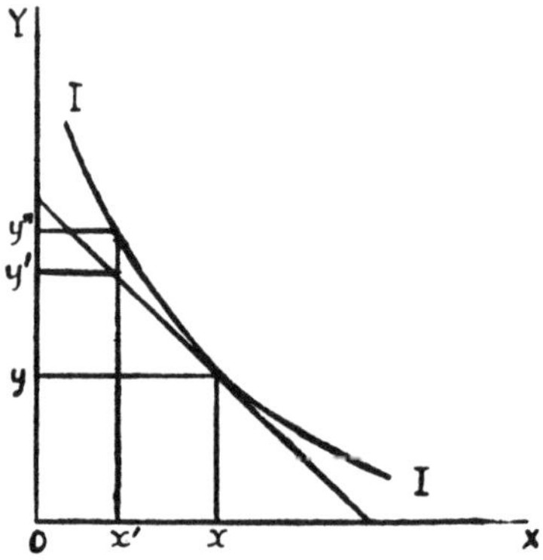

In a system, therefore, where rationing is in force the change in the cost of living, between any two periods, takes two forms: (i) the change due to the change in prices; (ii) the change due to the diversion of expenditure, through rationing. Only the first of these changes is measured by the index numbers currently in use, which, therefore, in times of rationing, necessarily understate the true change in the cost of living.[1] The method we propose attempts to isolate the effects of rationing from the effects of price changes, so that the change due to the former could be added to the latter (as measured by the usual index numbers) to give the total change in the cost of living.

3. The loss of satisfaction through the diversion due to rationing is the consumers' surplus on rationed goods taken as a group. As Marshall has

[1] The Measurement of Changes of Real Income under Conditions of Rationing. The REVIEW OF ECONOMIC STUDIES, February, 1941, p. 100.

[1] Some writers (cf. *The Economist*, May 31st, 1941, p. 731) suggest that they *overstate* it, insofar as rationing reduces the *actual* expenditure on rationed goods. This, however, is due to a wholly erroneous view as to the meaning of index numbers.

shown, if the marginal utility of money can be taken as constant—if, in other words the marginal satisfaction derived from unrationed goods is not reduced on account of the higher expenditure on them—the loss of consumers' surplus is half the difference between the " actual price " and the " free market price " (the price which would be established in a free market for the *given level* of consumption) multiplied by the reduction in consumption due to rationing (i.e. the difference between the actual consumption and what would be consumed in a free market at the " actual price "). It can, therefore, be expressed by the following equation :

$$P = \frac{1}{e} \cdot \frac{r^2}{2} \cdot \frac{E_r}{E_o}$$

where P is the percentage increase in the cost of living due to rationing, e the elasticity of demand for rationed goods taken as a group, r the percentage reduction in consumption due to rationing, and $\frac{E_r}{E_o}$ the expenditure on rationed goods, as a percentage of total expenditure prior to rationing. The formula can, moreover, be further generalised (the Marshallian condition about the constant marginal utility of money dropped) if by e we mean not the elasticity of demand, but the elasticity of substitution between rationed goods and unrationed goods.

4. On the rationing system at present in force in Britain (prior to the introduction of the rationing of clothing) $\frac{E_r}{E_o}$ is about 30 per cent of working-class expenditure (for food expenditure amounted to 45 per cent of the total, according to the 1937 Ministry of Labour budget enquiry, and rationed goods account for about two-thirds[1] of the total food expenditure), while r is about 50 per cent[1] (the average difference between present rations and the per capita consumption according to the same enquiry). e cannot be estimated so easily, but it is possible to fix reasonable limits within which it should fall. The elasticity of demand for *individual* foodstuffs was estimated by Schultz and found to be of the order of magnitude 0.5 to 1. The elasticity of demand for a *group* of foodstuffs (such as all rationed foods) is likely to be less, of course, than the elasticity of demand for individual goods. The *elasticity of substitution* between rationed foodstuffs as a group and all other goods has been estimated by Mr. Leser through a new method[1] and found to be between 0.6 and 0.8. We cannot be far wrong, therefore, if we estimate e as between 0.5 and 0.8. Hence P should be *between* 4.5 *and* 7.5 *per cent.*[2]

[1] This does not take into account goods which have disappeared from the market or are " unofficially rationed."

[1] To be published in the next number of this Review.

[2] This looks, on common sense grounds surprisingly moderate. The explanation may lie in the fact that both the elasticity of demand and elasticity of substitution are valid only for *marginal changes* and the " arc elasticities " for *large* changes (such as a 50 per cent reduction) might be considerably smaller.

As the official Ministry of Labour cost of living index is now (May, 1941) 28 per cent above 1938 (composed of food 22 per cent, rent 2.5 per cent, fuel and light 25 per cent, clothing 75 per cent, other items 29 per cent) the total increase in the cost of living since the war should be around 33 to 35 per cent.

London. NICHOLAS KALDOR.

[24]

INTERNATIONAL ECONOMIC REVIEW
Vol. 16, No. 1, February, 1975

THE HICKMAN-COEN ANNUAL GROWTH MODEL: STRUCTURAL CHARACTERISTICS AND POLICY RESPONSES

BY BERT G. HICKMAN, ROBERT M. COEN AND MICHAEL D. HURD[1]

1. INTRODUCTION

THIS PAPER DISCUSSES THE STRUCTURE and properties of the Hickman-Coen Annual Model of the U.S. economy. The model is designed to make conditional projections of the annual time paths of the major aggregative variables—actual and potential GNP; labor force, employment and unemployment; wages and prices—10 or more years into the future, under alternative assumptions about government policies and demographic and technological trends. It therefore incorporates those variables and processes which are most important for determining the movement of the economy over the long run, rather than emphasizing the minor (inventory-cycle) characteristics which primarily affect short-run stability.

The model combines elements of the Keynesian and neo-classical approaches to the determination of actual and potential output. The neo-classical strands are evident in the derivation of the factor demand equations from marginal productivity conditions incorporating relative factor prices and in the use of an explicit production function for potential output. The Keynesian constituents include an income-expenditure framework for the determination of effective demand in real terms and a specification that links the real and monetary sectors through interest rates. Money wages are proximately determined by changes in labor demand and wage expectations on a wage-adjustment hypothesis, whereas prices depend directly on long-run average cost and a markup which varies with the degree of capacity utilization.

The model is fitted to annual observations for the sample period 1924–40 and 1949–66. Where significant structural change has occurred, separate functions are estimated for prewar and postwar periods. It is a nonlinear system with a high proportion of logarithmic behavioral functions. The present version contains about 50 stochastic equations and 70 endogenous variables.

The principal novelties of the model include the introduction of interrelated demand functions for labor and capital; discrimination among concepts of potential, full employment, and capacity output; an integrated cost, production, and pricing framework; a long-run housing model featuring economic-demographic interactions in a disequilibrium framework; and an approach to wage determination utilizing elements of the search theory of unemployment rather than the Phillips curve approach commonly found in macroeconomic models.

[1] The authors gratefully acknowledge the assistance of Paul M. Harrigan, Andrea Kusko and Anthony K. Lima in preparing the computations for this paper. The research was supproted by the National Science Foundation under Grant No. GS41684.

We begin with a brief structural description of the model, pass on to an evaluation of ex-post prediction errors, and conclude with some multiplier analyses of fiscal and monetary policies in the short and long runs. The error and multiplier analyses are confined to the period after World War II. Similar studies of the prewar period will be reported in a later publication, together with ex-ante growth projections and other applications.

2. STRUCTURE OF THE MODEL

An overview of the model is presented in Table 1, which lists the principal equation blocs and endogenous variables. The first five blocs comprise the system of final demand equations, in which the principal arguments are real output and disposable personal income, relative prices, and interest rates. For given prices and interest rates, the income-expenditure loop is closed by the output, income, and tax-transfer blocs. Thus the first eight blocs together are basically a rather sophisticated and disaggregated version of the textbook multiplier-accelerator model. In itself this truncated system is inadequate for growth analysis, since it neglects supply constraints except in the housing sector.

The remainder of the model incorporates such constraints as they affect the growth of labor force, capital stock, potential output, and money supply. Real and monetary constraints are not treated as impenetrable ceilings, however, but rather as supply factors which interact with demand to determine the evolution of prices, production and employment.

Manpower constraints are modelled in the employment and labor force bloc, which contains equations for labor force participation and hours of work as functions of real wages, employment, and population. The labor input bloc consists entirely of a demand function for man-hours, with output and factor prices as the principal arguments. Together, these two blocs determine labor force, employment, unemployment, and hours worked as functions of population, output, and prices.

As mentioned earlier, wage changes depend primarily on changes in labor demand and wage expectations and prices are obtained as a variable markup on long-run average total cost. The money bloc contains a supply and demand model of the commercial banking sector to determine the money stock and Treasury bill rate as well as a term-structure model to relate short- and long-term interest rates. Finally, the utilization bloc contains equations to determine several measures of aggregate resource utilization. One or more feedback relations connects these blocs with each other and with the income, expenditure and employment system already described.

The foregoing overview of the model as a system built up from blocs incorporating the income and expenditure sides of the national accounts, production and employment relations, wage and price determination, and monetary factors is revealing in some aspects but not in others. In particular, it fails to highlight the unified view of firms' decision processes which connects the investment, employment, production and price equations. Enough space is available

TABLE 1

BLOC STRUCTURE OF HICKMAN-COEN MODEL

Bloc	Principal Endogenous Variables
1. CONS (Consumption)	1. Expenditures on automobiles; other durable goods; nondurable goods; services.
2. INV (Business investment)	2. Gross business fixed investment; stock of fixed business capital; inventory investment; inventory stock.
3. HOUS (Housing and residential construction)	3. Rent; nonfarm households; stock of nonfarm dwelling units; occupancy ratio; nonfarm housing starts; value per nonfarm housing start; residential construction expenditure.
4. GOVT (Government purchases of goods and services)	4. State and local government purchases of goods and services.
5. FORT (Foreign Trade)	5. Imports; exports.
6. OUT (Output)	6. GNP in current and constant prices; gross private nonresidential product in current and constant prices.
7. INC (Incomes)	7. Gross corporate profits; dividends; labor income; national income; personal income; disposable personal income.
8. TXTR (Taxes and transfers)	8. Unemployment compensation; unemployment contributions; contributions to social insurance; federal personal taxes; federal corporate taxes; indirect business taxes.
9. LBIN (Labor-input)	9. Private man-hours.
10. EMLF (Employment and labor force)	10. Labor force participation rate; average hours; labor force; employment; unemployment.
11. WAGE (money wages)	11. Change in aggregate wage rate.
12. PRIC (Product prices)	12. Implicit price deflators for: GNP; gross private nonresidential product; 12 final demand sectors.
13. MONY (Money stock and interest rates)	13. Currency; demand deposits; time deposits; commercial paper rate; average Moody's corporate bond rate.
14. UTIL (Resource utilization)	14. Levels and rates of utilization of capacity output; labor-optimizing output; full employment output; potential output. Full employment labor force; average hours at full employment; man-hours at full employment.

to summarize these relationships and also to comment on two other distinguishing features of the model—the wage equation and the housing sector—before turning to the simulation results.

2.1. *The production and factor demand functions.* Our approach stresses the interdependence of firms' decisions on labor and capital inputs. Imperfect competition is assumed in product markets, with product price set as a markup on average cost. For given product prices, output is demand-determined in the short run. Firms base their employment and investment decisions on output and factor prices in order to minimize production costs. The algebraic framework is as follows.

The production function is Cobb-Douglas:

$$(1) \qquad X_t = Ae^{\gamma t}(k_t K_{t-1})^{\alpha}(m_t M_t)^{\beta}, \qquad A, \alpha, \beta, \gamma > 0$$

where X_t is real output, k_t is an index of intensity of utilization of capital, K_t is observed capital stock in constant dollars at the end of period t, m_t is an index of intensity of utilization of labor, M_t is observed labor input in man-hours, and technical progress is assumed at the exponential rate γ. Under stationary[2] conditions, the measured inputs K_{t-1} and M_t would be fully adjusted to the desired or optimum levels K_t^* and M_t^*, and hence $k_t = k^* = 1$ and $m_t = m^* = 1$, where k^* and m^* are the long-run or normal utilization intensities. In the short-run, however, expectations lags and adjustment costs may cause k_t and m_t to diverge from normal, in which case the effective capital and labor inputs are $k_t K_{t-1}$ and $m_t M_t$.

Taking factor prices and output as exogenous insofar as investment and employment decisions are concerned, solution of the intertemporal cost minimization problem subject to (1) yields the following expressions for the desired inputs at normal intensities:

$$(2) \qquad M_t^* = \left[\left(\frac{\alpha}{\beta}\right)^{-\alpha} A^{-1}\right]^{(1/\alpha+\beta)} \left[\left(\frac{Q}{W}\right)_t^*\right]^{\alpha/(\alpha+\beta)} (X_t^*)^{1/(\alpha+\beta)} e^{-(\gamma/\alpha+\beta)t}$$

$$(3) \qquad K_t^* = \left[\left(\frac{\alpha}{\beta}\right)^{\beta} A^{-1}\right]^{(1/\alpha+\beta)} \left[\left(\frac{Q}{W}\right)_t^*\right]^{-\beta/(\alpha+\beta)} (X_t^*)^{1/(\alpha+\beta)} e^{-(\gamma/\alpha+\beta)t}.$$

In these expressions, the expected ratio of the rental price of capital (an implicit rental rate) to the money wage is denoted by $(Q/W)_t^*$ and the expected (long-run) output by X_t^*. Firms may not adjust immediately to variations in desired inputs, however, owing to adjustment costs. These costs are not explictly modelled, but are represented indirectly by the following partial adjustment hypotheses:

$$(4) \qquad \frac{M_t}{M_{t-1}} = \left(\frac{M_t^*}{M_{t-1}}\right)^{\lambda_1} \qquad 0 < \lambda_1 \leq 1$$

$$(5) \qquad \frac{K_t}{K_{t-1}} = \left(\frac{K_t^*}{K_{t-1}}\right)^{\lambda_2} \qquad 0 < \lambda_2 \leq 1.$$

Combining (2) and (4) with (3) and (5) yields our short-run factor demand functions:

$$(6) \quad M_t = \left\{\left[\left(\frac{\alpha}{\beta}\right)^{-\alpha} A^{-1}\right]^{(1/\alpha+\beta)} \left[\left(\frac{Q}{W}\right)_t^*\right]^{\alpha/(\alpha+\beta)} (X_t^*)^{(1/\alpha+\beta)} e^{-(\gamma/\alpha+\beta)t}\right\}^{\lambda_1} (M_{t-1})^{1-\lambda_1}$$

[2] The qualification is in order because the normal intensity indexes consistent with growth equilibrium exceed unity, as explained in [**6**].

$$(7)\quad K_t = \left\{\left[\left(\frac{\alpha}{\beta}\right)^{\beta} A^{-1}\right]^{(1/\alpha+\beta)} \left[\left(\frac{Q}{W}\right)_t^{*}\right]^{-(\beta/\alpha+\beta)} (X_t^*)^{(1/\alpha+\beta)}\, e^{-(\gamma/\alpha+\beta)t}\right\}^{\lambda_2} (K_{t-1})^{1-\lambda_2}.$$

Finally, expected factor prices and expected output are specified as weighted geometric averages of current and past levels of those variables, with weights determined by the data.

As explained in [**5**], equations (6) and (7) were estimated jointly and constrained to yield unique values for the production parameters (α, β and γ) common to both derived demand functions. In the version of the model used herein, the parameters α and β were also constrained to yield constant returns to scale. Thus the production function itself is not directly estimated, but instead is inferred from the estimated factor demand equations. This formulation has two properties which are highly desirable in a long-run model. First, since the factor demand equations share the same production parameters, the growth rates of the inputs cannot diverge from the appropriate values to maintain a viable production relationship as output grows even over long time spans. Second, the factor demand functions allow for capital-labor substitution over the long-run in response to changes in relative factor prices.

2.2. *The capacity and labor utilization indexes.* In the model, capacity is a cost-based concept referring to the output that would be produced if the existing capital stock were operated with the optimal input of labor for existing techniques and factor prices. Solution of the long-run cost minimization problem with both capital and labor as variable factors yields the following expression for capacity output:

$$(8)\qquad X_t^c = A\left(\frac{\beta}{\alpha}\right)^{\beta} e^{\gamma t}\left[\left(\frac{Q}{W}\right)_t^{*}\right]^{\beta} (K_{t-1})^{\alpha+\beta}.$$

Expression (8) may also be obtained by substituting actual for desired capital stock in equation (3) and solving for output. It can be shown that X_t^c is the point on the long-run average cost curve for a firm with a capital stock of size K_{t-1}.

We define an index of capacity utilization as the ratio $(X/X^c)_t$, where X is actual and X^c is capacity output. This utilization ratio may be used to correct measured capital stock in the production function (1) for variations in intensity of use. In particular, it is shown in [**6**] that

$$(9)\qquad k_t = \left(\frac{X}{X^c}\right)_t^{(1/\alpha+\beta)}.$$

An analogous index for labor input can be constructed by conceiving of labor as the limiting factor and inverting equation (2) to yield the expression for labor-optimizing output:

$$(10)\qquad X_t^m = A\left(\frac{\beta}{\alpha}\right)^{-\alpha} e^{\gamma t}\left[\left(\frac{Q}{W}\right)_t^{*}\right]^{-\alpha} (M_t)^{\alpha+\beta}.$$

This leads to an index of labor utilization which can be used to correct measured man-hours in the production function:

$$(11) \qquad m_t = \left(\frac{X}{X^m}\right)_t^{1/(\alpha+\beta)} .$$

Empirical estimates of production functions often use exogenous indexes of capacity utilization to correct capital stock for cyclical variations in the effective input of capital services, and similar adjustments are occasionally made for labor input. The novelty in our approach is that our indexes of capacity and labor utilization are inferred endogenously from the observed behavior of firms in adjusting measured inputs to the desired levels for long-run equilibrium. For a full discussion of these concepts and their rationale, the reader may consult **[6]**.

2.3. *Potential and full-employment output.* We distinguish between two measures of output at full employment of the labor force. Potential is defined as that output which could be produced with existing technology if the full employment supply of man-hours were combined with the existing capital stock irrespective of cost considerations, and hence it is estimated from the production function. In contrast, full-employment output is related to costs and is defined as the output which would have to be demanded in order to induce entrepreneurs to hire the full employment labor supply at existing factor prices. For either concept, the "full employment" supply of man-hours is calculated from equations for average hours and labor force participation on the conventional assumption that full employment occurs when four per cent of the labor force is unemployed.

The equation for full employment output is obtained by solving the labor demand function (6) for output and substituting current full-employment man-hours (M^f) for actual man-hours:

$$(12) \qquad X_t^f = A\left(\frac{\beta}{\alpha}\right)^{-\alpha}\left[\left(\frac{Q}{W}\right)_t^*\right]^{-\alpha} e^{rt}(M_t^f)^{(\alpha+\beta)/\lambda_1}(M_{t-1})^{-((1-\lambda_1)(\alpha+\beta)/\lambda_1)} .$$

Potential output is determined from the production function (1) by inserting full employment man-hours and measuring both labor and capital inputs at their normal utilization intensities k^* and m^*:[3]

$$(13) \qquad X_t^p = Ae^{rt}(k^*K_{t-1})^\alpha(m^*M_t^f)^\beta .$$

We base the estimate of potential output on the normal rates of capacity and labor utilization so that it changes over time only when available factor supplies and technology change, rather than varying from year to year as factors are used more or less intensively.

For details on labor force participation and average hours the reader is referred to **[3]** and **[4]**. The concepts of potential and full-employment output are

[3] As noted above, k^* and m^* exceed unity for a growing economy. The values of k^* and m^* are established by the method set forth in [**6**].

fully discussed in [**6**].

2.4. *Costs and prices,* We employ a variant of the markup hypothesis of price setting. Firms are assumed to base price on an estimate of normal or long-run average total cost,[4] but may vary the markup according to current demand pressures as measured by the rate of capacity utilization. Average cost is derived explicitly from the production function and factor prices by use of the following identity:

$$AC_t = A_0(Q_t)^{\alpha/(\alpha+\beta)}(W_t)^{\beta/(\alpha+\beta)}(X_t)^{(1-(\alpha+\beta))/(\alpha+\beta)}e^{-\gamma/(\alpha+\beta)t}\,. \tag{14}$$

The markup hypothesis is

$$\mu_t = \mu_0\left(\frac{X}{X^c}\right)_t^{\delta}. \tag{15}$$

Combining equations (14) and (15) and assuming partial adjustment of actual to desired price at the rate ε, yields the price equation:

$$P_t = \mu_0^{\varepsilon}\left(\frac{X}{X^c}\right)_t^{\delta\varepsilon}(AC)_t^{\varepsilon}(P_{t-1})^{1-\varepsilon}\,. \tag{16}$$

Equation (16) is used to predict the implicit price deflator for aggregate output in the model. Sectoral deflators for the various components of GNP are then linked to the aggregate deflator in auxiliary equations which also include capacity utilization and trend variables as proxies for systematic forces affecting relative prices.

2.5. *The wage equation.* The common justification for the Phillips curves which are found in most macroeconomic models is that wage changes depend on the excess demand for labor and that the unemployment rate is a proxy for excess demand. In our model it is specified that firms set wages in order to achieve the manpower level which minimizes costs of production. If manpower on hand is less than desired, firms will raise wages so that few or workers will quit and more job searchers will accept job offers. The wage increase necessary to achieve a particular manpower target depends on the perceived distribution of money wages, upon the pool of unemployed and upon the real wage: if people think that money wages are generally high, firms will have to offer high wages to reduce quits and increase job acceptances; if many people are unemployed, the flow into employment will be high given a fixed probability that each job searcher will accept employment; the real wage affects the flow into and out of the labor force and, therefore, affects the firms' wage offers. From these considerations a model is developed in which the level of money wages depends on the expected money wage, the difference between desired and actual manhours, the ratio of the unemployed to the employed, and the expected real wage. To explain expected wages, adaptive expectations are assumed, but it is found

[4] As Hymans has shown [**11**], in the Cobb-Douglas case a markup on average total cost is formally equivalent to a markup on unit labor cost.

that expectations on the rate of change of wages rather than on the level of wages fit the data better.

The theory, estimation technique and results may be found in [**10**]; however, since the findings differ substantially from the findings of other researchers, they will be briefly summarized. The estimated equation is an equation in the rate of change of wages. The difference between desired and actual manhours is found to have considerable effect on wage changes; the unemployment rate has a modest and transitory effect. It appears, therefore, that there is no long-run relationship between wage inflation and unemployment, at least none that could be discovered in the single equation estimates. It still might be found, of course, that in complete model simulations something like a Phillips curve for wages or prices will be traced out; however, as will be seen later in this paper, the complete model solutions indicate only a temporary and rapidly diminishing tradeoff between unemployment and price inflation.

2.6. *Household formation and residential construction.* The housing sector is another example of specification for long-run analysis in the model. Most recent econometric work on the sector has concentrated on the short-term fluctuations of residential construction in the postwar economy, and there is a general concensus that the contra-cyclical pattern of home construction is due to variations in credit conditions. This factor finds a place in our model, since new housing starts depend partly on credit availability to builders, as proxied by a variable measuring the spread between short and long-term interest rates. We are more concerned, however, with the factors governing the long-run trends of household formation, the housing stock, and new construction. The current demand for dwelling space is a function of population and its age distribution, the ratio of housing rent to the consumer price index, and real income. The short-run supply depends on the standing stock of dwelling units and the same price ratio. Together demand and supply determine the occupancy rate (ratio of nonfarm households to dwelling units) and rental level on the existing housing stock, with due allowance for market disequilibrium. These variables in turn affect the flow of new housing starts, along with external cost determinants. Current starts augment the stock of dwelling units in the next period, which in turn affects occupancies and rents, and so on. Thus, in the long-run the housing stock depends on population and income growth, but the stock-adjustment process involves complex interactions between the housing market and construction industry and is subject to lengthy lags.

The submodel for housing includes four behavioral equations to determine respectively the number of households, the rent level, housing starts, and the average value per housing start. Several identities are necessary to define the dollar volume of new residential construction and to relate the number and value of new housing starts to the stock of dwelling units and its value in constant dollars. The complete housing model has been documented and simulated in [**8**] and [**9**].

3. PREDICTION ERRORS

The builder of a long-run model faces something of a dilemma when it comes to evaluation of forecast error. His model is designed primarily with an eye for its growth or trend properties, and yet part of the evidence on which the model may be judged is its tracking ability over the sample period. In our case, the parameters of the model were estimated on data spanning the Great Depression, the Korean and Vietnam Wars, and several peacetime cycles of varying severity. Moreover, the annual time unit, while entirely appropriate for a long-run model, permits only a crude approximation to the short-term dynamics of the business cycle. Despite these circumstances real GNP was predicted with an average error of 2.1 per cent during the postwar portion of the sample period (1951–1966) and of 2.4 per cent during the post-sample years 1967–1972. Both figures are for complete dynamic simulations with initial conditions beginning respectively in 1951 and 1967.

Comparable error statistics are shown for the components of real GNP and several other variables of interest in Table 2. The error in the implicit GNP

TABLE 2

PREDICTION ERRORS FOR DYNAMIC SIMULATIONS

Variable	RMSE[a]		RMSE/MEAN[b]	
	1951-66	1967-72	1951-66	1967-72
GNP	9.6	27.1	2.0	2.8
Real GNP	10.0	17.6	2.1	2.4
Real consumption	4.9	8.1	1.6	1.7
Real business fixed investment	4.0	3.6	8.2	4.7
Real residential construction	2.7	3.8	12.6	15.2
Real inventory investment	2.9	5.1	67.2	95.8
Real state and local purchases	0.8	2.8	1.9	3.8
Real exports	0.9	2.0	3.3	3.9
Real imports	0.8	2.2	3.4	4.6
Implicit price deflator (1958=100)	2.7	4.7	2.7	3.6
Civilian labor force	0.5	2.1	0.7	2.6
Employment	1.1	1.4	1.6	1.8
Unemployment rate (per cent)	1.1	1.1	22.2	24.8
Wage rate	0.1	0.2	2.3	6.1
Labor income	6.1	30.8	2.3	5.9
Corporate profits before taxes	6.9	36.5	13.0	42.9
Commercial paper rate (per cent)	0.3	2.2	9.1	35.9
Corporate bond rate (per cent)	0.2	2.8	6.0	37.8
Money stock (M_2)	5.1	31.6	2.3	5.5

[a] Root mean square error.

[b] Root mean square error as a ratio to the mean of the variable.

deflator is greater than for real GNP, but these errors are largely compensating insofar as nominal GNP is concerned. Relatively small errors for the labor force and employment result in a much larger error for the unemployment rate, which is predicted as their difference. The post-sample errors for interest rates, money stock and corporate profits are sharply higher than in the sample period, probably because of the inflationary environment after 1966.

Inventory investment is badly predicted. This is largely irrelevant for a long-run model, however, since inventory investment is a small fraction of GNP and accounts for little of the change in GNP over spans of three or more years. If inventory investment is treated as exogenous in the dynamic simulations, incidentally, the error in real GNP is reduced from 2.1 to 1.5 per cent in the sample period and from 2.4 to 1.7 in 1967–1972.

4. POLICY SIMULATIONS

Cause and effect are impossible to specify in the model owing to its simultaneous structure. An exogenous change in a policy instrument has indirect as well as direct effects on the endogenous variables. The principal channels for the direct effects can be identified from the model's structure, but the total effect of a policy change can only be obtained by simulation of the complete system.

The model contains many policy instruments. The fiscal instruments include federal purchases of goods and services, federal employment, tax rates pertaining to personal, corporate and indirect business taxes and to contributions for social insurance, the investment tax credit, and parameters for tax depreciation policy. Incremental federal expenditures for goods purchased from the private sector are a direct contribution to aggregate demand, as are incremental expenditures for federal employment. Tax changes affecting receipts from personal or indirect taxes or from social security contributions affect incomes (and in the case of indirect taxes, prices) directly and consumer and housing demands indirectly. Changes in the various tax parameters affecting corporate income will directly influence business fixed investment expenditures and dividend contributions to personal incomes.

The monetary instruments include unborrowed reserves, regulation *Q*, the rediscount rate, and the required reserve ratios against demand and time deposits. Changes in these instruments affect the supply side of the money market and induce changes in the money stock and interest rates.[5] The money stock is not an argument in any of the final demand functions of the model, but interest rates enter the behavioral equations for residential construction and expenditures on consumer durables.

It is important to note that neither nominal nor real interest rates enter the factor demand equations for fixed capital and labor. Both factor demands depend on the relative price of capital and labor, with the former represented by the rental price of capital and the latter by the money wage (equations (6) and

[5] See Scadding [12] on the specification and estimation of the monetary sector.

(7)). The rental price of capital in turn is a complex function of several variables:

$$Q = p_k(e^r - 1 + \delta)\frac{[1 - s - u(1 - ms)B]}{1 - u}, \tag{17}$$

where p_k is the price index of newly produced capital goods, δ is the real depreciation rate, s is the rate of tax credit for gross investment expenditure, u is the rate of direct taxation on business income, m is the proportion of the investment tax credit which must be deducted from the depreciable base of assets on which the credit is claimed, B is the discounted value of the stream of depreciation charges for tax purposes generated by a dollar of current investment, and r is the discount rate or cost of capital. The specification and measurement of r is crucial for an evaluation of the direct impact of monetary policy on business fixed investment. We have experimented with three alternative measures of r: the nominal after-tax rate of interest on private long-term bonds, the corresponding real rate of interest (the nominal rate corrected for the expected rate of price inflation), and a constant, after-tax required rate of return of 10 per cent. The last assumption yields smaller errors of prediction of investment alone and better performance of the entire model and hence has been adopted herein.[6] Since neither the nominal nor real rate of interest after taxes has approached 10 per cent during the postwar period, this means that business fixed investment has been invariant to the *direct* effects of monetary policy in the model. Monetarist economists have argued that business fixed investment has been unrestrained by high nominal interest rates in recent years because inflationary expectations have kept the real rate from rising appreciably with the nominal rate, but it is also consistent with observed behavior to adopt our assumption of a high required rate of return which has insulated business investment from monetary constraints and thrown the main burden of tight money on residential construction and consumer durables.

Only a limited number of policy simulations can be presented in this paper. We evaluate the effects of an independent increase of federal expenditures and an independent decrease in federal personal income taxes, in both cases with and without an accomodating monetary policy to prevent crowding out of other expenditures. We also assay the effects of an autonomous monetary stimulus in the form of an increase in unborrowed reserves.

Apart from the two cases of accomodating monetary actions accompanying fiscal policies, we do not analyze policy packages comprising simultaneous changes in several instruments. Nor do we investigate the effects of direct tax inducements for investment spending and capital-labor substitution. Finally, we consider only the effects of once-for-all changes in the levels of the instrument variables, as contrasted with differential growth rates in the instruments.

Multiplier results for twelve key variables are presented in Tables 3–5. They

[6] A similar assumption—a constant before-tax rate of return of 20 percent in the evaluation of investment opportunities—has been used by Hall and Jorgenson in a study of the effects of tax policy on investment behavior [7].

TABLE 3

FISCAL AND MONETARY MULTIPLIERS FOR HICKMAN-COEN MODEL, SELECTED VARIABLES

Year	GNP (Current Prices)					REAL GNP (1958 Prices)				
	ΔG_1	ΔG_2	ΔT_1	ΔT_2	ΔM	ΔG_1	ΔG_2	ΔT_1	ΔT_2	ΔM
1	2.73	2.87	1.47	1.51	2.90	1.64	1.76	.87	.95	1.68
2	2.51	3.07	1.91	2.27	4.00	.92	1.06	.76	.89	1.65
3	2.93	3.21	2.36	2.54	2.51	1.10	1.15	.95	.97	.64
4	3.54	3.53	2.85	2.85	.40	1.59	1.59	1.28	1.30	−.30
5	3.73	3.89	3.06	3.25	.44	1.65	1.75	1.36	1.46	.12
6	3.55	3.79	2.89	3.10	.73	1.64	1.73	1.32	1.38	.44
7	3.59	3.77	2.95	3.12	.81	1.71	1.77	1.37	1.43	.44
8	3.87	3.85	3.26	3.26	.34	1.90	1.88	1.59	1.57	.09
9	3.87	3.95	3.28	3.39	1.08	1.98	2.03	1.66	1.72	.70
10	3.90	3.91	3.38	3.40	.31	2.11	2.12	1.81	1.81	.10
11	4.09	4.02	3.60	3.59	.06	2.19	2.13	1.90	1.88	.05
12	4.30	4.22	3.83	3.84	.10	2.25	2.15	1.96	1.94	.14
13	4.33	4.27	3.90	3.91	−.12	2.28	2.22	2.03	2.00	−.08
14	4.35	4.46	4.16	4.12	−.17	2.38	2.29	2.15	2.08	−.02
15	4.24	4.12	3.90	3.86	−.14	2.13	2.04	1.90	1.85	.01
16	4.25	4.15	4.00	3.96	.16	1.92	1.88	1.79	1.76	.12
	Implicit Price Index (1958=100)					Unemployment Rate (Per Cent)				
1	.34	.36	.20	.19	.36	−.12	−.13	−.07	−.07	−.12
2	.44	.54	.30	.37	.62	−.11	−.13	−.07	−.09	−.15
3	.47	.53	.36	.40	.47	−.12	−.13	−.09	−.10	−.10
4	.50	.51	.40	.41	.17	−.15	−.16	−.12	−.13	−.03
5	.50	.52	.41	.44	.07	−.17	−.18	−.14	−.15	−.01
6	.45	.49	.38	.41	.09	−.17	−.18	−.14	−.15	−.04
7	.43	.46	.36	.39	.10	−.17	−.18	−.14	−.15	−.05
8	.42	.42	.36	.37	.04	−.19	−.18	−.15	−.15	−.02
9	.40	.40	.34	.35	.09	−.19	−.19	−.16	−.16	−.05
10	.36	.37	.32	.33	.04	−.20	−.20	−.17	−.17	−.02
11	.35	.36	.32	.32	.00	−.20	−.20	−.17	−.17	−.01
12	.36	.35	.33	.33	.01	−.20	−.19	−.17	−.17	−.02
13	.33	.33	.31	.32	−.01	−.19	−.19	−.17	−.17	.00
14	.33	.32	.31	.31	−.02	−.19	−.18	−.17	−.17	.00
15	.30	.29	.28	.28	−.02	−.17	−.16	−.16	−.15	.00
16	.31	.31	.28	.29	.00	−.15	−.15	−.14	−.14	−.01

TABLE 4

FISCAL AND MONETARY MULTIPLIERS FOR HICKMAN-COEN MODEL, SELECTED VARIABLES

Year	Potential Output (1958 Prices)					Potential Utilization (Per Cent)				
	ΔG 1	ΔG 2	ΔT 1	ΔT 2	ΔM	ΔG 1	ΔG 2	ΔT 1	ΔT 2	ΔM
1	.08	.06	−.01	.06	.02	.52	.56	.29	.29	.55
2	.15	.02	.12	.01	.26	.24	.33	.20	.28	.44
3	.16	.09	.12	.10	.16	.29	.32	.25	.27	.15
4	.21	.18	.15	.13	.12	.40	.41	.33	.34	−.12
5	.28	.28	.22	.15	.23	.39	.42	.32	.37	−.04
6	.34	.35	.21	.20	.10	.35	.38	.30	.32	.09
7	.37	.39	.30	.26	.08	.35	.36	.28	.31	.09
8	.47	.52	.36	.36	.18	.36	.35	.31	.31	−.02
9	.49	.56	.39	.38	.11	.37	.36	.31	.33	.15
10	.58	.54	.43	.41	.16	.36	.38	.33	.33	−.01
11	.66	.62	.48	.50	.18	.35	.35	.33	.32	−.03
12	.68	.74	.52	.55	.04	.35	.31	.32	.31	.02
13	.74	.76	.61	.58	.08	.33	.31	.31	.31	−.03
14	.83	.84	.63	.64	.12	.32	.30	.31	.30	−.03
15	.82	.88	.74	.73	.09	.26	.23	.23	.22	−.02
16	.84	.76	.83	.71	.05	.21	.21	.18	.20	.01
	Federal Surplus (Current Prices)					Net Exports (Current Prices)				
1	.07	.12	−.42	−.42	1.16	−.10	−.11	−.06	−.05	−.11
2	.00	.20	−.27	−.10	1.57	−.11	−.13	−.07	−.09	−.15
3	.09	.18	−.12	−.06	.91	−.11	−.13	−.09	−.10	−.11
4	.16	.13	−.06	−.08	.07	−.14	−.15	−.11	−.12	−.04
5	.20	.25	−.01	.05	.14	−.15	−.16	−.12	−.14	−.02
6	.10	.19	−.10	−.02	.27	−.16	−.17	−.13	−.14	−.04
7	.11	.17	−.09	−.03	.31	−.16	−.17	−.13	−.14	−.04
8	.19	.18	.01	.01	.15	−.16	−.16	−.13	−.13	−.02
9	.17	.20	.00	.04	.44	−.16	−.16	−.13	−.14	−.04
10	.17	.17	.03	.03	.16	−.16	−.17	−.14	−.14	−.02
11	.23	.21	.10	.10	.09	−.17	−.17	−.14	−.15	−.01
12	.29	.27	.17	.18	.13	−.17	−.16	−.15	−.15	−.01
13	.29	.28	.18	.20	.06	−.17	−.16	−.15	−.15	.00
14	.30	.28	.22	.21	.06	−.17	−.17	−.16	−.16	.00
15	.15	.12	.08	.08	.10	−.35	−.33	−.31	−.31	.01
16	.19	.18	.14	.15	.24	−.40	−.39	−.36	−.37	−.01

TABLE 5

FISCAL AND MONETARY MULTIPLIERS FOR HICKMAN-COEN MODEL, SELECTED VARIABLES

Year	Real Consumption (1958 Prices)					Real Business Fixed Investment (1958 Prices)				
	ΔG 1	ΔG 2	ΔT 1	ΔT 2	ΔM	ΔG 1	ΔG 2	ΔT 1	ΔT 2	ΔM
1	.30	.32	.65	.69	.40	.19	.21	.11	.11	.21
2	.28	.29	.86	.87	.59	.13	.18	.11	.13	.22
3	.31	.31	1.00	1.01	.31	.16	.20	.14	.16	.12
4	.51	.50	1.21	1.21	−.01	.23	.25	.18	.20	−.01
5	.62	.65	1.35	1.37	.07	.25	.28	.20	.24	.01
6	.67	.71	1.40	1.43	.14	.25	.28	.21	.24	.06
7	.74	.77	1.47	1.50	.21	.26	.29	.21	.24	.08
8	.87	.86	1.60	1.59	.06	.28	.30	.24	.26	.03
9	.91	.93	1.65	1.66	.26	.30	.31	.26	.28	.11
10	1.01	.99	1.74	1.73	.09	.31	.33	.28	.30	.03
11	1.11	1.06	1.83	1.82	.03	.32	.34	.29	.31	.01
12	1.18	1.14	1.91	1.89	.01	.33	.33	.30	.32	.04
13	1.22	1.17	1.96	1.92	−.06	.34	.34	.32	.34	.01
14	1.32	1.26	2.04	2.00	−.05	.35	.35	.34	.34	.01
15	1.31	1.26	2.05	2.00	−.05	.32	.32	.30	.31	.01
16	1.28	1.21	2.04	1.98	.02	.30	.31	.27	.30	.03
	Real Inventory Investment (1958 Prices)					Real Residential Construction (1958 Prices)				
1	.33	.36	.19	.19	.35	.01	.07	.12	.15	1.12
2	−.07	−.04	−.01	.06	.04	−.06	.08	.12	.22	1.49
3	.05	.01	.07	.02	−.15	−.03	.08	.13	.22	.82
4	.12	.10	.09	.09	−.23	.09	.11	.19	.21	.02
5	.05	.06	.04	.07	.00	.08	.12	.13	.18	.06
6	.01	.01	.02	.00	.10	.02	.08	.04	.09	.22
7	.03	.02	.01	.01	.03	.01	.05	.02	.05	.24
8	.04	.01	.05	.02	−.10	.05	.04	.04	.05	.17
9	.04	.05	.04	.05	.13	.04	.05	.03	.05	.33
10	.04	.06	.05	.04	−.11	.05	.04	.04	.04	.15
11	.02	.01	.03	.02	−.04	.06	.04	.04	.04	.07
12	.03	−.01	.03	.02	.04	.06	.04	.04	.04	.08
13	.01	.02	.01	.02	−.06	.06	.03	.04	.03	.05
14	.02	.02	.04	.02	−.02	.05	.03	.04	.03	.04
15	−.04	−.05	−.06	−.06	.01	.04	.02	.03	.01	.05
16	−.06	−.02	−.06	−.02	.03	.01	−.01	.01	−.01	.10

are based on a sample period control solution for 1951–66 and hence cover 16 years. The two columns headed ΔG refer to the effects of a permanent increase in the level of Federal spending of one billion dollars per year at current prices. Variant 2 assumes an accomodating monetary policy to keep interest rates constant in the face of higher expenditures, whereas variant 1 does not. Similarly, the columns headed ΔT show multipliers for a sustained cut in personal income tax receipts of one billion dollars per year at current prices, with (2) and without (1) an accomodating monetary policy. Finally, ΔM refers to an expansionary monetary policy consisting of a permanent increase in the level of unborrowed reserves of one billion dollars per year. Note that the multipliers for constant-price variables are measured relative to autonomous changes in current-price variables in these calculations. If the autonomous increments were converted to constant prices, the resulting multipliers for the "real" variables would be moderately higher, owing to induced price increases which reduce the real values of the nominal increments.

The impact (first-year) multipliers for nominal GNP range between 1.5 and 2.9 and those for real GNP between 0.9 and 1.8 (Table 3). The impact effects of the expenditure and money shocks are about the same, whereas the tax multipliers are only about half as large. Over the long-run, however, the tax multipliers build to a peak nearly equal to the expenditure multipliers, whereas the monetary multipliers diminish toward zero or negative values for real and nominal GNP. Cyclical fluctuations occur over the 16 year span in all cases, but with considerable variation in timing and amplitude according to type of shock.

According to the model, a sustained exogenous increase in federal expenditures or reduction in tax receipts can permanently reduce the level of unemployment, with most of the potential reduction accomplished within five years. An expansionary monetary policy will reduce unemployment temporarily, but after two or three years the unemployment rate reverts to approximately the original level.

The tradeoff between prices and unemployment differs in the short and long runs. In the case of the expansionary fiscal policies, the price level is raised permanently, but the rate of inflation—the rate of change of prices—which is largest in the first year, diminishes in each subsequent year and turns negative after five years. The expansionary monetary policy also reduces unemployment at the expense of some inflation during the first two years, but prices fall thereafter as the decline of unemployment is reversed, and they eventually return to the original level. Thus neither the price nor unemployment levels are altered in the long run by monetary policy.

Both potential output and its rate of utilization are increased by the expansionary fiscal policies assumed in the simulations (Table 4). Potential output increases only slightly at first, but it continues to grow throughout the period as the capital stock gradually rises owing to the sustained induced increase in business fixed investment (Table 5). Because the utilization rate also rises, the multiplier for actual output is greater than for potential. The average unemployment rate during 1951–66 was 4.8 per cent, and with this degree of slack the model implies that output gains occur from higher utilization as well as from higher growth of potential output itself.

Some rise in potential also occurs under monetary stimulus, but it is quite limited. This is because monetary policy does not permanently increase gross business fixed investment and capital stock growth in the model, for reasons already discussed.

The direct effect of easier money is to stimulate residential construction and purchases of consumer durable goods by lowering interest rates. Since these expenditures involve stock-adjustment processes, the stimulus to actual output is largely spent within three years (Tables 3 and 5), and thereafter the rate of utilization of potential output is usually lower in most years than if the policy change had not occurred (Table 4).

In the absence of an explicit government budget constraint, the sources of deficit finance are merely implicit in the model.[7] In the first simulation, the initial increase in Federal expenditure is implicitly financed by borrowing from the public or from excess reserves of commercial banks. As a result, interest rates rise and residential construction is deterred, offsetting part of the expansionary stimulus of Federal spending. In the second simulation, an accomodating monetary policy is assumed, in the sense that the Federal Reserve allows unborrowed reserves to increase enough to prevent interest rates from rising, and hence partly finances the increased government spending through creation of high-powered money. An accomodating monetary policy increases the GNP multiplier comparatively little, however, since the degree of "crowding out" of residential construction is small when interest rates are allowed to risc (Tables 3 and 5). A similar observation holds for fiscal stimulus through tax reduction, as may be seen by comparing the third and fourth simulations. "Crowding out" would probably be more substantial at present (1974) levels of interest rates than in the simulation period, however.

It is important to note that the ex-ante deficit for the case of increased Federal spending is converted to an ex-post surplus even during the first year (Table 4). When allowance is made for the rise of tax receipts induced by income expansion, then, deficit financing is essentially transitory for this case. A deficit-financed personal tax reduction, in contrast, results in ex-post deficits of diminishing magnitude for five or six years before an ex-post surplus is generated. Even in this case, however, the ex-post deficit each year is considerably smaller than the amount of the exogenous tax reduction.

The injection of additional unborrowed reserves by the central bank occurs entirely in the first year of the fifth simulation, presumably through an open market purchase. The Treasury more than recovers the amount disbursed by the Federal Reserve during the same year owing to the induced expansion of tax revenue, however, and continues to benefit from induced surpluses during

[7] See [2] on the desirability of including the government budget constraint in econometric models.

the subsequent years.

With regard to net exports, the various policies reduce the surplus or increase the deficit on foreign account to the extent that they raise income and imports (Table 4). Any induced changes in the monetary base stemming from foreign transactions is assumed to be offset in the simulations by appropriate Federal Reserve actions to control unborrowed reserves.

In summary, these policy simulations support elements of both the monetarist and non-monetarist views of the influence of fiscal and monetary policy, but favor the latter view more than the former.[8] The monetarist view that the growth path of real output cannot be lastingly affected by monetary policy is broadly confirmed by the model. The model also implies, however, that in the long-run (after ten years) the price level is also neutral with respect to a once-for-all change in the monetary base, contrary to monetarist thought.[9]

Within the structure of the model, the path of potential GNP is largely invariant to monetary policy because the latter does not directly affect business fixed capital formation, and the indirect stimulus to business investment from increased activity in the housing and consumption sectors is short-lived. Fiscal policy can have a lasting effect on potential output because it can induce sustained capital stock growth by permanently raising aggregate demand. (Fiscal actions directly affecting the rental price of capital provide another channel for affecting the growth paths of capital stock and potential output, but that topic remains for future investigation.) Thus the monetarist view that fiscal policy unaccompanied by monetary expansion can affect real GNP only for a short period is rejected in this model.

Finally, the trade-off between unemployment and inflation in these complete model simulations is consistent with the non-monetarist view. A trade-off does exist in the first few years, but the inflation rate diminishes rapidly and the price level actually declines after five years, although not back to the original level in the case of fiscal stimuli. In the case of a monetary stimulus, prices eventually revert to the original level, but so also does unemployment.

Stanford University, U.S.A.,
Northwestern University, U.S.A., and
Stanford University, U.S.A.

REFERENCES

[1] ANDERSON, LEONALL C., "The State of the Monetarist Debate," *Review* of the Federal Reserve Bank of St. Louis, LV (September, 1973), 2–8.

[2] CHRIST, CARL F., "Econometric Models of the Financial Sector," *Journal of Money, Credit and Banking*, III, Part II (May, 1971) 419–449.

[8] See [1] for a summary of the monetarist debate.

[9] This is because in the long-run the income velocity of money is sufficiently diminished (by the reduction of interest rates which results from an expansion of unborrowed reserves in the model) to offset the induced expansion of the money stock.

[3] Coen, Robert M., "Aggregate Labor Supply in the United States Economy," Memorandum No. 117, Center for Research in Economic Growth, Encina Hall, Stanford University, (August, 1971).

[4] ———, "Labor Force and Unemployment in the 1920's and 1930's: A Re-Examina tion Based on Postwar Experience," *The Review of Economics and Statistics*, LV (February, 1973), 46–55.

[5] ——— and Bert G. Hickman, "Constrained Joint Estimation of Factor Demand and Production Functions," *The Review of Economics and Statistics*, LII (August, 1970), 287–300.

[6] ——— and ———, "Aggregate Utilization Measures of Economic Performance," Memorandum No. 140, Center for Research in Economic Growth, Encina Hall, Stanford University, (February, 1973).

[7] Hall, Robert E. and Dale W. Jorgenson, "Application of the Theory of Optimum Capital Accumulation," in Gary Fromm, ed., *Tax Incentives and Capital Spending* (Washington, D. C.: The Brookings Institution, 1971), 9–60.

[8] Hickman, Bert G., "What Became of the Building Cycle?" Paul A. David and Melvin W. Reder, eds., *Nations and Households in Economic Growth: Essays in Honor of Moses Abramovitz* (New York: Academic Press, 1974), 291–314.

[9] ———, Mary Hinz and Robert Willig, "An Economic-Demographic Model of the Housing Sector," Memorandum No. 147, Center for Research in Economic Growth, Encina Hall, Stanford University, (April, 1973).

[10] Hurd, Michael D., "Wage Changes, Desired Manhours and Unemployment," Memorandum No. 155, Center for Research in Economic Growth, Encina Hall, Stanford University, (October, 1974).

[11] Hymans, Saul H., "Prices and Price Behavior in Three U. S. Econometric Models," in *The Econometrics of Price Determination Conference*, October 30–31, 1970 (Washington, D. C.: Board of Governors of the Federal Reserve System, 1972).

[12] Scadding, John L., "An Annual Money Demand and Supply Model for the U. S.: 1924–1940/1949–1966," Memorandum No. 177, Center for Research in Economic Growth, Encina Hall, Stanford University, (October, 1974).

[25]

THE INFLUENCE OF THE RATE OF INTEREST ON PRICES.[1]

THE thesis which I humbly submit to criticism is this. If, other things remaining the same, the leading banks of the world were to lower their rate of interest, say 1 per cent. below its ordinary level, and keep it so for some years, then the prices of all commodities would rise and rise and rise without any limit whatever; on the contrary, if the leading banks were to *raise* their rate of interest, say 1 per cent. above its normal level, and keep it so for some years, then all prices would *fall* and fall and fall without any limit except Zero.

Now this proposition cannot be proved directly by experience, because the fact required in its hypothesis never happens.

The supposition was that the banks were to lower or raise their interest, *other things remaining the same*, but that, of course, the banks never do; why, indeed, should they? Other things remaining the same, the bank-rate is sure to remain the same too, or if, by any chance, *e.g.*, by mistake, it were altered, it would very soon come round to its proper level. My thesis is, therefore, only an abstract statement, and somebody, perhaps, will ask: what is the use of it then? But I venture to assert that it may be of very great use all the same. Everybody knows the statement of Newton that, if the attraction of the sun were suddenly to cease, then the planets would leave their orbits in the tangential direction; this, too, of course, is only an abstract proposition, because the solar attraction never ceases, but it is most useful nevertheless; indeed, it is the very corner-stone of celestial mechanics; and in the same way I believe that the thesis here propounded, if proved to be true, will turn out to be the corner-stone of the mechanics of prices, or rather one of its corner-stones, the influence of the supply of precious metals

[1] A paper read before the Economic Section of the British Association, 1906.

and of the demand for commodities from the gold-producing countries being the other.

Before going further, however, we must answer one more question. Our supposition might be not only unreal as to facts, but even logically impossible; and then, of course, its use would be *nil*. According to the general opinion among economists, the interest on money is regulated in the long run by the profit on capital, which in its turn is determined by the productivity and relative abundance of real capital, or, in the terms of modern political economy, by its *marginal productivity*. This remaining the same, as, indeed, by our supposition it is meant to do, would it be at all possible for the banks to keep the rate of interest either higher or lower than its normal level, prescribed by the simultaneous state of the average profit on capital?

This question deserves very careful consideration, and, in fact, its proper analysis will take us a long way towards solving the whole problem.

Interest on money and profit on capital are not the same thing, nor are they *immediately* connected with each other; if they were, they could not differ at all, or could only differ a certain amount at every time. There is no doubt *some* connecting link between them, but the proper nature and extent of this connection is not so very easy to define.

If we look only at credit transactions between individuals, without any interference of banks, the connection between interest and profit indeed seems obvious. If by investing your capital in some industrial enterprise you can get, after due allowance for risk, a profit of, say, 10 per cent., then, of course, you will not lend it at a much cheaper rate; and if the borrower has no recourse but to individuals in the same situation as you, he will not be able to get the money much cheaper than that.

But it is a very different thing with the modern forms of credit, which almost always imply the mediation of some bank or professional money-lender. The banks in their lending business are not only not limited by their own capital; they are not, at least not immediately, limited by any capital whatever; by concentrating in their hands almost all payments, they themselves create the money required, or, what is the same thing, they accelerate *ad libitum* the rapidity of the circulation of money. The sum borrowed to-day in order to buy commodities is placed by the seller of the goods on his account at the same bank or some other bank, and can be lent the very next day to some other person with the same effect. As the German author,

Emil Struck, justly says in his well-known sketch of the English money market : in our days demand and supply of money have become about the same thing, the demand to a large extent creating its own supply.

In a *pure* system of credit, where all payments were made by transference in the bank-books, the banks would be able to grant at any moment any amount of loans at any, however diminutive, rate of interest.

But then, what becomes of the connecting link between interest and profit? In my opinion there is no such link, except precisely *the effect on prices*, which would be caused by their difference.

When interest is low in proportion to the existing rate of profit, and if, as I take it, *the prices thereby rise*, then, of course, trade will require more sovereigns and bank-notes, and therefore the sums lent will *not* all come back to the bank, but part of them will remain in the boxes and purses of the public; in consequence, the bank reserves will melt away while the amount of their liabilities very likely has increased, which will force them to raise their rate of interest.

The reverse of all this, of course, will take place when the rate of interest has accidentally become too high in proportion to the average profit on capital. So far, you will easily remark, my proposition is quite in accordance with well-known facts of the money market. If it be not true, if, on the contrary, as Thomas Tooke asserted, and even Ricardo in his earlier writings seems to have believed, a low rate of interest, by cheapening, as they put it, one of the elements of production, would lower prices, and a high rate of interest raise them—a most specious argument, resting, however, on the unwarrantable assumption that the remuneration of the other factors of production could, under such circumstances, remain the same—then the policy of banks must be the very reverse of what it really is; they would lower their rates when prices were getting high and reserves becoming low, they would raise them in the opposite case.

A more direct proof of my thesis is required, however, and might be given in some such way as this. If as a merchant I have sold my goods to the amount of £100 against a bill or promissory note of three months, and I get it discounted at once by a bank or a bill broker, the rate of discount being 4 per cent. per annum, then in fact I have received a cash price for my goods amounting to £99. If, however, the bill is taken by the bank at 3 per cent., then the cash price of my goods have *ipso facto* risen, if only a quarter of 1 per cent.; very likely not even that, because competition probably will force me to cede part of my extra profit to the buyer of the goods. In other cases, however, when long-term credit comes into play, the immediate rise of prices might be very much greater than that. If the rate of discount remains low, the interest on long loans is sure to go down too; building companies and railway companies will be able to raise money, say at 4 per cent. instead of 5 per cent., and therefore, other things being the same, they can offer, and by competition will be more or less compelled to offer for wages and materials, anything up to 25 per cent. *more* than before, 4 per cent. on £125 being the same as 5 per cent. on £100.

But, further—and this is the essential point to which I would call your special attention—the upward movement of prices, whether great or small in the first instance, *can never cease* so long as the rate of interest is kept lower than its normal rate, *i.e.*, the rate consistent with the then existing marginal productivity of real capital. When all commodities have risen in price, a *new level of prices* has formed itself which in its turn will serve as basis for all calculations for the future, and all contracts. Therefore, if the bank-rate now goes up to its normal height, the level of prices will not go down; it will simply remain where it is, there being no forces in action which could press it down; and, consequently, if the bank-rate *remains lower* than its normal height, a new impetus towards forcing up the prices will follow, and so on. The opposite of all this will take place when the rate of interest has become too high in proportion to average profit, and so in both cases a difference between the two rates remaining, the movement of prices can never cease, just as the electric current never ceases as long as the difference of tension between the poles remains.

The proposition that a low rate of interest will raise prices, a high rate of interest lower prices, is in some respects anything but new; it has been stated more than once, but a formidable objection was always triumphantly brought against it in the shape of statistical facts; indeed, if you consider the figures given, *e.g.*, by Sauerbeck in his well-known tables in the *Journal of the Statistical Society*, you will generally find that high prices do not correspond with a low rate of interest, and *vice versa*; it rather comes the opposite way, interest and prices very often rising and falling together. But this objection quite loses its importance; nay, more, it turns into a positive support of our theory, as soon as we fix our eyes on the relativity of the conception of interest on money, its necessary connection with profit on capital. The rate of interest is never high or low in itself, but only in relation to the profit which people can make with the money in their hands, and this, of course, varies. In good times, when trade is brisk, the rate of profit is high, and, what is of great consequence, is generally expected to remain high; in periods of depression it is low, and expected to remain low. The rate of interest on money follows, no doubt, the same course, but not at once, not of itself; it is, as it were, dragged after the rate of profit by the movement of prices and the consequent changes in the state of bank reserve, caused by the difference between the two rates. In the meantime this difference acts on prices in just the same way as would be the case if, according to our original supposition, profit on capital were to remain constant, and interest on money were to rise or fall spontaneously. In one word, the interest on money is, in reality, very often low when it seems to be high, and high when it seems to be low. This I believe to be the proper answer to the objection stated above, as far as the influence of credit on prices is regarded; occasionally, of course, as in times of wild speculation or panics, the problem is complicated very much by the action of other factors, which need not here be taken into consideration.

Granted, then, our theory to be true in the main or in the abstract, what will be its practical consequences? to what extent would the leading money institutions be able to regulate prices?

A single bank, of course, has no such power whatever; indeed, it cannot put its rates, whether much higher or much lower than prescribed by the state of the market; if it did, it would in the former case lose all profitable business; in the latter case its speedy insolvency would be the inevitable consequence.

Not even all the banks of a single country united could do it in the long run; a too high or too low rate would influence its balance of trade, and thereby cause an influx or reflux of gold in the well-known way, so as to force the banks to apply their rates to the state of the universal money market.

But supposing, as, indeed, we have done, that all the leading banks of the commercial world were to follow the same course, then gold could have no reason to go to one place more than to another, and so the action exercised on prices would have its sway without any hindrance from the international movement of money. Still, even then it would, under the present circumstances, have its obvious limits. As I remarked at the outset, the influence of credit or the rate of interest is only one of the factors acting on prices; the other is the volume of metallic money itself, especially, in our times, the supply of gold, and so long as the gold itself remains the standard of value, this factor evidently will take the lead in the long run. Were the production of gold materially to diminish while the demand for money be unaltered, the banks no doubt, by lowering their rate of interest, might for a while profitably react against the otherwise inevitable pressure on prices, but only for a while, because, even if the rather unnecessary stiffness of present bank legislations could be slackened, the ever-growing demand for gold for industrial purposes would gradually reduce the bank stores, and could only be checked by raising the price of gold—that is, by lowering the average money prices.

The other extreme, which at present seems much more likely to occur: a plethora of gold supply, and the rise of prices thereby caused, could not be effectually met in any way, so long as free coinage of gold exists.[1]

On the other hand, if this most essential step on the way to a rational monetary system should be taken, if the free coining of gold, like that of silver, should cease, and eventually the bank-note itself, or rather the unity in which the accounts of banks are kept, should become the standard of value, then, and not till then, the problem of keeping the value of money steady, the

[1] It is not easy to describe or imagine the exact manner in which an excess or deficiency in the ordinary gold supply affects prices, although its ultimate effect on them cannot well be doubted. As in our days the new gold generally finds its way as soon as possible to the banks, the common impression seems to be that it by so much increases the loanable funds of the banks, and therefore in the first instance causes the rate of interest to go down. This, no doubt, would be true if the new gold in its totality were deposited by its owners as *capital* for lending purposes, and in so far as this may be the case it indeed affords an illustration, and the only practical one, of the lowering of bank rates effecting a rise of prices. But mostly, I suppose, the gold comes to us not as lending capital, but as payment for the imports of the gold-producing countries, and if so its acting on the prices will be much more immediate and its effect on the rate of interest very slight. It is even possible that the rise of prices, caused by the increased demand for commodities from the gold countries, will *forerun* the arriving of the gold, the necessary medium of exchange being in the meantime supplied by an extension of the credit, so that the rate of interest perhaps will rise from the beginning. In any case the *ultimate* effect of an increased gold supply will be a *rise*, not a fall, in the rate of interest (and *vice versa* with a lacking supply of gold), because the large mining enterprises and the buying up of gold by the non-producing countries have actually destroyed large amounts of real capital and thereby given the rate of profit a tendency to rise. This all may be the explanation of some rather perplexing features in economic history, a rise of prices even when apparently caused by a surplus of gold supply very seldom being accompanied by a low rate of interest, but generally by a high one.

average level of money prices at a constant height, which evidently is to be regarded as the fundamental problem of monetary science, would be solvable theoretically and practically to any extent. And the means of solving it need not be sought in some more or less fantastic scheme like that of a central issuing bank for all the world, as it is sometimes proposed, but simply in a proper manipulation of general bank-rates, lowering them when prices are getting low, and raising them when prices are getting high.

Nor would this system be at all artificial, because the point about which the rate of interest would then oscillate, and to which it would constantly gravitate, would be precisely what I have called above its normal level, that one prescribed by the simultaneous state of the marginal productivity of real capital, the alterations of which we, of course, cannot control, but only have to comply with.

P.S.—When this paper was read at the British Association meeting it was objected by Mr. Palgrave that the banks could not possibly be charged with the regulation of prices, their liberty of action—if I understood him right—being, in his view, restricted by the necessity of protecting their own reserves as well from getting too low in consequence of an unfavourable balance of trade, as from running to an unprofitable height by an influx of gold. This, no doubt, is true, but it must not be forgotten that the international rate policy of banks has, as it were, *two degrees of freedom*, in so far as the international movement of gold can be checked or modified, not only by raising the rate of discount in the country *from* which the metal flows, but also by lowering it in the country, or countries, *to* which gold is flowing. In other words, the action of the banks against each other, which has for its object the proper distribution of money, or the levelling of the *niveau* of prices between different countries, might logically be concomitant with a *common* action for the purpose of keeping the universal value of money and level of prices at a constant height, which, however, under present circumstances only can be done within the limits prescribed by the general supply of gold.

On the other hand, it was remarked by Professor Edgeworth that if the free coinage of gold be suppressed, the Governments themselves have in their hand the regulating of general prices. This, too, is true, at any rate so long as the present large production of gold persists; and even if it should cease,and gold become scarce, the Governments, no doubt, might supplant the lack in currency by a judicious emission of paper-money. But a single Government has in this respect only the choice between two alternatives: it may try to keep the value of its money steady *towards the commodities*, but then it necessarily sacrifices the parity of its exchanges; or else it may manage to keep its exchanges strictly at par, but then it has of itself no power over the level of prices. Some international agreement, either regarding the amount of gold to be coined by each country or else involving a common rate-policy of the banks as described above, must needs come into play, shall both those purposes—the steadiness of the average value of money and the parity of exchanges—be fulfilled together; and it seems to me, although I may be mistaken, that for several reasons such agreements could be far more easily and effectually made by the banks, with the support, that is, of the Governments, than by the Governments themselves exclusive of the banks.

For a more detailed analysis of the practical side of the question and of the whole argument, I must refer to my book, *Geldzins und Güterpreise* (Jena: Gustav Fischer, 1898; being the further development of an article in Conrad's *Jahrbücher*, Bd. 13, 1897), as well as to my printed *University Lectures* (Bd. I:2, 1906, in Swedish).

KNUT WICKSELL

[26]

"THE EQUATION OF EXCHANGE," 1896-1910.

In my book on *The Purchasing Power of Money*[1] I have endeavored to express in figures and diagrams the rise of prices in the United States and the causes of this rise for the period 1896-1909. When the book was about to go to press sufficient data were received to make it possible to include in an addendum the corresponding figures for 1910, but it was, of course, not possible to make the corresponding changes in the diagrams.

The object of the present paper is chiefly to reconstruct the principal diagram (figure 14) so as to include 1910. I shall take this opportunity to include also a correction for the year 1900 called to my attention through the kindness of Professor O. M. W. Sprague,—a correction which increases the figure for M′, deposits subject to check, from 4.24 to 4.44 and decreases the figure for V′, their velocity of circulation, from 40.1 to 38.3.

According to the theory of Ricardo, as algebraically expressed by Newcomb, Hadley and Kemmerer, and elaborated in *The Purchasing Power of Money*, the general level of prices (P) in any community is determined by five and only five factors; namely, M, the volume of money in circulation; V, the velocity of its circulation, (that is, the number of times that the money in circulation is "turned over" in a year, or what is sometimes called "the efficiency of money") ; M′, the volume of bank deposits subject to check; V′, their velocity of circulation, (that is, the number of times they turn over in a year, or what bankers sometimes call the "activity" of bank accounts) ; and T, the volume of trade, or the transactions effected by money and deposits. These five determining magnitudes and the sixth magnitude, P, determined by them, are connected by the "equation of exchange", namely $MV + M'V' = PT$.

In this equation, MV, the product found by multiplying the money in circulation by its velocity of circulation, expresses the total monetary circulation or the total expenditure of money per annum; and M′V′, the product found by multiplying the deposits subject to check by their velocity of circulation, expresses the total deposit circulation or the total expenditure by check per annum. Consequently the sum $MV + M'V'$, constituting the left side of the equation, represents the grand total expenditure in a year by both money and checks. The right side of the equation rep-

[1] The Macmillan Company, 1911.

resents the total value of the goods bought expressed as the product found by multiplying the price level by the volume of trade. The price level (P) is the index number of general prices for the year under consideration, e. g. 1910, relatively to 1909 taken as the base year; and the volume of trade (T) is the value of the trade in the year under consideration, e. g. 1910, reckoned at the prices, not of that year, but of the base year, 1909.[2]

Thus the equation of exchange merely expresses in form convenient for analysis the fact that the currency paid for goods is the equivalent of the value of the goods bought.

In Chapter VIII of my book I have endeavored to show that in the equation of exchange, P is in general the passive element or puppet of the other five factors which stand to it in the relation of cause to effect.[3]

From the equation of exchange we may evidently express the price level (P) in terms of the five factors which determine it, as follows:

$$P = \frac{MV + M'V'}{T}$$

In *The Purchasing Power of Money* statistical calculations were made for all five of the price-determining magnitudes; and from these calculated magnitudes the resultant value of P was derived. This value of P, as thus indirectly derived, was then compared with its actual value as directly calculated by index numbers. The discrepancies between the results of the direct and indirect methods of obtaining P imply statistical errors in the various calculations but these discrepancies proved to be remarkably small. In order to eliminate these small discrepancies thus found, slight revisions were next made in each of the six magnitudes in the equation of exchange. In other words, each of the six magnitudes, as inde-

[2] T may be conveniently regarded as the total *number of units* of goods exchanged when the units are expressed not in terms of tons, pounds, etc., in which they are usually expressed commercially, but in terms of specially constructed units, the unit for each commodity being the amount of that commodity which was worth one dollar in the base year (1909). Likewise P may conveniently be regarded as the average price per unit at which these goods are sold, these prices being stated, not in terms of tons, pounds, etc., but in terms of specially constructed units—namely, the "dollar's worth" for each good in the base year (1909).

[3] The cases in which (as during transition periods) this proposition is not strictly true are fully discussed in the book, but need not concern us here.

pendently calculated, was frankly altered in order to make all six exactly fit into the equation of exchange as the true figures necessarily must. The alterations thus necessary were extremely small, seldom exceeding 1 per cent; in more than six sevenths of the cases not exceeding 2 per cent; and reaching at the very utmost only 5 per cent. The final figures are as follows:[4]

[4] I shall not attempt here to explain in detail how these various magnitudes were calculated, as all details are given in *The Purchasing Power of Money*. For present purposes the following brief descriptions will suffice: M, the money in circulation, is taken from the estimates of the Director of the Mint and the Comptroller of the Currency, corrections being made for the errors now believed to have been committed in the earlier estimates for gold in circulation. By money in circulation is meant money standing ready for commercial purchases. It therefore excludes money in the United States Treasury and in banks. M′ is based on the reports of the Comptroller of the Currency for individual deposits, after adding the estimated unreported deposits and after deduction of all deposits in savings banks and exchanges for clearing houses, and estimated deposits not subject to check,—this last on the basis of calculations by the Monetary Commission for 1909, repeated at my request for 1896, 1899 and 1906. The velocity (V) of circulation of money was worked out by the method explained by me in the *Journal of the Royal Statistical Society* for December, 1909. ("A Practical Method of Estimating the Velocity of Circulation of Money"). The velocity (V′) of circulation of bank deposits was worked out by an analogous method. T, the volume of trade, was based on the statistics of internal commerce as published by the Bureau of Statistics in the Department of Commerce and Labor and includes also statistics of quantities of commodities exported and imported, sales of stocks, railroad tons carried, and postoffice letters carried. P, the price level, was based principally on the figures of the Bureau of Labor for the wholesale prices of two hundred and fifty-eight commodities, but partly also on prices of stocks and wages per hour.

FINALLY ADJUSTED VALUES OF ELEMENTS OF EQUATION OF EXCHANGE.

	M	M′	V	V′	P	T
1896	.88	2.71	18.8	36.6	60.3	191
1897	.90	2.86	19.9	39.4	60.4	215
1898	.97	3.22	20.2	40.6	63.2	237
1899	1.03	3.88	21.5	42.0	71.6	259
1900	1.18	4.44	20.4	38.3	76.5	253
1901	1.22	5.13	21.8	40.6	80.5	291
1902	1.25	5.40	21.6	40.5	85.7	287
1903	1.39	5.73	20.9	39.7	82.6	310
1904	1.36	5.77	20.4	39.6	82.6	310
1905	1.45	6.54	21.6	42.7	87.7	355
1906	1.58	6.81	21.5	46.3	93.2	375
1907	1.63	7.13	21.3	45.3	93.2	384
1908	1.62	6.57	19.7	44.8	90.3	361
1909	1.61	6.68	21.1	52.8	100.0	387
1910	1.64	7.23	21.0	52.7	104.0	399

The year 1909, taken as the base year, was the end of the period first under examination, 1896-1909, and affords a beginning for a new series for subsequent years.

There are various methods of representing visually the changes in each of the six magnitudes just given, but most of these methods fail to show the relations mutually existing between these magnitudes. The method of representation here employed is that given in *The Purchasing Power of Money*. It is based on the analogy between the equation of exchange and the mechanical balance or steelyard; for, in a sense, the expenditures of money and checks exactly balance the value of the goods bought.

The left and the right side of the balance symbolize respectively the left and the right side of the equation of exchange. The smaller weight at the left, symbolized by a purse, represents the money (M) in circulation in the United States. The larger weight at the left, symbolized by a bank book, represents the deposits (M′) subject to check. The distance to the left of the fulcrum at which the first weight (purse) is hung represents the efficiency of this money or its velocity (V) of circulation, and in like manner the distance to the left at which the bank book is hung represents the velocity (V′) of circulation of bank deposits subject to check. The volume of trade (T) is represented by a tray hanging on the right side and containing a miscellaneous assortment of goods symbolizing the total mass of goods exchanged in a year. The general average of prices (P) at which these goods are sold is represented by the distance to the right of the fulcrum at which the tray hangs. The equality between the two sets of magnitudes is symbolized by the equality or balance between the strains on the two sides of the fulcrum. Each weight exerts on its side a strain measured by the product found by multiplying that weight by its leverage or distance from the fulcrum. Thus, on the left, the purse exerts a strain measured by the product found by multiplying its weight (M) by its leverage (V); and the bank book exerts a strain measured by the product found by multiplying its weight (M′) by its leverage (V′); so that the total strain on the left is measured by $MV + M'V'$. This total strain is exactly balanced by the equal and opposite strain of the tray on the right—a strain measured by the product found by multiplying its weight (T) by its leverage (P).

Thus the equilibrium of the balance symbolizes clearly the equation

$$MV + M'V' = PT.$$

An increase in the weights or leverages on one side requires, in order to preserve equilibrium, a proportional increase in the weights or leverages on the other side. If, now, the velocities of circulation (left leverages) remain the same, and if the volume of trade (tray at the right) remains the same, then any increase in the nation's purse or bank account (left weights) will require a lengthening of the leverage at the right, representing prices.

In the figure this symbolism is repeated for each of the fifteen years for which the magnitudes involved have been calculated, and it is easy to trace with the eye the changes in the various magnitudes both singly and in their mutual relations.

We may in general summarize what has happened by stating that there has been a general *expansion*, that is, an increase of the hanging weights and a movement of them away from the center. The only exception to this general expansive movement worth mentioning was in the year 1908 following the crisis of 1907.

We observe that the nation's purse (M) grew steadily, approximately doubling in the fourteen years between 1896 and 1910, and that its velocity of circulation (V) changed but slightly; that the nation's bank-book (M′) grew more rapidly, approximately tripling in the fourteen years; and that the velocity of the deposit circulation (V′) or activity of bank accounts also increased rapidly and especially during the last few years; that the volume of trade (T), symbolized by the tray, doubled while general prices increased by three quarters.

The most noteworthy year represented is the crisis year, 1907, in which deposits reached a maximum,—their velocity of circulation having reached a maximum in the previous year. The last two years, 1909 and 1910, are also noteworthy because in those years the velocity of circulation of bank deposits has been unprecedentedly high. This high velocity means that the average man in the United States is now keeping an extremely small bank balance relatively to the large expenditures he is making; that is, he is leaning toward a spendthrift policy. This fact is especially interesting in view of the observation of Pierre des Essars that the activity of bank accounts in the continental banks of Europe increases rapidly prior to a crisis, usually reaching a maximum in the crisis year.

If we seek to explain the relative effect on prices of the changes in the five factors, we note that the changes in only four of them (the left factors M,M′,V,V′) have tended to produce a rise. The

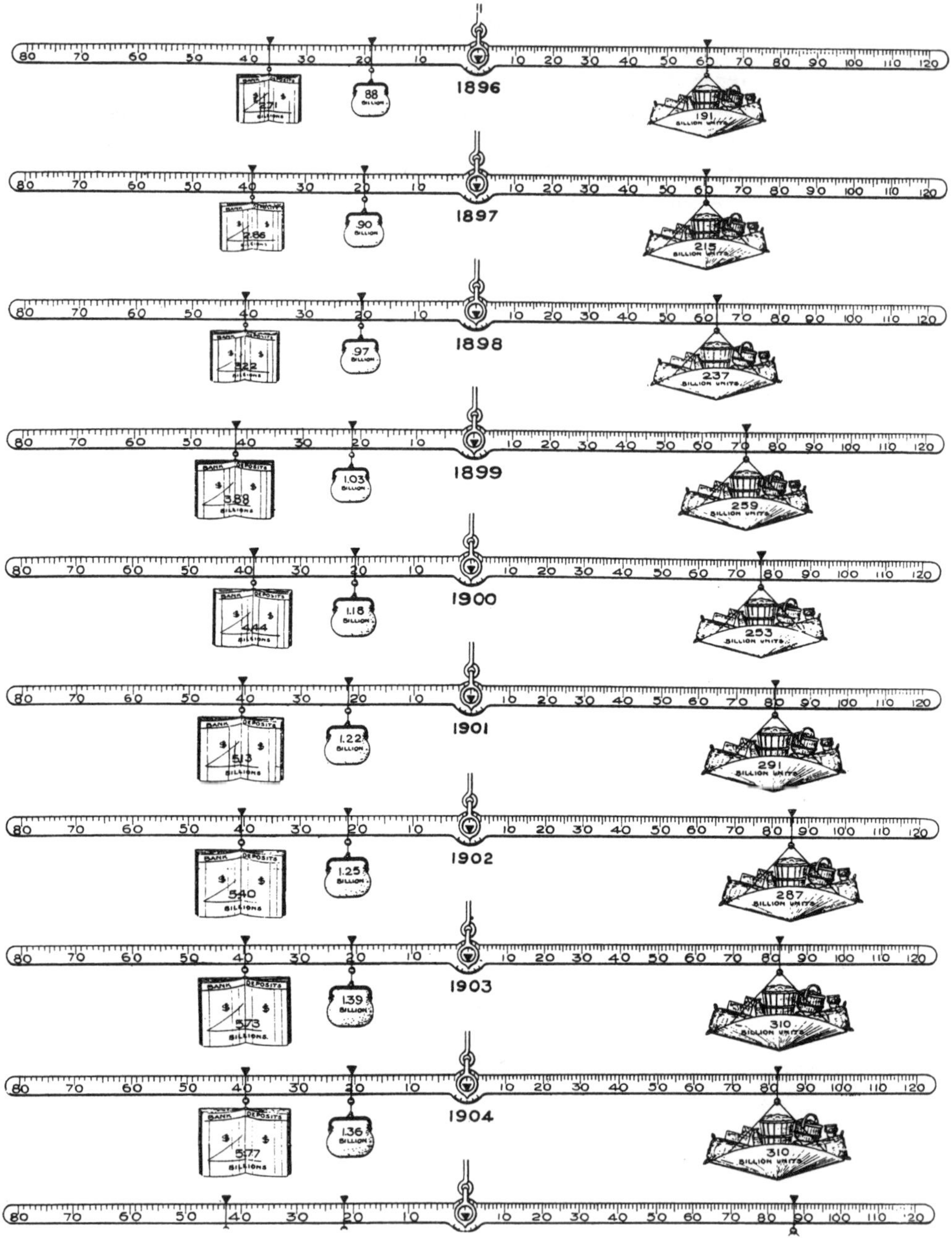

1896
2.71 BILLIONS
88 BILLION
191 BILLION UNITS
1897
2.66
90 BILLION
215 BILLION UNITS
1898
3.22 BILLIONS
.97 BILLION
237 BILLION UNITS
1899
BANK DEPOSITS
3.88 BILLIONS
1.03 BILLION
259 BILLION UNITS
1900
BANK DEPOSITS
4.44 BILLIONS
1.18 BILLION
253 BILLION UNITS
1901
BANK DEPOSITS
5.13 BILLIONS
1.22 BILLION
291 BILLION UNITS
1902
BANK DEPOSITS
5.40 BILLIONS
1.25 BILLION
287 BILLION UNITS
1903
BANK DEPOSITS
5.73 BILLIONS
1.39 BILLION
310 BILLION UNITS
1904
BANK DEPOSITS
5.77 BILLIONS
1.36 BILLION
310 BILLION UNITS

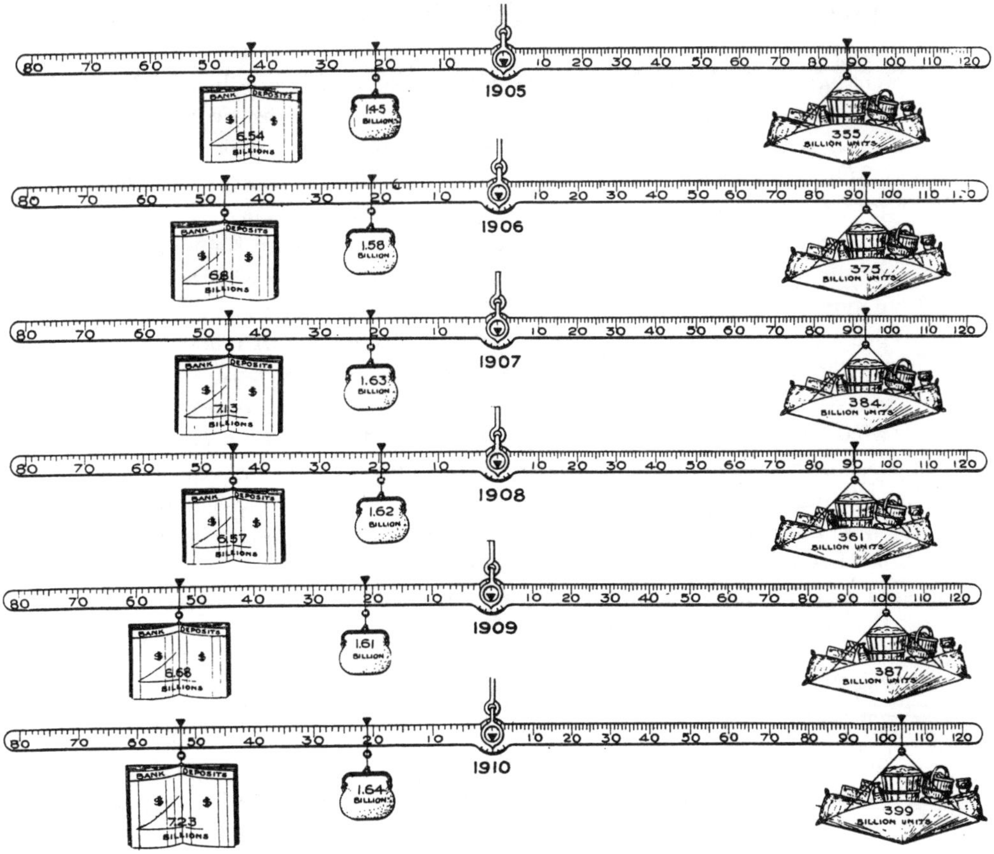
1905
BANK DEPOSITS
6.54 BILLIONS
1.45 BILLION
355 BILLION UNITS
1906
BANK DEPOSITS
6.81 BILLIONS
1.58 BILLION
375 BILLION UNITS
1907
BANK DEPOSITS
7.13 BILLIONS
1.63 BILLION
384 BILLION UNITS
1908
BANK DEPOSITS
6.57 BILLIONS
1.62 BILLION
361 BILLION UNITS
1909
BANK DEPOSITS
6.68 BILLIONS
1.61 BILLION
387 BILLION UNITS
1910
BANK DEPOSITS
7.23 BILLIONS
1.64 BILLION
399 BILLION UNITS

change in the fifth, the increase in the volume of trade, has tended to produce a fall. Of the four price-raising causes we find the most important *absolutely* to be the increase in bank deposits (M′). But if we measure these bank deposits (as they should be measured) *relatively* to the money in circulation, then their increase is found to be a less important price-raiser than the increase in the quantity of money. Fully as important as the increase of deposits is the increase in their velocity, V′. The least important price-raising factor is V, the velocity of circulation of money.

The relative importance of the four price-raising factors can be stated numerically if we compute from the equation of exchange what the rise of prices between 1896 and 1910 *would have been* had any particular one of the four price-raising factors, instead of increasing, remained unchanged, assuming of course that the other three factors and the volume of trade should have changed exactly as they did change.[5] We find that had it not been for the increase of M from .88 to 1.64, that is, if M had remained .88 throughout the period under consideration while the other factors had changed exactly as the facts show that they did, (namely, $\frac{M'}{M}$ from 3.1 to 4.4; V from 18.8 to 21; V′ from 36.6 to 52.7; T from 191 to 399), prices, instead of changing from 60.3 to 104.0, would have changed from 60.3 to about 56. In other words, prices, instead of rising as they did rise 72 per cent would have actually *fallen* 7 per cent. By similar calculations we find that had it not been for the relative increase in bank deposits, that is, for the increase of $\frac{M'}{M}$, prices, instead of rising 72 per cent, would have risen only 25 per cent. Again, had it not been for the increase in V, prices, instead of rising 72 per cent, would have risen only 71 per cent, and had it not been for the increase in V′, prices instead of rising 72 per cent would have risen only 24 per cent.

[5] Such a calculation is easily made by taking the formula $P = \frac{MV + M'V'}{T}$ or, transformed for our present purposes, $P = \frac{MV + \left[\frac{M'}{M}\right]MV'}{T}$, and substituting on the right hand side the statistical value for 1910 for T and for *all but one* of the four price-raising factors, M, $\frac{M'}{M}$, V, V′, their statistical values for 1910, and for the remaining one the statistical value for 1896.

Putting the matter in a slightly different way we may say that had it not been for the increase in money in circulation (M), prices for 1910 would have been 46 per cent lower than they were, while with similar calculations for $\frac{M'}{M}$, V' and V respectively the prices would have been lower by 28, 28 and 1 per cent. In other words of the four price-raising causes namely the increases in M, $\frac{M'}{M}$, V and V', the increase in money (M) is by far the most important and the increase in its velocity (V), by far the least important, while the other two—relative deposits $\left[\frac{M'}{M}\right]$ and their velocity (V')—stand approximately half-way between.

It need scarcely be noted that although these five factors fully account for all changes in the price level, yet other influences exist anterior to these factors. The proper mode of conceiving these other influences is to regard them as influencing prices, not directly, but indirectly by influencing one or more of the five factors (M, M', V, V', and T) on which, and on which alone, the price level (P) directly depends. Of these anterior or indirect influences on the price level the most important seem to be: first, the increase in the world's gold production, to which is chiefly due the increase in M noted; second, the concentration of population in cities, which has increased V'; third, the increase in banking facilities which has increased M'. Doubtless numerous other factors exist less important that the three mentioned. Gold is believed to be by far the most important factor. The changes in tariff laws have probably exerted some influence but that influence seems to be slight.[6]

It is noteworthy that in the year 1910 there has been little increase of money in circulation as compared with the previous year, and that the increase of prices during that year is almost solely due to the increase of bank deposits.

We cannot, however, infer that gold production played no part in the prices for 1910 as compared with 1909. The problem of price levels is an international one, and had it not been for the especially American fact of the increase of bank deposits, this country doubtless would have shared in the world's increased stock of money. The increase of deposits has tended to prevent what would have been the natural increase of money in the United

[6] See *Purchasing Power of Money,* pp. 312-314.

States. Putting the matter in a different light, we may say that if there had been no increase in the money of the world as a whole but only an increase in American deposits and if there had occurred the same increase in American deposits (relatively to money) there would have been an actual decrease in the money in the United States for the deposits would have expelled the money. Such expulsion was only prevented by the increase of money abroad. Consequently, while money in the United States is not very much greater than it was a few years ago, it is very considerably greater than it *would have been* had it not been for the increase of the world's money resulting from the increased production of gold. Had our currency been subjected to both inflations —that of money (M) and that of deposits (M′)—our prices would have risen disproportionately to foreign prices. It was, in fact, a tendency toward such a disproportionate rise in American prices that prevented the increase of our stock of money, for it made America a good country to sell in and a poor country to buy in, thus affecting the foreign exchanges.

What is the outlook for the future? Prediction is hazardous at all times, and especially now, as the present tendencies are not altogether simple and self-consistent and there exist currents and cross currents. Thus the sales of stocks and our exports and imports have declined during 1910 as compared with 1909, while our internal commerce has expanded. Again the prices of stocks have decreased while the prices of commodities have increased. Furthermore, the clearings, which are an indication of the payments by check (M′V′) have decreased in New York City while outside of New York City they have increased.

At the present writing the best indications seems to point to the conclusion that the year 1911 will show a general contraction; that is, a shrinkage of the weights in our mechanical balance (especially M′) and their movement toward the fulcrum—and this without a disturbance sufficiently acute to be called a crisis. However, it seems also probable, in view of all the circumstances[7] of the case, and especially of the progressive increase in the gold supply, that

[7] These include an inflation of land values, of bank loans and deposits based on these land values, and of the rates of interest on farm loans, an increased "slowness in collections" observed by credit men, continued great bank clearings outside of N. Y. City, increased failures and increased investments, as well as, on the other hand, slight falling off in building, in bank clearings in N. Y. City, in immigration, and in commodity prices.

the upward trend of prices and the tendency toward expansion of trade, and of money and deposits with their velocities, will be resumed within a year or two, continuing until the process does culminate in a crisis. In other words, in spite of the apparently impending recession, we are still in a period of incubation for a future crisis. The exact date of such a crisis, of course, it would be foolish to predict, but if it occurs at all, it would seem likely to occur between, say 1913 and 1916. This prognostication is, of course, purely tentative and based chiefly on the existence of the expansive tendency shown in the diagram and the fact that such a tendency led to the crisis of 1907 and, so far as our fragmentary knowledge allows us to judge, to the crises of 1857, 1866 and 1873.[8] The incubating period for such a crisis varies in different cases, but seems to be shorter when prices are rapidly rising than in other cases. The chief factor at work during the incubating period is, so far as the world in general is concerned, the increase in the supply of gold; and so far as conditions in this country in particular are concerned, it is the unprecedented extension of deposit banking.

The disproportionate growth of deposit banking and the consequent increase of the purchasing ability of the population is strikingly shown by the decreasing percentage which cash transactions (M′V′) bear to the total of all transactions, MV + M′V′, and the increasing percentage which the check transactions (M′V′) bear to the same total.

The calculations given above enable us to determine with considerable precision the relative importance of cash and check transactions during the fifteen years under consideration. They are as follows:

(1)	(2) $\frac{M'}{M}$	(3) $\frac{MV}{MV+M'V'}$ Per cent	(4) $\frac{M'V'}{MV+M'V'}$ Per cent
1896	3.1	14	86
1897	3.2	14	86
1898	3.3	13	87
1899	3.8	12	88

[8] This statement is in accordance with the facts and theories in Juglar's *Des Crises Commerciales*, Paris (Guillaumin), 1889; Thom's *Brief History of Panics in the U. S.*, New York (Putnam), 1893; Babson's *Business Barometers for Forecasting Conditions*, 1910, Wellesley Hills; and my *Purchasing Power of Money*.

1900........................	3.6	12	88
1901........................	4.2	11	89
1902........................	4.3	11	89
1903........................	4.1	11	89
1904........................	4.2	11	89
1905........................	4.5	10	90
1906........................	4.3	10	90
1907........................	4.4	10	90
1908........................	4.0	10	90
1909........................	4.1	9	91
1910........................	4.4	8	92

Here we notice, in column 2, that the ratio between bank deposits subject to check and money in circulation $\left[\frac{M'}{M}\right]$ has increased from 3.1 to 4.4; and that the percentage of cash transactions, $\frac{MV}{MV+M'V'}$, has declined from 14 per cent to 8 per cent while the percentage of check transactions has increased from 86 to 92 per cent.

Though we in America are accustomed to take pride in the fact that we use checks more than any other nation, this tendency may well give us pause. So extensive a use of checks must certainly tend to aggravate those periodic collapses in credit which follow a crisis.

But, while the instability of our purchasing power is aggravated by credit fluctuations, these fluctuations are usually initiated by alterations in the supply of our basic metal, gold. We cannot continue fanatically to defend gold as the best standard when it produces such violent and opposite fluctuations as we have witnessed—fluctuations first in the great rise of prices between 1850 and 1857, second in the great fall between 1873 and 1896, and third, in the great rise between 1896 and 1910. In fact the moral of the figures we have obtained seems to be that economists should turn their thoughts seriously to the question of controlling the purchasing power of money. I have attempted in *The Purchasing Power of Money* to discuss various plans for this purpose including a new and, I believe, safe and practicable proposal.

IRVING FISHER.

Yale University.

NOTES

THE BUSINESS CYCLE LARGELY A "DANCE OF THE DOLLAR"[1]

By Irving Fisher

Hitherto the effort to explain and forecast the "Business Cycle" has been chiefly empirical. I suspect that we shall, in the future, make greater progress by employing more analysis. Instead of beginning with actual historical "cycles" which are, in each case, a composite resultant of innumerable forces, we shall trace the action of the chief forces themselves. I further suspect that the principal force affecting the cycle is the *real* rate of interest, the sum of the *money* rate of interest and the rate of appreciation (positive or negative) of the purchasing power of the dollar.[2]

I here present some preliminary findings as to one only of the two components of the real rate of interest, namely, the appreciation (or depreciation) of the purchasing power of the dollar or, otherwise expressed, the rapidity of fall (or rise) of the price level.

The various business services which have sprung up during the last decade all seem to recognize that the price level is of vital importance, but its real rôle has been missed because the *price level* itself has been looked to instead of its rate of change.

They have made the mistake of treating the price curve like population, trade, etc., which grow with the growth of the country, and have attempted to discover a "secular trend" and estimate the oscillations about this trend. Some of these services, when the war wrought its havoc with prices, simply omitted the price curve altogether through the period of greatest disturbance although it was precisely under such circumstances that its rôle in disturbing business was most important and, as we shall see, most evident.

The distinction between a curve portraying the price level and a curve portraying its rapidity of change is the same sort of distinction as that between any mathematical function and its differential quotient or first derivative. It is exemplified by the distinction between dis-

[1] Expansion of remarks at the Annual Meeting of the National Monetary Association, June 7, 1923.

[2] This view was foreshadowed in my "Appreciation and Interest" (*Publications of the American Economic Association*, Vol. XI, No. 4, 1896, *e. g.* p. 410) and in subsequent writings. It was emphasized by me in the discussion at the dinner of the American Statistical Association, December 15, 1922.

tance and velocity, or velocity and acceleration, or energy and power, or the height of a hill and its steepness.

The distinction is shown graphically in Chart 1 where the upper curve, P, is taken as the plot (on the ratio scale) of the price level while the lower curve, P', plots (on the ordinary or arithmetical scale) the rapidity of change of the upper curve. In the first period the price level is rising at a constant rate. This is shown in P as a straight ascending line. The steepness of this line, *i. e.* the rapidity of its rise, say 2 per cent per annum, is shown as the height (2 units) of P' above

CHART 1

ILLUSTRATIVE PRICE LEVEL (P) AND ITS RAPIDITY OF CHANGE (P')

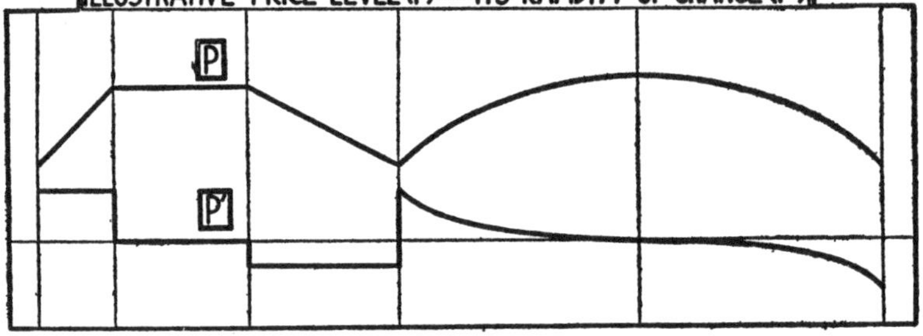

the zero line. As this height is constant throughout the first period, P' remains horizontal.

During the second period the price level remains constant so that the upper curve P is horizontal. Its slope is therefore zero so that the lower curve P' is (horizontal) on the zero line. During the third period prices are falling. Thus P slopes downward half as fast as the initial upward slope and P' is (horizontal) below zero (one unit).

Beyond this point P rises at first rapidly but with diminishing rapidity until at the top of the arch it stops rising entirely and begins falling with gradually increasing rapidity. The lower curve P' reflects these conditions by starting off at a high point and then gradually descending to the zero line, crossing it at a point under the arch of the upper curve, and then passing below zero.

In analyzing business conditions it is P' not P that helps. What concerns business is not whether prices are high or low but whether they are rising or falling. Thus rising prices stimulate business because the prices a producer can get outrun his expenses for interest, rent, salaries and wages, while falling prices depress trade.

Chart 1 is, of course, purely hypothetical to illustrate the simple types of a steadily rising, a constant, and a falling price level and a price level the rate of rise (or fall) of which gradually changes.

Chart 2, on the other hand, shows actual statistical facts. The upper curve P plots the index number of the United States Bureau of Labor Statistics while the lower, P', plots its rate of rise or fall.[1] It will be noted that the curve P', unlike P, oscillates about the zero line. We

CHART 2

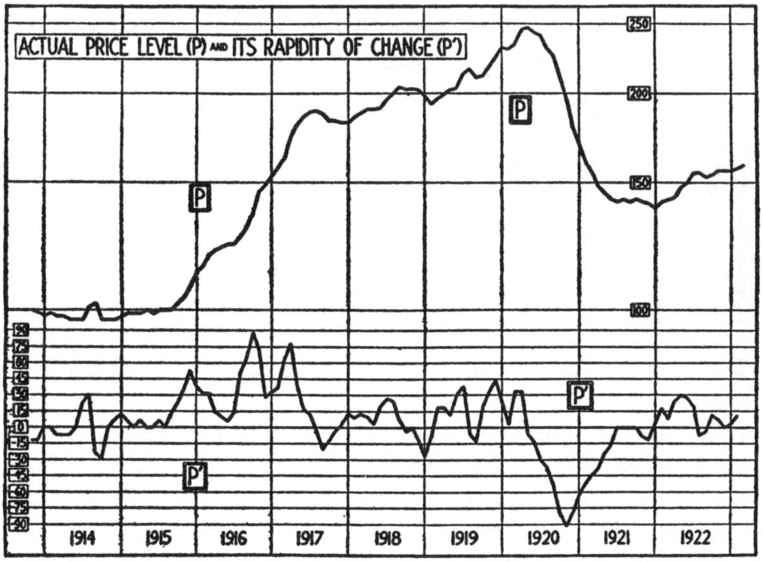

thus reach an oscillating barometer without the need of any of the usual corrections for secular and seasonal variations.

What is now needed is to correlate two curves namely: (1) a curve representing business—the physical volume of trade [2] (duly corrected for seasonal and secular changes), and (2) a curve (like P') representing the rapidity of change of the price level.

In Chart 3 these two curves are given. Curve T plots the business barometer of the American Telephone and Telegraph Company, which is the nearest approach, yet available,[3] to a barometer of physical volume of trade (duly corrected for secular trend and seasonal variation).

Curve $\overline{P}'$ is the curve plotting the rapidity of rise or fall of the price level. It is analogous to the lower curve in Charts 1 and 2. But in

[1] Found for each month by taking the two index numbers for the months following and preceding, dividing the former by the latter, and subtracting unity.

[2] The concept of "business conditions" has been very cloudy in most business barometers; for these often include indexes of values and even of the price level itself.

[3] Since this paper was prepared the Harvard Committee on Economic Statistics has prepared a more perfect barometer. It agrees closely however with the curve here used.

$\overline{P}'$ the minor irregularities of P' are smoothed out. That is, $\overline{P}'$ is a *moving average* of P', each ordinate being an average of eight consecutive ordinates of said "derivative", P'. Moreover it is a *weighted* average, the weights being 1, 2, 3, 4, 5, 6, 7, 8, for each eight consecutive ordinates of the "derivative" P'.

To better show the correspondence between Curves T and $\overline{P}'$ the ordinates of curve $\overline{P}'$ are plotted four months ahead of the date of the

CHART 3

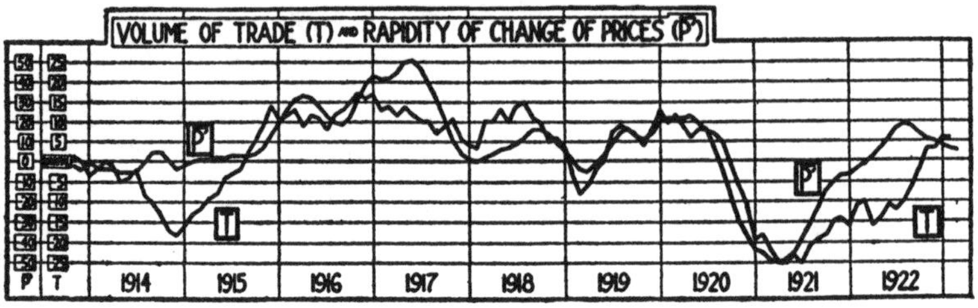

eighth or last of the ordinates of the "derivative" P' of which it is the average.

Taken in these relative positions the ordinates of curves $\overline{P}'$ and T are found to be correlated 79 per cent.

Since $\overline{P}'$ plots the rate of change of prices and so of the purchasing power of the dollar, we may say that it pictures the dance of the dollar while T pictures the dance of business. The 79 per cent correlation tells us that business dances attendance on the dollar.

The only case where the two curves widely diverge is during the months immediately following the sudden outbreak of war in 1914. A second but less pronounced case came in 1917 as the entrance of the United States into the War gradually hove into sight.

Thus we find that this one element, *rapidity of price movement*, during the period 1914–22 seems to account, almost completely, for the ups and downs of business, the chief exceptions being readily ascribable to other disturbances.

In the large swings of the last three years the "lag" between the dance of the dollar and the dance of business is greater than usual. By modifying the system of weighting the moving average $\overline{P}'$ according to probability principles, the two curves can, I think, be made to correspond more closely. The present paper is only a preliminary report made for the meeting of the National Monetary Association. I am now engaged, with the help of the Standard Statistics Co., in working through various lengthy calculations in the hope of finding the best methods of computing $\overline{P}'$.

After such an analysis, it may be possible to make a synthesis with the rate of interest and other factors by which we can not only better understand, but also better forecast business conditions—to say nothing of controlling them.

[28]

International Propagation of Business Cycles

I

It is a well-known fact that nearly every country is, in its economic position, highly dependent on these two factors: economic conditions in all other countries and the relative height of its currency in terms of other currencies; or, as we may express it, on the level of the wave of the business cycle abroad and the dyke-structure of the particular country that allows a smaller or larger amount of this fertilising wave to enter it.

Of both factors it may be very useful to have not only qualitative but also quantitative knowledge. To know how large an improvement in economic conditions may result from a devaluation of a country's currency of, say, 20 per cent, is almost a condition of a scientific exchange policy.

Knowledge about the degree in which the economic situation in one country is influenced by the cyclical position abroad, or, otherwise expressed, responds to and reflects these conditions, is indispensable for any general theory concerning the propagation of business cycles from one country to another. It is the aim of this paper to give an approximate answer to both questions.

II

The influence on a country's economic situation of an improvement in the world's economic position, and of a devaluation of its currency, work, to a considerable extent, along the same channels.

An improvement of the cyclical position abroad leads in the first place to an enlargement in the quantity of export products demanded. It is probable that, after some time, prices abroad will also rise in relation to home prices. The consequence is that export industries may sell more and at better prices, and that the industries working for the home market are less subject to foreign competition.

Devaluation immediately raises prices of imported and exported goods as far as they have world prices and allows exporters of those products that have no world prices to sell a larger quantity at a price that is not lower, perhaps even higher, than before, in terms of their own currency.

The favourable influence of both a revival abroad and a devaluation at home on industries producing for export or under foreign competition then gradually spreads through the whole economy of the country *via* higher pay rolls, larger raw material orders, higher dividends, etc.

It goes without saying that the reversed reasoning holds for a deterioration of conditions abroad and for a currency revaluation—or what comes to the same thing, *another* country's devaluation.

The following factors will chiefly affect the magnitude of the effects :

(a) The dependence of the country's economy on foreign influences ; the relative importance of its industries producing for the foreign market or competing with foreign industries on the home market. This factor should be quite sufficiently represented by the relation between foreign trade and national income.

(b) The character of its export products. A country exporting consumption goods will feel a cyclical variation in a lesser degree than one exporting production goods. If the demand for the exported goods is inelastic and the supply is not monopolised and is equally inelastic, the fluctuations will be strong. To what degree exports may be stimulated by a devaluation is in the same way strongly dependent on the character of the goods exported.

III

The theoretical arguments set out in the last section make it clear that it must be possible to find statistically :

(1) a *positive* correlation between the cycle of a country and that of the world ;

(2) a *negative* correlation between the cycle of a country and the price of its currency in terms of the curriencies of other countries.[1]

To verify this statement an attempt is made to " explain," by way of multiple correlation calculation, the national cycle of several countries, by :

(a) the world cycle ;

(b) the " exchange rate of the country's currency against the world."

(c) A trend (standing for the secular movement of the country's development and—perhaps—the degree in which changes in factor (b) are counteracted by adaptation).

The following material has been used in the calculations :[2]

(1) *World Cycle.* 1925–36. League of Nations : Index of industrial production and mining, world, incl. U.S.S.R. Extrapolated for the years 1920–4 on a comparable series from the Institut für Konjunkturforschung.

(2) *National Cycle.* Indices of industrial production and mining as published by the League of Nations, Institut für Konjunkturforschung, or, for Holland, of the Dutch Central Statistical Bureau.

(3) " *Exchange rate against the world.*" Relation between the price of the country's own currency (average quotation in New York, as published by Standard Statistics) and an average price of the currencies of ten important countries which had, in 1929, 55.1 per cent of world trade, weighted according to each country's part of world trade in 1929 (League of Nations data).

The result of the correlation calculations is given in Table I, and from

[1] Cf. R. A. Lester : " The Gold Parity Depression in Norway and Denmark, 1925–1928," *The Journal of Political Economy*, XLV, August, 1937.

[2] The figures are given in Appendix II.

charts 1–8 a visual synopsis may be had. All calculations are made in percentage deviations from average.

Column 3 in Table I shows the coefficients found for the world cycle in the explanation of the national cycles. To come to the real *influence* from the world cycle, this coefficient should be corrected for the weight with which the country's own cycle has been included in the world cycle (column 4, League of Nations data). Column 5 gives the result of this correction.

Similarly, column 6 gives the influence of the country's exchange rate against the world on its cycle. Here the coefficients are all but one negative, as is to be expected, indicating the beneficial influence of a low exchange rate.

Column 7 shows the coefficient for the trend and, finally, in column 8, the multiple correlation coefficient is given.

TABLE I

Country.	Period.	In percentage deviations from average. Calculated influence of World Cycle.	Weight in World Cycle.	Corrected influence of World Cycle.[1]	Calculated influence of Exchange Rate.	Calculated Trend	Correlation Coefficient R.
1	2	3	4	5	6	7	8
United States ..	1920–36	1.35	0.46	1.92	+0.29	−3.15	0.98
United Kingdom ..	,,	0.95	0.10	0.94	−0.63	+0.24	0.93
France	,,	0.37	0.08	0.35	−0.76	+0.09	0.92
Belgium	,,	0.71	0.02	0.70	−0.55	−3.22	0.97
Czechoslovakia ..	1921–36	0.86	0.02	0.86	−1.23	+1.82	0.83
Holland	,,	0.55	0.01	0.55	−0.81	+5.04	0.96
Sweden	1920–36	0.81	0.01	0.81	−0.45	+3.48	0.99
Norway	,, [2]	0.61	0.003	0.61	−0.17	+1.92	0.92

[1] This correction has been applied in the following way: Call the world cycle w, the observed cycle of any country k : o_k, the weight of k in the world index β_k, and the cycle of all other countries with the exception of k : w'_k; its weight in the world cycle will then be $1-\beta_k$:

$$w = \beta_k o_k + (1-\beta_k)w'_k \quad \text{(0.1)}$$

Call the coefficient found for k by the correlation calculus a''_k:

$$o_k = a''_k w \quad \text{(0.2)}$$

Substitute (0.1) in (0.2):

$$o_k = a''_k \beta_k o_k + a''_k (1-\beta_k) w'_k \quad \text{(0.3)}$$

or

$$o_k = \frac{a''_k(1-\beta_k)}{1-a''_k\beta_k} w'_k \quad \text{(0.4)}$$

where $\frac{\alpha''_k(1-\beta_k)}{1-\alpha''_k\beta_k}$ is equal to the corrected coefficient, which indicates the relation between the cycle of country k and that of the rest of the world.

[2] 1931 and 1932 corrected on account of big strike in 1931 : interpolated on Swedish figures between 1930 and 1933 ; trend difference eliminated.

IV

These results need cautious interpretation. The most remarkable fact is, perhaps, the very high correlation coefficient found in seven out of eight cases. This indicates that it is possible to give a very good explanation of the several countries' cycles by the variables included here.

Still the correlations are not perfect, as is also easily seen from the charts. This is not surprising. In every country special forces, apart from those accounted for in the correlations, come into play. They cause discrepancies between the observed and the calculated cycle—and, consequently, make somewhat uncertain the statistical determination of the regression coefficients.

Nevertheless, it may be taken as an indication that the coefficients we have found are not very far from the " true " ones, that the results do not show too heavy discrepancies for the different countries. All coefficients for the influence of the world cycle are positive and lie between 0.35 to 0.94. Under the coefficients for the exchange rate there is only one that is positive—and that is the coefficient of the United States, where one would have expected, as a consequence of the small relative importance of their foreign trade, a coefficient only slightly below 0. The spread of the other coefficients is, indeed, somewhat larger (from —0.17 to —1.23) than it was in column 5 (when the United States coefficient is left out of account).

The imperfection of the correlations, and, consequently, the considerable margin of error in the coefficients does not allow, I think, of attributing a very high importance to the coefficients found for any particular country ; and, therefore, I do not think one should try to explain these coefficients by the special properties of the country (relative importance of foreign trade, character of products exported, etc.).[1]

But much more confidence may be placed in the total of the observations. As for countries that are roughly similar in structure, the true coefficients must certainly be roughly the same, an *average* of the coefficients found for Holland,

[1] The exceptional case of the United States is treated in Section VI.

Note to Charts 1–8.—Charts 1–8 represent the result of the correlation between the cycle of a country (O) on the one hand ; and the world cycle (W), the relative price of the country's currency (r), and a trend (t), on the other.

The three influencing factors are shown already multiplied by their respective " influence coefficients " (see Table 1). The three influences are added up in O' (in every chart $O' = aW+br+ct$), which is the explanation of the " own " cycle (continuous line), while O is the observed series (dotted line).

All charts are at about the same scale, one point in the O curve indicating roughly 1 per cent of its average.

II. UNITED KINGDOM

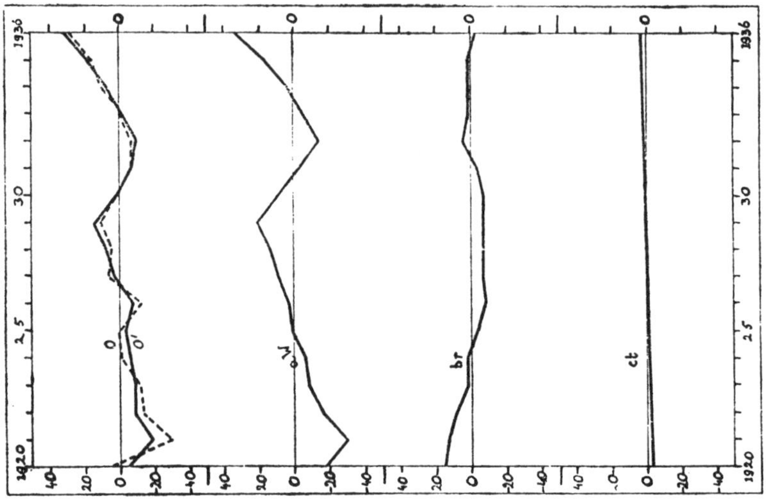

I. UNITED STATES

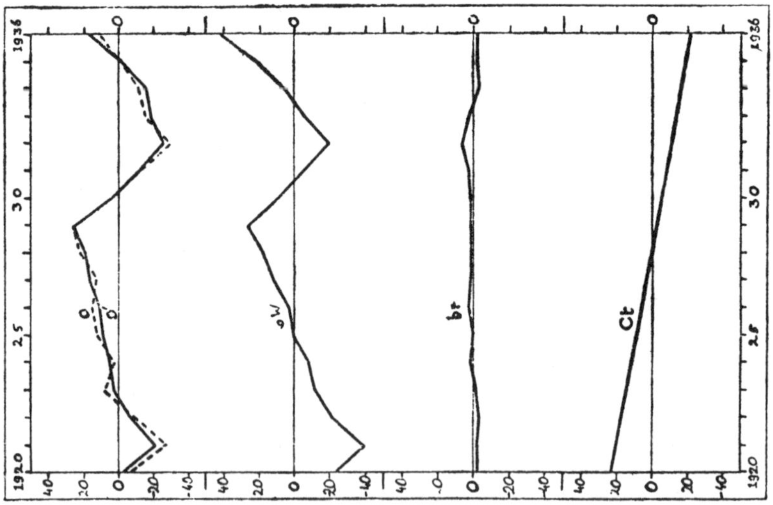

III. France

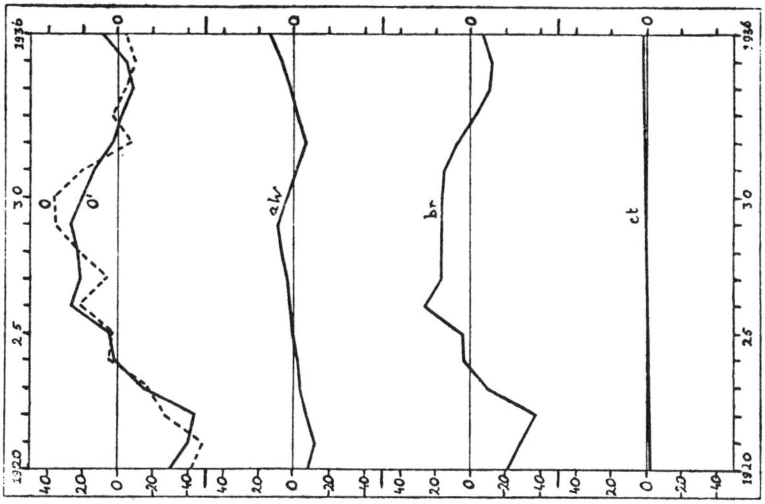

IV. Belgium

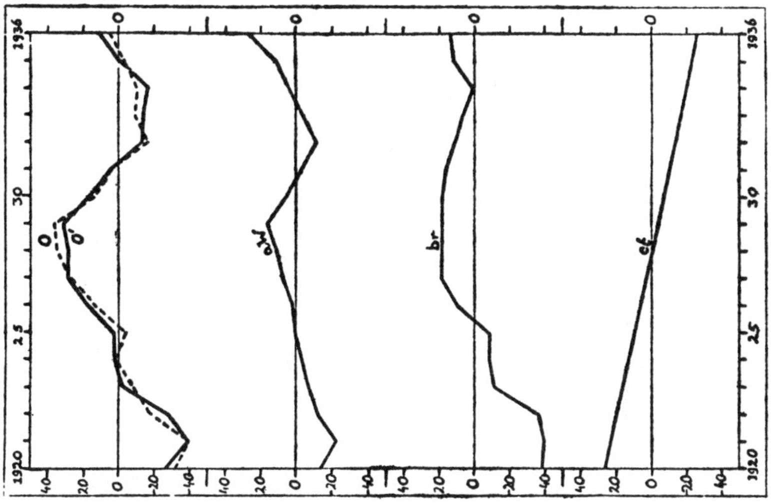

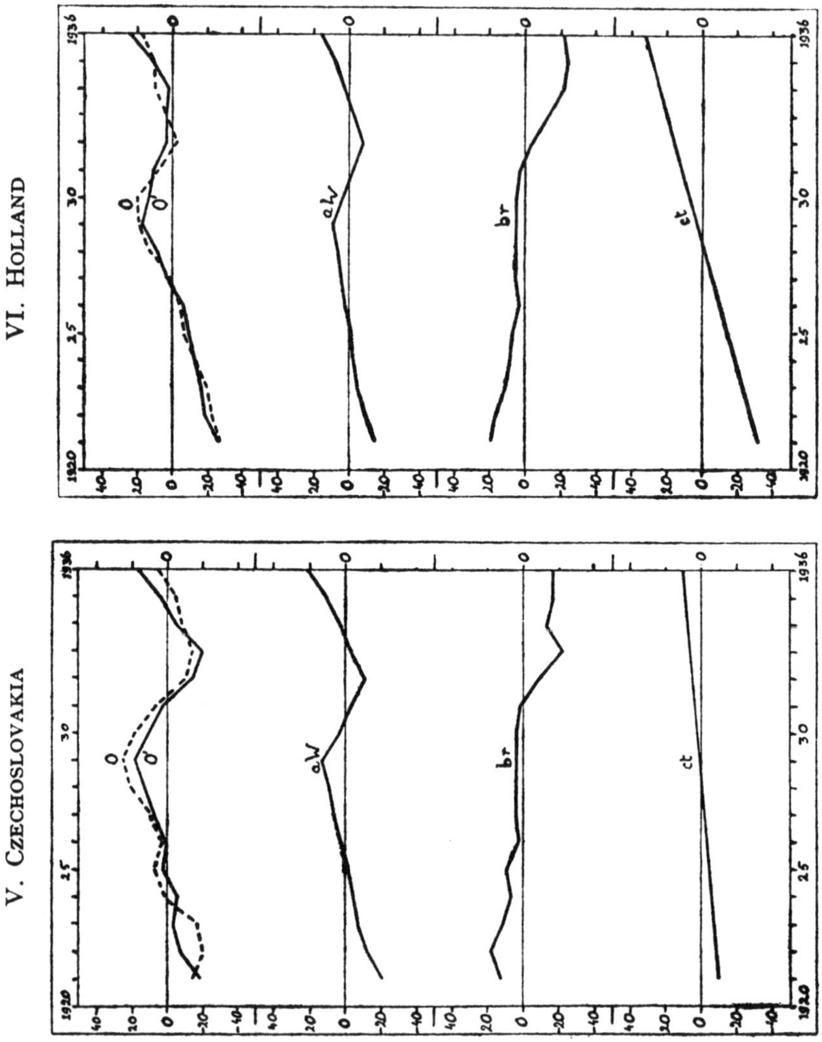
VI. HOLLAND
V. CZECHOSLOVAKIA

VII. SWEDEN

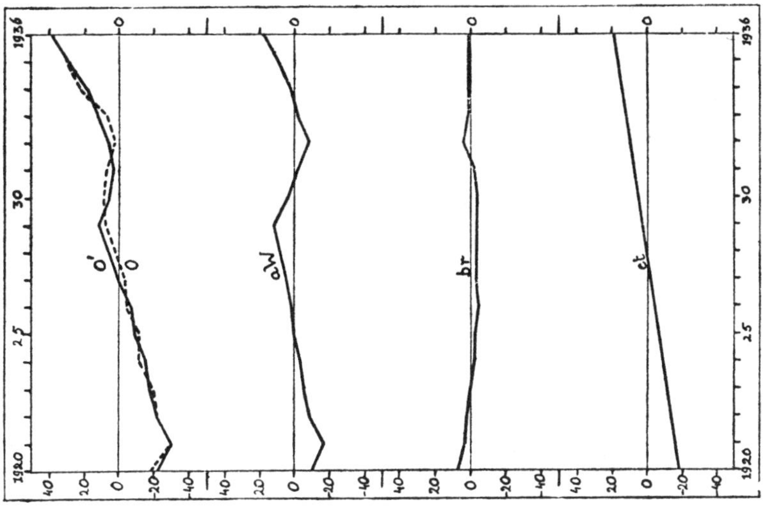

VIII. NORWAY

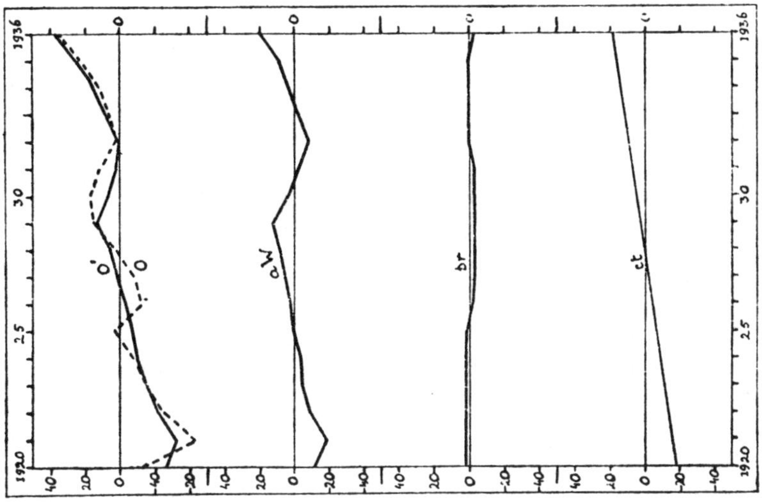

Belgium, Norway, Sweden, and Czechoslovakia may be regarded as much nearer to the true coefficients for countries of this kind.

In doing so we find—

a coefficient for the world cycle of 0.70

a coefficient for the exchange rate of −0.64

meaning that such a country's economic activity rises by about 14 per cent as a consequence of a 20 per cent rise in world activity and by about 13 per cent as a consequence of a 20 per cent devaluation of the country's currency. It is not necessary to repeat that these are only rough estimates for an " average country " of the type just mentioned.

However, with regard to the first of these coefficients, more confidence may be placed upon it than for the mere reason that the inaccuracies of particular coefficients tend to neutralise each other in an average. For all coefficients obtained for the " influence of the world cycle " are *together* open to a check which does not exist for each of them separately ; this check may prove the figure of 0.70 to be reliable as an average for all countries other than the United States. For this proof we repeat the formula used on page 81 :

$$o_k = \alpha''_k w \qquad (0.2)$$

where o_k is the cycle of country k, w the world cycle, and α''_k the coefficient found (Table I, column 3). By definition

$$w = \Sigma\beta_k o_k \qquad (0.5)$$

(the world cycle is equal to the sum of the cycles of each country, multiplied by their respective weights). Multiplying all o_k's in (0.2) by their weights and adding up, we find :

$$\Sigma\beta_k o_k = w\Sigma\beta_k\alpha''_k \qquad (0.6)$$

The combination of (0.5) and (0.6) gives us :

$$w = w\Sigma\beta_k\alpha''_k \qquad (0.7)$$

or

$$\Sigma\beta_k\alpha''_k = 1 \qquad (0.8)$$

Now we know the α'''s of eight countries, and the β's of all. When we make a reasonable assumption about the unknown α'''s we may see whether formula (0.8) holds—i.e. whether the eight coefficients we found are, as a whole, reliable.

It would not be reasonable to suppose that the α'''s we have not determined are equal to the average of those we have determined ; this would overlook the fact that we have especially analysed the larger countries. It would be better to assume

(a) that the countries not analysed have α'''s like the average of the eight countries analysed, with the exception of the United States ; or

(b) that they have α'''s like the average of these eight countries, with the exception of the United States, United Kingdom, and France.

Both possibilities have been calculated in Table II (as an alternative to weighted averages, medians have also been calculated). The result is quite satisfactory: the expected theoretical figure (in italics in column 5) is reached within a very narrow margin. This proof relates to the figures of column 3; as the correction applied in column 5 is very small for countries with a small weight, we may also conclude that the figure 0.70 is a very reliable estimate for the influence of the world cycle on the cycle of a small country.

TABLE II

	Country.	Coefficient (Table I, Col. 3).	Weight (Table I, Col. 4).	Col. 3 × Col. 4.
1	2	3	4	5
1	United States	1.35	0.46	0.621
2	United Kingdom	0.95	0.10	0.095
3	France	0.37	0.08	0.030
4	Belgium	0.71	0.02	0.014
5	Czechoslovakia	0.86	0.02	0.017
6	Holland	0.55	0.01	0.006
7	Sweden	0.81	0.01	0.008
8	Norway	0.61	0.003	0.002
9*a*	Sum 2–8	0.71[1]	0.24	0.17
10*a*	"Other countries"	0.71[2]	0.30	0.21
11a	*All countries (1+9a+10a)*		*1.00*	*1.00*
9*b*	Sum 4–8	0.74[1]	0.063	0.047
10*b*	"Other countries"	0.74[2]	0.297	0.222
11b	*All countries (1+2+3+9b+10b)*		*1.00*	*1.01*
9*c*	Median 4–8[3]	0.71		
10*c*	"Other countries"	0.71	0.297	0.213
11c	*All countries (1+2+3+9b+10c)*		*1.00*	*1.00*

V

The causal mechanism that is supposed to lie behind the above correlations may be analysed in somewhat more detail for a country for which research in this direction has been carried out sufficiently, viz. Holland. Such an analysis may both give some evidence on the relative importance of the different influences mentioned in Section II, and yield a possibility of testing the coefficients found in correlating the Dutch cycle with the world cycle and the "exchange rate of the guilder against the world."

For this purpose, the mechanism described in rather general terms in Section II will be split up into the following stages:

(i) the influence of the world cycle on the quantity of Dutch exports;

[1] Col. 5÷Col. 4. [2] As in preceding line. [3] For 2–8 median equal to weighted average.

(ii) the influence of a relative appreciation or depreciation of the guilder on the quantity of Dutch exports;

(iii) the influence of a relative appreciation or depreciation of the guilder on Dutch production for the home market in competition with foreign producers:

(a) consumption goods,
(b) production goods;

(iv) the propagation of the effects under (i) to (iii) through the whole of the Dutch economy.

(i) The quantity of Dutch exports is determined by the following equation:[1]

$$u_A = z + 2.23(p_W)_{-0.25} - 1.26 p_A \quad \text{(T.6) (1.1)}$$

where

u_A = exports (quantity), in "guilders of 1923–33";
z = world exports (quantity), index, 1929 = 100;
p_W = world price level (here lagged by 0.25 of a year);
p_A = Dutch export price index

(all measurements are in absolute deviations from average).

When we correlate world exports, included in this equation, with the series for world production (w) used above, we find

$$z = 1.00w,^{2} \ (R = 0.940) \quad (1.2)$$

both measured in percentage deviations from average.

The average of u_A is 88, of z, 85; this yields, in percentage deviations from average, when we combine (1.1) and (1.2):

$$u_A = 0.96w + \text{(some other terms treated separately under (ii))}. \quad (1.3)$$

Thus the dependence of Dutch exports on the world cycle is established.

(ii) We may find the influence of a relative depreciation of the guilder on the quantity exported by starting from an equation, the graph of which has been published in *De Nederlandsche Conjunctuur*[3]:

$$\frac{u_A}{z} = -2.16\frac{p_A - p_W}{p_A}, \ (R = 0.903) \quad (2.1)$$

indicating that the ratio of Dutch exports to world exports is negatively influenced by the margin between Dutch prices — world prices.

[1] J. Tinbergen: Paper read before the Vereeniging voor Staathuishoudkunde en Statistiek, The Hague, 1936 (Dutch). The numbers of Tinbergen's equations quoted are indicated by (T . . .).

[2] Here, as in the following correlations in this section, the coefficients found have been divided by the total correlation coefficient in order to obtain coefficients that are not reduced as a consequence of imperfect correlation. The correlation coefficients obtained are given with every regression equation.

[3] J. Tinbergen: "La disparité des prix et le commerce extérieur," *De Nederlandsche Conjunctuur*, May, 1936, lower graph on p. 19. Professor Tinbergen has kindly put the figures at my disposal. The series p_A is not identical with that used in (2.1), but this is of no relevance in this connection.

This equation may be transformed into

$$\frac{u_A}{z} = -2.16+2.16\frac{p_W}{p_A} \quad \text{(2.2)}$$

or, neglecting a constant :

$$\frac{u_A}{z} = 2.16\frac{p_W}{p_A} \quad \text{(2.3)}$$

This may be interpreted that, *given a certain* z, we may write :

$$u_A = 2.16\frac{p_W}{p_A} \quad \text{(2.4)}$$

It is to be expected that $\frac{p_W}{p_A}$ depends on the relation between the guilder and other currencies r :

$$\frac{p_W}{p_A} = -0.43r \quad (R = 0.970) \quad \text{(2.5)}$$

(with an important trend in favour of Dutch exports).

Combining (1.3), (2.4), and (2.5) we find :

$$u_A = 0.96w-0.93r \quad \text{(2.6)}$$

(iii) (a) We start from the following three equations taken from Tinbergen's paper mentioned above : [1]

$$(1)\ x'_A-0.71u'_A = -0.42p+0.39p'_A \quad \text{(T.12) (3.1)}$$

where

x'_A = quantity of raw materials for consumption goods imported,
u'_A = quantity of finished consumption goods imported,
p = price of home-produced consumption goods,
p'_A = price of imported consumption goods.

This is a competition equation, indicating that, the higher the margin between Dutch prices and import prices, the more finished consumption goods and the less raw materials will be imported.

$$(2)\ a-b = 0.20u'_A+0.98x'_A \quad \text{(T.9) (3.2)}$$

employment in consumption goods industries $(a-b)$ increases about five times as much when there is an additional import of *raw materials* for consumption goods as when *finished* consumption goods are imported.

$$(3)\ u = 1.72u'_A+4.35x'_A \quad \text{(T.11) (3.3)}$$

The quantity of consumption goods delivered (u) is determined by the same factors as is $(a-b)$, the value added to raw materials being two and a half times as large as the value added to imported finished consumption goods.

Elimination of two of these three equations gives :

$$a-b = 0.19u+0.066p'_A-0.072p \quad \text{(3.4)}$$

[1] They are also to be found in J. Tinbergen : *An Econometric Approach to Business Cycle Problems*, Paris, 1937.

Here employment in consumption-goods industries is expressed as a function of consumption and the margin between import prices and Dutch prices.

Now p is slightly dependent on p'_A, and on raw material prices r'_A :

$$p = 0.04p'_A + 0.15r'_A + \dots \text{(some irrelevant terms)} \quad \text{(T.2)} \quad (3.5)$$

As r'_A may be approximated by $1.46p'_A$, we find

$$p = 0.26p'_A \quad (3.6)$$

and, consequently,

$$a-b = 0.19u + 0.066p'_A - 0.019p'_A$$

$$a-b = 0.19u + 0.047p'_A \quad (3.7)$$

The average of $(a-b) = 76.2$, of $u = 335$, and of $p'_A = 100$; so the equation becomes, in percentage deviations from average,

$$a-b = 0.84u + 0.06p'_A \quad (3.71)$$

Now p'_A is determined by many causes. There is, however, in this context, only one of them that interests us, *viz.* the cause that makes p'_A (measured in guilders) in Holland different from the price level for the same goods abroad. Evidently, this cause is the relation between the guilder and other currencies, i.e. r. The higher the guilder in relation to other currencies, the cheaper will be imported goods. Given the smallness of the Dutch market, the change may be taken to be proportional, so that we may replace $0.06p'_A$ by $-0.06r$.

We still have to pass from quantity of labour $(a-b)$ to volume of production (u). We may take, therefore, the average relation found in equation (3.7), and so, finally, put

$$u = -0.07r \quad (3.8)$$

(iii) (b) In principle, the same procedure might be followed to determine the importance of a devaluation on the competitive production of capital goods for the home market. It may, however, be easily shown, that a devaluation cannot cause much systematic difference between the price of imported capital goods (q'_A) and the price of those produced at home (q). For :

$$q = 0.74q'_A + 0.16s'_A + \dots \text{etc.} \quad \text{(T.4)} \quad (3.9)$$

where s'_A is the price of raw materials for capital goods. Now s'_A fluctuates about one and a half times as much as q'_A, so that approximately

$$q = q'_A \dots \text{etc.} \quad (3.10)$$

The competition term $0.86(q'_A - q)$ in Tinbergen's equation (T.13) is, therefore, systematically independent of q'_A, and consequently of r.

(iv) What we have found so far are only the *primary* effects of a change in conditions of Holland *vis-à-vis* the world. These effects spread, of course, through the economy, thereby causing the total effects to be considerably larger than the primary ones. The relation between the former and the latter may be expressed as a " multiplier." [1]

[1] I should like to stress the difference between this multiplier and Mr. Harrod's " foreign trade multiplier " (*The Trade Cycle*, p. 146), by which total production is related to the volume of foreign investment.

Foreign investment is, I think, perhaps the worst phenomenon to link up to total activity

The best evidence on the magnitude of this multiplier may, I think, be obtained from a calculation on the basis of a complete system of equations, describing all important relations in Dutch economic life. With such a system, the consequences of certain changes, e.g. a public works policy, may be determined over any period of time one likes. Thus, in Table III, we compare employment when a policy of additional investment of 14 units every year is followed during three consecutive years, with employment that would exist *without* this policy. The difference is taken over so many units of time (ten years) as to take into account all after-effects of the policy: in the tenth year there is no longer any difference. The total of the difference, taken over

TABLE III

Calculated Employment in Holland

A. When a policy of additional investment is followed during years 1, 2, 3.
B. When no special policy is followed.
C. A−B: additional employment through the adoption of policy A.

Year.	0	1	2	3	4	5	6	7	8	9	10	Total.
A	−15.6	−12.2	−10.3	−10.5	−16.5	−19.1	−19.5	−20.5	−20.8	−20.8	−21.0	
B	−15.6	−18.6	−19.2	−20.1	−20.4	−20.8	−20.9	−20.9	−21.1	−21.0	−21.0	
C	0	6.4	8.9	9.6	3.9	1.7	1.4	0.4	0.3	0.2	0	32.8

Lines A and B from *Tinbergen, An Econometric Approach, etc.*, p. 60, for years 0 to 7, from that point using formula given on p. 61 until C becomes 0.

these ten years is the total employment caused by the works. 42 units of additional primary investment turn out to cause 32.8 units of employment. The equivalent primary employment was 21 units (labour cost amounting to 50 per cent of total cost). Hence the multiplier $= \frac{32.8}{21} = 1.56$. It should be noted that this figure is remarkably close to some other employment multipliers that have been calculated for Holland: 1.50–1.75 by Mr. Van Mill, 1.48 by Mr. Reuchlin, and 1.42 in the Dutch *Labour Plan*.[1]

We now assume the effects of additional investment on employment to

by a multiplier. True, in any *static* position there is a definite relation between the two; and this may be of interest for some studies of long-run changes. But there is nothing like £1,000,000 of additional foreign investment causing £2,000,000 of additional income when the multiplier is 2. The causation actually runs like this: additional exports ⟶ additional income ⟶ additional imports. It is not much use, then, to compare the difference between the additional exports and the additional imports (i.e. *ceteris paribus*, net foreign investment) with additional home production.

On the other hand, there is, in many cases, a practically independent one-sided causation between exports and home production. There may, indeed, be some reaction via rising prices—but in many cases this will be almost negligible. The case, therefore, seems to be nearly an ideal one to treat with the multiplier procedure—much better than the relation between investment and total production.

[1] See a summary of these calculations—J. J. Polak: *Public Works as a Form of Business Cycle Policy*, The Hague, 1938 (Dutch), p. 18.

be the same as the effects of additional production for exports—an assumption that is certainly not too far from reality. So multiplying the coefficients of (2.6) by 1.56 and then by the relation of the average of u_A to the average of total production [1] to return to percentage deviations from the average, we find :

(a) Total production $= 0.344w - 0.333r$ . . . . (4.1)

To this should be added the result of equation (3.8), treated in the same way :

(b) . . . . $- 0.095r$ . . . . (4.2)

or

(a)—(b) : Total production $= 0.344w - 0.428r$ . . . . (4.3)

Finally, the fact must be taken into account that the index of industrial activity fluctuates much more than total production, as the latter also includes such rather stable components as agriculture and retail trade. The relation of the fluctuations was found to be 1.96 ($R = 0.967$). When multiplying the right-hand member of (4.3) by this factor, we find :

Industrial production $= 0.68w - 0.85r$ . . . . (4.4)

The result of directly correlating the series was (cf. Table I), after division by $R = 0.96$:

Industrial production $= 0.56w - 0.84r$ . . . . (4.5)

When we take into account the quite considerable margin of error involved in the numerous correlation and elimination processes that lead to (4.4), both results are, I think, sufficiently close to regard the one as a proof of the other.

VI

This test of the coefficients obtained for one small country may also give some support to the coefficients of about the same magnitude obtained for countries of roughly the same economic structure. In this group we might perhaps even include the United Kingdom, since it has in common with the other countries the important rôle of international trade in her economy.

The United States, on the other hand, has such an exceptionally small international trade in comparison to total production (5–10 per cent), that one would expect to find for that country coefficients that are distinctly lower. This expectation is, indeed, partly fulfilled : the influence of a change in the exchange rate proved to be too small to be clearly observable and the correlation calculation even gave a small positive coefficient (+0.29). The coefficient representing the influence of the rest of the world's cycle proved, on the contrary, to be by far the largest found in all countries analysed : 1.92. *Does* this coefficient actually represent the influence of the cycle of all other countries on that of the United States ?

It is a generally held opinion that no country in the world has such strong

[1] According to Tinbergen's approach, total production is found as $u + 2b$.

endogenous business cycles as the United States, and that these cycles play a large part in causing the alternation of prosperity and depression elsewhere. It would seem, then, that the large coefficient is due to the influence of the United States cycle on that of other countries, rather than the other way round. In the following an attempt is made to prove this proposition.

To this purpose we make the extreme, but perhaps not very unrealistic, assumption that the United States is the only country with an endogenous cycle; and that, consequently, the cyclical waves in all other countries are nothing but the result of various repercussions of the American cycle. What information does this give us on the meaning of the coefficient 1.92?

We call—

c an original cyclical disturbance in the United States;

$a_1, a_2 \ldots a_n$ the openness of the non-American (for simplicity: European) countries 1, 2 ... n, i.e. the degree in which their economic systems react to changes in economic conditions abroad;

$\beta_1, \beta_2 \ldots \beta_n$ their relative importance, or, in statistical terms, their weight in an index of production;

a the openness of the United States—for which we want to see whether the figure 1.92 is confirmed;

b the relative importance of United States production.

From this it follows that in an index of world production

$$\beta_1+\beta_2+ \ldots +\beta_n+b = 1 \qquad (5.1)$$

An increase in the United States cycle from zero[1] to c will, according to these definitions, cause an increase in the world production index of bc. Hence, in any European country k production will rise to

$$a_k bc \qquad (5.2)$$

But this is only the first stage of the propagation, for country k will then receive the repercussions of the changes in production in the other European countries; these changes are multiplied by the weights (β's) of the respective countries and then reduced through k's openness. Hence, we get in k, as a provisional total change:

$$a_k bc+a_k(\beta_2 a_2 bc+\beta_3 a_3 bc+ \ldots +\beta_{k-1}a_{k-1}bc+\beta_{k+1}a_{k+1}bc+ \ldots +\beta_n a_n bc) \qquad (5.3)$$

or

$$a_k bc(1+\Sigma_{(k)}a\beta) \qquad (5.4)$$

where $\Sigma_{(k)}$ indicates summation over all countries except k.

To simplify our calculations we may at once make the approximation that

$$\Sigma_{(1)}a\beta \cong \Sigma_{(2)}a\beta \cong \ldots \cong \Sigma_{(n)}a\beta \cong \Sigma a\beta \qquad (5.5)$$

and define

$$\Sigma a\beta = A \qquad (5.6)$$

This approximation seems reasonable when the number of countries (n)

[1] As the calculations have been made in deviations from average, a zero position indicates the average.

is large, the weight of each country is relatively small, and the α's of the various countries are not too different.

As, further, a has been found to be <1 for all European countries, and $\Sigma\beta$ is <1 according to (5.1), we may take it that

$$A<1 \qquad (5.7)$$

Equation (5.6) allows us to simplify (5.4) to

$$a_k bc(1+A) \qquad (5.8)$$

When one compares this formula to (5.1), it becomes clear that, as the result of one more European repercussion, the position in country k will be:

$$a_k bc(1+A+A^2) \qquad (5.9)$$

and after r repercussions:

$$a_k bc(1+A+ \ . \ . \ . \ +A^r) \qquad (5.10)$$

As a consequence of (5.7) the series of repercussions is decreasing and (5.10) may be written as

$$a_k bc\frac{1}{1-A} \qquad (5.11)$$

This formula holds for any country; so for the whole of Europe we find:

$$bc\frac{1}{1-A}\,.\,\Sigma\alpha\beta \quad \text{or} \quad bc\,\frac{A}{1-A}. \qquad (5.12)$$

We have not yet taken into account the repercussions back from Europe to America, and *vice versa*. This may easily be done by observing that each wave from the European production via American production back to European production is multiplied by four factors:

(i) the American openness a;
(ii) the American weight b;
(iii) the openness of any European country a_k; and
(iv) its weight β_k.

Hence, the addition to a wave w is, after one "journey,"

$$ab\Sigma\alpha\beta\,.\,w \quad \text{or} \quad abAw\,. \qquad (5.13)$$

This, too, continues as a geometrical series, the sum of which is

$$\frac{w}{1-abA}. \qquad (5.14)$$

This repercussion process of each European wave may be directly applied to the whole increase in production calculated before. We may put w equal to (5.12) and find as the final result for the European part in the world cycle:

$$\frac{bcA}{(1-A)\,(1-abA)}. \qquad (5.15)$$

The total American cycle may now easily be determined. It is equal to the original c *plus* a $\times$ every element of the (weighted) European cycle, or:

B

$$c+\frac{abcA}{(1-A)(1-abA)}= \qquad (5.16)$$

$$=c\,.\,\frac{1-A+abA^2}{(1-A)(1-abA)}. \qquad (5.17)$$

When we wish to compare the American cycle with the non-American cycle, both in percentage deviations from average, we have to divide the latter by its weight in the world cycle, by which it is multiplied in (5.15). This weight is $\Sigma\beta$, or, according to (5.1): $(1-b)$. Hence, the factor of proportionality between the American and the non-American cycle is, in our units,

$$\frac{(1-A+abA^2)(1-b)}{bA} \qquad (5.18)$$

This form is evidently equal to the apparent openness of the United States: 1.92. Inserting, moreover, $b=0.46$ (cf. Table I), we may express a (the real openness) as a function of A; this yields:

$$a=\frac{5.74A-2.17}{A^2} \qquad (5.19)$$

This gives the following values for a with given values for A (Table IV).

TABLE IV

Values calculated for a *according to* (5.19) *with given values for* A

A	a
1.00	3.6
0.80	3.8
0.76	3.8 (max.)
0.60	3.5
0.50	2.8
0.40	0.8
0.39	0.5
0.38	0.1
0.37	−0.4
0.30	−5.0
0.20	−25.5

It is seen that a is very much dependent on the value we choose for A. Luckily, A may be determined rather accurately. It is, according to (5.6), the weighted average of the openness of "all other countries." Though we have analysed only seven of these other countries, we may nevertheless (on the basis of the reasoning on page 87) take the figure of 0.70 as a good estimate for the average openness [1] of *all* other countries. The sum of the weights to be

[1] This is, indeed, not the average *real*, but the average *apparent* openness of these countries. The difference between the two is, however, not very large; this proposition will be proved in Appendix I.

applied to this coefficient is not 1, but 0.54 (cf. equation (5.1)). Hence, we find for A : 0.38, and for a : 0.1. This figure shows a very good harmony with the coefficient we expected to find on the basis of *a priori* reasoning : a very low positive figure.

Geneva.

J. J. POLAK.

APPENDIX I

RELATION BETWEEN "REAL" AND "APPARENT" OPENNESS OF SMALL COUNTRIES

We consider the repercussions between one small country k and all other countries. We call the combined cycle of the latter C—which takes into account all repercussions between these countries.

The weight of the cycle of k is β_k ; accordingly that of all other countries is $(1-\beta_k)$.

The real openness of k is a_k, its apparent openness a'_k. For the real openness of the other countries we may take : (i) for the United States : 0, the approximate *a priori* coefficient which has been confirmed in Section VI [1]; weight 0.46 ; (ii) for the other "other countries" the average *apparent* openness of 0.70 ; weight $(0.54-\beta_k)$; as we shall prove that the real openness is only slightly different from the apparent one, it has no appreciable influence on our calculations to make a distinction between the two here.[2]

Hence, the openness of all "other countries," which we shall use in our calculations, is $\dfrac{0.70(0.54-\beta_k)+0\times 0.46}{1-\beta_k}=\dfrac{0.38-0.70\beta_k}{1-\beta_k}$.

According to the line of thought developed above (cf. (5.2) etc.), we find that C is reflected in country k as

$$a_k(1-\beta_k)C \qquad (6.1)$$

After one repercussion to and from all other countries it will be

$$a_k(1-\beta_k)C\left(1+a_k\beta_k(1-\beta_k)\frac{0.38-0.70\beta_k}{1-\beta_k}\right) \qquad (6.2)$$

and after an infinite series of repercussions

$$\frac{a_k(1-\beta_k)C}{1-a_k\beta_k(0.38-0.70\beta_k)} \qquad (6.3)$$

As the second term of the denominator is very small as compared to 1, (0.3) may approximately be written as

$$C\,.\,a_k(1-\beta_k)[1+a_k\beta_k(0.38-0.70\beta_k)] \qquad (6.4)$$

As β_k is small, we may neglect all terms with β_k^2 and β_k^3, and accordingly simplify (6.4) to

$$C\,.\,a_k(1-\beta_k+0.38a_k\beta_k) \qquad (6.5)$$

The form that multiplies C in (6.5) is equal to what we would have found by correlating C with the cycle of country k. Hence :

$$a'_k = a_k[1-\beta_k(1-0.38a_k)] \qquad (6.6)$$

As a_k in the right-hand side of this equation is multiplied by the very small factor $0.38\beta_k$, we may replace it by a'_k. We then find, once more approximating a quotient by a product (cf. (6.4)) :

$$a_k = a'_k[1+\beta_k(1-0.38a'_k)] \qquad (6.7)$$

---

[1] This assumption tends to overstate the difference to be found between a and a'. If we assumed the United States real openness to be 0.5 instead of 0, we should find a 4 per cent difference instead of one of 5 per cent.

[2] This may easily be seen in equation (6.7) below.

Hence, considering the difference between the real and apparent openness for the average " non-American " country, with $\alpha' = 0.70$ and $\beta = 0.07$,[1]—this case is especially relevant for the calculation of A—we should find α to be about 5 per cent [2] higher than α'.

Appendix II

STATISTICAL MATERIAL USED

I. Indices of Production in Manufacturing and Mining Industries

Country.	*1920*	*1921*	*1922*	*1923*	*1924*	*1925*	*1926*	*1927*	*1928*	*1929*	*1930*	*1931*	*1932*	*1933*	*1934*	*1935*	*1936*
United States ..	87	67	85	101	95	104	108	106	111	119	96	81	64	76	80	90	105
United Kingdom	105	71	87	90	100	101	88	|107	106	112	103	94	93	98	110	118	130
France	62	55	78	88	109	108	126	110	127	139	140	124	96	107	99	94	99
Belgium	72	63	84	96	105	100	118	131	138	139	117	105	87	93	92	100	108
Czechoslovakia ..	—	60	55	58	76	79	77	89	96	100	89	81	64	60	67	70	80
Holland	—	58	59	62	69	75	78	80	95	100	102	91	80	86	92	91	98
Sweden	96	75	87	96	109	112	123	127	134	151	150	144	136	145	|175	192	208
Norway	103	73	91	100	108	117	104	107	118	131	133	127[3]	117[3]	123	128	140	151
World	66	56	68	74	77	|82	84	90	94	100	88	79	69	78	85	96	110

Sources : *Statistical Yearbook of the League of Nations ; Statistisches Handbuch der Weltwirtschaft ; De Nederlandsche Conjunctuur.*

In some cases, indicated by a |, it was necessary to go over from one series to another. This procedure is always somewhat arbitrary. It is believed, however, that another choice would not materially influence the results.

II. Part of World Trade in 1929

Country.	*Per cent of Total World Trade.*
United States	14.4
United Kingdom	13.6
France	6.5
Canada	3.8
India	3.2
Japan	3.0
Italy	2.8
Belgium	2.9
Holland	2.9
Australia	2.0
Total	55.1

Source : *Review of World Trade*, League of Nations.

Principle of selection : All countries having at least 2 per cent of world trade in 1929, except Germany (9.8 per cent) and Argentina (2.6 per cent) for which representative currency quotations could not easily be obtained.

---

[1] This figure has been found as the weighted average of *all* weights in the League of Nations' World Production Index, with the exception of that of the United States ; it covers twenty-three countries. Formula : $\frac{\Sigma\beta^2}{\Sigma\beta}$.

[2] Cf. note [1] on preceding page.

[3] See note to Table I above.

III. Exchange Rates in Terms of Dollars, 1929 = 100.

Country.	*1920*	*1921*	*1922*	*1923*	*1924*	*1925*	*1926*	*1927*	*1928*	*1929*	*1930*	*1931*	*1932*	*1933*	*1934*	*1935*	*1936*
United States ..	100	100	100	100	100	100	100	100	100	100	100	100	100	100	100	100	100
United Kingdom	75	79	91	94	91	99	100	100	100	100	100	93	72	87	104	101	102
France	179	191	209	155	134	124	83	100	100	100	100	100	100	128	168	168	156
Canada	90	90	99	99	100	101	101	101	101	100	101	97	89	93	101	100	101
India	106	73	79	86	88	100	100	100	100	100	100	93	73	88	104	102	104
Japan	109	104	104	105	89	89	102	101	100	100	107	106	61	55	64	62	63
Italy	95	82	91	88	83	76	74	99	100	100	100	100	98	127	164	157	139
Belgium	265	268	276	188	167	172	118	100	100	100	100	100	100	128	168	133	122
Holland	86	84	94	97	95	100	100	100	100	100	100	100	100	128	168	168	160
Australia.. ..	75	79	92	96	94	102	101	101	101	100	96	75	58	70	84	82	83
World ..	110	110	117	108	102	104	98	100	100	100	100	97	87	99	117	114	111
Czechoslovakia ..	100	100	100	100	100	100	100	100	100	100	100	100	100	129	143	140	136
Sweden	77	85	98	99	99	100	100	100	100	100	100	94	69	82	97	94	95
Norway	62	56	66	63	52	67	84	98	100	100	100	94	68	80	95	93	94

Source : *Standard Statistics*, New York ; 1929 figures made equal to 100.

World : indices of ten first-mentioned countries multiplied by percentages from Table II, then added up, and total for 1929 made equal to 100.

[29]

A Theory of Demand for Products Distinguished by Place of Production

Paul S. Armington *

I. Introduction and Summary

INTERNATIONAL TRADE flows are commonly identified and classified on the basis of three characteristics: the kind of merchandise involved, the country (or region) of the seller, and the country (or region) of the buyer. In theories of demand for tradable goods, it is frequently assumed that merchandise of a given kind supplied by sellers in one country is a perfect substitute for merchandise of the same kind supplied by any other country. This assumption implies—leaving aside any factors that lead buyers to spend more for a given item than necessary—that elasticities of substitution between these supplies are infinite and that the corresponding price ratios are constants. While the importance of lags in buyers' responses, and other such "imperfections" in buyers' behavior, need not be overlooked, an appeal to them as the sole basis for changes in relative prices of directly competing merchandise would appear to be neither realistic nor attractive theoretically. A preferable approach would be to recognize explicitly that any world model of feasible dimensions would identify few, if any, kinds of merchandise for which the perfect-substitutability assumption is tenable.

Accordingly, this paper presents a general theory of demand for products that are distinguished not only by their kind—e.g., machinery, chemicals—but also by their place of production. Thus French machinery, Japanese machinery, French chemicals, and Japanese chemicals might be 4 different products distinguished in the model. Such products are distinguished from one another in the sense that they are assumed to be imperfect substitutes in demand. Not only is each good, such as chemicals, different from any other good but also each good is assumed to be differentiated (from the buyers' viewpoint) according to the suppliers' area of residence. If the model distinguished 10 goods and

* Mr. Armington, economist in the Current Studies Division of the Research Department, is a graduate of Swarthmore College and the University of California at Berkeley. Before joining the Fund in 1965, he was a Research Fellow in Economics at the Brookings Institution.

20 supplying areas, the number of products distinguished in the model would be 200.[1]

The geographic areas that serve as a basis for distinguishing products by origin are also used as a basis for identifying different sources of demand. For example, if France is identified as 1 of the 20 supplying areas, the model would contain a function expressing French demand for each of the 200 products. There would be 10 French demands for domestic products and 190 French import demands. Conversely, for each French product, there would be 1 domestic demand and 19 export demands.

The problem confronted in this paper is that of systematically simplifying the product demand functions to the point where they are relevant to the practical purposes of estimation and forecasting.[2] Starting with the general Hicksian model, the exposition runs through a sequence of progressively more restrictive assumptions leading to a specification of the product demand functions which, though highly simplified, preserves the relationships between demand, income, and prices that are apt to be quantitatively significant.

The fundamental modification of the basic Hicksian model is the assumption of independence—an assumption whose implications have already been explored in other branches of demand theory and in capital theory.[3] In its present application, the assumption of independence states, roughly, that buyers' preferences for different products of any given kind (e.g., French chemicals, Japanese chemicals) are independent of their purchases of products of any other kind.[4] By this assumption, for example, an increase in purchases of French machinery does not change the buyers' relative evaluation of French chemicals and Japanese chemicals. Given the assumption of independence, the quantity of each good demanded by each country (e.g., French demand

[1] In the second paragraph of Section I and throughout the rest of the paper, a distinction is made between "goods" and "products." "Goods" are distinguished only by kind (that is, by the kinds of wants or needs they serve), whereas "products" are distinguished both by kind and by place of production. The geographic and commodity dimensions of the model are spelled out more formally in Section II.

[2] See Section VI, pages 170–71.

[3] Seminal contributions were made by Robert M. Solow, "The Production Function and the Theory of Capital," *The Review of Economic Studies,* Vol. XXIII (1955–56), pp. 101–108, and by R. H. Strotz, "The Empirical Implications of a Utility Tree," *Econometrica,* Vol. 25 (April 1957). A fuller development is given by I. F. Pearce, Chapters 4 and 5, in his *A Contribution to Demand Analysis* (Oxford University Press, 1964), pp. 133–230. H.A.J. Green provides a good review of the relevant literature in his book, *Aggregation in Economic Analysis* (Princeton University Press, 1964).

[4] The assumption of independence is stated in more precise terms in Section III, page 164.

for chemicals-in-general) can in principle be measured unambiguously.[5] In other words, there exist demands for *groups* of competing products. Following conventional terminology, each such demand can be called a market. There would be, for example, the French market for chemicals; and chemicals supplied by different countries or areas (including France, of course) could be said to compete in that market. Moreover, demand for any particular product (e.g., French demand for Japanese chemicals) can be rigorously expressed as a function of the size of the corresponding market (e.g., French demand for chemicals-in-general) and of relative prices of the competing products.

It is next assumed that each country's market share is unaffected by changes in the size of the market as long as relative prices in that market remain unchanged. On this additional assumption, the size of the market is a function of money income and of the prices of the various goods (e.g., the price of chemicals-in-general, the price of machinery-in-general).[6] Combining this function with the product demand function described above, the demand for any product becomes a function of money income, the price of each good, and the price of that product relative to prices of other products in the same market. (Prices of products competing in other markets are influential only insofar as they determine the prices of goods.)

If there are a large number of products competing in the market (in other words, if the number of supplying areas identified in the model is large), then further ways of simplifying the product demand functions are needed if they are to be of much relevance to practical research. The approach suggested in this study (Section IV) is to assume that (a) elasticities of substitution between products competing in any market are constant—that is, they do not depend on market shares, and (b) the elasticity of substitution between any two products competing in a market is the same as that between any other pair of products competing in the same market. These assumptions yield a specific form for the relation between demand for a product, the size of the corresponding market, and relative prices; and the only price parameter in this function is the (single) elasticity of substitution in that market.

Differentiation of the demand functions yields an analysis of changes in demand for any given product (Section V). The percentage change in demand for any product depends additively on the growth of the market in which it competes and on the percentage change in the product's share in that market. The change in the product's market

[5] See page 164.
[6] See pages 165–66.

share will depend in a specific way on the change in the product's price relative to the average change in prices of products in the market. The growth of the market will depend mainly on the change in income and on the income elasticity of demand for the respective good (i.e., the class of products of which the given product is a member). In order that market growth depend exclusively on this income effect (and not on the prices of goods), certain additional assumptions are needed (see p. 170). The study concludes with a brief discussion of the relevance of demand theory to some of the current research in the area of trade analysis and forecasting.

II. Geographic and Commodity Dimensions of the Model

Any large model of the world economy would make use of some vector of countries or other geographic areas, $C=(C_1,C_2, \ldots ,C_m)$, as well as some vector of goods, $X=(X_1,X_2, \ldots ,X_n)$. The present demand model stipulates, in addition, that each good is differentiated in use (e.g., in demand) according to where it is produced. Any "good," X_i, refers to a group of "products," each supplied by a different country or area; that is, $X_i=(X_{i1},X_{i2}, \ldots ,X_{im})$, where X_{ij} is assumed to be an imperfect substitute for $X_{ik}(j \neq k)$ from the viewpoint of buyers in any country or area, C_i. For later reference, it will be useful to set out these specifications in the following format:

$$\begin{aligned} X= &(X_{11},X_{12}, \ldots ,X_{1m},X_{21},X_{22}, \\ &\ldots ,X_{2m}, \ldots ,X_{n1},X_{n2}, \ldots ,X_{nm}) \\ \equiv &(X_1,X_2, \ldots ,X_n), \text{ where} \\ X_i\equiv &(X_{i1}, X_{i2}, \ldots ,X_{im}), \text{ for } i=1,2, \ldots ,n. \end{aligned} \tag{1}$$

The top line of this formulation, which may be called the product vector, can also be presented as a product matrix:

goods ↓ \ supplying countries →	1	2	. . . .	m
1	X_{11}	X_{12}	. . . .	X_{1m}
2	X_{21}	X_{22}	. . . .	X_{2m}
.	.	.	. . . .	.
.	.	.	. . . .	.
.	.	.	. . . .	.
n	X_{n1}	X_{n2}	. . . .	X_{nm} .

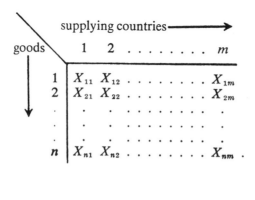

The country vector $C=(C_1,C_2, \ldots ,C_m)$ also lists the various sources of demand. The demand of buyers in any country, C_i, for any product, X_{ij} is here called a product demand, and the demand side of the model is described by all such functions. Since there are m demands for each product, and since there are mn products, the demand side of the model is comprised of m^2n product demands, of which mn are domestic demands and $mn(m-1)$ are export (or import) demands. (Import demands are not residual demands, depending on domestic supply functions, as is the case in models which presume that goods are homogeneous over different sources of supply. In the present model, the analysis of *ex ante* demand—domestic, import, and export—requires no particular assumptions about supply functions.)

III. Market Demands and Product Demands: An Application of the Assumption of Independence

Ex ante demand functions state relationships that must exist among certain variables if buyers are to be satisfied. Buyers' satisfaction entails getting the most for their money, given the available selection of products and their prices. Demand functions may thus be viewed as statements of conditions under which an index of buyers' satisfaction is as high as limited incomes and given prices permit. Given such an index, U, these conditions or demand functions can be derived by maximizing U subject to a budget constraint.[7]

The general approach to the derivation of the product demand functions identified in the previous section is to express U as a function of all mn products; that is, using (1), $U=U(X)$.[8] Then, given a corresponding price vector,

$$P=P_{11},P_{12}, \ldots ,P_{1m},P_{21},P_{22}, \ldots ,P_{2m}, \ldots ,P_{n1},P_{n2}, \ldots ,P_{nm}, \quad (2)$$

and national money expenditure, D, $U(X)$ is maximized subject to the budget constraint $D=PX'$. Once U is specified, the first-order condi-

[7] Each of the four simplifying assumptions introduced in Section I can be interpreted as a certain restriction on, or specification of, the index U. Thus, by using the maximization procedure to derive the product demand functions, a formal link is established between general demand functions and the highly simplified relationships mentioned in Section I.

[8] The rest of this paper deals with the demand of any single country and does not consider the aggregation of demands across markets. Hence, no notation is attached to U, or to other variables mentioned later, to identify the country whose demand is referred to.

tions, together with the budget constraint, imply this country's *mn* demand functions, each one having the general form

$$X_{ij}=X_{ij}(D,P_{11},P_{12}, \ldots ,P_{1m},P_{21},P_{22}, \ldots ,$$
$$P_{2m}, \ldots ,P_{n1},P_{n2}, \ldots ,P_{nm}), \tag{3}$$

for all *i* and all *j*.

Of course, the close association between products of the same kind is not reflected at all in the general form of (3). The problem at hand is to specify *U* in such a way that the information implicit in the product classification scheme is fully utilized, to the end that the product demand functions may be appropriately simplified. The first and most fundamental step is to specify *U* in such a way that the demand for any good, X_i, can be measured unambiguously.

Professor Solow asked the question (albeit in a rather different context),[9] Under what condition can *U* be "collapsed" in the following way?

$$U= U(X_{11},X_{12}, \ldots ,X_{1m},X_{21},X_{22},$$
$$\ldots ,X_{2m}, \ldots ,X_{n1},X_{n2}, \ldots ,X_{nm}) \tag{4}$$
$$\equiv U'(X_1,X_2, \ldots ,X_n), \text{ where}$$
$$X_i\equiv \phi_i(X_{i1},X_{i2}, \ldots ,X_{im}), \text{ for } i=1,2, \ldots ,n.$$[10]

If *U* can be so collapsed, all combinations of $X_{i1},X_{i2}, \ldots ,X_{im}$ which yield any given value of X_i are equally good, and that given value is a specific quantity of X_i-in-general. In other words, if (4) is true, demands for goods—here called market demands—can be measured unambiguously. The necessary and sufficient condition for collapsing *U* is that marginal rates of substitution between any two products of the *same* kind must be independent of the quantities of the products of all *other* kinds.[11] In other words, buyers' relative evaluation (at the margin) of different products competing in a given market must not be affected by their purchases in other markets. This is the assumption of independence.[12]

[9] See Solow, *op. cit.*
[10] Compare with equation (1).
[11] The proof is in Solow, *op. cit.*, and in an early work by Leontief referred to in the Solow article.
[12] In theory, the assumption of independence might be viewed as tautological; for independence could well be taken as a *defining* characteristic of products distinguished by their kind (that is, by the kind of want or need they serve). Following this approach, an alternative, more basic assumption would be necessary, namely, that products can be rigorously classified by kind in the first place. In practice, however, goods must be identified within the framework of some available classification scheme (such as the Standard International Trade Classification). Given this constraint, independence is not necessarily tautological. How far the

Given the assumption of independence, which leads to (4), demand for any particular product X_{ij} can be written as a function of X_i and of relative product prices in the ith market.[13] If the demand for X_i can in turn be related to income and appropriate price variables, then a manageable specification of (3) is within reach.

The price variables on which X_i will depend are, naturally, the prices of goods, or P_i $(i=1,2, \ldots, n)$, and P_i is a function of prices of products in the ith market, just as X_i is a function of quantities of these products. But P_i cannot be just any function of product prices; the prices of goods must be such that the demand for the ith good, which they explain, is consistent with the optimum selection of products in the ith market. More exactly, the demand for X_i as determined by income and prices of goods must be the same as the value of ϕ_i implied by all demands for products in the ith market as determined by direct reference to income and product prices.

This condition is fulfilled if

$$P_i = P_{i1} \div \frac{\partial \phi_i}{\partial X_{i1}} = P_{i2} \div \frac{\partial \phi_i}{\partial X_{i2}} = \ldots = P_{im} \div \frac{\partial \phi_i}{\partial X_{im}}, \quad \text{for } i=1,2, \ldots, n. \tag{5}$$

[14]

Note that (5) implies that

$$\frac{P_{i1}}{P_{i2}} = \frac{\dfrac{\partial \phi_i}{\partial X_{i1}}}{\dfrac{\partial \phi_i}{\partial X_{i2}}}, \quad \text{and} \quad \frac{P_{i2}}{P_{i3}} = \frac{\dfrac{\partial \phi_i}{\partial X_{i2}}}{\dfrac{\partial \phi_i}{\partial X_{i3}}}, \quad \text{etc.,}$$

which are the first-order conditions for optimum mix of products in the ith market.

It is not clear from inspection of (5) that P_i depends only on product prices. In fact, to ensure that P_i is independent of X_i, it must be assumed that ϕ_i is linear and homogeneous. Then the partial derivatives in (5) depend only on ratios of quantities of products demanded in the ith

assumption restricts the realism of the model depends on the extent to which the different items in the goods vector correspond to more or less discrete wants or needs. Within the limitation imposed by the available classification scheme, the analyst may attempt to select a vector of goods that renders the independence assumption as realistic as possible. It should be noted, however, that supply factors may suggest to him a rather different choice of goods. The identification of goods, for purposes of a complete model, cannot be guided in practice by any single criterion.

13 The function may be derived from the conditions for minimizing the money cost of purchasing any given volume of X_i, given some specification of ϕ_i. The derivation is analogous to that of the demand for a factor of production as a function of output and relative factor prices.

14 See Solow, *op. cit.*

market, and these ratios in turn depend only on ratios of the product prices; hence, P_i is only a function of $P_{i1}, P_{i2}, \ldots, P_{im}$. The assumption that the quantity index functions are linear and homogeneous is the second restriction (the first being the assumption of independence) that has been placed on U. This second restriction means that market shares must depend only on relative prices of the products in the market; shares must not depend on the size of the market itself.

An important property of P_i as given in (5) is that $P_iX_i = \sum_{k=1}^{m} P_{ik}X_{ik} =$ money expenditure in the ith market.[15] This fact leads directly to the budget constraint,

$$D \equiv \sum_{i=1}^{n}\sum_{k=1}^{m} P_{ik}X_{ik} = \sum_{i=1}^{n} P_iX_i,$$

which, along with U' in (4), determines the demand for X_i. To summarize, the demand for any good, X_i, can be obtained by maximizing $U'(X_1, X_2, \ldots, X_n)$ subject to the constraint $D = \sum_{i=1}^{n} P_iX_i$. Then, the demand for any product, X_{ij}, can be obtained by minimizing the cost of purchasing the volume of X_i just determined; that is, the expression $\sum_{k=1}^{m} P_{ik}X_{ik}$ is minimized subject to the constraint $X_i = \phi_i(X_{i1}, X_{i2}, \ldots, X_{im})$. The resulting demand functions are

$$X_i = X_i(D, P_1, P_2, \ldots, P_n), \text{ where } X_i \text{ is any good, and} \tag{6}$$

$$X_{ij} = X_{ij}\left(X_i, \frac{P_{ij}}{P_{i1}}, \frac{P_{ij}}{P_{i2}}, \ldots, \frac{P_{ij}}{P_{im}}\right), \text{ where } X_{ij} \text{ is any product.} \tag{7}$$

[15] Equation (5) implies that

$$P_{i1}X_{i1} = P_i\frac{\partial\phi_i}{\partial X_{i1}}X_{i1};$$

$$P_{i2}X_{i2} = P_i\frac{\partial\phi_i}{\partial X_{i2}}X_{i2};$$

$$\vdots \qquad \vdots$$

$$P_{im}X_{im} = P_i\frac{\partial\phi_i}{\partial X_{im}}X_{im}.$$

Therefore,

$$\sum_{k=1}^{m} P_{ik}X_{ik} = P_i\sum_{k=1}^{m}\frac{\partial\phi_i}{\partial X_{ik}}X_{ik} = P_iX_i,$$

using the assumption that ϕ_i is linear and homogeneous, together with Euler's theorem.

By substituting (6) into (7), a particular reformulation of (3) is obtained. In this reformulation the role of prices is handled by only $m+n$ variables, compared with mn variables in (3): product prices outside the ith market affect X_{ij} only insofar as they determine price levels in other markets (that is, $P_1, P_2, \ldots, P_{i-1}, P_{i+1}, \ldots, P_n$). This, specifically, is the sense in which the two restrictions on U serve to utilize the information implicit in (1). And these restrictions—both very mild—open the door to more powerful simplifying assumptions, such as those discussed below.

IV. Product Demand Functions Assuming a Single, Constant Elasticity of Substitution in Each Market

If many countries or areas were identified in the model, equations (7), in the above form, would probably be too complicated to be of practical use. A way to simplify them is to introduce the assumptions that (a) elasticities of substitution in each market are constant and (b) the elasticity of substitution between any two products competing in a market is the same as that between any other pair of products competing in the same market. In terms of the index U (equation 4), these assumptions are equivalent to the specification that the ϕ_i's are constant-elasticity-of-substitution (CES) functions, having the general form

$$X_i \equiv \phi_i(X_{i1}, X_{i2}, \ldots, X_{im})$$

$$= \left[b_{i1}X_{i1}^{-\rho_i} + b_{i2}X_{i2}^{-\rho_i} + \ldots + b_{im}X_{im}^{-\rho_i} \right]^{-\frac{1}{\rho_i}}.\text{[16]} \tag{8}$$

Given (8), it can be shown that equations (7) have the form

$$X_{ij} = b_{ij}^{\sigma_i} X_i \left(\frac{P_{ij}}{P_i} \right)^{-\sigma_i}, \tag{9}$$

where σ_i is the elasticity of substitution in the ith market and b_{ij} is a constant.[17]

In equation (9) and in all those that follow, X_{ij} can be interpreted either as the demand for the ith good supplied by country j or as the demand for the ith good supplied by the jth *group* of countries. For example, the jth group could be all foreign countries; in this instance, (9) would express the demand for total imports of the ith good (X_{ij}) as a function of demand for the ith good wherever produced (X_i) and of the ratio of the average import price (P_{ij}) to the average price level in the market (P_i). This flexible interpretation of the variables in (9) is the

[16] This function is linear and homogeneous, as required.
[17] The derivation of (9) from (8) is in Part I of the Appendix.

consequence of two properties of ϕ_i as specified in (8): (a) the marginal rate of substitution between any pair of products competing in the ith market is independent of demand for any other product(s) in that market, so that ϕ_i in (8) can be "collapsed" in the manner of equation (4); (b) ϕ_i in (8) is linear and homogeneous, so that the index functions appearing in any "collapsed" form of (8) must be linear and homogeneous also. Hence there exists an unambiguous demand for any subset of products in the ith market, and this demand can be related to the over-all market demand just as X_i, under strictly analogous conditions, can be related to total income.

Equation (9) can be written in a variety of useful ways; for example,

$$P_{ij}X_{ij}=b_{ij}^{\sigma_i}(P_iX_i)\left(\frac{P_{ij}}{P_i}\right)^{1-\sigma_i}, \tag{10}$$

which relates money demand for X_{ij} to the size of the corresponding market measured in value terms, and

$$\frac{X_{ij}}{X_i}=b_{ij}^{\sigma_i}\left(\frac{P_{ij}}{P_i}\right)^{-\sigma_i}, \text{ or} \tag{11}$$

$$\frac{P_{ij}X_{ij}}{P_iX_i}=b_{ij}^{\sigma_i}\left(\frac{P_{ij}}{P_i}\right)^{1-\sigma_i}, \tag{12}$$

which expresses the market share as the dependent variable. As is clear from (12), value shares are constant if $\sigma_i=1$. (In this special case, ϕ_i is a Cobb-Douglas function with parameters b_{ik}.) If $\sigma_i>1$, a relative fall (or increase) in P_{ij} yields an increase (or decrease) in the market share of X_{ij}. The reverse is true if $\sigma_i<1$. Ordinarily, it would be expected that σ_i exceeds unity: an "improvement in competitiveness" should yield an increased share, and vice versa. But the logic of the model (as distinct from some particular interpretation of the variables) places no such restriction on this elasticity.

V. Analysis of Changes [18]

Total differentiation of the market demand function (6) and the product demand function (9) yields the following relation between the percentage change in demand for X_{ij}, in value terms, and percentage changes in income and price variables:

[18] The argument of this section is more fully developed in Part II of the Appendix.

$$\frac{d(P_{ij}X_{ij})}{P_{ij}X_{ij}} = \epsilon_i \frac{dD}{D} - (\eta_i - 1)\frac{dP_i}{P_i} + \sum_{k \neq i} \eta_{i/k} \frac{dP_k}{P_k} - (\sigma_i - 1)\left(\frac{dP_{ij}}{P_{ij}} - \frac{dP_i}{P_i}\right), ^{19} \quad (13)$$

where ϵ_i is the income elasticity of demand for X_i, η_i is the direct price elasticity of demand for X_i, and $\eta_{i/k}$ is the cross elasticity of demand for X_i with respect to P_k $(k=1,2, \ldots ,i-1,i+1, \ldots ,n)$. The first three terms together measure the growth of the market (in value) for X_{ij}, while the fourth term measures the percentage change in X_{ij}'s share of the market.

The change in demand for X_{ij} can also be analyzed in more traditional terms by replacing the price level in the ith market with product prices and market shares. As is demonstrated in the Appendix,[20] one of the properties of P_i is that the percentage change in this variable is equal to an average of changes in component product prices, weighted by market shares; specifically,

$$\frac{dP_i}{P_i} = \sum_{k=1}^{m} S_{ik} \frac{dP_{ik}}{P_{ik}}, \text{ where } S_{ik} = \frac{P_{ik}X_{ik}}{P_iX_i}.$$

Substituting this summation for $\frac{dP_i}{P_i}$ in the second and fourth terms of (13), one obtains (after a little shuffling of terms) the following result:

$$\frac{d(P_{ij}X_{ij})}{P_{ij}X_{ij}} = \epsilon_i \frac{dD}{D} - \Big[(1 - S_{ij})(\sigma_i - 1) + S_{ij}(\eta_i - 1) \Big] \frac{dP_{ij}}{P_{ij}} + \sum_{k \neq j} \Big[S_{ik}(\sigma_i - 1) - S_{ik}(\eta_i - 1) \Big] \frac{dP_{ik}}{P_{ik}} + \sum_{k \neq i} \eta_{i/k} \frac{dP_k}{P_k}. \quad (14)$$

Here, the growth of demand for X_{ij} is divided into the following components: an income effect (first term), an "own price" effect (second term), the effect of prices of closely related products (third term), and the effect of all other prices (fourth term). The bracketed coefficient of $\frac{dP_{ij}}{P_{ij}}$ is the direct price elasticity of demand for X_{ij}, in value terms, while the bracketed coefficient of $\frac{dP_{ik}}{P_{ik}}$ represents the cross elasticity of demand for X_{ij} with respect to the price of any other product competing in the

---

[19] $\sum_{k \neq i}$ indicates summation over all k, for $k = 1,2, \ldots ,i-1,i+1, \ldots ,n$.

[20] See page 174, footnote 29.

same market. Conversely, of course, the cross elasticity of demand for X_{ik} with respect to P_{ij} would be given by $[S_{ij}(\sigma_i - 1) - S_{ij}(\eta_i - 1)]$.

The analysis of changes into market-expansion factors and share-adjustment factors (equation 13) is of greater relevance to current research than the more conventional breakdown shown in (14)—see Section VI. On the other hand, (14) is useful because it focuses attention on how changes in individual product prices affect trade, and in particular on the role played by market shares.[21]

In the event that equations (13) or (14) are yet too complicated to suit practical purposes, the feasibility of introducing two further simplifying assumptions may be considered. The first of these is that the elasticity of demand for X_i (η_i) equals unity, and the second is that the third term of (13), or the fourth term of (14), is small enough to be ignored. The first of these assumptions, which implies that expenditure on the ith class of products is independent of price changes in the ith market, focuses attention on the effects of changes in *relative* prices in the market and abstracts from any (presumably small) effects of changes in the general *level* of prices in the market. The second assumption would not be unreasonable if changes in price levels in other markets are very small, or if such changes are apt to have offsetting effects on demand for X_i.[22] On these additional assumptions, (13) and (14) reduce to the relatively simple formula

$$\frac{d(P_{ij}X_{ij})}{P_{ij}X_{ij}} = \epsilon_i \frac{dD}{D} - (\sigma_i - 1)\left(\frac{dP_{ij}}{P_{ij}} - \frac{dP_i}{P_i}\right). \qquad (15)$$

VI. Conclusion

In much of the current research in the area of trade analysis and forecasting, the change in any particular trade flow is viewed as the sum

[21] See pages 174–75 of the Appendix. This role of market shares is examined in detail by the author in "The Geographic Pattern of Trade and the Effects of Price Changes," which will be published in a subsequent issue of *Staff Papers.* The partial elasticities in (14) formally resemble the formulas derived by Hicks and Allen. (See J. R. Hicks and R. G. D. Allen, "A Reconsideration of the Theory of Value: Part II.—A Mathematical Theory of Individual Demand Functions," *Economica,* New Series, Vol. I (1934), pp. 201–202 and 208–11.) Similar formulas have been derived and applied in the context of international trade by Professor P. J. Verdoorn. For his early work in this area, see Annex A of his contribution to the annual papers of the Dutch Economic Society, 1952, and also Appendix A of "The Intra-bloc Trade of Benelux," in *Economic Consequences of the Size of Nations,* ed. by E. A. G. Robinson (London, 1960), pp. 319–21.

[22] One might be tempted to assume that the cross elasticities, $\eta_{i/k}$, are zero. However, if $\eta_{i/k} = 0$ and $\eta_i = 1$, then ϵ_i must equal unity, since, by definition, $\eta_i = \sum_{k \neq i} \eta_{i/k} + \epsilon_i$. See Paul Anthony Samuelson, *Foundations of Economic Analysis* (Harvard University Press, 1961), p. 105. Ordinarily, it would be intolerably restrictive to assume that the income elasticity is perforce equal to 1.

of two components: the change that would occur if the given seller country were to maintain its share in the market (that is, its share of total sales to the given buyer country in the given commodity class), and the deviation of actual sales from constant-shares sales. Within this framework, forecasting of trade is essentially a two-step process in which (a) forecasts of growth in the various markets, together with a base-period matrix, yield a constant-shares matrix for the projection period, and (b) this constant-shares matrix is modified to take account of factors expected to yield gains or losses in shares. In retrospective analysis, the role of these factors is evaluated by comparing actual sales in particular markets—or, more frequently, groups of markets—with constant-shares sales. This general approach to trade analysis and forecasting might conveniently be called the modified-shares approach.[23]

Is the breakdown of changes in trade flows into the two components merely a matter of accounting that seems useful for certain purposes but which has no causal significance, no roots in buyers' behavior? Or can the traditional theory of buyers' behavior provide a satisfactory rationalization of the modified-shares approach? Can a few assumptions tie theory and practice together?

This paper shows that the modified-shares approach does not require any radical departures from the traditional theory of buyers' behavior. Starting with the fundamental assumption that products of different countries competing in the same market are imperfect substitutes, the study shows how a powerful and reasonably realistic specialization of the function describing buyers' behavior—the specialization indicated by equations (4) and (8)[24]—leads to quite simple demand relationships embodying the constant-share and share-adjustment components. The modified-shares approach may find foundations on the demand side that are different from those proposed in this paper, including the market imperfections referred to at the outset. But the assumption that products are distinguished by place of production is a very convenient point of departure toward a rigorous theory of market growth and share adjustment.

[23] For an introduction to the research in this area, together with an appraisal of alternative frameworks for the analysis of international trade, see Grant B. Taplin, "Models of World Trade," *Staff Papers*, Vol. XIV (1967), pp. 433–55. Forecasting methods involving the modified-shares approach are currently being developed at the International Monetary Fund and elsewhere. Regarding retrospective analysis, studies of export performance measured by changes in average export shares appear from time to time in recent Fund Annual Reports.

[24] See pages 164 and 167.

MATHEMATICAL APPENDIX

I. Derivation of Product Demands Assuming a Single, Constant Elasticity of Substitution in Each Market

Section IV introduces the simplifying assumption that any given quantity-index function, ϕ_i, has the generalized CES form;[25] that is (to repeat),

$$X_i = \phi_i(X_{i1}, X_{i2}, \ldots, X_{im}) = \left[b_{i1}X_{i1}^{-\rho_i} + b_{i2}X_{i2}^{-\rho_i} + \ldots + b_{im}X_{im}^{-\rho_i}\right]^{-\frac{1}{\rho_i}}, \quad (8)$$

where $\sum_{k=1}^{m} b_{ik} = 1$, and where ρ_i is a constant greater than -1. The demand for any product competing in the ith market, X_{ij}, can then be expressed as a specific function of X_i and of relative prices (see equation 9). The derivation of this function is given below.

If any given quantity of the ith good is to be obtained at least money cost, the following conditions must hold:

$$\frac{\dfrac{\partial \phi_i}{\partial X_{ij}}}{\dfrac{\partial \phi_i}{\partial X_{ik}}} = \frac{b_{ij}}{b_{ik}}\left(\frac{X_{ik}}{X_{ij}}\right)^{1+\rho_i} = \frac{P_{ij}}{P_{ik}}, \qquad k = 1,2, \ldots, m.^{26} \quad (16)$$

That is, marginal rates of substitution between competing products must equal the corresponding ratios of their prices.

Solving (16) for X_{ik},

$$X_{ik} = X_{ij}\left(\frac{b_{ik}P_{ij}}{b_{ij}P_{ik}}\right)^{\frac{1}{1+\rho_i}}, \qquad k = 1,2, \ldots, m. \quad (17)$$

Using this equation, (8) can be expressed as a relation between X_i, X_{ij}, and the prices. Rearrangement of this relation, to show X_{ij} as the dependent variable, yields the desired product demand function. First, however, (17) might conveniently be rewritten in terms of the elasticity of substitution. By rearranging (17),

$$\frac{X_{ij}}{X_{ik}} = \left(\frac{b_{ik}}{b_{ij}}\right)^{-\frac{1}{1+\rho_i}}\left(\frac{P_{ij}}{P_{ik}}\right)^{-\frac{1}{1+\rho_i}}, \qquad k = 1,2, \ldots, m,$$

from which it follows that the elasticity of substitution between X_{ij} and any other product competing in the market is equal to the constant $\frac{1}{1+\rho_i}$.[27] To simplify

[25] The CES form has been used elsewhere in the literature in a somewhat similar framework; see, for example, Harry G. Johnson, "The Costs of Protection and Self-Sufficiency," *The Quarterly Journal of Economics*, Vol. LXXIX (1965), pp. 358–62.

[26] There are, of course, only $m - 1$ nontrivial first-order conditions. To except the trivial case where $j = k$ would unduly complicate the notation.

[27] The elasticity of substitution between X_{ij} and X_{ik} is, by definition,

$$-\frac{\partial\left(\dfrac{X_{ij}}{X_{ik}}\right)\left(\dfrac{P_{ij}}{P_{ik}}\right)}{\partial\left(\dfrac{P_{ij}}{P_{ik}}\right)\left(\dfrac{X_{ij}}{X_{ik}}\right)}.$$

notation, let $\frac{1}{1+\rho_i} \equiv \sigma_i$, the elasticity of substitution in the ith market. Equation (17) then becomes

$$X_{ik} = X_{ij}\left(\frac{b_{ik}P_{ij}}{b_{ij}P_{ik}}\right)^{\sigma_i}, \qquad k = 1,2, \ldots ,m, \tag{18}$$

where $0 < \sigma_i < \infty$. (The limiting cases have the following interpretations: if $\sigma_i = 0$, the products are perfect complements; if $\sigma_i = \infty$, the products are perfect substitutes.)

Now, substituting (18) into (8), and writing ρ_i in terms of σ_i

$$X_i = \left\{\sum_{k=1}^{m} b_{ik}\left[X_{ij}\left(\frac{b_{ik}P_{ij}}{b_{ij}P_{ik}}\right)^{\sigma_i}\right]^{\frac{\sigma_i - 1}{\sigma_i}}\right\}^{\frac{\sigma_i}{\sigma_i - 1}} \tag{19}$$

$$= b_{ij}^{-\sigma_i}X_{ij}\left[\sum_{k=1}^{m} b_{ik}^{\sigma_i}\left(\frac{P_{ij}}{P_{ik}}\right)^{\sigma_i - 1}\right]^{\frac{\sigma_i}{\sigma_i - 1}}.$$

Then, solving (19) for X_{ij}

$$X_{ij} = b_{ij}^{\sigma_i}X_i\left[\sum_{k=1}^{m} b_{ik}^{\sigma_i}\left(\frac{P_{ij}}{P_{ik}}\right)^{\sigma_i - 1}\right]^{\frac{\sigma_i}{1-\sigma_i}}. \tag{20}$$

Equation (20) may be viewed as a particular specification of (7).

Simplification of (20) can be effected by relating the complex, relative-price term to the price level in the market, P_i. P_i has a particular form, corresponding to the specification of ϕ_i. Using (5) and (8),

$$P_i = P_{ij} \div \frac{\partial \phi_i}{\partial X_{ij}} = P_{ij}b_{ij}^{-1}X_{ij}^{\frac{1}{\sigma_i}}X_i^{-\frac{1}{\sigma_i}}.$$

Then, substituting from (19)

$$P_i = P_{ij}b_{ij}^{-1}X_{ij}^{\frac{1}{\sigma_i}}b_{ij}X_{ij}^{-\frac{1}{\sigma_i}}\left[\sum_{k=1}^{m} b_{ik}^{\sigma_i}\left(\frac{P_{ij}}{P_{ik}}\right)^{\sigma_i - 1}\right]^{\frac{1}{1-\sigma_i}} \tag{21}$$

$$= P_{ij}\left[\sum_{k=1}^{m} b_{ik}^{\sigma_i}\left(\frac{P_{ij}}{P_{ik}}\right)^{\sigma_i - 1}\right]^{\frac{1}{1-\sigma_i}}.$$

Therefore,

$$\left(\frac{P_{ij}}{P_i}\right)^{-\sigma_i} = \left[\sum_{k=1}^{m} b_{ik}^{\sigma_i}\left(\frac{P_{ij}}{P_{ik}}\right)^{\sigma_i - 1}\right]^{\frac{\sigma_i}{1-\sigma_i}}. \tag{22}$$

Substituting (22) into (20), equation (9) is obtained. To repeat,

$$X_{ij} = b_{ij}^{\sigma_i}X_i\left(\frac{P_{ij}}{P_i}\right)^{-\sigma_i}, \tag{9}$$

where X_{ij} is any country's demand for any product, expressed in volume.

II. Analysis of Changes

Total differentiation of (9) and (6) yields the relationship between changes in X_{ij} and changes in the explanatory variables. Starting with (9),

$$dX_{ij} = \frac{\partial X_{ij}}{\partial X_i} dX_i + \frac{\partial X_{ij}}{\partial P_{ij}} dP_{ij} + \frac{\partial X_{ij}}{\partial P_i} dP_i$$

$$= \frac{\partial X_{ij}}{\partial X_i} dX_i - \sigma_i X_{ij} P_{ij}^{-1} dP_{ij} + \sigma_i X_{ij} P_i^{-1} dP_i.$$

Dividing through by X_{ij},

$$\frac{dX_{ij}}{X_{ij}} = \frac{\partial X_{ij} X_i}{\partial X_i X_{ij}} \frac{dX_i}{X_i} - \sigma_i \frac{dP_{ij}}{P_{ij}} + \sigma_i \frac{dP_i}{P_i} \tag{23}$$

$$= \frac{dX_i}{X_i} - \sigma_i \left(\frac{dP_{ij}}{P_{ij}} - \frac{dP_i}{P_i} \right),$$

noting that the partial elasticity of X_{ij} with respect to X_i equals unity. The first term represents the growth of the market for X_{ij}; the second term represents the percentage change in X_{ij}'s share of the market. The growth of the market can, of course, be analyzed by differentiating (6).

$$\frac{dX_i}{X_i} = \epsilon_i \frac{dD}{D} - \eta_i \frac{dP_i}{P_i} + \sum_{k \neq i} \eta_{i/k} \frac{dP_k}{P_k},\text{[28]} \tag{24}$$

where ϵ_i is the income elasticity of demand for X_i, η_i is the direct price elasticity of demand for X_i, and $\eta_{i/k}$ is the cross elasticity of demand for X_i with respect to P_k $(k = 1,2, \ldots, i-1, i+1, \ldots, n)$. And substituting (24) into (23),

$$\frac{dX_{ij}}{X_{ij}} = \epsilon_i \frac{dD}{D} - \eta_i \frac{dP_i}{P_i} + \sum_{k \neq i} \eta_{i/k} \frac{dP_k}{P_k} - \sigma_i \left(\frac{dP_{ij}}{P_{ij}} - \frac{dP_i}{P_i} \right). \tag{25}$$

It can be shown that $\frac{dP_i}{P_i} = \sum_{k=1}^{m} S_{ik} \frac{dP_{ik}}{P_{ik}}$, where $S_{ik} = \frac{P_{ik} X_{ik}}{P_i X_i}$ = the market share of X_{ik} in value terms.[29] Thus the effects on X_{ij} of changes in prices of products

[28] $\sum_{k \neq i}$ indicates summation over all k, for $k = 1,2, \ldots, i-1, i+1, \ldots, n$.

[29] Since ϕ_i in (8) is linear and homogeneous,

$$X_i = \sum_{k=1}^{m} \frac{\partial \phi_i}{\partial X_{ik}} X_{ik} = \sum_{k=1}^{m} \frac{P_{ik}}{P_i} X_{ik}, \text{ using (5).}$$

Therefore,

$$P_i = \sum_{k=1}^{m} \frac{X_{ik}}{X_i} P_{ik}.$$

Then

$$\frac{dP_i}{P_i} = \sum_{k=1}^{m} \frac{P_{ik} X_{ik}}{P_i X_i} \frac{dP_{ik}}{P_{ik}} + \sum_{k=1}^{m} \frac{P_{ik} X_{ik}}{P_i X_i} \frac{d\left(\frac{X_{ik}}{X_i}\right)}{\frac{X_{ik}}{X_i}}, \text{ and}$$

the second term, a weighted average of percentage changes in market shares, is zero.

competing in the ith market depend not only on σ_i and η_i but also on market shares. This role of market shares can be seen more clearly if the second and fourth terms of (25) are expanded in the following way:

$$-\sigma_i\left(\frac{dP_{ij}}{P_{ij}}-\frac{dP_i}{P_i}\right)-\eta_i\frac{dP_i}{P_i}=-\sigma_i\left(\frac{dP_{ij}}{P_{ij}}-\sum_{k=1}^{m}S_{ik}\frac{dP_{ik}}{P_{ik}}\right)-\eta_i\sum_{k=1}^{m}S_{ik}\frac{dP_{ik}}{P_{ik}}$$

$$=-\sigma_i\left(\frac{dP_{ij}}{P_{ij}}-S_{ij}\frac{dP_{ij}}{P_{ij}}-\sum_{k\neq j}S_{ik}\frac{dP_{ik}}{P_{ik}}\right)-\eta_i\left(S_{ij}\frac{dP_{ij}}{P_{ij}}+\sum_{k\neq j}S_{ik}\frac{dP_{ik}}{P_{ik}}\right)$$ [80]

$$=-(1-S_{ij})\sigma_i\frac{dP_{ij}}{P_{ij}}+\sum_{k\neq j}S_{ik}\sigma_i\frac{dP_{ik}}{P_{ik}}-S_{ij}\eta_i\frac{dP_{ij}}{P_{ij}}-\sum_{k\neq j}S_{ik}\eta_i\frac{dP_{ik}}{P_{ik}}$$

$$=-\Big[(1-S_{ij})\sigma_i+S_{ij}\eta_i\Big]\frac{dP_{ij}}{P_{ij}}+\sum_{k\neq j}\Big[S_{ik}\sigma_i-S_{ik}\eta_i\Big]\frac{dP_{ik}}{P_{ik}}.$$

Substituting into (25),

$$\frac{dX_{ij}}{X_{ij}}=\epsilon_i\frac{dD}{D}-\Big[(1-S_{ij})\sigma_i+S_{ij}\eta_i\Big]\frac{dP_{ij}}{P_{ij}}+\sum_{k\neq j}\Big[S_{ik}\sigma_i-S_{ik}\eta_i\Big]\frac{dP_{ik}}{P_{ik}}$$

$$+\sum_{k\neq i}\eta_{i/k}\frac{dP_k}{P_k}. \qquad (26)$$

The bracketed coefficient of $\frac{dP_{ij}}{P_{ij}}$ in (26) is the direct, partial elasticity of demand for X_{ij}, and the bracketed coefficient of $\frac{dP_{ik}}{P_{ik}}$ is the cross elasticity of demand for X_{ij} with respect to the price of any other product in the ith class. The direct elasticity of demand for X_{ij} is inversely related to its market share (assuming that $\sigma_i > \eta_i$). Intuitively, the more important is X_{ij} in the market, the smaller will be the percentage gain or loss from the substitution associated with a given change in its price—and the larger the percentage change in demand for all other products in the market. By the same token, the cross elasticity of demand for X_{ij}, with respect to the price of any other product in the same market, is directly related to the market share of that product (again, if $\sigma_i > \eta_i$).

The two bracketed coefficients in (26) each have two terms, reflecting the fact that a change in the price of a product affects demand for that product, or any other product in the same market, in two different ways. First, the price change alters *relative* prices of products in that market, bringing about a substitution effect measured by the first term. Second, the price change alters the price *level* in the market, bringing about a change in the size of the market itself, and this market-expansion effect is measured by the second term. In (25), market-expansion factors and share-adjustment factors are clearly separated, while in (26) they are scrambled in such a way as to focus attention on the effects of particular price changes.

The percentage change in demand for X_{ij} in value terms may be obtained by adding $\frac{dP_{ij}}{P_{ij}}$ to both sides of (25) or (26). After considerable manipulation it is found that this change, $\frac{d(P_{ij}X_{ij})}{P_{ij}X_{ij}}$, is the same as shown in (25) or (26) except that σ_i and η_i are replaced by $(\sigma_i - 1)$ and $(\eta_i - 1)$, respectively.

---

[80] $\sum_{k\neq j}$ indicates summation over all k, for $k = 1,2, \ldots, j-1, j+1, \ldots, m$.

In some practical applications, it may be feasible to introduce the further simplifying assumptions that $\eta_i = 1$ and that the fourth term of (26), or the third term of (25), is quantitatively insignificant. In this event, the percentage change in demand for X_{ij} in value terms reduces to a relatively simple formula. Starting from (26)

$$\frac{d(P_{ij}X_{ij})}{P_{ij}X_{ij}} = \epsilon_i \frac{dD}{D} - (1 - S_{ij})(\sigma_i - 1)\frac{dP_{ij}}{P_{ij}} + \sum_{k \neq j} S_{ik}(\sigma_i - 1)\frac{dP_{ik}}{P_{ik}}$$

$$= \epsilon_i \frac{dD}{D} - (\sigma_i - 1)\left(\frac{dP_{ij}}{P_{ij}} - \sum_{k=1}^{m} S_{ik}\frac{dP_{ik}}{P_{ik}}\right) \tag{27}$$

$$= \epsilon_i \frac{dD}{D} - (\sigma_i - 1)\left(\frac{dP_{ij}}{P_{ij}} - \frac{dP_i}{P_i}\right).$$

The first term represents the growth of the market for X_{ij}, in value terms, and the second term represents the percentage change in the product's value share of the market. Of course, this result can also be derived directly from (25).

[30]

On an Empirical Law Governing the Productivity of Labor, P. J. VERDOORN, Centraal Planbureau, 's-Gravenhage, The Netherlands.

FOR THE purpose of making long term estimates of the future development of the productivity of labor, a comparison has been made in a number of cases between: (*i*) the rate of increase of labor productivity, and (*ii*) the corresponding increase of the volume of output. As a result of these investigations for industry as a whole, a fairly constant relationship has been found between the two rates of increase just mentioned. For the United States, the United Kingdom, The Netherlands, etc., regression equations have been computed showing the average relationship between the increase of productivity and output in a number of different branches of industry, when measured over long periods. The type of regression equation used was $x/a = x^{\alpha}e^{\beta t}$.

The statistician, impressed by this apparent dependency of the development of the productivity of labor on the growth of production, may feel inclined to formulate his findings in the form of an empirical law, in the same manner as Pareto sixty years ago formulated his famous law of the distribution of income. In this case the "law" would read that productivity as a rule has been increasing as the square root of the volume of output. As a matter of fact, however, a law of this type describes only the behavior pattern of the industrial entrepreneur and therefore cannot even be regarded as one of J. S. Mill's *axiomata media*, unless per chance a satisfactory explanation by means of technical conditions or the more general economic laws becomes feasible.

Using a model of long term structural equations, where the known Cobb-Douglas function is adopted, the elasticity of labor productivity with regard to output can be bound to significant parameters of the labor and capital supply, etc. A rigidly constant relation between the rates of increase of productivity and output appears not to be a necessary consequence of the model; nevertheless, the assumption of a constant elasticity, if not an ideal working hypothesis, might serve well as one of the criteria for judging the consistency of the existing long-term plans with the experience of the past.

DISCUSSION: We must not disclaim the great importance of empirical laws, which are often incentives to theoretical developments and necessary tools for their application. The results obtained would perhaps be improved by using productivity and employment as variables instead of productivity and output (since output = productivity × employment). It is hard to attribute in general a homogeneity of first degree to a production function: compensations can occur in certain cases between increasing and decreasing industrial costs, and so on, but these should be factual ascertainments rather than a priori general assumptions. Homogeneity, however, does not present one of the general assumptions of that analysis.

[31]

COMPLEMENTARITY AND LONG-RANGE PROJECTIONS

BY P. J. VERDOORN

This article studies the implications of complementarity on the problem of the long-term forecast. The conditions for maintaining long-run equilibrium between factor demand and factor supply are derived and illustrated with the help of a three-factor model, so as to bring out the particular problem of foreign trade. Equilibrium for all of the three factors appears possible only if the parameters of the system satisfy a set of specific relations or certain policy variables are introduced. Finally the complete system as used by the Central Planning Bureau is presented, together with the numerical values chosen for the parameters.

1. SOME IMPLICATIONS OF COMPLEMENTARITY

1.1. FOR THE PURPOSE of long-range projections a choice must be made as to the nature of the production function. Two extreme assumptions are possible, viz., perfect substitutability and strict complementarity. Most long-range projections published hitherto are based explicitly or implicitly upon the hypothesis of complementarity. Some of the implications of this hypothesis will be discussed in the first and second sections of this paper. In the third a model based on complementarity as has been used by the Central Planning Bureau for projections covering the period 1950–1970 will be presented.

1.2. The type of model to be considered will cover a period of only one to three decades. It is, moreover, not concerned with the cyclical variations of the variables nor with problems of a really secular character such as those studied by Haavelmo.[1] Furthermore, the implications of disequilibria due to a disproportionate development as between sectors of the economy will be ignored.[2]

The main problem to be dealt with is therefore the question of equilibrium for the macro variables in the medium-long run. As compared with economic statics the equilibrium concept should obviously be widened so as to allow for the dynamics of long-run development. In the following equilibrium will be defined as a development that is compatible with the equality of demand and supply for each of the factors of production. Neither stable values of the endogenous variables nor constancy of the policy parameters is required. Defined in this way, long-term equilibrium does not necessarily imply optimal development. Unless only one development-equilibrium is possible, restrictions other than that of equilibrium are necessary to guarantee the best development, however defined.

1.3. *Equilibrium and substitutability.*

Perfect substitution presupposes a production function of the form

[1] Haavelmo, T., *A Study in the Theory of Economic Evolution*, Amsterdam, 1954.

[2] Hawkins, D., "Some Conditions of Macroeconomic Stability," *Econometrica*, 16, 4 (Oct., 1948), p. 309 ff.

(1) $$y = y(x_1, \cdots, x_n),$$

where y is national product and $x_1, \cdots, x_n$ are factors with continuous partial derivatives, $\partial y/\partial x_i$, $i = 1, \cdots, n$.

Assuming perfect competition, factor prices will equal marginal product. Given n factors of production, there will be n demand equations:

(2) $$p_i = \partial y/\partial x_i,$$

where $p_1, \cdots, p_n$ are the factor prices.

Let there be n supply equations:

(3) $$x_i = x_i(p_i, \bar{x}_{ir}),$$

where $\bar{x}_{ir}$ represents a group of exogenous variables with $r = 1, \cdots, m$. Thus, there are $2n + 1$ equations and $2n + 1$ endogenous variables. Equilibrium as defined in Section 1.2 is therefore guaranteed whatever the development of the exogenous variables in (3). Equilibrium is even maintained if the price elasticities of factor supply have zero values. Factor prices then are determined by (2) and the entire supply will be employed, since (1) allows for every imaginable combination of factors.

Only in the case where for some factors the price elasticity of supply is infinite will the equality of demand and supply for these factors, and hence equilibrium, not be possible, although the system can nevertheless be solved for y for any set of fixed factor prices.

The implications of perfect substitutability between capital and labour have been investigated by Tinbergen,[3] who used the Cobb-Douglas function. Linear forms of this function have been dealt with by Haavelmo.[4] Recently Klein and Goldberger used a linear form for their new business cycle model[5] and Vail used one for his statistically tested long-term model covering the period 1869–1953.[6]

1.4. *Equilibrium and complementarity.*

In the absence of a waste process, under complementarity as opposed to substitutability, only one factor combination is admissible at each level of national product:

(4) $$x_i = x_i(y)$$

where $x_i(y)$ may represent any function that relates x_i uniquely to y.

Since (4) does not allow for partial derivatives with respect to p_i, it must be considered as specifying factor demand.

[3] Tinbergen, J., "Zur Theorie der langfristigen Wirtschaftsentwicklung," *Weltwirtschaftliches Archiv*, 55, 3 (Mei, 1942), p. 511 ff.

[4] Haavelmo, T., *loc. cit.*

[5] Klein, L. R. and Goldberger, A. S., *An Econometric Model of the United States, 1929–1952*, Amsterdam, 1955.

[6] Valavanis-Vail, S., "An Econometric Model of Growth, U.S.A.: 1869–1953." *American Economic Review*, XLV, 2 (May, 1955), p. 208 ff.

Assuming free competition, decisions as to y are determined by maximum profits at given factor prices. Let

$$z = y - \sum_1^n x_i p_i \tag{5}$$

be profits.

Profits are maximal if $dz/dy = 0$; hence if:

$$1 - \sum_1^n f_i(y) p_i = 0 \tag{6}$$

where

$$f_i(y) = dx_i/dy. \tag{7}$$

Corresponding to the n demand equations there are again n supply equations

$$x_i = x_i(p_i\,,\, \bar{x}_i). \tag{3}$$

Equilibrium requires that factor demand should equal factor supply, that is to say, that the right-hand sides of (3) and (4) should be equal. Given equilibrium, p_i is therefore uniquely related to y and to the exogenous factors:

$$p_i = p_i(\bar{x}_i\,,\, y), \tag{8}$$

this equation being subject to the condition that there exist partial derivatives of (3) with respect to p_i,

$$0 \neq \partial x_i/\partial p_i \neq \infty. \tag{9}$$

If every factor ($i = 1, \cdots, n$) satisfies (9), the equilibrium value of y can be determined by substituting (8) in (6).

In the case where one or more elasticities of supply equal infinity, i.e., if prices are exogenous (e.g., fixed institutionally), equation (6) can still be solved

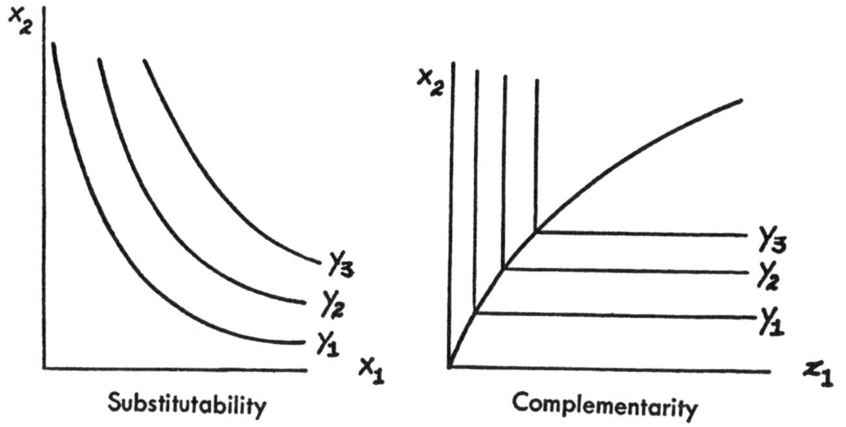

FIGURE 1

for y if, at least, either one of the factor prices satisfies (8) or one of the first derivatives (7) of the production functions (4) is a function of y. Although in this case the system is determined, there is no guarantee that the solution will satisfy equilibrium conditions. Consequently (6) cannot be solved for y. Apart from the fact that there is no equilibrium value for y, y itself becomes indeterminate.

Apparently, this is the fundamental difference between the assumptions of complementarity and substitutability. Assuming the latter, the total supply of each factor will be exhausted so long as free competition prevails, i.e., so long as prices corresponding to marginal productivity are accepted. In an economy where complementarity prevails permanent disequilibrium cannot be avoided and even national product becomes indeterminate, if for one or more factors supply is independent of price.[7]

This impossibility of adjustment to equilibrium in the case of $\partial x_i/\partial p_i = 0$ holds whether or not output decisions are taken according to the rules of free competition.

The obvious consequence of complementarity coexisting with zero elasticities of supply is to have prices fixed institutionally. The conclusion seems therefore unavoidable that given one or more zero elasticities of supply free competition as to factors of production is not compatible with complementarity.

1.5. Long-range projections, as a rule, presuppose capital coefficients, labour productivity, etc. to be either constant or to depend on time. Apparently, then, complementarity of production is assumed and the conclusions of the last section are not without relevance.

Let us suppose that h out of n factors of production have zero elasticities of supply. In order to ascertain whether or not long-run equilibrium will be possible, it is necessary that a number of new assumptions be made, viz., with respect to

(i) the way in which national product will be determined, since equation (8) is no longer valid and (6) cannot be used to solve y;

(ii) the way in which the supply of each of those h factors will possibly satisfy the values required by the demand relation $x_h = x_h(y)$.

In this connection it should be noted that y can be determined either independently of the equilibrium requirements of any of the h factors with zero elasticities or it can be geared to the rate of development of one of those factors. But in the first case the supply of each of the h factors has to satisfy the values required by the demand relation $x_h = x_h(y)$ for any specific value of y, since according to the nature of the complementary production function there exists for each level of y one and only one permissible combination of factors. In the second case the supply of only $h - 1$ factors has to be adapted to that value of y which is compatible with the supply of the remaining hth factor with zero

[7] It should be noted that this conclusion does not follow as unambiguously for an economy that is segmentized into different sectors with non-zero cross elasticities of demand for the products concerned. The author is indebted to Professor D. B. J. Schouten for this suggestion.

elasticity. Finally, the adjustment of supply must result in both cases from the use of other parameters than factor prices.

No attempt has been made in this paper to specify the assumptions as required under (i). Our only concern has been to investigate the conditions under which equilibrium as defined in section 1.2 will be possible and whether or not there exists an optimal rate of development. National product is then supposed to conform automatically to whatever rate of growth is required by the equilibrium conditions under different assumptions as to factor supply.

1.6. The parameters that are ultimately responsible for the maintenance of equilibrium will be called *instruments*. For our purpose it does not matter whether their adaptation to equilibrium values is effectuated by the interested parties themselves (e.g., employers or trade unions), the government, or otherwise. It should further be noted that these parameters, were they not instruments, would mostly be variables which, if left alone, would have had an autonomous value of their own. Let us take as an example the increase of working population, u. Its autonomous value $\tilde{u}$ depends, e.g., upon the natural rate of increase of population in the working ages, $e^{\pi t}$. Therefore, if u is used as an instrument (e.g., by the expediencies of birth control, migration, etc.) the absolute impact, φ, of adapting u to its equilibrium value u' can be measured by the difference between the equilibrium and the autonomous value of u (viz., by the number of people that must immigrate or emigrate, etc.):

$$u' = \tilde{u}(e^{\pi t}) + \varphi. \tag{10}$$

The smaller the difference between u' and $\tilde{u}$, the greater, therefore, is the chance that equilibrium can be realized in practice. This holds particularly if u is subjected to boundary conditions ($u_1 < u < u_2$).

1.7. The projection models under discussion pretend to describe the time shape of the variables over a period of about twenty years. The complementary demand curves (4) must consequently be defined over a considerable range. As the kind of interaction considered here is in the long run multiplicative rather than additive, the exponential relation

$$x_i = \alpha y^{\beta} \tag{11}$$

is no doubt the best suited to allow for changes in factor productivity as output increases.

This holds particularly with respect to labour demand. According to recent studies in the U. S. A. the unit cost of labour and hence productivity are uniquely related to the cumulated volume of output[8]:

$$y/a = \alpha\left(\int_0^t y dt\right)^{\beta}, \tag{12}$$

where a is labour.

[8] Hirsch, W. Z., "Manufacturing Progress Functions," *Review of Economics and Statistics*, XXXIV (May, 1952), p. 143–156 ff. and literature cited; "Firm Progress Ratios," *Econometrica*, 24, 2 (April, 1956), pp. 136 ff.

Since we are interested only in the trend values of variables and since the rate of increase of output as a whole changes but little if fairly long periods are considered, y can be approximated by, e.g.,

$$y_t = \gamma e^{\zeta t}. \tag{13}$$

Substituting this value for y in the right-hand side of (12), we find

$$y/a = \alpha \left(\frac{y - \gamma}{\zeta} \right)^{\beta}. \tag{14}$$

As t becomes large, y/a will approach the expression

$$y/a = \alpha \zeta^{-\beta} y^{\beta}. \tag{15}$$

We may therefore expect a rather stable long-run relation between productivity and the level of national product. Statistical verification of (15) shows, as a matter of fact, that the values for β are comparatively stable, and vary from industry to industry in different countries between 0.45 and 0.6.[9]

The same mechanism that explains relation (15), viz.,

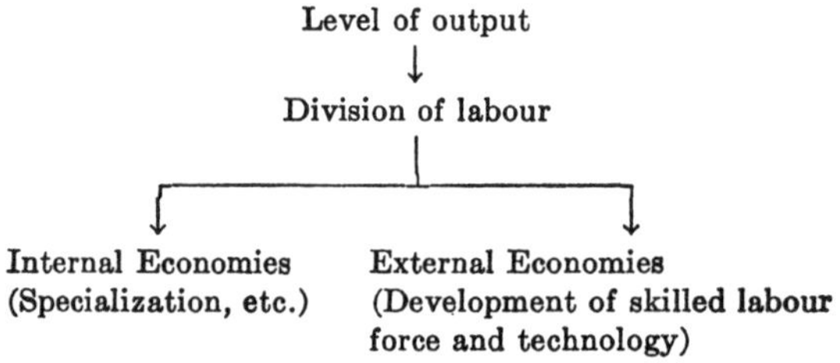

justifies the use of (11) also in the case of the capital stock, c, for a certain industry. If, however, the capital requirements of the economy as a whole are studied, the possibility of stable and even perhaps declining capital coefficients (c/y) should be taken into account. Nevertheless, as has been shown by Mr. Colin Clark, there is also in this case a unique relation between capital and real income per head, given by[10]

$$y = 2{,}000x + 5{,}450 \quad (1 - e^{-2.5x}) \tag{16}$$

where x is real income per man hour and y is reproducible capital per person in work, both in International Units.

Formula (11), then, can be considered as an approximation to (16) for the relevant interval of y.

Finally, in the case of imports (11) should be preferred to simple proportionality if natural resources cannot keep pace with national product. An exponent somewhat greater than one is then indicated in equation (11).

[9] Verdoorn, P. J., "Fattori che regolano lo sviluppo della produttività del lavoro," *L'Industria*, 1949, 1; *Preadvies Vereeniging voor Staathuishoudkunde*, (The Hague: Martinus Nijhoff), 1952.

[10] Colin Clark, *Review of Economic Progress*, Jan., 1950.

2. COMPLEMENTARITY AND ECONOMIC POLICY

2.1. *The single factor case.*

Let capital be the only factor of production and its price elasticity of supply equal to zero. Since in this case we have no relation that describes the behaviour pattern of entrepreneurial demand, the point raised in Section 1.5 can readily be illustrated by the Harrod-Domar theorem.[11]

Let α be the propensity to save. Since investment equals savings, the annual supply of net investment can be related to the existing level of national income:

(17) $$\dot{k}_t = \alpha y_t .$$

On the other hand, capital demand, i.e., the capital stock required to produce y_t, is given by

(18) $$k_t = \kappa y_t^{\chi}.$$

The capital stock actually available at t is, however, determined by all previous investments:

(19) $$k_t = \int_0^t \alpha y_t dt + k_0 .$$

In the absence of any "waste process" or actual shortage of capital, the equilibrium condition for capital is found by equating the right-hand sides of (18) and (19):

(20) $$\kappa y_t^{\chi} = \int_0^t \alpha y_t dt + k_0 .$$

Differentiating with respect to t we find

(21) $$\dot{y}/y = \frac{\alpha}{\kappa\chi} y^{1-\chi},$$

and

(22) $$y_t = \left[y_0^{\chi-1} + \frac{\alpha(\chi - 1)}{\kappa\chi} t \right]^{1/\chi-1} .$$

In the case where $\chi = 1$, however, a more elegant expression results from (21):

(23) $$y_t = y_0 e^{\alpha t/\kappa}.$$

It should be noted that so far nothing in this system guarantees that the equilibrium condition for capital as expressed by (21) is fulfilled. As a matter of fact, since the price elasticity of capital supply is assumed to be zero, investment must be considered as an exogenous variable determined by entrepreneurial expectations as to future output, thus

(24) $$\dot{k} = u_t$$

[11] Cf. Domar, E. D., "Capital Expansion, Rate of Growth and Employment," *Econometrica*, 14, 2 (April, 1946), p. 139 ff.

where u is an exogenous factor. Hence national income is determined by (17) and (24),

$$y_t = \frac{1}{\alpha} \dot{k}_t = \frac{1}{\alpha} u_t, \tag{25}$$

and its rate of increase will not necessarily satisfy (21).

Maintenance of equilibrium therefore requires that either $\dot{y}/y$ will be adapted to a level that is compatible with the existing values of α, κ and χ, or that these parameters are adjusted to the prevailing level of $\dot{y}/y$. According to the complementarity hypothesis κ and χ are considered as technical data. For this reason our choice is restricted either to adapting α to $\dot{y}/y$ or, conversely, to regulating $\dot{y}/y$ in accordance with the accepted level of α.

In the following it shall tacitly be assumed that $\dot{y}/y$ will be adapted one way or another to any given level of α (e.g., by means of monetary measures or other instrument variables that are not incorporated in the equations of the system).

2.2. *The two-factor case (closed economy).*

If labour is to be the second factor of production and supposing its price elasticity to equal either 0 or ∞, we have two demand and two supply equations:

$$k = \kappa y^{\chi}, \tag{26}$$

$$a = y^{\rho}, \tag{27}$$

$$\dot{k} = \alpha y, \tag{28}$$

$$a = e^{\pi t} \qquad (a = y = 1 \text{ for } t = 0), \tag{29}$$

where a is labour, π is the rate of increase of population in working ages, y, k, and a are endogenous variables, and χ, ρ, and π are constants. α is considered as an instrument of economic policy.

Equilibrium requires again that full employment be maintained with respect to labour and capital. The solution requires the conditions:

$$\kappa\chi y^{\chi-1}\dot{y} = \alpha y, \tag{30}$$

$$y^{\rho} = e^{\pi t}. \tag{31}$$

It should be noted that as a consequence of complementarity the required rate of growth of national product follows directly from (31) and is independent of (30):

$$\dot{y}/y = \pi/\rho \tag{32}$$

and

$$y_t = e^{\pi t/\rho}. \tag{33}$$

Substitution of (33) in (30) gives the required propensity to save

$$\alpha_t = \kappa\chi\frac{\pi}{\rho}\, e^{(\pi/\rho)(\chi-1)t}. \tag{34}$$

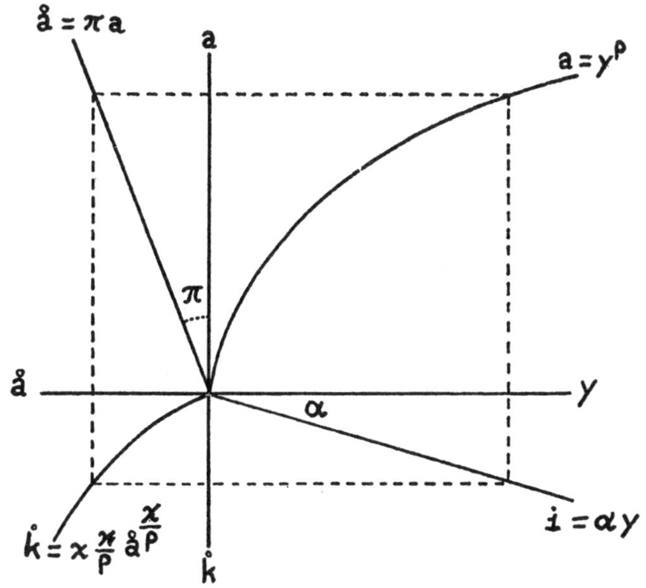

FIGURE 2.—Diagrammatic Representation of the Two-Factor Case ($y_0 = a_0 = 1$)

As π and the other coefficients in the right-hand side of (34) are constant, α is not invariant as against time so long as $\chi \neq 1$. In the special case where $\chi = 1$, the factor with e vanishes from the right-hand side and

(35) $$\alpha = \kappa\pi/\rho,$$

where κ represents the capital coefficient.

In this simplified case of a closed economy, the required rate of saving varies:

(i) proportionately with the rate of growth of the working population and the capital coefficient;

(ii) inversely with the elasticity of labour with respect to output, i.e., inversely with the relative increase of the working force corresponding to a growth in output of one per cent.

This is not too far removed from common sense expectations. Nevertheless, two particular consequences of the complementarity hypothesis should be stressed. As long as ρ and χ are considered inflexible, e.g., when they are dictated by technology or entrepreneurial behaviour patterns:

(i) the whole burden of the adaptation to equilibrium falls on α; and

(ii) consequently, one and only one pattern of growth is compatible with the requirements of long-run equilibrium. No room is left for choosing maximum positions.

2.3. *A three-factor case: the open economy.*

2.3.1. As compared with a closed economy using only capital and labour the model has to allow for:

(i) international trade, imports being the third factor of production;

(ii) the possibility of migration of labour and capital.

The introduction of international trade implies moreover:

(i) a third equilibrium condition concerning the equality of the supply and demand for imports, i.e., equilibrium on the balance of payments (in this simplified model capital exports will be neglected); and

(ii) a balance equation, since real national income may deviate from physical output as a consequence of variations in the terms of trade.

In the following, import prices will be used as numéraire.

Thus the model consists of three equations representing the equilibrium conditions for each of the factors of production, one balance equation and four definitional equations (see Table I).

2.3.2. The variables entering the equilibrium conditions of the factors of production are summarized below.

	Demand		Supply	
	Endogenous		Exogenous	Instrument
k	v	y	.	α
m	v	.	β	γ
a	v	.	.	π

α, γ and π are already reputed to have been manipulated by public policy, viz.,

α, by monetary policy and government saving;

γ, by monetary policy, wages and price control; and

π, by measures to stimulate or control external migration.

These three variables will therefore be considered as the instruments of a long-term economic policy. Since there are nine variables and only eight equations, the value of one of the instruments can be chosen freely. Consequently, several equilibrium positions are possible and one of the instruments can be chosen in such a way as to maximize economic welfare, e.g., real national income per head.

2.3.3. Because of complementarity, the possibilities of adaptation by means of the instruments are rather restricted:

(i) Since the demand for each of the factors is uniquely determined by total production, only the employment level for one of the factors can be chosen freely. The employment of the other factors has to be adapted accordingly.

(ii) The choice of a certain value for one of the instruments determines the other instrument variables. This is particularly clear in the case of export prices, $e^{\gamma t}$ and of working population, $e^{\pi t}$.

Upon equating the right-hand sides of (III) and (IV), substitution of VI, VII, and VIII gives

$$\gamma = \frac{1}{\epsilon + 1}\left(\frac{\pi}{\rho}\mu - \beta\right). \tag{36}$$

TABLE I

EQUATIONS OF THREE-FACTOR MODEL

Balance equation	Volume of output:	$v = c + i + b - m$
	Real national income:	$y = c + i + bp - m$
I. $y = v - b + bp$		
Capital	Demand:	$k = \kappa v;\ \dot{k} = \kappa \dot{v} = i$
	Supply:	$i = \alpha y$
II. $\dot{v} = \frac{\alpha}{\kappa} y$		
Imports	Demand:	$m = m_0\, v^{\mu}$
	Supply:	$m = bp = b_0 \tilde{b}\, p^{\epsilon+1}$
	Assuming $v_0 = p_0 = 1$, it follows that	
III. $v = (\tilde{b}\, p^{\epsilon+1})^{1/\mu}$		
Labour	Demand:	$a = a_0 v^{\rho}$
	Supply:	$a = a_{00}\, e^{\pi t}$
	Assuming $a_0 = v_0 = 1$, it follows that	
IV. $v = a^{1/\rho}$		
Definitional equations		
V. Volume of exports:		$b = b_0 b\, p^{\epsilon}$
VI. Autonomous export demand:		$\tilde{b} = e^{\beta t}$
VII. Export price:		$p = e^{\gamma t}$
VIII. Labour supply:		$a = e^{\pi t}$
Endogenous variables:		$y, v, b, \tilde{b}, a, p.$
Instruments:		α = propensity to save
		γ = rate of change of the ratio between export prices and import prices
		π = net rate of increase of working population (allowance being made for external migration)
Constant parameters:		ϵ = price elasticity of export demand
		β = rate of increase of autonomous export demand
		κ = capital coefficient
		ρ = elasticity of labour with respect to total production

More complicated is the relation between γ and α if α is chosen as a given constant. Assuming $\mu = 1$ and solving the system with respect to γ the following expression is found:

$$b_0\, e^{-\gamma t} + \gamma(\epsilon + 1)\frac{\kappa}{\alpha} = 1 + b_0 - \frac{\kappa}{\alpha}\beta \qquad (\mu = 1). \tag{37}$$

Conversely, if γ is considered given and constant and $\mu = 1$, α is given by:

$$\alpha = \frac{\kappa\{\beta + \gamma(\epsilon + 1)\}}{1 + b_0(1 - \bar{e}^{\gamma t})} \qquad (\mu = 1). \tag{38}$$

It follows that a constant value for γ (and π) is incompatible with a constant value of α and vice versa. Exception should be made for the special case where $\gamma = 0$, and

$$\alpha = \kappa\beta/\mu \qquad (\gamma = 0; \mu \neq 1). \tag{39}$$

Since according to (36)

$$\beta = \pi\mu/\rho, \qquad (\gamma = 0; \mu \neq 1), \tag{40}$$

(39) can be written as

$$\alpha = \kappa\pi/\rho \qquad (\gamma = 0; \mu \neq 1). \tag{41}$$

This result is consistent with that found for the closed economy (sec. 2.2, formula (35)) with the restraint, however, that

$$\pi = \beta\rho/\mu \tag{42}$$

(χ has been assumed to equal one in both cases).

Stable values for the propensity to save (α_t constant) and export prices ($\gamma = 0$) are therefore only compatible with equilibrium so long as π, the rate of net population increase, satisfies (42) and, moreover, $\chi = 1$.

2.4. *The case of optimal development.*

This problem can be dealt with under several aspects. Often it arises in a very simple manner when a projection is required for the period $t_1, t_2, \cdots, t_n$ under the condition that real national income per head should be maximized in the final year of the period. Since imports are the only factor that is governed on the supply side by an exogenous variable (β), maximization of y/a with respect to γ is indicated.

Writing the right-hand side of the balance equation as a function of $p(\gamma)$ and dividing by $a(\gamma)$, differentiation with respect to $p(\gamma)$ results in the form

$$\frac{1-\rho}{\mu}\tilde{b}^{(1/\mu)-1}p^{[(1-\mu)/\mu)](1+\epsilon)} - b_0\left(\frac{\epsilon}{\epsilon+1} - \frac{\rho}{\mu}\right)p^{-1} + b_0\left(1 - \frac{\rho}{\mu}\right) = 0. \tag{43}$$

This equation can be solved for p only by way of approximation. Nevertheless, the conditions under which real national income per head is already maximal can easily be found. This will be the case if the value of b_0 and the other constants is such that $p = 1$ and consequently a change in p would result in a lower income per head.

In (43) μ and ρ are technical constants; also ϵ is constant. However, b_0 is an initial datum since it stands for the share of exports in national income, as $y_0 = v_0 = 1$. Accordingly b_0 is a function of the absolute level of export prices (in terms of world market prices). By giving p the value 1 and solving (43) for b_0, that export share is found that allows for the highest possible income per head:

$$b_0\tilde{b}^{1-(1/\mu)} = -(1-\rho)(\epsilon+1)/\mu \qquad (y/a \text{ max.}). \tag{44}$$

Since $b = b_0 \bar{b} p^{\epsilon}$, $v = (\bar{b} p^{\epsilon+1})^{1/\mu}$, and $p(y/a \text{ max.}) = 1$, the left-hand side of this equation represents the share of exports in national product, and, since $p = 1$, their share in national income. Hence we can write generally:

$$b_t/y_t = -(1 - \rho)(\epsilon + 1)/\mu \qquad ((y/a)_t \text{ max.}). \tag{45}$$

The rationale of this optimum condition can be seen clearly in the special case where $\epsilon = -2$ and $\mu = 1$:

$$b/y = b_0 = (1 - \rho) \qquad (y/a \text{ max.}; \epsilon = -2; \mu = 1). \tag{46}$$

Income per head is maximal, if export prices are decreased to the level where marginal output per head with respect to export prices equals marginal loss on the balance of payments due to the deterioration of the terms of trade. (This loss is defined as $b_0 p(1 - p)$.) If export prices are lowered be one per cent, the value of exports will rise also by one per cent, since $\epsilon = -2$. Imports and national product are thus rising by one per cent. The consequent increase of output per head equals the productivity increase, i.e., $1 - \rho$ per cent.

On the other hand the *real* loss on the balance of payments is represented by b_0 times the percentage decrease in price. In this case, since $\epsilon = -2$ and $\mu = 1$, it corresponds with the expansion of total output, i.e., with one per cent. Hence maximum income is reached as exports are pushed up to the level where $b_0 = 1 - \rho$.

In this special case, the total price change necessary to maximize real maximal income per head at the end of the period ($t = n$) is found to be

$$e^{\gamma t} = b_0(2 - \rho)/(1 + b_0)(1 - \rho) \qquad ((y/a)_t \text{ max.}; \epsilon = -2; \mu = 1; t = n), \tag{47}$$

and

$$\gamma = \frac{1}{t} \log \frac{b_0(2 - \rho)}{(1 - b_0)(1 - \rho)}. \tag{48}$$

The corresponding values of α for the period considered are given by

$$\alpha_t = \frac{\kappa(\beta - \gamma)}{1 + b_0(1 - e^{-\gamma t})}. \tag{49}$$

Finally, it is not without interest to investigate the conditions that permit the optimum situation, once it is realized, to continue indefinitely. Since the optimum conditions are defined by (43), their maintenance requires that (43) shall be an identity for all values of t.

Differentiation of (43) with respect to t gives therefore the rate of change of $p(\gamma)$ that satisfies the condition $(y/a)_t$ max. if t changes from $t = n$ to $t = n + 1$.

As the value of b_0 is already defined by (45) and we are free in the choice of units for p and $\bar{b}$ in the initial year, we put $p_0 = \bar{b}_0 = 1$. It then follows that:

$$\gamma = \frac{-\beta(1 - \mu)}{(\epsilon + 1)(1 - \mu + \rho) - \epsilon\mu}. \tag{50}$$

The elasticity of imports with respect to national product differs as a rule but a fraction from 1. For the Netherlands, e.g., a value of 1.15 seems plausible. The influence of the rate of increase β of autonomous exports on the optimal level of export prices appears therefore to be negligible, if the period considered is not too long and the numerical value of ϵ exceeds unity appreciably.

The same holds true if the influence of β on the permissible rate of increase π of working population is considered. Substitution of (50) in (36) gives:

$$\pi = \frac{\rho\beta}{\mu}\left(1 - \frac{(1-\mu)}{(1-\mu+\rho-\mu(\epsilon/\epsilon+1))}\right). \tag{51}$$

The factor $\rho\beta/\mu$ is therefore decisive for the value of π that is compatible with the maintenance of maximum income per head.

Denoting the natural rate of increase of working population by π', the rate of migration required to keep income per head on its maximum level is approximately

$$\varphi \cong \frac{\rho}{\mu}\beta - \pi'. \tag{52}$$

If $\varphi(y/a \text{ max.})$ happens to surpass the boundary conditions set to external migration, then either

(i) continuous changes in export prices have to be accepted, or

(ii) disequilibrium on the labour market has to be tolerated. In the case of a negative value for φ this means unemployment or a shorter working week. In the opposite case, however, v falls automatically below the level indicated by $\gamma = 0$ and a growing surplus on the balance of payments becomes unavoidable as long as export prices are not increased.

In both cases income per head is reduced below its virtual maximum.

2.5. *Appraisal of the complementarity hypothesis.*

It is a strange world indeed into which we are led by strict complementarity—strange at least from the point of view of traditional theory that sees the world as an ever-continuing process of substitution of each factor by all other factors and vice versa. Those who are thinking in the terms of input-output analysis or linear programming and who define reality in terms of a finite series of discrete technical processes and inflexible boundary conditions will, however, probably feel more at home with this view. The crucial question, therefore, remains: Which of the two highly one-sided pictures, perfect substitutability or strict complementarity, can pride itself on the higher content of reality?

Particularly with respect to the open economy, it should be pointed out that complementarity must lead in many cases to pessimistic conclusions with respect to the possibilities of durable equilibrium. This is because if our definition of equilibrium is widened, so as to allow for the side conditions

$$\gamma = 0,$$

$$\pi = \pi',$$

long-term equilibrium with respect to the outside world is only possible if, according to formula (36),

$$\pi' = \frac{\rho}{\mu}\beta, \tag{53}$$

unless population increase is to create unemployment.

This picture presents perhaps some basic tendencies of the economic structure. Witness the classical difficulties of countries such as Italy, Germany, and Japan. Nevertheless, it tends to underestimate the possibilities of adaptation which are available in reality.

This is not to say that the complementarity hypothesis should be regarded as unduly unrealistic for projections that cover a period that is sufficiently long to cancel out the effect of cyclical fluctuation but not too long to be affected by changes in economic structure of a more secular character. As a matter of fact, the relation representing capital demand

$$k = \kappa y^{\chi} \tag{54}$$

seems sufficiently stable and realistic.

Also the coefficient ρ of the labour demand relation

$$a = v^{\rho} \tag{55}$$

has shown itself of sufficient stability to be used for projections covering one or two decades. In those cases, however, where the rate of increase of the working population is comparatively low, special allowance should perhaps be made for an autonomous increase in productivity.

In those cases (55) can be replaced by

$$a = v^{\rho}e^{\psi t}. \tag{56}$$

Although the curvilinear approach to complementarity as used in the foregoing is certainly more satisfying from a theoretical point of view than the simple linear approach, its main drawback is still the complete lack of any allowance for substitutability. Nevertheless, since perfect substitutability tends to exaggerate the possibilities of adjustment, the complementarity approach should perhaps be preferred from a purely pragmatic point of view when making long-term projections. Exactly because of its rigidity, possibilities of tension and discrepancies may be discovered, whereas substitutability tends to conceal them altogether.

It stands to reason that the extremely simplified model, as given in Table I, should be considered only as the bare frame upon which the definitive model to be used for projection purposes has to be developed. The economic structure and institutional conditions vary from country to country and consequently the possibilities of adaptation to equilibrium are different. The additional relations that are to be incorporated in the model and the choice of the instruments should, therefore, differ as to the country considered.

As will be seen in Section 3, this process of refining the model may mitigate the severe rigidity imposed by strict complementarity.

TABLE II

PROJECTION MODEL OF THE CENTRAL PLANNING BUREAU

Balance Equations	
(1) Gross national product	$v = c + i + d + b - m$
(2) National income	$y = c + i + bp - m$
I	$y = v - d - b(1 - p)$
Capital	
(3) Demand	$k = \kappa v^{\chi}$
(4) Definition	$\dot{k} + i' = i + d$
(5) Replacements	$i' = \omega d$
(6) Depreciation	$d = d_0^* k^{\nu}$
(7) Definition	$i = \alpha y - b'$
II	$\frac{\dot{v}}{v} = \frac{1}{\chi k} \{\alpha y + (1 - \omega) d_0^* k^{\nu} - b'\}$
Labour	
(8) Demand (man-hours)	$a = v^{\rho}$
(9) Supply (do)	$a = a_0^* \left(\frac{y}{N}\right)^{\psi} e^{(\pi - \varphi) t}$
(10) Total population	$N = e^{(\pi - \varphi) t}$
III	$v = v_0^* y^{\psi / \rho} e^{1/\rho (\pi - \varphi)(1 - \psi) t}$
Imports	
(11) Demand	$m = m_0^* \left(\frac{b}{v}\right)^{\eta} v^{\mu} e^{\sigma t}$
(12) Supply	$m = qb \frac{p}{p'}$
(13) Capital exports	$b' = (1 - q) bp$
(14) Definition	$q = q_0 e^{\lambda t}$
(15) Exports	$b = b_0 e^{\beta t} \{1 + \epsilon(\frac{p}{p''} - 1)\}$
(16) Export prices	$p = p'' e^{\gamma t}$
(17) Prices competing exports	$p'' = p' e^{\delta t}$
IV	$v = \{1 + \varepsilon(e^{\gamma t} - 1)\}^{(1 - \eta)/(\mu - \eta)} e^{[\beta(1 - \eta) + \gamma - \sigma + \delta + \lambda]/(\mu - \eta) t}$

3. THE PROJECTION OF THE CENTRAL PLANNING BUREAU

3.1. Work on the forecast covering the period 1950–1970 was started in 1950. The final results were published in November, 1955.[12]

The model underlying these results is given in Table II; the variables and parameters used, together with the numerical values of the initial data and constants are given in Table III. Finally, Table IV gives the actual results for the three main alternative possibilities of the development.

3.2. *The model (Table II).*

The model has been built along the main general lines as the simple three-factor model for an open economy (Table I). It shows therefore the same sub-

[12] *Een verkenning der economische toekomstmogelijkheden van Nederland 1950–1970* (Dutch), Government Publishing Office, The Hague, 1955.

TABLE III

VARIABLES AND CONSTANTS

(All value variables are deflated)

	Values of initial data and constants
A. *Endogenous*	
y: national income	.91
v: gross national product	1.00
c: consumption	.77
i: net investments	.17
d: depreciation	.09
b: exports	.41
m: imports	.44
k: capital stock	5.00
i': replacement investments	—
a: man hours worked	1.00
N: total population	1.00
b': capital exports	−.03
q: ratio of imports to exports (current prices)	1.07
p: export prices	1.00
p'': prices of competing exports	1.00
B. *Exogenous*	
π: rate of increase of total population and of population in working ages	.012
β: rate of increase of autonomous export demand	.039
δ: rate of increase of the ratio p''/p'	−.0025
p': import prices ($p' = 1$ for all values of t)	1.00
C. *Instruments*	
α: propensity to save	—
φ: rate of emigration (net)	—
γ: rate of change of relative export prices	—
σ: rate of import substitution	—
D. *Structural coefficients*	
χ: elasticity of capital with respect to GNP	.80
ω: ratio of replacements to depreciation	.80
ν: elasticity of depreciation with respect to capital stock	1.20
ρ: elasticity of labour with respect to GNP	.275
μ: elasticity of imports with respect to GNP	1.15
η: elasticity of m with respect to b/v	0.26
ϵ: price elasticity of export demand	−2.00
ψ: price elasticity of labour supply	−.25
E. *Other constants*	
κ	5.00
d_0^*	.013
a_0^*	.98
v_0^*	.93
m_0^*	.55
F. *Target variables*	
Flexible target: $(y/N)_t$ max.	
Unconditional target: $b_t'(\lambda)$	

division of equations into three headings as to factors of production. By successive elimination it proves possible to obtain for each factor a final equation as printed in heavy type. A few comments are in order regarding certain equations.

Equation (3): χ, the elasticity of demand for capital with respect to GNP, is a weighted average for the main branches of activity for which coefficients have been found *inter alia* from empirical data for the United States[13] covering the period 1899–1929. The weights have been derived by means of input-output analysis (see below).

Equations (4) and (5): A distinction has been made between depreciation and replacements so as to take into account the influence of steady growth upon the financial requirements of new investments.[14] The coefficient ω has been given a priori the value of .80.

Equation (6): The coefficient ν has also been found by means of input-output analysis.

Equation (7): This equation has been refined as compared with the corresponding equation in Table I so as to allow for the impact of capital exports on the savings available for net investments.

Equation (8): The elasticity of labour demand in terms of man hours on the volume of output has been estimated at .275. This coefficient represents essentially the combined result of two different partial elasticities:

(i) The weighted elasticity of man years (weekly hours being constant) for different branches of activity with respect to output. The separate elasticities have been estimated empirically.[15] The average elasticity appears to be already rather low since branches of industry that are non-labour-intensive happen to be the same branches where expansion is largest and the weights given to output are relatively heavy.

(ii) The elasticity of productivity per man hour with respect to average daily hours. Since national income per head increases, weekly hours will be reduced (equation (9)) on the average by about 6%. Consequently productivity per man hour will increase, although less than 6%. For this reason labour requirements in terms of man hours are lower than might be expected if no reduction of daily hours had been effectuated.

Equations (9) and (10): The value of $-.25$ for the price elasticity of labour supply consists again of two partial elasticities:

(i) The elasticity of hours worked with respect to income per head.[16]

(ii) The average elasticity of supply in man years for different age classes with respect to income per head as estimated from a cross section analysis between different cities in the Netherlands (1947).

[13] Verdoorn, P. J., *Preadvies Vereeniging voor Staathuishoudkunde*, (The Hague: Martinus Nijhoff), 1952, Appendix D.

[14] Domar, E. D., "Depreciation, Replacement and Growth," *The Economic Journal*, March, 1953.

[15] Verdoorn, *op. cit.*, Appendix C.

[16] Douglas, D. H., *The Theory of Wages*, 1934, pp. 309 ff.

Since the natural rate of increase of the working population and of total population are approximately the same, π represents the expected net rate of increase for both variables. The net rate of emigration φ has been represented separately as an instrument variable.

Equation (11): The most important parameter in the demand equation for imports μ represents the relative increase of imports as a consequence of the increase in GNP (v). Since the marginal propensity to import is dependent upon the degree of liberalization in international trade, the share of exports in GNP has been taken into account as a second explaining variable. The two parameters considered have been estimated by means of a time series analysis for the Netherlands (1921–1954). Since substitution of imports went ahead gradually in the inter-war period, a trend term $e^{\sigma t}$ has been added. As the rate of import substitution in turn is also not independent of the international division of labour and hence of the degree of liberalization, the coefficient σ has been assumed to have different values in the different data-alternatives giving the rate of increase of world export demand.

Equations (12), (13), and (14): The ability to import is not only dependent on exports (b) but also on capital exports (b'). Capital exports in this model are considered as an unconditional target since in the year 1950 the balance of payments still showed a considerable gap between imports and exports. This gap is assumed to diminish gradually in the course of time ($e^{\lambda t}$) so as to provide in the year of projection the required amount of capital exports (transfer of foreign debts, technical aid, financial support of emigrants).

Equations (16) and (17): Since prices of industrial manufactures tend in the long run to decline gradually as compared with those of raw materials, prices of competing exports (p'') will slowly decrease ($e^{\delta t}$) as compared with import prices (p'). In equation (16) the trend ratio (γ) of export prices is considered as an instrument of economic policy.

Equation (15): Export demand is supposed to vary linearly with export prices, the elasticity of the relevant interval of the curve being -2.

3.3. *Alternative possibilities of development.*

There are fifteen endogenous variables and four instruments, viz:

α, propensity to save;
φ, rate of net emigration;
γ, rate of change in relative export prices; and
σ, rate of import substitution.

Since there are seventeen equations, two degrees of freedom, therefore, remain. Two of these four instruments may therefore be chosen in such a way as to ensure optimal development, i.e., to maximize national income per head in the year of projection (1970). The two selected are:

(a) the rate of import substitution has been chosen in accordance with the level of expected world demand for exports, since for a low level of autonomous exports a relative high rate of substitution of imports seems probable and vice versa;

(b) the level of the export prices relative to competitive prices abroad (p/p'') has been chosen so as to maximize real income per head. From this optimal ratio of p/p'' some conclusions can be drawn as to the required level of the nominal wage rate with respect to productivity of labour and import prices (these relations are not incorporated in the model).

Since the rate of autonomous increase in export demand is, as a matter of fact, uncertain, export demand has been computed on the basis of three main alternative assumptions as to the data.

3.4. *Graphical representation of the main results.*

For each of these three alternatives and for different values of the rate of import substitution, $e^{\sigma t}$, the optimal value of export prices, $e^{\gamma t}$, has been determined graphically. Because of the hypothesis of complementarity of factors of production, there corresponds for each of these optimum values of $e^{\gamma t}$ only one re-

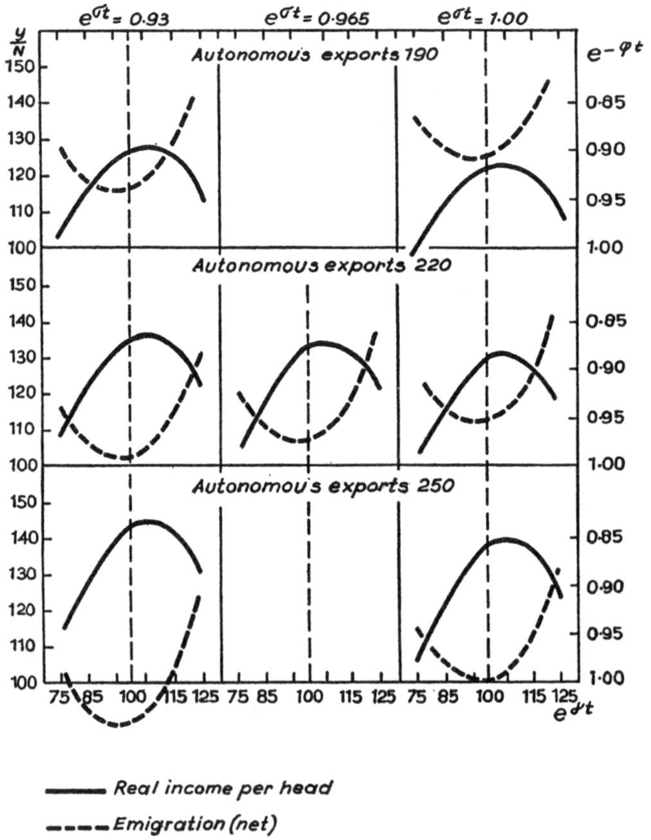

FIGURE 3.—Real Income per Head and Emigration vs. Relative Export Prices, 1970

quired rate of net emigration, $e^{\varphi t}$, if unemployment is to be avoided. As a matter of fact, the model only allows for normal unemployment (3.4 per cent of the dependent working population), the surplus of labour supply over labour demand being assumed to emigrate.

In all cases the optimal level of export prices remains very near to the initial level (1953), as already found in the simplified case of the three-factor models (Section 2.4, equation (50)). Here again the optimal value of γ is virtually independent of the rate of autonomous export increase, β. The graph shows at the same time the required effect of net emigration for various values of β, σ, and γ. The location of the minimum, which also in this case is practically independent of β, nearly coincides with the optimal value of $e^{\gamma t}$.

TABLE IV
TABLE OF RESULTS (1970)

	Symbol	Unit	Alternative estimates, 1970		
			A	B	C
Exogenous variables:					
autonomous volume of exports	$b_0e^{\beta t}$	1950 = 100	190	220	250
total population (before deduction of emigration)	N	"	127	127	127
Instruments:					
net rate of emigration (annual averages 1950–1970)		thousands	32	15	2
import substitution	$e^{\sigma t}$	—	0.93	0.965	1.00
export prices relative to prices of competing exports	p/p''	1953 = 100	100	100	100
rate of saving		%	9	10	10
Results:					
real income per head	y/N	1950 = 100	128	134	139
real private consumption per head	c/N	"	138	144	148
productivity of labour per man-year in industries	—	"	135	140	145
employment in industries (man-years)	—	"	120	124	127
volume of output in industries	—	"	161	174	185
of which:					
metals	—	"	194	212	226
chemicals	—	"	200	221	241
textiles and clothing	—	"	158	169	176
food and beverages	—	"	138	149	158
public utilities	—	"	190	204	215
mining	—	"	110	110	110
building and construction	—	"	137	152	164
other manufacturing industries	—	"	165	180	194
agriculture	—	"	125	125	125
transportation	—	"	183	205	227
other services	—	"	166	180	193

3.5. *Numerical results.*

The numerical results are presented in Table IV. They describe three alternative cases that are characterized by different levels of autonomous export demand (190, 220, and 250; 1950 = 100) and the corresponding values of import substitution ($e^{\sigma t}$ = .93, .965, and 1.00).

The table also gives estimates for the output of different branches of industry. These results have been obtained by input-output analysis.[17] The advantage of the breakdown of the results appeared to be threefold: In the first place, it was possible to give more complete results. Secondly, the breakdown proved a valuable check on the plausibility of the results obtained and allowed one to take into account the existence of bottlenecks in agriculture and mining. Thirdly, input-output analysis provided the possibility of a more refined weighting of the micro-coefficients for the structural parameters to be used in the macro model.

Central Planning Bureau, The Hague

[17] Van den Beld, C. A., "Input-output Analysis as a Tool for Long-term Projections,' (paper presented at the International Seminar for Input-output Analysis, Varenna, 1954).

[32]

NOTES AND MEMORANDA

INCOME ELASTICITY OF DEMAND, A MICRO-ECONOMIC AND A MACRO-ECONOMIC INTERPRETATION

THE concept of income elasticity of demand has been used with two entirely different meanings: a micro- and a macro-economic one.

The micro-economic interpretation refers to the relation between income and outlay on a certain commodity *for a single person or family.*

The macro-economic interpretation is derived from the corresponding relation between total income and total outlay *for a large group of persons or families* (social strata, nations, etc.).

If we make the assumption that an individual family's outlay c on a certain commodity is wholly determined by its income i and a number of other factors (size of family, tastes, etc.), it is possible to ascribe an unambiguous sense to the (micro-economic) income elasticity ε, viz.—

$$\varepsilon = \frac{i}{c} \cdot \frac{\partial c}{\partial i} \quad . \quad . \quad . \quad . \quad . \quad . \quad . \quad . \quad (1)$$

Our empirical knowledge of the micro-economic relation is very limited. This relation might be determined statistically by comparing the simultaneous fluctuations of income and outlay in time. As, however, other factors also may be expected to play a rôle, it would be necessary to apply the method of multiple correlation. As far as I know, this method has not yet been used for individual families. Our statistical knowledge of the micro-economic relation is up to now wholly based on the results of family budget inquiries.[1] From these data we may, at best, derive an average micro-economic relation, because we generally lack data on a number of determining factors (tastes, etc.). Moreover, we must assume that outlay is not dependent on the rate of increase of income, and that the reaction of income on outlay is not lagged (it would be impossible to derive such dynamic relations from the data of budget inquiries, unless these data refer to the expenditures of the same families during at least two different periods).

[1] Cf. *Family Expenditure,* by R. D. G. Allen and A. L. Bowley, London, 1935.

Although the statistical determination of the micro-economic relation is thus not free from difficulties, the relation itself, as has been shown, has a perfectly clear meaning, and the same holds true of the income elasticity derived from it. It is not so simple, however, to give an unassailable definition of the macro-economic income elasticity E. If we know the micro-economic relation between outlay and income, total outlay will be determined as soon as we know the income distribution. This may be described by a function $F(i)$ of i, telling us the number of families $F(i)di$ with incomes between i and $i + di$. If the total number of families is denoted by N, total income by I and total outlay on the considered commodity by C we have the following relations :

$$N = \int_0^\infty F(i)di \quad . \quad . \quad . \quad . \quad . \quad . \quad . \quad (2)$$

$$I = \int_0^\infty iF(i)di \quad . \quad . \quad . \quad . \quad . \quad . \quad (3)$$

$$C = \int_0^\infty c(i).F(i)di \quad . \quad . \quad . \quad . \quad . \quad (4)$$

(If $F(i)$ proves to vanish outside a certain range $\alpha-\beta$, the limits of integration 0 and ∞ may be replaced by α and β without altering the meaning of the integrals.) In general it is not possible to study the relation between C and I given by (3) and (4), without making some assumption about the character of $F(i)$. There is, however, one exception : viz. *when $c(i)$ is a linear function of i :*

$$c(i) = a + bi \quad . \quad . \quad . \quad . \quad . \quad . \quad . \quad (5)$$

a and b being constants.

In this case (4) immediately reduces to :

$$C = aN + bI \quad . \quad . \quad . \quad . \quad . \quad . \quad . \quad (6)$$

Now, generally, N and I will be independent variables (in most cases N will practically be constant or show a slight trend), and therefore E may be put equal to :

$$E = \frac{I}{C} \cdot \frac{\partial C}{\partial I} = b\frac{I}{C} \quad . \quad . \quad . \quad . \quad . \quad . \quad . \quad (7)$$

In all other cases we must know the properties of $F(i)$, in order to be able to perform the transition from ε to E.

Now there are practically no theories about the shape of the income distribution function. But nevertheless we may assume that such a theory would lead to a mathematical expression for the distribution function, containing a number of constants or parameters λ, μ, ν . . ., depending on the economic structure of the group of families. We shall denote this general expression by $F(i;\ \lambda,\ \mu,\ \nu\ .\ .\ .)$. We have already observed that the number of families may be considered as practically a constant. If we assume that this holds rigorously, we may eliminate one of the parameters, say λ. Instead of F we will then obtain a function $f(i;\ \mu,\ \nu\ .\ .\ .)$.

Now we are able to prove that, if f contains only one parameter, it is possible to generalise the definition of ε to the macro-economic case.

Equations (3) and (4) will then take on the following forms:

$$I = \int_0^\infty if(i;\ \mu)di \quad . \quad . \quad . \quad . \quad . \quad . \quad (8)$$

$$C = \int_0^\infty c(i)\,.f(i;\ \mu)di \quad . \quad . \quad . \quad . \quad . \quad (9)$$

I and C both become functions of μ. If μ is kept constant, I and C are constant too. (The variable i has disappeared after the process of integration.) If μ changes, I and C will change at the same time, and their fluctuations are uniquely connected with the fluctuations of μ.

Consequently C may be considered as a function of I, and the derivative $\frac{\partial C}{\partial I}$ may be calculated with the help of the ordinary function of a function rule:

$$\frac{\partial C}{\partial I} = \frac{\partial C}{\partial \mu} : \frac{\partial I}{\partial \mu} \quad . \quad . \quad . \quad . \quad . \quad . \quad . \quad (10)$$

and E becomes:

$$E = \frac{I}{C} \cdot \frac{\partial C}{\partial \mu} : \frac{\partial I}{\partial \mu} \quad . \quad . \quad . \quad . \quad . \quad . \quad . \quad (11)$$

As soon as, however, the number of parameters of f becomes greater than one, it is no longer possible to reason in the same way. Suppose that f contains two parameters μ and ν, consequently I and C will also become functions of these parameters. The variations of C are now no longer uniquely connected with the variations of I. We may, for instance, compare the simultaneous changes ΔC of C and ΔI of I brought about by changes of μ, keeping ν constant, or, on the contary, caused by variations of ν, treating μ as a constant. More generally we may vary μ and ν together, keeping constant a certain relation between them: $\phi(\mu,\ \nu) =$ constant. The quotient $\frac{\Delta C}{\Delta I}$ will be different for the different choices, and the derivative $\frac{\partial C}{\partial I}$ as well as E becomes wholly arbitrary. The same holds true *a fortiori*, if f contains three or more parameters. In such cases we have still more freedom to choose the variations of the parameters (we have to introduce more than one constant function ϕ between the parameters in order to obtain a definite value for $\frac{\partial C}{\partial I}$). We may still arrive at an unambiguous definition, by restricting ourselves to a given ϕ (or generally a number of ϕ's equal to the number of parameters of f minus one), *it will, however, always be necessary clearly to state which quantities ϕ are assumed to be constant.* It will perhaps be best to illustrate this by some examples.

Pareto's well-known distribution function is characterised by three constants. If we state Pareto's law in the following form : the number of persons (families) with incomes exceeding a given number i may be represented by Ki^{-a}, these constants are K, a and i_0, the minimum income (i_0 cannot be put equal to 0, as in this case the total number of persons would become infinite). The function f would consequently contain two parameters—say K and α (i_0 being eliminated with the help of (2)). Now we may consider one (macro-economic) income elasticity with the additional condition α is constant, another with the condition K is constant, etc. The value of these concepts is, however, very much reduced, as we lack a theory telling us the economic meaning of changes of the income distribution for which a (or K) is constant.

The second example refers to a paper of Staehle,[1] in which he tries to improve the relation between total consumption outlay (on all commodities) and total income of German workers by introducing a coefficient β connected with the concentration of incomes (due to Mendershausen). His result reads as follows :

$$C = aI + b\beta + c \quad . \quad . \quad . \quad . \quad . \quad (12)$$

a, b and c being constants. Here again we can derive a formula for E :

$$E = a\frac{I}{C} \quad . \quad . \quad . \quad . \quad . \quad . \quad . \quad (13)$$

If we are allowed to assume that the distribution function F in this case contains only two parameters (of which one can be eliminated, whereas the other is β), the condition which has to be added in order to ascribe a definite sense to (13) is : β is constant. But there is no reason at all to make this assumption; on the contrary, Staehle introduces the coefficient β, instead of Pareto's a, to enable him to apply his methods to distributions for

[1] Hans Staehle : "Short-Period Variations in the Distribution of Incomes," *Review of Economic Statistics*, August 1937.

which Pareto's law does not hold and which will generally be characterised by a greater number of parameters. *In this case the theoretical meaning of the income elasticity derived from* (12) *becomes rather vague.*

From the preceding we learn that, with two exceptions, it is not possible to define the macro-economic income elasticity in an unambiguous way. In the general case the definition refers to a special type of variations of the distribution function, and this type must be carefully specified. As a general theory of income distribution is still lacking, there are no theoretical grounds to prefer a particular definition, and it seems hardly possible to avoid ambiguity.

Sometimes, however, a particular definition intrudes itself upon us on practical grounds. Suppose we know that the income distribution for a certain country in different years can be described by a function $f(i;\ \mu, \nu)$ with two parameters (we presume that this function has already been chosen so as to satisfy the condition: N is constant). If we now observe that the time series of μ and ν (and consequently also the series of μ and I and of ν and I) are highly correlated, it is allowed to consider μ as a function $\phi(\nu)$ of ν (at least for the variations which occurred in the past). Strictly speaking, *there is now only one parameter*, and we already know that in this case an unambiguous definition can be given. It will be obvious that the additional definition in this case must be: ϕ is constant. Moreover, the income elasticity, corresponding to this definition, is the only one which can statistically be determined, as, according to our supposition, all our observations refer only to variations for which ϕ has been constant.

A high degree of interrelatedness of the parameters seems to occur rather frequently. For the Netherlands 1921–38 Pareto's α is highly correlated with I; the same is true for the United States 1919–32.[1] If the other parameters show corresponding relations (this has not yet been verified), we are justified in applying the last-mentioned definition in these two cases. When using this definition we should, however, remember the following two points:

(1) It is meaningless to introduce a parameter of the distribution as a separate factor in order to improve the result of a correlation calculation between C and I;

(2) the income elasticity calculated according to it should

[1] J. Tinbergen, *Business Cycles in the United States of America, 1919–1932* League of Nations, 1939.

not be applied to cases in which the condition of a constant volume for ϕ is probably not fulfilled—*e.g.*, to study the effect of a sudden and heavy change of the progressivity of income tax, etc.

P. DE WOLFF

Central Bureau of Statistics,
The Hague, The Netherlands.

[33]

A MODEL OF INCOME DISTRIBUTION

Summary

In the models discussed in this paper the distribution of incomes between an enumerable infinity of income ranges is assumed to develop by means of a stochastic process. In most models the stochastic matrix is assumed to remain constant through time. Under these circumstances, and provided certain other conditions are satisfied, the distribution will tend towards a unique equilibrium distribution dependent upon the stochastic matrix but not on the initial distribution. It is found that under fairly general conditions, provided the prospects of change of income as described by the matrix are in a certain sense independent of income for incomes above some limit then the Pareto curve of the equilibrium distribution will be asymptotic to a straight line. This result is preserved even when some of the effects of age on income are allowed for, and also when allowance is made for the effect of an occupational stratification of the population. Some consideration is also given to the fact that changes in the income distribution may cause the stochastic matrix itself to change. Some discussion is also given of cases where the Pareto curve of the equilibrium distribution is not asymptotic to a straight line.

§ 1. Introduction

In a recent article [1] instructions were given for graduating the distribution of personal incomes before tax by means of the distribution function

$$(1.1) \qquad F(t) = \frac{N}{\theta} \tan^{-1} \frac{\sin \theta}{\cos \theta + (t/t_0)^{\alpha}}$$

where $F(t)$ is the number of incomes exceeding t, and N, α, t_0 and θ are fitted parameters. For high incomes this formula closely approximates the form

$$(1.2) \qquad F(t) = Ct^{-\alpha}$$

with

$$C = \frac{N\pi}{180} t_0^{\alpha} \sin \theta$$

which is the form predicted by Pareto's law.

It has been frequently claimed that actual distributions do

[1] Champernowne [3]. See references at the end of this article.

approximate closely to this form for high income levels, and it is the purpose of this note to seek theoretical reasons for this. I am indebted to Mr. M. Crum of New College, Oxford, for critical advice and enabling me to correct several inaccuracies. Needless to say, he is in no degree responsible for any mis-statements which may remain.

§ 2. The Development of Income Distribution Regarded as a Stochastic Process

The forces determining the distribution of incomes in any community are so varied and complex, and interact and fluctuate so continuously, that any theoretical model must either be unrealistically simplified or hopelessly complicated. We shall choose the former alternative but then give indications that the introduction of some of the more obvious complications of the real world does not seem to disturb the general trend of our conclusions.

The ideas underlying our theoretical model have been briefly indicated in an earlier publication,[1] but a more complete statement may be conveniently put forward at the present time, since recent developments in the theory of stochastic processes involving infinite matrices have enabled more rigorous and neater formulation to be made than was previously found possible.

We shall suppose that the income scale is divided into an enumerable infinity of income ranges, which, for reasons to be later explained, we shall assume to have uniform proportionate extent. For example, we might consider the ranges of income per annum to be £50–£100, £100–£200, £200–£400, £400–£800, . . . although a finer graduation would be more interesting. We shall regard the development through time of the distribution of incomes between these ranges as being a stochastic process, so that the income of any individual in one year may depend on what it was in the previous year and on a chance process. In reality new income-receivers appear every year and old ones pass away, but an obvious and fruitful simplifying assumption to make is that to every " dying " income-receiver there corresponds an heir to his income in the following year, and vice versa. This assumption will imply that the number of incomes is constant through time and that the incomes live on individually, although their recipients are transitory. Not very much difficulty would be involved in allowing more or less than one heir to each dying

[1] Champernowne [1], [2].

person, but on the whole the loss of simplicity would be likely to outweigh the advantages due to the gain in verisimilitude.

Under such assumptions any historical development of the distribution of incomes could be summarily described in terms of the following vectors and matrices, $X_r(0)$, telling us the number $X_r(0)$ of the income-receivers in each range R_r, $r = 1, 2 \ldots$ in the initial year Y_0 and a series of matrices $p'_{rs}(t)$ telling us in each year Y_t, the proportions of the occupants of R_r who are shifted to range R_s in the following year Y_{t+1}. With these definitions the income distributions $x_r(t)$ in the successive years will be generated according to

$$X_s(t+1) = \sum_{r=0}^{\infty} X_r(t)p'_{rs}(t) \tag{2.1}$$

If we suppose, as is convenient, that the income ranges are paraded in order of size (there being a lowest income range R_0), then there will be some advantage in defining a new set of matrices

$$p_{ru}(t) = p'_{r,\,r+u}(t) \tag{2.2}$$

and rewriting (2.1) in the form

$$X_s(t+1) = \sum_{u=-\infty}^{s} X_{s-u}(t)p_{s-u,\,u}(t) \tag{2.3}$$

$p_{ru}(t)$ then tells us the proportion in Y_t of the occupants in R_r who shift up by various numbers u of ranges.

The advantage arises from the fact that in the real world the sizes of such shifts from year to year are mostly fairly limited, so that each $p_{ru}(t)$, regarded as a frequency distribution in u, is likely to be centred round $u = 0$.

In order to make simple models, we should like to be able to assume that the $p_{ru}(t)$ regarded as a frequency distribution in u differed very little in form for variations over a wide range of values of r and t.

When we consider the practical counterpart to this suggestion we see that it means that the prospects of shifts upwards and downwards along the ladder of income ranges differ little as between the occupants of different income ranges, and differ little from year to year.

This obviously cannot apply to all income ranges. For example, a rich man's income must be allowed some risk through death or misadventure of being degraded to a lower range in the following year; but the incomes in the lowest range cannot by definition be allowed this possibility. Again the *absolute* changes in income are liable to be much higher for incomes of £1,000,000 than for incomes of £100, so that the ranges must have a greater absolute width for high than for low incomes if our simplification is to have any plausibility. The obvious choice of ranges is that indicated above whereby each range has equal proportionate extent, for then any universal effects, such as price and interest movements, which are likely to alter income prospects for widely different ranges R_r and R_q in approximately the same manner proportionately, will affect the various functions $p_{ru}(t)$ and $p_{qu}(t)$ in roughly the same fashion.

Our other assumption that the functions $p'_{r,\,r+u}(t) = p_{ru}(t)$ remain constant as t changes through time, takes us far from reality: but an essential preliminary to the study (not here attempted) of the dynamic equilibrium with moving $p'_{rs}(t)$ is to examine the static equilibrium generated by a fixed set of functions $p'_{rs}(t)$.

For it is known that under very general conditions the repeated application of the same set of income-changes represented by an irreducible matrix $p'_{rs}(t)$ will make *any* initial income distribution eventually approach a unique equilibrium distribution which is determined by the matrix $p'_{rs}(t)$ alone. Considerable interest may therefore be found in the question of the type of income distribution which will correspond to the repeated operation of the changes represented by any realistic form of the matrix $p'_{rs}(t)$.

It would be a great advantage in constructing models of income distribution if we had empirical evidence about the matrices $p'_{rs}(t)$ describing actual movements of income in modern

TABLE I

Gross income 1951, £:	0–199	200–399	400–599	600–999	1000 and over
1952 income as percentage of 1951 income.	Proportion of cases per hundred.				
150 and over	7·53	2·62	0·99	0·70	0·36
125 to 149	4·65	5·47	1·90	3·87	0·89
115 to 124	4·68	6·50	6·68	5·64	6·57
105 to 114	24·53	20·69	23·36	23·87	20·35
101 to 104	7·67	16·16	18·13	14·40	7·00
100 exactly	46·51	36·53	30·33	29·57	43·55
96 to 99	0·27	0·96	2·36	2·61	1·10
86 to 95	1·47	4·93	6·69	4·12	5·61
76 to 85	0·74	2·23	5·69	6·93	6·52
57 to 75	1·95	2·41	2·81	7·06	7·32
50 and under	—	1·35	1·06	1·21	0·72
Not available	—	0·14	—	—	—
All ratios	100·00	100·00	100·00	100·00	100·00

communities. Some such evidence could presumably be compiled from the records of the income-tax authorities, but this information has not been tapped for such a purpose. The only figures available to the writer have been kindly supplied by the Institute of Statistics at Oxford and are a by-product of their survey of savings. Unfortunately these figures are regarded as unreliable by the authors of the survey, and they can therefore merely be given in illustration of the discussion which is to follow.

Table I gives a summary of the estimates provided by the Institute of Statistics. With comparatively little manipulation, these figures can be used to provide an estimate of the elements in the matrix $p'_{rs}(t)$ for low values of s and t. Taking for R_0 the range £89–£111, and in general for R_r the range £$10^{1\cdot 95+r/10}$ to £$10^{2\cdot 05+r/10}$, the resulting estimates for $p'_{rs}(t)$ for $r = 0$–11, $s = 0$–14 are shown in Table II.

This table shows some degree of regularity in the figures in each diagonal, with a tendency for the lowest incomes to shift upwards by rather more ranges on the average than the high incomes. The reader may find it useful to refer back to it later when considering some of the simplifying assumptions which we will use in constructing our models.

It is unfortunate, however, that the figures tell us virtually nothing about the changes among the incomes of the rich : it is with these that our basic postulate will be mainly concerned.

§ 3. A Simple Model Generating an Exact Pareto Distribution

As an expository device it will be convenient at this stage to consider what will result from very simple assumptions indeed about the matrix $p'_{rs}(t)$ and the corresponding distributions $p_{ru}(t) = p'_{r,\,r+u}(t)$. Although the assumptions of this section do not approach reality at all, the results they lead to will resemble reality in one respect, and this will assist an understanding of one possible explanation of this aspect of actual distributions.

Let us assume, then, that for every value of t and r, and for some fixed integer n

$$(3.1) \qquad p'_{r,\,r+u}(t) = p_{r,\,u}(t) = 0 \text{ if } u > 1 \text{ or } u < -n$$

This means that no income moves up by more than one income range in a year, or down by more than n income ranges in a year,

$$(3.2) \qquad p'_{r,\,r+ru}(t) = p_{r,\,u}(t) = p_u > 0$$

if $\qquad -n \leqslant u \leqslant 1 \text{ and } u > -r.$

TABLE II

Estimates of Some Elements in the Matrix p'_{rs} *for England and Wales* 1951–52

Income range.	$s =$	0	1	2	3	4	5	6	7	8	9	10	11	12	13	14
	$r =$	p'_{rs}.														
£89–£111	0	n.a.	n.a.	n.a.	n.a.	n.a.	—	—	—	—	—	—	—	—	—	—
£112–£141	1	0·020	0·672	0·202	0·083	0·023	—	—	—	—	—	—	—	—	—	—
£142–£177	2	0·015	0·020	0·674	0·204	0·068	0·019	—	—	—	—	—	—	—	—	—
£177–£221	3	0·007	0·014	0·030	0·676	0·205	0·053	0·015	—	—	—	—	—	—	—	—
£222–£281	5	—	0·012	0·015	0·040	0·672	0·207	0·043	0·011	—	—	—	—	—	—	—
£282–£354	5	—	—	0·016	0·017	0·052	0·666	0·209	0·033	0·007	—	—	—	—	—	—
£355–£445	6	—	—	—	0·015	0·018	0·075	0·666	0·200	0·023	0·004	—	—	—	—	—
£446–£562	7	—	—	—	—	0·013	0·020	0·096	0·658	0·198	0·013	0·002	—	—	—	—
£563–£707	8	—	—	—	—	—	0·016	0·035	0·100	0·632	0·200	0·015	0·002	—	—	—
£708–£892	9	—	—	—	—	—	—	0·018	0·049	0·104	0·607	0·205	0·015	0·002	—	—
£893–£1119	10	—	—	—	—	—	—	—	0·017	0·050	0·106	0·625	0·190	0·010	0·002	—
£1120–£1409	11	—	—	—	—	—	—	—	—	0·015	0·051	0·108	0·646	0·178	0·005	0·001

We may refer to this equation (3.2), and to later modifications of it, as our *basic postulate*. It here means that the prospects of shifts upwards and downwards along the ladder of income ranges are distributed in a manner independent of present income, apart from the limitations imposed by the impossibility of descending below the bottom rung of the ladder. This is the postulate which we shall retain in some modified form in nearly all our models, and which always leads to an income distribution which obeys Pareto's law at least asymptotically for high incomes.

We also need to assume that for each value of r and t

$$(3.3) \qquad \sum_{s=0}^{\infty} p'_{rs}(t) = \sum_{u=-r}^{\infty} p_{ru}(t) = 1$$

which by (3.2) also implies

$$(3.3a) \qquad \sum_{u=-n}^{1} p_u = 1.$$

This assumption (3.3) expresses the fiction that all incomes preserve their identity throughout time in the manner described in Section 2 above.

One other assumption must be introduced in order to ensure that the process is not dissipative, *i.e.*, that the incomes do not go on increasing indefinitely without settling down to an equilibrium distribution. Let us denote

$$(3.4) \qquad g(z) \equiv \sum_{u=-n}^{1} p_u z^{1-u} - z$$

then our stability assumption is that

$$(3.5) \qquad g'(1) \equiv -\sum_{u=-n}^{1} u p_u \text{ is positive.}$$

This means that for all incomes, initially in any one of the ranges R_n, R_{n+1}, R_{n+2} . . ., the average number of ranges shifted during the next year is negative.

This completes the list of assumptions for our first model and when $n = 5$ they give rise to a matrix of Diagram 1.

Now we may determine the equilibrium distribution corresponding to any matrix $p'_{r,\,r+u}(t) = p_{r,\,u}(t)$ conforming to our assumed rules. Owing to the uniqueness theorem mentioned above in Section 2, it will be sufficient to find any distribution which remains exactly unchanged under the action of the matrix $p'_{rs}(t)$ for one year. For this distribution when found must (apart from an arbitrary multiplying constant) be the unique distribution which will be approached by all distributions under

$s =$	0	1	2	3	4	5	6	7	8 . . . .
$r =$	$p'_{rs}(t)$								
0	$1 - p_1$	p_1	0	0	0	0	0	0	0 . . . .
1	$1 - p_0 - p_1$	p_0	p_1	0	0	0	0	0	0 . . . .
2	$p_{-5} + p_{-4} + p_{-3} + p_{-2}$	p_{-1}	p_0	p_1	0	0	0	0	0 . . . .
3	$p_{-5} + p_{-4} + p_{-3}$	p_{-2}	p_{-1}	p_0	p_1	0	0	0	0 . . . .
4	$p_{-5} + p_{-4}$	p_{-3}	p_{-2}	p_{-1}	p_0	p_1	0	0	0 . . . .
5	p_{-5}	p_{-4}	p_{-3}	p_{-2}	p_{-1}	p_0	p_1	0	0 . . . .
6	0	p_{-5}	p_{-4}	p_{-3}	p_{-2}	p_{-1}	p_0	p_1	0 . . . .
7	0	0	p_{-5}	p_{-4}	p_{-3}	p_{-2}	p_{-1}	p_0	p_1 . . . .
8	0	0	0	p_{-5}	p_{-4}	p_{-3}	p_{-2}	p_{-1}	p_0 . . . .
.	.	.	.	.	.	.	.	.	.
.	.	.	.	.	.	.	.	.	.
.	.	.	.	.	.	.	.	.	.
.	.	.	.	.	.	.	.	.	.

DIAGRAM 1

the repeated action of the matrix multiplier $p'_{rs}(t)$ year after year.

Our assumptions (3.1) to (3.5) have deliberately been chosen so as to make the solution obvious. Indeed, if X_s is the desired equilibrium distribution, we need by (2.3), (3.1) and (3.2)

$$X_s = \sum_{-n}^{1} p_u X_{s-u} \quad \text{for all } s > 0 \tag{3.6}$$

and

$$X_0 = \sum_{-n}^{0} q_u X_{-u} \quad \text{where } q_u = \sum_{v=-n}^{u} p_r. \tag{3.7}$$

We need only satisfy (3.6), since (3.6), (3.1), (3.2) and (3.3) ensure the satisfaction of (3.7) as well.

Now an obvious solution of (3.6) is

$$X_s = b^s \tag{3.8}$$

where b is the real positive root other than unity of the equation

$$g(z) = \sum_{u=-n}^{1} p_u z^{1-u} - z = 0 \tag{3.9}$$

where $g(z)$ was already defined in (3.4) above.

Descartes' rule of signs establishes the fact that (3.9) has no more than two real positive roots : since unity is one root, and $g(0) = p_0 > 0$, and $g'(1) > 0$ by (3.5), the other real positive root must satisfy

$$0 < b < 1. \tag{3.10}$$

Hence the solution (3.8) implies a total number of incomes given by

$$N' = \frac{1}{1 - b} \tag{3.11}$$

and, to arrange for any other total number N, we need merely modify (3.8) to the form

(3.8a) $$X_s = N(1 - b)b^s.$$

Now suppose that the proportionate extent of each income range is 10^h, and that the lowest income is $y_{min.}$: then X_s is the number of incomes in the range R_s whose lower bound is given by

(3.12) $$y_s = 10^{sh}y_{min.} \text{ whence } \log_{10}y_s = sh + \log_{10}y_{min.}$$

By summing a geometrical progression, using (3.8a), we now find that in the equilibrium distribution the number of incomes exceeding y_s is given by

(3.13) $$F(y_s) = Nb^s \text{ whence } \log_{10}F(y_s) = \log_{10}N + s\log_{10}b$$

Now put

(3.14) $$\alpha = \log_{10}b^{-1/h} \text{ and } \gamma = \log_{10}N + \alpha\log_{10}y_{min.}$$

Then it follows from (3.12) and (3.13) that

(3.15) $$\log_{10}F(y_s) = \gamma - \alpha\log_{10}y_s$$

This means that for $y = y_0, y_1, y_2 \ldots$, the logarithm of the number of incomes exceeding y is a linear function of y. This states Pareto's law in its exact form.

Thus if all ranges are of equal proportionate extent, our simplifying assumptions ensure that any initial distribution of income will in the course of time approach the exact Pareto distribution given by (3.14), (3.15).

The very simple model discussed in this section brings out clearly the tendency for Pareto's law to be obeyed in a community where, above a certain minimum income, the prospects of various amounts of percentage change of income are independent of the initial income.

Most of the remainder of the article will be spent in generalising this very simple model so that it is less unrealistic.

In actual income distributions, Pareto's law is not even approximately obeyed for low incomes: if logarithm of income is measured along the horizontal axis, the frequency distributions found in practice are not J-shaped like that obtained in our model, but single humped and moderately symmetrical. The first modification which we make to our model is to remove the assumption that there is a lowest income range R_0 and to set up conditions which lead to a two-tailed distribution, one for the poor and one for the rich.

In these simple models, Pareto's law is obeyed exactly, not merely asymptotically. We next introduce two generalisations which limit observance of the law to the occupants of high income groups and render it no longer exact but asymptotic. These generalisations consist in :

(i) allowing incomes to shift upwards by more than one range in a year;

(ii) limiting our basic assumption (3.2) that the prospects of various amounts of percentage change of income are independent of initial income to apply to higher incomes only.

These two generalisations bring our model much closer to the conditions indicated by Table II above.

In real life a man's age has a great influence on his prospects of increasing his income. Our next generalisation takes this into account. We now allow a man's prospects of change of income to depend on his age. Finally, we use the same technical device to allow a man's occupation to influence his prospects of change of income.

Despite these generalisations of the model, it is still found that the Pareto curve must be asymptotic to a straight line. Is it then possible that the approximate linearity over high income ranges of the Pareto curves found for many modern communities is due to the approximate fulfilment in the real world of our basic assumption? This question is briefly discussed in the final sections of the paper.

§ 4. A Model Generating a Two-tailed Income Distribution Obeying Pareto's Law

The simple model described in the last section generated a distribution with only one Pareto tail. The essential modifications required to introduce a two-tailed distribution are the following :

(i) We drop the assumption that there is a lowest income-range R_0, and adopt an infinite sequence of income ranges R_r, of equal proportionate extent, allowing r to run from minus infinity to plus infinity.

(ii) We adopt assumptions about that part of the matrix $p'_{rs}(t)$ for which r is negative analogous to those adopted about that part for which r is positive.

(iii) We allow for some movement of incomes to and fro between ranges R_r for which r is positive and those for which r is negative.

In particular, we assume as in (3.1)

(4.1) $p'_{r,r+u}(t) = p_{ru}(t) = 0$ when $r \geqslant 0$ and $u \geqslant 1$ or $u < -n$

and we retain our basic postulate (3.2)

(4.2) $p'_{r,r+u}(t) = p_{ru}(t) = p_u > 0$ if $-n \leqslant u \leqslant 1$ and $u > -r$

We further assume that

(4.3) when $r \geqslant 0$ and $u < -r$, and when $r < 0$
and $u > r$, $u < -1$ or $u > v$,
$p'_{r,r+u}(t) = p_{ru}(t) = 0$

We now introduce a positive integer r and non-negative constants $\pi_{-1}\, \pi_0\, \pi_1 \ldots \pi_v$ and satisfying

(4.4) $\pi_{-1} > 0 \;\; \pi_0 > 0 \;\; \pi_1 > 0 \;\; \pi_v > 0 \;\; \lambda > 0 \;\; \sum_{s=1}^{v} \pi_s = 1 \;\; \sum_{u=1}^{v} u\pi_u > 1$
$1 - \lambda - \pi_{-1} > 0 \;\; 1 - \lambda - p_1 > 0$

and put

(4.5) $p_{ru}(t) = \pi_u$ when $r < 0$ and $u < -r - 1$
and $-1 \leqslant u \leqslant v$
$p_{0,-1}(t) = p_{-1,2}(t) = \lambda \quad p_{00}(t) = 1 - \lambda - p_1 > 0$
$p_{-10}(t) = 1 - \lambda - \pi_{-1} > 0$

and assume as before that for all r

(4.6) $$\sum_{u=-\infty}^{\infty} p_{ru}(t) = 1 \text{ and } p'_{r,r+u}(t) = p_{ru}(t).$$

These assumptions can best be understood by considering their effects when n and v take particular values. Thus when $n = 3$ and $v = 2$, they give rise to a matrix for $p'_{rs}(t)$ whose centre is of the following form :

$s =$	-4	-3	-2	-1	0	1	2	3	4	5
$r =$										
-5	π_1	π_2	0	0	0	0	0	0	0	0
-4	π_0	π_1	π_2	0	0	0	0	0	0	0
-3	π_{-1}	π_0	π_1	π_2	0	0	0	0	0	0
-2	0	π_{-1}	π_0	$1 - \pi_0 - \pi_{-1}$	0	0	0	0	0	0
-1	0	0	π_{-1}	$1 - \lambda - \pi_{-1}$	λ	0	0	0	0	0
0	0	0	0	λ	$1 - \lambda - p_1$	p_1	0	0	0	0
1	0	0	0	0	$1 - p_0 - p_1$	p_0	p_1	0	0	0
2	0	0	0	0	$p_{-3} + p_{-2}$	p_{-1}	p_0	p_1	0	0
3	0	0	0	0	p_{-3}	p_{-2}	p_{-1}	p_0	p_1	0
4	0	0	0	0	0	p_{-3}	p_{-2}	p_{-1}	p_0	p_1
5	0	0	0	0	0	0	0	p_{-3}	p_{-1}	p_0
6	0	0	0	0	0	0	0	p_{-3}	p_{-2}	p_{-1}

DIAGRAM 2

We retain our assumption (3.5) that

(4.7) $$g'(1) = -\sum_{u=-n}^{1} up_u \text{ is positive}$$

and introduce the analogous assumption that

$$\gamma'(1) = -\sum_{v=-1}^{m} v\pi_v \text{ is negative} \tag{4.8}$$

where

$$\gamma(z) \equiv \sum_{v=-1}^{1} \pi_v z^{1-v} - z \tag{4.9}$$

Then, by an argument analogous to that of Section 3, the equation

$$\gamma(z) = 0 \tag{4.10}$$

must have a single real root β satisfying

$$\beta > 1 \tag{4.11}$$

It may be easily verified that the distribution

$$\begin{aligned} X_s &= Ab^s \text{ when } s \geqslant 0 \\ X_s &= A\beta^{s+1} \text{ when } s < 0 \end{aligned} \tag{4.12}$$

satisfies the equilibrium condition

$$X_s = \sum_{r=-\infty}^{\infty} p'_{rs}(t) X_r \tag{4.13}$$

Hence for some value of A, this must be the equilibrium distribution towards which any actual distribution must tend under the repeated action of the multiplying matrix $p'_{rs}(t)$ determined by the various assumptions of this model.

To secure any total number of incomes, N say, we need only put

$$A = \frac{(1-b)(\beta-1)N}{2\beta - b\beta - 1} \tag{4.14}$$

In this solution there are two Pareto tails, one relating to high incomes and one to low incomes. The distribution is kept stable by the two conditions (4.7), (4.8), which ensure that for large incomes the expected change u is negative and for small incomes it is positive. This pair of conditions is needed to offset the continual dispersal of incomes due to the variance of the frequency distributions in u, p_u and π_u.

This example has been hand-picked so as to yield a crystal-clear solution, but one essential feature of this solution, namely the conformity to Pareto's law of the distribution, will be found to be approximately preserved through a series of modifications and relaxations of our simplifying assumptions. The basic postulate which leads to the approximate obedience of this law was retained in assumption (4.2), which determines that the functions of type $p_{ru}(t)$ should be the same for all values of r relating to high income ranges.

One minor generalisation which can be made to the above example without essentially altering the form of the solution is to enlarge the channels of communication between income ranges with $r \geqslant 0$ and those with $r < 0$, hitherto limited to the flow of a proportion λ from each of R_{-1} and R_0. We may adjust the values of $p'_{r,-1}(t)$ and $p'_{r0}(t)$ in such a manner as to allow the flow of incomes from each of $R_0R_1 \ldots R_{n-1}$ to R_{-1} and from each of $R_{-1}R_{-2} \ldots R_{-r}$ to R_0 without altering the solution further than to the form

$$(4.15) \qquad x_s = Bb^s \text{ when } s \geqslant 0$$
$$x_{-s} = B\beta^{s-1} \text{ when } s < 0$$

where the ratio between β and B will now depend on the value of $p'_{r,-1}(t)$ and $p'_{r0}(t)$, and need no longer be unity.

§ 5. A More General Model Generating a Distribution Asymptotic to a Pareto Distribution

One of the most restrictive assumptions in the example we have discussed was that

$$p_{ru}(t) = 0 \text{ when } u > 1 \text{ and } r \geqslant 0$$

The abandonment of this assumption destroys the complete simplicity of the solution.

In order to concentrate attention on the new generalisation, let us first restore the assumption that R_0 is the minimum income range so that we shall only have to consider one tail of the distribution. Then let us replace the assumption (3.1) by

(5.1) $p_{ru}(t) = 0$ if $u > m$ a given positive integer or $u < -n$ and modify (3.2) to the form

(5.2) $p_{ru}(t) = p_u$ (defined for $u = -n, 1-n, \ldots, m$)

if $u + r \geqslant m$ where $\sum_{u=-n}^{m} p_u = 1$ and no p_u is negative.

We may retain assumptions (3.3), (3.4) and (3.5) (extending the summation in (3.4) and (3.5) from $-n$ to m) and add the additional assumption, $p_m > 0$.

The assumptions made so far have defined $p'_{rs}(t)$ for $s \geqslant m$ and determined $\sum_{s=0}^{m-1} p'_{rs}(t)$ for each $r = 0, 1, \ldots, n$ and $\sum_{s=r-n}^{m-1} p'_{rs}(t)$ for each $r = n+1, \ldots, n+m-1$. But the individual values $p'_{rs}(t)$ for $r = 0, 1, \ldots, n+m-2$ and $r - n \leqslant s < m$ are, subject to these linear restraints, still at our disposal. We shall make no further assumption about these individual values, except that none are negative and that when $|r - s| \leqslant 1$, $p'_{rs}(t)$ is positive.

The effect of these assumptions in the case $n = 2$ $m = 3$ is to give the matrix $p'_{rs}(t)$ the following form :

$p'_{00}(t)$	$p'_{01}(t)$	$p'_{02}(t)$	p_1	0	0	0	0 . . . .
$p'_{10}(t)$	$p'_{11}(t)$	$p'_{12}(t)$	p_2	p_3	0	0	0 . . . .
$p'_{20}(t)$	$p'_{21}(t)$	$p'_{22}(t)$	p_1	p_2	p_3	0	0 . . . .
0	$p'_{31}(t)$	$p'_{32}(t)$	p_0	p_1	p_2	p_3	0 . . . .
0	0	p_{-2}	p_{-1}	p_0	p_1	p_2	p_3 . . . .
0	0	0	p_{-2}	p_{-1}	p_0	p_1	p_2 . . . .
0	0	0	0	p_{-2}	p_{-2}	p_0	p_1 . . . .
0	0	0	0	0	p_{-2}	p_{-1}	p_0 . . . .
.	.	.	.	.	.	.	.
.	.	.	.	.	.	.	.

DIAGRAM 3

subject to the conditions :

(i) that the sum of the elements in each row are unity;

(ii) that the elements in the three central diagonals are all positive, and no elements are negative.

In the general case where m is some positive integer, the equation

$$g(z) = \sum_{\theta=0}^{m+n} p_{m-\theta} z^{\theta} - z^m = 0 \tag{5.3}$$

will still have just one positive root b_1 less than unity, provided we retain our assumption (3.5) in the form

$$g'(1) = - \sum_{u=-n}^{m} u p_u > 0. \tag{5.4}$$

This assumptions ensures, by a theorem due to Mr. F. G. Foster,[1] that the matrix $p'_{rs}(t)$ is "non-dissipative," and hence that a unique finite non-zero equilibrium distribution will be approached in the limit under the repeated application of the changes embodied in this matrix.

Let the $m + n$ roots of (5.3) be $b_1 b_2 \ldots b_{m+n}$; and let x_s $(s = 0, 1, 2 \ldots)$ denote the equilibrium distribution, which must satisfy the equilibrium equations

$$\begin{cases} x_s = \sum_{r=0}^{\infty} p'_{rs}(t) x_r \qquad s = 0, 1, 2 \ldots \\ \sum_{s=0}^{\infty} x_s = N \end{cases} \tag{5.5}$$

[1] Foster [4].

This set of equations may be subdivided into

$$(5.6) \qquad x_s = \sum_{r=0}^{\infty} p'_{rs}(t)x_r \qquad s = 0, 1, 2 \ldots m - 1$$

$$(5.7) \qquad x_s = \sum_{u=-n}^{m} p_u x_{s-u} \qquad s = m, m + 1, m + 2 \ldots$$

$$(5.8) \qquad \sum_{s=0}^{\infty} x_s = N$$

The solution is known, because of Foster's theorem, to exist: hence there exist coefficients $B_1 \ldots B_{m+n}$ such that

$$(5.9) \qquad x_s = \sum_{k=1}^{m+n} B_k b_k^s \qquad s = 0, 1, 2 \ldots m + n - 1$$

It will then follow from (5.3) and (5.7) that

$$(5.10) \qquad x_s = \sum_{k=1}^{m+n} B_k b_k^s \qquad s = m + n, m + n + 1, \ldots$$

Amongst those roots whose coefficients in (5.10) are not zero there will be one (at least) whose modulus is not exceeded by that of any other. Let its modulus be b: then for large s, (5.10) will reduce to the form

$$(5.11) \qquad x_s = b^{-s}\{B'_1 + B'_2(-1)^s + \sum_{k=3}^{k} B'_k \cos(s\theta_k + \phi_k) + o(1)\}$$

Since no x_s can be negative

$$(5.12) \qquad B'_1 > 0$$

and b itself must be one root of (5.3). But since all the coefficients of non-zero powers of z in the expansion of $z^{-m}g(z)$ are positive, there can then be no other root of modulus b than b itself. Hence (5.11) may be reduced to

$$(5.13) \qquad x_s = b^{-s}\{B'_1 + o(1)\}$$

It follows from (5.8), (5.12) and (5.13) that $|b| < 1$ and hence

$$(5.14) \qquad x_s = b_1^{-s}\{B_1 + o(1)\}$$

where b_1 is the real root lying between 0 and 1. (5.14) expresses the fact that the Pareto curve for the equilibrium distribution is asymptotic to a straight line.

It is always possible to find the coefficients B_k in the exact solution (5.9), (5.10) by finding b_1 and the roots $b_2 \ldots b_m$ of modulus less than b_1 and fitting B_1 to B_k so as to satisfy (5.6).

It is perhaps of some interest to state that by a suitable choice of the elements $p'_{rs}(t)$ in the top left-hand corner of the matrix illustrated in Diagram 3, which were left with arbitrary values, it is always possible to arrange that all the terms except the first vanish in the expansion for x_s so that in this case Pareto's law is exactly obeyed throughout the whole income scale as in the example of Section 3. A variety of such suitable choices is available, but the result has so little practical relevance that it may be left to the curious reader to verify it if he so wishes.

It is now convenient to relax our assumption (5.2) so that the distribution $p_{ru}(t)$ need only conform to the standard form p_u for high incomes. We replace (5.2) by

$$(5.15) \quad p_{ru}(t) = p_u \text{ defined for } u = -n, 1-n, \ldots, m \quad \text{if } u + r \geqslant m + w$$

where w is a non-negative integer

$$\sum_{u=-n}^{m} p_u = 1 \text{ and no } p_u \text{ is negative.}$$

The $p_{ru}(t)$ thus freed from the restriction (5.3) are those for which $m - r \leqslant u \leqslant m + w - r$ and $-n \leqslant u \leqslant m$, and these may be left free, apart from the usual requirements that no $p_{ru}(t)$ is negative, all $p_{r1}(t)$, $p_{r0}(t)$ and $p_{r-1}(t)$ are positive and the survival assumption (5.2).

In the case $n = 1$ $m = 2$ $w = 2$, the effect of these assumptions on the appearance of the matrix $p'_{rs}(t)$ is shown below.

$r =$	0	1	2	3	4	5	6
$s =$							
0	$p'_{00}(t)$	$p'_{01}(t)$	$p'_{02}(t)$	0	0	0	0
1	$p'_{10}(t)$	$p'_{11}(t)$	$p'_{12}(t)$	$p'_{13}(t)$	0	0	0
2	0	$p'_{21}(t)$	$p'_{22}(t)$	$p'_{23}(t)$	p_2	0	0
3	0	0	$p'_{32}(t)$	$p'_{33}(t)$	p_1	p_2	0
4	0	0	0	$p'_{43}(t)$	p_0	p_1	p_2
5	0	0	0	0	p_{-1}	p_0	p_1
6	0	0	0	0	0	p_{-1}	p_0

DIAGRAM 4

The reader may compare this diagram with the figures of Table II.

The effect of the change in our model on the solution is in principle not very great. As before, we find $b_1 \ldots b_m$ those m roots of (5.3) which have modulus less than unity and we try solutions of the form (5.9) for $x_w x_{w+1} \ldots$

But we can no longer expect $x_0 x_1 \ldots x_{w-1}$ to conform to the rule (5.9), and we need w more equations to determine these w further unknowns. These equations are provided by extending the equations (5.6) to cover $s = 0, 1, \ldots, m + w - 1$.

Subject to these modifications, the solution is exactly the same as before, and again the Pareto curve for high incomes must be asymptotic to a straight line.

The extension of these results to the case where there are two tails in a generalised form of the example discussed in Section 4 above involves no difficulty in principle.

§ 6. A Model Making Allowance for Some Effects of Age- and Occupation-Structure

An obvious objection to a theory based on the constancy over time of the movement matrices $p_{rs}(t)$ is the fact that age and death play such an important part in determining the changes in an income. In this section we shall modify our assumptions so as to go some way towards meeting this difficulty.

Our method will be to suppose that our population is divided between C "colonies," and that income-receivers can migrate from one colony to another, the prospects of change of income varying from colony to colony. When we wish to discuss the effect of age on income distribution, the "colonies" will represent age-groups: if the width of the age-groups exceeds one "year," then an income attached to one individual may either remain in that age-group or pass on to the next age-group above, or if the individual dies, pass with an appropriate reduction in size to the age-group containing the heir.

But the method could be used also to study the effects on income distribution of the tendency for families to remain in the same occupation: for this purpose we would make the "colonies" represent occupations. As in occupations, the income prospects in some colonies would be better than in others: most incomes would remain in one colony, but there would again be some movement between colonies.

We shall find that provided within each colony the $p_{ru}(t)$ functions have a form independent of the income range, for all large incomes the asymptotic approach of the Pareto curve to a straight line will be preserved under these far more general assumptions.

We now set down formally the notation for our model modified to include colonies.

Let $${}_{cd}p'_{rs}(t) = {}_{cd}p_{rs-r}(t)$$

denote the proportion of the incomes in range R_r in colony c in year t which move into range R_s in colony d in year $t + 1$.

If ${}_{c}x_r(t)$ denotes the number of incomes in range R_r in colony c in year t, then by definition

$$(6.1) \qquad {}_{d}x_s(t+1) = \sum_{c-1}^{c} \sum_{r-0}^{\infty} {}_{cd}p'_{rs}(t) {}_{c}x_s(t)$$

and if an equilibrium distribution ${}_dx_s$ exists it must satisfy the condition

$$(6.2) \qquad {}_dx_s = \sum_{c=1}^{C} \sum_{r=0}^{\infty} {}_{cd}p'_{rs}(t)_c x_r$$

for every $d = 1, 2, \ldots C$ and $s = 0, 1, 2, \ldots$

The assumptions for our model can now be set down in a form closely analogous to those of the simpler model of Section 5, We assume

$$(6.3) \qquad {}_{cd}p_{rs}(t) = {}_{cd}p'_{r,\,r+s}(t) = 0$$

when $s > m_d$ or $s < -n_d$

where m_d and n_d are positive integers $d = 1, 2, \ldots C$

$$(6.4) \qquad {}_{cd}p_{ru}(t) = {}_{cd}p'_{r,\,r+u}(t) = {}_{cd}p_u \geqslant 0$$

if $s = r + u \geqslant m_d + w_d$

and $m_d \geqslant u \geqslant -n_d$

where the w_d are non-negative integers for $d = 1, 2, \ldots C$, and the ${}_{cd}p_u$ are constants satisfying for each $c = 1, 2, \ldots C$, the survival condition

$$(6.5) \qquad \sum_{d=1}^{c} \sum_{u=-n_d}^{m_d} {}_{cd}p_u = 1$$

It is convenient at this stage to introduce the notion of the accessibility of one income range R_s in one colony C_d from the income range R_r in colony C_c.

Range R_s in C_d will be called accessible in one step from range R_r in C_c if ${}_{cd}p'_{rs}(t)$ is positive : it will be called accessible in two steps from R_r in C_c if it is accessible in one step from any range in any colony which itself is accessible from R_r in C_c in one step. In general, the definition may be extended one by one to any larger number of steps, by always defining R_s in C_d to be accessible in n steps from R_r in C_c, if it is accessible in one step from any range in any colony, which itself is accessible from R_r in C_c in $(n - 1)$ steps.

Finally, R_s in C_d will be termed accessible from R_r in C_c if for any n it is thus accessible in n steps.

We now make the further assumption

(6.6) Each range in any colony is accessible from each range in every colony.

The purpose of this assumption is to ensure that the equilibrium income distribution is unique.

The survival postulate now takes the form

$$(6.7) \qquad \sum_{d=1}^{c} \sum_{u=-n_d}^{m_d} {}_{cd}p_{ru}(t) = 1$$

and we require one further postulate in order to rule out solutions involving periodic fluctuations from one distribution to another. This postulate may take the form that

(6.8) There is some pair of ranges R_s in C_d and R_r in C_c and some integer n such that R_s in C_d is accessible from R_r in C_c both in n steps and in $(n + i)$ steps.

The effect of these assumptions on the matrices $_{cd}p'_{rs}(t)$ may be illustrated by a numerical example with $C = 3$. In this example, the three colonies represent the young, middle-age and old-age groups 20–35, 35–50 and 50–65 years, and the unit of time during which the matrix $_{cd}p'_{rs}(t)$ operates once is taken as fifteen calendar years. It is supposed that all the young survive to middle-age, but half the middle-aged die and their incomes pass with suitable reduction to young heirs in the next period, while the other half reappear as the old in the next period, then to die and transmit their incomes to the young in the following period.

We arrange $m_1 = 0 \quad m_2 = 1 \quad m_3 = 1 \quad C = 3$

$w_1 = 1 \quad w_2 = 0 \quad w_3 = 0$

and choose the following nine matrices $_{cd}p'_{rs}(t)$ for $c = 1, 2, 3$ and $d = 1, 2, 3$.

We put identically equal to zero those five of the matrices for which either $c = d$ or $c = 1$ and $d = 3$, or $c = 3$ and $d = 2$. The other four matrices we choose as follows :

$$
{}_{12}p'_{rs}(t) = \begin{array}{lllll} 0{\cdot}1 & 0{\cdot}9 & 0 & 0 & \text{etc.} \\ 0 & 0{\cdot}1 & 0{\cdot}9 & 0 & \text{etc.} \\ 0 & 0 & 0{\cdot}1 & 0{\cdot}9 & \text{etc.} \\ 0 & 0 & 0 & 0{\cdot}1 & \text{etc.} \\ & & \text{etc.} & & \end{array}
\qquad
{}_{23}p'_{rs}(t) = \begin{array}{lllll} 0{\cdot}1 & 0{\cdot}4 & 0 & 0 & \text{etc.} \\ 0 & 0{\cdot}1 & 0{\cdot}4 & 0 & \text{etc.} \\ 0 & 0 & 0{\cdot}1 & 0{\cdot}4 & \text{etc.} \\ 0 & 0 & 0 & 0{\cdot}1 & \text{etc.} \\ & & \text{etc.} & & \end{array}
$$

$$
{}_{21}p'_{rs} = \begin{array}{lllll} 0{\cdot}5 & 0 & 0 & 0 & \text{etc.} \\ 0{\cdot}4 & 0{\cdot}1 & 0 & 0 & \text{etc.} \\ 0{\cdot}2 & 0{\cdot}2 & 0{\cdot}1 & 0 & \text{etc.} \\ 0 & 0{\cdot}2 & 0{\cdot}2 & 0{\cdot}1 & \text{etc.} \\ 0 & 0 & 0{\cdot}2 & 0{\cdot}2 & \text{etc.} \\ & & \text{etc.} & & \end{array}
\qquad
{}_{31}p'_{rs} = \begin{array}{llllll} 1 & 0 & 0 & 0 & 0 & \text{etc.} \\ 0{\cdot}9 & 0{\cdot}1 & 0 & 0 & 0 & \text{etc.} \\ 0{\cdot}8 & 0{\cdot}1 & 0{\cdot}1 & 0 & 0 & \text{etc.} \\ 0{\cdot}5 & 0{\cdot}3 & 0{\cdot}1 & 0{\cdot}1 & 0 & \text{etc.} \\ 0 & 0{\cdot}5 & 0{\cdot}3 & 0{\cdot}1 & 0{\cdot}1 & \text{etc.} \\ 0 & 0 & 0{\cdot}5 & 0{\cdot}3 & 0{\cdot}1 & \text{etc.} \\ & & \text{etc.} & & & \end{array}
$$

DIAGRAM 5

It may be noted that R_0 in C_1 is accessible from R_0 in C_2 both in one step and in two steps. Thus the matrices satisfy the postulate (6.8).

In any generalised model of this type we shall have C sets of equilibrium equations to be satisfied by the equilibrium distributions $_dx_s$, namely

$$(6.9) \qquad {}_dx_s = \sum_{c=1}^{C} \sum_{r=0}^{\infty} {}_{cd}p'_{rs}(t)\,{}_cx_r \qquad d = 1, 2, \ldots C$$

For $s > m_d + w_d$, these conditions become

$$(6.10) \qquad {}_dx_s = \sum_{c=1}^{c} \sum_{u=-n_d}^{m_d} {}_{cd}p_u \, {}_dx_{s-u} \qquad d = 1, 2, \ldots C$$

We are thus led to investigate the C simultaneous equations

$$(6.11) \qquad A_d = \sum_{c=1}^{c} \sum_{u=-n_d}^{m_d} {}_{cd}p_u A_c z^{-u} \qquad d = 1, 2, \ldots C$$

which we may write again as

$$(6.12) \qquad \sum_{c=1}^{c} P_{cd}(z) A_c = 0 \qquad d = 1, 2, \ldots C$$

where

$$(6.13) \qquad P_{cd}(z) = \left\{ \sum_{u=-n_d}^{m_d} {}_{cd}p_u z^{-u} - 1 \right\} \text{ if } c = d$$

$$= \sum_{u=-n_d}^{m_d} {}_{cd}p_u z^{-u} \qquad \text{if } C \neq d$$

Elimination of the coefficients A_c leads to

$$(6.14) \qquad \text{Det.}|P_{cd}(z)| = G(z), \text{ say } = 0$$

This function $G(z)$ can be expressed in the form

$$(6.15) \qquad G(z) = \sum_{u=-n}^{m} p_u z^{-u} \qquad m = \sum_{c=1}^{C} m_c \quad n = \sum_{c=1}^{c} n_c$$

and plays a similar role in the theory to the function $g(z)$ in earlier sections. In particular, if we postulate

$$(6.16) \qquad G'(1) = - \sum_{u=-n}^{m} u p_u > 0$$

it can be proved by an application of Foster's theorem that the process is non-dissipative and that a unique equilibrium distribution exists.

We can again prove by the methods of Section 5 that for large s, where x_s is the equilibrium distribution

$$(6.17) \qquad x_s = b_1^s \{B_1 + o(1)\}$$

where b_1 is a real positive root of (6.14).

Thus again the Pareto curve is asymptotic to a straight line in the region of high incomes.

The procedure for finding an exact solution is the following. First find b_1 the largest real positive root and $b_2 \ldots b_m$ the roots of lesser modulus. Let B_{ce} denote the co-factor of $P_{c1}(b_e)$ in the determinant $G(z)$. Then

$$(6.18) \qquad \sum_{c=1}^{C} B_{ce} P_{c1}(b_e) = G(b_e) = 0 \qquad e = 1, 2 \ldots m$$

and (6.12) will clearly be satisfied, provided

(6.19) $A_c = \sum_{e=1}^{m} B_{ce}\lambda_e$, where λ_e are any numbers.

We have still to determine not only the m values λ_e but also those values ${}_dx_s$ for which $s < w_d$: the number of these is given by

$$(6.20) \qquad w = \sum_{d=1}^{c} w_d$$

We have thus $(w + m)$ unknowns to find. To discover them we have the $w + m$ equations determining the equilibrium of those ${}_cx_s$ for which $s < m_c + w_c$: namely (6.2) for these values of c and s. These equations are not linearly independent, and only determine the ratios between the $w + m$ unknowns. Apart from a scale factor, this is sufficient to determine all the ${}_cx_s$, and the scale factor can then be found if we know the original total population.

It can be proved exactly as before that the distribution

$$(6.21) \qquad x_s = \sum_{c=1}^{C} {}_cx_s$$

so determined is the unique equilibrium distribution and that the term involving $b_1{}^s$ will dominate the whole value of x_s for sufficiently large s. Thus the Pareto curve for sufficiently large incomes will preserve its property of being asymptotic to a straight line, despite the greater generalisation introduced in this model.

As in simpler models, we could remove the restriction that there is a minimum income range R_0 and elaborate the model so as to secure an equilibrium distribution with two Pareto tails, one for the poor and one for the rich. The exposition is tedious, and since our conclusions would not be substantially affected, this refinement is eschewed.

§ 7. Numerical Example Involving the Effect of Age-structure on Income Distribution

The general method of solution indicated in the last section can be made much clearer by applying it to the numerical example described above in Diagram 4.

In this example, $C = 3$, $m = 2$, and the determinant of $P_{cd}(z)$ is

$$(7.1) \quad G(z) = \begin{vmatrix} -1 & 0{\cdot}9z^{-1} + 0{\cdot}1 & 0 \\ 0{\cdot}1 + 0{\cdot}2z + 0{\cdot}2z^2 & -1 & 0{\cdot}4z^{-1} + 0{\cdot}1 \\ 0{\cdot}1 + 0{\cdot}1z + 0{\cdot}3z^2 & 0 & -1 \\ +0{\cdot}5z^3 & & \end{vmatrix}$$

$$= 0{\cdot}36z^{-2} + 0{\cdot}139z^{-1} - 0{\cdot}688 + 0{\cdot}420z + 0{\cdot}088z^2 + 0{\cdot}005z^3$$

By differentiation

$$G'(1) = 0{\cdot}4 > 0 \tag{7.2}$$

so that, since $m = 2$, the equation $G(z) = 0$ must have just two roots of modulus less than unity. These may be found by Horner's method

$$\text{as } b_1 = 0{\cdot}4563136 \qquad b_2 = -\ 0{\cdot}1453788 \tag{7.3}$$

The six co-factors B_{ce} of $p_{c1}(b_e)$ in the determinants $D(b_e)$ are

$$B_{1e} = 1 \quad B_{2e} = 0{\cdot}9b_e^{-1} + 0{\cdot}1$$
$$B_{3e} = (0{\cdot}9b_e^{-1} + 0{\cdot}1)(0{\cdot}4b_e^{-1} + 0{\cdot}1) \quad e = 1, 2 \tag{7.4}$$

and their numerical values are

$$B_{11} = 1 \quad B_{21} = 2{\cdot}072\ 327 \quad B_{31} = 2{\cdot}023\ 814$$
$$B_{12} = 1 \quad B_{22} = -\ 6{\cdot}090\ 724 \quad B_{32} = -\ 6{\cdot}310\ 8 \tag{7.5}$$

We now put

$$\begin{cases} {}_1x_s = \lambda_1 b_1^s + \lambda_2 b_2^s & \text{for } s = 1, 2, 3 \ldots \\ {}_2x_s = \lambda_1 B_{21} b_1^s + \lambda_2 B_{22} b_2^s & \text{for } s = 0, 1, 2 \ldots \\ {}_3x_s = \lambda_1 B_{31} b_1^s + \lambda_2 B_{32} b_2^s & \text{for } s = 0, 1, 2 \ldots \end{cases} \tag{7.6}$$

and we still have to determine λ_1, λ_2 and ${}_1x_0$.

We have available for this purpose the three equations

$$\begin{cases} {}_1x_0 = 0{\cdot}5\,{}_2x_0 + 0{\cdot}4\,{}_2x_1 + 0{\cdot}2\,{}_2x_2 + {}_3x_0 + 0{\cdot}9\,{}_3x_1 \\ \qquad\qquad + 0{\cdot}8\,{}_3x_2 + 0{\cdot}5\,{}_3x_3 \\ {}_2x_0 = 0{\cdot}1\,{}_1x_0 \\ {}_3x_0 = 0{\cdot}1\,{}_2x_0 \end{cases} \tag{7.7}$$

Fortunately, any two equations contain all the fresh information provided by the three, and we accordingly take the two simple ones and rewrite them as

$$\begin{cases} \lambda_1 B_{21} + \lambda_2 B_{22} = 0{\cdot}1\,{}_1x_0 \\ \lambda_1 B_{31} + \lambda_2 B_{32} = 0{\cdot}1(\lambda_1 B_{21} + \lambda_{22} B_{22}) \end{cases} \tag{7.8}$$

If we leave aside the scale factor we may arbitrarily put $\lambda_1 =$ 10,000 and, substituting our numerical values for $B_{21} B_{22} B_{31}$ and B_{32}, we then find from the second equation that

$$\lambda_2 = 3185{\cdot}939 \tag{7.9}$$

and then from the first equation that

$${}_1x_0 = 13185{\cdot}939 \tag{7.10}$$

Using our equations (7·6) for the other ${}_cx_s$ we may now obtain the numerical values of as many ${}_cx_s$ as we please. Here are the first few values, with λ_1 put equal to 10000 :

TABLE III

	Young.	Middle-aged.	Old.	Total.	Income range.
S	${}_1X_s$	${}_2X_s$	${}_3X_s$		
0	13,186	1,319	132	14,637	£125– £200
1	4,100	12,277	1,755	18,132	£200– £316
2	2,150	3,995	5,301	11,356	£316– £500
3	940	2,028	1·765	4,734	£500– £800
4	435	890	901	2,225	£800–£1250
5	198	411	397	1,006	£1250–£2000
6	90	187	183	460	£2000–£3160
7 and over	75	157	153	385	£3160–
TOTAL :	21,174	21,174	10,687	52,935	

The income scale put in on the extreme right assumes that the minimum income is £125 and that the upper limit of each income range is nearly 60% greater than the lower limit.

It will be noted that although the equilibrium distributions of incomes for young, middle-aged and old are very different for small incomes, yet already at income levels of £1,250 and over each is rapidly approaching a Pareto distribution with

$$(7.11) \qquad a = -\frac{\log_{10}b_1}{\log_{10} 1{\cdot}58} = -5\log_{10}b_1 = 1{\cdot}7041$$

This is well brought out by Chart 1 which shows for each age group and for all ages the following cumulative totals plotted on the double logarithmic paper.

TABLE IV

Income level.	Number of incomes exceeding this level.			
	Young.	Middle-aged.	Old.	Total.
£125	21,174	21,174	10,587	52,935
£200	7,988	19,855	10,455	38,298
£316	3,888	7,578	8,700	20,166
£500	1,738	3,674	3,399	8,810
£800	798	1,645	1,634	4,076
£1250	363	755	733	1,851
£2000	165	344	336	845
£3160	75	157	153	385

We may read off from the chart that the median incomes in the three age-groups differ considerably : they are £175, £280 and £410 approximately. Yet for incomes over £500 it is clear from Chart 1 that the *proportionate* distributions are almost identical for the three age-groups.[1]

[1] For similar charts of actual distributions see Lydall [5].

§ 8. Numerical Example Involving the Effect of Occupational Structure on Income Distribution

In our last model we made the assumption that every income range in every colony was accessible from every other. If we relax this assumption to state that within a certain group G of

Chart I

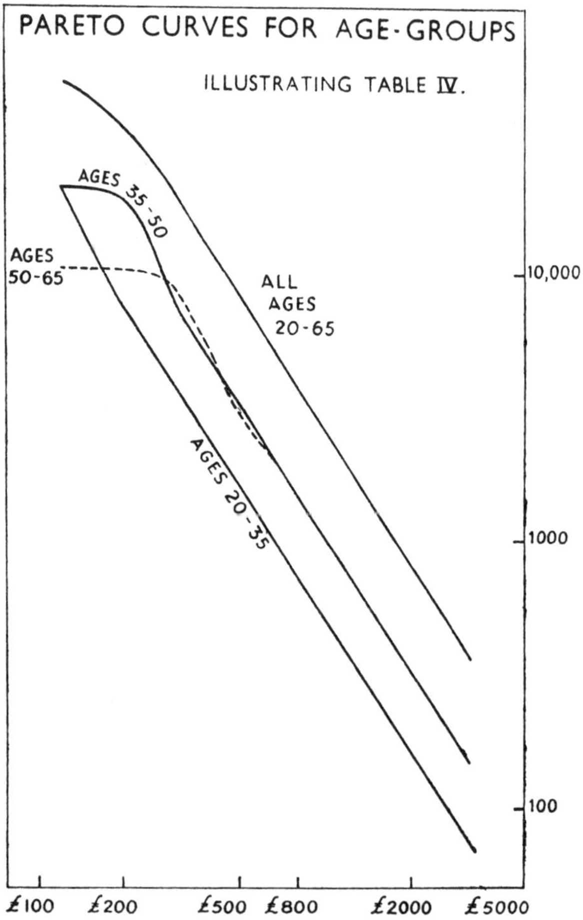

pairs (rc) every R_r in every colony c is accessible from every other, then our results will still hold, provided that the initial distribution was confined to this group.

If we maintain our other assumptions, then the effective new possibility introduced by this relaxation is the inclusion of colonies where there is an upper limit to the possible income.

This is useful when our colonies represent groups of occupations. Thus, let our society be composed of persons classified according to their main sources of income into :

1. Unskilled labour.
2. Semi-skilled work ; skilled work and clerical.
3. Salaries and professional.
4. Profits, land, property.

Then we might assume that there was an effective ceiling on the incomes of classes 1 and 2, and 3. If for simplicity we ignore the complication of age considered in our last example and take broad income groups so that group R_r extends from 2^{r-3} thousand pounds to 2^{r-2} we might set up the following model within our relaxed assumption (see Diagram 6).

It is assumed that no one can obtain incomes higher than £500 in occupation 1, or higher than £1000 in occupation 2. It will be seen that ${}_{33}p'_{rs}$, ${}_{34}p'_{rs}$, ${}_{43}p'_{rs}$ and ${}_{44}p'_{rs}$ assume repetitive forms when r becomes large : we might therefore expect to find the Pareto curves for occupations 3 and 4 to be asymptotic to straight lines.

It will be noted that ${}_{43}p'_{r2} > 0$ for all $r > 0$ so that (6.3) is not satisfied for finite n_3 when $c = 4$ $d = 3$ $s = 2$. Nevertheless, a solution can be found by the following method, which is similar to that of Section 7.

The matrix $P_{rs}(z)$ for this example is only concerned with the values 3 and 4 of r and s. It is

$$(8.1)\quad P_{rs}(z) = \begin{vmatrix} 0{\cdot}020z^{-1} - 0{\cdot}218 + 0{\cdot}180z & 0{\cdot}000139z^{-1} + 0{\cdot}01786 \\ 0 & 0{\cdot}030z^{-1} - 0{\cdot}115 + 0{\cdot}075z \end{vmatrix}$$

The survival condition (6·5) is not, however, satisfied, since 1% of those in each income group $s > 3$, in C_4, escape each year into income group R_2 of C_3. Consequently, writing

$$(8.2)\quad G(z) = \text{Det}|P_{rs}(z)| = 0{\cdot}00060z^{-2} + 0{\cdot}0088z^{-1} + 0{\cdot}03197 - 0{\cdot}03705z + 0{\cdot}01350z^2$$

we find that $G(1) \neq 0$ and that the non-dissipative condition (6.15) is not satisfied.

Nevertheless, two real positive roots of $G(z) = 0$ of modulus less than unity can be found and the usual method of solution proves adequate. The two roots are

$$(8.3)\qquad b_1 = 0{\cdot}333\ 333 \qquad b_2 = 0{\cdot}100\ 000$$

	$_{11}p'_{rs}$.		$_{12}p'_{rs}$.		
$r =$ \ $s =$	0	1	0	1	2
0	0·856	0·144	0	0	0
1	0·250	0·593	0·057	0·110	0

	$_{21}p'_{rs}$.		$_{22}p'_{rs}$.			$_{23}p'_{rs}$.				$_{24}p'_{rs}$.			
$r =$ \ $s =$	1	2	0	1	2	0	1	2	2	0	1	2	2
0	0·050	0·100	0·750	0·100	0	0	0	0	0	0	0	0	0
1	0·050	0·220	0·075	0·640	0·025	0	0·010	0	0	0	0	0	0
2	0	0·075	0	0·125	0·500	0	0	0·250	0	0	0	0·050	

	$_{32}p'_{rs}$.				$_{33}p'_{rs}$.						
$r =$ \ $s =$	0	1	2	2	0	1	2	3	4	5	6
0	0·482	0	0	0	0·132	0·1875	0	0	0	0	0
1	0·02657	0·075	0	0	0·025	0·500	0·250	0	0	0	0
2	0	0	0·05	0	0·00486	0·055	0·79956	0·020	0	0	0
3	—	—	—	—	0	0	0·180	0·782	0·020	0	0
4	—	—	—	—	0	0	0	0·180	0·782	0·020	0
5	—	—	—	—	0	0	0	0	01·80	0·782	0·020
6	—	—	—	—	0	0	0	0	0	0·180	0·782
						etc.			etc.		

	$_{34}p'_{rs}$.							
$r =$ \ $s =$	0	1	2	3	4	5	6	
0	0·100	0·120	0	0	0	0	0	
1	0·0025	0·050	0·07075	0	0	0	0	etc.
2	0	0·010	0·060	0·000139	0	0	0	
3	0	0	0	0·01786	0·000139	0	0	
4	0	0	0	0	0·01786	0·000139	0	
5	0	0	0	0	0	0·01786	0·000139	
				etc.				

	$_{43}p'_{rs}$.			
$r =$ \ $s =$	0	1	2	>2
0	0·500	0·050	0	0
1	0·050	0·300	0·150	0
2	0	0·0081	0·010	0
3	0	0	0·010	0
4	0	0	0·010	0
	0	0	0·010	0

	$_{44}p'_{rs}$.							
$r =$ \ $s =$	0	1	2	3	4	5	6	
0	0·250	0·200	0	0	0	0	0	
1	0·100	0·370	0·030	0	0	0	0	etc.
2	0	0·010	0·8519	0·030	0	0		
3	0	0	0·075	0·885	0·030	0	0	etc.
4	0	0	0	0·075	0·885	0·030	0	
5	0	0	0	0	0·075	0·885	0·030	
			etc.		etc.			etc.

$_{13}p'_{rs} = {}_{14}p'_{rs} = 0$ for all $r.s.$
$_{31}p'_{rs} = {}_{41}p'_{rs} = {}_{42}p'_{rs} = 0$ for all $r.s.$

DIAGRAM 6

and we calculate

$$(8.4)\qquad \begin{aligned} B_{3e} &= 0{\cdot}30b_e^{-1} - 0{\cdot}115 + 0{\cdot}075b_e \\ B_{4e} &= -\,0{\cdot}000139b_e^{-1} - 0{\cdot}01786 \qquad e = 1, 2 \end{aligned}$$

to give

$$B_{31} = 0 \quad B_{32} = 0{\cdot}1925 \quad B_{41} = -\,0{\cdot}18278 \quad B_{42} = -\,0{\cdot}01925$$

Hence we are led to try solutions of the form

$$(8.5)\qquad \begin{aligned} {}_3x_s &= 0{\cdot}1925\lambda_2 10^{-s} \qquad s = 2, 3, 4 \ldots \\ {}_4x_s &= -\,0{\cdot}18278\lambda_1 3^{-s} - 0{\cdot}01925\lambda_2 10^{-s} \quad s = 3, 4, 5 \ldots \end{aligned}$$

It will slightly simplify the algebra to fix the scale arbitrarily at this stage by choosing λ_2 so that

$$(8.6)\qquad \begin{aligned} {}_3x_s &= 10^{8-s} \qquad s = 2, 3, 4 \ldots \\ {}_4x_s &= \lambda'_1 3^{-s} - 10^{7-s} \qquad s = 3, 4 \ldots \end{aligned}$$

λ'_1 is still undetermined and we also have still to find ${}_4x_0$, ${}_4x_1$, ${}_3x_0$, ${}_3x_1$, ${}_2x_0$, ${}_2x_1$, ${}_2x_2$, ${}_1x_0$ and ${}_1x_1$.

To find these ten constants we have the eleven equations associated with the equilibrium of ${}_1x_0$, ${}_1x_1$, ${}_2x_0$, ${}_2x_1$, ${}_2x_2$, ${}_3x_0$, ${}_3x_1$, ${}_3x_2$, ${}_4x_0$, ${}_4x_1$ and ${}_4x_2$, namely

$$(8.6)\qquad \begin{cases} {}_1x_0 = 0{\cdot}856\,{}_1x_0 + 0{\cdot}250\,{}_1x_1 + 0{\cdot}050\,{}_2x_0 + 0{\cdot}050\,{}_0x_1 \\ {}_1x_1 = 0{\cdot}144\,{}_1x_0 + 0{\cdot}593\,{}_1x_1 + 0{\cdot}100\,{}_2x_0 \\ \qquad\qquad + 0{\cdot}200\,{}_2x_1 + 0{\cdot}075\,{}_2x_2 \\ \qquad\qquad \text{(seven equations omitted)} \\ {}_4x_1 = 0{\cdot}120\,{}_3x_0 + 0{\cdot}050\,{}_3x_1 + 10^4 + 0{\cdot}200\,{}_4x_0 \\ \qquad\qquad + 0{\cdot}370\,{}_4x_1 + 0{\cdot}010\{\lambda'_1 3^{-2} - 10^5\} \\ \lambda' 3^{-2} - 10^5 = 0{\cdot}7075\,{}_3x_1 + 6000 + 0{\cdot}030\,{}_4x_1 \\ \qquad\qquad + 0{\cdot}0852\{\lambda'_1 3^{-2} - 10^5\} + 0{\cdot}075\{\lambda'_1 3^{-3} - 10^4\} \end{cases}$$

Only ten of these equations provide independent information: any one is implied by the other ten. The solution of ten simultaneous equations is no mean undertaking, but in this example the solution can be found as

$$(8.7)\qquad \begin{cases} \lambda'_1 = 7{\cdot}29 \,.\, 10^6 & {}_1x_0 = 10^7 \\ {}_1x_1 = 5 \,.\, 10^6 & {}_2x_0 = 2{\cdot}10^6 \\ {}_2x_1 = 1{\cdot}8 \,.\, 10^6 & {}_2x_2 = 2.10^5 \\ {}_3x_0 = 2.10^4 & {}_3x_1 = 2{\cdot}10^5 \\ {}_4x_0 = 10^4 & {}_4x_1 = 5{\cdot}10^4 \end{cases}$$

The values of ${}_3x_s$ and ${}_4x_s$ for $s > 1$ may now be found from the equations

$$(8.8)\qquad \begin{aligned} {}_3x_s &= 10^{3-s} \\ {}_4x_s &= 3^{6-s}10^4 - 10^{7-s} \end{aligned}$$

CHART II

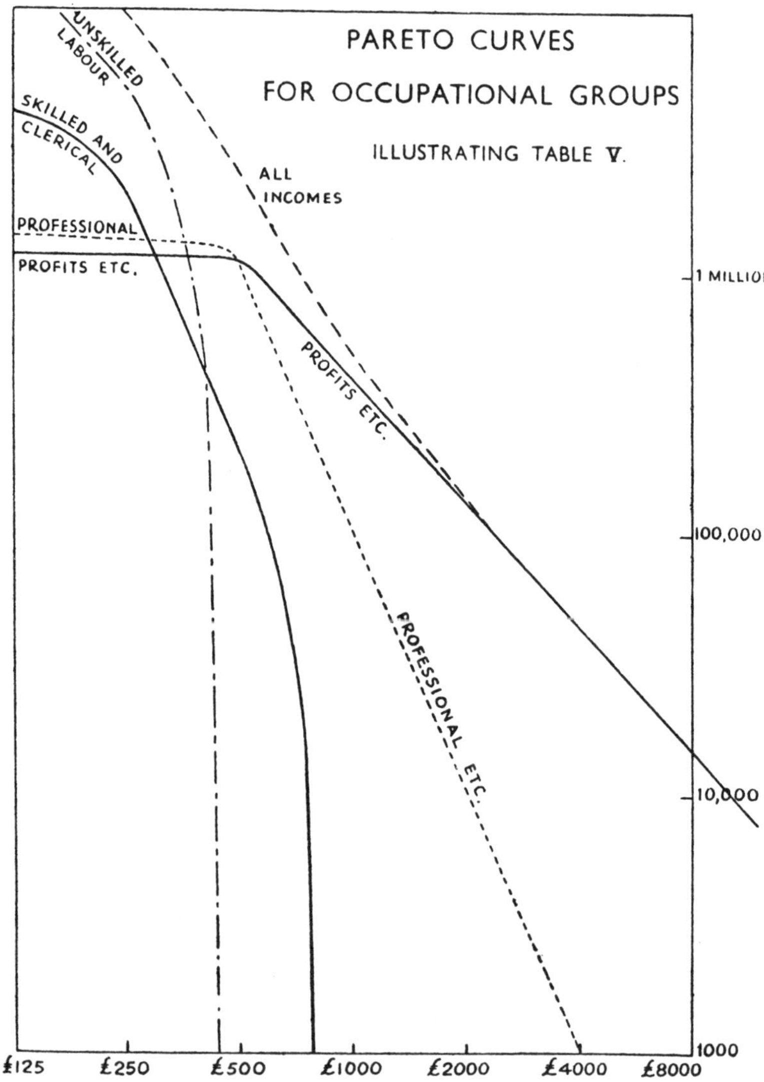
PARETO CURVES
FOR OCCUPATIONAL GROUPS
ILLUSTRATING TABLE V.
UNSKILLED LABOUR
SKILLED AND CLERICAL
ALL INCOMES
PROFESSIONAL
PROFITS ETC.
PROFITS ETC.
PROFESSIONAL ETC.
1 MILLION
100,000
10,000
1000
£125
£250
£500
£1000
£2000
£4000
£8000

From the complete set of ${}_{c}x_{s}$ thus obtained, it is a quick matter to compile the following table showing for each occupation the number with incomes exceeding various levels.

TABLE V

Income level.	Number of incomes exceeding this level.				
	Unskilled labourers.	Skilled workers and clerical.	Salaried and professional.	Profits, land, etc.	Total.
£125 . .	15,000,000	4,000,000	1,331,111	1,163,889	21,495,000
£250 . .	5,000,000	2,000,000	1,311,111	1,153,889	9,465,000
£500 . .	0	200,000	1,111,111	1,103,889	2,415,000
£1,000 . .	0	0	111,111	393,889	505,000
£2,000 . .	0	0	11,111	133,889	145,000
£4,000 . .	0	0	1,111	44,889	46,000
£8,000 . .	0	0	111	14,989	15,100
£16,000 .	0	0	11	4,999	5,010
£32,000 .	0	0	1	1,667	1,668

The corresponding Pareto curves are shown in Chart 2. An interesting feature of this solution is that the slopes of the Pareto lines for occupations 3 and 4 are not the same, that for the professional and salaried classes being much steeper than that for those whose income came from profits, land, etc. It is the latter distribution, of course, which determines the slope of the Pareto line for all incomes.[1]

§ 9. A MODEL GENERATING A DISTRIBUTION IN WHICH PARETO'S LAW IS NOT OBEYED

The above examples are probably sufficient to illustrate the theory that the approximate observance of Pareto's law which has so often been remarked upon is not an illusion or coincidence, but has its explanation in a similarity at different high income-levels of the prospects of given proportionate changes of income.

They can do little more than illustrate the theory, since they are built on the artificial simplifying assumption that these prospects of change remain constant through time at each income level. It will be readily appreciated that any model catering for prospects which are not constant through time is much more complicated and the results obtainable are far less clear: the investigation of such models must form the subject of another article than this. The importance of such change in prospects has already been hinted at in the suggestion that changes in the

[1] For similar charts of actual distributions see Lydall [5].

income distribution affect the influence described by the matrices $p'_{rs}(t)$ just as much as the influence affect the incomes.

Another gap in our discussion so far has been any consideration

CHART III

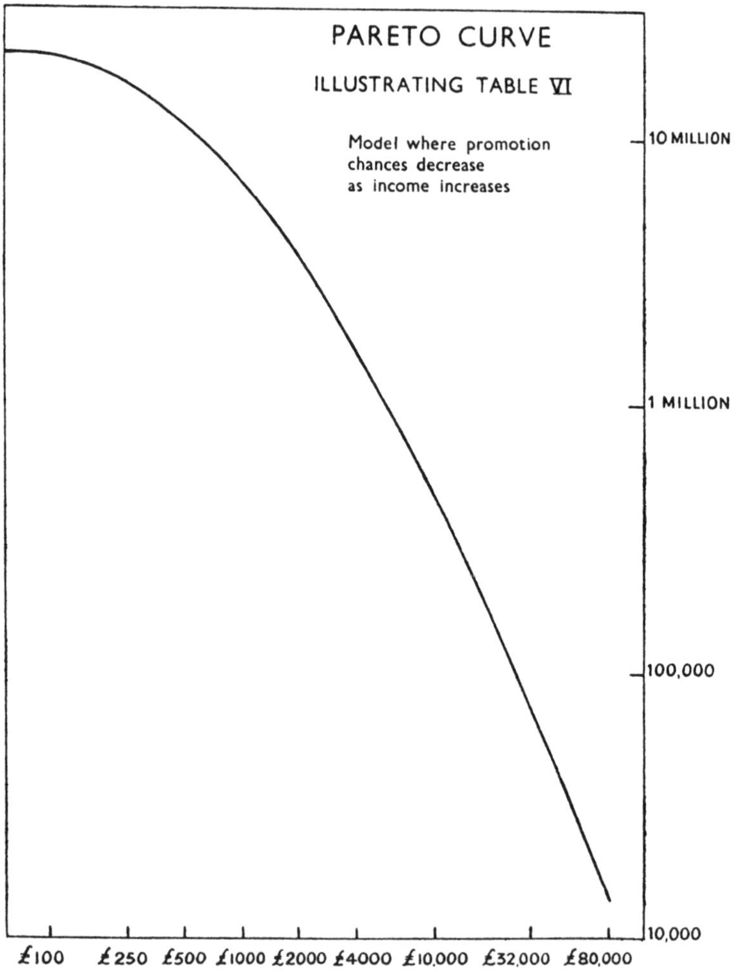

of models which do *not* lead to a Pareto distribution. There is a noticeable tendency recently for the Pareto curves of the United Kingdom and other countries to curve very slightly downwards at the tail, and it would be interesting to have a model illustrating how this could come about. The explanation is probably that the prospects of increasing are proportionately less rosy nowadays for the very large incomes than for the large incomes. This is not necessarily because the owners of vast incomes are any less abstemious and accumulative than their forerunners used to be, but may be because income tax and death duties are now at a level which makes the piling up of huge fortunes a more gradual and less-rewarding undertaking.

A very simple model will suffice to illustrate the effect on the Pareto curve that would result from a progressive worsening of the chance of (say) doubling the income as one considered larger and larger incomes.

We shall suppose that R_0, R_1, R_2 . . . are the income ranges £62 10*s*.–£125, £125–£250, £250–£500, etc., etc. We shall suppose that the chance of going *down* one range is the same in all ranges (except R_0), and is 10%. In R_0 the chance of going *up* one range is 30%, but in R_1 it is only 15%, in R_2 it is 10%, and in general in R_r it is only $\frac{30\%}{r+1}$.

The equilibrium condition for this model is

$$(9.1) \qquad x_r = \frac{0{\cdot}3x_{r-1}}{r} + \left\{0{\cdot}9 - \frac{0{\cdot}3}{r+1}\right\} x_r + 0{\cdot}1x_{r+1}$$

It can easily be checked that the solution is $r = 1, 2 \ldots$

$$(9.2) \qquad x_r = \frac{3^r x_0}{r} \quad r = 1, 2, \ldots$$

The cumulative distribution corresponding to $x_0 = 10^6$ is given in Table VI, and the corresponding Pareto curve is shown in Chart 3. As one would expect, the steadily worsening prospects of income-promotion that are found as consideration passes up the income scale are reflected in a continuous downward curvature of the Pareto curve.

TABLE VI

Income.	Number of incomes exceeding x.
x	(Fx) (thousands)
£62 10*s*.	20,085
£125	19,085
£250	16,085
£500	11,585
£1,000	7,085
£2,000	3,710
£4,000	1,685
£8,000	673
£16,000	239
£32,000	76·4
£64,000	22·1
£135,000	5·9

This example has been chosen so as to provide a very simple solution. In general, it will be difficult to obtain the equilibrium solutions in models where the promotion prospects, as reflected in the matrix $p_{ru}(t)$, vary throughout the income scale.

§ 10. A Model Illustrating the Reaction of Changes in the Income Distribution on the Matrix Depicting the Influences Shaping that Distribution

In conclusion, a warning must be given that although the models discussed above throw some light on the reasons why an approximate obedience of Pareto's law is so often found in actual income distributions, they do not throw much light on the mechanism determining the actual values observed for Pareto's α. It is tempting to draw conclusions from the fact that in equilibrium

$$\alpha = \frac{-\log b_1}{\log(1+h)} \qquad (10.1)$$

where b_1 is the positive root of the equilibrium equation

$$\sum_{u=-n}^{m} p_u z^{-u} = 1 \qquad (10.2)$$

and h is the proportionate width of each income range. One might suppose that one had only to estimate the p_u corresponding to various economic situations in order to deduce the slopes of the Pareto lines in the consequent income distributions. But it would be just as sensible to guess at the consequent income distributions and deduce how much the p_u functions would have to be modified before that equilibrium was reached.

The point may be illustrated by a final model. Suppose that initially the income distribution is

$$x_s = 2^{23-s} \qquad (10.3)$$

where R_s is the range $2^{s/2}$ £100 to $2^{s+1/2}$ £100; then the total income will be approximately 2^{25} £100.

Now suppose that the real income of the community is held constant and that the $p_{ru}(t)$ are given by

$$p_{ru}(t) = p_u, \quad r = 1, 2, 3 \ldots$$
$$p_{01}(t) = p_1 \quad p_{00}(t) = 1 - p_1 \qquad (10.4)$$

where $\quad p_{-1} = 0{\cdot}3 \; p_0 = 0{\cdot}5 \; p_1 = 0{\cdot}2$ other $p_u = 0$.

The corresponding value of b_1 is $2/3$, so that the equilibrium distribution must be

$$x^s = \frac{2^{24}}{3}\left(\frac{2}{3}\right)^s \qquad (10.5)$$

which involve a total income of approximately $\frac{2^{24}}{1-\theta}$ £100 where

$$(10.6) \qquad \theta = \frac{\log 2}{\log 9 - \log 4} = 0{\cdot}8547$$

The numerical value of this total income is about $3{\cdot}44 \times 2^{25}$ £100. Thus money income will have to rise in ratio 3.44, so that if total real income is to remain constant, prices must rise in ratio 3.44, so that the real income of those in R_0 will be only about 30% of what it was originally in R_0.

Now suppose that originally an income at the lower end of R_0 represented the subsistence level. Then directly prices tend to rise some policy must be adopted to subsidise those in R_0: let us suppose that prices are subsidised at the expense of prospects of increasing income. More precisely

$$(10.7) \quad p_{-1} = 0{\cdot}3 + T \quad p_0 = 0{\cdot}5 \quad p_1 = 0{\cdot}2 - T \quad p_{01}(t) = p_1 p_{00}(t) = 1 - p_1$$

where T is continually adjusted so as to keep prices and total money income stable.

It is intuitively plausible that this policy will lead eventually to an equilibrium distribution.

The corresponding value of b_1 is given by

$$(10.8) \quad (0{\cdot}3 + T)b_1^2 + 0{\cdot}5b_1 + (0{\cdot}2 - T) = b_1$$

whence since $b_1 \neq 1$

$$(10.9) \qquad b_1 = \frac{0{\cdot}2 - T}{0{\cdot}3 + T}$$

The total income will be $\frac{2^{24}}{1-\theta}$ £100

where

$$\theta = \frac{+\log 2}{-2\log b_1},$$

and in order that this should be equal to the initial total income of 2^{25} £100 so as to obviate the need for higher prices we need $\theta = \frac{1}{2}$ and hence $b_1 = \frac{1}{2}$ and hence $T = 0{\cdot}1$.

When we work out the equilibrium distribution we find, of course, that it is simply the initial distribution unchanged. Hence, it is truer, under our extreme simplifying assumptions, that the initial distribution determined the $p_{ru}(t)$ than that the $p_{ru}(t)$ determined the equilibrium distribution.

Had we allowed some increase in total real income, a lower value of T would, of course, have been necessary, and had we allowed for a continuous expansion of real income an altogether more advanced model with a shifting $p_{ru}(t)$ function for low values of r would have been required.

These illustrations remind one of the impossibility of drawing any simple conclusions about the effect on Pareto's a of various redistributive policies by *merely* considering the effects of these policies on the functions $p_{ru}(t)$ representing the prospects of increase of income.

D. G. CHAMPERNOWNE

Nuffield College,
Oxford.

References

[1] D. G. Champernowne. "The Distribution of Income between Persons," 1937. Unpublished fellowship thesis deposited in the Library of King's College, Cambridge.

[2] D. G. Champernowne, "Notes on Income Distribution," *Econometrica*, 1937. Report of Econometric Conference at New College in 1936.

[3] D. G. Champernowne, "The Graduation of Income Distribution," *Econometrica*, October, 1952.

[4] F. G. Foster, "Some Problems in the Mathematical Theory of Probability." Unpublished D.Phil.Thesis deposited in Bodley's Library, Oxford University.

[5] H. Lydall. Reports on Savings Survey published in Bulletin of Oxford Institute of Statistics, Feb.–March, 1953 and other issues.

[34]

THE TRANSACTIONS DEMAND FOR CASH: AN INVENTORY THEORETIC APPROACH

By William J. Baumol

A stock of cash is its holder's inventory of the medium of exchange, and like an inventory of a commodity, cash is held because it can be given up at the appropriate moment, serving then as its possessor's part of the bargain in an exchange. We might consequently expect that inventory theory and monetary theory can learn from one another. This note attempts to apply one well-known result in inventory control analysis to the theory of money.[1]

I. A Simple Model

We are now interested in analyzing the transactions demand for cash dictated by rational behavior, which for our purposes means the holding of those cash balances that can do the job at minimum cost. To abstract from precautionary and speculative demands let us consider a state in which transactions are perfectly foreseen and occur *in a steady stream.*

Suppose that in the course of a given period an individual will pay out T dollars in a steady stream. He obtains cash either by borrowing it, or by withdrawing it from an investment, and in either case his interest cost (or interest opportunity cost) is i dollars per dollar per period. Suppose finally that he withdraws cash in lots of C dollars spaced evenly throughout the year, and that each time he makes such a withdrawal he must pay a fixed "broker's fee" of b

1. T. M. Whitin informs me that the result in question goes back to the middle of the 1920's when it seems to have been arrived at independently by some half dozen writers. See, e.g., George F. Mellen, "Practical Lot Quantity Formula," *Management and Administration*, Vol. 10, September 1925. Its significant implications for the economic theory of inventory, particularly for business cycle theory, seem to have gone unrecognized until recently when Dr. Whitin analyzed them in his forthcoming *Inventory Control and Economic Theory* (Princeton University Press) which, incidentally, first suggested the subject of this note to me. See also, Dr. Whitin's "Inventory Control in Theory and Practice" (elsewhere in this issue, *supra*, p. 502), and Kenneth J. Arrow, Theodore Harris, and Jacob Marschak, "Optimal Inventory Policy," *Econometrica*, Vol. 19, July 1951, especially pp. 252–255. In addition to Dr. Whitin, I am heavily indebted to Professors Chandler, Coale, Gurley, Lutz, Mr. Turvey, and Professor Viner, and to the members of the graduate seminar at Harvard University, where much of this paper was first presented.

dollars.[2] Here T, the value of transactions, is predetermined, and i and b are assumed to be constant.

In this situation any value of C less than or equal to T will enable him to meet his payments equally well provided he withdraws the money often enough. For example, if T is \$100, he can meet his payments by withdrawing \$50 every six months or \$25 quarterly, etc.[3] Thus he will make $\frac{T}{C}$ withdrawals over the course of the year, at a total cost in "brokers' fees" given by $\frac{bT}{C}$.

In this case, since each time he withdraws C dollars he spends it in a steady stream and draws out a similar amount the moment it is gone, his average cash holding will be $\frac{C}{2}$ dollars. His annual interest cost of holding cash will then be $\frac{iC}{2}$.

The total amount the individual in question must pay for the use of the cash needed to meet his transaction when he borrows C dollars at intervals evenly spaced throughout the year will then be the sum of interest cost and "brokers' fees" and so will be given by

$$\frac{bT}{C} + \frac{iC}{2}. \tag{1}$$

2. The term "broker's fee" is not meant to be taken literally. It covers all non-interest costs of borrowing or making a cash withdrawal. These include opportunity losses which result from having to dispose of assets just at the moment the cash is needed, losses involved in the poor resale price which results from an asset becoming "secondhand" when purchased by a nonprofessional dealer, administrative costs, and psychic costs (the trouble involved in making a withdrawal) as well as payment to a middleman. So conceived it seems likely that the "broker's fee" will, in fact, vary considerably with the magnitude of the funds involved, contrary to assumption. However, *some* parts of this cost will not vary with the amount involved — e.g., postage cost, bookkeeping expense, and, possibly, the withdrawer's effort. It seems plausible that the "broker's fee" will be better approximated by a function like $b + kC$ (where b and k are constants), which indicates that there is a part of the "broker's fee" increasing in proportion with the amount withdrawn. As shown in a subsequent footnote, however, our formal result is completely unaffected by this amendment.

We must also extend the meaning of the interest rate to include the value of protection against loss by fire, theft, etc., which we obtain when someone borrows our cash. On the other hand, a premium for the risk of default on repayment must be deducted. This protection obtained by lending seems to be mentioned less frequently by theorists than the risk, yet how can we explain the existence of interest free demand deposits without the former?

3. In particular, if cash were perfectly divisible and no elapse of time were required from withdrawal through payment he could make his withdrawals in a steady stream. In this case he would never require any cash balances to meet his payments and C would be zero. However, as may be surmised, this would be prohibitive with any b greater than zero.

Since the manner in which he meets his payments is indifferent to him, his purpose only being to pay for his transactions, rationality requires that he do so at minimum cost, i.e., that he choose the most economical value of C. Setting the derivative of (1) with respect to C equal to zero we obtain[4]

$$-\frac{bT}{C^2}+\frac{i}{2}=0,$$

i.e.,

$$C=\sqrt{\frac{2bT}{i}}. \tag{2}$$

Thus, in the simple situation here considered, the rational individual will, given the price level,[5] demand cash in proportion to the square root of the value of his transactions.

Before examining the implications of this crude model we may note that, as it stands, it applies to two sorts of cases: that of the individual (or firm) obtaining cash from his invested capital and that of the individual (or firm) spending out of borrowing in anticipation of future receipts. Since our problem depends on non-coincidence of cash receipts and disbursements, and we have assumed that cash disbursements occur in a steady stream, one other case seems possible, that where receipts precede expenditures. This differs from the first case just mentioned (living off one's capital) in that the individual now has the option of withholding some or all of his receipts from investment and simply keeping the cash until it is needed. Once this withheld cash is used up the third case merges into the first: the individual must obtain cash from his invested capital until his next cash receipt occurs.

We can deal with this third case as follows. First, note that any receipts exceeding anticipated disbursements will be invested, since, eventually, interest earnings must exceed ("brokerage") cost of investment. Hence we need only deal with that part of the cash influx which is to be used in making payments during the period

4. This result is unchanged if there is a part of the "broker's fee" which varies in proportion with the quantity of cash handled. For in this case the "broker's fee" for each loan is given by $b + kC$. Total cost in "broker's fees" will then be

$$\frac{T}{C}(b+kC)=\frac{T}{C}b+kT.$$

Thus (1) will have the constant term, kT, added to it, which drops out in differentiation.

5. A doubling of *all* prices (including the "broker's fee") is like a change in the monetary unit, and may be expected to double the demand for cash balances.

between receipts. Let this amount, as before, be T dollars. Of this let I dollars be invested, and the remainder, R dollars, be withheld, where either of these sums may be zero. Again let i be the interest rate, and let the "broker's fee" for withdrawing cash be given by the linear expression $b_w + k_w C$, where C is the amount withdrawn. Finally, let there be a "broker's fee" for investing (depositing) cash given by $b_d + k_d I$ where the b's and the k's are constants.

Since the disbursements are continuous, the $R = T - I$ dollars withheld from investment will serve to meet payments for a fraction of the period between consecutive receipts given by $\frac{T-I}{T}$. Moreover, since the average cash holding for that time will be $\frac{T-I}{2}$, the interest cost of withholding that money will be $\frac{T-I}{T} i \frac{T-I}{2}$. Thus the total cost of withholding the R dollars and investing the I dollars will be

$$\frac{T-I}{2} i \frac{T-I}{T} + b_d + k_d I.$$

Analogously, the total cost of obtaining cash for the remainder of the period will be

$$\frac{C}{2} i \frac{I}{T} + (b_w + k_w C) \frac{I}{C}.$$

Thus the total cost of cash operations for the period will be given by the sum of the last two expressions, which when differentiated partially with respect to C and set equal to zero once again yields our square root formula, (2), with $b = b_w$.

Thus, in this case, the optimum cash balance after the initial cash holding is used up will again vary with the square root of the volume of transactions, as is to be expected by analogy with the "living off one's capital" case.

There remains the task of investigating $R/2$, the (optimum) average cash balance before drawing on invested receipts begins. We again differentiate our total cost of holding cash, this time partially with respect to I, and set it equal to zero, obtaining

$$-\frac{T-I}{T} i + k_d + \frac{Ci}{2T} + \frac{b_w}{C} + k_w = 0,$$

i.e.,

$$R = T - I = \frac{C}{2} + \frac{b_w T}{Ci} + \frac{T(k_d + k_w)}{i},$$

or since from the preceding result, $C^2 = 2Tb_w/i$, so that the second term on the right hand side equals $C^2/2C$,

$$R = C + T\left(\frac{k_w + k_d}{i}\right).$$

The first term in this result is to be expected, since if *everything* were deposited at once, C dollars would have to be withdrawn at that same moment to meet current expenses. On this amount two sets of "broker's fees" would have to be paid and no interest would be earned — a most unprofitable operation.[6]

Since C varies as the square root of T and the other term varies in proportion with T, R will increase less than in proportion with T, though more nearly in proportion than does C. The general nature of our results is thus unaffected.[7]

Note finally that the entire analysis applies at once to the case of continuous receipts and discontinuous payments, taking the period to be that between two payments, where the relevant decision is the frequency of investment rather than the frequency of withdrawal. Similarly, it applies to continuous receipts and payments where the two are not equal.

II. Some Consequences of the Analysis

I shall not labor the obvious implications for financial budgeting by the firm. Rather I shall discuss several arguments which have been presented by monetary theorists, to which our result is relevant.

The first is the view put forth by several economists,[8] that in a

6. Here the assumption of constant "brokerage fees" with $k_d = k_w = 0$ gets us into trouble. The amount withheld from investment then is never greater than C dollars only because a strictly constant "broker's fee" with no provision for a discontinuity at zero implies the payment of the fee even if nothing is withdrawn or deposited. In this case it becomes an overhead and it pays to invest for any interest earning greater than zero.

For a firm, *part* of the "broker's fee" may, in fact, be an overhead in this way. For example, failure to make an anticipated deposit will sometimes involve little or no reduction in the bookkeeping costs incurred in keeping track of such operations.

7. If we replace the linear functions representing the "broker's fees" with more general functions $f_w(C)$ and $f_d(I)$ which are only required to be differentiable, the expression obtained for R is changed merely by replacement of k_w, and k_d by the corresponding derivatives $f_w'(C)$ and $f_d'(I)$.

8. See, e.g., Frank H. Knight, *Risk, Uncertainty and Profit* (Preface to the Re-issue), No. 16 in the series of Reprints of Scarce Tracts in Economic and Political Science (London: The London School of Economics and Political Science, 1933), p. xxii; F. Divisia, *Économique Rationelle* (Paris: G. Doin, 1927), chap. XIX and the Appendix; and Don Patinkin, "Relative Prices, Say's Law and the Demand for Money," *Econometrica*, Vol. 16, April 1948, pp. 140–145. See also, P. N. Rosenstein-Rodan, "The Coordination of the General Theories of Money and Price," *Economica*, N. S., Vol. III, August 1936, Part II.

stationary state there will be no demand for cash balances since it will then be profitable to invest all earnings in assets with a positive yield in such a way that the required amount will be realized at the moment any payment is to be made. According to this view no one will want any cash in such a stationary world, and the value of money must fall to zero so that there can really be no such thing as a truly static monetary economy. Clearly this argument neglects the transactions costs involved in making and collecting such loans (the "broker's fee").[9] Our model is clearly compatible with a static world and (2) shows that it will generally pay to keep some cash. The analysis of a stationary monetary economy in which there is a meaningful (finite) price level does make sense.

Another view which can be reëxamined in light of our analysis is that the transactions demand for cash will vary approximately in proportion with the money value of transactions.[1] This may perhaps even be considered the tenor of quantity theory though there is no necessary connection, as Fisher's position indicates. If such a demand for cash balances is considered to result from rational behavior, then (2) suggests that the conclusion cannot have general validity. On the contrary, the square root formula implies that

9. It also neglects the fact that the transfer of cash takes time so that in reality we would have to hold cash at least for the short period between receiving it and passing it on again.

It is conceivable, it is true, that with perfect foresight the difference between money and securities might disappear since a perfectly safe loan could become universally acceptable. There would, however, remain the distinction between "real assets" and the "money-securities." Moreover, there would be a finite price for, and non-zero yield on the former, the yield arising because they (as opposed to certificates of their ownership) are not generally acceptable, and hence not perfectly liquid, since there is trouble and expense involved in carrying them.

1. Marshall's rather vague statements may perhaps be interpreted to support this view. See, e.g., Book I, chap. IV in *Money, Credit and Commerce* (London, 1923). Keynes clearly accepts this position. See *The General Theory of Employment, Interest and Money* (New York, 1936), p. 201. It is also accepted by Pigou: "As real income becomes larger, there is, prima facie, reason for thinking that, just as, up to a point, people like to invest a larger proportion of their real income, so also they like to hold real balances in the form of money equivalent to a larger proportion of it. On the other hand, as Professor Robertson has pointed out to me, the richer people are, the cleverer they are likely to become in finding a way to *economize* in real balances. On the whole then we may, I think, safely disregard this consideration . . . for a close approximation. . . . ." *Employment and Equilibrium*, 1st ed. (London, 1941), pp. 59–60. Fisher, however, argues: "It seems to be a fact that, at a given price level, the greater a man's expenditures the more rapid his turnover; that is, the rich have a higher rate of turnover than the poor. They spend money faster, not only absolutely but relatively to the money they keep on hand. . . . We may therefore infer that, if a nation grows richer per capita, the velocity of circulation of money will increase. This proposition, of course, has no reference to *nominal* increase of expenditure." *The Purchasing Power of Money* (New York, 1922), p. 167.

demand for cash rises less than in proportion with the volume of transactions, so that there are, in effect, economies of large scale in the use of cash.

The magnitude of this difference should not be exaggerated, however. The phrase "varying as the square" may suggest larger effects than are actually involved. Equation (2) requires that the average transactions velocity of circulation vary exactly in proportion with the quantity of cash, so that, for example, a doubling of the stock of cash will *ceteris paribus*, just double velocity.[2]

A third consequence of the square root formula is closely connected with the second. The effect on real income of an injection of cash into the system may have been underestimated. For suppose that (2) is a valid expression for the general demand for cash, that there is widespread unemployment, and that for this or other reasons prices do not rise with an injection of cash. Suppose, moreover, that the rate of interest is unaffected, i.e., that none of the new cash is used to buy securities. Then so long as transactions do not rise so as to maintain the same proportion with the square of the quantity of money, people will want to get rid of cash. They will use it to demand more goods and services, thereby forcing the volume of transactions to rise still further. For let ΔC be the quantity of cash injected. If a proportionality (constant velocity) assumption involves transactions rising by $k \Delta C$, it is easily shown that (2) involves transactions rising by more than twice as much, the magnitude of the excess increasing with the ratio of the injection to the initial stock of cash. More precisely, the rise in transactions would then be given by[3]

$$2k \Delta C + \frac{k}{C} \Delta C^2.$$

Of course, the rate of interest would really tend to fall in such circumstances, and this would to some extent offset the effect of the influx of cash, as is readily seen when we rewrite (2) as

$$T = C^2 i/2b. \tag{3}$$

Moreover, prices will rise to some extent,[4] and, of course, (3) at best

2. Since velocity equals $\frac{T}{C} = \frac{i}{2b} C$ by (2).

3. This is obtained by setting $k = C\,i/2b$ in (3), below, and computing ΔT by substituting $C + \Delta C$ for C.

4. Even if (2) holds, the demand for cash may rise only in proportion with the money value of transactions when all prices rise exactly in proportion, the rate of interest and transactions remaining unchanged. For then a doubling of all prices and cash balances leaves the situation unchanged, and the received argument holds. The point is that b is then one of the prices which has risen.

is only an approximation. Nevertheless, it remains true that the effect of an injection of cash on, say, the level of employment, may often have been underestimated.[5] For whatever may be working to counteract it, the force making for increased employment is greater than if transactions tend, *ceteris paribus*, toward their original proportion to the quantity of cash.

Finally the square root formula lends support to the argument that wage cuts can help increase employment, since it follows that the Pigou effect and the related effects are stronger than they would be with a constant transactions velocity. Briefly the phenomenon which has come to be called the Pigou effect[6] may be summarized thus: General unemployment will result in reduction in the price level which must increase the purchasing power of the stock of cash provided the latter does not itself fall more than in proportion with prices.[7] This increased purchasing power will augment demand for commodities[8] or investment goods (either directly, or because it is used to buy securities and so forces down the rate of interest). In any case, this works for a reduction in unemployment.

Now the increase in the purchasing power of the stock of cash which results from fallen prices is equivalent to an injection of cash with constant prices. There is therefore exactly the same reason for suspecting the magnitude of the effect of the former on the volume of transactions has been underestimated, as in the case of the latter. Perhaps this can be of some little help in explaining why there has not been more chronic unemployment or runaway inflation in our economy.

III. The Simple Model and Reality

It is appropriate to comment on the validity of the jump from equation (2) to conclusions about the operation of the economy. At

5. But see the discussions of Potter and Law as summarized by Jacob Viner, *Studies in the Theory of International Trade* (New York, 1937), pp. 37–39.

6. See A. C. Pigou, "The Classical Stationary State," *Economic Journal*, Vol. LIII, December 1943.

7. Presumably the "broker's fee" will be one of the prices which falls, driven down by the existence of unemployed brokers. There is no analogous reason for the rate of interest to fall, though it will tend to respond thus to the increase in the "real stock of cash."

8. The term "Pigou effect" is usually confined to the effects on consumption demand while the effect on investment demand, and (in particular) on the rate of interest is ordinarily ascribed to Keynes. However, the entire argument appears to antedate Pigou's discussion (which, after all, was meant to be a reformulation of the classical position) and is closely related to what Mr. Becker and I have called the Say's Equation form of the Say's Law argument. See our article "The Classical Monetary Theory; the Outcome of the Discussion," *Economica*, November 1952.

best, (2) is only a suggestive oversimplification, if for no other reason, because of the rationality assumption employed in its derivation. In addition the model is static. It takes the distribution of the firm's disbursements over time to be fixed, though it is to a large extent in the hands of the entrepreneur how he will time his expenditures. It assumes that there is one constant relevant rate of interest and that the "broker's fee" is constant or varies linearly with the magnitude of the sum involved. It posits a steady stream of payments and the absence of cash receipts during the relevant period. It deals only with the cash demand of a single economic unit and neglects interactions of the various demands for cash in the economy.[9] It neglects the precautionary and speculative demands for cash.

These are serious lacunae, and without a thorough investigation we have no assurance that our results amount to much more than an analytical curiosum. Nevertheless I offer only a few comments in lieu of analysis, and hope that others will find the subject worth further examination.

1. It is no doubt true that a majority of the public will find it impractical and perhaps pointless to effect every possible economy in the use of cash. Indeed the possibility may never occur to most people. Nevertheless, we may employ the standard argument that the largest cash users may more plausibly be expected to learn when it is profitable to reduce cash balances relative to transactions. The demand for cash by the community as a whole may then be affected similarly and by a significant amount. Moreover, it is possible that even small cash holders will sometimes institute some cash economies instinctively or by a process of trial and error not explicitly planned or analyzed.

2. With variable b and i the validity of our two basic results — the non-zero rational transactions demand for cash, and the less than proportionate rise in the rational demand for cash with the real volume of transactions, clearly depends on the nature of the responsiveness of the "brokerage fee" and the interest rate to the quantity of cash involved. The first conclusion will hold generally provided the "broker's fee" never falls below some preassigned level, e.g., it never falls below one mill per transaction, and provided the interest rate, its rate of change with C and the rate of change of the "broker's fee" all (similarly) have some upper bound, however large, at least when C is small.

9. I refer here particularly to considerations analogous to those emphasized by Duesenberry in his discussion of the relation between the consumption functions of the individual and the economy as a whole in his *Income, Saving and the Theory of Consumer Behavior* (Cambridge, Mass., 1950).

The second conclusion will not be violated persistently unless the "brokerage fee" tends to vary almost exactly in proportion with C (and it pays to hold zero cash balances) except for what may roughly be described as a limited range of values of C. Of course, it is always possible that this "exceptional range" will be the one relevant in practice. Variations in the interest rate will tend to strengthen our conclusion provided the interest rate never decreases with the quantity of cash borrowed or invested.[1]

It would perhaps not be surprising if these sufficient conditions for the more general validity of our results were usually satisfied in practice.

3. If payments are lumpy but foreseen, cash may perhaps be employed even more economically. For then it may well pay to obtain cash just before large payments fall due with little or no added cost in "brokers' fees" and considerable savings in interest payments. The extreme case would be that of a single payment during the year

1. For people to want to hold a positive amount of cash, the cost of cash holding must be decreasing after $C = 0$. Let b in (1) be a differentiable function of C for $C > 0$ (it will generally be discontinuous and equal to zero at $C = 0$). Then we require that the limit of the derivative of (1) be negative as C approaches zero from above, where this derivative is given by

$$\text{(i)} \; -b\frac{T}{C^2} + \frac{T}{C}b' + \frac{i + i'C}{2}.$$

Clearly this will become negative as C approaches zero provided b is bounded from below and b', i, and i' are all bounded from above.

The second conclusion, the less than proportionate rise in minimum cost cash holdings with the volume of transactions, can be shown, with only b not constant, to hold if and only if $b - b'C + b''C^2$ is positive. This result is obtained by solving the first order minimum condition (obtained by setting (i), with the i' term omitted, equal to zero) for $\frac{T}{C}$ and noting that our conclusion is equivalent to the derivative of this ratio with respect to C being positive.

Now successive differentiation of (i) with the i' term omitted yields as our second order minimum condition $2(b - b'C) + b''C^2 > 0$ (note the resemblance to the preceding condition). Thus if our result is to be violated we must have

$$\text{(ii)} \; b - Cb' \leqq -b''C^2 < 2(b - Cb'),$$

which at once yields $b'' \leqq 0$. Thus if b' is not to become negative (a decreasing *total* payment as the size of the withdrawal increases!) b'' must usually lie within a small neighborhood of zero, i.e., b must be approximately linear. However we know that in this case the square root formula will be (approximately) valid except in the case $b = kC$ when it will always (by (i)) pay to hold zero cash balances. Note incidentally that (ii) also yields $b - Cb' \geqq 0$ which means that our result must hold if ever the "brokerage fee" increases more than in proportion with C.

Note, finally, that if i varies with C the first order condition becomes a cubic and, provided $\infty > i' > 0$, our conclusion is strengthened, since T now tends to increase as C^3.

which would call for a zero cash balance provided the cash could be loaned out profitably at all. Cash receipts during the relevant period may have similar effects, since they can be used to make payments which happen to be due at the moment the receipts arrive. Here the extreme case involves receipts and payments always coinciding in time and amounts in which case, again, zero cash balances would be called for. Thus lumpy payments and receipts of cash, with sufficient foresight, can make for economies in the use of cash, i.e., higher velocity. This may not affect the rate of increase in transactions velocity with the level of transactions, but may nevertheless serve further to increase the effect of an injection of cash and of a cut in wages and prices. With imperfect foresight, however, the expectation that payments may be lumpy may increase the precautionary demand for cash. Moreover, the existence of a "broker's fee" which must be paid on lending or investing cash received during the period is an added inducement to keep receipts until payments fall due rather than investing, and so may further increase the demand for cash.

4. The economy in a single person's use of cash resulting from an increase in the volume of his transactions may or may not have its analogue for the economy as a whole. "External economies" may well be present if one businessman learns cash-economizing techniques from the experiences of another when both increase their transactions. On the diseconomies side it is barely conceivable that an infectious liquidity fetishism will permit a few individuals reluctant to take advantage of cash saving opportunities to block these savings for the bulk of the community. Nevertheless, at least two such possible offsets come to mind: (a) The rise in the demand for brokerage services resulting from a general increase in transactions may bring about a rise in the "brokerage fee" and thus work for an increase in average cash balances (a decreased number of visits to brokers). If cash supplies are sticky this will tend to be offset by rises in the rate of interest resulting from a rising total demand for cash, which serve to make cash more expensive to hold. (b) Widespread cash economizing might require an increase in precautionary cash holdings because in an emergency one could rely less on the ability of friends to help or creditors to be patient. This could weaken but not offset the relative reduction in cash holdings entirely, since the increase in precautionary demand is contingent on there being some relative decrease in cash holdings.

5. A priori analysis of the precautionary and the speculative demands for cash is more difficult. In particular, there seems to be

little we can say about the latter, important though it may be, except that it seems unlikely that it will work consistently in any special direction. In dealing with the precautionary demand, assumptions about probability distributions and expectations must be made.[2] It seems plausible offhand, that an increase in the volume of transactions will make for economies in the use of cash for precautionary as well as transactions purposes by permitting increased recourse to insurance principles.

Indeed, here we have a rather old argument in banking theory which does not seem to be widely known. Edgeworth,[3] and Wicksell[4] following him, suggested that a bank's precautionary cash requirements might also grow as the square root of the volume of its transactions (!). They maintained that cash demands on a bank tend to be normally distributed.[5] In this event, if it is desired to maintain a fixed probability of not running out of funds, precautionary cash requirements will be met by keeping on hand a constant multiple of the standard deviation (above the mean). But then the precautionary cash requirement of ten identical banks (with independent demands) together will be the same as that for any one of them multiplied by the square root of ten. For it is a well-known result that the standard deviation of a random sample from an infinite population increases as the square root of the size of the sample.

William J. Baumol.

Princeton University

2. See Arrow, Harris and Marschak, *op. cit.* for a good example of what has been done along these lines in inventory control analysis.

3. F. Y. Edgeworth, "The Mathematical Theory of Banking," *Journal of the Royal Statistical Society*, Vol. LI (1888), especially pp. 123–127. Fisher (*loc. cit.*) points out the relevance of this result for the analysis of the cash needs of the public as a whole. The result was independently rediscovered by Dr. Whitin (*op. cit.*) who seems to have been the first to combine it and (2) in inventory analysis.

4. K. Wicksell, *Interest and Prices* (London, 1936), p. 67.

5. The distribution would generally be approximately normal if its depositors were large in number, their cash demands independent and not very dissimilarly distributed. The independence assumption, of course, rules out runs on banks.

The Rate of Interest and the Optimum Propensity to Consume

By Oskar Lange

1. By introducing liquidity preference into the theory of interest Mr. Keynes has provided us with an analytical apparatus of great power to attack problems which hitherto have successfully resisted the intrusion of the economic theorist. In this paper I propose first to elucidate the way in which liquidity preference co-operates with the marginal efficiency of investment and with the propensity to consume in determining the rate of interest and to point out how both the traditional and Mr. Keynes's theory are but special cases of a more general theory. Further I propose to show how the analytical apparatus created by Mr. Keynes can be used to handle the problem which bothered the under-consumption theorists since the time of Malthus and Sismondi.

2. The economic relations by which the rate of interest is determined can be represented by a system of four equations.[1]

The first of these equations is the function relating the amount of money held in cash balances to the rate of interest and to income. This is the liquidity preference function. If M is the amount of money held by the individuals, Y their total income and i the rate of interest we have[2]:

$$M=L(i,\ Y) \qquad (1)$$

It is convenient to take M and Y as ***measured in terms of wage-units***, or of any other ***numéraire***. Thus Y is the real income while M is the real value of the cash balances, both

[1] A similar system of equations has been given for the first time by Reddaway, "The General Theory of Employment, Interest and Money," *The Economic Record*, June, 1936, p. 35. While writing this there has come to my notice a forthcoming paper of Dr. Hicks on "Mr. Keynes and the Classics," in the meanwhile published in *Econometrica*, April, 1937, which treats the subject in a similar and very elegant way. The form chosen in my paper seems, however, more adapted for the study of the problems it is concerned with. Cf. also Harrod, "Mr. Keynes and Traditional Theory," *Econometrica*, January, 1937.

[2] This function is obtained by summation of the liquidity preference functions of the individuals in the same way as a market demand function is obtained from the demand functions of the individuals. It holds only for a given distribution of incomes.

in terms of the *numéraire* chosen. This presupposes, of course, that the ratio of the price of each commodity or service to the price of the commodity or service which is chosen as the *numéraire* is given. These ratios may be thought of as determined by the Walrasian or Paretian system of equations of general economic equilibrium. Thus index numbers are *not* involved in this procedure. We assume that the real value, as defined, of cash balances decreases (or, in the limiting case, remains constant) in response to an increase of the rate of interest and that it increases (or, in the limiting case, remains constant) in response to an increase of real income, i.e., $L_i \leq 0$ and $L_Y \geq 0$.

The second equation expresses the propensity to consume. The total expenditure on consumption depends on the total income and, possibly, on the rate of interest. Denoting by C the total expenditure on consumption during a unit of time, we have the function[1] :

$$C = \phi(Y, i) \qquad (2)$$

where C and Y are measured in wage-units (or in some other *numéraire* chosen). The expenditure on consumption increases in response to an increase of income, though less than the income, i.e., $0 < \phi_Y < 1$, while no general rule can be stated as to the reaction of this expenditure to a change in the rate of interest, so that $\phi_i \gtreqless 0$.

The investment function which relates the amount invested per unit of time to the rate of interest and to the expenditure on consumption provides us with a third equation. If I is the investment per unit of time the function is :

$$I = F(i, C) \qquad (3)$$

Both I and C are measured in wage-units. The investment function is based on the theorem that the amount of investment per unit of time is such as to equalise the rate of net return on that investment (the marginal efficiency in Mr. Keynes' terminology) to the rate of interest. This rate of net return is derived from the rate of net return (marginal efficiency) on capital but it is not identical with it.[2] The

[1] This function is the sum of the functions expressing the propensity to consume for each individual. It holds only for a given distribution of incomes.

[2] They are frequently confused. However, the marginal efficiency of capital relates the rate of net return to a *stock* of capital while the marginal efficiency of investment relates it to a *stream* of investment per unit of time. As to how the marginal efficiency of investment is related to the marginal efficiency of capital cf. a forthcoming paper by Mr. Lerner. It also ought to be observed that the investment function holds only for a given capital equipment and for a given distribution of the expenditure for consumption between the different industries.

lower the rate of interest the larger the investment per unit of time, i.e., $F_i < 0$. Investment per unit of time depends, however, not only on the rate of interest but also on the expenditure on consumption. For the demand for investment goods is *derived* from the demand for consumers' goods. The smaller the expenditure on consumption the smaller is the demand for consumers' goods and, consequently, the lower is the rate of net return on investment. Thus, the rate of interest being constant, investment per unit of time is the larger the larger the total expenditure on consumption, i.e., $F_c > 0$.

Finally we have the identity:

$$Y \equiv C + I \qquad (4)$$

which provides us with the fourth equation.[1]

If the amount of money M (in wage-units) is given these four equations determine the four unknowns, i, C, I and Y. Alternatively, i may be regarded as given (for instance, fixed by the banking system) and M as determined by our system of equations. These equations determine also the income-velocity of circulation of money which is $\frac{Y}{M}$.[2] It must, however, be remembered that C, I and Y are measured in terms of a *numéraire* (wage-units). If we want them to be expressed in money we need an additional equation which expresses the money price of the commodity or service chosen as *numéraire* (a unit of labour in our case). If w is this money price and Q the quantity of money we have:

$$Q = wM \qquad (5)$$

which is equivalent to the traditional equation of the quantity theory of money.

3. The process of determination of the rate of interest according to the four equations above is illustrated by the three following diagrams.

Fig. 1 represents the relation between the demand for cash balances and the rate of interest. The quantity of

[1] This identity is the sum of the budget equations of the individuals. It can also be written in the form $Y - C \equiv I$ which expresses the equality of investment and the excess of income over expenditure on consumption, i.e., saving. The identical equality of investment and saving holds for investment and saving actually performed. Investment or saving *decisions* can be different. The identity above states, however, that, whatever the decisions, income is bound to change so as to make equal saving and investment actually realised.

[2] It is interesting to notice that the income-velocity resulting from these equations is the "hybrid" corresponding to the definition of Professor Pigou (cf. *Industrial Fluctuations*, 1927, p. 152) and of Mr. Robertson (*Money*, new edition, 1932, p. 38) and not the ratio of income to income deposits only which Mr. Keynes calls income-velocity (cf. *A Treatise on Money*, Vol. II, pp. 24–25).

money (in wage-units) being measured along the axis *OM* and the rate of interest along the axis *Oi*, we have a *family*

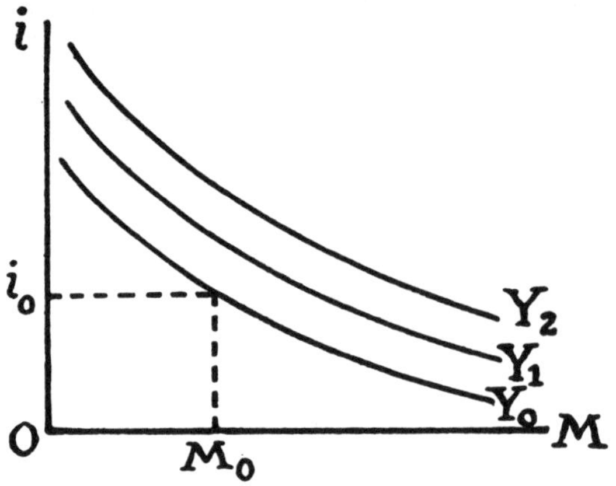

Fig. 1

of liquidity preference curves: one for each level of total income (measured in wage-units). The greater the total income the higher up is the position of the corresponding curve.

Further we have a family of curves (one for each rate of interest) representing the relation between income and expenditure on consumption (Fig. 2). Income is measured along *OY* and expenditure on consumption along *OC*.

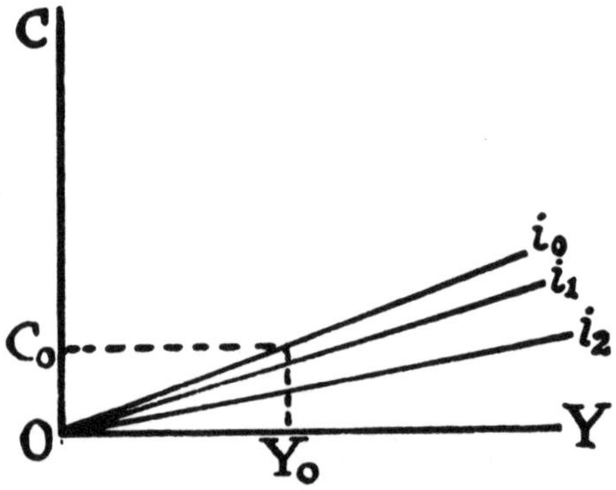

Fig. 2

The relation between investment and the rate of interest is represented by Fig. 3. Measuring investment per unit of time along the axis *OI* and the rate of interest along *Oi* we have a family of curves indicating the investment corresponding to each value of the rate of interest.

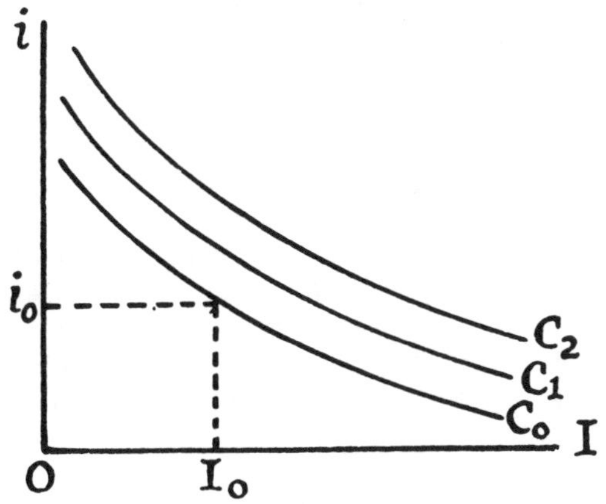

Fig. 3

These curves represent the marginal net return (marginal efficiency) of each amount of investment per unit of time. It is important to notice that there is a separate curve for each level of expenditure on consumption. The greater the expenditure on consumption the higher up is the position of the corresponding curve.

To study the process of determination of the rate of interest let us start with a given amount of money (OM_0 in Fig. 1) which is kept constant throughout the process and with a given initial income Y_0. The position of the liquidity preference curve being determined by the level of income (in Fig. 1 the curve corresponding to the income Y_0), the amount of money determines the rate of interest, say i_0. This rate of interest determines the position of the curve in Fig. 2 representing the propensity to consume. This position being determined, we get the expenditure on consumption C_0 corresponding to the initial income Y_0. The expenditure on consumption being given, the position of the marginal efficiency curve in Fig. 3 is determined (i.e., the curve corresponding to C_0). When this position is determined the rate of interest i_0 determines the amount I_0 of investment per unit of time. We have thus the expenditure on consumption and the amount of investment.

But the sum of these two is equal to the total income (*vide* equation 4). If it happens so that $C_o + I_o$ is equal to the initial income Y_o the system is in equilibrium. Otherwise the liquidity preference curve in Fig. 1 changes its position so as to correspond to the new level of income $C_o + I_o$. This gives us a new rate of interest. As a result of this and of the changed income we get a new level of expenditure on consumption. This in turn changes the position of the marginal efficiency curve in Fig. 3 and the new rate of interest determines another amount of investment which, together with the expenditure on consumption, determines a third level of total income. As a result the liquidity preference curve shifts again, etc. This process of *mutual adjustment* goes on until the curves in our three diagrams have reached a position compatible with each other and with the quantity of money given, i.e., until equilibrium is attained.[1]

4. Let us now consider how changes in the curves of the marginal efficiency of investment and in the curves representing the propensity to consume affect the rate of interest.

If the marginal efficiency curves are all shifted upwards (which, ultimately, must be due to an increase of the marginal net productivity of capital), then a larger amount of investment corresponds to any given rate of interest and expenditure on consumption. Therefore total income increases and the curve of liquidity preference in Fig. 1 shifts upwards. This causes a rise of the rate of interest. Thus, just as in the traditional theory, an increase in the marginal productivity of capital is accompanied by a rise of the rate of interest. The reverse happens when the marginal productivity of capital declines.

On the other hand, a decrease in the propensity to consume (or, in other words, an increase in the propensity to save) is accompanied by a fall of the rate of interest. For with a given initial income and a given rate of interest the expenditure on consumption is now lower. This causes the marginal efficiency curve in Fig. 3 to shift downward and a lower quantity of investment corresponds to any given rate of interest. Total income decreases both as a direct result of the decreased expenditure on consumption and

[1] If this process of adjustment involves a time lag of a certain kind a cyclical fluctuation, instead of equilibrium, is the result. Cf. Kalecki, "A Theory of the Business Cycle," *Review of Economic Studies*, February, 1937.

because of the diminished quantity of investment. Thus a downward shift of the liquidity preference curve in Fig. 1 takes place. The consequence is a fall of the rate of interest. In a similar way an increase in the propensity to consume raises the rate of interest.

Thus the two traditional statements that the rate of interest rises together with the marginal net productivity of capital, and vice versa, and that it moves in the opposite direction to the propensity to save, hold fully in our generalised theory. Two limiting cases, however, deserve special attention.

The theory put forward is quite general and formal. The actual reactions, however, depend on the concrete shape of the functions (1), (2) and (3). We are concerned at present with the consequences of different shapes of the liquidity preference function. For the general case it has been assumed that the demand for liquidity is a decreasing function of the rate of interest and an increasing function of total income. The demand for liquidity (i.e., for cash balances) has thus two elasticities: an interest-elasticity which is negative and an income-elasticity which is positive. These two elasticities determine the reaction of the rate of interest to changes in the marginal efficiency of investment (which is correlated to the marginal net productivity of capital) and in the propensity to consume; for the reaction of the rate of interest to these is due to the influence which the change of income caused by them exerts upon liquidity preference. The greater the income-elasticity of the demand for liquidity the more the curve of liquidity preference is shifted when income changes and, consequently, the greater is the reaction of the rate of interest. The shift of the liquidity preference curve changes the demand for liquidity corresponding to any given rate of interest. If, however, the amount of money (in wage-units) is fixed, the rate of interest must change so as to equalise the demand for liquidity to the quantity of money available. The change of the rate of interest which thus follows is the greater the smaller the interest-elasticity of the demand for liquidity. Therefore, the reaction of the rate of interest is the greater the smaller the interest-elasticity of the demand for liquidity.

In the special case in which the income-elasticity of the demand for liquidity is zero the rate of interest does not react at all to changes other than in the quantity of money (measured in wage-units). The demand for liquidity is in this case a function of the rate of interest alone:

$$M = L(r) \qquad (1a)$$

There is but one curve of liquidity preference and the amount of money determines the rate of interest independently of the level of total income. Changes in the marginal efficiency of investment and in the propensity to consume do not affect the rate of interest at all. The whole brunt of such changes has to be borne by the other variables of the system (i.e., expenditure on consumption, investment and income). The same result is also reached when the interest-elasticity of the demand for liquidity is infinite. In this case, too, the rate of interest does not react to changes in the marginal efficiency of investment or in the propensity to consume. For the change of the rate of interest which is necessary to balance a given change in the demand for liquidity caused by a change of total income is nil in this case. This is Mr. Keynes' theory. Since Mr. Keynes recognises *expressis verbis* the dependence of the demand for liquidity on total income[1] it is obviously the last case he must have in mind.

The other special case is when the interest-elasticity of the demand for liquidity is zero. The demand for cash balances is in this case a function of income alone:

$$M = L(Y) \qquad (1b)$$

Both Y and M being measured in wage-units (or in any other *numéraire*, for instance, wheat[2]) this equation states simply the proportion of their real income people hold in cash (in real balances). If this proportion is regarded as constant our function becomes:

$$M = kY$$

(where k is a constant) which is the well known Cambridge equation of the quantity theory of money. Taking into account equation (5) this can be written $Q = kYw$, or $Q = wL(Y)$ in the more general case, where Q is the quantity of money and w is the money price of the commodity or service which has been chosen as *numéraire*. The latter being given, the total income is determined by the quantity of money. Total income being given, the rate of interest is determined exclusively by the equations (2), (3) and (4),

[1] Cf. *The General Theory of Employment, etc.*, pp. 171–172 and pp. 199 *et seq.*

[2] The reader will be reminded that Marshall and Professor Pigou have used wheat as a *numéraire* in this connection. *Vide* Marshall, *Money Credit and Commerce*, p. 44, and Pigou, *Essays in Applied Economics*, p. 177.

i.e., by the propensity to consume, by the marginal efficiency of investment (which in turn depends on the marginal net productivity of capital), and by the condition that investment is equal to the excess of income over expenditure on consumption (i.e., saving). This is the traditional theory of interest.

Thus both the Keynesian and the traditional theory of interest are but two limiting cases of what may be regarded to be the general theory of interest.

5. It is a feature of great historical interest that the essentials of this general theory are contained already in the work of Walras.

Indeed, the demand for liquidity appears in Walras as the *encaisse désirée*. Walras is quite explicit about the fact that the demand for liquidity is a function of the rate of interest. This dependence is expressed as early as in the second edition of his *Eléments d'économie politique pure* which was published in 1889. "In a society—he writes—where money is kept in cash from the moment when it is received until the day when it is given into payment or loaned out, money renders few services and those who keep it, producers or consumers, lose needlessly the interest on the capital which it represents." ("Dans une société où on garde la monnaie en caisse depuis le moment où on la reçoit jusqu'au jour où on la donne en paiement ou jusqu'au jour où on la prête, la monnaie rend peu de services, et ceux qui la détiennent, producteurs ou consommateurs, perdent inutilement l'intérêt du capital qu'elle représente.")[1] This is emphasised even more in his *Théorie de la Monnaie* where we read about the service yielded by a given *encaisse monétaire*: "its satisfaction is obtained at the price of interest and this is why the effective demand for money is a decreasing function of the rate of interest" ("sa satisfaction se paie au prix d'un intérêt et c'est pourquoi la demande effective de monnaie est une fonction décroissante du taux d'intérêt").[2] He goes on, to quote again from the second edition of the *Eléments*, saying: "Suppose that on a certain day the existing quantity of money Q_u has diminished or that the demand for cash H which represents the utility of money has increased . . . . Equilibrium will be re-established on the next day on the market at a new

[1] P. 382.

[2] P. 95 of the reprint in *Etudes d'économie politique appliquée* (published in Lausanne in 1898). This passage does not occur in the original edition in form of a separate book which was published in 1886 (Lausanne).

and higher rate of interest at which the demand for cash will be reduced." (" Supposons qu'un jour la quantité existante de monnaie Q_u ait diminué ou que l'encaisse désirée H représentant l'utilité de la monnaie ait augmenté . . . L'équilibre ne s'établirait, le lendemain, sur le marché, qu'à un nouveau taux d'intérêt plus élevé auquel l'encaisse desirée se reduirait.")[1]. Walras also uses the device of expressing the demand for cash balances in real terms. It is a certain real purchasing power over which the individual wants to have command and he expresses it in terms of a *numéraire*.[2] If H is the demand for liquidity in terms of the *numéraire* chosen and Q_u is the amount of money in existence, then the price p_u of money in terms of the *numéraire* is determined by the equation $Q_u p_u = H$, which is analogous to the equation (5) above.[3] Walras fails, however, to indicate whether the *encaisse désirée* depends also on the level of real income. But whatever the shortcomings of his presentation, the liquidity preference function has been indicated clearly by Walras.

Our remaining three equations are also contained in the system of Walras. There is, first of all, the propensity to save (instead of our propensity to consume). Saving is defined, as by Mr. Keynes, as the excess of income over consumption (l'excédent du revenu sur la consommation).[4] Now this excess of income over consumption is conceived by Walras to be a function of both the rate of interest and income. He expresses the propensity to save by an equation and states explicitly that this equation " gives the excess of income over consumption as a function of the prices of the productive services and of consumers' goods and of the rate of interest " (" donnant *l'excédent* du revenu sur la consommation en fonction des *prix* des services et des produits consommables et du *taux* du revenu net ").[5] By introducing the prices of all commodities he brings income

[1] P. 383. In the last editions of the *Eléments* the exposition, though put into mathematics, is somewhat obscure. Walras introduces also the question of liquidity (i.e., of stocks) in other commodities. Of each commodity a stock is kept which renders a " *service d'approvisionnement* " (service of storage). The rate of interest is the cost of this service. Cf. *Eléments*, 4th ed., 1900, pp, 179, 298, 303.

[2] Pp. 377–78 of 2nd ed. and *Théorie de la Monnaie* (as reprinted in *Etudes d'économie politique appliquée*), p. 95.

[3] P. 378 and p. 383 of 2nd ed.

[4] P. 281 of first edition published in 1874 (p. 269 of second ed. and p. 249 of final ed.). Walras uses throughout the term *excédent* and the word *épargne* is reserved to denote net saving. Cf. p. 282 of first ed. (p. 270 of 2nd ed. and p. 250 of final ed.).

[5] P. 271 of 2nd ed. " Taux du revenu net " must be translated by " rate of interest " in this connotation.

indirectly into the equation expressing the propensity to save. His equation thus corresponds to our equation (2). As a counterpart to our investment function Walras has an equation which determines the total value of "*capitaux neufs*" produced. This value is determined by the condition that the selling price of the *capitaux neufs* (which is equal to the capitalised value of their net returns) is equal to their cost of production.[1] This equation determines the total volume of investment corresponding to any given rate of interest. Unfortunately, Walras fails to indicate on what the net return of the *capitaux neufs* depends. He takes it just for granted and as a consequence there is no relation between their net return and the expenditure on consumption.

Finally Walras expresses in a separate equation the equality of the value of the *capitaux neufs* and the excess of income over consumption.[2] This, however, is *not* equivalent to our equation (4) which states the equality of investment and the excess of income over consumption. For there is an important difference. In our system, as in the theory of Mr. Keynes, equation (4) is an identity. Whatever the investment and saving *decisions* are, the volume of total income always adjusts itself so as to equalise saving and investment *actually performed*.[3] This is a simple budget relationship, for the individuals' incomes are equal to the sum of expenditure on consumption and investment. Walras, however, treats the equality of investment and saving not as an identity but as a genuine equation which holds true only in a position of equilibrium. Hence his investment (value of the *capitaux neufs*) and saving (excess of income over consumption) are to be interpreted as *decisions* which finally are brought into equilibrium by a change in the rate of interest and in total income.[4] But this equation does not show how total income changes so as to bring saving actually performed always into equality with investment.

This is done by our identity (4) which corresponds to

[1] Cf. p. 284 of first ed. (pp. 246–7 and p. 253 of final ed.).

[2] P. 284 of first ed. (p. 252 of final ed.).

[3] It ought to be mentioned here that this has been recognised by many economists before Mr. Keynes. If investment decisions exceed saving decisions "forced saving" takes place according to a widely accepted doctrine. And Mr. Robertson has pointed out (cf. *Money*, London, 1928, pp. 93–97) that if saving decisions exceed investment decisions the excess cannot be saved. It becomes "abortive."

[4] Pp. 286–7 of 2nd ed. (pp. 266–67 of final ed.). In the process of *tâtonnements* described by Walras all the prices change and thus total income changes, too.

the sum of the budget equations in the Walrasian system and shows how expenditure on consumption and investment *determine* the total income. When this budget relationship is taken account of, there is no need any more for a separate equation indicating the equilibrium of saving and investment decisions based on some *given* income, however defined. All the relevant relations are expressed by our equations (2), (3) and (4). Thus Mr. Keynes' apparatus involves a considerable simplification of the theory.

6. Having investigated the consequences which the introduction of liquidity preference has for the formulation of the theory of interest, let us see how the general theory outlined above can be applied to solve the problem which is the concern of all theories of underconsumption. Mr. Keynes has scarcely done justice to what is the core of the argument of those theories. " Practically—he writes—I only differ from these schools of thought in thinking that they may lay a little too much emphasis on increased consumption at a time when there is still much social advantage to be obtained from increased investment. Theoretically, however, they are open to the criticism of neglecting the fact that there are *two* ways to expand output."[1] Mr. Keynes treats investment and expenditure on consumption as two *independent* quantities and thinks that total income can be increased indiscriminately by expanding *either* of them. But it is a commonplace which can be read in any textbook of economics that the demand for investment goods is *derived* from the demand for consumption goods. The real argument of the underconsumption theories is that investment *depends* on the expenditure on consumption and, therefore, cannot be increased without an adequate increase of the latter, at least in a capitalist economy where investment is done for profit.

Few underconsumption theorists ever maintain that *any* saving discourages investment.[2] Generally they maintain that up to a certain point saving encourages investment while it discourages it if this point is exceeded.[3] This is the theory of oversaving. If people would spend their whole income on consumption, investment would obviously

[1] *The General Theory of Employment, etc.*, p. 325.
[2] The most prominent among those who did so was Rosa Luxemburg in her famous book *Die Akkumulation des Kapitals* (Berlin, 1912).
[3] *Vide*, for instance, Hobson, *The Industrial System*, London, 1910, pp. 53–54.

be zero, while the demand for investment would be zero too, if they consumed nothing. Thus mere common sense suggests that there must be somewhere in between an *optimum* propensity to save which maximises investment. But no underconsumption theorist ever has shown what this optimum is and how it is determined. The problem, however, was put forward with unsurpassed clarity already by Malthus: "No considerable and continued increase in wealth could possibly take place without that degree of frugality which occasions, annually, the conversion of some revenue into capital, and creates a balance of produce over consumption; but it is quite obvious . . . that the principle of saving, pushed to excess, would destroy the motive to production . . . If consumption exceeds production, the capital of the country must be diminished, and its wealth must be gradually destroyed from its want of power to produce; if production be in great excess above consumption, the motive to accumulate and consume must cease from the want of will to consume. The two extremes are obvious; and it follows that there must be some intermediate point, though the resources of political economy may not be able to ascertain it, where taking into consideration both the power to produce and the will to consume, the encouragement to the increase of wealth is greatest."[1]

The general theory of interest outlined in this paper enables us to solve this problem and to determine the optimum propensity to save which maximises investment. Since investment per unit of time is a function of both the rate of interest and expenditure on consumption a decrease of the propensity to consume (increase in the propensity to save) has a twofold effect. On the one hand the decrease of expenditure on consumption discourages investment, but the decrease in the propensity to consume also causes, as we have seen, a fall of the rate of interest which encourages investment on the other hand. The optimum propensity to consume is that at which the encouraging and the discouraging effect of a change are in balance.

The condition of such a balance is easily found. A change of the propensity to consume is mathematically a change of the *form* of the function (2) in our equations. We want to discover the conditions this function has to satisfy in

[1] *Principles of Political Economy*, London, 1820, pp. 8–9 (Introduction). Cf. also pp. 369–70.

order to maximise investment. Let δC be the variation of expenditure on consumption and δi the variation of the rate of interest which are caused by the change of the propensity to consume. Recalling the investment function (3), which is $I=F(i, C)$, the condition that investment be a maximum is then:

$$\delta I = F_i \delta i + F_c \delta C = 0 \tag{6}$$

where δI is the corresponding variation of investment.

From equation (4) we derive the variation of total income caused by the change of the propensity to consume:

$$\delta Y = \delta C + \delta I$$

and since $\delta I = 0$ when investment is a maximum we have in the maximum position:

$$\delta Y = \delta C \tag{7}$$

Now the change of the rate of interest due to the change of the propensity to consume can be obtained from equation (1), i.e., from the liquidity preference function. We have[1]:

$$\delta M = L_i \delta i + L_Y \delta Y \tag{8}$$

If the sum of real balances available, i.e., the quantity of money measured in wage-units or in any other *numéraire*, is assumed to be constant[2] this reduces to:

$$L_i \delta i + L_Y \delta Y = 0 \tag{8a}$$

whence:

$$\delta i = -\frac{L_Y}{L_i} \delta Y \tag{9}$$

By substitution of (9) and (7) in (6) we arrive at the equation:

$$-F_i \frac{L_Y}{L_i} \delta C + F_c \delta C = 0$$

[1] The liquidity preference function holds only for a given distribution of incomes (cf. footnote 2 on p. 12 above). Similarly the investment function holds only for a given distribution of the expenditure for consumption between the different industries, for even if the total expenditure on consumption remains unchanged a shift of expenditure from goods requiring less to goods requiring more capital to produce, or vice versa, necessarily affects investment. Equations (6) and (8) in the text presuppose, therefore, that changes in the distribution of incomes and in the direction of consumers' expenditure to different industries are either absent, or that their effect on total investment and on the total demand for liquidity is of second order magnitude and can thus be neglected. Since a change of the propensity to consume certainly produces changes in the distribution of incomes and of consumers' expenditure the second assumption is the only realistic one. A more precise theory would have to take into account the effect of these changes, too.

[2] If the money wage (or, more generally, the money price of the *numéraire* chosen) is constant, this means that the nominal quantity of money is constant, too. If not, the nominal quantity of money has to change proportionally to the money price of the *numéraire*. If, however, labour is not regarded as a homogeneous factor the use of labour-units as *numéraire* involves really the use of a particular index number, i.e., the labour standard, and our assumption amounts to assuming that the purchasing power of money in terms of the labour standard is constant.

which can be transformed into:

$$-\frac{L_Y}{L_i} = -\frac{F_c}{F_i} \qquad (10)$$

This equation, together with the equations (1), (3) and (4) of our system, determines the optimum propensity to consume under the assumption that the amount of money (measured in wage-units) is constant.[1]

Only such forms of the function representing the propensity to consume which satisfy this equation provide a maximum investment. A very simple economic interpretation can be given to the equation obtained. The right hand side of the equation is the marginal rate of substitution between a change of the rate of interest and a change of the expenditure on consumption as inducements to invest. The left hand side is the marginal rate of substitution between a change of the rate of interest and a change of real income as determining the demand for liquidity. The optimum propensity to consume is thus determined by the condition that *the marginal rate of substitution between the rate of interest and total income as affecting the demand for liquidity is equal to the marginal rate of substitution between the rate of interest and expenditure on consumption as inducements to invest.*[2]

[1] If the amount of money (as defined in the text) is allowed to change a more general condition is obtained. For this purpose we must add to our system of equations a supply function of money. Let this function be:

$$M = \psi(i, Y)$$

where M and Y are measured in terms of wage-units. We have then:

$$\delta M = \psi_i \delta i + \psi_Y \delta Y$$

and taking into account equation (8) in the text we obtain:

$$\psi_i \delta i + \psi_Y \delta Y = L_i \delta i + L_Y \delta Y$$

which can be written in the more convenient form:

$$(\psi_Y - L_Y)\delta Y = (L_i - \psi_i)\delta i$$

whence we get:

$$\delta i = \frac{\psi_Y - L_Y}{L_i - \psi_i}\delta Y$$

Substituting this and (7) in (6) we arrive at:

$$F_i \frac{\psi_Y - L_Y}{L_i - \psi_i}\delta C + F_c \delta C = 0$$

which is, finally, transformed into:

$$\frac{\psi_Y - L_Y}{L_i - \psi_i} = -\frac{F_c}{F_i} \qquad (10a)$$

This is the most general form of the equation which determines the optimum propensity to consume. Equation (10) obtained in the text is a special case of it when $\psi_Y = 0$ and $\psi_i = 0$.

[2] The economic interpretation of equation (10a) is similar to that of equation (10), only the left hand side is here the marginal rate of substitution not along a curve of equal liquidity (isoliquidity curve; *vide* below) but along the curve corresponding to the equation:

$$\psi(i, Y) = L(i, Y)$$

Thus the left hand side of (10a) is the marginal rate of substitution between the changes

It is convenient to have a graphic illustration of this condition. On Fig. 4 we draw a family of indifference curves indicating the possible variations of the rate of interest and of the expenditure on consumption which do not change the level of investment per unit of time. We

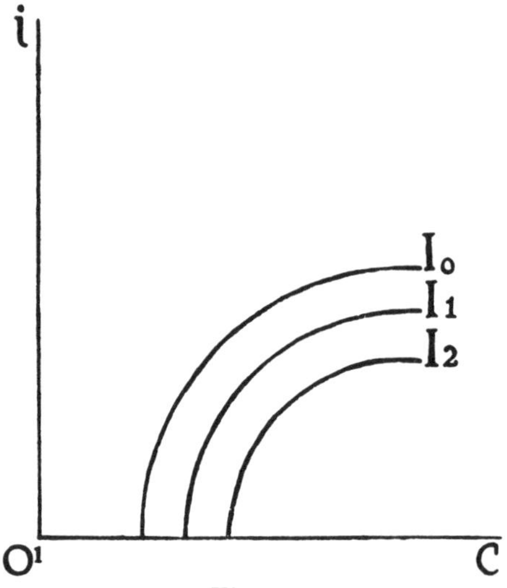

Fig. 4

may call them *isoinvestment curves.* The expenditure on consumption being measured along the axis $O'C$ and the rate of interest along $O'i$ these curves slope upward[1] and the greater the level of investment the more to the right is the position of the corresponding isoinvestment curve[2]. The curves can be expected to be concave downwards, for the stimulus to invest exercised by each successive increment of expenditure on consumption is weaker. This is explained by the increasing prices of the factors of production which diminish the net return derived by entrepreneurs from successive increments of expenditure on consumption (the curves of marginal efficiency of investment in Fig. 3 are

of the rate of interest and of total income which are compatible with the maintenance of the equality of the supply of and the demand for money. The supply function of money depends on the behaviour of the monetary system.

[1] The slope of these curves is $-\frac{F_c}{F_i}$. Since $F_c > 0$ and $F_i < 0$ the slope is positive.

[2] There are certain combinations of the expenditure on consumption and of the rate of interest at which the existing capital is just maintained by replacement. They determine the curve corresponding to zero investment (i.e., the curve I_0 in Fig. 4). All curves to the right of it correspond to positive and all to the left correspond to negative investment.

shifted upwards less and less). Thus the greater the expenditure on consumption the greater is the increment of it which is necessary to compensate a given rise of the rate of interest. Finally, we reach a point where a further increase of the expenditure on consumption fails entirely to stimulate investment. This happens when the elasticity of supply of the factors of production has become zero, so that an increase of the expenditure on consumption only raises their prices. Thus the isoinvestment curves become horizontal to the right of a certain critical value of the abscissa.[1]

On Fig. 5 we draw an indifference curve which represents all the variations of the rate of interest and of total income which do not affect the demand for liquidity (total income and the demand for liquidity being expressed in wage-units). We may call it the *isoliquidity curve*. Since the

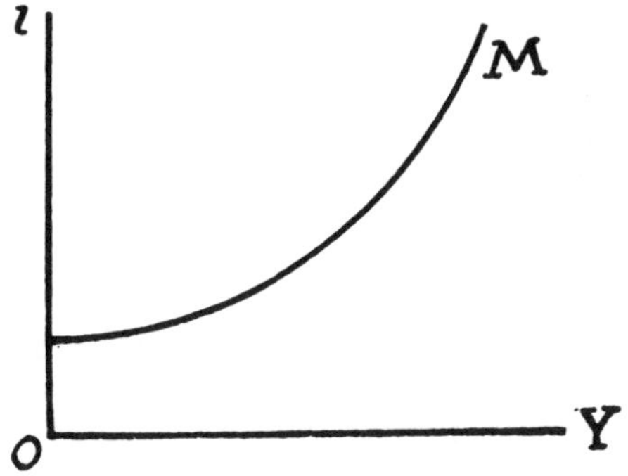

Fig. 5

amount of money is assumed to be given we have only one such curve (the curve M in Fig. 5). It slopes upward[2] and generally it may be expected to be convex downward, for as real income increases its marginal utility decreases and the less felt is the loss of interest income due to keeping money in cash balances. Therefore the increase of the rate of interest which is necessary to compensate the effect

[1] $-\frac{F_c}{F_i} = 0$ when $F_c = 0$.

[2] The slope of the curve is $-\frac{L_Y}{L_i}$. It is positive because $L_Y > 0$ and $L_i < 0$. In the limiting cases, however, where either $L_Y = 0$ or $L_i = 0$ we have either $-\frac{L_Y}{L_i} = 0$ or $-\frac{L_Y}{L_i} = \infty$ and the isoliquidity curve degenerates into a horizontal or vertical straight line.

a given increment of real income has on the demand for liquidity is the greater the greater the income.

The optimum propensity to consume can now be determined in a simple way by combining the diagrams of Fig. 4 and Fig. 5. Equation (10) states that the slope of the isoliquidity curve has to be equal to the slope of the isoinvestment curve (*vide* the point P in Fig. 6). But the position of the origins O and O' in the combined diagram

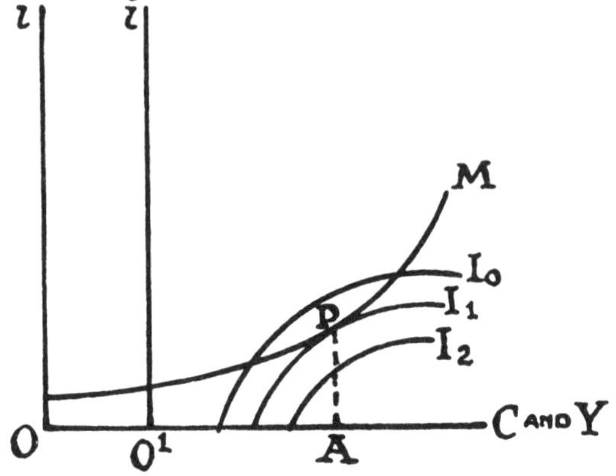

Fig. 6

is not arbitrary. For OO' is the difference between total income and expenditure on consumption, i.e., represents the level of investment. Thus to each level of investment there belongs a special length of OO'. The optimum propensity to consume is, therefore, obtained by superimposing Fig. 5 upon Fig. 4 (as in Fig. 6) and moving it horizontally until the isoliquidity curve becomes tangent to the isoinvestment curve whose index (i.e., level of investment) is equal to the length of OO'. OO' is then the maximum investment, $O'A$ and OA are the expenditure on consumption and the total income which correspond to it. If the isoinvestment curves are concave and the isoliquidity curve is convex downward there exists only one isoinvestment curve which satisfies this condition and the solution is unique[1].

[1] The graphic solution indicated in Fig. 6 is also applicable to the general case where the quantity of money (in terms of wage-units) is not constant. As shown in the footnotes 1 and 2 on p. 26 the equation (10a) is substituted in this case for the equation (10). Instead of the isoliquidity curve we get a curve corresponding to the equation $\psi(i, Y) = L(i, Y)$. It is a projection on the Yi plane of the curve resulting from the intersection of the two

From Fig. 6 we obtain the expenditure on consumption $O'A$ and the total income OA which correspond to maximum investment and which are, as we have seen, uniquely determined. Plotting them on a diagram (*vide* Fig. 7) we obtain a point R through which the curve representing the propensity to consume has to pass. Thus the function

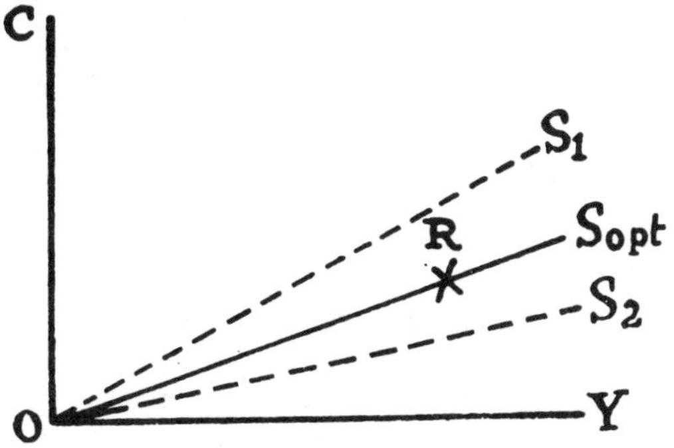

Fig. 7

expressing the optimum propensity to consume is determined only by *one* point through which it has to pass. *Any* function which passes through the point R maximises investment. Any function, however, which does not pass through R makes total investment smaller. Generally we may expect that a decrease of the propensity to consume (i.e., an increase of the propensity to save) leads us from curves which pass above R to curves which pass below R (e.g., the curves S_1 and S_2 in Fig. 7). As long as they pass above R the propensity to consume is above optimum, when they pass below R it is below optimum. Maximum investment is attained when we hit upon a curve which passes through R (e.g., the curve S_{opt} in Fig. 7). This is a curve of optimum propensity to consume. Any change of the shape of the curve which does not affect its passing through R is irrelevant.

7. Let us now apply the result obtained to two special cases.

When either the income-elasticity of the demand for liquidity is zero or the interest-elasticity of the demand

surfaces representing the supply and the demand for money respectively (the isoliquidity curves are a special case of it obtained when the supply surface of money is a plane parallel to the Yi plane). The shape of the curve depends now also on the form of the supply function of money. The graphic solution is obtained as in the text by moving the diagram of this curve horizontally until the curve becomes tangent to the isoinvestment curve corresponding to the level of investment equal to OO'.

for liquidity is infinite, which is the case corresponding to Mr. Keynes' theory, we have either $L_Y = 0$ (and $L_i \neq 0$) or $L_i = \infty$ (and $L_Y \neq 0$). It follows immediately from equation (10) that $F_c = 0$ in either case.[1] The economic interpretation is simple. As we have seen, in this case a change in the propensity to consume does not affect the rate of interest at all. The rate of interest remaining constant, the optimum propensity to consume is *when the expenditure on consumption is such that a further increase does not any more increase the marginal efficiency of investment.* It has been mentioned already that this happens when the elasticity of supply of factors of production becomes zero, so that an increase of the expenditure on consumption only raises their prices but cannot increase investment. This implies the absence of even voluntary unemployment of factors of production. If involuntary unemployment of a factor is defined by its supply being infinitely elastic, it is absent whenever the elasticity of supply is finite. A zero elasticity of supply, however, means that there are no more factors which would offer their services if the remuneration were greater, i.e., are voluntarily unemployed. Until this stage is reached any increase in the propensity to consume stimulates investment.[2] This fits well into the scheme of Mr. Keynes' theory.

The other special case is when the interest-elasticity of the demand for liquidity is zero which is, as we have seen, the case of the traditional theory. Then $L_i = 0$ (and $L_Y \neq 0$) and by rewriting equation (10) in the form:

$$-\frac{L_i}{L_Y} = -\frac{F_i}{F_c}$$

we obtain $F_i = 0$ for this case. ***Any decrease in the propensity to consume stimulates investment*** by causing an appropriate fall of the rate of interest. The propensity to save can never be excessive, for the rate of interest falls always sufficiently to make room for additional investment. The only limit is when a further decrease of the rate of interest stops increasing investment ($F_i = 0$), i.e., when

[1] It seems, however, highly doubtful that $L_i = \infty$ over the whole range of the liquidity preference function.

[2] In the general case where the quantity of money is allowed to vary the same result is reached when $\psi_Y = L_Y$ (*vide* equation (10a)). In this case the income elasticity of supply of money is equal to the income-elasticity of the demand for liquidity; each change of total income is balanced by exactly such a change of the supply of money that the rate of interest remains constant.

the net return on investment becomes zero and the rate of interest is zero, too.

In the general case the optimum propensity to save is somewhere between these two limits and *it is the greater the greater the income-elasticity and the smaller the interest-elasticity of the demand for liquidity.* For the fall of the rate of interest due to an increase in the propensity to save is the greater the greater is the first and the smaller is the second of these two elasticities. The optimum propensity to save is also the greater the greater the elasticity of investment with respect to the rate of interest and the smaller the elasticity of investment with respect to expenditure on consumption.

Thus we arrive at the result that, with the exception of the special case covered by the traditional theory of interest, there exists an optimum propensity to save which depends on the shape of the liquidity preference and of the investment functions. This imposes a maximum limit on investment per unit of time and any attempt to exceed it by raising the propensity to save above its optimum frustrates itself by leading to a diminution of investment. In a society where the propensity to save is determined by the individuals there are no forces at work which keep it automatically at its optimum and it is well possible, as the underconsumption theorists maintain, that there is a tendency to exceed it. Whether this is actually the case is a matter for empirical investigation and cannot be answered by the economic theorist.

The optimum propensity to save is, however, defined only with regard to a given quantity (or more generally: to a given supply function) of money. Therefore, if the propensity to save does exceed its optimum it need not be curbed to avoid its evil consequences. It can be made to benefit economic progress by an appropriate monetary policy which increases the quantity of money sufficiently to reduce the rate of interest so as to compensate the discouraging effect a high propensity to save has on investment.[1] How far such a policy is possible depends on the structure of the monetary and of the whole economic system.

[1] The requirement of an increase of the quantity of money to counteract an excessive propensity to save is *not* in contradiction with the teaching of Professor Davidson, Professor Hayek and Mr. Robertson that technical progress does not require an increase of the quantity of money to avoid deflation. If the increase in the propensity to save is accompanied by technical progress which increases the marginal efficiency of investment, investment is not discouraged and no increase of the quantity of money is necessary.

[36]

FUNCTIONAL FINANCE AND THE FEDERAL DEBT

BY ABBA P. LERNER

APART from the necessity of winning the war, there is no task facing society today so important as the elimination of economic insecurity. If we fail in this after the war the present threat to democratic civilization will arise again. It is therefore essential that we grapple with this problem even if it involves a little careful thinking and even if the thought proves somewhat contrary to our preconceptions.

In recent years the principles by which appropriate government action can maintain prosperity have been adequately developed, but the proponents of the new principles have either not seen their full logical implications or shown an over-solicitousness which caused them to try to save the public from the necessary mental exercise. This has worked like a boomerang. Many of our publicly minded men who have come to see that deficit spending actually works still oppose the permanent maintenance of prosperity because in their failure to see *how* it all works they are easily frightened by fairy tales of terrible consequences.

I

As formulated by Alvin Hansen and others who have developed and popularized it, the new fiscal theory (which was first put forward in substantially complete form by J. M. Keynes in England) sounds a little less novel and absurd to our preconditioned ears than it does when presented in its simplest and most logical form, with all the unorthodox implications expressly formulated. In some cases the less shocking formulation may be intentional, as a tactical device to gain serious attention. In other cases it is due not to a desire to sugar the pill but to the fact that the writers themselves have not seen all the unorthodox implications—perhaps subconsciously compromising with their own orthodox education. But now it is these compromises that are under fire. Now more than ever it is necessary to pose the theorems in the purest form. Only thus will it be possible to clear the air of objections which really are concerned with awkwardnesses that appear only when the new theory is forced into the old theoretical framework.

Fundamentally the new theory, like almost every important discovery, is extremely simple. Indeed it is this simplicity which makes the public suspect it as too slick. Even learned professors who find it hard to abandon ingrained habits of thought have complained that it is "merely logical" when they could find no flaw in it. What progress the theory has made so far has been achieved not by simplifying it but by dressing it up to make it more complicated and accompanying the presentation with impressive but irrelevant statistics.

The central idea is that government fiscal policy, its spending and taxing, its borrowing and repayment of loans, its issue of new money and its withdrawal of money, shall all be undertaken with an eye only to the *results* of these actions on the economy and not to any established traditional doctrine about what is sound or unsound. This principle of judging only by *effects* has been applied in many other fields of human activity, where it is known as the method of science as opposed to scholasticism. The principle of judging fiscal measures by the way they work or function in the economy we may call *Functional Finance.*

The first financial responsibility of the government (since nobody else can undertake that responsibility) is to keep the total rate of spending in the country on goods and services neither greater nor less than that rate which at the current prices would buy all the goods that it is possible to produce. If total spending is allowed to go above this there will be inflation, and if it is allowed to go below this there will be unemployment. The government can increase total spending by spending more itself or by reducing taxes so that the taxpayers have more money left to spend. It can reduce total spending by spending less itself or by raising taxes so that taxpayers have less money left to spend. By these means total spending can be kept at the required level, where it will be enough to buy the goods that can be produced by all who want to work, and yet not enough to bring inflation by demanding (at current prices) *more* than can be produced.

In applying this first law of Functional Finance, the government may find itself collecting more in taxes than it is spending, or spending more than it collects in taxes. In the former case it can keep the difference in its coffers or use it to repay some of the national debt, and in the latter case it would have to provide the difference by borrowing or printing money. In neither case should the government feel that there is anything especially good or bad about this result; it should merely concentrate on keeping the total rate of spending neither too small nor too great, in this way preventing both unemployment and inflation.

An interesting, and to many a shocking, corollary is that taxing is *never* to be undertaken merely because the government needs to make money payments. According to the principles of Functional Finance, taxation must be judged only by its effects. Its main effects are two: the taxpayer has less money left to spend and the government has more money. The second effect can be brought about so much more easily by printing the money that only the first effect is significant. Taxation should therefore be imposed only when it is desirable that the taxpayers shall have less money to spend, for example, when they would otherwise spend enough to bring about inflation.

The second law of Functional Finance is that the government should borrow money only if it is desirable that the public should have less money and more government bonds, for these are the *effects* of government borrowing. This might be desirable if otherwise the rate of interest would be reduced too low (by attempts on the part of the holders of the cash to lend it out) and induce too much investment, thus bringing about inflation. Conversely, the government should lend money (or repay some of its debt) only if it is desirable to increase the money or to reduce the quantity of government bonds in the hands of the public. When taxing, spending, borrowing and lending (or repaying loans) are governed by the principles of Functional Finance, any excess of money outlays over money revenues, if it cannot be met out of money hoards, must be met by printing new money, and any excess of revenues over outlays can be destroyed or used to replenish hoards.

The almost instinctive revulsion that we have to the idea of printing money, and the tendency to identify it with inflation, can be overcome if we calm ourselves and take note that this printing does not affect the amount of money *spent*. That is regulated by the first law of Functional Finance, which refers especially to inflation and unemployment. The printing of money takes place only when it is needed to implement Functional Finance in spending or lending (or repayment of government debt).[1]

In brief, Functional Finance rejects completely the traditional doctrines of "sound finance" and the principle of trying to balance the budget over a solar year or any other arbitrary period. In their place it prescribes: first, the adjustment of total spending (by everybody in the economy, including the government) in order to eliminate both unemployment and inflation, using government spending when total spending is too low and taxation when total spending is too high; second, the adjustment of public holdings of money and of government bonds, by government borrowing or debt repayment, in order to achieve the rate of interest which results in the most desirable level of investment; and, third, the printing, hoarding or destruction of money as needed for carrying out the first two parts of the program.

II

In judging the formulations of economists on this subject it is difficult to distinguish between tact in smoothing over the more stag-

[1]Borrowing money from the banks, on conditions which permit the banks to issue new credit money based on their additional holdings of government securities, must be considered for our purpose as printing money. In effect the banks are acting as agents for the government in issuing credit or bank money.

gering statements of Functional Finance and insufficient clarity on the part of those who do not fully realize the extremes that are implied in their relatively orthodox formulations. First there were the pump-primers, whose argument was that the government merely had to get things going and then the economy could go on by itself. There are very few pump-primers left now. A formula similar in some ways to pump-priming was developed by Scandinavian economists in terms of a series of cyclical, capital and other special budgets which had to be balanced not annually but over longer periods. Like the pump-priming formula it fails because there is no reason for supposing that the spending and taxation policy which maintains full employment and prevents inflation must necessarily balance the budget over a decade any more than during a year or at the end of each fortnight.

As soon as this was seen—the lack of any guarantee that the maintenance of prosperity would permit the budget to be balanced even over longer periods—it had to be recognized that the result might be a continually increasing national debt (if the additional spending were provided by the government's borrowing of the money and not by printing the excess of its spending over its tax revenues). At this point two things should have been made clear: first, that this possibility presented no danger to society, no matter what unimagined heights the national debt might reach, so long as Functional Finance maintained the proper level of total demand for current output; and second (though this is much less important), that there is an automatic tendency for the budget to be balanced in the long run as a *result* of the application of Functional Finance, even if there is no place for the *principle* of balancing the budget. No matter how much interest has to be paid on the debt, taxation must not be applied unless it is necessary to keep spending down to prevent inflation. The interest can be paid by borrowing still more.

As long as the public is willing to keep on lending to the government there is no difficulty, no matter how many zeros are added to the national debt. If the public becomes reluctant to keep on lending, it must either hoard the money or spend it. If the public hoards, the government can print the money to meet its interest and other obligations, and the only effect is that the public holds government currency instead of government bonds and the government is saved the trouble of making interest payments. If the public spends, this will increase the rate of total spending so that it will not be necessary for the government to borrow for this purpose; and if the rate of spending becomes too great, *then* is the time to tax to prevent inflation. The proceeds can then be used to pay interest and repay government debt. In every case Functional Finance provides a simple, quasi-automatic response.

But either this was not seen clearly or it was considered too shocking or too logical to be told to the public. Instead it was argued, for example by Alvin Hansen, that as long as there is a reasonable ratio between national income and debt, the interest payment on the national debt can easily come from taxes paid out of the increased national income created by the deficit financing.

This unnecessary "appeasement" opened the way to an extremely effective opposition to Functional Finance. Even men who have a clear understanding of the mechanism whereby government spending in times of depression can increase the national income by several times the amount laid out by the government, and who understand perfectly well that the national debt, when it is not owed to other nations, is not a burden on the nation in the same way as an individual's debt to other individuals is a burden on the individual, have come out strongly against "deficit spending."[2] It has been argued that "it would be impossible to devise a program better adapted to the systematic undermining of the private-enterprise system and the hastening of the final catastrophe than 'deficit spending.'"[3]

These objections are based on the recognition that although every dollar spent by the government may create several dollars of

[2]An excellent example of this is the persuasive article by John T. Flynn in *Harper's Magazine* for July 1942.

[3]Flynn, *ibid.*

income in the course of the next year or two, the effects then disappear. From this it follows that if the national income is to be maintained at a high level the government has to keep up its contribution to spending for as long as private spending is insufficient by itself to provide full employment. This might mean an indefinite continuation of government support to spending (though not necessarily at an increasing rate); and if, as the "appeasement" formulation suggests, all this spending comes out of borrowing, the debt will keep on growing until it is no longer in a "reasonable" ratio to income.

This leads to the crux of the argument. If the interest on the debt must be raised out of taxes (again an assumption that is unchallenged by the "appeasement" formulation) it will in time constitute an important fraction of the national income. The very high income tax necessary to collect this amount of money and pay it to the holders of government bonds will discourage risky private investment, by so reducing the net return on it that the investor is not compensated for the risk of losing his capital. This will make it necessary for the government to undertake still more deficit financing to keep up the level of income and employment. Still heavier taxation will then be necessary to pay the interest on the growing debt—until the burden of taxation is so crushing that private investment becomes unprofitable, and the private enterprise economy collapses. Private firms and corporations will all be bankrupted by the taxes, and the government will have to take over all industry.

This argument is not new. The identical calamities, although they are now receiving much more attention than usual, were promised when the first income tax law of one penny in the pound was proposed. All this only makes it more important to evaluate the significance of the argument.

III

There are four major errors in the argument against deficit spending, four reasons why its apparent conclusiveness is only illusory.

In the first place, the same high income tax that reduces the return on the investment is deductible for the loss that is incurred if the investment turns out a failure. As a result of this the *net* return on the risk of loss is unaffected by the income tax rate, no matter how high that may be. Consider an investor in the $50,000-a-year income class who has accumulated $10,000 to invest. At 6 percent this would yield $600, but after paying income tax on this addition to his income at 60 cents in the dollar he would have only $240 left. It is argued, therefore, that he would not invest because this is insufficient compensation for the risk of losing $10,000. This argument forgets that if the $10,000 is all lost, the net loss to the investor, after he has deducted his income tax allowance, will be only $4,000, and the rate of return on the amount he actually risks is still exactly 6 percent; $240 is 6 percent of $4,000. The effect of the income tax is to make the rich man act as a kind of agent working for society on commission. He receives only a part of the return on the investment, but he loses only a part of the money that is invested. Any investment that was worth undertaking in the absence of the income tax is still worth undertaking.

Of course, this correction of the argument is strictly true only where 100 percent of the loss is deductible from taxable income, where relief from taxation occurs at the same rate as the tax on returns. There is a good case against certain limitations on permissible deduction from the income tax base for losses incurred, but that is another story. Something of the argument remains, too, if the loss would put the taxpayer into a lower income tax bracket, where the rebate (and the tax) is at a lower rate. There would then be some reduction in the net return as compared with the potential net loss. But this would apply only to such investments as are large enough to threaten to impoverish the investor if they fail. It was for the express purpose of dealing with this problem that the corporation was devised, making it possible for many individuals to combine and undertake risky enterprises without any one person having to risk all his fortune on one venture. But quite apart from corporate investment, this problem would be met almost entirely if the maximum rate of income tax were reached at a relatively low level, say at $25,000 a year (low, that is, from the point of view of the rich men who are the supposed source of risk capital). Even if all income in excess of $25,000 were taxed at 90 percent there would be no discouragement in the investment of any part of income over this level. True, the net return, after payment of tax, would be only one-tenth of the nominal interest payments, but the amount risked by the investors would also be only ten percent of the actual capital invested, and therefore the net return on the capital actually risked by the investor would be unaffected.

In the second place, this argument against deficit spending in time of depression would be indefensible even if the harm done by debt were as great as has been suggested. It must be remembered that spending by the government increases the *real* national income of goods and services by several times the amount spent by the government, and that the burden is measured not by the amount of the interest payments but only by the inconveniences involved in the process of transferring the money from the taxpayers to the bondholders. Therefore objecting to deficit spending is like arguing that if you are offered a job when out of work on the condition that you promise to pay your wife interest on a part of the money earned (or that your wife pay it to you) it would be wiser to continue to be unemployed, because in time you will be owing your wife a great deal of money (or she will be owing it to you), and this might cause matrimonial difficulties in the future. Even if the interest payments were really lost to society, instead of being merely transferred within the society, they would come to much less than the loss through permitting unemployment to continue. That loss would be several times as great as the *capital* on which these interest payments have to be made.

In the third place, there is no good reason for supposing that the government would have to raise all the interest on the national debt by current taxes. We have seen that Functional Finance permits taxation only when the *direct* effect of the tax is in the social interest, as when it prevents excessive spending or excessive investment which would bring about inflation. If taxes imposed to prevent inflation do not result in sufficient proceeds, the interest on the debt can be met by borrowing or printing the money. There is no risk of inflation from this, because if there were such a risk a greater amount would have to be collected in taxes.

This means that the absolute size of the national debt does not matter at all, and that however large the interest payments that have to be made, these do not constitute any burden upon society as a whole. A completely fantastic exaggeration may illustrate the point. Suppose the national debt reaches the stupendous total of ten thousand billion dollars (that is, ten trillion, $10,000,000,-000,000), so that the interest on it is 300 billion a year. Suppose the real national income of goods and services which can be produced by the economy when fully employed is 150 billion. The interest alone, therefore, comes to twice the real national income. There is no doubt that a debt of this size would be called "unreasonable." But even in this fantastic case the payment of the interest constitutes no burden on society. Although the real income is only 150 billion dollars the money income is 450 billion—150 billion in income from the production of goods and services and 300 billion in income from ownership of the government bonds which constitute the national debt. Of this money income of 450 billion, 300 billion has to be collected in taxes by the government for interest payments (if 10 trillion is the legal debt limit), but after payment of these taxes there remains 150 billion dollars in the hands of the taxpayers, and this is enough to pay for all the goods and services that the economy can produce. Indeed it would do the public no good to have any more money left after tax payments, because if it spent more than 150 billion dollars it would merely be raising the prices of the goods bought. It would not be able to obtain more goods to consume than the country is able to produce.

Of course this illustration must not be taken to imply that a debt of this size is at all likely to come about as a result of the application of Functional Finance. As will be shown below, there is a natural tendency for the national debt to stop growing long before it comes anywhere near the astronomical figures that we have been playing with.

The unfounded assumption that current interest on the debt must be collected in taxes springs from the idea that the debt must be kept in a "reasonable" or "manageable" ratio to income (whatever that may be). If this restriction is accepted, *borrowing* to pay the interest is eliminated as soon as the limit of "reasonableness" is reached, and if we further rule out, as an indecent thought, the possibility of *printing* the money, there remains only the possibility of raising the interest payments by taxes. Fortunately there is no need to assume these limitations so long as Functional Finance is on guard against inflation, for it is the fear of inflation which is the only rational basis for suspicion of the printing of money.

Finally, there is no reason for assuming that, as a result of the continued application of Functional Finance to maintain full employment, the government must always be borrowing more money and increasing the national debt. There are a number of reasons for this.

First, full employment *can* be maintained by printing the money needed for it, and this does not increase the debt at all. It is probably advisable, however, to allow debt and money to increase together in a certain balance, as long as one or the other has to increase.

Second, since one of the greatest deterrents to private investment is the fear that the depression will come before the investment has paid for itself, the guarantee of permanent full employment will make private investment much more attractive, once investors have got over their suspicions of the new procedure. The greater private investment will diminish the need for deficit spending.

Third, as the national debt increases, and with it the sum of private wealth, there will be an increasingly yield from taxes on higher incomes and inheritances, even if the tax rates are unchanged. These higher tax payments do not represent reductions of spending by the taxpayers. Therefore the government does not have to use these proceeds to maintain the requisite rate of spending, and it can devote them to paying the interest on the national debt.

Fourth, as the national debt increases it acts as a self-equilibrating force, gradually diminishing the further need for its growth and finally reaching an equilibrium level where its tendency to grow comes completely to an end. The greater the national debt the greater is the quantity of private wealth. The reason for this is simply that for every dollar of debt owed by the government there is a private creditor who owns the government obligations (possibly through a corporation in which he has shares), and who regards these obligations as part of his private fortune. The greater the private fortunes the less is the incentive to add to them by saving out of current income. As current saving is thus discouraged by the great accumulation of past savings, spending out of current income increases (since spending is the only alternative to saving income). This increase in private spending makes it less necessary for the government to undertake deficit financing to keep total spending at the level which provides full employment. When the government debt has become so great that private spending is enough to provide the total spending needed for full employment, there is no need for any deficit financing by the government, the budget is balanced and the national debt automatically stops growing. The size of this equilibrium level of debt depends on many things. It can only be guessed at, and in the very roughest manner. My guess is that it is between 100 and 300 billion dollars. Since the level is a result and not a principle of Functional Finance the latitude of such a guess does not matter; it is not needed for the application of the laws of Functional Finance.

Fifth, if for any reason the government does not wish to see private property grow too much (whether in the form of government bonds or otherwise) it can check this by taxing the rich instead of borrowing from them, in its program of financing government spending to maintain full employment. The rich will not reduce their spending significantly, and thus the effects on the economy, apart from the smaller debt, will be the same as if the money had been borrowed from them. By this means the debt can be reduced to any desired level and kept there.

The answers to the argument against deficit spending may thus be summarized as follows:

The national debt does not have to keep on increasing;

Even if the national debt does grow, the interest on it does not have to be raised out of current taxes;

Even if the interest on the debt is raised out of current taxes, these taxes constitute only the interest on only a fraction of the benefit enjoyed from the government spending, and are not lost to the nation but are merely transferred from taxpayers to bondholders;

High income taxes need not discourage investment, because appropriate deductions for losses can diminish the capital actually risked by the investor in the same proportion as his net income from the investment is reduced.

IV

If the propositions of Functional Finance were put forward without fear of appearing too logical, criticisms like those discussed above would not be as popular as they now are, and it would not be necessary to defend Functional Finance from its friends. An especially embarrassing task arises from the claim that Functional Finance (or deficit financing, as it is frequently but unsatisfactorily called) is primarily a defense of private enterprise. In the attempt to gain popularity for Functional Finance, it has been given other names and declared to be essentially directed toward saving private enterprise. I myself have sinned similarly in previous writings in identifying it with democracy,[4] thus joining the army of salesmen who wrap up their wares in the flag and tie anything they have to sell to victory or morale.

Functional Finance is not especially related to democracy or to private enterprise. It is applicable to a communist society just as well as to a fascist society or a democratic society. It is applicable to any society in which money is used as an important element in the economic mechanism. It consists of the simple principle of

[4] In "Total Democracy and Full Employment," *Social Change* (May 1941).

giving up our preconceptions of what is proper or sound or traditional, of what "is done," and instead considering the *functions* performed in the economy by government taxing and spending and borrowing and lending. It means using these instruments simply as instruments, and not as magic charms that will cause mysterious hurt if they are manipulated by the wrong people or without due reverence for tradition. Like any other mechanism, Functional Finance will work no matter who pulls the levers. Its relationship to democracy and free enterprise consists simply in the fact that if the people who believe in these things will not use Functional Finance, they will stand no chance in the long run against others who will.

[37]

INTEREST THEORY–SUPPLY AND DEMAND FOR LOANS OR SUPPLY AND DEMAND FOR CASH

ABBA P. LERNER

New School for Social Research

WHEN I, as a Keynesian, say that the rate of interest is determined by the supply and demand for cash, i.e. the *stock* of cash and the quantity of cash that the public wishes to *hold* at various rates of interest, I do not, of course, mean to deny that in the economic universe everything is to a greater or less degree dependent on everything else. The whole system of Walrasian equations is necessary to describe the determination of the equilibrium of the economic system as a whole. Nevertheless, it seems to me that there is more meaning in my statement than is admitted by critics like Dr. Fellner and Dr. Somers,[1] who prefer to say that the rate of interest is determined by the supply and demand for loans and who declare that my statement is correct only on the assumption that all the other prices and quantities in the Walrasian scheme are given. This means that "the rate of interest equates the demand and supply of cash only in the sense in which the shoe price can also be said to perform this function if all other prices are given." [2]

It cannot be denied that the rate of interest, being the price paid for a loan, must be at the level where the demand for loans is equal to the supply of loans. But to say that the rate of interest is determined by the supply and demand for loans is unsatisfactory, because such a formulation, unlike most partial analyses of this kind, does not even give the first approximation provided by a statement like "the price of shoes is determined by the supply and demand for shoes." [3]

In the case of shoes, such a simplification from the Walrasian formulation of general equilibrium is permissible because an increase in the demand for shoes (say because a shortage of rubber makes people walk more) does not as a rule have a very important effect on the supply of shoes. In the case of *loans* this relative independence does not hold. When there is an increase in the demand for loans, say because business men want to borrow more money in order to spend it, there is likely to result from this an increase in the supply of loans. The increased spending on the construction of new factories or in the purchase of additional consumption goods will increase incomes, and part of these incomes will be saved and offered on the loan market. The part of these incomes that is not saved but spent will increase incomes still further and part of these further additions to income will be saved and offered on the loan market. Such induced increases in the supply of loans may partly or wholly offset the effect of the increase in the demand for loans. (Similarly, if there is a decrease in the supply of loans because some lenders decide to spend their money instead of lending it, this will increase the amount of money in the hands of those from whom the purchases are made, and these may directly or indirectly increase the supply of loans; or the money spent by the erstwhile lenders may flow into the hands of erstwhile borrowers who will now decrease their demand for loans.)

There may be delays in the working out of these effects. Some may argue that any increase in demand for loans can increase the supply only in a degree smaller than the increase in demand. Others may argue that the supply would increase in an equal degree and in some circumstances in a greater degree. These complications, important as they are for other purposes, are not significant for the present issue. As long as the change in demand for loans *may* have an important effect on the supply of loans (or a change in the supply of loans may have an important effect on the demand for loans, or a change in demand or supply by some can have an important effect on the demand or supply by others), we cannot use this partial analysis. We are then faced with the

[1] "Alternative Monetary Approaches to Interest Theory," this REVIEW, XXIII (1941), pp. 43–48.

[2] *Ibid.*, p. 48.

[3] The proposition that the rate of interest is determined by the supply and demand for loans is often called the "Loanable Funds" theory of interest. This phrase seems to be ideally suited to cloud the distinction between the supply and demand for *loans* and the supply and demand for the *cash* (funds) in which the loans are made.

question of whether we can find some way of correcting this fault in the partial analysis or whether we must give it up and go back to the correct but not very illuminating statement of general analysis that the rate of interest, like any other price, depends on everything in the entire economy.

One solution is to construct simplified Walrasian or general equilibrium schemes in which there are a small number of variables representing composite quantities, such as output of consumption goods in general or output of investments goods in general. Perhaps the most enlightening of these schemes and the easiest for the non-mathematical economist to understand is that constructed by Professor Oscar Lange.[4] The schemes, although they raise difficulties of their own in the unavoidable implications of some sort of homogeneity in the really non-homogeneous entities to which they refer (like the output of consumption goods or the output of investment goods or even the output of goods in general), are of great value in elucidating some of the more complex interrelationships between the different variables. But they are much more difficult to understand than the simple supply and demand partial analyses to which all of us are accustomed.

Many economists and all non-economists still do not feel quite satisfied when they are shown that there are *n* equations to determine *n* unknowns, and are not much happier when they are shown a simplified account which they do not fully understand and which they suspect of all kinds of skulduggery even though there are only six unknowns and six equations. Is it not possible to apply something like the familiar supply and demand analysis and yet give not too inaccurate an account of the determination of the rate of interest?

The partial supply and demand analysis can be salvaged. The clue to this lies in noticing that the disturbing effects of a change in demand on the supply (and vice versa) arise only in those cases where the increase in demand for loans is not for the purpose of holding the extra cash but for the purpose of spending it. To the extent that the borrower increases his own holding of cash his borrowing cannot indirectly increase the supply of loans. And even when he does spend the money he borrows, there can be no increase in the supply of loans if the person who receives the money from him keeps it and adds it to *his* previous stock of cash. In fact, if we consider all such increases of cash in the hands of all the members of society who receive any of this money in the course of its wanderings through the economy, we can say that the money which people in general wish to add to their stores of cash cannot come on to the loan market again as an additional supply of loans resulting from the original increase in demand for loans, but that the money which nobody wishes to add to his store of cash keeps on moving until it is offered again on the market for loans.[5]

Thus by bringing in the demand for cash to hold (and in parallel fashion the supply of cash), we can eliminate the effects of demand on supply (and of supply on demand) which threatened to frustrate the attempt at partial analysis. In the demand for loans we must count only that part of the demand which the borrowers, or the other people who indirectly receive the borrowed money, wish to add to their stock of cash. Similarly, in the supply of loans we must count only those loans which come from new issues of money or which the lenders are able to supply because they wish to decrease their holdings of cash. Any other loans indicate a withdrawal of cash by the lenders from other parts of the economy (where the lenders would have spent it if they had not loaned it out) and the withdrawals have the effect of increasing the demand for loans or decreasing the supply of loans in these other parts of the economy. When this is done, the corrected demand for loans consists of the demand for additional cash to be held by the borrower or by those who directly or indirectly receive the money from the borrowers when they spend their borrowings. The corrected supply of loans consists of newly created cash *plus* the cash set free by the lenders (who may

[4] "The Rate of Interest and the Optimum Propensity to Consume," *Economica*, V (N. S., 1938), pp. 12–32.

[5] It is not necessary for this to attempt to follow the adventures of the identical dollars that start the train of additional spendings and receipts. This is impossible anyway, even theoretically, unless all the money in the economy is hard cash and there is no credit whatever. We merely mean the increases in anybody's payments (and therefore in every case in somebody's receipts) which are induced directly or indirectly by the initial increase in spending by the borrowers of the new loans or by the erstwhile lenders who spend the money instead of lending it.

be lending only indirectly, spending the spare cash which eventually finds its way into the hands of the actual lenders). The demand for loans is nothing but the demand for additional cash and the supply of loans is nothing but the supply of additional or spare cash. If we add the stock of cash actually in existence to both sides of this supply and demand, and subtract the decrease in demand for cash from both sides (i.e. the cash set free and loaned out, directly or indirectly), we have the demand for loans translated into the demand for cash and the supply of loans translated into the supply of cash.

We are then tempted to deny that we have a supply-and-demand-for-loans theory of interest and to say that the rate of interest is determined by the supply and demand for the stock of cash, since it is this supply and demand for cash which determines the equilibrium of the supply and demand for loans. It is only when the supply or stock of cash is equal to the demand for it that the supply of loans is equal to the demand for them.

It cannot be overemphasized that the supply and demand for cash refers to the *stock* of cash while the supply and demand for loans refers to the *flow* of lending and borrowing which is measured as so much *per period of time.* If the stock of cash in existence is in accord with the stock that people wish to hold, there will be no attempt by individuals to increase their holdings of cash by increasing the rate of borrowing (or reducing the rate of lending) and there will be no attempt by individuals to decrease their holdings of cash by increasing the rate of lending (or decreasing the rate of borrowing). The equilibrium of the supply and demand for the stock of cash is therefore a necessary and sufficient condition for the equilibrium of the supply and demand for the flow of loans. The actual rate of borrowing must be equal to the actual rate of lending (since these are merely different aspects of the same phenomenon), and there is no desire on the part of borrowers or lenders to vary these rates of borrowing or lending.

In saying that the "cash" theory of interest is preferable to the "loans" theory, I do not deny that the actual rate of interest is in fact agreed upon by the suppliers and demanders for loans. I only mean to assert that in estimating the effect of any event on the rate of interest we are likely to be misled unless we take into account the effects of the event on the supply and demand for the stock of cash. For example, the simple "loans" theory might lead to the conclusion that an increase in the profitability of investment in new capital goods, by increasing the demand for loans, must raise the rate of interest. But if the investors and others are led by the same increase in the profitability of investment to reduce their own holdings of saving by investing or spending out of their previous stocks of cash, the supply of loans will increase more than the demand for loans and the rate of interest will fall. This is liable to be overlooked if we concentrate on the effect on the demand for loans, but is seen at once if attention is directed to the effects of the initial event on the supply and demand for the stock of cash.

It might be argued that the "loans" analysis is adequate if we consider a short period in which there is no time for the increased spending by the borrowers to bring about the increase in lending by those whose income will be increased.[6] It is true that in this case an increase in the demand for loans will have the effect of raising the rate of interest, but even then we cannot say that the rate of interest is a function of the supply and demand for loans. Rather is it a function of the *rate of change* in the supply (or demand) for loans. If there is a once for all increase in the demand for loans of this nature, there will at first be an increase in the demand for loans without any increase in the supply. After some delay, the increased spending by the lenders will increase incomes and savings. The part of the increased income which is not saved will be spent and will increase other incomes. In this way saving *immediately* increases by the amount of increase in investment (since that is the amount by

[6] For this it is necessary to assume that the increase in the profitability of investment or in the attractiveness of consumption which brings about the increase in the demand for loans (or the decrease in the supply of loans) does not induce the borrowers (or the erstwhile lenders) to increase their expenditure out of their previous holdings of cash in anticipation of the forthcoming borrowings (or reduced lendings out of their income). If there should be such an anticipatory increase in spending, the increased lending to which it gives rise may come about even before the increased demand for loans, leading to a (temporary) *fall* in the rate of interest.

which income increases in relation to consumption), and the supply of loans *gradually* expands (as the increased rate of investment raises income to the corresponding higher level) until it has increased as much as the demand for loans. After this both the supply and the demand for loans will be greater than before in the same degree and there is no reason why the rate of interest will be maintained at the higher level only if the *rate at which the demand for loans increases* continues at the higher level. The rate of interest in this case is raised not by the greater *demand* for loans but by the greater rate of increase in the demand for loans.[7]

Of course, a higher level of economic activity will probably bring with it a need for more cash to be held in connection with the greater volume of transactions, and the increase in the demand for cash will tend to raise the rate of interest. This looks something like the proposition criticized in the preceding paragraph, but there is no reason for believing that the greater need for cash that accompanies the greater volume of transactions is the same as the cash temporarily absorbed by the borrowing (which may initiate an increased volume of transactions) in the interval between the initial borrowing and the time when it results in increased income saving and lending. The increased *transactions* demand for cash may be greater or less than this transitional increase in the demand for cash, and in any case it fits perfectly into the formula that the rate of interest is determined by the supply and demand for cash.

Methodologically, Lord Keynes' contribution was to point out that partial analysis can be made a little more complicated, bringing in three or four variables instead of the Marshallian two, and yet remain manageable. For some economists who are accustomed to black and white of either the very simplest kind of partial analysis with only two variables, or else the complete Walrasian general equilibrium with everything depending on everything else, this point of Lord Keynes seems difficult to grasp. The liquidity preference theory of interest is an example of this kind of more complicated partial analysis, bringing in the supply and demand for cash to support the supply and demand for loans. Perhaps some difficulty has been caused by the shorthand method of expressing it which may seem to imply that borrowing and lending have nothing to do with the rate of interest.[8]

[7] If the demand had previously been constant, the rate of increase in the demand for loans was zero, and now during the change it is positive. When the demand for loans is stabilized at the higher level, the rate of increase in the demand for loans is again zero and the rate of interest falls to the previous level.

[8] In the article referred to above, Fellner and Somers conceive of the supply of cash as consisting of (a) the cash demand for securities, (b) the cash demand for goods, and (c) the stock of cash (considered as the supply by the owners of the cash to themselves). In parallel fashion, the demand for cash is conceived as consisting of (a) the supply of securities against cash, (b) the supply of goods against cash, and (c) the stock of cash (considered as the owners' demand of cash from themselves). In equating this supply and demand for cash the items (c) can be eliminated because being identical they are always equal to each other. The items (b) can be eliminated if we assume that the supply of each commodity is equal to its demand. This leaves only the items (a) which may indifferently be called the supply and demand for loans or the supply and demand for cash. On this interpretation it is true that the rate of interest can be considered as determined by the supply and demand for cash only if all the other prices are given,—namely in items (a).

Unfortunately the same criticism applies to the proposition that the rate of interest is determined by the supply and demand for loans. This is inevitable where the supply and demand for cash is defined so as to mean the same thing as the supply and demand for loans.

It should be observed that this account of the "loans" theory is not subject to the criticism made above of the partial or simple supply and demand analysis which was upset because the supply and the demand were not independent. Here the interdependences are taken account of only too well. It should further be observed that this account of the "cash" theory is also quite different from the partial Keynesian "cash" theory (which is defended in the present article) and indeed misses its essential feature. In the Keynesian theory, the supply and demand for cash refers to the *stock* of cash and to the desire to *hold* cash, sometimes called liquidity preference. In Fellner and Somers' article, the supply and demand for cash refers to the *flows* of cash currently offered and demanded for goods and securities. Even the existing stock of cash seems to be translated into a flow by supposing it to be offered by its owners to themselves each period. Fellner and Somers' strictures are applicable only to this "flow" account of the "cash" theory of interest. It is fitting that their strictures should be equally applicable to the theory they favor.

[38]

The American Economic Review

VOLUME XXXVIII MARCH, 1948 NUMBER ONE

ARE THERE LAWS OF PRODUCTION?*

By PAUL H. DOUGLAS

I. *Introduction*

A century and a third ago, in 1815, Malthus[1] and Sir Edward West[2] simultaneously pointed out that if successive combined doses of labor and capital were applied to a given piece of land, the amount of the product would increase by diminishing increments. Two years later this principle was adopted by Ricardo in his *Principles of Political Economy* as the basis for his theory of distribution. The joint return to labor and capital was declared by Ricardo to be governed by and to be equal to the amount of product added by the last combined dose of labor and capital, while the owners of land received as rent all sums in excess of these amounts. Since the quantities of labor and capital were not supposed to vary in relation to each other but were instead bound together in fixed and unvarying proportions, there was no way of isolating the specific contributions of these two factors as a means of determining the rates of wages and of interest. These rates were instead presumed to be regulated by cost-of-supply factors, namely, the Malthusian forces governing population which would keep wages down to a fixed minimum which was at least close to basic subsistence and the low minimum needed to compensate savers and investors. Such was the classical theory of distribution which dominated economic thinking for over sixty years.

Meanwhile, in Germany, during the 1840's, Von Thünen had theoretically broken up the combined dose of labor and capital and had pointed out that when each of the factors was separately increased but the others held constant, the product increased by diminishing

* Presidential address delivered at the Sixtieth Annual Meeting of the American Economic Association, Chicago, Illinois, December 29, 1947.

[1] T. R. Malthus, *Nature and Progress of Rent,* p. 61.

[2] Edward West, *The Application of Capital to Land* (Hollander ed., 1815) p. 54. Prior to Malthus and West, Turgot had pointed out in 1768 that successive applications of labor to land yielded diminishing increments to product. Turgot, *Oeuvres* (1844 ed.), pp. 420-21.

increments.[3] Von Thünen went on to state that the rates of wages and of interest were equal to the amounts of the product added by the last increments of each. He was thus the real discoverer of marginal productivity. Nor was this all. He reasoned that the product added by each equal increment of a factor was a constant fraction of the preceding increment of product, namely two-thirds, in the case of labor and nine-tenths, in the case of capital. This meant that it would be necessary to increase a factor in a given geometric ratio in order to increase the product by equal arithmetic amounts. This is precisely the law of the soil which Mitscherlich and W. J. Spillman later discovered,[4] and it is strikingly similar to the so-called Weber-Fechner law of physiological response. It would be most interesting to find out whether these conclusions of Von Thünen were merely happy hypotheses or whether, like so much of his work, they were based upon experimentation. Von Thünen's work, unfortunately, never had the influence which it deserved. The British, with their customary insularity of thought, virtually ignored it. The Germans, dominated by the fact-grubbing historical school, while lavishing attention upon Von Thünen's theory of location and his advocacy of $\sqrt{ap}$ as a just wage, almost completely neglected his discovery of the curve of the diminishing increment as the guiding principle for both production and distribution. Indeed, schooled as they were to believe in the relativity of economic principles, they naturally averted their gaze from what gave every evidence of being an economic law, which was independent of time and place.

It is to the glory of American economics that it was one of our own number, John Bates Clark, who at a meeting of our Association in 1888, fifty-nine years ago tonight, announced what was in effect the rediscovery of the marginal productivity principle. Clark, who had studied in Germany, had possibly been unconsciously influenced by Von Thünen, but certainly he was not consciously following him when he stated:[5]

An increasing amount of labor applied to a fixed amount of pure capital goods yields a smaller and smaller rate of return. . . . Let there be ten thousnd dollars worth of productive instruments and ten men to use them. Let each man be supposed to create by the operation a product worth three dollars

[3] J. H. Von Thünen, *Der Isolirte Staat; Zweiter Teil,* pp. 507-557-59.

[4] W. J. Spillman, *The Law of Diminishing Returns* (1924).

[5] John Bates Clark, "The Possibility of a Scientific Law of Wages," *Publications, American Economic Association,* Vol. IV (March, 1889). pp. 39-63. It was at this same session that Stuart Wood, the economist-businessman, also developed the marginal productivity theory of wages and interest and indeed went somewhat further by developing the principle of elasticity of substitution. Stuart Wood, "The Theory of Wages," *op. cit.,* pp. 5-35.

a day. Raise now the number of workmen to twenty and let the capital remain the same and each man will create less than before. A day's product will be 3−X dollars. Each successive unit of labor employed in connection with a fixed amount of pure capital produces less than any of its predecessors. . . . General wages tend to be equal to the actual product created by the last laborer that is added to the social working force.[6]
The earnings of capital are subject to identically the same law as those of labor; they are fixed by the product of the last increment that is brought into the field. . . . Let the labor supply remain fixed and let capital increase and each increment of the latter, as it enters the productive field finds that it can create less than any of its predecessors. The general law of diminishing returns is two-sided.[7]

During the next decade Clark completed his theory in a series of subtle articles, and in 1899 gave it final expression in his book *The Distribution of Wealth.*

In the meantime, in 1894, the extraordinarily gifted Philip Wicksteed showed in his pathbreaking little essay, *The Coordination of the Laws of Distribution,* that if production were characterized by a homogeneous linear function of the first degree (that is, if when each and all of the factors of production were doubled or tripled, product would increase in the same proportion), then with each factor receiving its marginal product, the total product would be absorbed in payments to the factors without either surplus or deficit. This essay of Wicksteed's fluttered the mathematical dovecotes. Edgeworth, who in his *Mathematical Psychics,* had attempted to prove, by quotations from Owen Meredith's *Lucille,* that men should receive larger incomes than women, now dismissed with elegant irony the theory that production followed a homogeneous linear function. Pareto's attempted refutation was almost pure sophistry in which, by limiting the market, he sought to prove that product would not increase in proportion to the factors. It remained for Wicksell to give the most sensible treatment of this subject when he pointed out that while the homogeneous production function could not be expected to apply over the whole range of output within a plant, nevertheless under perfect competition, each firm would tend to carry its scale of output to the point where neither increasing nor decreasing returns prevailed but where instead the rate of return was constant.[8] Since industries were merely aggregates of firms and the economy as a whole was an aggregate of industries, it was presumed that the linear function tended, therefore, to be true of society

[6] *Publications, American Economic Association* (Mar., 1889), p. 49.

[7] *Ibid.,* p. 53.

[8] Knut Wicksell, *Lectures on Political Economy,* Vol. I, pp. 101-33.

as a whole at its growing points. Under these conditions, Wicksteed's conclusion held that the payment of the marginal products to each unit of the respective factors of production exactly distributed the product.

At this point, the theoretical discussion of marginal productivity was largely allowed to lapse, except for the clarifications and refinements which were introduced by our chairman, Professor Carver and by F. M. Taylor.

Over the course of the decades which followed, two tendencies in economic teaching became fairly evident. The first was a form of split personality or scientific schizophrenia, which developed in our economics departments. In the classes in economic theory, the principles of pure marginal productivity were taught, uncontaminated by any idea that there might be imperfect competition in either the product or the factor markets, or that there might be unemployment for reasons other than a wage rate in excess of social marginal productivity. This group taught that labor received the amount which its last unit added to the total product multiplied by the number of workers, while the return to capital was similarly determined. Neither trade union nor governmental action was needed to give to labor its own marginal product under conditions of full employment. All that was required was for the employers to bid competitively against each other for labor and this condition was commonly assumed to exist. But if government and unions disturbed the system of *laissez-faire* by raising wage rates above the social margin, this could only be effected by decreasing the numbers employed and hence creating unemployment.

In the classes which dealt with labor economics, however, a different doctrine was taught. Here marginal productivity was muted and the theory of the Webbs, as developed in *Industrial Democracy,* was stressed. It was the pressure of the market competition for lower prices which, weighing more heavily upon the successive levels of sellers because of their heavier overhead costs, tended to drive down wages and to worsen working conditions. Unions and governmental legislation operating through the imposition of common rules, could not only protect the workers from this competition but could raise the general standard of living.

It would be a fascinating task to analyze the differences between these two sets of theories; one dealing primarily with real and the other, with money wages; one assuming the relative absence and the other, the presence of unemployment; one postulating free and perfect competition between employers and between workers; the other absorbed by the power struggles of combinations of employers and workers. But such is not our present task. It is enough to point out, that both of these two widely conflicting doctrines have been taught within our economics departments with little effort made by either set of protagonists to determine the relative truth of either, or their compatability. So far has this confusion of doctrine gone, that I have known professors, who teaching both theory and labor economics, have instilled the pure doctrine of John Bates Clark during one hour, and then during the next hour have taught as economic gospel the bargain theories of Sidney and Beatrice Webb!

The effect upon our students of this dualism in the winds of doctrine has been most unfortunate. It has caused some to shrug their shoulders and to dismiss all economic teaching with the words of Omar, so beloved by sophomores,

> Myself when young, did eagerly frequent
> Doctor and Saint, and heard great argument
> About it and about; but evermore
> Came out by the same door where in I went.

Others, like chameleons, have given diametrically different answers to identical questions, depending on which instructor asked them. But to every candidate for the Ph.D. degree, there has loomed the nightmare of that dreaded hour when in his oral examination, he must face both sets of teachers and know that the answers which would be judged right by one school would be judged wrong by the other. Such a state of affairs is at once both ridiculous and scandalous, and as long as it continues, there is little hope for scientific progress or even sound mental health among economists.

But within the ranks of the theorists themselves, a serious intellectual slovenliness, unfortunately, set in. Convinced that the marginal productivity curves of the factors were negatively inclined, they contented themselves with drawing the curves as sloping downwards and to the right, but took apparently little interest in trying to determine what the positions and slopes of these curves actually were. Thus I have seen an experienced instructor on successive days draw widely differing marginal productivity curves for labor, one declining very gradually, one at an angle of 45°, and the third plunging sharply downward. Moreover, this instructor gave every evidence of not realizing that there was any significant difference between these curves nor did he indicate whether he was drawing the curves upon an arithmetic or a double logarithmic scale. Indeed, the slope of the curve seemed to be determined partly by chance, partly by the stance of the instructor, and partly by the degree to which he happened to bend his arm!

The orthodox theorists may urge in self defense that they do not have the statistical information which would permit them to approximate the production function, the elasticities of the marginal productivity curves, or to determine the degree to which the actual distribution of the product conforms to what one would expect from the nature of the production function itself. But the sad truth of the matter is that they have made little effort to find out and have instead turned their backs upon inductive research and have, in effect, been school men living within ivy-clad towers.

II. *The Early Studies of the Cobb-Douglas Production Function*

It was twenty years ago last spring that, having computed indexes for American manufacturing of the numbers of workers employed by years from 1899 to 1922, as well as indexes of the amounts of fixed capital in manufacturing deflated to dollars of approximately constant purchasing power, and then plotting these on a log scale together with the Day index of physical production for manufacturing, I observed that the product curve lay consistently between the two curves for the factors of production and tended to be approximately a quarter of the relative distance between the curve of the index for labor, which showed the least increase over the period, and that of the index for capital which showed the most. Since I was lecturing at Amherst College at the time, I suggested to my friend, Charles W. Cobb, that we seek to develop a formula which would measure the relative effect of labor and capital upon product during this period. We were both familiar with the Wicksteed analysis and Cobb was, of course, well versed in the history of the Euler theorem. At his suggestion, therefore, the sum of the exponents was tentatively made equal to unity in the formula

$$P = bL^kC^{1-k} \tag{1}$$

Here it was only necessary to find the values of b and k. This was done by the method of least squares and the value of k was found to be .75. This was almost precisely what we had expected because of the relative distance of the product curve from those of the two factors. The value of the capital exponent, or $1-k$, was, of course, then taken as .25. Using these values, we then computed indexes of what we would theoretically have expected the product to be in each of the years had it conformed precisely to the formula. We found that the divergencies between the actual and theoretical product were not great since in only one year did they amount to more than 11 per cent, and that except for two years, the deviation of the differences was precisely what we would expect from the imperfect nature of the indexes of capital and labor. Since our index of capital measured the quantities which were *available for,* rather than their relative *degree of use,* it did not make allowance for the idle capital in periods of depression nor for the more intensive use of capital during years of prosperity. Similarly, our index of labor did not make allowance for failures to work full time in the bad years, nor for overtime hours which were worked in the good years. It was, therefore, to be expected that the actual product (P) would exceed the theoretical product (P') in years of prosperity and would fall below it in years of depression. So in fact it did in every year except the war years of 1918 and 1919. Professor Cobb and I, therefore, regarded these deviations as additional evidence of the general validity of the formula for normal times.

Still another striking bit of evidence was found in the fact that under perfect competition with a production formula of this type we would expect a factor to receive as its share of the product, the proportion indicated by its exponent. From the income studies of the National Bureau of Economic Research, we found that labor's share of the net value product of manufacturing during the decade 1909-1918, was estimated at 74.1 per cent, or almost precisely the value of the exponent for labor.

Professor Cobb and I embodied the results of our inquiries in a paper which we read before this Association exactly twenty years ago tonight.[9] We then determined to analyze more of such time series. Cobb computed indexes of labor, capital, and product in Massachusetts manufacturing for the period 1890-1926, and found the value of k to bc .743. Interestingly enough, it was also found that the average of labor's share of the net value of the product in that state for that period was .74, or a virtual identity with the value of k.[10] A similar study, which was made in Chicago by Mr. Director for New South Wales manufacturing for the period 1901-1927, found k to have a value of .65.

There the matter more or less rested when my book, *The Theory of Wages,* appeared in 1934. Three years later, with the aid of Mrs. Marjorie Handsaker, I resumed our analysis of time series, and after working up data for Victorian manufacturing for the period 1907-1929, we found the value of k under the k and $1\text{-}k$ formula to be .71.[11] Labor's share of the net product or W/P was found to be .61 for this period.

We then introduced two important new features into our investiga-

[9] C. W. Cobb and Paul H. Douglas, "A Theory of Production," *Am. Econ. Rev.*, Suppl., Vol. XVIII (Mar., 1928), pp. 139-65.

[10] See Douglas, *The Theory of Wages,* pp. 159-66.

[11] Handsaker and Douglas, "The Theory of Marginal Productivity as Tested by Data for Manufacturing in Victoria," *Quart. Jour. Econ.*, Vols. LII and LIII (Nov., 1937 and Feb., 1938), pp. 1-36 and 215-54.

tions. An able young American scholar, David Durand,[12] had published in 1937, an excellent critical article of the earlier material, and had urged that the restricted function of

$$P = bL^kC^{1-k} \quad (1)$$

be abandoned for one in which the exponent for capital was independently determined. As he correctly pointed out, the use of the k and $1\text{-}k$ function assumed the existence of an economic law which it should be one of the tasks of science to test, namely, the assumption of true constant returns. If we permitted the exponent for capital to be independently determined, it would then be possible for the sum of the exponents to be either greater or less than unity and hence to show true increasing and decreasing as well as constant returns to scale. We therefore decided that Durand's suggestion should be adopted and that we should try to find the values in terms of the formula:

$$P = bL^kC^j \quad (2)$$

The second change was to broaden our fields of investigation. Hitherto, we had dealt only with time studies and had found the values of our exponents from index numbers of labor, capital, and product within a given economy, with each year serving as a separate observation. Here we measured the effect upon total physical product, of changes in the physical quantities of labor and of capital and from these we derived curves of diminishing incremental physical productivity of the classical type. We now determined to open up another field for investigation and to make cross-section analyses between industries in a given economy for specific years. Thus the annual statistics of manufacturing for the British Dominions (although not the British Census of Production itself) and the decennial and quinquennial *Censuses for Manufacturing* for the United States up until 1921 showed aggregates for each of a wide variety of industries from which it was possible to compute: (1) aggregates of the average numbers employed, including wage earners, clerical and salaried employees, officials and generally firm members and working proprietors (L), (2) aggregates of capital (C) expressed in terms of dollars including both fixed and working capital, and (3) aggregates of the *net* value of product added by manufacturing expressed in terms of dollars (P).

In these studies, differences between industries in the quantities of their net value product were presumed to be a function of the total

[12] David Durand, "Some Thoughts on Marginal Productivity with Special Reference to Professor Douglas' Analysis," *Jour. Pol. Econ.*, Vol. XLV (Dec., 1937), pp. 740-58.

number of employees and of the total quantities of fixed and working capital with each industry serving as a separate observation. This is obviously a somewhat different production function from that which is based on the time series. The quantities of labor used are physical quantities and though capital is expressed in value terms, these are also rough measurements of relative physical amounts. But since product is also expressed in value terms, this is the result not only of: (a) changes in the increments to the total physical product but also of (b) changes in the exchange value, or the relative price per unit of the products of an industry. The net values turned out by the respective industries will, therefore, be affected in these cases not only by the quantities produced but also by the respective demand curves for the products. Changes in each of these variables will affect the total exchange value produced.

Some critics will, of course, object that this second type of study, since it includes both quantities and prices, does not measure production at all and is in no sense a test of marginal productivity theory. It is certainly a somewhat different type of production function from that which is based on index numbers of quantities. But marginal productivity theory has always implicitly dealt in terms of values as well as of physical quantities since it assumes that the supplies of labor and capital in each of the various industries are regulated by the principle that the respective marginal laborers will produce equal amounts of value as will the marginal units of capital. In the apportionment of resources within an economy, therefore, the principle of diminishing incremental value productivity is an essential part of economic theory and is worthy of consideration. There is no reason why a production function which deals with it should not also be worthy of consideration and treatment.

Although interrupted by the war, we now have completed six cross-section or inter-industry studies for American manufacturing, namely, for the years 1889, 1899, 1904, 1909, 1914, and 1919; four cross-section studies for Canada covering the years 1923, 1927, 1935, and 1937; three studies for Victoria for the years 1910-11, 1923-24, and 1927-28; one study for New South Wales for 1933-34, and five studies for the Commonwealth of Australia, namely, 1912, 1922-23, 1926-27, 1934-35, and 1936-37. Two of my students, Messrs. G. Brinegar and K. O. Campbell, have just finished such a study for Queensland for 1937-38, and two more, Messrs. B. Solomon and N. A. Deif, are completing another study for New Zealand for 1926-27. In all, therefore, twenty-one cross-section studies have been carried through by our Chicago group to add to our previous four time studies, namely, for the United States, Massachusetts, New South Wales, and Victoria. In addition, two New Zealand economists, Max Brown[13] and J. W. Williams,[14] have carried through two time studies for New Zealand while the latter has also carried through a cross-section study for that country, as has G. W. G. Browne[15] for South Africa. We have, therefore, records for a total of twenty-nine inductive studies of the production function instead of the three which were reported upon thirteen years ago in *The Theory of Wages*.

In these investigations which have been carried out over the last two decades, we have had the assistance of a devoted and, I believe, competent group of associates, and in the aggregate many tens of thousands of hours have been spent upon the work. I am deeply indebted to this group, and while I am solely responsible for any errors which may lie within the work, my associates are chiefly entitled to any credit which may be forthcoming.[16]

Since these studies were carried out over a period of many years and since there were differences between countries and between years within a country in the basic data used, and since we were also constantly trying to improve our methods, it was inevitable that some dissimilarities should have developed in the precise content of the categories used and in the methods of attack. We have now ironed out a great many of these differences, and I believe that with a few exceptions which will be later noted, the results have now been made roughly comparable. It is hoped that in the next few months they may be made completely so.

III. *The Main Results of the Study of the Production Function in Manufacturing*

We can summarize the main results of these studies in three tables. Table I brings together the main results for manufacturing in the

[13] See an unpublished Ph.D. thesis at Cambridge by Max Brown, *The Relation Between Capital and Labour in New Zealand*.

[14] J. W. Williams, "Professor Douglas' Production Function," *Econ. Record*, Vol. XXV (1945), pp. 55-63.

[15] G. W. G. Browne, "The Production Function for the South African Manufacturing Industry," *So. African Jour. Econ.*, Vol. XI (Dec., 1943), pp. 258-68.

[16] First, of course, I am indebted to my chief associate during this period, namely, Grace Gunn, and after her to Marjorie L. Handsaker, Patricia Ogburn, Martin Bronfenbrenner, Ernest Olson, and Estelle Mass. But we have also had the faithful aid of numerous research assistants, computers, and draftsmen, among whom have been Yetta Abend, Helen Butcher, Julia Elliott Lewis, Oscar Seltzer, K. Sanow, H. Minsky, B. Nimer, William L. Slayton, Betty Roth, Donna Allen, Mitchell Locks, Y. K. Wong and Margaret Labadie. My colleague H. G. Lewis has also been most helpful in his criticisms and suggestions, as have John H. Smith and Colin Clark.

United States, as does Table II, for Australia; while Table III covers the investigations for the three British Dominions of New Zealand, South Africa, and Canada.

We may properly begin with a consideration of the American results, which include four time series studies for the period 1899-1922, and six cross-section or inter-industry investigations for the various census years from 1889 to 1919. It is unfortunate that the statistics of capital were omitted from the *United States Census of Manufactures* after 1919 and that we have been unable to continue our analysis of American data beyond the dates stated. Fortunately, the British Dominions in their admirable annual *Censuses of Production* have continued to collect statistics on the amounts of capital invested and this has permitted us to carry on studies for these countries in more recent times.

The four sets of time studies for the United States show somewhat differing results because of the differences which exist between the series of index numbers for labor and product. The precise nature of these series is described in the footnotes to Table I. It is believed that Series II, III, and IV, are appreciable improvements over the original Cobb-Douglas series or Series I. It will be observed that Series II and III, which use total man years (including clerical employees as well as wage earners) and total standard man hours respectively, as the measure of labor, show *k's* with values of .78 and .73 respectively. Series IV, which eliminates secular trends from each of the three basic series and expresses each observation as a percentage of its respective trend, gives *k* a value of .63. The value of *j* varies from .15 under Series II to .30 under Series IV. On the whole, Series II is the one in which the definition of the factors of production is most comparable to that of the cross-section or inter-industry studies, but Series IV avoids the dangers connected with the downward bias of the index of production and also eliminates the factor of time.

Five of the six inter-industries studies show lower values for *k* than do Series I, II, and III of the time studies. The *k*'s average .63 for the six cross-section years with the average of the *j*'s amounting to .34. The values of *k* and *j* for the initial and terminal years of 1889 and 1919, however, deviate appreciably from this average. Those for the earlier years have lower values of *k* and higher values of *j*, while in 1919 this tendency is reversed. The values of the exponents during the four middle years of 1899, 1904, 1909, and 1914, however, do exhibit a marked stability around the general average, with the *k*'s ranging between .61 and .65, and the *j*'s between .31 and .37.

It will be observed that in three cross-section studies, the values of *k* and *j* are many times their respective standard errors, the *k*'s from

TABLE I.—THE VALUES OF THE PRODUCTION FUNCTION FOR AMERICAN MANUFACTURING 1889–1922

Years		$P=bL^kC^j$						$P=bL^kC^{1-k}$	
		k	σ_k	j	σ_j	$k+j$	b	k	σ_k
A. Time series									
Series I[a]	1899–1922	.81	±.15	.23	±.06	1.04	.84	.75	±.04
Series II[b]	1899–1922	.78	±.14	.15	±.08	.93	1.38	.90	±.04
Series III[c]	1899–1922	.73	±.12	.25	±.05	.98	1.12	.76	±.04
Series IV[d]	1899–1922	.63	±.15	.30	±.05	.93	1.35	.69	±.05
B. Cross-section or inter-industry studies based on industry aggregates[e]									
Year	N								
1889	363	.51	±.03	.43	±.03	.94	58.34	.53	±.03
1899	332	.62	±.02	.33	±.02	.95	106.43	.66	±.02
1904	336	.65	±.02	.31	±.02	.96	107.40	.68	±.21
1909	258	.63	±.02	.34	±.02	.97	90.99	.66	±.02
1914	340	.61	±.03	.37	±.02	.98	81.66	.63	±.02
1919	556	.76	±.02	.25	±.02	1.01	244.21	.75	±.02
Average		.63		.34		.97		.65	

[a] The original Cobb-Douglas series of Labor, Capital, and Product as published in the original paper in 1927, were as follows: (1) Labor (L) = average number of employed wage earners only. Salaried employees, officials, working proprietors, etc., were *not* included; (2) Capital (C) = value of plant, buildings, and tools and machinery reduced to dollars of constant purchasing power with annual increments of investment divided by a specially constructed index of the relative cost of capital goods in which the wholesale prices of metals and metal products, of building materials, and of wages were given the respective weights of 4, 2, and 3; (3) Product (P) = the original Day index of physical production as published in the *Review of Economic Statistics*, Vol. II (1920), pp. 328–29, and Vol. VI (1923), p. 201. For a fuller description see Cobb and Douglas, "A Theory of Production," *Am. Econ. Rev.*, Vol. XVIII, Suppl. (Mar., 1928), pp. 139–65.

[b] The basic data used in Series II differ from those in Series I in that (1) labor now includes clerical and salaried workers as well as wage earners; (2) The basic index of physical production used was the Day-Thomas revision as it appeared in *The Growth of Manufactures, 1899–1923*, Census Monograph VIII, instead of the earlier Day study which was used in Series I. Values for the intercensal years were interpolated by the use of the earlier Day series, while I constructed a new index for leather. See Douglas, *The Theory of Wages*, pp. 174–76. The Day-Thomas index gave slightly lower values for P for the terminal years than the earlier index.

[c] The main difference which distinguishes Series III from Series II is that Labor (L) is defined to be the *relative total standard man hours* worked in the various years by the combined force of wage earners and clerical and salaried employees. This was obtained by multiplying (a) the indexes of employment for the various years by (b) the indexes of the length in manufacturing of the standard working week. For data and methods see Douglas, *Real Wages in the United States*, pp. 546–47.

[d] The essential distinguishing feature of Series IV is that the factor of time was eliminated from the basic data, not from the logs of data. This was done by fitting trends to each of the three series and expressing each index for a given year as a percentage of its trend. The basic data themselves were, however, identical with those used in Series II.

[e] The series of Labor, Capital, and Product in the six cross-section studies have now been reduced to an almost completely comparable basis: (1) Labor (L) = average number of wage

17 to 38 times their standard errors and the *j*'s from 12 to 18 times as great as their standard errors.

On the whole, we should not be surprised by the fact that we obtain higher values for *k* and lower values for *j* in our first three time series studies than we do for the cross-section studies. For as we have pointed out, the two functions are, in fact, somewhat different and we should not necessarily expect identical results. Moreover, in the time studies, there tends to be a systematic downward bias to the index of production which keeps it closer to the index of labor than it should be in reality and hence gives an excessive value to *k*. This downward bias is caused by two factors: (1) Since the indexes are primarily based on the quantities of raw material produced, they do not include the increased fabrication and reworking of these materials which is a pronounced, although not a universal, tendency of industry. (2) It is in practice not possible to include with sufficient rapidity the new products which are continually pushing themselves forward, nor to drop in adequate time the products which are becoming obsolete. The net result is to keep the index numbers of Product (*P*), particularly during the latter years of a given period, closer to Labor (*L*) than in reality they should be and hence *k* is raised above and *j* is depressed below their "true" values.

This weakness is absent from the cross-section or inter-industry studies, which are made for a given year, and we would, therefore, expect the *k*'s to be lower and the *j*'s to be higher in this group of studies. Such is, in fact, exactly the case.

It may be of some significance that when the factor of time is eliminated from each of the three basic series of Labor, Capital, and Product, and the deviations from the trends are studied (as in Series IV), that the true value of *k* for the period of 1899-1922 is reduced to .63. This is identical with the average value of *k* for the six years for which inter-industry studies were made.

It may also be of some significance that in three of the four time

earners, salaried employees, supervisory officials, firm members, and working proprietors; (2) Capital (*C*) = total fixed and working capital; (3) Product (*P*) = gross sales value minus (a) cost of raw materials, (b) cost of fuel, heat, power, and rent, (c) taxes and insurance payments, (d) amounts paid to contractors, (e) cost of repairs, (f) sundries. No deduction has been made for the depreciation of fixed capital except that included under the heading of "repairs." For earlier studies on four of these years see Gunn and Douglas, "The Production Function for American Manufacturing for 1919," *Am. Econ. Rev.*, Vol. XXXI (Mar., 1941) pp. 67–80; Gunn and Douglas, "The Production Function for American Manufacturing for 1914," *Jour. Pol. Econ.*, Vol. L (Aug., 1942), pp. 595–602; Bronfenbrenner and Douglas, "Cross-Section Studies in the Cobb-Douglas Function," *Jour. Pol. Econ.*, Vol. XLVII (Dec., 1939), pp. 761–85; Daly, Olson and Douglas, "The Production Function for Manufacturing in the United States in 1904," *Jour. Pol. Econ.*, Vol. LI (Feb., 1943), pp. 61–65. A more complete description of the methods and results for 1889 will shortly be published by Miss Estelle Mass.

studies and in five of the six cross-section studies, the sum of k and j is slightly less than unity. While this by no means establishes the reality of true diminishing returns, since the differences between $k + j$ and unity are well within the range of the standard errors, there is at least a faint suggestion to that effect. It is possible that American manufacturing industry during this period may have exceeded the optimum size and that the desire for the power and prestige which is attached to bigness may have caused firms to be conducted on a larger scale than that which was justified by the most efficient combination of the factors of production.

While all due caution in drawing conclusions should be observed, it would seem that the most likely long-run norm for k during the period covered was between .63 and .64; and for j was approximately .34. This would mean that a change of one per cent in the quantity of labor (unaccompanied by any change in the quantity of capital) would normally result during this period in a change in the same direction of about sixty-three or sixty-four hundredths of one per cent in the quantity of product, and that similarly a change of one per cent in quantity of capital (unaccompanied by any change in the quantity of labor) would normally result, during this period, in a change in the same direction of about thirty-four hundredths of one per cent. If both factors of production were increased by one per cent, then the total product would normally increase during this period by from ninety-seven to ninety-eight hundredths of one per cent.

If we disregard the slight suggestion of decreasing returns and treat the most probable sum of the exponents as equal to unity, then an increase of one per cent in the quantities of both labor and capital would normally result in a corresponding increase of one per cent in product. A one per cent increase in the quantity of labor alone would normally be accompanied, during this period, by an increase of approximately two-thirds of one per cent in product and an increase of one per cent in the quantity of capital alone would normally be accompanied by an approximate increase of one-third of one per cent in the product. Perhaps this is as close a tentative conclusion as we should draw for this period although further studies may lead to some revision of these results.

Since under these conditions (*i.e.*, $k + j = 1.0$) the elasticity of the marginal productivity curves for a given factor is equal to the reciprocal of the exponent for the other factors, that is $e_L = \frac{1}{1\text{-}k}$ and $e_C = \frac{1}{1\text{-}j}$, it follows that the approximate elasticity of the normal marginal productivity curve for labor during this period would seem to be not far from 3.0, and for capital, to be around 1.5[17]

Let us now turn to the examination of the two time series and nine cross-section studies which have been made for Australia, and which are summarized in Table II, with its accompanying notes. In the Victorian time study, k has a value of .84 and j of .23, while in the New South Wales study, the value of k is .78, and that of j is .20. It should be noticed, however, that the respective standard errors of k and j are quite high and that the values of k under the original formula ($P = bL^kC^{1-k}$) vary somewhat from those obtained under the second formula.

As we would expect from the reasons which have been given, the values of k in the nine cross-section studies for Australia are somewhat lower. The combined average of the k's was .60 and of the j's was .37. Their average sum was, therefore, .97. Here it will be observed that we get identical results with either formula since the average of the k's under formula (1) is also .60. It should also be noted that the values of k are from 8 to 14 times and the j's from 3 to 10 times their standard errors.

The results for the five Commonwealth studies differ somewhat from those for the separate states, having somewhat lower k's and higher j's. Thus, in the Commonwealth, the average of the k's is .55, with a spread in individual years between .49 and .64, while the average for the four state studies is .65. On the other hand, the j's average .43 in the Commonwealth, as contrasted with .20 in the state studies.[18] After the text

[17] The marginal productivity of labor is

$$\frac{\partial P}{\partial L} = \frac{k}{L} P = \frac{k}{L} bL^{k}C^{j} = MP_L.$$

The elasticity of the marginal productivity curve for labor is then defined as

$$\eta = \frac{1}{\frac{(MP_L)}{L}} \cdot \frac{MP_L}{L} = \frac{1}{\frac{k(k-1)P}{L^2}} \cdot \frac{\frac{kP}{L}}{L},$$

then

$$\eta = \frac{1}{k-1}.$$

The flexibility of the marginal productivity curve for labor is defined as the reciprocal of the elasticity of this curve or

$$\phi_L = \frac{1}{\eta} = k - 1.$$

[18] The values of k and j are each relatively large in relation to their standard errors.

TABLE II.—THE VALUES OF THE PRODUCTION FUNCTION FOR MANUFACTURING IN AUSTRALIA

Years	N	$P=bL^kC^j$						$P=bL^kC^{1-k}$	
		k	σ_k	j	σ_j	$k+j$	b	k	σ_k
A. Time series							.71		
Victoria[a] 1907–29	22	.84	±.34	.23	±.17	1.07	.71	.71	±.07
New South Wales[b] 1901–27	26	.78	±.12	.20	±.08	.98	1.14	.86	±.05
B. Cross-section or inter-industry studies									
Australia[c] 1912	85	.52	±.05	.47	±.05	.99	15.87	.52	±.04
Australia[c] 1922–23	87	.53	±.05	.49	±.05	1.02	16.49	.52	±.05
Australia[c] 1926–27	85	.59	±.05	.34	±.04	.93	77.26	.64	±.05
Australia[c] 1934–35	138	.64	±.04	.36	±.04	1.00	39.79	.64	±.04
Australia[c] 1936–37	87	.49	±.04	.49	±.04	.98	21.57	.50	±.04
Victoria[d] 1910–11	34	.74	±.08	.25	±.11	.99	42.87	.75	±.08
Victoria[d] 1923–24	38	.62	±.08	.31	±.10	.93	96.93	.61	±.08
Victoria[d] 1927–28	35	.59	±.07	.27	±.09	.86	207.49	.60	±.05
New South Wales[d] 1933–34	125	.65	±.04	.34	±.03	.99	53.70	.66	±.03
Average all Commonwealth and state studies		.60		.37		.97		.60	
Average Commonwealth studies only		.55		.43		.98		.56	
Average state studies only		.65		.29		.94		.66	

[a] The Victorian index numbers for Labor, Capital, and Product from which the results were computed, were constituted as follows: (1) Labor (L) = average number of persons employed including wage earners, salaried employees, supervisory officials, and working employers; (2) Capital (C) = fixed capital reduced to dollars of constant purchasing power but excluding land values and working capital; (3) Product (P) = index of physical production using 1911 value weights. See Handsaker and Douglas, "The Theory of Marginal Productivity Tested by Data for Manufacturing in Victoria," *Quart. Jour. Econ.*, Vol. LII (Nov., 1937), pp. 1–36.

[b] The New South Wales study is based on series for Labor, Capital, and Product, which are virtually identical in their definition with those of Victoria. The capital index differs from that constructed earlier by Mr. Director in that it does not provide for the replacement at differing price levels for the estimated depreciation on capital. For the Director study, see Douglas, *The Theory of Wages*, pp. 167–172.

[c] In the Commonwealth cross-section studies, the terms are defined as follows: (1) Labor (L) = average number employed of wage earners and salaried employees but generally excluding working proprietors (except in 1934–35); (2) Capital (C) = value of plant and machinery, buildings, and land, but excluding working capital. The exclusion of working capital is the chief dissimilarity between this series and the definition of total capital used in the case of the United States and Canadian cross-section studies. We will try to revise the Australian capital figures to include working capital but this may be difficult. (3) Product (P) = value added by manufacturing. For all the years except 1934–35, this was defined as gross sales value minus (a) cost of materials used, (b) cost of fuel and light, and (c) cost of replacing tools and repairs to plants. In the 1934–35 study estimated deductions were made for fire insurance and workmen's compensation premiums, and also for estimated depreciation rates on the various types of capital goods used based on the rates estimated in the Production Bulletin, No. 29, *Commonwealth Bureau of Census and Statistics*. For a further discussion of these issues, see Gunn

for this article had been prepared, Keith Campbell and George Brinegar, in their Queensland study for 1937-38, found *k* to have a value of .58 and *j* one of .45.[19]

Since the sum of the exponents tends to be slightly less than unity, there is an added slight suggestion of true diminishing returns. But here again, since the difference is less than the standard errors of estimate, we should be chary about drawing definite conclusions.

If we choose .60 as the most probable "normal" value of *k* and .37 as the corresponding value of *j*, this would mean that the approximate elasticity of the marginal productivity curve in Australia for labor was somewhere around 2.7 and for capital of about 1.7.

The third set of results which we should consider are those for New Zealand, Canada, and South Africa. These are shown in Table III. Using the formula of *k* and 1-*k*, Max Brown found for New Zealand a value of .51 for *k* for the period 1915-1935,[20] and when we reworked the Brown series with the second formula, we found values of .42 for *k* and .49 for *j*. It is interesting that in the single cross-section study which has been made for New Zealand, namely, that made by Williams for 1938-39, *k* has a value of .46 and *j* of .51.[20a] In the four Canadian studies which we made for so-called "normal" years, the *k*'s range between .43 and .50, with an average of .47, and the *j*'s between .48 and .58, with an average of slightly more than .52. There is a considerable degree of steadiness in these results, which seem to indicate an elasticity of the marginal productivity curve for labor in that country as slightly less than 2.0 for the years studied and of capital as slightly more than that figure.

One of the most interesting studies which has been made is that by G. W. G. Browne for South Africa for 1937-38. Taking the seventeen main groups of industry and treating all labor as homogeneous, Browne

---

and Douglas, "The Production Function for Australian Manufacturing," *Quart. Jour. Econ.*, Vol. LVI (Nov., 1941), pp. 108–129.

[d] The definitions of terms in the studies for the separate Australian states were substantially similar to those in the four Commonwealth studies, except that (1) working proprietors were included in the definition of labor; (2) the estimated value of land was deducted from the capital figures; (3) deductions were made from the value of product for (a) the estimated cost of local and state and federal taxes, (b) estimated fire insurance and workmen's compensation premiums, and (c) allowances for depreciation upon buildings, plant, and machinery. These were also the methods used in the Commonwealth Study of 1934–35. See Gunn and Douglas, "Further Measurements of Marginal Productivity," *Quart. Jour. Econ.*, Vol. LIV (May 1940), pp. 399–428.

[19] See an unpublished manuscript study by Keith O. Campbell and George K. Brinegar, *The Production Function for Queensland Manufacturing in 1937-38* (1947).

[20] Brown omitted the war years of 1916-17 and 1917-18.

[20a] In the cross-section study just completed for New Zealand, 1926-27, *k* has a value of .48 and *j* of .53.

TABLE III.—THE VALUES OF THE PRODUCTION FUNCTION FOR MANUFACTURING IN NEW ZEALAND, CANADA, AND SOUTH AFRICA

Years		N	$P=bL^kC^j$						$P=bL^kC^{1-k}$	
			k	σ_k	j	σ_j	$k+j$	b	k	σ_k
A. Time studies										
New Zealand[a] (Brown)	1915–16 1918–35	18	.42	±.11	.49	±.03	.91	2.03	.51	±.03
New Zealand[b] (Williams)	1923–40	18	—	—	—	—	—	—	.54	±.02
B. Cross-section or inter-industry studies										
South Africa[c] (Browne)	1937–38	17	.66	±.08	.32	±.08	.98	54.48	—	—
South Africa[d] (Browne)	1937–38	85	.65	—	.37	±.08	1.02	55.25	—	—
Canada[e]	1923	167	.48	±.04	.48	±.04	.96	48.53	.52	±.04
Canada[e]	1927	163	.46	±.04	.52	±.04	.98	33.04	.48	±.04
Canada[e]	1935	165	.50	±.04	.52	±.04	1.02	22.23	.48	±.04
Canada[e]	1937	164	.43	±.04	.58	±.04	1.01	15.42	.42	±.04
New Zealand[f] (Williams)	1938–39	61	.46	—	.51	—	.97	.73	—	—

[a] Dr. Max Brown, in his study, *The Relation Between Capital and Labour in New Zealand* (an unpublished doctoral dissertation at Cambridge University), defined Product (P) as the total money value of production divided by the price index of locally produced goods. His index of Labor (L) was one of total *man-hours* worked, *i.e.*, numbers employed multiplied by the length of the standard working week plus or minus the hours of overtime worked or short time suffered in the various years. The index of Capital (C) was the value of buildings, plant, and machinery (*i.e.*, fixed capital) with the annual increments of investment deflated by a price index of the cost of capital goods. We have fitted the function $P=bL^kC^j$ to the Brown data as well as the $P=bL^kC^{1-k}$ formula which Brown originally used.

[b] Professor Williams computed his indexes as follows: (1) Product (P) = (a) value added by manufacturing (*i.e.*, gross value minus cost of materials, fuel, and power), divided by (b) the price index of locally produced goods; (2) Capital (C) = initial value (1919–20) of land, buildings, machinery, and plant *minus* depreciation actually written off each year, and *plus* the money value of additions to capital in each year adjusted for changes in the index, number of prices for buildings and construction; (3) Labor (L) = number of persons employed. See J. W. Williams, "Professor Douglas' Production Function," *Econ. Record*, Vol. XXI (1945), pp. 55–63.

[c] Professor Browne defined his units as follows: (1) Product (P) = net value added by manufacturing or the gross value of output minus cost of materials, fuel, light, and power; (2) Labor (L) = average number of employees, including wage earners, salaried staff, managers, accountants, working proprietors, and persons regularly employed in their homes; (3) Capital (C) = the value of land, buildings, machinery, plant, and tools (*i.e.*, *fixed* capital only, with working capital excluded). See G. W. G. Browne, "The Production Function for South African Manufacturing Industry," *South African Jour. Econ.*, Vol. XI (1943), p. 259.

[d] This study differed from the former in that it was based on a more minute classification of industries and that it also separated white and black laborers and treated each as a separate factor of production. The value of k given is the sum of the k for white labor (.45) and for native labor (.20). See Browne, *op. cit.*, pp. 260–61. The value of σ_k could not be obtained by adding the σ_k of the exponents for native and white labor.

[e] The statistical series used were: (1) Labor (L) = average number of employed wage earn-

found the value of *k* was .66, and that for *j*, .32. When he made white and black labor separate factors of production and broke manufacturing down into eighty-five industries, the sum of the two exponents for labor amounted to .65. While we cannot rely too much upon only one study, it is of interest that his results were substantially the same as those which we obtained on the average for the United States for the period 1889-1919 and not far from the Australian results. This would be equivalent to an elasticity of approximately 3.0 for the marginal productivity curve for labor and of 1.5 for the marginal productivity curve for capital.

If we try to summarize our results, we do find a relatively close agreement between the values of *k* and *j* which we obtain from the cross-section studies for the United States, Australia, and South Africa. But we also find differences in the values of *k* and *j* (1) between Canada and New Zealand, on the one hand, and the United States, upon the other, with the former having lower *k*'s and higher *j*'s than the United States, and (2) between years within the same country. This is to be expected, as I pointed out long ago in a section of my *Theory of Wages*.[21] But underneath all these differences, it is submitted that there has been *for the periods studied,* a substantial core of stability within countries and that differences in technique, differences in the relative importance of given industries, and differences in the ratios of capital to labor may account for such deviations in the values of the exponents as exist.[22]

[21] Douglas, *The Theory of wages,* pp. 203-4.

[22] The economic and statistical meaning of *b* deserves to be considered.

A. In the four time series for the United States, the values of *b* under formula (1) are closely approximate to unity. For the United States the values are the same for each of the four series.

	b		*b*
Series I	1.01	Series III	1.01
Series II	1.01	Series IV	1.01

(Footnote 22 continued on next page)

ers, salaried workers, etc.; (2) Capital (*C*) = total capital used, *i.e.*, (a) fixed capital in the form of land, buildings, plant, tools, and machinery plus (b) working capital including materials, goods in process, and goods in storage. The inclusion of working capital makes the results comparable with the cross-section studies for the United States but differentiates them from the series used in Australia, New Zealand, and South Africa. (3) Product (*P*) = gross sales value *minus* cost of materials, fuel, electricity, etc., used. See Patricia Daly (Ogburn) and Paul H. Douglas, "The Production Function for Canadian Manufactures," *Jour. Am. Stat. Assoc.*, Vol. XXXVIII (1943), pp. 178–86.

[f] Professor Williams defined his terms as follows: (1) Labor (*L*) = number of persons engaged; (2) Capital (*C*) = value of land, buildings, plant, and machinery, *i.e.*, *fixed* capital. (3) Product (*P*) = gross sales value of product minus cost of materials, fuel, and power. See J. W. Williams, *op. cit.*, p. 59.

It is submitted that the results are, on the whole, corroborative. If they were purely accidental, as some have charged, they would show widely varying results. The fact that on the basis of fairly wide studies there is an appreciable degree of uniformity, and that the sum of the

For Victoria, the value of b was .97 and for New South Wales, 1.02. In all these cases, b represents the value of the intercept with the functional plane of theoretical product merely moved up or down by the small difference between the values of b and unity. In the time series, of course, we are dealing with index numbers which show relative changes, not absolute values.

B. Under formula (2) (*i.e.*, $P = bL^kC^j$) b deviates in a greater degree from unity because of the greater degree of freedom given to the exponent for capital. Here the values for the United States are:

	b		b
Series I	.84	Series III	1.12
Series II	1.38	Series IV	1.35

For Victoria b is .71 and for New South Wales, .97.

C. In the cross-section or inter-industry studies, b still represents the intercept but it is also a conversion factor which translates the number of employees and dollars of invested capital into *dollars* of net value product. As in the case of the time series based on index numbers, b is generally higher under formula (2) when the values of j are independently determined than under formula (1). It also tends to move in some direct ratio with changes in the general price level, being generally higher in those years when the price level is higher and *vice versa*. There are, however, occasional exceptions to this rule. These tendencies are shown in the following tables for the United States:

Year	Values of b Formula (1)	Formula (2)
1889	28.58	58.34
1899	69.66	106.43
1904	79.62	120.23
1909	98.63	90.99
1914	66.22	81.66
1919	258.82	244.21

For the Commonwealth of Australia the corresponding values are

Year	Values of b Formula (1)	Formula (2)
1912	14.79	15.87
1922-23	19.72	16.49
1926-27	41.50	77.26
1934-35	37.15	39.79
1936-37	17.99	21.57

It will, of course, be remembered that Australian prices and values are expressed in terms of pounds.

For Canada, the values are

Year	Values of b Formula (1)	Formula (2)
1923	38.55	48.53
1927	28.51	33.04
1935	24.38	22.23
1937	16.48	15.42

I hope to give a fuller treatment of the significance of the b term in the regression equations in a book on *The Theory of Production* which I hope shortly to publish with Miss Grace Gunn.

exponents approximates unity, fairly clearly suggests that there are laws of production which can be approximated by inductive studies and that we are at least approaching them.

And yet it is proper to chronicle the fact that we have obtained some negative results. One persistent area of difficulty in these last months has been the Massachusetts time series. We tried to improve on Professor Cobb's series of capital and product with the result that the more we refined the basic series, the more nonsensical the results became. We are still working on this problem, but at the moment we certainly do not see the light. Secondly, it is disconcerting to observe that if we shorten our time periods by dropping off a number of terminal years, we appreciably alter our results. We observed this fact earlier, as did Professor Williams in New Zealand, but this paradox has been most manifest when we omit the war years from 1916 on, in our United States time series. Finally, we have attempted various inter-spatial studies in which we use individual states as separate observations. We have personally had no success with these attempts. The most ambitious study of this latter nature has, however, been made by my friend and former associate, Ernest Olson, and will be presented to this Association later in these meetings. I do not wish to anticipate the results of his paper, but I think it is proper to say that Mr. Olson has been able to develop a formula which makes differences between countries in their *real* national income a mathematical function of (1) the total energy used, (2) the numbers of the working population, (3) the quantity of livestock reduced to comparable units, and (4) the amount of land—and he has derived exponents which indicate the comparative importance of each. There is still much to be done in this direction and some hard puzzles remain to be solved, but Mr. Olson's comparative success offers us some hope that we may not face a completely blank wall in working with this third method for deriving the laws of production.

Finally, I should like to point out that in the case of the United States, we were compelled because of lack of capital figures, to stop with 1922 in our time series and with 1919 in our cross-section studies. We have, therefore, not been able to cover the very perplexing period of 1920-40. I am doubtful for two reasons whether we can develop a satisfactory production function for the United States during this period: (a) In spite of the excellent work of the National Bureau of Economic Research, we still lack adequate data for this period on the capital *available* for use; and (b) there was wide variation between the decades in the degree to which the available capital was *actually used*. During the 'twenties, capital was quite fully employed, but during the 'thirties a large proportion of this equipment lay idle. Variations in the degree to which available capital was utilized created some difficulties within the ordinary business cycles which prevailed between 1899 and 1919 when each of the four phases of the cycle did not last for more than one or two years. But the period between the two wars was quite extraordinary in that we had high prosperity from 1922 to the fall of 1929 and that we did not fully recover from the collapse which then set in until 1941. It was this fundamental difficulty which prevented one of my students, Mr. Leonard Felsenthal, from developing a satisfactory production function for Germany in the inter-war period. I shall, therefore, await with sympathetic interest the paper on this subject which Mr. Burton Wall is to give tomorrow.

IV. *The Production Function as Based on Plant Averages Rather than Industry Aggregates*

The inductive values which have thus far been developed in the cross-section or inter-industry studies have been based on industry aggregates, namely the totals of workers, capital, and net values added by manufacturing in each industry. This method is somewhat disconcerting to those who are accustomed in their *a priori* reasoning to start with the theory of production for the individual firm and who then move to a model for a given industry but who shy away from developing a theory of production for the economy as a whole or from the manufacturing sector of that economy. Such theorists probably believe that we are starting at the wrong end and that we should begin instead with the individual firm rather than the whole manufacturing sector of the economy and that we should consider the production function within these units rather than deal with inter-industry and aggregate functions.

There are two answers to this position. The first is that I should be very glad indeed to make studies of individual firms if the necessary data were available. But statistics on the changing quantities of labor and capital which are used over a period of time by individual firms, and the amounts of product which are thus turned out by them, are some of the most carefully guarded secrets of business. I am reluctant to believe that we should stop all our investigations until all of these facts are forthcoming for a multitude of firms.

Secondly, I personally see no reason why we cannot approach this problem from either end and study the macrocosm as well as the microcosm. No one, for example, in the physical sciences would propose that we give up using the telescope because the microscope had not yielded all its secrets. Why should we not, therefore, study the economy as a whole as well as speculate about the individual firm, particularly since a knowledge of the former throws a great deal of light upon the problems of the latter?

In the meantime, however, we should all welcome such brilliant studies of the production function for individual firms as that which will shortly be published by my friend and colleague, Professor William H. Nicholls, for a meat-packing plant.[22a] Moreover, if we could get the figures for specific firms and plants *within* given industries for a specific year, we would then be able to develop production functions for each of the main industries with each firm serving as an observation. But the census has always been obligated to conceal the identity of the specific firms which report to it and can only publish totals by industries and geographical subdivisions. This fact prevents us, at present, from developing such studies, although it is barely possible that either the Census Bureau itself or employers' associations could carry them on, were they once convinced of their value. This cannot, however, be done at present.

To my mind, therefore, we are at present forced to work primarily with industry aggregates. But there is one important refinement which we can and should introduce. That is to divide the total number of workers, the aggregate amounts of capital, and the total net value of the product in each of the various industries by the number of plants in that industry. This will give us *plant averages* for given industries rather than industry aggregates as the individual observations[23] and from these we can derive another variant of the production function.

We have made such studies for each of the six years which were covered for American manufacturing and for two of the Australian studies and these results are embodied in Table IV.

It will thus be seen that while we obtained closely similar results in Australia by the two methods, nevertheless, clear differences developed in the case of the United States. In every year the value of k in our American studies was substantially less under the method of plant averages than it was under the method of industry aggregates. The amount of this difference ranged between 5 and 6 points, as in 1904 and 1909, to 15 points in 1889. On the other hand, the values of j were always higher under the methods of plant averages than under that of industry aggregates but the amounts of these differences were much less. As a result, the combined values of $k + j$ are less by from 3 to 8 points

[22a] William H. Nicholls, *Labor Productivity Functions in Meat Packing,* to be published by University of Chicago Press, 1948.

[23] This is not quite the same as the so-called "representative" firm because many firms operate multiple plants.

on the plant average basis than they are when industry aggregates are used and, indeed, average only .92. This gives an unmistakable indication of true diminishing returns so far as the size of individual

TABLE IV.—A COMPARISON OF THE VALUES OF k AND j OBTAINED BY THE METHOD OF PLANT AVERAGES WITH THOSE OBTAINED BY THE METHOD OF INDUSTRY AGGREGATES ($P=bL^kC^j$)[a]

Year	Values According to Method of Plant Averages			Difference (In Points) from Those Obtained by Methods of Industry Aggregates		
	k	j	$k+j$	k	j	$k+j$
United States						
1889	.36	.50	.86	−.15	+.07	−.08
1899	.52	.36	.88	−.10	+.03	−.07
1904	.60	.32	.92	−.05	+.01	−.04
1909	.57	.37	.94	−.06	+.03	−.03
1914	.52	.41	.93	−.09	+.04	−.05
1919	.66	.32	.98	−.10	+.07	−.03
Australia Commonwealth						
1934–35[b]	.60	.38	.98	+.04	−.04	.00
Victoria						
1910–11	.76	.26	1.02	+.02	+.01	+.03

[a] The formula, $P=bL^kC^{1-k}$, gives identical results using aggregate and per plant data.

(1) $$P = bL^kC^{1-k}$$

(2) $$\frac{P}{N} = b\left(\frac{L}{N}\right)^k\left(\frac{C}{N}\right)^{1-k} = b\frac{L^k}{N^k}\frac{C^{1-k}}{N^{1-k}}$$

$$\frac{P}{N} = \frac{b}{N}L^kC^{1-k}.$$

Multiplying both sides by N, we get formula (1).

[b] Figures refer to Commonwealth of Australia 1934-35 A, which used the studies of C. H. Wickens, "The Commonwealth Statistical Allocation of Factory Output," *Econ. Record* (1929), pp. 226-33. The values of k and j for the industry aggregates were .56 and .42, respectively. The results of the plant averages for the Commonwealth for the years 1912, 1922-23, 1926-27, 1936-37 were previously published. It was found that the values of k and j did not change greatly. Only one value of k, that for 1922-23, differed from the aggregate k, by an amount greater than σ_k. For further discussion, see Gunn and Douglas, "The Production Function for Australian Manufacturing," *Quart. Jour. Econ.*, Vol. LVI (Nov., 1941), pp. 108-29.

plants is concerned. While much more study is needed to develop and to clarify this point, it is suggested that quite possibly American plants during this period were in practice developed beyond the point of maximum efficiency. Whether or not the differences between the respective $k+j$'s can be taken as a coefficient of managerial megalomania, I shall have to leave to the psychiatrists.[24]

[24] If this is a psychiatric problem, we can take consolation in the fact that the disease was apparently less acute in 1919 than in 1889.

V. *Do the Deviations of the Actual Products from Those Which We Would Theoretically Expect from the Formula Tend to Strengthen or Weaken Belief in the Validity of the Production Function?*

An important test of our function is the degree to which the values of the product which we would expect from the quantities of labor

CHART I—DEVIATIONS OF ACTUAL FROM THEORETICAL VALUES OF LOG P
UNITED STATES MANUFACTURING 1889

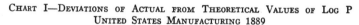

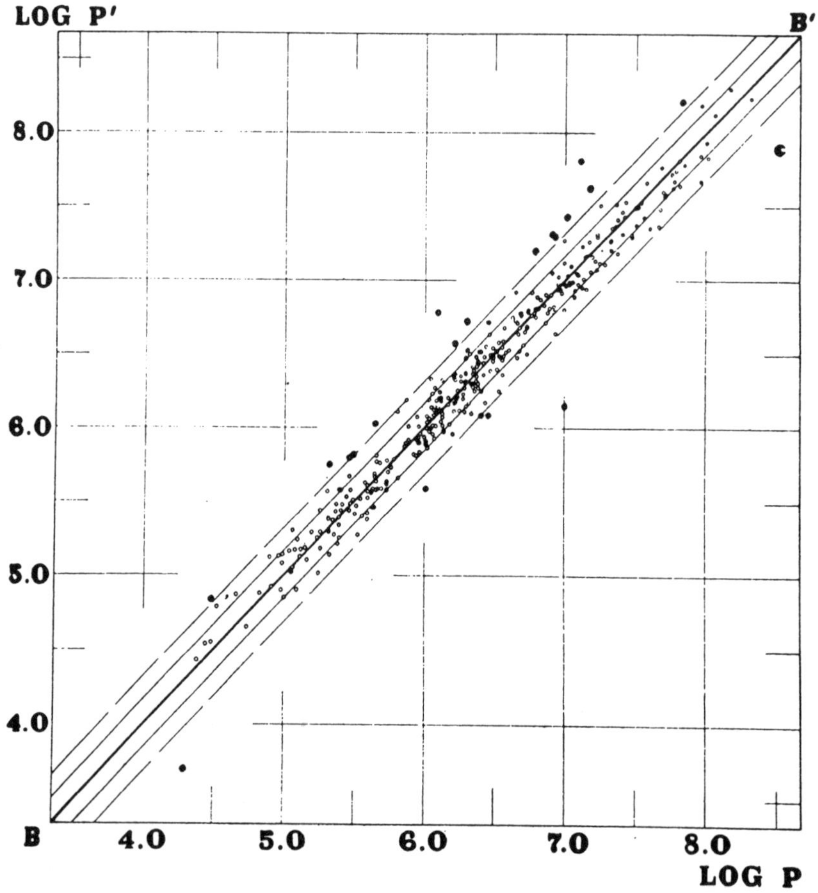

and capital available, tend in practice to be realized in terms of actual product in each of the various industries during the given years. We have made these tests and I should like to present our results in a series of charts and summary tables. As a first step, we computed the standard errors of estimate (S) for each study. Under a normal distribution of cases with the only departures of the actual from theoretical values being those caused by random errors of measurement and of sampling, we would expect that in 68.3 per cent of the cases

CHART II—DEVIATIONS OF ACTUAL FROM THEORETICAL VALUES OF LOG P
UNITED STATES MANUFACTURING 1899

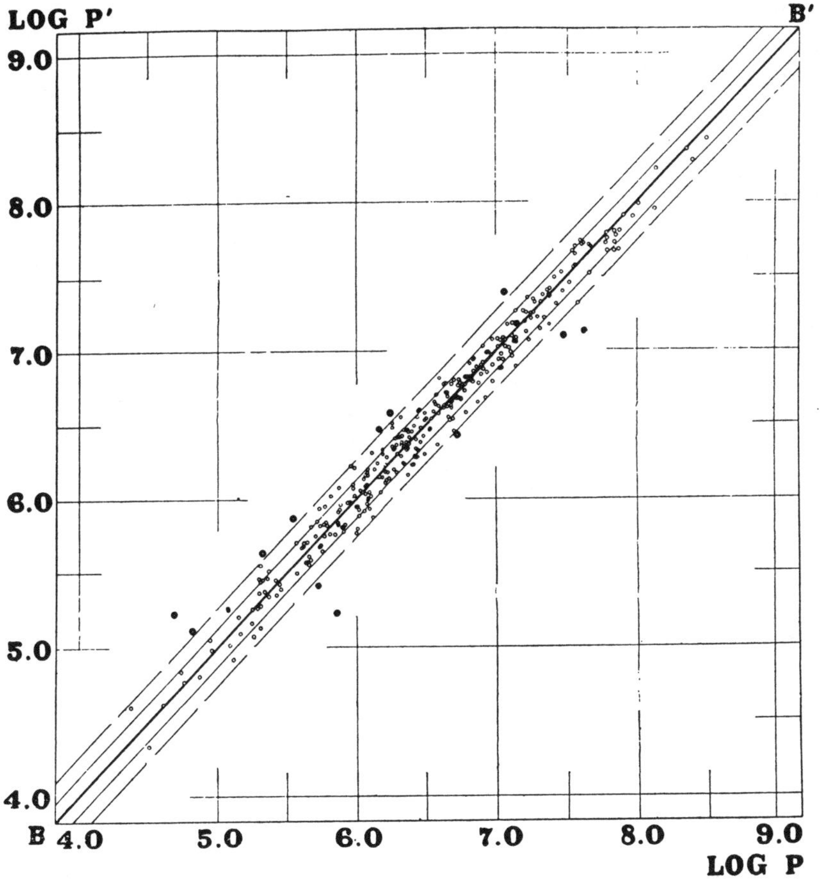

the actual values would deviate from the theoretical values by less than one standard error of estimate, and that in 95 per cent of the cases the actual values would deviate from the theoretical values by less than two such standard errors. In only one per cent of the cases would the actual values deviate by more than three standard errors of estimate. Then in our charts of the cross-section or inter-industry studies, we have plotted the logs of the theoretical or expected products on the vertical scale and of the actual products on the horizontal scale. Since the values of scale are the same on both axes, the line BB′ (with a slope of unity) is the locus of all those points for which the theoretical

CHART III—DEVIATIONS OF ACTUAL FROM THEORETICAL VALUES OF LOG P
UNITED STATES MANUFACTURING 1904

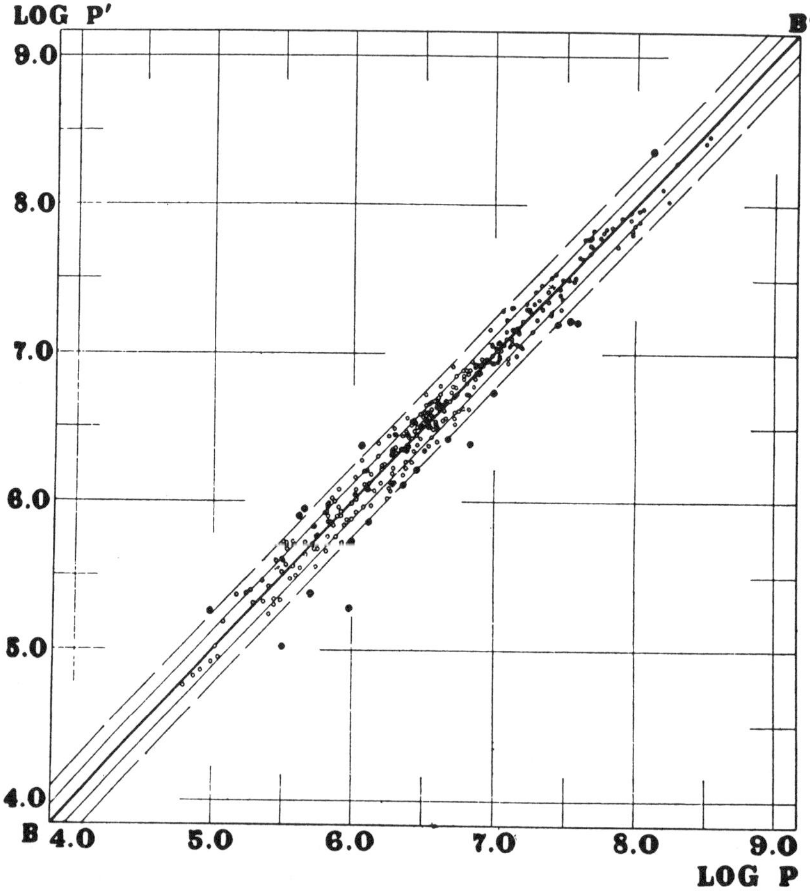

values of the product are identical with the actual values. In these studies for a given year, it will be remembered that each industry constitutes a separate observation.

The degree of departure of the actual from the theoretical values is, therefore, shown by either the horizontal or the vertical distance of a given point from the line BB′. We have, therefore, marked out on each side of the line BB′ two other pairs of lines at the respective distances of one and two standard errors of estimate. An inspection of these charts for American manufacturing for the years 1889, 1899, 1904, 1909, 1914, and 1919, (Charts I, II, III, IV, V, and VI) show that in practice the actual values tend to be close to the line BB′, and a statistical analysis of these variations is given in Table V. Here it will be seen that in every year more than 70 per cent of the actual values were within one standard error of estimate of the values which we would

TABLE V.—DEGREE OF DEVIATION OF ACTUAL FROM THEORETICAL VALUES OF PRODUCT IN AMERICAN MANUFACTURING INDUSTRIES 1889–1919

Census Year	Number of Industries or Observations—N	Deviation of Actual Product (P) from Theoretical Product (P') in Terms of Standard Errors of Estimate					
		Number			Per Cent		
		Less than 1σ	1–2 σ	Over 2σ	Less than 1σ	1–2 σ	Over 2σ
1889	363	280	63	20	77.0	17.0	6.0
1899	332	250	70	12	75.0	21.0	4.0
1904	336	236	82	18	70.0	25.0	5.0
1909	258	215	38	5	83.0	15.0	2.0
1914	340	243	83	14	72.0	24.0	4.0
1919	556	453	85	18	82.0	15.0	3.0
Total	2185	1677	421	87	—	—	—
Averages	—	—	—	—	76.5	19.5	4.0

theoretically expect under the formula and that in two of the six years, over 80 per cent of the cases were within this range.

Taking the 2185 industry observations in the United States as a whole, we find that in 76.5 per cent of the cases, the actual products were within one standard error of estimate of the theoretical products, whereas under a normal distribution we would only expect a little over 68 per cent of the cases to lie within this range. Moreover, in only one year did the number of observations whose actual products varied from the theoretical values by more than two standard errors of estimate come to as much as 6 per cent of the total while the average for all 2185 observations was 4 per cent as compared with the 5 per cent which we would normally expect.[25]

In our American studies, the distribution of the actual values about

[25] Incidentally, instead of 22 cases or 1.0 per cent of the total, which would normally expect to deviate by more than three standard errors of estimate, we find only 16 observations or three-quarters of one per cent in this class.

the theoretical values is, therefore, somewhat *closer* than what we would normally expect on the basis of random errors of sampling and of measurement. Belief in the reliability of the formula as a description of production during this period is, therefore, strengthened, rather than weakened.

TABLE VI.—DEGREE OF DEVIATION OF ACTUAL FROM THEORETICAL VALUES OF PRODUCT IN MANUFACTURING INDUSTRIES OF BRITISH DOMINIONS FOR SPECIFIC YEARS

Country and Year	Number of Industries (*N*)	Deviation of Actual Product (*P*) from Theoretical Product (*P'*) in Terms of Standard Errors of Estimate (σ)					
		Number			Per Cent		
		Less than 1σ	1–2 σ	More than 2σ	Less than 1σ	1–2 σ	More than 2σ
Canada							
1923	167	116	41	10	69.0	25.0	6.0
1927	163	115	40	8	71.0	24.0	5.0
1935	165	113	45	7	69.0	27.0	4.0
1937	164	122	33	9	74.0	20.0	6.0
Commonwealth of Australia							
1912	85	66	13	6	78.0	15.0	7.0
1922–23	87	66	15	6	76.0	17.0	7.0
1926–27	85	65	17	3	76.0	20.0	4.0
1934–35	138	110	23	5	80.0	17.0	3.0
1936–37	87	70	9	8	81.0	10.0	9.0
Australian States							
New South Wales 1933–34	125	98	22	5	78.0	18.0	4.0
Victoria 1910–11	34	26	7	1	76.0	21.0	3.0
Victoria 1923–24	38	32	4	2	84.0	11.0	5.0
Victoria 1927–28	35	26	6	3	74.0	17.0	9.0
Total	1373	1025	275	73	—	—	—
Average	—	—	—	—	74.7	20.0	5.3

Let us see from Table VI if these results are confirmed by an analysis of the deviations of the actual from the theoretical values in the thirteen cross-section studies which we have thus far made for the Dominions within the British Commonwealth of Nations. It will be noticed that out of the total of 1373 observations, 1025, or over 74 per cent deviated by less than one standard error of estimate from the theoretical values, and that between 94 and 95 per cent deviated by less than two standard errors of estimate. The distribution of the observations in this sample is, therefore, somewhat better than that which we would expect

CHART IV—DEVIATIONS OF ACTUAL FROM THEORETICAL VALUES OF LOG P
UNITED STATES MANUFACTURING 1909

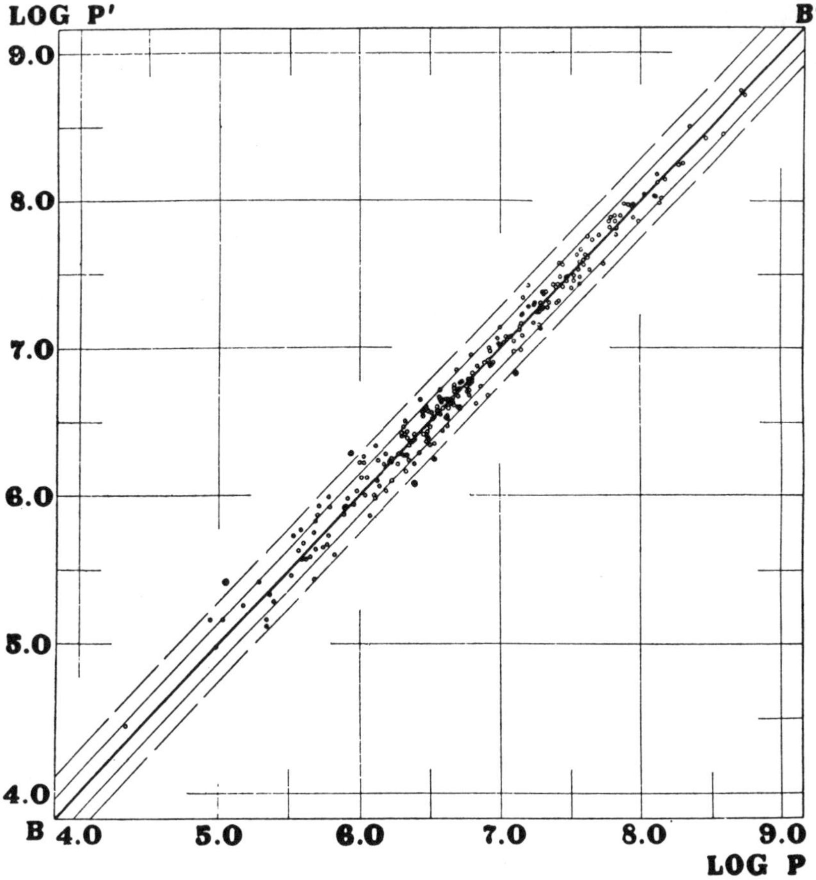

under normal conditions of random error. Credence in the production function would seem to be further reinforced.[25a]

The fact that we have, therefore, in practice, a somewhat closer distribution of the actual values about the line of the theoretical values

[25a] While charts showing the distribution of the individual products about the line of theoretical relationship have been prepared for the British Dominion, these are not published in this article because of considerations of space and expense. They were, however, shown in connection with the address.

under the formula than we would normally expect, is all the more striking in view of the fact that the values of the production function need not be the same within all industries or allied groups of industries.

CHART V—DEVIATIONS OF ACTUAL FROM THEORETICAL VALUES OF LOG P
UNITED STATES MANUFACTURING 1914

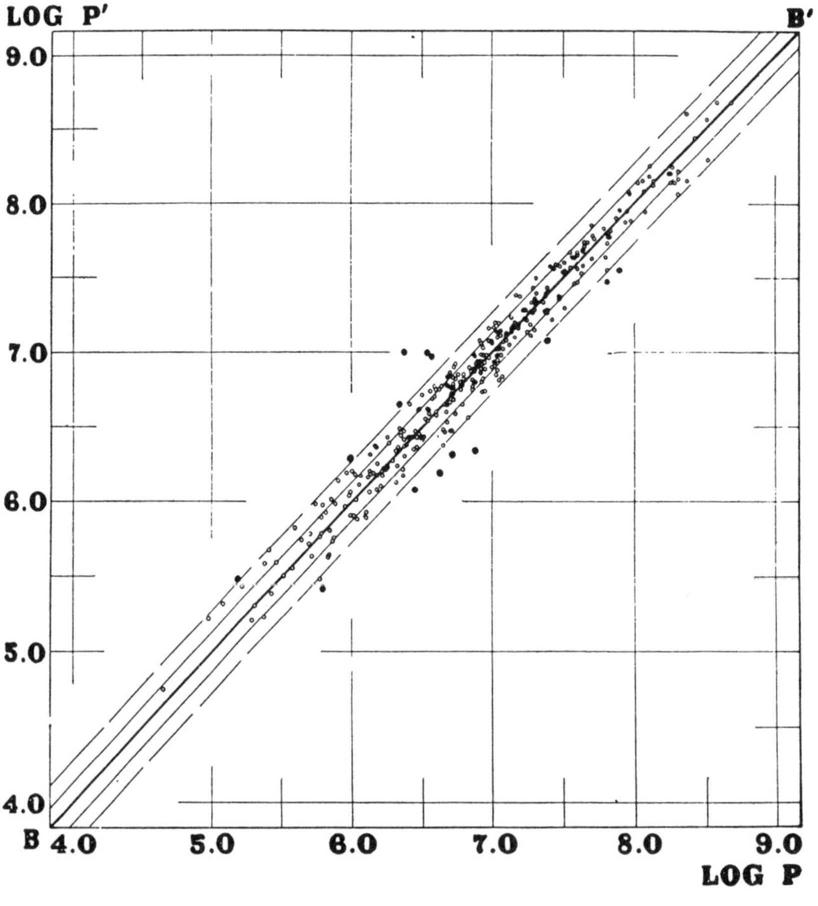

As I have constantly pointed out during the last twenty years, there is no reason why the exponents of capital and labor should be constant for all periods and economies. As a matter of fact, we have already seen that they are not and that there is some variation between countries and years in the values of k and j. We would similarly expect some variation to exist as between groups of industries within a country at any given time. Thus the values of the production function for the textile industries need not be the same as for the clothing group, while these might well differ from those prevailing in the food industries and be appreciably different from those in the iron and steel and heavy metals industries, etc. If, therefore, we could compute separate values

CHART VI—DEVIATIONS OF ACTUAL FROM THEORETICAL VALUES OF LOG P
UNITED STATES MANUFACTURING 1919

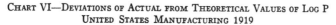

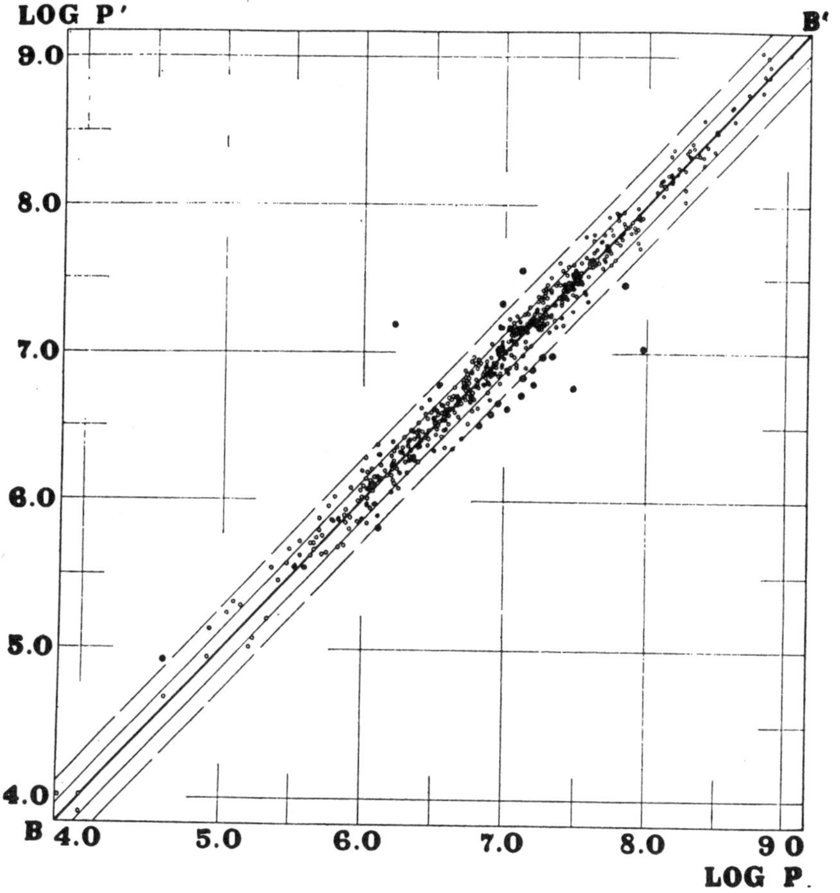

of *k* and *j* for each of the various main groups of manufacturing and compare the actual with the resulting theoretical products, we could doubtless find the resulting deviations to be appreciably less than those obtained when we treat all manufacturing as a whole. The fact that we do get such a good fit when we treat all of the industries as homogeneous is, therefore, all the more remarkable. It seems, further, to suggest that to the degree that the values of *k* and *j* do differ between groups of industries, such differences tend to be more or less symmetrically distributed around the "normal" values which we have found in the given years for manufacturing as a whole.

A further analysis of the plus and minus deviations offers interesting suggestions. We would expect industries characterized by monopoly and by highly imperfect competition to have a value product which would be appreciably greater than that which we would expect from the production formula itself, and from the quantities of labor and capital which are available. This would be caused by the control over supplies and prices exercised by the dominant firms and by their ability to control or to limit entrance into the monopolized industries. Conversely, in the industries which may be characterized by "excessive" competition into which large numbers of workers and also in some cases, relatively large quantities of capital are forced and which consequently lower the marginal productivity of one or both factors appreciably below their general levels, we would expect the value product per unit of labor and possibly also of capital, to be below the general average for society as a whole.

Similarly, we would expect that the industries which are rapidly expanding because of an increase in demand or in the disposition of consumers income, or because of great technical progress, will have value products which are in excess of those derived from the formula. Conversely, again, we would expect that the contracting industries, which are suffering from a decrease in demand and an obsolescence of technique, would produce less value product than that which our formula would predict.

There are, moreover, a considerable number of industries which probably can best be described as "sweated." These are industries which have had large supplies of cheap labor, sometimes caused, as in the past, by an influx of immigrants or by the presence of a large number of women and juveniles who are forced to seek work because of the low earnings of the male heads of households. The average earnings in these industries tends to be appreciably below the national average, and if there is a normal degree of competition at work, these low earnings will commonly be translated into a lower sales price for the product than would normally be the case. The value product in these industries will, therefore, tend to be less than what would be shown under the formula for manufacturing as a whole.

We can test the relative truth of these hypotheses both by statistical analysis and also by identifying the specific industries where the deviations of the actual from the theoretical values are great. In analyzing the American deviations by years, as in Table VII, certain marked differences appear between the results for the earliest year of 1889 and the years from 1904 on. From 1904 on, and particularly in 1914 and 1919, the big deviations were predominantly on the plus, and the minor deviations on the minus, side. Thus, in 1919, of the 18 industries where the deviations amounted to more than two standard errors of

TABLE VII.—AN ANALYSIS OF THE COMPARATIVE DEGREES OF PLUS AND MINUS DEVIATIONS OF ACTUAL FROM THEORETICAL PRODUCTS IN AMERICAN MANUFACTURING INDUSTRIES 1889–1919

Year	Number of Industries with Deviations of Less Than Two Standard Errors of Estimate		Number of Industries with Deviations of More Than Two Standard Errors of Estimate	
	Plus	Minus	Plus	Minus
1889	190	153	4	16
1899	166	154	5	7
1904	144	174	11	7
1909	122	131	3	2
1914	152	174	10	4
1919	230	308	16	2

estimate, 16 had their actual products in excess of the theoretical values, while in only two cases did they fall below. On the other hand, of the 538 industries in 1919 where the deviations amounted to less than two standard errors, 308 or nearly three-fifths, were below what would have been expected under the formula. For the three census years of 1909, 1914, and 1919, there were 29 industry observations where the actual products were more than two standard errors of estimate greater than the theoretical values and only 10 industry observations which were more than two standard errors less. Conversely, in these three years there were only 504 industries which had actual products which exceeded the theoretical values up to two standard errors as contrasted with 613 industries where the actual products fell below the theoretical by these amounts.

The general framework of these later results is approximately what we would expect on theoretical grounds. The monopolistic and expanding industries tend to absorb large quantities of purchasing power at the expense of the rest of the economy. They would, therefore, be expected to show wider profit margins than the general average and each combined dose of labor and capital would consequently tend to yield a greater dollar value than would normally be the case. The withdrawal of this purchasing power would, moreover, exert a slight depressing influence upon each of the remaining industries so that we would expect the number of industries where the actual product fell below the theoretical to exceed in number those where it was greater. This was exactly what happened from 1904 to 1919. Why the opposite result should have occurred in 1889 and to a much lesser degree in 1899, however, merits further study.

Even more important, however, is an analysis of each of the 87 American cases where the deviations were more than two standard errors of estimate from the theoretical values and I only regret that lack of time prevents a full analysis of these instances. Let us first consider the forty in which the deviations were of a minus nature. In no less than ten cases, these were in the flax, hemp, linen, jute and oakum family of industries, which has always been one of the most "sweated" groups in all industrial countries. Two were in allied "sweated" industries, namely nets and seines (1904) and hammocks (1889), while three more were connected with cotton which has generally been a sub-standard industry. Three more, charcoal, waste, and canning oysters, have been distinctly disagreeable and badly "sweated" industries, while several others, such as grindstones, millstones, hooks and eyes, etc., were instances of contracting demand.

On the other hand, the vast majority of the plus deviations which amounted to more than two standard errors of estimate can be explained as caused by (1) some form of quasi-monopoly or imperfect competition, or (2) by expanding demand, or (3) by both factors. Examples of the first are wood engraving, gold and silver reducing, lapidary work, music publishing, glucose, starch, linseed oil, patent medicines, tin plate, brass, and lead. These in themselves accounted for nineteen of the markedly plus deviations.

Illustrations of the second group, namely those caused by an expanding demand, were cordials and flavoring syrups (1909, 1914, 1919), oleomargarine (1914), perfumery (1919), and washing machines (1919).

There is also a third class of plus deviations which was probably affected both by imperfect competition and by expanding demand. Illustrations of this group are airplanes (1914), chewing gum (1919), cigars and cigarettes (1919), fountain pens (1914), photographic supplies and equipment (1904, 1909, 1914), cash registers (1889), smelting and refining copper (1899, 1904), typewriters and supplies (1889).

A very large majority of the major deviations so far as the United States is concerned, were, therefore, precisely what we would expect on *a priori* grounds. Belief in the function as a description of "normal" relationships is, therefore, still further strengthened.

VI. *To What Degree Do the Shares Which Labor and Capital Receive of the Product Approximate the Proportions Which We Would Expect from the Values of the Production Function?*

We now come to one of the most important features of the theory of production and of distribution, namely, the relative degree to which the actual shares received by labor and capital approximate those

TABLE VIII.—A COMPARISON BY YEARS OF THE VALUES OF THE EXPONENTS OF LABOR AND CAPITAL IN THE PRODUCTION FUNCTION FOR AMERICAN MANUFACTURING (k AND j) WITH THE UNWEIGHTED AVERAGE OF THE SHARES OF THE NET VALUE PRODUCT RECEIVED BY LABOR (W/P)

Year	N	k		$\frac{k}{k+j}$	$\frac{W}{P}$	Degree to which W/P differs from k and $\frac{k}{k+j}$ in terms of standard errors: $\frac{\frac{W}{P}-k}{\sigma_k}$	$\frac{\frac{W}{P}-\frac{k}{k+j}}{\sigma_k}$
1889	363	.51	.43	.54	.60	+ 3	+ 2
1899	332	.62	.33	.65	.58	− 2	−3–4
1904	336	.65	.31	.68	.64	−0–1	− 2
1909	258	.63	.34	.65	.63	0	− 1
1914	340	.61	.37	.62	.59	−0–1	− 1
1919	556	.76	.25	.75	.59	−8–9	− 8
Average	—	.63	.34	.65	.605	—	—

which we would expect from the values of the production function. As my associates and I have demonstrated mathematically a number of times, we would expect, under conditions of (1) true constant returns where the sum of the exponents is equal to unity and (2) perfect competition, that each factor of production would receive that fraction of the total product which is indicated by its exponent.[26]

[26] The share which labor receives:

Let $W =$ the amount of wages received.

Marginal productivity of labor $= k\,\frac{P}{L}$

$$W = L\,k\,\frac{P}{L} = kP$$

$$W = kP$$

$$k = W/P$$

Similarly, for capital.

Let us, therefore, compare the actual share which wages and salaries formed of the net value product (*i.e.*, W/P) in the various years with the values of k. It will also be instructive to compare W/P with the ratio of $\frac{k}{k+j}$ since the latter is a rough measure of what we would approximately expect to occur if the total product were to be divided between labor and capital so as to eliminate either net residual profits or losses.

This is shown for the United States cross-section studies in Table VIII. From an examination of this table, it will be seen that in five of the six years there was a very close agreement between the values of k and of W/P. In one year (1909), there was precise agreement between the two; in two of the years (1904 and 1914), the differences were approximately only one standard error, while in two more (1889 and 1899), they amounted to two to three standard errors. The biggest difference was in 1919 when W/P was less than k by over eight standard errors.[27]

Taking the average for the six years as a whole, we find that k averages .63, $\frac{k}{k+j}$ equals .65, and labor's actual share or W/P was .605. There was, therefore, a close average agreement for the period between what we would have theoretically expected the distribution of the product to be under conditions of perfect competition and that which actually occurred. It should be remembered, moreover, that due to our inability to deduct allowances for depreciation in specific industries, the true values of W/P are probably understated by approximately 3 percentage points,[28] and that, therefore, the average

[27] The year 1919 was one in which prices rose with great rapidity. It would be expected, therefore, that wages would lag behind in such a period.

[28] On the basis of Dr. Fabricant's estimate of depreciation totals for manufacturing as a whole in 1919, it appears that these amounted to approximately five per cent of the value added by manufacturing in that year. If this had been deducted, labor's share would, therefore, have been raised in 1919 by about three percentage points, or to approximately .62. Thus, Fabricant's careful allowance for depreciation in 1919 was 1151 millions of dollars. (Solomon Fabricant, *Capital Consumption and Adjustment*, pp. 260-61.) The total value added by manufacturing in that year, (*i.e.*, value of product minus cost of raw material minus rent and taxes minus cost of contract work) was 22,486 millions of dollars. This comes to a depreciation rate in terms of net value of product of 5.1 per cent. If we deduct such estimated charges, we would raise labor's share by almost precisely 3 points (*i.e.*, $^{59}/_{95}$ = .62). Due to the smaller quantity of capital used per unit of product, in the earlier years the additional "loading" required to approximate labor's share would then have been somewhat less, and for 1889 and 1899 would probably have been nearer two percentage points.

ratio of W/P was probably very close to .63 or the exact average value of k.

I submit, therefore, that the degree of agreement between the values of k and of W/P is most striking and that the results conform to what normally would be expected to occur under competitive productivity theory. Hence, this constitutes a still further reinforcement to the productivity function itself.

It should, however, be frankly recognized that there is a further problem of reconciling these results with the known facts of imperfect competition, oligopoly and monopoly. Such conditions, as has been abundantly developed in our meetings, do exist, and, in fact, characterize a large sector of our economy. It is, therefore, puzzling to find labor's share approximately equal to that which we would expect under conditions of perfect competition. A further investigation of this subject is much needed. In the meantime, I would merely suggest that perhaps one answer to the paradox may be that the quasi-monopolies and oligopolies may have shared with their workers the excess gains which they have made at the expense of the consumers.

We can make a further test of the degree to which W/P approximates k and $\frac{k}{k+j}$ by examining the results for the British Dominions of Australia, New Zealand, and Canada. This is done in Table IX.

Taken in the large, the agreement in the cross-section studies for Australia between the values of W/P and k are indeed striking. In each and all of the five inter-industry studies for the Commonwealth, the differences never exceeded one standard error of k. For the five years as a whole, the average value of k and W/P were both .55. The average value of $\frac{k}{k+j}$ was .56. It would scarcely be possible to have a closer agreement than this.

In the case of the four studies for the Australian states, the differences in the case of Victoria were not great, never exceeding two standard errors of k and being slightly reduced if the comparisons are made between W/P and $\frac{k}{k+j}$.[29] For the three years as a whole, the differences are largely ironed out since the average values of k are .65 and of W/P .66. The average value of $\frac{k}{k+j}$ was .70.

[29] In the Queensland study the value of W/P was .614 or less than one standard error more than the value of k.

TABLE IX.—A COMPARISON BY YEARS OF THE VALUES OF THE EXPONENTS OF LABOR AND CAPITAL IN THE PRODUCTION FUNCTION FOR THE BRITISH DOMINIONS (k AND j) WITH THE UNWEIGHTED AVERAGE OF THE SHARES OF THE NET VALUE PRODUCT RECEIVED BY LABOR (W/P)

Dominion and Year	N	k	j	$\frac{k}{k+j}$	$\frac{W}{P}$	Differences between W/P and k in terms of standard error: $\frac{\frac{W}{P}-k}{\sigma_k}$	$\frac{\frac{W}{P}-\frac{k}{k+j}}{\sigma_k}$
I. Australian time series							
Victoria							
1907–1929	22	.84	.23	.79	—	—	—
New Zealand (Brown)							
(1915–16)–(1934–35)	18	.42	.49	.46	.52[a]	+0–1	+0–1
New Zealand (Williams)							
1923–1940[b]	18	.54	—	—	.54	—	—
II. Cross-section studies							
Australia							
1912	85	.52	.47	.53	.54	+0–1	+0–1
Australia							
1922–23	87	.53	.49	.52	.54	+0–1	+0–1
Australia							
1926–27	85	.59	.34	.63	.57	−0–1	−1–2
Australia							
1934–35	138	.64	.36	.64	.61	+0–1	−0–1
Australia							
1936–37	87	.49	.49	.50	.51	+0–1	+0–1
Victoria							
1910–11	34	.74	.25	.75	.64	−1–2	−1–2
Victoria							
1923–24	38	.62	.31	.67	.65	+0–1	−0–1
Victoria							
1927–28	35	.59	.27	.69	.68	+1–2	−0–1
New South Wales							
1933–34	125	.65	.34	.66	.51	−3–4	−3–4
Average All Commonwealth and State Studies		.60	.37	.62	.58		
Average Commonwealth Studies Only		.55	.43	.56	.55		
New Zealand							
1938–39	61	.46	.51	.47	.57	—	—
Canada							
1923	167	.48	.48	.50	.50	+0–1	0
Canada							
1927	163	.46	.52	.47	.48	+0–1	+0–1
Canada							
1935	165	.50	.52	.49	.40	−2–3	−2–3
Canada							
1937	164	.43	.58	.43	.52	+2–3	+2–3
Average Canadian Studies	—	.47	.52	.47	.48	—	—

[a] For the years 1924–1935 only.
[b] In the Williams study, the values of k were computed using formula (1). All other values were computed under formula (2).

In the one cross-section study which was carried through for New South Wales, the differences were greater, amounting to between 3 and 4 standard errors of estimate. In the case of Canada, however, the *average* degree of agreement was very close. The average value of k for the four years was .47, and similarly, $\frac{k}{k+j}$ was .47; while the average ratio of W/P was .48. This is an almost precise agreement. This agreement was also true of the years 1923 and 1927 when they are considered individually. The years 1935 and 1937, however, exhibit opposing tendencies. In the former year, k exceeded W/P by an appreciable amount; in the latter year, which was marked by great wage advances in the United States, which were reflected to some degree in Canada, this situation was exactly reversed. The two differences, however, almost precisely offset each other. The case of South Africa does, however, merit special mention. As I have pointed out, Professor Browne found that the combined exponents for black and white labor in 1937-38 were .65, but he also found that both groups of labor received only a total of .46 per cent of the net value added. While Professor Browne does not draw such a conclusion, perhaps this is a case where a highly monopolized set of industries which are largely run by foreign employers or by men whose cultural interests are elsewhere, do not give to the laborers that which in a competitive society they would obtain.

VII. *Summary*

After working on this problem for the better part of twenty years, I think I am aware of the many difficulties which are involved. In a few cases, the method apparently breaks down and in other cases incongruous results are obtained. I should like to suggest, however, that the following tentative conclusions seem justified.

1. That within a given country for the periods studied, there is a substantial and indeed a surprising degree of agreement in the values of k and of j which we obtain for various years.

2. There is also a surprising degree of agreement between the results for the United States, Australia, and South Africa.

3. It is hard to believe that these results can be purely accidental, as some critics have maintained.[30] Time studies for the period between

[30] It would be interesting to work out the mathematical possibility that these results are purely accidental. I believe that it would only be one out of many millions. It is theoretically possible, as Bertrand Russell has pointed out, that all the books in the British Museum were written by monkeys pounding typewriters at random. But we know that they were not!

the two great wars are, however, likely to present difficulties.

4. The deviations of the actual or observed values from those which we would theoretically expect to prevail under the formula are not large and indeed are slightly less than we would expect under the random distribution of errors of sampling and of measurement. It is submitted that the total number of observations, namely over 3,500, is sufficiently large so that if the results had been purely accidental, this degree of agreement would not have occurred.

5. The instances of large deviations of the actual from the theoretical values can in most cases be explained as being caused by imperfect competition and by expanding demand in the case of the plus deviations and by contracting demand, "sweating," and possibly "excessive" competition in the case of the minus industries. This would indicate that if these complications could be eliminated, the agreement between the actual and theoretical products would be greater.

6. That, taken in the large, there is an almost precise degree of agreement between the actual share received by labor and that which, according to the theory of marginal productivity, we would expect labor to obtain.

In conclusion, may I emphasize again that there is much work which remains to be done on this question and that a lifetime would be all too short to probe the many problems which present themselves. Is it too much to hope that the succeeding twenty years may see further progress along this line and that if the older generation finds it impossible to carry on such studies, the younger economists may find such lines of inquiry a challenge to their ingenuity and abilities?[31] I have always been struck by the old Hindu saying, "This is no door but only a little window that opens out upon a great world." Since this is peculiarly applicable to the studies which I have attempted, upon that note I shall end.

[31] Some of the studies which badly need to be carried out are (1) to develop the production function for each and every year over a long period, say 1910-1940, for Australia, New Zealand, and Canada; (2) to carry on studies of the production function for a large number of specific firms and *within* specific industries and hence connect the theory of the firm and of the industry with that of the economy; (3) to carry on further studies, along the lines of Mr. Olson, on inter-spatial variations in real income and the factors affecting them; and (4) to develop production functions for agriculture, mining, and public utilities.

In order to bring our analysis down to date in the larger countries, it is highly desirable that statistics on the quantities of capital be collected for Great Britain, Sweden, and the United States.

[39]

THE ECONOMIC JOURNAL

MARCH 1997

The Economic Journal, **107** (*March*), 297–321. Published by Blackwell Publishers, 108 Cowley Road, Oxford OX4 1JF, UK and 238 Main Street, Cambridge, MA 02142, USA.

BRINGING INCOME DISTRIBUTION IN FROM THE COLD*

A. B. Atkinson

I. INTRODUCTION: THE SUBJECT OF INCOME DISTRIBUTION

The title of this Presidential Address is chosen to highlight the way in which the subject of income distribution has in the past been marginalised. For much of this century, it has been very much out in the cold. There are signs that in the 1990s it is being welcomed back, and I shall be referring to recent research, but I would like to use this occasion to give further impetus to the re-incorporation of income distribution into the main body of economic analysis.

The peripheral nature of income distribution has long been a concern. In 1920, Hugh Dalton wrote in the Preface to his book *Some Aspects of The Inequality of Incomes in Modern Communities* that:

> 'While studying economics at Cambridge in 1909–10, I became specially interested in those [parts] which set out to discuss the distribution of income. I gradually noticed, however, that most "theories of distribution" were almost wholly concerned with distribution as between "factors of production". Distribution as between persons, a problem of more direct and obvious interest, was either left out of the textbooks altogether, or treated so briefly, as to suggest that it raised no question, which could not be answered either by generalisations about the factors of production, or by plodding statistical investigations, which professors of economic theory were content to leave to lesser men.' (1920), p. vii).

Of course, income distribution was a subject of central importance to classical economists. There is the famous quotation from Ricardo in which he told Malthus that Political Economy should be

* Presidential Address to the Royal Economic Society, Swansea April 1996. This Address is dedicated to the memory of Professor James Meade, who sadly died on 22 December 1995. From him I first learned how economic analysis can help us understand the distribution of income and can contribute to raising the seriousness of public debate.

I should like to thank the many people with whom I have worked on this subject, and on whose research, including our joint writings, I have drawn heavily. In particular, I owe especial thanks to (in alphabetical order) François Bourguignon, Andrea Brandolini, Frank Cowell, Alan Harrison, John Hills, Stephen Jenkins, Mervyn King, John Micklewright, Brian Nolan, Lee Rainwater, Amartya Sen, Tim Smeeding, Nick Stern, Joe Stiglitz, Holly Sutherland, and Chris Trinder. I am most grateful to the following for their helpful comments on an earlier version of this text: Philippe Aghion, Kenneth Arrow, Patrick Bolton, Andrea Brandolini, Stephen Jenkins, Holly Sutherland, and Steven Webb.

'an enquiry into the laws which determine the division of the produce of industry amongst the classes who concur in its formation' (1951 edition, p. 278).

This was the functional, or factor, distribution of income, and much of what can be found today in textbooks under the heading of the 'Theory of Distribution' is concerned with the determinants of payments to factors (labour, land and capital). In mainstream economic theory, the competitive theory of factor pricing determines the division of national income between wages, profit and rent. Competitive theory has been criticised, with alternatives proposed, such as the Cambridge theory based on the accumulation relationships, or the Kaleckian theory based on imperfect competition, but it is these ideas which form the main component of the theory of distribution. However, as Dalton observed, the relationship of the factor distribution with the personal distribution of income is typically not spelled out. Statements about the division of national income between wages and profits do not tell us directly what determines the share of the top 20% or the bottom 20% of income recipients. The factor distribution is certainly part of the story, but it is only part, and the other links in the chain need to receive attention.

Nor has the personal distribution of income been a central subject for research in the economics profession. An analysis of the contents of this JOURNAL over the past 50 years indicates that, on average, the JOURNAL published one and a half articles a year on income distribution, out of an average of 38 articles per year. In other words, about 4% of the articles dealt with income distribution (broadly interpreted), as shown by the nine-year moving average in Fig. 1. As a basis for comparison, I took international

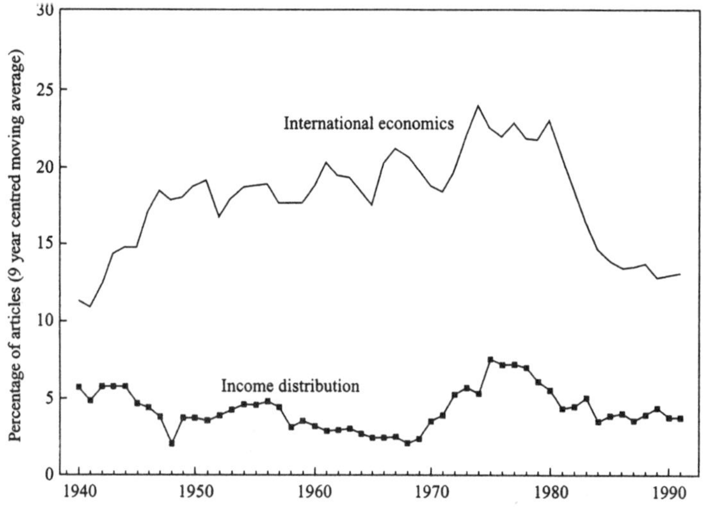

Fig. 1. Articles in this JOURNAL on income distribution and international economics.

economics, which is another significant field, of central importance for the United Kingdom. Here the corresponding average is six and a half articles per year – or about four times as many.

Taking all journals and books together, there is, of course, a large number of articles on income distribution. If one types in the key words 'income distribution' to the EconLit database 1969–6/1995, then one comes up with 4,549 entries. (In contrast, 'international trade' generates twice as many entries.) But if one examines these, one discovers that a large proportion deal with development economics. This is clearly of great importance, but here I am concerned with OECD countries. A sizeable number deal with the impact of income distribution on other variables. There are articles on the statistical evidence about distribution and about the measurement of inequality; there are articles on the redistribution of income and social security. But what I missed when I read through these entries is research which ties income distribution centrally into analysis as to how the economy works. What is the connection between income inequality and the macro-economic variables that are centre stage in most economic debate? What is the inter-relationship between economic performance and income distribution? How can we use economic theory to explain what is happening to the incomes of individuals, families and households?

II. EMPIRICAL POINTS OF DEPARTURE

In setting the scene for an analysis of the economics of personal income distribution, I begin with empirical evidence about the distribution of disposable household income in the United Kingdom and other OECD countries.[1] I should stress that I am not here attempting to set out the strengths and weaknesses of the evidence on income inequality. There are many limitations to the data presented. They tell us nothing about expenditure, only about income; they omit important sources of income such as fringe benefits or capital gains or undisclosed earnings from the informal economy; they omit the benefits of government spending other than cash or near-cash transfers; they relate to the household and do not explore what happens within the family. When I compare changes over time in income inequality in different countries, the figures are drawn from national studies of income inequality which are not designed for purposes of international comparison. They are not necessarily based on the same concepts of income or method of calculation or period of time, although I have chosen those series which give a reasonable span of years and which are themselves intended to be consistent over time. (I have also in some cases linked series; the sources are listed in the Appendix.)

The data, nonetheless, tell an interesting story. In particular:

(i) the United Kingdom stands out for the sharpness of the rise in recorded income inequality in the 1980s;

[1] For fuller information about recent trends in income distribution in OECD countries, see Gardiner (1993), Atkinson (1996*a*), Atkinson *et al.* (1995), and Hills (1996). On the United Kingdom, see Coulter *et al.* (1994), Goodman and Webb (1994), and Jenkins (1995).

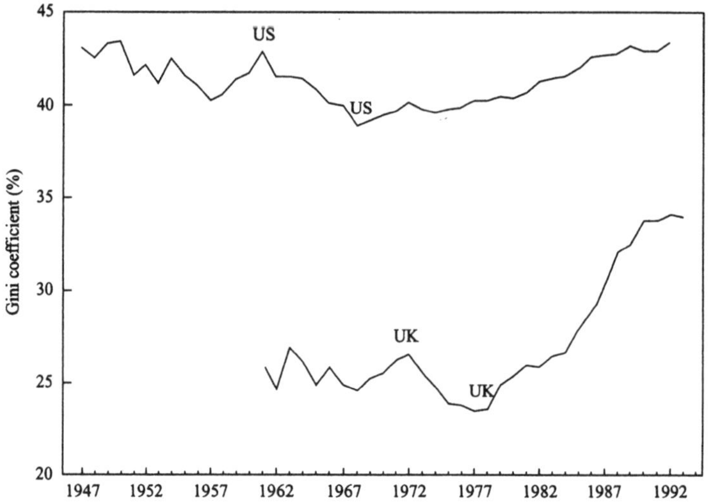

Fig. 2. Income inequality in the United Kingdom and the United States. US 1947–92; UK 1961–93.

(ii) changes in the personal distribution are large enough to affect our view of aggregate economic performance;
(iii) changes in inequality may be better described as 'episodic' rather than as long-run 'trends'.

Whether one finds the rise in inequality a matter for concern is a matter of personal judgement. In this paper, I follow conventional practice and refer to income differences as 'income in equality', but whether any difference is actually considered an injustice is a matter both of judgement and of interpretation. I am, for example, largely concentrating on snapshots of the distribution – such as income in 1993 or what people earned in the month of April 1995 – whereas in assessing equity we may be concerned with income mobility. We may want to adopt a lifetime or even dynastic perspective, leading us to view the distribution either more or less favourably.

II.A. *Unparalleled Rise in United Kingdom Income Inequality in the* 1980*s*

One of the most durable of stylised facts in the field of income distribution is the celebrated 'Kuznets curve', relating income inequality to the process of industrialisation. Kuznets (1955) considered a two sector economy in which overall inequality depends on the proportion employed in each sector, on the degree of inequality within sectors, and on the difference between the mean incomes in the two sectors. A rise in the proportion employed in the higher income industrial sector could, on certain assumptions, lead first to rising and then falling overall inequality. Kuznets saw the turning point in his tentatively suggested 'long secular swing in income inequality' as coming in the last

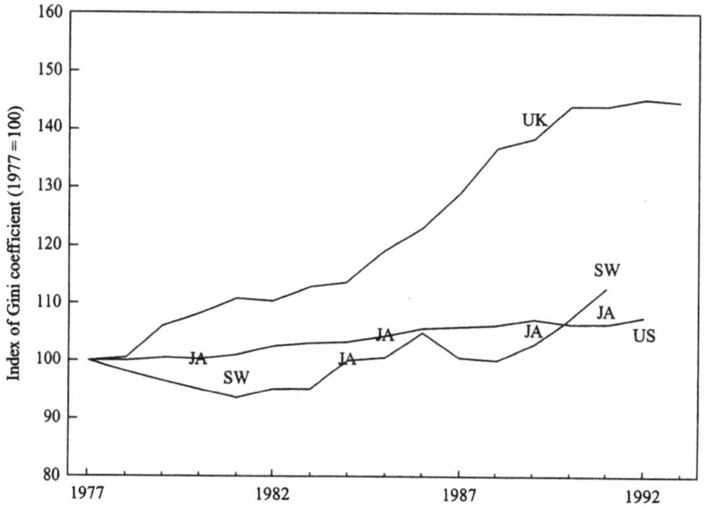

Fig. 3. Income inequality 1977 = 100. UK, US, Sweden (SW) and Japan (JA) (1980 = 100).

quarter of the nineteenth century in England, and somewhat later in the United States and Germany. He was writing in the 1950s, but there continued to be a widespread belief that income inequality in countries such as the United Kingdom and the United States would continue to fall, steadily, if not spectacularly (see, for example, Tinbergen, 1975).

As we now know, income inequality did not continue to fall. In the United States, the Gini coefficient of inequality for household incomes rose between 1968 and 1992 by three and a half percentage points, which more or less took the coefficient back to the level before the decline in the 1960s – see Fig. 2. This is a significant increase, but if you want to see a *big* increase then it is to the United Kingdom that one has to look. Between 1977 and 1991, the United Kingdom Gini coefficient rose by 10 percentage points (these are the estimates of Goodman and Webb, 1994).

Inequality has of course risen in a number of other countries. Fig. 3 shows the change in recorded income inequality since 1977 for Sweden and Japan, in addition to the United States and the United Kingdom. Inequality rose sharply in Sweden at the end of the 1980s, but for a much shorter period than in the United Kingdom. It increased in Japan (shown by isolated points marked JA) but not to the same degree. Nor did inequality rise in all countries over this period. Fig. 4 shows the position for the three large members of the European Union. One clear conclusion is that the United Kingdom stands out for the sharpness of the rise in recorded income inequality in the 1980s. This was unparalleled in the countries examined.

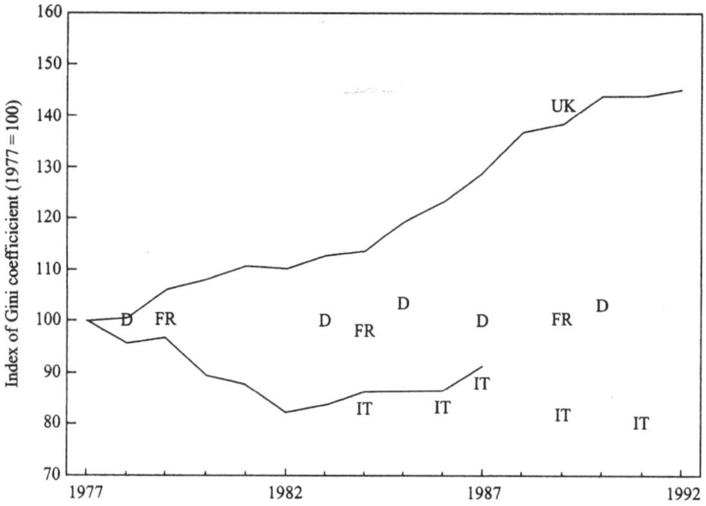

Fig. 4. Income inequality 1977 = 100. UK, (FR) France (1979 = 100), (D) West Germany (1978 = 100) and (IT) Italy.

II.B. *Rising Inequality Matters*

In the past, changes in income distribution have often been dismissed as too insignificant to be worth attention. But this can no longer be done. Changes in the distribution of the magnitude observed in the United Kingdom in the 1980s can affect our view of aggregate economic performance.

The impact of rising inequality does of course depend on judgements of value. A person who is indifferent to changes in the distribution of income is content to measure performance by mean income. The solid line in Fig. 5 shows the trend in mean household equivalent disposable income since 1961, using the estimates of Goodman and Webb (1994). On the other hand, for a person concerned about income inequality, the assessment of the outcome depends on their distributional preferences. The dashed line in Fig. 5 shows the distributionally adjusted real income measure proposed by Sen (1976) on the basis of rank order weights (mean income times (one minus the Gini coefficient)). The distributionally adjusted measure tracks the mean income closely until 1973; it then does a little better until 1979; and after that it falls progressively behind. The Gini adjustment is only one of many possible, but it shows that taking account of distributional changes can give a different picture of the growth performance: the record of the 1980s looks less impressive.[2]

[2] Distributional corrections to the UK growth rate have been made by Beckerman (1980) and by Crafts (1993) in his evaluation of the 'Thatcher Experiment'. In the United States, Klasen has shown how distributionally-weighted growth rates 'shed a much more favorable light on improvements in well-being during the 1960s, particularly compared to the 1980s' (1994, p. 270).

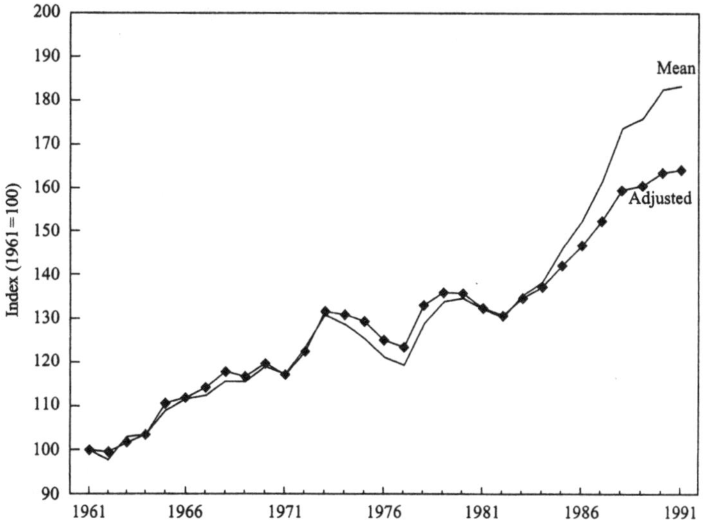

Fig. 5. UK mean income and distributionally adjusted income using Gini coefficient.

II.C. *Episodes not Trends*

Not only has the 'Kuznets curve' been confounded by recent events, but it has also become clear that it is misleading to talk of 'trends' when describing the postwar evolution of the income distribution. The evidence in Figs. 2–4 suggests that it may be better for a number of countries to think in terms of 'episodes' when inequality fell or increased. Returning to Fig. 2, we can see that there was an episode of declining inequality in the United States during the Kennedy/Johnson years (1961–8, marked by US–US), followed by a period of increase from 1969. In the United Kingdom, there appears to have been a decline post-1972 (marked by UK–UK), which may, or may not, be associated with incomes policies (see below); and the post-1977 period divides into three sub-periods, with a faster rise in the Gini coefficient after 1984, and possibly a flattening in the 1990s. Here I should note that the most recent figures from the Central Statistical Office (CSO) show 1991 as being the highwater mark of inequality in the United Kingdom.[3]

What I am suggesting is not new. Those used to working with macro-economic time series will recognise that I am describing a segmented trend model (Perron, 1989), which does indeed seem to provide a reasonable

[3] The CSO estimates differ in definition from those of Goodman and Webb (1994) used in Fig. 2, in that they are weighted by households, are not re-weighted for differential non-response or for the under-representation of high incomes, and in annualising their data in some respects.

The CSO estimates show the Gini coefficient for household equivalent disposable income rising from 27% in 1979 to 34% in 1989 (Central Statistical Office, 1994, p. 123). The CSO estimates for later years differ in including the benefit from company cars and from beneficial loans for house purchase from employers; they show a Gini coefficient of 34% for 1992 and 1993/4 and 33% for 1994/5 (same source and Central Statistical Office, 1995, p. 46).

description of the data. My emphasis on the episodic nature of change in the income distribution has parallels elsewhere. In his account of wage differentials, Reder notes that

> 'The long-run decline in the skill margin in advanced countries has not occurred slowly and steadily. Instead, the skill margin appears to have remained constant for relatively long periods of time and then to have declined sharply within a very few years' (1962, p. 408).

The analysis by Donohue and Heckman (1991) of the status of black Americans concludes that

> 'the story of black economic progress is not one of uniform secular advance, but rather of episodic change.' (1991, p. 1604).

More generally, one advantage of rejecting an evolutionary approach in favour of an 'episodic' characterisation, is that as described by Giddens, it

> 'helps free us from the tendency...to analyse societal development in terms of "stages", and from the influence of "unfolding models" of change' (Giddens, 1981, pp. 82–3).

I should emphasise that episodic change in inequality may be in either direction: the recent United Kingdom experience could be reversed. It also has important implications for the possible lines of explanation, to which I turn in Sections IV–VI. It means that we have to consider not just the long-run equilibrium properties of the distribution, but also the explanations of these episodic departures, if possible making these endogenous.[4]

III. THE SOURCES OF INEQUALITY

One could describe the textbook economic approach as starting from the underlying economic forces and working back to how they impinge on individuals and families. In principle, the line of argument leads from the factor distribution to the personal distribution of income. The trouble is that it often does not seem to get there. The link is not made: we are left wondering about the implications for the personal distribution.

I therefore want to start from the other end: with the sources of household income. According to the *Family Expenditure Survey*, which is the origin of the United Kingdom data I have been using, the bulk of household income comes from work (employment and self-employment), but the proportion has been falling: from 83% in 1973 to 75% in 1983 and 73% in 1993.[5] Recorded household income from capital rose from 1973 to 1993 (from 7% to 11%), but this has come increasingly through the route of annuities and private pension

[4] Among the factors which may be associated with episodes of distributional change are shifts in demographic structure. These are not discussed here, but see, in a United Kingdom context, Mookherjee and Shorrocks (1982) and Jenkins (1995).

[5] These figures are from Central Statistical Office (1994), Chart 8.1, page 85. It should be noted that in these figures people away from work without pay for 13 weeks or less are treated as continuing to receive their normal wage or salary. Although the series over time is shown as continuous by the CSO in this graphic, there is a break in the series in 1983 – see Atkinson (1993).

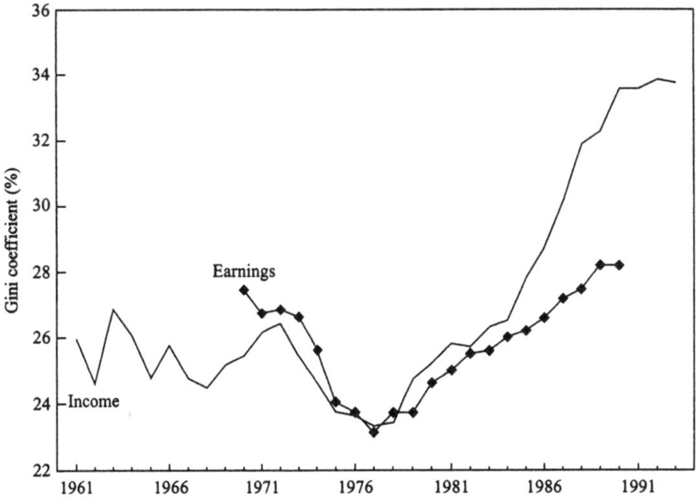

Fig. 6. Incomes and Earnings. Inequality of household incomes and individual earnings.

benefits, which have doubled from 3 to 6%. Finally, one has to remember that the second largest source of income is social security benefits. This accounted for 14% in 1993, although the proportion fell between 1983 and 1993, after having increased greatly between 1973 and 1983 (from 9% to 16%).

These three sources – earnings, capital income and transfers – will be my focus throughout the rest of the paper.

III.A. *Earnings Dispersion*

When one talks about income inequality, most people think of rising earnings dispersion, and this is indeed the aspect which has received most attention from the economics profession. In the United Kingdom there is plain evidence of widening differentials in the distribution of wage income (see Gosling *et al.* 1996): for all workers, paid for a full week, the real earnings of the bottom decile, deflated by the retail prices index, grew by 11% between April 1979 and April 1995, compared with 50% for the top decile.[6]

Fig. 6 shows the movement in earnings dispersion for individual employees and the comparison with the household income inequality series we have been using. The two series appear to move together over the 1970s and early 1980s, but from 1984 to the end of the 1980s there was a divergence, with the income coefficient rising more sharply. The rise in earnings dispersion is a powerful contributing factor but only part of story. Inequality among those in work has to allow for the self-employed, whose importance in the distribution has been stressed by Goodman and Webb (1994), Jenkins (1995) and Parker (1996). But

[6] These figures are from the *New Earnings Survey* (1979, p. A34 and 1995, p. A1.1), and relate to adult male full-time workers whose pay was not affected by absence. They are adjusted for the change in definition of adult workers in 1983. The price index used is the all items retail prices index.

there was also, particularly between 1975 and 1985, a large rise in the proportion of families without incomes from work: from 20% to 30% (Atkinson, 1993, table 5). As has been stressed by Gregg and Wadsworth (1996), there has been a divergence between the employment rates of individuals and of households, with a rise in both workless and two-income families.

III.B. *Incomes without Work: Capital Income and Transfers*

The rise in the proportion of families without income from work is important because this group not only has a lower average income but also exhibits considerable inequality. It is commonly believed, especially given the largely flat-rate benefit structure, that there is much less inequality within this group, but being without work income does not reduce everyone to the same level: for family units, in 1985 the Gini coefficient was virtually the same as for those with work income (Atkinson, 1993, table 5). This makes it of particular interest to examine the position of this group.

One element is capital income. Real rates of interest increased in the early 1980s and remained high a decade later (see Blanchard, 1993); real dividends increased, and share prices rose still faster. The implications of these changes for the observed distribution of household income are, however, far from transparent: it is money income, rather than real income, which appears in the statistics, and allowance has to be made for financial and other intervening institutions, such as pension funds – see Atkinson (1996*b*). Here I simply note for future reference that the rise in expected real interest rates (Scott, 1993) may well have affected household decisions, an aspect to which I return when discussing investment in human capital.

The main source of income for those not in work is in fact social security, and this brings me to the distributional impact of the government, a subject which goes back at least to Jevons who wrote a memorandum for the Treasury in 1869 (Roseveare, 1973). The present day counterpart is the *Economic Trends* study published by the Central Statistical Office (1995). This shows the difference between 'private income' (i.e. earnings plus capital income plus private transfers) and post-tax income allowing for social security transfers received, and direct and indirect taxes paid. We cannot draw any conclusions from this difference as to the actual incidence of the government budget, but it is, nonetheless, interesting that the *Economic Trends* study shows that in the first half of the 1980s the Gini coefficient for private income (not including transfers) increased sharply, with a much more moderate increase in the coefficient for post-tax and benefit income. At first sight, at least, the welfare state appears to have moderated the rise in pre-transfer incomes. After 1984 the situation reverses: the Gini coefficient for original incomes rose by one percentage point from 1984 to 1989 but that for post-tax income increased by seven percentage points.

The apparent fall in the redistributive impact of transfers and direct taxes since the mid-1980s is circumstantial evidence that policy changes have contributed to the rise in income inequality. Redmond and Sutherland (1995) have calculated that application of the 1978/9 tax and benefit system, indexed in line with per capita GDP, to the 1994/5 distribution of household incomes would have reduced the tax burden for all decile groups except the top; and the Gini coefficient would have been lower by about five percentage points. At a more detailed level, Atkinson and Micklewright (1989) list seventeen distinct changes in unemployment insurance between 1979 and 1988, the majority of which reduced the level or coverage of benefit.

To sum up, it is not just the dispersion of labour income that we need to understand – important though that is – and it is not just private incomes that need to be considered. The determinants of public redistribution are part of what has to be explained. Do they reflect shifts in the constraints faced by governments (for example, on account of fiscal competition)? How far are they the outcome of changes in the prevailing ideology? I return to these questions in Section VI.

IV. DIFFERENT EXPLANATIONS OF EARNINGS DISPERSION

As already indicated, there is at present limited connection between economic theory and the explanation of personal income distribution. This is not to suggest that there is *no* connection, and I begin with one of the areas which has been most discussed in recent years: the explanation of earnings dispersion.

This recent literature is remarkable both for its liveliness and for the extent to which supply and demand considerations hold sway. There appears to be widespread agreement on a straightforward explanation of rising earnings dispersion: there has been a shift in demand away from unskilled labour in favour of skilled workers. In the United States and the United Kingdom this has led to a fall in the relative wage of unskilled workers, and hence a rise in dispersion.

IV.A. *Supply and Demand for Skill*

Increased dispersion is explained therefore by the simplest of economic tools: supply and demand. Suppose that we consider just two kinds of labour (skilled and unskilled). If the premium for skilled workers increases at a time when the relative number of skilled workers in employment rises (as has been the case – see Levy and Murnane, 1992, and Gregg and Machin, 1994), then there must have been a rise in the relative demand for skilled labour. Why should the demand curve have shifted? One much-discussed explanation is the liberalisation of international trade and increased competition from the countries where unskilled labour is abundant: the growth of North–South trade in manufactures, as emphasised by Wood (1994). The precise contribution of trade has been debated (see Burtless, 1995, for a recent review), and other explanations have been advanced, notably that technical change has been biased towards skilled labour with the introduction of automation and Information Technology (IT). Moreover, it is possible that trade and technical change interact.

Whether based on trade or on technology, the supply and demand story sounds an attractive one, not least because it can be readily explained to a lay audience:

> 'factory workers in developed countries face the twin threat of robots filling in job applications, as well as long lines of overseas suppliers offering to produce goods at a fraction of the cost' (Leamer, 1995, p. 6).

It can also explain why there may be episodes of rising or falling differentials. If, for instance, government education and training policy were to lead to an expansion of the supply of skilled workers, then we would expect the wage premium to fall over a period. If there is major technological innovation, such as the introduction of IT, then this may cause a once-for-all shift in the opposite direction.

The proponents of the skill-based explanation stress that it is not just a matter of observable job characteristics, but also of unobserved skill components. This extension is necessary in view of what Krugman (1994) has called the 'fractal' quality of increased dispersion: however narrowly one defines groups, one still finds an increase in dispersion. Evidence for the United Kingdom is provided by Robinson (1994), who reports that the dispersion of male earnings, measured by the decile ratio (ratio of top to bottom decile), widened significantly between 1979 and 1990 for all occupational groups except III (Professional and related in education, welfare and health) and IX (Security and protective service). The more detailed occupational data are shown in Fig. 7, where I have taken the 38 detailed KOS occupations where there were more

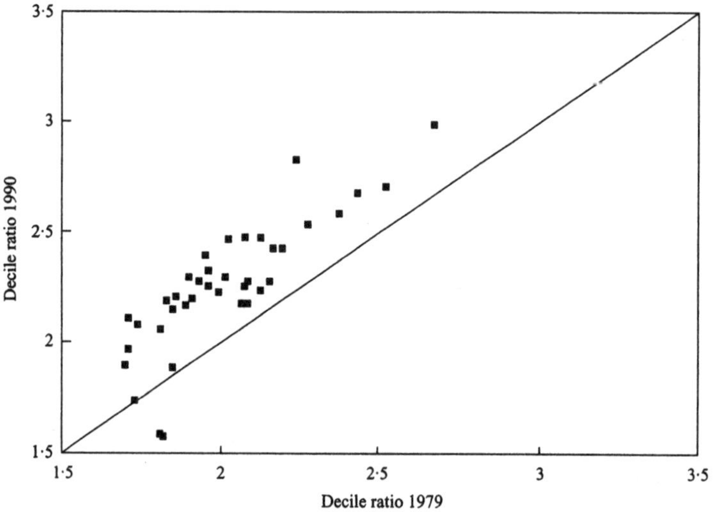

Fig. 7. Occupational groups. Decile ratio of individual earnings within occupational groups.

than 500 employees in 1979 and followed them to 1990, which is the date when the classification was changed.[7] The figures refer to adult men paid for the full week (no adjustment is made for the change in the definition of 'adult' in 1983). The overall decile ratio was 2·38 in 1979 and 3·11 in 1990. There are two observations below the 45° line: policemen and secondary school teachers. There are two close to the line: further education teachers and bus and coach drivers. But the great majority show increased dispersion even within narrowly defined occupational groups.

Faced with such a fractal picture of differences within narrowly-defined occupational or educational groups, some researchers have concluded that it too is a matter of skill differences: according to Murphy

> 'the increase in within-group variation is generated by the same forces leading to greater wage inequality across groups (i.e., the general growth in the demand for skill)' (1995, p. 56).

Others may conclude that the increased dispersion within occupational groups is a reason for seeking additional explanations.

IV.B. *Alternative Explanations*

The present-day hegemony of the supply and demand story contrasts markedly with earlier writing on wage differentials, where there has been a creative tension between market force and alternative explanations of wage differentials. Phelps Brown, for instance, opened his *The Inequality of Pay* (1977) by contrasting the 'economist's' approach to pay determination with that of the 'sociologist': the economist sees people as engaged in rational, impersonal transactions; the sociologist sees people interacting as members of a society.

In part, social interactions are institutionalised through collective bargaining and government intervention. The simple competitive model has to be modified to allow for trade union/employer negotiations and for the impact of government, both on collective bargaining and directly on wage determination. If it is the case that unions lead to lower earnings dispersion, then one possible cause of the rise in dispersion in the United Kingdom is the decline in union power and coverage; and there is evidence that part (but only part) can be explained in this way. Gosling and Machin (1993), using establishment data on semi-skilled earnings, conclude that decline in unionisation accounted for around 15–20% of increased earnings dispersion in the 1980s. A similar result is reached by Bell and Pitt (1995) using Family Expenditure Survey data on individual male earnings.

The direct impact of government in the 1980s has included the removal of 'fair wages' requirements for government contractors and the abolition of Wages Council protection for lower-paid workers. Dickens *et al.* (1994), using New Earnings Survey data, find that Wages Councils significantly compressed the distribution of earnings in Wages Council industries. More generally, in the

[7] The KOS data have been examined by Bell *et al.* (1990). For instance, they show for engineering technicians that over the period 1973–82 there was first a fall then a rise in dispersion which was less pronounced than, but mirrored, the overall change.

1970s Government incomes policies were explicitly concerned to tilt pay settlements in favour of the less well paid (for a summary, see Goodman and Webb, 1994, p. 17). The Conservative Stage Two in 1973 set a group pay limit of £1 plus 4%, with an individual maximum increase of £250 a year. Labour's *Attack on Inflation* in 1975 restricted increases to £6 a week, with no increase for those earning more than £8,500 a year.

Incomes policies are examples of what I mean by 'episodes'. If we were to carry out a time series analysis of the earnings dispersion series, then the imposition and ending of incomes policy would provide natural points at which to introduce a break in the trend. However, the extent to which incomes policies in fact achieved their redistributive aims has been the subject of debate. While some argue that reduced earnings dispersion in the 1970s was, at least in part, the result of incomes policy (see Chater, 1981, for a case study of the engineering industry), and that the subsequent reversal reflects its abandonment (Adams, 1988), others have been more sceptical, pointing to the lack of correspondence between the particular policy stages and the observed narrowing (Dean, 1978) and to the failure to observe the same outcome at the level of individual settlement groups (Ashenfelter and Layard, 1979). Brown (1976 and 1979) has argued that the levelling during the 1970s was more associated with high rates of inflation, combined with concepts of 'fairness' involving absolute rather than relative positions.

IV.C. *Social Custom and Norms*

Trade union bargaining and statutory wage determination may be incorporated into the supply and demand framework, or the economists' approach, and the same applies to monopsonistic behaviour by employers. More of a challenge is the view that supply and demand only place limits on the possible wage differentials, with other factors such as social norms determining where between these limits wages actually lie. Such a 'range theory' of wage differentials was advanced by Lester (1952) and has long been implicit in much institutional writing on labour economics, even if it has received less attention in recent years. Within this range, there is scope for notions of fairness or equity, as has been investigated by, among others, Wood (1978), and Carruth and Oswald (1989).

It seems to me that these alternative approaches have merits which have been too hastily discounted by supply and demand theorists. There are good grounds to try and build bridges. Such an approach has been well illustrated by the research of Akerlof and of Solow on involuntary unemployment. From their work, one can draw the lesson that observance of social norms can be consistent with individual rationality, even where it may appear to conflict with economic advantage. Akerlof (1981) describes a model where individual utility depends not only on income but also on reputation and, for those who believe in the social code, on conformity with the code. The loss of reputation depends on the proportion who believe in the code, which is undermined if people cease to observe it. He shows that there may be a long-run equilibrium with the persistence of a 'fair', rather than market-clearing, wage. Solow

(1990) uses a repeated game model to argue that it may be individually rational for unemployed workers not to undercut the wages of those in employment.

In this way, we are not suspending supply and demand as much as enriching the behaviour which lies behind these relations. Looked at this way, widening wage dispersion can result not just from shifts in the demand for skill but also from changes in social norms. It may, for exogenous reasons, have become socially acceptable to have larger wage differentials within the workplace. Or the exogenous shift in demand may have interacted with the endogenous determination of social norms. As more people are remunerated outside the conventional norms, so adherence to these norms becomes weaker, or the socially acceptable range widens. There may be multiple equilibria. The demand shift may have caused a movement from a low differential equilibrium to a high differential equilibrium. This line of explanation seems to me to repay further consideration, drawing on sociological and psychological theories of social norms.[8]

V. OTHER PARTS OF THE PUZZLE

The account given so far may be criticised as partial/partial analysis. It is partial in the sense that it has focused on the labour market, and not considered the general equilibrium of the economy as a whole. It is partial/partial in that relatively little has been said about the supply side. If differentials widen on account of demand shifts (or changes in social norms), what effect will this ultimately have on the supply of workers with different skills?

The potential importance may be seen from a simple model. Suppose that ability differences affect earnings equally in skilled and unskilled jobs, that there are no other costs of training apart from the time spent acquiring the skill, that everyone can borrow at an interest rate r, and that the working life is the same. Then for the skilled wage, w_s, to compensate exactly for the delayed entry into work, it has to be the case that $w_s e^{-rS} = w_u$ where the length of training is S, and w_u is the unskilled wage. In terms of the supply and demand for skill diagram, the relative supply curve in terms of relative wages is horizontal; in the long-run, where the wage differential (w_s/w_u) is equal to e_{rS}, people are indifferent between skilled and unskilled jobs. In the long-run, shifts in demand affect the number of skilled workers but not the wage differential.

In such a case, the differential exactly compensates for the cost of education (delayed earnings). This has two important implications. First, no lifetime inequality is introduced. This simple observation is often overlooked in the public debate. It is indeed striking how much the recent discussion has focused exclusively on wage differentials and not asked whether such differences are associated with inequality. This re-inforces the warning given earlier that, although concentrating on a snapshot of the distribution, we need to bear in mind the lifetime perspective. Secondly, the compensating wage differential depends on the rate of interest, so that if real interest rates have risen this may

[8] An alternative approach is to make endogenous people's beliefs about the relation between their actions and economic rewards – see Piketty (1995*b*).

explain part of the observed widening in the wage distribution. This takes us outside the labour market. We are led to ask how people are differentially affected by a rise in the interest rate, which in turn depends on their initial endowments of capital.

V.A. *The Capital Market and General Equilibrium*

One of the important contributions of James Meade to our understanding of income distribution is that he set the acquisition of marketable skills in the wider context of home background and the transmission of advantage from generation to generation, through both human capital and material inheritance. In *Efficiency, Equality and the Ownership of Property* (1964), he described a model of intergenerational transmission, later developed in 'The Inheritance of Inequalities' (1973). Among other elements, educational attainment was assumed to be affected by parental income and wealth, moderated by stochastic elements ('luck') and social contacts. Property was accumulated through saving and inheritance, and the rate of return to savings was assumed to be an increasing function of wealth on the grounds that the fixed costs of acquiring information could be spread. This illustrates the 'positive feedback' emphasised by Meade:

> 'self-reinforcing influences which help to sustain the good fortune of the fortunate and the bad fortune of the unfortunate' (Meade, 1976, p. 155).

Meade's microeconomic analysis of income distribution was not explicitly related to the macro-economy, but Stiglitz (1969) set the model in the framework of neoclassical growth, where factor returns depend on the stock of capital. With the specific assumptions made (including a proportional savings function and the equal division of estates), Stiglitz proved that, in the absence of intrinsic differences between people, of imperfections in the capital market, and of stochastic elements, the distribution converges to equality. Convergence to long-run equality of wealth is guaranteed by the steady state condition that the rate of return is less than the rate of growth. This result depends on the assumptions. Convergence does not necessarily follow where consumption decisions are based on maximising the infinite stream of dynastic utility (Bliss, 1995). Stiglitz showed that unequal inheritance in the form of primogeniture could lead to sustained inequality. Bourguignon (1981) demonstrated how non-convexity in the accumulation relationship can lead to a two-class equilibrium, with persistent inequality despite people being intrinsically identical.

Non-convexity has been introduced in a different way in a recent interesting series of papers on the macro-economics of income distribution by Aghion and Bolton (1992, 1993), Banerjee and Newman (1991, 1993), Galor and Zeira (1993), and Piketty (1994).[9] Suppose that we combine the earlier supply and demand model of skill differentials (involving an indivisible investment in training) with a model of imperfections in the capital market, and the transmission of wealth from generation to generation. For this purpose, I

[9] For a review of these, and other contributions, see Brandolini and Rossi (1995), and Piketty (1995*a*).

simplify by assuming away stochastic elements, as is done by Galor and Zeira (1993), whose work I am following closely. There are, as in the model of Meade, a sequence of dynasties, although I do not allow for marriage, so that everyone reproduces unaided (and has one child). There are overlapping generations,[10] with bequests made at the end of the second period, so that each dynasty inherits in middle age. Bequests passed on to the next generation are determined as a fraction of lifetime wealth, based on the maximisation of a lifetime utility function where the amount bequeathed enters (a 'warm-glow' version of the bequest motive).

People are identical on birth in all respects except for their anticipated bequest; this does, however, affect their decision whether or not to acquire skills. The capital market is imperfect in that people can lend freely at a (continuous) rate of interest r but can only borrow against collateral. In the case of educational finance, expected bequests serve as a collateral. There is a critical level of bequest received below which people cannot afford to finance their consumption during education; moreover, this is an increasing function of the interest rate.[11,12] It is assumed that we are in a small economy open to world capital and product markets; the interest rate is therefore the world interest rate, but the wages are determined in the labour market where the demand is that of profit-maximising firms with identical production functions (assumed to be Cobb–Douglas).

The outcome depends on the various parameters. Fig. 8 shows a situation like that in the Galor and Zeira analysis where there is a long-run equilibrium with two groups, with different amounts of capital, where the richer group are skilled workers and the poorer are unskilled workers. The initial level of inherited wealth, i, is shown on the horizontal axis in the right hand quadrant. Those with more than i^* have sufficient collateral to invest in education. The lower right hand quadrant shows the distribution in a specified generation of people with wealth below i. If investment in skill is rationed by the capital market constraint, then the proportion below i^* determines the proportion of unskilled workers, denoted by l_u.

The wages for skilled and unskilled labour are shown in the bottom left quadrant as functions of the proportion of unskilled workers. (These functions are derived from the profit-maximising conditions of firms, and depend negatively on the rate of interest.) Comparing w_u with $w_s e^{-rS}$, we can see whether or not people would choose education if unconstrained. The diagram has been drawn in such a way that the constraint is binding, so that the supply

[10] All education and work takes place in the first period, and all work for the same length of time. Skilled workers spend the first fraction, S, of the period being trained, and then work for the remaining ($1-S$) of the first period. Unskilled workers work for the first fraction ($1-S$) of the first period, and then retire early. All workers are retired for the second period. The Galor and Zeira model has been adapted in this way to study the impact of pension schemes by Alessandra Casarico of Brasenose College, Oxford, in her M.Phil dissertation.

[11] It is assumed that there is a minimum level of consumption which has to be financed by the individual during training, which grows during the training period at exponential rate r.

[12] In Banerjee and Newman (1993) and Aghion and Bolton (1993), people borrow against collateral to invest in entrepreneurship; in both cases the minimum wealth level to make the investment is an increasing function of the rate of interest on a safe asset. See also Ferreira (1995).

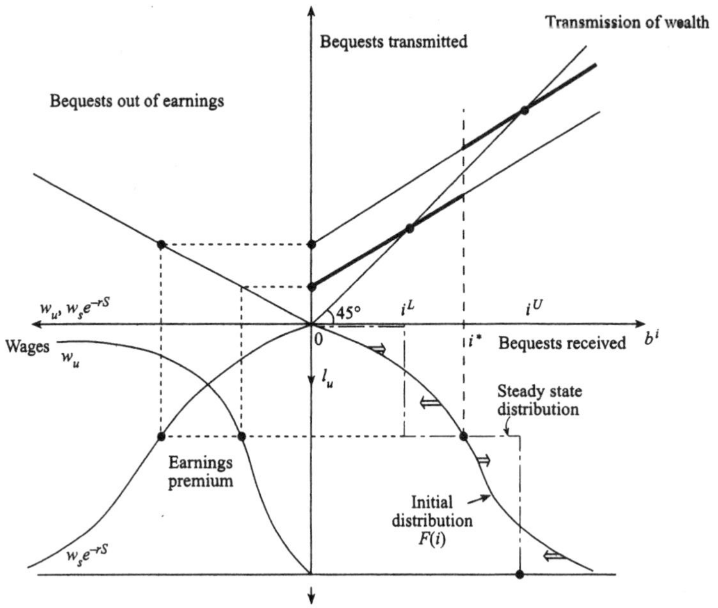

Fig. 8. Distribution of income with imperfect capital market. ⇐ shows evolution of distribution across generations.

of skilled labour consists of those who can borrow to finance the acquisition of education, and the wage premium exceeds the compensating differential.

The wage premium gives an advantage to skilled workers in terms of lifetime earnings which feeds into the determination of bequests out of earned income in the top left hand quadrant. In turn, this determines the intercept in the overall bequest relationship, and hence the wealth inherited by the next generation – see the top right hand quadrant in Fig. 8. From this, we can see how the distribution evolves over time. With the combination of parameters shown, the initial class division is maintained, with people initially below i^* converging to i^L and people initially above i^* converging to i^U (shown by the dashed and dotted lines).

My object in this paper has been to incorporate income distribution into the mainstream of economics, and what could be more mainstream than a four-quadrant diagram? Moreover, as in other branches of economics, it yields interesting comparative statics and dynamics. For instance, we can follow through the general equilibrium implications of technical change affecting the relative demand for skilled and unskilled labour, which would shift apart the curves in the bottom left hand quadrant. The model can be used to investigate the consequences of a rise in the real interest rate. It affects the demand for labour, shifting the w_u and w_s curves inward (we are moving round the factor/price frontier). The rise in r increases the compensating wage premium

e^{rS}. In the top left hand quadrant, the propensity to bequeath rises, as does the slope in the top right hand quadrant. At the same time, the rise in r increases the necessary collateral, and hence i^*.

Or to take a simpler exercise, suppose that we start, not from Fig. 8, but from Fig. 9. Here the cost of education is lower, so that i^* now lies below the value at which the unskilled class are in equilibrium. The unskilled are subject to the capital market constraint, so the wage premium exists, but over generations their wealth is rising, so that eventually the point is reached where the capital market ceases to be a constraint and the wage differential is at the equilibrium level. We are heading towards a situation where there is only one class.

Suppose now that this benign process (benign not least because ultimately the capital market imperfection ceases to be operative) is interrupted by an upward shift in the cost of education (for example, as a result of eliminating state subsidies). If sufficiently large, then this could transform the dynamic evolution, with people in the lower class unable to accumulate sufficient collateral. They would become trapped, as in Fig. 8. The whole nature of the distribution would change.

The model just described falls well short of incorporating all the rich detail of Meade's account of the determination of incomes (there is no marriage in the model, nor differential family size, nor genes, nor social contacts) and it does not do justice to important strands in the recent literature.[13] It does however, cast light on a number of current issues, including the phenomenon noted in the 1995 OECD survey of the United Kingdom that

> 'economic inequality in general hampers education and training reform. Income distribution has widened significantly since 1979. High income inequality can act to constrain pupil achievements in the lower tail of the distribution: learning can be a struggle for pupils from households which lack the resources to support their learning.' (OECD, 1995, pp. 81–2).

VI. PUBLIC CHOICE

The importance of state transfers in the distribution of personal income means that, as I have argued elsewhere (Atkinson, 1993), we need to go beyond purely economic explanations and to look for an explanation in the theory of public choice, or 'political economy'. We have to study the behaviour of the government, or its agencies, in determining the level and coverage of state benefits. The government's actions cannot be treated as purely exogenous.

There has been a recent resurgence of interest amongst economists in the politics of income redistribution, stemming particularly from concern with the relationship between income inequality and the rate of growth, including Alesina and Rodrik (1991), Bertola (1993), Perotti (1992, 1993), Persson and Tabellini (1994), and Saint-Paul and Verdier (1992). The models differ in their treatment of the link between distribution and growth, but they share a

[13] For instance, Brandolini (1992) has cast the relation between factor and personal distributions in terms of 'entitlement rules', which determine individual claims on the income from production. A second example of important work not referred to here is that on neighbourhood effects and human capital formation – see for example Durlauf (1996) and Bénabou (1996).

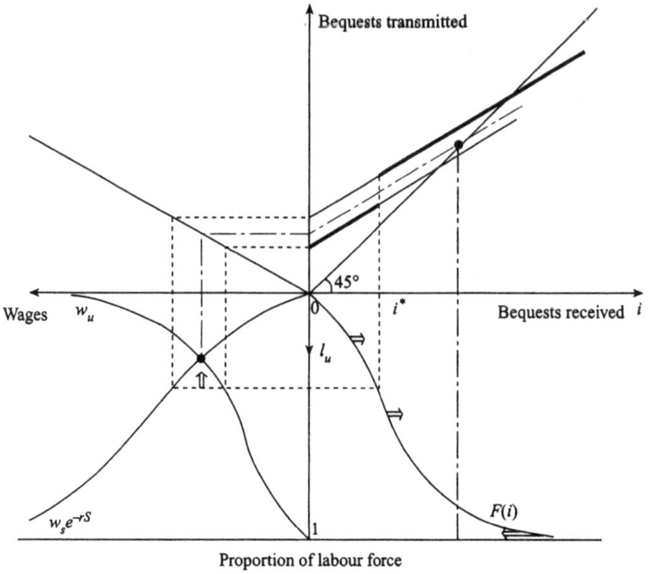

Fig. 9. Evolution towards one class society. ⇐ shows evolution of distribution across generations.

common approach to the determination of political equilibrium. As explained by Perotti in his review of this literature,

> 'one only needs to specify the political mechanism. In all cases, this is essentially some version of the standard median-voter result.' (1992, p. 312).

In my view, this understates what economists can usefully learn from political scientists (who may be a little offended by the word 'only'). The median voter theory is far from being 'standard'. It seems to me important to see how far the findings depend on whether the outcome is governed by the preferences of the median voter, or by the ideology or preferences of political parties, or by political pressure from different interest groups, or by bureaucratic control of civil servants or agencies. There has been relatively little research by economists which has set side by side different possible explanations of income redistribution, and examined the sensitivity of the conclusions to the choice of model.

Even if we accept that the preferences of voters are decisive, the modelling is a matter of some subtlety, as may be illustrated if we consider a concrete example and ask why has the response to higher unemployment in Britain been to reduce the relative level, and the coverage, of unemployment benefit? Then the median voter model can be interpreted in at least two different ways.

Suppose first that policy towards unemployment benefit reflects the wishes of the majority of the electorate who are in regular employment and who are assumed to have some degree of concern for the level of welfare of the unemployed. They maximise a function of their own net income and of the level of (flat-rate) unemployment benefit. This may be seen as a welfare function based on solidarity: people in employment are willing to pay a contribution towards unemployment benefit. We may now ask what happens if a labour market shock causes the cost of this policy to rise: for example where there is a rise in the number of beneficiaries, reducing the benefit per head for a given tax rate. This may well lead to a fall in the replacement rate preferred by the majority in work. On the other hand, it is easy to construct examples where the voter would choose the same replacement rate: there is an equi-proportionate reduction in benefits and net earnings (Atkinson, 1990 and 1996*a*, Chapter 9).

An alternative version of the median voter model is that where concern for the unemployed stems from a prudential, insurance motive, where the employed recognise that they themselves may be future recipients. The idea that voters determine their policy choices behind a genuine 'veil of ignorance', rather than a hypothetical veil as with the solidaristic welfare function, may provide an explanation as to why political support for unemployment compensation declined with the onset of recession. During the years of full employment of the 1950s and 1960s, support for the Welfare State persisted since, when unemployment was low, people remained uncertain whether they would be affected if we returned to unemployment of the level of the 1930s. By the time that the rise in unemployment in the 1980s had levelled off, however, people had a much better idea as to whether or not they were likely to be at risk and what was the probability of finding another job. The veil had been lifted. The majority found that they were not at risk, and they ceased to give as much weight to the risk of unemployment in their objective function. (This may of course have changed recently if there has been a rise in job insecurity.)

This is speculation. The main point to be made is that the explanation of trends in the income distribution cannot be complete without an analysis of public choice, and this cannot be treated simply as a routine application of a well-tried theory.

VII. CONCLUSIONS: BRINGING IT TOGETHER

My principal purpose here has been to argue that the economic analysis of the distribution of income is in need of further development before we can hope to give a definitive answer to the questions in which the ordinary person is interested – such as what determines the extent of inequality and why has inequality increased? This does not mean that current economic theory has nothing to contribute. It certainly offers insights into parts of the story, but what is required is for the different elements to be brought together. We need an overall framework, both conceptual and empirical, within which to fit the different mechanisms. The skill shift explanation for wage differentials is valuable, but it is only part of the story. The labour market cannot be seen as totally independent from the capital market. Both economic and political economy explanations have their place.

About 20 years ago, there was a spate of Presidential Addresses which were full of gloom about the state of economics. Since I began by criticising the profession for what I feel to have been its neglect of a central subject, I would like to end on a positive note. The first ground for optimism is the upsurge of interest in the recent past. The contributions which I have mentioned, and others not covered, are a welcome indication that income distribution is beginning to receive again the attention which it merits. The second is that there is evidence that economics is beginning to learn in this area from other disciplines. I have touched on social norms, where we can learn from the sociology of labour markets and from social psychology. I have discussed public choice, where we can learn from political science. A subject so central to social science as income distribution is unlikely to be one that we can solve on our own, and I take a receptiveness to outside ideas to be a sign of a discipline in good health.

Nuffield College

References

Adams, M. (1988). *The distribution of earnings 1973 to 1986.* Research Paper No. 64. London: Department of Employment.

Aghion, P. and Bolton, P. (1992). 'Distribution and growth in models of imperfect capital markets.' *European Economic Review*, vol. 36, pp. 603–11.

Aghion, P. and Bolton, P. (1993). 'A theory of trickle-down growth and development.' Nuffield College and LSE.

Akerlof, G. A. (1981). 'A theory of social custom, of which unemployment may be one consequence.' *Quarterly Journal of Economics*, vol. 95, pp. 749–75.

Alesina, A. and Rodrik, D. (1994). 'Distributive politics and economic growth.' *Quarterly Journal of Economics*, vol. 109, pp. 465–90.

Ashenfelter, O. and Layard, R. (1983). 'Incomes policy and wage differentials.' *Economica*, vol. 50, pp. 127–43.

Atkinson, A. B. (1990). 'Income maintenance for the unemployed in Britain and the response to high unemployment.' *Ethics*, vol. 100, pp. 569–85.

Atkinson, A. B. (1993). 'What is happening to the distribution of income in the UK?' *Proceedings of the British Academy*, vol. 82, pp. 317–51.

Atkinson, A. B. (1996*a*). *Incomes and the Welfare State.* Cambridge: Cambridge University Press.

Atkinson, A. B. (1996*b*). 'Seeking to explain the distribution of income.' In *New Inequalities* (ed. J. Hills). Cambridge: Cambridge University Press.

Atkinson, A. B. and Micklewright, J. (1989). 'Turning the screw: benefits for the unemployed 1979–1988.' In *The Economics of Social Security* (ed. A. Dilnot and I. Walker). Oxford: Oxford University Press.

Atkinson, A. B. and Micklewright, J. (1992). *Economic Transformation in Eastern Europe and the Distribution of Income.* Cambridge: Cambridge University Press.

Atkinson, A. B. Rainwater, L. and Smeeding, T. (1995). *Income Distribution in OECD Countries: the Evidence from the Luxembourg Income Study.* Paris: OECD.

Banerjee, A. and Newman, A. (1991).'Risk-bearing and the theory of income distribution.' *Review of Economic Studies*, vol. 58, pp. 211–35.

Banerjee, A. and Newman, A. (1993). 'Occupational choice and the process of development.' *Journal of Political Economy*, vol. 101, pp. 274–98.

Beckerman, W. (1980). 'Comparative growth rates of "measurable economic welfare": some experimental calculations.' In *Economic Growth and Resources*, volume 2: *Trends and Factors* (ed. R. C. O. Matthews). London: Macmillan.

Bell, B. D. and Pitt, M. K. (1995). 'Trade union decline and the distribution of wages in the UK: evidence from kernal density estimation.' Nuffield College Economics Discussion Paper 107.

Bell, D., Hunter, L. and Danson, M. (1990). 'The distribution of earnings'. In *A Portrait of Pay, 1970–1982* (ed. M. B. Gregory and A. W. J. Thompson). Oxford: Clarendon Press.

Bénabou, R. (1996). 'Equity and efficiency in human capital investment: the local connection.' *Review of Economic Studies*, vol. 63, pp. 237–64.

Bertola, G. (1993). 'Factor shares and savings in endogenous growth.' *American Economic Review*, vol. 83, pp. 1184–98.

Blanchard, O. J. (1993). 'Movements in the equity premium.' *Brookings Papers on Economic Activity*, no. 2, pp. 75–118.

Bliss, C. J. (1995). 'Capital mobility, convergence clubs and long-run economic growth.' Nuffield College Economics Discussion Paper 100.

Bourguignon, F. (1981). 'Pareto superiority of unegalitarian equilibria in Stiglitz' model of wealth distribution with convex saving function.' *Econometrica*, vol. 49, pp. 1469–75.

Bourguignon, F. and Martinez, M. (1995). 'A decomposition analysis of the evolution of the family income distribution: France 1979–89.' Paris: DELTA.

Brandolini, A. (1992). 'Nonlinear dynamics, entitlement rules, and the cyclical behaviour of the personal income distribution.' Centre for Economic Performance Discussion Paper 84, London School of Economics.

Brandolini, A. and Rossi, N. (1995). 'Growth, inequality and social institutions.' Paper presented at International Economic Association Congress, Tunis, 1995.

Brandolini, A. and Sestito, P. (1994). 'Cyclical and trend changes in inequality in Italy, 1977–1991.' Servizio Studi, Banca d'Italia.

Brown, W. A. (1976). 'Incomes policies and pay differentials.' *Oxford Bulletin of Economics and Statistics*, vol. 38, pp. 27–49.

Brown, W. A. (1979). 'Engineering wages and the social contract 1975–77.' *Oxford Bulletin of Economics and Statistics*, vol. 41, pp. 51–61.

Burtless, G. (1995). 'International trade and the rise in earnings inequality.' *Journal of Economic Literature*, vol. 33, pp. 800–16.

Carruth, A. A. and Oswald, A. J. (1989). *Pay Determination and Industrial Prosperity*. Oxford: Clarendon Press.

Central Statistical Office. (1994). *Family Spending: A report on the 1993 Family Expenditure Survey*. London: HMSO.

Central Statistical Office. (1995). 'The effects of taxes and benefits on household income, 1994/95.' *Economic Trends*, no. 506, pp. 21–59.

Chater, R. E. J. (1981). 'The differential dilemma.' In *Incomes Policy* (ed. R. E. J. Chater, A. J. H. Dean and R. F. Elliott). Oxford: Clarendon Press.

Coulter, F. A. E., Cowell, F. A. and Jenkins, S. P. (1994). 'Family fortunes in the 1970s and 1980s.' In *The Measurement of Household Welfare*. (ed. R. Blundell, I. Preston, and I. Walker). Cambridge: Cambridge University Press.

Crafts, N. F. R. (1993). 'Was the Thatcher experiment worth it?' In *Explaining Economic Growth* (ed. A. Szirmai, B. Van Ark and D. Pilat). Amsterdam: Elsevier.

Dalton, H. (1920). *Some Aspects of the Inequality of Incomes in Modern Communities*. London: Routledge.

Dean, A. J. H. (1978). 'Incomes policies and differentials.' *National Institute Economic Review*, August, pp. 40–8.

Dickens, R., Machin, S. and Manning, A. (1994). 'Estimating the effect of minimum wages on employment from the distribution of wages: a critical review.' Centre for Economic Performance Discussion Paper No. 203, London School of Economics.

Donohue, J. H. III and Heckman, J. (1991). 'Continuous versus episodic change: the impact of civil rights policy on the economic status of blacks.' *Journal of Economic Literature*, vol. 29, pp. 1603–43.

Durlauf, S. N. (1996). 'A theory of persistent income inequality.' *Journal of Economic Growth* (forthcoming).

Ferreira, F. H. G. (1995). 'Roads to equality: wealth distribution dynamics with public-private capital complementarity.' STICERD Discussion Paper No. TE/95/286, London School of Economics.

Galor, O. and Zeira, J. (1993).'Income distribution and macroeconomics.' *Review of Economic Studies*, vol. 60, pp. 35–52.

Gardiner, K. (1993). 'A survey of income inequality over the last twenty years – how does the UK compare?' STICERD Welfare State Programme, Discussion Paper WSP/100, LSE.

Giddens, A. (1981). *A Contemporary Critique of Historical Materialism*, vol. 1, *Power, Property and the State*. London: Macmillan.

Goodman, A. and Webb, S. (1994). *For Richer, For Poorer*. London: Institute for Fiscal Studies, Commentary No. 42.

Gosling, A. and Machin, S. (1993). 'Trade unions and the dispersion of earnings in UK establishments, 1980–90.' Discussion paper 93-05. University College, London.

Gosling, A., Machin, S. and Meghir, C. (1996). 'What has happened to the wages of men since 1966?' In *New Inequalities* (ed. J. Hills). Cambridge: Cambridge University Press.

Gregg, P. and Machin, S. (1994). 'Is the UK rise in inequality different?' In *The UK Labour Market* (ed. R. Barrell). Cambridge: Cambridge University Press.

Gregg, P. and Wadsworth, J. (1996). 'More work in fewer households?' In *New Inequalities* (ed. J. Hills). Cambridge: Cambridge University Press.

Gustafsson, B. and Palmer, E. E. (1993). 'Changes in Swedish inequality: a study of equivalent income 1975–1991.' University of Gothenburg.

Hauser, R. and Becker, I. (1993). 'The development of the income distribution in the Federal Republic of Germany during the seventies and eighties.' University of Frankfurt.

Hills, J. (editor) (1996). *The New Inequalities*. Cambridge: Cambridge University Press.

Jenkins, S. P. (1995). 'Accounting for inequality trends: decomposition analyses for the UK, 1971–86.' *Economica*, vol. 62, pp. 29–63.

Klasen, Stephan, (1994). 'Growth and well-being: introducing distribution-weighted growth rates to reevaluate U.S. Postwar economic performance.' *Review of Income and Wealth*, series 40, pp. 251–72.

Krugman, Paul. (1994). 'Past and prospective causes of high unemployment.' In *Reducing Unemployment: Current Issues and Policy Options*. Jackson Hole Symposium. Kansas City: Federal Reserve Bank of Kansas City.

Kuznets, S. (1955). 'Economic growth and income inequality.' *American Economic Review*, vol. 45, pp. 1–28.

Leamer, E. (1995). *ANU Reporter*, 2 August 1995.

Lester, R. A. (1952). 'A range theory of wage differentials.' *Industrial and Labor Relations Review*, vol. 5, pp. 483–500.

Levy, F. and Murnane, R. J. (1992). 'U.S.earnings levels and earnings inequality: a review of recent trends and proposed explanations.' *Journal of Economic Literature*, vol. 30, pp. 1333–81.

Meade, J. E. (1964). *Efficiency, Equality and the Ownership of Property*. London: Allen and Unwin.

Meade, J. E. (1973). 'The inheritance of inequalities: some biological, demographic, social, and economic factors.' *The Proceedings of the British Academy*, vol. 59, pp. 355–81.

Meade, J. E. (1976). *The Just Economy*. London: Allen and Unwin.

Mookherjee, D. and Shorrocks, A. F. (1982). 'A decomposition analysis of the trend in UK income inequality.' ECONOMIC JOURNAL, vol. 92, pp. 886–902.

Murphy, K. (1995). 'Comment', National Bureau of Economic Research. *Macroeconomics Annual 1995* (ed. B. S. Bernanke and J. J. Rotemberg), pp. 54–9. Cambridge, Mass.: MIT Press.

Nelson, C. T. (1994). 'Levels and changes in the distribution of U.S. income.' In *The Changing Distribution of Income in an Open U.S. Economy* (ed. J. H. Bergstrand *et al.*). Amsterdam: Elsevier.

OECD (1995). *OECD Economic Surveys: United Kingdom 1995*. Paris: OECD.

Parker, S. C. (1996). 'The distribution of self-employment income in the UK, 1976–1991.' University of Durham.

Perron, P. (1989). 'The Great Crash, the oil price shock, and the unit root hypothesis.' *Econometrica*, vol. 57, pp. 1361–401.

Perotti, R. (1992). 'Income distribution, politics, and growth.' *American Economic Review*, vol. 82, Papers and Proceedings, pp. 311–6.

Perotti, R. (1993). 'Political equilibrium, income distribution, and growth.' *Review of Economic Studies* vol. 60, pp. 755–76.

Persson, T. and Tabellini, G. (1994). 'Is inequality harmful for growth?' *American Economic Review*, vol. 84, pp. 600–21.

Phelps Brown, E. H. (1977). *The Inequality of Pay*. Oxford: Oxford University Press.

Piketty, T. (1994). 'The dynamics of the wealth distribution and the interest rate with credit-rationing.' MIT Discussion Paper.

Piketty, T. (1995*a*). 'Social mobility and redistributive politics.' *Quarterly Journal of Economics*, vol. 100, pp. 551–84.

Piketty, T. (1995*b*). 'Income distribution theory: a survey of selected recent contributions.' Paper presented at International Economic Association Congress, Tunis.

Reder, M. W. (1962). 'WAGES : structure.' *International Encyclopedia of Social Sciences*, pp. 403–14.

Redmond, G. and Sutherland, H. (1995). 'How has tax and social security policy changed since 1978? A distributional analysis.' Microsimulation Unit Discussion Paper MU9508, Department of Applied Economics, Cambridge.

Ricardo, D. (1951). *The Works and Correspondence of David Ricardo*, vol. VIII, (ed. P. Sraffa.) Cambridge: Cambridge University Press.

Robinson, P. (1994). 'Is there an explanation for rising pay inequality in the UK?' CEP Discussion Paper 206, LSE.

Roseveare, H. (1973). *The Treasury*. London: Allen and Unwin.

Saint-Paul, G. and Verdier, T. (1993). 'Education, democracy and growth.' CEPR Discussion Paper 613.

Scott, M. (1993). 'Real interest rates: past and future.' *National Institute Economic Review*, no. 143, pp. 54–71.

Sen, A. K. (1976). 'Real national income.' *Review of Economic Studies*, vol. 43, pp. 19–39.

Solow, R. M. (1990). *The Labour Market as a Social Institution*. Oxford: Basil Blackwell.

Stiglitz, J. E. (1969). 'Distribution of income and wealth among individuals.' *Econometrica*, vol. 37, pp. 382–97.

Tinbergen, J. (1975). *Income Distribution*. Amsterdam: North-Holland.

U.S. Department of Commerce (1993). *Money Income of Households, Families, and Persons in the United States: 1992*. Current Population Reports, Series P-60, No. 184, Washington DC.

Wood, A. (1978). *A Theory of Pay*. Cambridge: Cambridge University Press.

Wood, A. (1994). *North–South Trade, Employment and Inequality*. Oxford: Clarendon Press.

Appendix: sources for figures

Figure 2

United States

1947–67 for family (excluding unrelated individuals) gross income, unadjusted for family size, with family weights, from Nelson (1994), Table 2·1, linked at 1967 to 1967–92 for household gross income, unadjusted for household size, with household weights, from U.S. Department of Commerce (1993), Table B-3.

United Kingdom

1961–91 for equivalent household disposable income, with person weights, from Goodman and Webb (1994), page A2 (BHC); I am grateful to Alissa Goodman and Steven Webb for supplying comparable figures for 1992 and 1993.

Figure 3

United States and United Kingdom as above.

Japan

1980–91 supplied by Management and Coordination Agency, see Atkinson *et al.* (1995), Chapter 5.

Sweden

1975–91 for equivalent disposable income, with person weights, from Gustafsson and Palmer (1993), Annex.

Figure 4

France

1979, 1985 and 1989 for equivalent household (excluding households with retired head) disposable income, with person weights, Bourguignon and Martinez (1995).

Germany

1978, 1983, 1985, 1987 and 1990 for equivalent household (excluding households with non-German head) disposable income, with person weights, from Hauser and Becker (1993), Table 7, linked at 1983.

Italy

1977–91 for equivalent household disposable income, with household weights, from Brandolini and Sestito (1994), Table 2*a*; I am grateful to Andrea Brandolini for supplying a comparable figure for 1993.

Figure 5

Goodman and Webb (1994), pp. A2, A14 and A26.

Figure 6

Income as Fig. 2; earnings from Atkinson and Micklewright (1992), Table BE1. The earnings series covers all full-time workers.

Figure 7

New Earnings Survey 1979, Table 96, and *1990*, Table 8 in Part A.

[40]

Econometrica, Vol. 28, 2 (April 1960)

ECONOMIC EXPANSION AND THE INTEREST RATE IN GENERALIZED VON NEUMANN MODELS[1]

BY MICHIO MORISHIMA

In this paper, we explicitly introduce consumption into the von Neumann models of economic growth and show that the two alternative Marx-von Neumann and Walras-von Neumann models—in both of which the effects of prices, the rate of interest, and the real wage rate on the consumption coefficients are allowed—have balanced growth solutions. The relation between the rate of interest and the rate of balanced growth is discussed also. It should be noted, however, that the models possess one degree of freedom; once the real wage rate is given, all prices, the rate of interest, and the rate of growth are determined. The rate of growth thus determined is a variant of Harrod's warranted rate of growth. The real wage rate is fixed at the level where the warranted rate and the natural rate of growth are equal.

INTRODUCTION

VON NEUMANN'S DYNAMIC model [**7**] is based on the following assumptions: (a) there are constant returns to scale; (b) the primary factor of production (labour) can be expanded indefinitely; (c) wages are held at the subsistence level; (d) all capitalists' income is automatically reinvested. In this paper we shall relax the last three assumptions and deal with two generalized models, both of which assume that (b′) the working population grows at a finite rate, (c′) workers' demand for consumption goods depends not only on wage income, but also on prices, and (d′) capitalists consume a constant proportion of their income, and their demand for consumption goods is such as to allow substitution in response to price changes. Professors Kemeny, Morgenstern and Thompson have been concerned with a similar problem in a section of their joint article [**4**]. They have shown that the introduction of a final demand for goods decreases the rate of expansion, in step with an equal rate of interest. Unfortunately, however, this result seems unsatisfactory, because the way in which final demand is introduced into the von Neumann model is rather peculiar. The conclusion of the present paper is that, barring negative expansion, the rate of expansion will be equal to the product of the interest rate and capitalists' average propensity to save.

[1] I am greatly indebted to Dr. N. Kaldor of King's College, Cambridge, Dr. F. Seton of Nuffield College, Oxford, and Professor H. Nikaidô of Osaka University for valuable suggestions and criticisms. I have also benefited from Professor G. L. Thomspon's paper entitled "A Generalization of the von Neumann Dynamic Model" (unpublished). The method of proof of the theorem in Section 2 below is similar to the method used by Professor Thompson, although the theorems proved are different. Needless to say, the author alone is responsible for any errors which may be found in this paper.

As for the unit cost of production there are at least two definitions which are historically important; the first is Marx's definition and the second Walras's. In Section 1 we are concerned with a model in which the Marxian assumption of equal rates of profit (based on his definition of unit cost) is satisfied, while in Section 3 we deal with a model where the Walrasian definition prevails. The first model may be regarded as a restatement of Marx's reproduction scheme [**5**, Vol. II, Chap. XX and XXI] in terms of the von Neumann apparatus, and the second as a von Neumann version of Walras's theory of capital formation and credit [**10**, pp. 267–312]. Section 2 offers a proof for the existence of economic solutions to the model presented in Section 1.

1. A MODEL OF AN EXPANDING CAPITALIST ECONOMY: MARX-VON NEUMANN

Let us consider an economy in which there are a finite number m of technically possible processes of production operating at discrete time intervals and producing n different goods with a lag of one time period of production. Let A be a matrix of material-input coefficients whose element a_{ij} (in the ith row and the jth column) denotes the quantity of good j used up per unit level of process i; and let L be a column vector of labour-input coefficients, the ith element (l_i) of which represents labour employed per unit level of process i. Finally, the element, b_{ij}, in the ith row and the jth column of the output-coefficient matrix B represents the quantity of good j produced per unit level of process i.

In this paper we make the following assumptions concerning the technological coefficients A, B, and L:

(i) $$A \geqslant 0 \quad \text{and} \quad B \geqslant 0$$

(ii) $$L > 0$$

(iii) $$v(B) > 0\,,$$

where $v(B)$ is the value of the matrix game B in which the maximizing player controls the rows and the minimizing player controls the columns. It should be noted that although the assumption $v(-A) < 0$ made in [**4**] is economically plausible, we do not assume it in this paper.

The meaning of the first assumption is quite obvious. The second assumption implies that every process must consume a positive amount of labour. The third assumption made by Professors Kemeny, Morgenstern and Thompson [**4**] is stated more intuitively as follows: there is no good which cannot be produced by at least one process.

Next, let $\beta(t)$ be the interest factor in period t ($= 1 +$ the rate of interest in period t), and $w(t)$ the money wage rate in the same period. An m dimensional row vector $q(t) = [q_1(t), \ldots, q_m(t)]$ and an n dimensional column vector $P(t) = \{P_1(t), \ldots, P_n(t)\}$ represent the intensity and price vectors (in period t), respectively. Of course, $\beta(t)$, $w(t)$, $q(t)$ and $P(t)$ are nonnegative.

At the position of equilibrium no process must yield positive supernormal profits, i.e.,

$$BP(t+1) \leqslant \beta(t)\,[AP(t) + w(t)L]\,. \tag{1}$$

$AP(t)$ and $w(t)L$ are the Marxian "constant capital" and "variable capital," respectively. It is worth mentioning that the unit cost of production includes not only the interest charge on constant capital but also the interest charge on variable capital. Note also that (1) is an *in*equation interpretation of Marx's assumption of general equality in the rates of profit.[2] Following von Neumann and others, we assume that if process i is unprofitable, it will not be used and its intensity $q_i(t)$ equals zero; therefore we find

$$q(t)BP(t+1) = \beta(t)q(t)\,[AP(t) + w(t)L]\,. \tag{2}$$

Capitalists' income in period $t+1$ is now equal to $E(t+1) \equiv q(t)\,[BP(t+1) - AP(t) - w(t)L] = [\beta(t) - 1]q(t)\,[AP(t) + w(t)L]$, which may be positive or negative. In what follows it is assumed that when capitalists' income is nonpositive, their consumption is zero and when it is positive, it is proportional to their income. We shall denote by c (or s) capitalists' average propensity to consume (or to save) in case of positive incomes. Of course $0 < c < 1$ and $c + s = 1$.

Let $d(t)$ be an n dimensional row vector, the jth element of which represents capitalists' consumption of good j in period t; then we have the capitalists' consumption function,

$$cE(t) = d(t)P(t)\,,$$

providing that capitalists' income in period t, $E(t)$, is assumed to be positive. According to the pure theory of consumer's behaviour, $d(t)$ is a homogeneous function of degree zero in the variables $P(t)$ and $E(t)$; so that $d(t)$ can be written in the form:

$$d(t) = d\left(y(t), \frac{E(t)}{\sum_{j=1}^{n} P_j(t)}\right)$$

where $y(t)$ stands for the normalized price vector, i.e.,

$$\frac{1}{\sum_{j=1}^{n} P_j(t)} P(t)\,.$$

There is no a priori knowledge of consumer's behavior that specifies the dependency of $d(t)$ on $y(t)$ and $E(t)/\sum_{j=1}^{n} P_j(t)$; but we assume in this

[2] Cf. Samuelson [**9**, p. 887].

paper that the Engel-elasticity of capitalists' consumption of each good is unity. Then $d(t)$ is of the following simple form:

$$d(t) = \frac{E(t)}{\sum_{j=1}^{n} P_j(t)} f(y(t)) ,$$

where $f(y)$ is an n dimensional row vector such that $f(y)y = c$.

Next let an n dimensional row vector $e(t)$ represent workers' consumption of goods in period t. If we assume that workers do not save, we obtain

$$W(t) = e(t)P(t) ,$$

where $W(t)$ designates workers' income, $q(t)w(t)L$, in period t. Of course, $e(t)$ is a homogeneous function of degree zero in $P(t)$ and $W(t)$; and if we assume for simplicity that $e(t)$ is of the following form:

$$e(t) = \frac{W(t)}{\sum_{j=1}^{n} P_j(t)} g(y(t)) ;$$

then we find at once that $g(y)y = 1$.

As for $f(y)$ and $g(y)$ we assume that

(iv) $f(y)$ and $g(y)$ are nonnegative and continuous for all y in the set $\{y \mid y_j \geqslant 0, / \sum_{j=1}^{n} y_j = 1\}$.

Goods are used up either in the processes of production or through workers' or capitalists' consumption. The demand for goods for production in period t is $q(t)A$, and for workers' consumption is $e(t)$. Remembering that capitalists' consumption, $d(t)$, does not take place when their income is nonpositive, we find that the total consumption of goods amounts to $q(t)A + e(t) + \max\ (0, E(t) / \sum_{j=1}^{n} P_j(t))\ f(y(t))$, where "$\max\ (0, E(t) / \sum_{j=1}^{n} P_j(t))$" means the larger of the numbers in parentheses. Since no more goods can be consumed during any time period than were produced during the preceding one, we obtain:

$$q(t-1)\ B \geqslant q(t)A + e(t) + \max\left(0, E(t) \Big/ \sum_{j=1}^{n} P_j(t)\right) f(y(t)) . \tag{3}$$

We assume that if there is excess production of good j, its price $P_j(t)$ becomes zero, and therefore, taking into account that $g(y)y = 1$ and $f(y)y = c$, we can conclude from (3) that

$$q(t-1)BP(t) = q(t)AP(t) + W(t) + \max\ (0, E(t))\ c . \tag{4}$$

The final condition requires that the total value of all goods produced must be positive, i.e.,

$$q(t-1)BP(t) > 0 . \tag{5}$$

Let us now assume that the money wage-rate $w(t)$ is adjusted so as to maintain a given level, Ω, of the real wage rate, and let units be chosen in such a way that $w(t) / \sum_{j=1}^{n} P_j(t)$ is equal to Ω. Throughout the following analysis we concentrate our attention on the state of balanced growth where each component of the intensity vector q increases (or decreases) by a constant percentage per unit of time, i.e., $q(t) = \alpha q(t-1)$, and the interest factor β and all the prices P are constant over time. Considering $E(t) = [\beta(t-1) - 1]\, q(t-1)\, [AP(t-1) + w(t-1)L]$ and $W(t) = q(t)w(t)L$, we can easily find that our expressions (1) — (5) now become

(1′) $$By \leqslant \beta[Ay + \Omega L]\,,$$

(2′) $$xBy = \beta x[Ay + \Omega L]\,,$$

(3′) $$xB \geqslant \alpha[xA + x\Omega Lg(y)] + \max(0, \beta - 1)\,(xAy + x\Omega L)f(y)\,,$$

(4′) $$xBy = [\alpha + \max(0, \beta - 1)c]\,(xAy + x\Omega L)\,,$$

(5′) $$xBy > 0\,,$$

where x and y are the normalized intensity vector, $\frac{1}{\sum_{i=1}^{m} q_i} q$, and the normalized price vector, $\frac{1}{\sum_{j=1}^{n} P_j} P$, respectively.

2. RELATION BETWEEN INTEREST FACTOR AND EXPANSION FACTOR

In order to prove the existence of solutions to (1′)—(5′), given assumption (i)—(iv), we shall consider the following auxiliary system:

(1″) $$By \leqslant \gamma M(y, \alpha)y\,,$$

(2″) $$xBy = \gamma xM(y, \alpha)y\,,$$

(3″) $$xB \geqslant \alpha xM(y, \alpha)\,,$$

(4″) $$xBy = \alpha xM(y, \alpha)y\,,$$

(5″) $$xBy > 0\,,$$

where $x \varepsilon X$ (the set of all m dimensional nonnegative vectors with unit sums), $y \varepsilon Y$ (the set of all n dimensional nonnegative vectors with unit sums) and

$$M(y, \alpha) = A + \Omega Lg(y) + \max\left(0, \frac{\alpha - 1}{\alpha s}\right)(Ay + \Omega L)\, f(y)\,.$$

LEMMA 1. *If x, y, α and γ are solutions of (1″)—(5″), then $\alpha = \gamma > 0$.*

PROOF: From (2″), (4″) and (5″) we see $\alpha xM(y, \alpha)y = \gamma xM(y, \alpha)y > 0$. Since $xM(y, \alpha)y \geqslant 0$, we obtain $\alpha = \gamma > 0$ at once.

Let x, y and $\alpha = \gamma$ be solutions of (1″)—(5″); and define β as $\alpha + \max(0, (\alpha - 1)/s)c$. We can easily show that these x, y, α, and β are solutions of

(1′)—(5′); thus the problem is completely solved if we can prove the existence of a solution to (1″)—(5″).

By Lemma 1 we need look only for solutions in which α equals γ. Under the assumption that $\alpha = \gamma$, equations (2″) and (4″) are direct consequences of (1″) and (3″) and of the fact that $x \varepsilon X$ and $y \varepsilon Y$; hence we have

$$[B - \alpha M(y, \alpha)]\, y \leqslant 0 \,,$$
$$x[B - \alpha M(y, \alpha)] \geqslant 0 \,,$$
$$xBy > 0 \,.$$

If we divide $B - \alpha M(y, \alpha)$ by $1 + \alpha$ and set $\lambda = \alpha/(1 + \alpha)$, the above expressions become

(1‴) $$[(1 - \lambda)B - \lambda N(y, \lambda)]\, y \leqslant 0 \,,$$

(3‴) $$x[(1 - \lambda)B - \lambda N(y, \lambda)] \geqslant 0 \,,$$

(5‴) $$xBy > 0 \,,$$

where

(6) $$N(y, \lambda) = A + \Omega\, Lg(y) + \max\left(0, \frac{2\,\lambda - 1}{\lambda\, s}\right)(Ay + \Omega\, L)f(y) \,.$$

From assumptions (i)—(iv) we find at once:

(i′) $B \geqslant 0$; and for all (y, λ) in the set $S = \{(y, \lambda)\,|y_j \geqslant 0,\ \Sigma_{j=1}^{n} y_j = 1$ and $0 \leqslant \lambda \leqslant 1\}$ the inequalities $N(y, \lambda) \geqslant 0$ hold.

(ii′) $L > 0$.

(iii′) $v(B) > 0$.

(iv′) $N(y, \lambda)$ is continuous for all (y, λ) in S.

In the inequalities (1‴) and (3‴) the matrix $N(y, \lambda)$ of the "augmented input coefficients" is dependent on y and λ. Let us choose a point (y^*, λ^*) in the set S and consider the following expressions:

(7) $$[(1 - \lambda)B - \lambda N(y^*, \lambda^*)]\, y \leqslant 0$$

(8) $$x[(1 - \lambda)B - \lambda N(y^*, \lambda^*)] \geqslant 0 \,.$$

Since (i′) and (iii′) hold, we can easily show that there is at least one λ such that

(9) $$v[(1 - \lambda)B - \lambda N(y^*, \lambda^*)] = 0$$

and $0 < \lambda \leqslant 1$. Therefore a solution exists for inequalities (7) and (8). Now let $T(y^*, \lambda^*)$ be the following set:

$$T(y^*, \lambda^*) = \{(y, \lambda) \mid (7) \text{ and } (9) \text{ hold}\} \,.$$

We can establish

LEMMA 2.[3] *The mapping* $(y^*, \lambda^*) \rightarrow T(y^*, \lambda^*)$ *is an upper semicontinuous*

[3] I am indebted to Professor H. Nikaidô for the following proof of this lemma.

mapping of $Y \times [0, 1]$ *(the cartesian product of* Y *and* $[0, 1]$*) into itself. Furthermore* $T(y^*, \lambda^*)$ *is contractible.*

PROOF: Let (y^k, λ^k) and $(\bar{y}^k, \bar{\lambda}^k)$ be any sequences of points in $Y \times [0, 1]$ that converge to the points (y^*, λ^*) and $(\bar{y}, \bar{\lambda})$, respectively. Let $(\bar{y}^k, \bar{\lambda}^k) \varepsilon T(y^k, \lambda^k)$. The continuity assumption (iv′) implies that $\lim_{k\to\infty} N(y^k, \lambda^k) = N(y^*, \lambda^*)$. Since $v[(1 - \bar{\lambda}^k)B - \bar{\lambda}^k N(y^k, \lambda^k)] = 0$ and $[(1 - \bar{\lambda}^k)B - \bar{\lambda}^k N(y^k, \lambda^k)]\bar{y}^k \leqslant 0$ for every k imply $v[(1 - \bar{\lambda})B - \bar{\lambda}N(y^*, \lambda^*)] = 0$ and $[(1 - \bar{\lambda})B - \bar{\lambda}N(y^*, \lambda^*)]\bar{y} \leqslant 0$, we find that $(\bar{y}, \bar{\lambda}) \varepsilon T(y^*, \lambda^*)$.

Let both (y', λ) and (y'', λ) belong to $T(y^*, \lambda^*)$. It is clear that $[(1 - t)y' + ty'', \lambda] \varepsilon T(y^*, \lambda^*)$ for all t in the interval $0 \leqslant t \leqslant 1$. Next let λ^0 (or λ^1) be the largest (or the smallest) λ such that $v[(1 - \lambda)B - \lambda N(y^*, \lambda^*)] = 0$, and let $(y, \lambda) \varepsilon T(y^*, \lambda^*)$. From Lemma 2 proved by Kemeny, Morgenstern, and Thompson [**4**, p. 120] it follows that $(y, (1 - t)\lambda + t\lambda^0) \varepsilon T(y^*, \lambda^*)$ for all t in the interval $0 \leqslant t \leqslant 1$.

Now let $(y^1, \lambda^1) \varepsilon T(y^*, \lambda^*)$, and let (y, λ) be any pair in $T(y^*, \lambda^*)$. Consider the following operator:

$$F[(y, \lambda), t] = (1 - t)\,(y, \lambda) + t(y^1, \lambda^0)\,,$$

where $0 \leqslant t \leqslant 1$. From the above argument it is clear that $[(1 - t)y + ty^1, (1 - t)\lambda + t\lambda^0] \varepsilon T(y^*, \lambda^*)$. Hence $T(y^*, \lambda^*)$ is deformable into the point $(y^1, \lambda^0) \varepsilon T(y^*, \lambda^*)$.

Now we can prove the

THEOREM: *A solution exists for inequalities* (1‴), (3‴) *and* (5‴).

PROOF: By the Eilenberg-Montgomery fixed point theorem [**1**] the mapping, $(y^*, \lambda^*) \to T(y^*, \lambda^*)$, defined in Lemma 2, has a fixed point, say $(y^*, \lambda^*) \varepsilon T(y^*, \lambda^*)$. Let $U(y^*, \lambda^*)$ be the set $\{x \mid x[(1 - \lambda^*)B - \lambda^* N(y^*, \lambda^*)] \geqslant 0\}$, and let $x^* \varepsilon U(y^*, \lambda^*)$; then (x^*, y^*, λ^*) satisfies (1‴) and (3‴), so that we have

$$x^*[(1 - \lambda^*)B - \lambda^* N(y^*, \lambda^*)]y^* = 0\,.$$

Together with (6), this leads to

$$\frac{(1 - \lambda^*)}{\lambda^*} x^* B y^* = x^* A y^* + x^* \Omega L g(y^*) y^* + \max\left(0, \frac{2\lambda^* - 1}{\lambda^* s}\right) (x^* A y^* + x^* \Omega L) f(y^*) y^*\,.$$

In view of $x^* \varepsilon X$, $y^* \varepsilon Y$, $g(y^*)y^* = 1$, $f(y^*)y^* = c$, $A \geqslant 0$, $\Omega L > 0$, and $0 < \lambda^* \leqslant 1$, we obtain $x^* B y^* > 0$; hence (5‴) holds; and $\lambda^* < 1$.

It is immediately obvious that x^*, y^*, and $\alpha^* = \gamma^* = \lambda^*/(1 - \lambda^*)$ satisfy inequalities (1″)—(5″). Let

$$\beta^* = \alpha^* + \max\left(0, \frac{\alpha^* - 1}{s} c\right). \tag{10}$$

Clearly, x^*, y^*, α^* and β^* satisfy our original inequalities (1′)—(5′).

It follows from (10) that if $\beta^* - 1 \leqslant 0$, then $\alpha^* - 1 = \beta^* - 1$, and that if $\beta^* - 1 > 0$, then $\alpha^* - 1 = s(\beta^* - 1)$. Consequently, we make the following statement: *If the rate of interest is nonpositive, the output of each commodity decreases (or remains unchanged) by a constant percentage per unit time equal to the rate of interest; if the rate of interest is positive, the output of each commodity increases by a constant percentage equal to the product of the rate of interest and capitalists' average propensity to save.*

The thick line in Figure 1 represents the relation between the interest factor and the expansion factor. For comparison we also show the original von Neumann relation in the form of a dotted line.

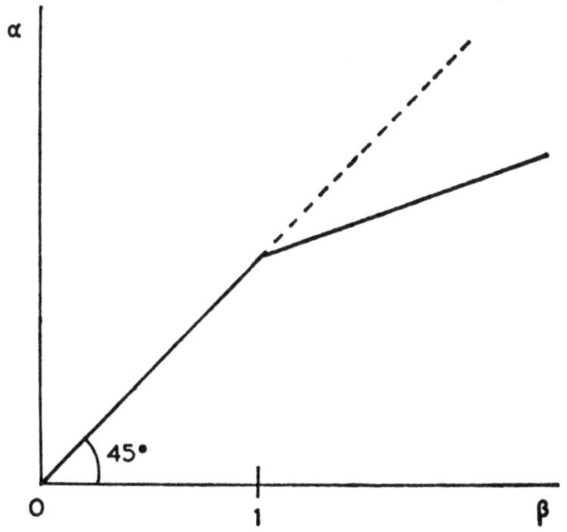

FIGURE 1

Let us write xAy as the Marxian "constant capital" C, $x\Omega L$ as "variable capital" V, and $xBy - xAy - x\Omega L$ as "surplus value" S. Then it follows from (2′) that

$$\beta - 1 = \frac{S}{C + V} \equiv \text{the Marxian "rate of profit."}$$

Since capitalists spend cS for consumption and sS for capital accumulation, s represents the ratio of capital accumulation to surplus value. Thus the conclusion above can be stated in terms of Marx's terminology as follows:

In the case of expanded reproduction, the rate of growth of the economy equals the rate of profit multiplied by the ratio of capital accumulation to surplus value.[4]

So far we have found that x^*, y^*, α^* and β^* are determined corresponding to a given real wage rate Ω. It remains to determine the rate Ω that makes the demand for and the supply of labour equal. This problem will be solved by an argument which is identical to that discussed in Section 3 below.

3. ALTERNATIVE MODEL: WALRAS-VON NEUMANN

We shall now turn from Marx's reproduction scheme to Walras's theory of capital formation and credit. Let a_{ij} be the quantity of good j used per unit level of process i, and let τ_{ij} be the length of life of good j (when used by process i); then the Walrasian unit cost is written:[5] $\sum_{j=1}^{n} (a_{ij}/\tau_{ij})P_j(t) + (\beta(t) - 1) \sum_{j=1}^{n} a_{ij}P_j(t) + w(t)L$. It should be noted that the unit cost defined by Walras does not include the interest charge on the working capital $w(t)L$. Assume now that all τ's are equal to unity and that workers spend their whole income of period $t-1$ for consumption in period t. Then our equations (1)—(5) are modified as follows:

$$BP(t+1) \leqslant \beta(t)AP(t) + w(t)L, \tag{11}$$

$$q(t)BP(t+1) = \beta(t)q(t)AP(t) + q(t)w(t)L, \tag{12}$$

$$q(t-1)B \geqslant q(t)A + e(t) + \max\left(0, E(t)/\sum_{j=1}^{n} P_j(t)\right) f(y(t)), \tag{13}$$

$$q(t-1)BP(t) = q(t)AP(t) + W(t-1) + \max(0, E(t))\, c, \tag{14}$$

$$q(t-1)BP(t) > 0, \tag{15}$$

where workers' demand for goods, $e(t)$, is of the form

$$e(t) = \frac{W(t-1)}{\sum_{j=1}^{n} P(t)} g(y(t))$$

and $E(t)$ stands for capitalist income, $q(t-1)BP(t) - q(t-1)AP(t-1) - q(t-1)w(t-1)L$, of period t.

In the state of balanced growth on which our thoughts are now fixed, we have $P(t+1) = P(t)$, $\beta(t) = \beta(t-1)$, and $q(t) = \alpha q(t-1)$. Write βP as p; then we find:

$$y_i \equiv \frac{P_i}{\sum_{j=1}^{n} P_j} \equiv \frac{p_i}{\sum_{j=1}^{n} p_j},$$

[4] A similar result was obtained by Morishima [**6**, pp. 179–184].

[5] τ is the reciprocal of the sum of Walras's μ and ν. Using his equations (8) on page 281 in [**10**], his equations (6) on page 280 can be rewritten in our form.

$$\Omega \equiv \frac{w}{\sum_{j=1}^{n} P_j} \equiv \beta \frac{w}{\sum_{j=1}^{n} p_j} \equiv \beta\omega ,$$

$$W(t-1) \equiv q(t-1)wL \equiv q(t-1)\omega L\left(\sum_{j=1}^{n} p_j\right) ,$$

$$e(t) \equiv \frac{W(t-1)}{\sum_{j=1}^{n} P_j} g(y) \equiv \beta q(t-1)\omega L g(y) .$$

By virtue of (12), we can easily find that $E(t) = [\beta(t-1) - 1]q(t-1)AP(t-1)$, so that we obtain

$$\frac{E(t)}{\sum_{j=1}^{n} P_j} \equiv \frac{(\beta - 1)q(t-1)\,AP}{\sum_{j=1}^{n} P_j} = (\beta - 1)q(t-1)\,Ay .$$

Therefore (11)—(15) can be written in the form:

(11′) $By \leqslant \beta[Ay + \omega L)$,

(12′) $xBy = \beta x[Ay + \omega L]$,

(13′) $xB \geqslant \alpha xA + \beta x\omega Lg(y) + \max(0, \beta - 1)xAyf(y)$,

(14′) $xBy = \alpha xAy + \beta x\omega L + \max(0, \beta - 1)xAyc$,

(15′) $xBy > 0$,

where x stands for the normalized intensity vector.

Let us suppose for a while that ω is a given constant. Consider the following auxiliary system:

(11″) $By \leqslant \gamma M(y, \alpha)y$,

(12″) $xBy = \gamma xM(y, \alpha)y$,

(13″) $xB \geqslant \alpha xM(y, \alpha)$,

(14″) $xBy = \alpha xM(y, \alpha)y$,

(15″) $xBy > 0$,

where

$$M(y, \alpha) = A + \omega Lg(y) + \max\left(0, \frac{\alpha - 1}{\alpha s} c\right)\omega Lg(y) + \max\left(0, \frac{\alpha - 1}{\alpha s}\right)Ay\ f(y) .$$

Since $A \geqslant 0$, $B \geqslant 0$, $L > 0$, and $v(B) > 0$ hold, we can show, by the same argument as in Section 2, that the system (11″)—(15″) has at least one solution $(x^*, y^*, \alpha^*, \gamma^*)$ such that $x^* \varepsilon X$, $y^* \varepsilon Y$ and $\alpha^* = \gamma^* > 0$. Let

(16) $$\beta^* = \alpha^* + \max\left(0, \frac{\alpha^* - 1}{s} c\right) .$$

Taking account of the fact that $c + s = 1$, we easily find that x^*, y^*, α^* and β^* satisfy the original inequalities (11')—(15'). Clearly, from (16) it follows that if $\beta^* - 1 \leqslant 0$, then $\alpha^* - 1 = \beta^* - 1$, and that if $\beta^* - 1 > 0$, then $\alpha^* - 1 = s(\beta^* - 1)$.

Let us now write $xBy - xAy - x\Omega L$ as "profit" P and xAy as "capital" K. Since $\Omega = \beta\omega$, we have from (12') that $\beta - 1 = P/K$. Hence we can conclude that: *Barring negative expansion, the economy grows at a rate equal to the product of the capitalists' average propensity to save and the rate of profit on capital.* This conclusion is identical to that reached in Dr. Kaldor's recent model of economic growth.[6]

In the above we started from an arbitrarily given constant ω and then determined the β^* corresponding to the ω. If the rate of growth of population were a passive factor, the real wage rate would be equal to $\beta^*\omega$; but in reality the growth of population is an independent datum. It remains, therefore, to solve one more problem about how the real wage rate Ω is determined.

Let us now make a simple assumption that the real wage rate is determined by the demand for and the supply of labour. Suppose the supply of labour in period t is $\varrho^t N$ where the rate of growth of population (or labour force) ϱ is assumed constant. Since the demand for labour in period t is $q(t)\, L (\equiv \alpha^t[\sum_{i=1}^m q_i(0)]xL)$, the demand-supply equilibrium for the labour force is described by

$$\alpha^t \left(\sum_{i=1}^{m} q_i(0)\right) xL = \varrho^t N \qquad \text{for all } t,$$

which is equivalent to the following two equations:

$$\left(\sum_{i=1}^{m} q_i(0)\right) xL = N, \tag{17}$$

$$\alpha = \varrho. \tag{18}$$

It is worth mentioning that α is a variant of Mr. Harrod's "warranted rate of growth"[7] and ϱ a variant of his "natural rate" (under the hypothesis of no technological progress.)[7] Our equation (18) implies that the "natural" and the "warranted" rates are equal.

In view of the fact that x, y and α are solutions to equations (11')—(15') we can find that they depend on ω in an upper semicontinuous way. It can also be proved that even if ω tends to zero, $\alpha(\omega)$ remains positive and if ω tends to infinity, $\alpha(\omega)$ tends to zero. Hence if the set $\alpha(\omega)$ is convex for every ω and if $0 < \varrho \leqslant \max \alpha(\omega)$, the equation, $\alpha(\omega) = \varrho$, has a solution $\hat{\omega}$. Let $\hat{\alpha}$ be $\alpha(\hat{\omega})$ and let $\hat{\beta}$ be $\hat{\alpha} + \max\,(0, (\hat{\alpha}-1)/s)c$. The $\hat{\Omega}$, being equal to $\hat{\beta}\hat{\omega}$, is

[6] See Kaldor [3 pp. 613–614].

[7] See [2, pp. 63–100].

the real wage rate at which the "natural" and the "warranted" rates of growth are equal. The solution $(x(\hat{\omega}), y(\hat{\omega}), \hat{\alpha}, \hat{\beta})$ corresponds to the state which Mrs. Robinson describes as a golden age, and the absolute level of activity in the initial period can be derived with the aid of equation (17) as $N/x(\hat{\omega})L$.

If $\varrho > \max \alpha(\omega)$, there exists no golden age solution; the real wage rate will be pushed down to the subsistence level, and unemployment of labour is inevitable.

Osaka University

REFERENCES

[1] Eilenberg, S., and D. Montgomery: "Fixed Point Theorems for Multi-Valued Transformations," *American Journal of Mathematics*, 68, 1946, pp. 214–222.

[2] Harrod, R. F.: *Towards a Dynamic Economics*, New York: Macmillan, 1952, 169 pp.

[3] Kaldor, Nicholas: "A Model of Economic Growth," *Economic Journal*, 67, 1957, pp. 591–624.

[4] Kemeny, John G., Oskar Morgenstern, and Gerald L. Thompson: "A Generalization of the von Neumann Model of an Expanding Economy," *Econometrica*, 24, 1956, pp. 115–135.

[5] Marx, Karl: *Capital*, Chicago: Charles Kerr and Company, 1933.

[6] Morishima, Michio: "An Analysis of the Capitalist Process of Reproduction," *Metroeconomica*, VIII, 1956, pp. 171–185.

[7] von Neumann, John: "A Model of General Economic Equilibrium," *Review of Economic Studies*, 13, 1945–46, pp. 1–9.

[8] Robinson, Joan, *The Accumulation of Capital*, London: Macmillan, 1956, 440 pp.

[9] Samuelson, Paul A.: "Wages and Interest: A Modern Dissection of Marxian Economic Models," *The American Economic Review*, XLVII, 1957, pp. 884–912.

[10] Walras, Léon: *Elements of Pure Economics*, translated by W. Jaffé, Homewood: Richard D. Irwin, Inc., 1954, 620 pp.

Name Index